BOOKS BY N. RICHARD NASH

NOVELS

East Wind, Rain
The Last Magic
Dragonfly
Cry Macho
Radiance
Aphrodite's Cave
Behold the Man
The Wildwood

PLAYS

See the Jaguar
Handful of Fire
Echoes
Girls of Summer
The Rainmaker
The Young and Fair
Second Best Bed
Everybody, Smile!
Breaking the Tie
Alchemy
Bluebird of Happiness
The Green Clown

LIBRETTI

110 in the Shade
Wildcat
The Happy Time
Yes, Tom, Yes!

NON-FICTION

The Wounds of Sparta
The Athenian Spirit

UNDER THE PSEUDONYM "JOHN ROC"

Winter Blood (a novel)
Fire! (a play)
The Loss of D-Natural (a play)

N. RICHARD NASH

Selected Plays

A GREENHOUSE AND KIRBY BOOK

Greenhouse and Kirby, Publishers
P.O. Box 939
Planetarium Station
New York, NY 10024-0546

First Edition, June, 1996
10 9 8 7 6 5 4 3 2 1

Jacket design by Amelia Copeland

Jacket figure by Stacie Simmons

Library of Congress Cataloging-in-Publication Data
N. Richard Nash
    (Plays)
        Selected Plays of N. Richard Nash.—1st ed.
                Contents: The Rainmaker; Everybody, Smile!; Breaking the Tie; Alchemy; Yes, Tom, Yes!; Bluebird of Happiness; The Green Clown; The Loss of D-Natural.
            ISBN 1-888825-02-2

Dedicated to My Son and Daughters

CONTENTS

THE RAINMAKER

A Romantic Comedy in Three Acts

CHARACTERS

(In order of appearance)

H. C. Curry
Noah Curry
Jim Curry
Lizzie Curry
File
Sheriff Thomas
Bill Starbuck

SCENES

The play takes place in a Western state on a summer day in a time of drought

ACT ONE
Day

ACT TWO
That evening

ACT THREE
Later the same night

FOREWORD

When drought hits the lush grasslands of the richly fertile West, they are green no more and the dying is a palpable thing. What happens to verdure and vegetation, to cattle and livestock can be read in the coldly statistical little bulletins freely issued by the Department of Agriculture. What happens to the people of the West—beyond the calculable and terrible phenomena of sudden poverty and loss of substance—is an incalculable and febrile kind of desperation. Rain will never come again; the earth will be sere forever; and in all of heaven there is no promise of remedy.

Yet, men of wisdom like H. C. Curry know to be patient with heaven. They know that the earth will not thirst forever; they know that one day they will again awaken to a green morning. Young people like Lizzie, his daughter, cannot know this as certainly as he does. Bright as she is, she cannot know. She can only count the shooting stars, and hope.

The play is set in such a drought-beset region in the moment when Lizzie's hope is faltering. Because the hopes of Lizzie and H. C., of Jim and Starbuck and File are finally brought to blessing, because the people of the play are deserving and filled with love of one another—and most important, because it is not always that the hopes of deserving, loving human beings *are* blessed—this play is a comedy and a romance. It must never be forgotten that it is a romance, never for an instant by the director, the actors, the scenic designer or the least-sung usher in the theater.

In this regard there must be, without eschewing truth, a kind of romantic beauty in the relationships of all the characters with one another. Especially so in the Curry family, even when Noah is laying down the stern law of a rigid God who, to Noah, looks rather like an irate Certified Public Accountant. There must be love in the house, or somewhere a benign promise.

This same felicity in the sets. True, the Curry ranch house—the living and dining rooms, the kitchen—is a place where people scratch their heads and take their shoes off, where woodwork has to be scrubbed and pots scoured. But more important, it is a place where beauty is made out of affection and all manner of gentleness. The tack room, if seen realistically, might be a dust bin attractive only to the termites and the rodents of the night. But if the designer sees it romantically—as Lizzie might see it, with all its memorabilia of childhood—it will tell the hopeful promise intended. Or File's office—it is not an office really, although File's roll-top desk is there and his old-fashioned telephone—it is File's secret hiding place from the world, the island where he errantly believes he can bring balm to his loneliness.

Despite the mention of many playing areas, it is essential that this be a one-set play. The center stage area should be the house—the living room or "parlor" as they called it in those days, combined with dining and kitchen areas into one large playing space, taking up perhaps half the stage. Down right, File's office, approximately a quarter of the stage—and down left, the tack room, the remaining quarter. It is essential that it be a one-set play—not for reasons of production economy, although economies will fortuitously flow from it—but because the designer can best serve the unity intended if the visual effects seem to be closely related and unified. And in the same regard—to avoid time separations as well as spatial ones—there must be no lowering of a curtain between scenes—merely a dimming of light in one area and a lift in light in another.

If there is incidental music in the play, it should sing on the romantic instruments and forswear brass and tympani. It should lament on strings and woodwinds and promise sweet melody.

Perhaps the best rule of thumb in direction, acting, scenery, music is this oversimplification: Let us not use the panoramic lenses. Let us focus closely, but through a romantically gauzed lens, on the face of Lizzie's loneliness, and on her hope. Life can be seen deeply through small lenses. And truthfully even through gauze.

Act One

T HE LIGHTS COME UP SLOWLY to reveal the center area of the stage which is the interior of the Curry house. The Curry ranch is a prosperous one and the house is a place where gentle, kindly people who have an uneducated but profoundly true sense of beauty have lived in love of one another. It is strongly masculine in its basic structure—brick and hand-hewn beams and such—but it shows Lizzie's hand in many of its appointments. We see a comfortable kitchen on the left; the rest of the downstairs living area is a combination of living and dining room. One of the earliest telephones on the wall; a gramophone with a horn; a primitive radio, a crystal set which, when operated, sets up a fearful screech of static. There are stairs to the bedrooms; a rear door to the ranch proper and to the barn and tack room; and a larger, more imposing front door to the private road that leads to the main highway.

It is early morning of a scorching, drought-ridden day. Already the blazing sun has taken over the house.

When the lights are up we see H. C. Curry making breakfast. He is in his mid-fifties, powerfully set, capable, a good man to take store in. But he's not all prosaic efficiency—there is deep vision in him.

A moment, then his oldest son, Noah, comes in from outdoors. Noah is somewhat like his father, without H. C.'s imagination. As a matter of fact, he has little imagination at all—a somewhat self-righteous man, rigidly opinionated.

NOAH: That you, Pop?

H.C.: Yeah. Mornin', Noah.

NOAH: I heard somebody fussin' around in the kitchen—I was hopin' it was Lizzie.

H.C.: She was so dead beat after her trip I figured I'd let her sleep.

NOAH: Yeah. I heard her walkin' her room last night until hell knows when. (*Looking at his pocket watch*) Gettin' late. Maybe I better wake her up. (*He starts for the stairs.*)

H.C.: No, don't do that, Noah. She must of had a pretty rough time. Let her sleep it off.

NOAH: Well, if she had a rough time—it was your idea. . . . I was sure hopin' she'd cook breakfast. (*Then, quickly, with a half smile, so as not to offend H.C.*) But I guess if we didn't croak after a week of your cookin', we can live through another meal.

(*Noah goes to the radio and fiddles with it. It screeches.*)

H.C.: Noah, Jimmy just fixed that thing—don't you go breakin' it again.

NOAH: If that kid's gonna waste his money on a darnfool crystal set—why can't we get some good out of it? Can't hear a thing.

H.C.: What do you want to hear?

NOAH: Thought somebody'd say somethin' about the drought.

H.C.: Only one thing to say. No rain.

NOAH: (*Switching off the set*) And no sign of it, neither. (*He goes to the calendar alongside of which hangs a pencil on a string*) Well, cross out another day.

H.C.: Noah, I wish you wouldn't do that—you and that damn calendar. Why'n't you stop countin'? When it rains, it rains!

NOAH: I'd sure like to take it easy like you and Jim. You know what I seen this mornin'? Three more calves down and out—and a couple of heifers! And you know what I had to do? I had to give Sandy and Frank their time.

H.C.: (*Disturbed*) You mean you fired them?

NOAH: No—I just laid 'em off—till the drought's over.

H.C.: You shouldn't of done that, Noah.

NOAH: Listen, Pop—if you want to take over the bookkeepin', you're welcome to it. (*Taking two large black ledgers off the desk*) Here's the books—you can have 'em!

H.C.: (*With a smile*) Now, I wouldn't do that to you, Noah. You'd be lost without Accounts Receivable and Debit and Credit. (*As Noah bridles*) Don't get mad, Noah. What I mean is—I can't make head or tail out of your new-style system!

NOAH: All right then. Let's stick to the deal—the rest of you do the dreamin', I'll do the figurin'.

H.C.: Yeah, but we said figures—not people.

NOAH: People are figures! Sandy and Frank are *red* figures! I don't like to lay nobody off any more'n you do—but it's gotta be done!

H.C.: How do you want your eggs?

NOAH: What's the best way you can't ruin 'em?

H.C.: Raw.

NOAH: I'll take 'em raw.

(*Noah goes into the kitchen and comes back quickly with a couple of eggs. Almost simultaneously, Jim Curry comes racing downstairs. Jim is the youngest in the family, in his early twenties—but he's big and broad-shouldered and looks older until he opens his mouth, and then he's a child. He has been convinced that he isn't very bright and this is his great cross. He is filled with inchoate longing. At the moment he is agog with excitement, as he nearly always is; but right now his frenzy has to do with universal catastrophe.*)

JIM: Mornin'! Mornin', Pop!

H.C. AND NOAH: Mornin', Jimmy . . . Mornin'.

JIM: Pop! Pop, it's like I said yesterday—just like I told you!

H.C.: What'd you tell me, Jim?

JIM: I said to you like this, I said: "Pop the whole world's gonna blow up!" I said: "The world's gonna get all s-w-o-l-e up—and bust right in our faces!"

H.C.: You sure of that, Jimmy?

JIM: You bet I'm sure! And I ain't the only one thinks that way! Last night— at the dance—Gil Demby and the boys, they say to me: "Jim, whatta you think of this drought?" And I says to them: "The world's gonna blow up! It's gonna get all swole up and bust in our faces!" And you know what? They all said: "Jim Curry, you hit it right on the head!"

H.C.: (*Gently, affectionately*) They were kiddin' you, Jimmy.

JIM: No, they weren't! Gil Demby—he's been to college—and he said it's all got to do with the sun! You gotta understand, Pop—you see, the sun—it's got a lot of spots on it. And them spots is growin'. And one of these days them spots is gonna get so big the sun won't be able to shine through. And then, brother—bang!

NOAH: You keep thinkin' about that you're gonna miss your breakfast.

JIM: Yeah. Ain't no good thinkin' about it—it just gets me all upset. (*Noticing Noah's food*) Holy mackerel, Noah—them eggs is raw!

NOAH: What of it?

JIM: What's the matter—you sick?

NOAH: No, I ain't sick.

JIM: You sure must be sick if you're eatin' raw eggs.

H.C.: He's all right, Jim. He just don't like my cookin'.

JIM: Why? You cook better'n Lizzie. I like the way you cook, Pop. Everything slides down nice and greasy.

H.C.: (*Wryly accepting the dubious compliment*) Thanks, Jim. How do you want your eggs?

JIM: Oh, any old way.

H.C.: How many?

JIM: (*Casually*) I guess five or six'll do.

NOAH: He ain't so hungry today.

(*Jim has already begun to gorge on bread and jam.*)

NOAH: Jimmy . . .

JIM: (*Bolting his food—not looking up*) Huh?

NOAH: Jimmy, if you'll come up for a minute, I got somethin' to say to you.

JIM: What?

NOAH: Last night . . . You coulda got yourself into a hatful of trouble.

JIM: (*Embarrassed to discuss it in front of his father*) Do we have to talk about it now?

H.C.: What kind of trouble, Noah?

NOAH: (*Distastefully*) A certain girl named Snookie.

H.C.: Oh—was Snookie at the dance?

NOAH: Was she at the dance? You'da thought nobody *else* was there! She comes drivin' up in a brand-new five-cylinder Essex car! And her hair is so bleach-blonde . . .

JIM: It ain't bleached!

NOAH: Don't tell me! Gil Demby says she comes into the store and buys a pint of peroxide every month.

JIM: What's that? I use peroxide for a cut finger.

NOAH: If she got cut that often she'd bleed to death.

JIM: You just don't like her 'cause she smokes cigarettes.

NOAH: Right in front of people!

H.C.: (*Quietly*) What happened, Jim?

NOAH: I'll tell you what happened. Along about nine-thirty I look around. No Jim—and no Snookie. That dumb kid—he walked outta that barn dance without even tippin' his hat. And he went off with that hot-pants girl.

JIM: I didn't go off with her—I went off by myself. I walked outside and I was lookin' at that Essex. And pretty soon she comes out and she's kinda starin' me up and down. And I says to her: "How many cylinders has this Essex got?" And she says: "Five." And then she says to me: "How tall are you?" And I says: "Six." And before you know it we're ridin' in the Essex and she's got that car racin' forty miles an hour. Man, it was fast!

NOAH: Everything about her is fast.

JIM: (*Rearing*) Whatta you mean by that, Noah?

NOAH: Just what I said! (*To H.C.*) When the dance was over—when we were all supposed to go pick Lizzie up at the depot—I had to go lookin' for him. And you know where he was? He was sittin' in that girl's car—parked outside of Demby's store—and the two of them—I never seen such carryin's on! They were so twisted up together, I couldn't tell where he left off and Snookie began. If I hadn't of come along, hell knows what would of happened.

JIM: (*Tragically*) Yeah . . . hell knows . . . I could of come home with her little red hat.

H.C.: With her what?

NOAH: She wears a little red hat.

H.C.: Well, why would you come home with her little red hat?

JIM: Nothin'—nothin'.

NOAH: Go on—tell him.

JIM: Noah—you quit it!

NOAH: Well, I'll tell him. She always wears this little red hat. And last night, Dumbo Hopkinson says to her: "Snookie, you gonna wear that little red hat all your life?" And she giggles and says: "Well, I hope not, Dumbo! I'm gonna give it to some handsome fella—when, as and if!" (*As H.C. smiles*) It ain't funny, Pop! (*To Jim*) Do you know what trouble you can get yourself into with a girl like that? A dumb kid like you—why, pretty soon she's got you hog-tied and you have to marry her!

JIM: Why don't you let me alone?

NOAH: (*Outraged*) Did you hear that, Pop?

H.C.: Maybe it's a good idea, Noah.

NOAH: What's good idea?

H.C.: To let him alone.

JIM: Maybe it is!

NOAH: (*Hurt; in high dudgeon*) All right! If you want me to let you alone— kid, you're alone!

JIM: (*Withdrawing a little*) I don't know what you're gettin' so mad about.

NOAH: You don't, huh? You think I like lookin' out for you? Well, I don't! Taggin' after me all your life! "How do I tie my shoelaces? How do I do long division?" Well, if you don't want me to give you no advice—if you think you're so smart, you just go and get along by yourself!

JIM: I ain't sayin' I'm so smart. Heck, I don't mind you tellin' me how to do and how to figure things out . . .

NOAH: (*Bitingly*) Thanks!

JIM: What I mean—I appreciate it. (*Bellowing*) I just wish you wouldn't holler!

H.C.: All right—that's enough, boys! (*A moment. H.C. goes to the thermometer*) A hundred and one degrees.

NOAH: If only it'd cool off at night.

JIM: I don't mind a hot night. (*Longingly*) Somethin' about a hot night . . . Gets you kind of—well—all stirred up inside. . . . Why don't Lizzie come down and make our breakfast, Pop?

H.C.: Let her sleep. She didn't sleep much last night.

JIM: Yeah. Gets off the train—comes home—and starts cleanin' up her bedroom in the middle of the night. Hell, there was no need for that. I cleaned her room up real nice.

H.C.: (*Quietly*) Jimmy, when some girls ain't happy, they cry. . . . Lizzie works.

JIM: Yeah. Well, what are we gonna do about her?

H.C.: (*Worriedly*) I don't know.

JIM: We gotta do *somethin'*, Pop. We gotta at least talk to her. Mention!

H.C.: Who's gonna mention it to her?

JIM: Well . . . you're her father.

H.C.: I don't see bein' her father's got everything to do with it. I could say you're her brothers.

NOAH: I told you, Pop—I'm not gonna mention it to her.

JIM: Me neither. I'm not gonna mention.

H.C.: Stop sayin' exactly what Noah's sayin'. Speak for yourself.

JIM: I say what Noah is sayin' because I agree with him. When I don't, I spit in his eye.

H.C.: Then why won't you talk to her?

JIM: Because if we do, she'll think we're tryin' to get rid of her.

H.C.: She'll sure think the same if *I* do it.

NOAH: Maybe.

JIM: May *be*.

H.C.: So there you are!

JIM: But you're her father and comes a time when a father's gotta mention.

H.C.: I can't! I can't just speak up and say: "Lizzie, you gotta get married!" She knows she's gotta get married. We all know it.

NOAH: Well then—seems there's no point to mention anything.

(*Lizzie Curry comes down the stairs. At first glance, she seems a woman who can cope with all the aspects of her life. She has the world of mate- riality under control; she is a good housekeeper; pots and pans, needles and thread—when she touches them, they serve. She knows well where she fits in the family—she is daughter, sister, mother, child—and she en- joys the manifold elements of her position. She has a sure ownership of her own morality, for the tenets of right and wrong are friendly to her— and she is comfortably forthright in living by them. A strong and integral woman in every life function—except one. Here she is, twenty-seven years old, and no man outside the family has loved her or found her beautiful. And yet, ironically, it is this one unfulfilled part of Lizzie that is the most potentially beautiful facet of the woman, this yearning for romance, this courageous searching for it in the desert of her existence. . . . But she is at great pains to conceal these hungers—by an open display of good humor, by laughter at herself—and by behaving, in a western world of men, as if she were as much a man as any of them. Lizzie, the Tomboy. But if some day a man should find her, he will find no tomboy but a full and ready woman, willing to give herself with the totality of her rich being.*)

LIZZIE: Morning, Pop—Noah—Jimmy.

H.C.: Mornin', honey.

NOAH AND JIM: Mornin', Lizzie . . . Hi, Liz.

LIZZIE: Sure good to be home again.

H.C.: Just what the boys were sayin'—sure good to have Lizzie home again.

LIZZIE: No sign of rain yet, is there?

H.C.: Not a cloud nowhere.

LIZZIE: I dreamed we had a rain—a great big rain!

H.C.: Did you, Lizzie?

LIZZIE: Thunderstorm! Rain coming down in sheets! Lightning flashed—thunder rolled up and down the canyon like a kid with a big drum! I looked up and I laughed and yelled . . . I (*With a laugh*) Oooh, it was wonderful!

NOAH: Drought's drought—and a dream's a dream.

LIZZIE: But it was a nice dream, Noah—and nearly as good as rain.

NOAH: Near ain't rain!

H.C.: It's too bad we picked you up at the depot so late last night, Lizzie. Didn't have much time to talk about your trip.

NOAH: Looks like it perked you up real good. Yeah, you were lookin' all dragged out by the heat. What was it like in Sweetriver?

LIZZIE: Hotter'n hell.

(*Pop and Jim laugh.*)

NOAH: I don't see nothin' funny in her talkin' like a cowhand.

LIZZIE: Sorry, Noah. That's about all the conversation I've heard for a week.

H.C.: How's Uncle Ned, Lizzie? And Aunt Ivy?

JIM: And how's all them boys?

LIZZIE: (*Muscularly*) Big.

H.C.: If they take after Aunt Ivy I bet they talked your ear off.

LIZZIE: No, they take after Uncle Ned. They just grunt.

NOAH: Who got to be the best-lookin' of the boys, Lizzie?

LIZZIE: Oh—I guess Pete.

H.C.: Never could get those boys straight. Which one is Pete?

LIZZIE: He's the one with the yellow hair.

NOAH: (*Quickly*) Yella hair's nice in a man!

JIM: It's honest!

LIZZIE: Oh, Pete was honest all right.

JIM: The way you said that I bet you liked him the best.

LIZZIE: Oh, I'm crazy about Pete—he asked me to marry him.

(*A moment.*)

H.C.: Is that true, Lizzie?

JIM: (*Agog*) He did? What did you tell him?

LIZZIE: I told him I would—as soon as he graduates from grammar school. (*Silence.*)

JIM: Grammar school! Is he that dumb?

LIZZIE: No . . . (*With a laugh*) He's only nine years old. (*Seeing the stricken look on their faces*) Pop—let's not beat around the bush. I know why you sent me to Sweetriver. Because Uncle Ned's got six boys. Three of them are old enough to get married—and so am I. Well, I'm sorry you went to all that expense—the railroad ticket—all those new clothes—the trip didn't work. Noah, you can write it in the books—in red ink.

H.C.: What happened at Sweetriver, Lizzie?

LIZZIE: (*Emptily*) Nothing—just nothing at all.

H.C.: What did you do? Where'd you go?

LIZZIE: Well, the first three or four days I was there—I stayed in my room most of the time.

NOAH: What'd you do that for?

LIZZIE: Because I was embarrassed!

NOAH: Embarrassed about what?

LIZZIE: Noah, use your head! I knew what I was there for—and the whole family knew it too. And I couldn't stand the way they were looking me over. So I'd go downstairs for my meals—and rush right back to my room. I packed—I unpacked—I washed my hair a dozen times—I read the Sears, Roebuck catalog from cover to cover. And finally I said to myself: "Lizzie Curry, snap out of this!" Well, it was a Saturday night—and they were all going to a rodeo dance. So I got myself all decked out in my highest heels and my lowest cut dress. And I walked down to that supper table and all those boys looked at me as if I was stark naked. And then for the longest while there wasn't a sound at the table except for Uncle Ned slurping his soup. And then suddenly—like a gunshot—I heard Ned Junior say: "Lizzie, how much do you weigh?"

H.C.: What'd you say to that?

LIZZIE: (*Squaring off*) I said, "I weigh a hundred and nineteen pounds, my teeth are all my own and I stand seventeen hands high."

NOAH: That wasn't very smart of you, Lizzie. He was just tryin' to open the conversation.

LIZZIE: (*Wryly*) Well, I guess I closed it . . . . Then, about ten minutes later little Pete came hurrying in to the supper table. He was carrying a geography book and he said: "Hey, Pop—where's Madagascar?" Well, everybody ventured an opinion and they were all dead wrong. And suddenly I felt I had to make a good impression and I heard my own voice talking as if it didn't belong to me. I said: "It's an island in the Indian Ocean off the coast of Africa right opposite Mozambique." (*With a wail*) Can I help it if I was good in geography?

H.C.: What happened?

LIZZIE: Nothing. Not a doggone thing. Everything was so quiet it sounded like the end of the world. Then I heard Ned Junior's voice: "Lizzie, you fixin' to be a schoolmarm?"

H.C.: Oh, no!

LIZZIE: Yes. And suddenly I felt like I was way back at the high school dance—and nobody dancing with me. And I had a sick feeling that I was wearing eyeglasses again the way I used to. And I knew from that minute on that it was no go. So I didn't go to the rodeo dance with them—I stayed home and made up poems about what was on sale at Sears, Roebuck's.

H.C.: You and little Pete?

LIZZIE: Yes . . . And the day I left Sweetriver little Pete was bawling. And he said: "You're the beautifulest girl that ever was!"

H.C.: And he's right! You are!

LIZZIE: (*More pain than pleasure*) Oh, Pop, please . . .!

H.C.: *We* see you that way—*he* saw you that way . . .

LIZZIE: But not his big brothers!

H.C.: Because you didn't *show* yourself right.

LIZZIE: I tried, Pop—I tried!

H.C.: No, you didn't! You hid behind your books. You hid behind your glasses that you don't even wear no more. You're *afraid* of bein' beautiful.

LIZZIE: (*In an outburst*) I'm afraid to *think* I am when I *know* I'm *not*! (*Her intensity stops the discussion. Then:*)

H.C.: Lizzie . . .?

LIZZIE: Yes?

H.C.: Me and the boys—we put our heads together—and we thought we'd mention somethin' to you.

LIZZIE: What?

H.C.: (*Uncomfortably, to Noah*) You want to tell her about it, Noah?

NOAH: Nope. It's your idea, Pop.

H.C.: Well, the boys and me—after we get some work done—we figure to ride into Three Point this afternoon.

LIZZIE: Well?

H.C.: We're goin' to the sheriff's office and gonna talk to his deputy.

LIZZIE: (*Alert now*) File?

H.C.: Yes—File.

LIZZIE: Pop, that's the craziest idea . . .

H.C.: I'm just gonna invite him to supper, Lizzie.

LIZZIE: If you do, I won't be here.

H.C.: I can invite a fella to supper in my own house, can't I?

LIZZIE: I don't want you to go out and lasso a husband for me!

H.C.: I won't do anything of the kind. I won't even say your name. We'll start talkin' about a poker game maybe—and then we'll get around to supper—and before you know it, he'll be sittin' in that chair.

LIZZIE: No!

H.C.: Lizzie, we're goin'—no matter what you say!

NOAH: Hold on, Pop. I'm against this. But if Lizzie says it's okay to go down there and talk to File—I'll go right along with you. But one thing—we won't do it if Lizzie says no.

LIZZIE: And that's what I say—no!

H.C.: Don't listen to Noah! Every time you and Jim have to scratch your back, you turn and ask Noah.

LIZZIE: Because he's the only sensible one around here, Pop. The three of us—we get carried away and then—

H.C.: (*Interrupting hotly*) For once in your life—*get* carried away! It won't hurt you—not a bit!

NOAH: That's the dumbest advice I ever heard.

H.C.: Noah, any time something comes up that you can't figure on paper— you say it's dumb! What's so dumb about it?

NOAH: It's a matter of pride!

H.C.: What the hell *is* pride anyway?

NOAH: Well, if you don't know what it is, I ain't gonna try to tell you. But me and Lizzie—we know what it is. Don't we, Lizzie?

(*As Lizzie turns away, H.C. sees her rejection of "pride" as a reason for not going through with the plan. Now he confronts her with the question.*)

H.C.: Is that why you say no, Lizzie? *Pride?*

LIZZIE: (*Avoiding the confrontation*) Pop, if you want to invite somebody to supper—go ahead—but not File!

H.C.: For Pete sake, why not?

LIZZIE: Because File—he doesn't even know I'm on earth!

H.C.: (*With a quiet smile*) He knows, Lizzie—he knows.

LIZZIE: No, he doesn't. Whenever we ride into town, File's got a great big hello for you and Noah and Jim—but he's got nothing for me. He just barely sneaks his hat off his head—and that's all. He makes a *point* of ignoring me.

H.C.: (*Quietly*) When a man makes a *point* of ignorin' you, he ain't ignorin' you at all. (*As she looks at him quickly*) How about it, Lizzie? File for supper?

LIZZIE: (*In an outburst*) No—I don't like him!—no!—no!

H.C.: If you don't really like him—one no is enough. . . . And you can say it quiet.

LIZZIE: (*Controlling herself—quietly, deliberately*) All right—I don't like him. I don't like the way he tucks his thumbs in his belt—and I don't like the way he always seems to be thinking deep thoughts.

H.C.: (*Secretly amused*) I thought you liked people with deep thoughts.

LIZZIE: Not File.

H.C.: (*Gently—soberly*) Lizzie—when you were a kid—if I ever thought you were lyin'—I'd say to you: "Honest in truth?" And then you'd never lie. Well, I'm sayin' it now. . . . You don't like File—honest in truth?

LIZZIE: (*Flustered*) Oh, Pop, that's silly!

H.C.: I asked you a question. Honest in truth?

LIZZIE: (*Chattering evasively*) Pop, that's a silly childish game and all you'll get is a silly childish answer and I refuse—I simply refuse to—to . . . (*But suddenly she puts the brakes on. In an outburst*) Oh, for God sake, go on and invite him!

H.C.: (*With a whooping shout*) O-kaaay! Come on, boys! (*At the doorway*) You go ahead and cook a great supper, Lizzie!

(*The men hurry out. For an instant, Lizzie is unnerved, alarmed at what she has let herself in for. Then suddenly, her spirits rising with expectancy, she goes about clearing the breakfast dishes. When Lizzie is happy she dances as she works. Lizzie is dancing. The lights fade.*)

(*The lights come up to disclose the inside of the Sheriff's office. There is an ancient roll-top desk with an old-style telephone on it. On the wall, a*

bulletin board with various "Wanted" posters featuring the faces of crim-
inals. A door leading to a washroom which, with its Franklin stove and
homemade ice box, serves as File's kitchen. His bed is a well-worn leather
couch in the corner of the office proper. The walls are warmly stained
knotty pine. The office is empty a moment, then File enters, followed by
Sheriff Thomas. File's thumbs, as Lizzie described them, are tucked in his
belt. He is a lean man, reticent, intelligent, in his late thirties. He smiles
wryly at the world and at himself. Perhaps he is a little bitter; if so, his
bitterness is leavened by a mischievous humor. He and the Sheriff are deep
in argument. Actually, it is the Sheriff who is arguing; File is detached, hu-
moring the Sheriff's argument. The men are obviously fond of each other.)

SHERIFF: I won't *charge* you nothin' for it, File.

FILE: (*With a smile*) That's nice of you, Sheriff—but right now I don't want
no dog.

SHERIFF: How do you know you don't want him until you see him?

FILE: Well, I seen dogs before.

SHERIFF: Not this one—he's different. I tell you, File—you see this little fella
and you'll reach out and wanta hug him to death.

FILE: (*Humoring him*) Think I will, huh?

SHERIFF: Yes, you will. You know what he does? There's five little puppies
in that litter, but him—he's the smartest. When my wife feeds those other
puppies, they stampede to the first bowl she fills. But not him. He lets
them fight and scrounge for the *first* bowl—and he eats every speck out
of the other four. Now whattaya think of that?

FILE: I think he's gonna bust right open.

SHERIFF: No, he ain't. I'll tell you another thing. He's real lovin'. If you're
sittin' in your bare feet, he'll come over and lick your big toe. And pretty
soon, there he is—dead asleep—right across your feet. How about it, File?

FILE: (*Hesitating*) Well . . . that sounds real homey—but I'll do without him.

SHERIFF: File, you make me disgusted. It ain't right for you to shack up all
by yourself—with a coffee pot and a leather sofa. Especially once you been
married. When you lose your wife, the nights get damn cold. And you
gotta have somethin' warm up against your backside.

FILE: Well, last night was a hundred and four degrees.

SHERIFF: All right—if you don't want the dog—if you're the kind of fella
that don't like animals . . .

FILE: (*Amused*) I like animals, Sheriff.

SHERIFF: If you liked animals, you'd have animals.

FILE: Oh, I've had 'em.

SHERIFF: (*Disbelievingly*) I'll bet! What kind?

FILE: Well, back in Pedleyville—I went out and got myself a raccoon.

SHERIFF: A raccoon ain't a dog!

FILE: (*With a smile*) No—I guess it ain't. But I liked him. He was awful
clean. You give him a banana, and he'd wash it ten times. He was a crazy
little fella—made me laugh.

SHERIFF: Yeah? Whatever happened to him?

FILE: I don't know. One day he took to the woods and never came back, the little bastard.

SHERIFF: (*Triumphantly*) There! See? Now can you figure a *dog* doin' that? No, sir! I tell you, File, if you never had a dog . . .

FILE: Oh, I had a dog.

SHERIFF: (*Defensively*) When did you have a dog?

FILE: When I was a kid.

SHERIFF: (*Testing for the truth of it*) What kind of dog was it?

FILE: Mongrel. Just a kid's kind.

SHERIFF: What'd you call him?

FILE: Dog.

SHERIFF: No, I mean what was his name?

FILE: Dog!

SHERIFF: (*Exasperated*) Didn't you have no name for him?

FILE: Dog! That was his name—Dog!

SHERIFF: That ain't no fittin' name for a dog!

FILE: I don't see why not!

SHERIFF: (*Shocked*) You don't see why not?

FILE: Nope. He always came when I called him.

SHERIFF: (*Almost apoplectic*) Hell, man, you couldn't of liked him much if you didn't even give him a name.

FILE: Oh, I liked him a lot, Sheriff. Gave him everything he wanted. Let him break it up—rip things to pieces. Took good care of him too—better than he took care of himself.

SHERIFF: Why? What happened to him?

FILE: Dumb little mutt ran under a buckboard.

SHERIFF: Well, hell—you figure everything's gonna run away—or get run over?

FILE: (*With a smile*) Oh, I dunno . . . I just don't want a dog, Sheriff. Not that I ain't obliged.

SHERIFF: All right . . . Maybe you'll change your mind.

FILE: I don't think so.

SHERIFF: Stubborn bastard . . . Well, I guess I'll have a look around—see what's doin'.

FILE: (*As the Sheriff goes to the door*) Yeah . . . Sleeps on your feet, does he?

SHERIFF: (*Laughing*) Right on my feet! Right on my big old stinkin' feet! See you later, File.

(*He goes out. File stretches and, as he does, he notes a rip under his sleeve. He goes to the desk, pulls out an old cigar box, opens it and takes out a needle and thread from his makeshift sewing kit. He threads the needle and starts to mend the rip when the telephone rings. He lets the needle and thread dangle from his shirt as he answers the phone.*)

FILE: Hello . . . No, Sheriff Thomas just left. I'll take it—I'm his deputy. Name of what? Tornado Johnson? Yeah, I got it. What's he wanted for?

(*Writing on a pad*) Is he armed? I say is he got a gun? All right . . . Yeah, send us a picture as soon as you get it.

(*As he hangs up, the three Curry men enter. They are embarrassed about their errand, and, although they have plotted a plan of action, they're nervous about its outcome. Noah is sullenly against this whole maneuver.*)

FILE: Hey, H.C. Hey, boys.

H.C., NOAH AND JIM: Hey, File . . . Hey, File . . . Hey, File.

FILE: Ridin' over, you boys see any sign of rain?

NOAH: Not a spit.

FILE: (*With a trace of a smile, but not unkindly*) What's it like in Sweetriver?

NOAH: (*Tensing a little*) How'd we know? We ain't been to Sweetriver.

FILE: Sheriff says that Lizzie's been to Sweetriver.

H.C.: Yeah.

FILE: What's it like?

NOAH: Dry.

FILE: How'd Lizzie like it in Sweetriver?

NOAH: (*Sensing that their legs are being pulled*) Fine—she liked it fine!

JIM: Yeah—she liked it fine! Three barn dances, a rodeo, a summer fair and larkin' all over the place.

(*He laughs loudly. Noah squirms as he realizes that File sees through them. And H.C. feels queasy. Then, jumping in:*)

H.C.: How's your poker, File?

FILE: My what?

H.C.: Poker.

FILE: Oh, I don't like poker much.

JIM: You don't? Don't you like Spit in the Ocean?

FILE: Not much.

H.C.: We figured to ask you to play some cards.

FILE: I gave cards up a long time ago, H.C.

JIM: (*Stymied*) You did, huh?

FILE: Mm-hm.

(*Silence. An impasse. Suddenly Jim sees the needle hanging down from File's shirt.*)

JIM: File, what's that hangin' down from your shirt?

FILE: (*A little self-consciously*) Kinda looks like a needle.

H.C.: It sure does.

JIM: What's the matter—your shirt tore?

FILE: Looks like it.

JIM: Fix it yourself, do you?

FILE: Sure do.

JIM: (*Clucking in sympathy*) Tch-tch-tch-tch-tch-tch.

FILE: (*Suppressing the smile*) Oh, I wouldn't say that, Jim. I been fixin' my own shirts ever since I became a widower back in Pedleyville.

JIM: Lizzie fixes all my shirts.

FILE: Well, it sure is nice to have a sister.

JIM: (*Significantly*) Or somethin'!

FILE: That's right.

(*Silence. Another impasse.*)

JIM: (*Abruptly*) Yessir! Sure is great what a great time Lizzie had in Sweetriver!

H.C.: Great!

FILE: Did—uh—did Lizzie come back by herself?

NOAH: (*Tensing*) Sure! She went by herself, didn't she?

FILE: (*With a dry smile*) That don't mean nothin'. I rode down to Leverstown to buy myself a mare. I went by myself but I came back with a mare!

JIM: (*Getting to the point; starting to lose his temper*) Well, she didn't go to buy nothin'! Get it, File—nothin'!

FILE: (*Evenly*) Don't get ornery, Jim. I just asked a friendly question.

NOAH: (*To Jim—with hidden warning*) Sure! Just a friendly question—don't get ornery.

H.C.: (*Baiting the trap for File*) I always say to Jim—the reason you ain't got no real friends is 'cause you're ornery! You just don't know how to make friends!

JIM: (*Hurt and angry*) Sure I do—sure I do!

H.C.: No, you don't! (*Meaningfully*) Do you ever ask a fella out to have a drink? No! Do you ever say to a fella: Come on home and have some supper?

JIM: (*Suddenly remembering the objective; not sure how to spring the trap*) I guess you're right. I'm sorry, File. Didn't mean to get ornery. Come on out and have a drink.

NOAH: (*Reflexively*) Supper!

JIM: (*Quickly, realizing his error*) Yeah—come on home and have some supper.

FILE: (*Aware of the trap*) Guess I'll say no to the supper, boys. (*With a flash of mischief*) But I'll be glad to go out and have a drink with you.

NOAH: We don't have time for a drink. But we been figurin' to ask you to supper one of these days.

FILE: Be glad to come—one of these days.

H.C.: How about tonight?

FILE: Don't have the time tonight. Seems there's some kind of outlaw comin' this way. Fella named Tornado Johnson. Have to stick around.

NOAH: You don't know he'll come this way, do you?

FILE: They say he's Three Point bound.

H.C.: But you don't know he'll be here tonight.

FILE: I don't know he won't be here tonight.

JIM: Why, he might be down at Pedleyville or Peak's Junction. He might even be over at our place.

FILE: (*Quietly*) Well, I won't be over at your place, Jim.

JIM: (*Riled—to H.C.*) You said for me to be friendly. Well, I'm tryin' but he don't want to be friendly.

FILE: (*Evenly*) I want to be friendly, Jim—but I don't want to be married. (*A flash of tense silence.*)

JIM: (*Exploding*) Who says we're invitin' you over for Lizzie? You take that back!

FILE: Won't take nothin' back, Jim.

JIM: Then take somethin' else.

(*Jim's fist flashes out but File is too quick for him. He parries the single blow and levels off one of his own. It connects squarely with Jim's eye and Jim goes down. The fight is over that quickly.*)

NOAH: (*Tensely, to File*) If I didn't think he had it comin', I'd wipe you up good and clean!

FILE: He had it comin'.

(*An instant. Noah is the most humiliated of all of them.*)

NOAH: (*To H.C. more than to File*) I guess we all did. (*To Jim*) Come on, turtlehead, let's go home.

(*Noah goes out quickly, followed by Jim. But H.C. remains with File. Silence. File speaks quietly.*)

FILE: I shouldn't of hit him, H.C.

H.C.: Oh, that's all right. Only thing is—you know you lost that fight.

FILE: What?

H.C.: Yeah. It wouldn't of hurt you to come to supper. It mighta done you some good.

FILE: We weren't talkin' about supper!

H.C.: (*Meeting the confrontation squarely*) That's right. We were talkin' about Lizzie. And she mighta done you some good too.

FILE: I can mend my own shirts.

H.C.: Seems to me you need a lot more mendin' than shirts.

FILE: What do you mean by that?

H.C.: Just what I said. You need mendin'.

(*H.C. starts for the door.*)

FILE: Wait a minute, H.C.! You don't drop a word like that and just leave it.

H.C.: All right—what'd you hit him for?

FILE: He threw a punch.

H.C.: Yeah—and you ducked it fine. He wouldn't of thrown another one— we'da stopped him. What'd you hit him for?

FILE: I'm sorry! I got angry!

H.C.: That's the point—why? We come around here and say we like you enough to have you in our family. Is that an insult?

FILE: I don't like people interferin'.

H.C.: Interferin' with what?

FILE: I'm doin' all right—by myself!

H.C.: You ain't doin' all right! A fella who won't make friends with no-body—who locks himself in against a whole town that wants to like him— he ain't doin' all right! And if he says he is, he's a liar!

FILE: Take it easy, H.C.

H.C.: I said a liar and I mean it! You talk about yourself as bein' a widower. And, because we all got respect for your feelin's, we all say: "Okay, if he wants us to call him widower, that's what we'll call him." But you ain't a widower—and everybody in this town knows it!

FILE: (*Losing his temper*) I am a widower! My wife died six years ago—back in Pedleyville!

H.C.: Your wife didn't die, File—she ran out on you! And you're a divorced man. But we'll all go on calling you a widower as long as you want us to. Hell, it don't hurt us none—to us it's only a little lie. But to you . . .! A fella who shuts himself up with that lie—he needs mendin'! (*A moment*) Want to throw any more punches?

(*File slowly turns away from him. H.C. goes out. Brooding, File goes back to his desk. He resumes the mending of his shirt but his mind is not on it; his thoughts are turned inward. The lights fade.*)

(*The lights come up on the Curry house again. Lizzie is just finishing the supper preparations. She works competently, quickly, bubbling with excitement. A quick survey of the kitchen—everything is fine. Now she has to dress. She hurries to the dining room and notices there are only four chairs around the table. She shoves two chairs apart, gets another one and pushes it up against the table to make the fifth. The sight of five chairs instead of the customary four is exhilarating to her. Singing, she hurries toward the stairs. At this moment, Noah comes in. He is in low, disgruntled spirits—but seeing Lizzie, he tries to smile.*)

LIZZIE: You all back so soon? (*Chattering excitedly*) Now don't walk heavy because the lemon cake will fall! You told File six o'clock, I hope.

NOAH: Uh—we didn't tell him no exact time.

LIZZIE: (*In a spate of words*) Now that's real smart! Suppose he comes at seven and all the cooking goes dry? I got the prettiest lemon cake in the oven—and a steak and kidney pie as big as that table. Oh, look at me—I better change my dress or I'll get caught looking a mess!

(*As she starts up the stairs he tries to stop her.*)

NOAH: Lizzie . . .

(*Just then the phone rings.*)

LIZZIE: Answer the telephone, will you, Noah?

(*Lizzie rushes upstairs. The phone rings again and Noah answers it.*)

NOAH: Hello!

(*Jim enters. He has an effulgent black eye.*)

NOAH: (*Into phone—annoyed at the instrument*) Hello—hello! No, this ain't Jim—it's Noah. Who's this? (*To Jim—darkly*) It's Snookie Maguire.

JIM: Hot dog!

(*He catapults across the room and reaches for the receiver. But Noah with one hand over the mouthpiece, withholds the receiver from Jim with his other hand.*)

NOAH: What exactly do you mean—hot dog?

JIM: (*Lamely*) Just hot dog, Noah.

NOAH: What are you gonna say to her?

JIM: I don't know what she's gonna say to me.

NOAH: Well, watch out.

JIM: (*Into phone—he coos lovingly*) Hello . . . Hello, Snookie . . . Oh, I'm fine—I'm just fine and dandy! How are you? Fine and dandy? Well, I'm sure glad you're fine and dandy too!

NOAH: (*Muttering disgustedly*) Fine-and-dandy-my-big-foot!

JIM: (*So sweetly*!) I was gonna telephone you, Snookie. But you telephoned me, di'n't you? Ain't that the prettiest coincidence?

NOAH: (*Nauseated*) Jimmy, for Pete sake!

JIM: (*Into phone*) What? . . . You mean it, Snookie? You mean it? Gee, I sure hope you mean it!

NOAH: What's all that you mean it about?

JIM: (*To Noah—in raptures*) She says: "It's a hot night and the moon looks like the yoke of an egg—and the Essex is sayin', 'Chug-chug, where's little Jimmy?'"

NOAH: Well, you tell her chug-chug, little Jimmy's gonna sit home on his little fat bottom!

JIM: Now wait a minute, Noah . . . !

NOAH: Don't say wait a minute! If you wanta get mixed up with poison, you go right ahead! But I wash my hands!

JIM: (*Unhappily—into phone*) Hello, Snookie . . . I just can't tonight . . . (*Confused*) Well, I don't know why exactly. Anyway, I can't talk now . . . Oh, Snookie—(*Longingly*)—are you still wearin' your little red hat? (*Relieved*) That's fine, Snookie—you take care of that! . . . Good-bye, Snookie.

(*He hangs up.*)

NOAH: See that? What'd I tell you! You go out with her once and she starts chasin' you.

JIM: Well, I don't see what's wrong with that, Noah.

NOAH: (*Shocked*) You don't?

JIM: No! She wants a date with me she calls me on the phone. Lizzie wants a date with File—we go down and try and fetch him.

NOAH: Well, if you remember, I didn't approve of goin' down to see File neither.

JIM: Why not? People want to get together—they oughta get together. It don't matter how, does it?

NOAH: Now, you ask yourself if it don't really matter—go on and ask yourself, Jimmy.

JIM: (*Suddenly lost when he has to figure it out for himself*) Well, maybe it does . . . Holy mackerel, I sure wish I could figure things out. (*At the radio*) You think I could get Kansas City this time of the night?

NOAH: I don't think you could get Kansas City any time of the day or night!

JIM: Yeah? Well, maybe I got it and I didn't know it! Last night—when everybody went to bed, I couldn't sleep. So I come downstairs and I fiddled with that crystal set and suddenly I hear a sound like the prettiest music. And I says to myself: "Sonofagun, I got Kansas City!"

NOAH: Static—that's all—just static.

JIM: I knew you'd say that, Noah. And I figured the answer to it: If it feels like Kansas City, it is Kansas City!

NOAH: Then why don't you make it feel like Africa?

JIM: On that little crystal set? (*A moment. Then, longingly*) I sure wish I could get *somethin'*!
(*H.C. comes in.*)

H.C.: Where's Lizzie? Did you tell her?

NOAH: No—she ran upstairs to get dressed.
(*Lizzie comes hurrying down the stairs. She is all dressed up and in a flurry of anticipation.*)

LIZZIE: Well, folks, how do I look?

H.C.: Beautiful.

LIZZIE: You know, Pop—I really think I am!—if you don't look too close! (*Exuberantly*) When do you suppose File will get here? I ought to know some time we can start eating!

H.C.: (*Quietly*) We can start any time you say.

LIZZIE: Any time? (*She looks at him quickly—and quickly gets the point. Then, pretending that life goes on unchanged, even pretending to see some advantage in File's not coming, she rattles on with studied casualness*) Well, you better wash up—and we can have more room at the table and . . . (*She has gone to the table to remove File's fifth chair, but she cannot bring herself to do it*) . . . File's not coming . . .

H.C.: No.

LIZZIE: I see.

JIM: (*Quickly*) Not that he didn't want to come! He wanted to—a lot!

LIZZIE: He did, huh?

JIM: Sure! Pop said: "Come to supper tonight, File." And when Pop said that—(*Quickly, to H.C.*)—did you notice how his face kinda—well—it lighted up? Did you notice that?

H.C.: (*Lamely*) Yeah.

JIM: And then File said: "Sure—sure I'll come! Glad to come!" And then suddenly he remembered.

LIZZIE: (*Quietly—not at all taken in*) What did he remember, Jimmy?

JIM: Well, he remembered there's some kind of outlaw runnin' around. And he figured—bein' Sheriff's deputy—he better stick around and pay attention to his job. Business before pleasure. (*Pleased with himself*) That's just what he said—business before pleasure. Yessir, File was real friendly!

LIZZIE: Friendly, huh? What happened to your eye?

JIM: It kinda swole up on me.

NOAH: File hit him.

LIZZIE: You mean you fought to get him to come here?

JIM: It was only a little fight, Lizzie.

LIZZIE: (*Trying to laugh*) Why didn't you make it a big one—a riot! Why didn't you all just pile on and slug him!

JIM: Lizzie, you're seein' this all wrong.

LIZZIE: I'm seeing it the way it happened! He said: "She might be a pretty good cook—and it might be a good supper—but she's plain! She's as plain as old shoes!"

H.C.: He didn't say anything like that!

JIM: He didn't say nothin' about shoes!

H.C.: Lizzie—we made a mess out of it.

NOAH: If you'da taken my advice there wouldn't of been a mess.

H.C.: (*Annoyed*) Noah, you're always right!

NOAH: I said don't go down and talk to File—nobody listened. I said don't send her to Sweetriver—nobody listened. So what happens? Disappointments!

H.C.: We gotta take a risk, Noah.

NOAH: No, we don't! We gotta figure things out so there ain't no risk! We gotta see things the way they are! (*Angry, unhappy*) Hell, I'm tired of talkin' like this! I don't like to say no to everything. And I don't like to be right all the time! But for God's sake . . .!

H.C.: Well, Noah, I'm stumped. If you were Lizzie's father, what would you do?

NOAH: Who says we gotta do anything? We been pushin' her around—tryin' to marry her off! Why? What if she don't get married? Is that the end of everything? She's got a home! She's got a family—she's got bed and board and clothes on her back and plenty to eat!

LIZZIE: That's right. From now on we listen to Noah.

H.C.: No! Don't you dare listen to him!

NOAH: Why not? She's got everything she needs!

H.C.: You mean she's got everything you can tote up in your bookkeepin' books! But she ain't got what'll make her happy!

JIM: And she ain't gonna get it! (*As they all look at him in surprise*) Because she's goin' at it all wrong!

LIZZIE: How, Jimmy? How am I going at it wrong?

JIM: Because you don't talk to a man the way you oughta! You talk too serious! And if there's anything scares hell out of a fella it's a serious-talkin' girl!

H.C.: Well, that's the way Lizzie is—and she can't be anything else.

JIM: Yes, she can! She's as smart as any of them girls down at the Ladies' Social Club. She can go down to the Social on Wednesday nights—and she can giggle and flirt as good as any of them.

H.C.: What do you want her to turn into—Lily Ann Beasley?

JIM: Lily Ann Beasley gets any man she goes for. Why, I saw her walk up to Phil Mackie one mornin'—and she wiggled her hips like a cocker spaniel and she said: "Phil Mackie, how many toes have you got?" And he said, "Well, naturally—I got ten." And she said, "Why, that's just the right number of toes for a big strong man to have!" And pretty soon he was cooked! He started followin' her around—and she got him so nervous, he bust right out with the shingles.

LIZZIE: Well, if she wants Phil Mackie she can have him—shingles and all.

JIM: And how about that livestock fella from Chicago . . . ?

LIZZIE: Jimmy! Can I treat a man the way she treated him? (*Imitating Lily Ann*) "My—a polka-dot tie! I just adore a man with a polka-dot tie! Those little round dots go right to my heart!"

JIM: Yeah—and that poor fella—the blood rushed out of his face and I thought he'd keel right over in the horse trough.

LIZZIE: I don't want a man to keel over. I want him to stand up straight— and I want to stand up straight *to* him. Without having to trick him. (*With a cry*) Isn't that possible with a man? Isn't it *possible?*

NOAH: (*Quietly*) No, it ain't.

H.C.: Yes, it is, Lizzie!

NOAH: No! For once in his life, Jim said somethin' sensible. (*Confronting Lizzie quietly*) If it's a man you want, you gotta get him *the way a man gets got*!

LIZZIE: If that's the way a man gets got, I don't want any of them!

H.C.: Lizzie . . .

LIZZIE: No! To hell with File! To hell with all of them!

NOAH: Don't use that language!

LIZZIE: Hell—hell—hell! To hell with all of them!

(*It is an outcry straight from the heart—rebellious but aching—and they can do nothing to help her. Suddenly, the outside door swings open, screaming on its hinges, whacking the wall like a pistol shot. Everybody turns to the door but all they can see is a vista of sky—no one is there.*)

NOAH: Who opened that door?

JIM: Musta been the wind!

(*Bill Starbuck steps into the doorway. He is a big man, lithe, agile—a loud braggart, a gentle dreamer. He carries a short hickory stick—it is his weapon, his magic wand, his pride of manhood. He hears Jim's line about the wind.*)

STARBUCK: Wind? Did you say wind? There's not a breath of wind anywhere in the world!

NOAH: Who are you?

STARBUCK: The name's Starbuck! Starbuck is the name! (*He espies Lizzie and his whole manner changes. He doffs his hat and his bow is part gallantry, part irony*) Lady of the house—hello!

LIZZIE: (*Involuntarily*) Hello.

STARBUCK: That's a mighty nice dress—it oughta go to a party.

LIZZIE: (*Not charmed*) Don't you knock on a door before you come in?

STARBUCK: If I'da knocked any harder, I'da broken the door down.

H.C.: What is it? What can we do for you?

STARBUCK: You're askin' the wrong question. The question is what can I do for you?

NOAH: I don't remember we called for anybody to do anything.

STARBUCK: You should have, Mister—you sure should have! You need a lot of help. You're in a parcel of trouble. You lost twelve steers on the north range and sixty-two in the gully. The calves are starvin' and the heifers are down on their knees.

JIM: You know a heckuva lot about our herd!

STARBUCK: (*Noticing Jim's black eye*) Man, that sure is a shiner! (*To H.C.*) Your ranch, Mister?

NOAH: He owns it—I run it.

STARBUCK: (*To Noah*) Well, I guess I'll talk to *you*. You got a look of business about you, Mister. You got your feet apart—and you stand solid on the ground. And I know while you're standin' that way, everything's in its right place—and the earth ain't gonna dare to move! That's the kind of a man I like to talk to! Well, what are you gonna do about them cattle?

NOAH: If you know we lost the cattle, you oughta know what killed them. Drought! Ever hear of it?

STARBUCK: Hear of it! That's *all* I hear! Wherever I go, there's drought ahead of me. But when I leave—behind me there's rain—*rain*!

LIZZIE: I think this man's crazy!

STARBUCK: Sure! That's what I am! Crazy! I woke up this mornin'—I looked at the world and I said to myself: The world's gone completely out of its mind. And the only thing that can set it straight is a first-class, A-number-one lunatic! Well, here I am, folks—crazy as a bedbug! Did I introduce myself? The name is Starbuck—*Rainmaker*!

H.C.: (*Doubtfully*) I've heard about rainmakers.

NOAH: I read about a rainmaker—I think it was Idaho.

STARBUCK: What'd you read, Mister?

NOAH: I can't remember whether they locked him up or ran him out of town.

STARBUCK: Might be they strung him up on a sycamore tree.

NOAH: Look, fella, the idea is—we don't believe in rainmakers.

STARBUCK: What do you believe in, Mister—dyin' cattle?

JIM: You really mean you can bring rain?

LIZZIE: He talks too fast—he can't bring anything.

JIM: I asked him. Can you bring rain?

STARBUCK: It's been done, brother—it's been done!

JIM: (*Excitedly*) Where? How?

STARBUCK: (*With a flourish of his stick*) How? Sodium chloride! Pitch it up high—right up to the clouds. Electrify the cold front. Neutralize the warm front. Barometricize the tropopause. Magnetize occlusions in the sky.

LIZZIE: (*Confronting him quietly*) In other words—bunk!

(*Realizing he will have to contend with Lizzie and Noah, he suddenly and shrewdly reverses his field—he agrees with her.*)

STARBUCK: Lady, you're right! You know why that sounds like bunk? Because it *is* bunk! Bunk and hokey pokey! And I tell you, I'd be ashamed to use any of those methods.

JIM: What method do you use?

STARBUCK: My method's like my name—it's all my own. You want to hear my deal?

LIZZIE: We're not interested.

NOAH: Not one bit!

H.C.: What is it?

NOAH: Pop, you're not listenin' to this man . . .?

H.C.: (*Quietly to Starbuck*) Any charge for listenin'?

STARBUCK: No charge—free!

H.C.: Go ahead. What's the deal?

STARBUCK: One hundred dollars in advance—and inside of twenty-four hours you'll have rain!

JIM: (*In a dither*) You mean it? Real rain?

STARBUCK: Rain is rain, brother! It comes from the sky. It's a wetness known as water. Aqua pura. Mammals drink it, fish swim in it, little boys wade in it, and birds flap their wings and sing like sunrise. Water! I recommend it!

JIM: (*Convinced*) Pay him the hundred, Noah!

LIZZIE: Noah, don't be a chump!

NOAH: Me?—don't worry—I won't!

JIM: We got the drought, Noah! It's rain, Lizzie—we need it!

LIZZIE: We won't get a drop of it! Not from him!

H.C.: (*Quietly*) How would you do it, Starbuck?

STARBUCK: Now don't ask me no questions.

LIZZIE: Why? It's a fair question! How will you do it?

STARBUCK: What do you care how I do it, sister, as long as it's done? But I'll tell you how I'll do it. I'll lift this stick and take a long swipe at the sky and let down a shower of hailstones as big as canteloupes. I'll shout out some good old Nebraska cusswords and you turn around and there's a lake where your corral used to be. Or I'll just sing a little tune maybe and it'll sound so pretty and sound so sad you'll weep and your old man will weep and the sky will get all misty-like and shed the prettiest tears you ever did see. How'll I do it? Girl, I'll just do it!

NOAH: Where'd you ever bring rain before?

LIZZIE: What town? What state?

STARBUCK: Sister, the last place I brought rain is now called Starbuck—they named it after me! Dry? I tell you, those people didn't have enough damp to blink their eyes. So I get out my big wheel and my rolling drum and my yella hat with three little feathers in it. I look up at the sky and I say: "Cumulus!" I say: "Cumulo-nimbus! Nimbulo-cumulus!" And pretty soon—way up there—there's a teeny little cloud lookin' like a white-washed chicken house. And then I look up and there's a herd of white buffalo stampedin' across the sky. And then, sister-of-all-good-people, down comes the rain! Rain in buckets, rain in barrels, fillin' the lowlands, floodin' the gullies. And the land is as green as the valley of Adam. And when I rode out of there I looked behind me and I see the prettiest colors in the sky—green, blue, purple, gold—colors to make you cry. And me? I'm ridin' right through that rainbow!—Well, how about it? Is it a deal?

H.C.: Well . . .

LIZZIE: (*Seeing her father's indecision*) Pop—no! He's a liar and a con man!

H.C.: (*Reluctantly*) Yep, that's what he is all right—a liar and a con man!

STARBUCK: Hurts me to hear you say that, Mister! Well, so long to you—so long for a sorry night!

(*He starts for the door.*)

H.C.: Wait a minute!

STARBUCK: You said I was a con man!

H.C.: You're a liar and a con man—but I didn't say I wouldn't take your deal!

LIZZIE: Pop . . .

H.C.: (*Quickly, to Lizzie*) I didn't say I *would*, neither!

NOAH: Pop, you ain't gonna throw away a hundred bucks!

H.C.: It's my hundred, Noah!

NOAH: How do I write it in the books?

H.C.: Write it as a gamble, Noah! I've lost more'n that in poker on a Saturday night!

LIZZIE: You get an even chance in poker!

H.C.: Lizzie, I knew an old fella once—and he had the asthma. He went to every doctor and still he coughed and still he wheezed. Then one day a liar and a con man come along and took the old man for fifty dollars and a gold-plated watch. But a funny thing . . .! After that con man left, the old boy never coughed one minute until the day he was kicked by a palomino!

LIZZIE: That's a crazy reason!

STARBUCK: I'll give you better reasons, Lizzie-girl! You gotta take my deal because once in your life you gotta take a chance on a con man. You gotta take my deal because there's dyin' calves that might pick up and live. Because a hundred bucks is only a hundred bucks—but rain in a dry season is a sight to behold. You gotta take my deal because it's gonna be a hot night—and the world goes crazy on a hot night—and maybe that's what a hot night is for.

H.C.: (*Suddenly*) Starbuck, you got you a deal!

STARBUCK: (*With a quick smile*) Tell you: I knew I had a deal the minute I walked into this house!

JIM: How'd you know that?

STARBUCK: I see four of you and five places set for supper. And I says to myself: Starbuck, your name's written right on that chair!

H.C.: (*With a laugh*) Let's eat!

(Starbuck tosses his hat up on the rack, throws his leg over the back of one of the dining chairs and in one movement—before the others can approach it—he is seated at the table. As the others sit down to supper . . .)

END OF ACT ONE

Act Two

INSIDE THE CURRY HOUSE, a short while after supper. Noah is paying Starbuck his fee, counting out the money on the dining table. H.C. is watching quietly; Jim, with keyed excitement. Lizzie is clearing the supper dishes, hostile to the whole situation.

NOAH: (*Fuming as he counts out the bills*) Seventy—eighty—eighty-five . . .! I'm against this, Pop.

H.C.: (*Quietly*) Keep countin', Noah.

NOAH: Ninety—ninety-five—one hundred. There's your hundred bucks.

STARBUCK: Thank you, Noah.

NOAH: Don't thank me—thank him. (*Going to his ledger*) I'm writin' that down in my book. One hundred dollars—thrown away.

STARBUCK: No—don't write that, Noah. Write it like this, Say: On August the twenty-seventh, a man come stompin' through our doorway. We bid him time of night, we fed him a supper fit for a king and we gave him one hundred honest notes on the fair government of the United States of America. And in return for that hospitality he did us one small favor—he brought rain! (*With a smile*) You got that? Write it!

NOAH: I don't see no rain yet.

STARBUCK: I still got twenty-three hours to bring it.

NOAH: Well, you better get busy.

JIM: (*Eagerly*) Yeah, Starbuck, you better knuckle down.

STARBUCK: Now let's not get nervous. Rain, my friends, rain comes to the man that ain't nervous! (*Getting down to work*) Now, what kind of rain would you like?

JIM: You mean we can choose our kind?

STARBUCK: Sure, you can choose your kind. And brother, there's all kinds! There's mizzle and there's drizzle—but you wouldn't want that. I generally give that away as a free sample. There's trickle and there's sprinkle! But that's for the little flower gardens of little pink old ladies. There's April showers that I can bring in April—but I can sometimes bring 'em in May. There's rain with thunder and rain with hail! There's flash floods—and storms that roll down the shoulder of the mountain. But the biggest of all—that's deluge! (*Modestly*) But don't ask me for deluge—that takes a bit of doin'.

JIM: What kind do we get for a hundred bucks?

STARBUCK: You choose it and I'll bring it.

LIZZIE: He brags so loud he gives me a pain in the neck.

STARBUCK: Look, folks, if you all act like she does, it's gonna make it mighty tough for me to do my job! Because when there's suspicion around, it's a *d-r-y* season!

LIZZIE: I don't doubt it.

STARBUCK: Well, she don't believe in me. How about the rest of you?

NOAH: What do you mean believe in you? We certainly don't!

STARBUCK: Then I changed my mind! I don't want your money—take it back! (*In a temper he slams the money on the table. They are stunned.*)

H.C.: Noah—please. We made a bargain—it's settled. Now be a good sport.

NOAH: (*Exasperated*) Good sport? What's he expect me to say?

STARBUCK: I'll explain it to you, Noah. Makin' rain—it takes a lot of confidence. And if you have doubts about me—I get doubts about myself.

NOAH: Oh, I see! If you don't bring rain, you're gonna blame it on us. We didn't have confidence. Well, I'll tell you how far my confidence goes. We're losin' cattle. So I figure we'll lose a hundred bucks—that's no more than the price of a well-fed steer. And maybe—one chance in a million, thanks to you bein' *lucky*—there'll be rain and we'll *save* a few cattle. But believe in you?—not a word!

LIZZIE: You can steal our money—but that's *all* you can steal.

STARBUCK: (*In a temper*) That's not the right attitude!

JIM: (*Manfully*) I got the right attitude—take back your dough!

STARBUCK: No! What if I need some help?

JIM: I'll help you—so will Pop!

STARBUCK: But not him!

NOAH: Darn right I won't!

H.C.: (*Shrewdly*) Look, Noah—suppose he takes the hundred bucks. You gotta account for it in the books *some* way. Well, if there's a Chinaman's chance you can account for it as a profitable investment . . .?

NOAH: (*To Starbuck*) What kind of help?

STARBUCK: Nothin' you can't do. How about you, lady? Any confidence?

LIZZIE: No confidence.

JIM: We don't need her, Starbuck—here's your dough. (*As Starbuck takes it*) Now—what's the first step?

STARBUCK: Well, what I'm gonna ask you to do—it ain't gonna make sense. But what's sensible about a flash of lightnin'? What's sensible about cyclones, blizzards, flood and hurricane?

JIM: Nothin'!

STARBUCK: Right! Now—what I want you to do: (*He hurries to the window and points out*) You see that little old wagon of mine? On that wagon I got me a big bass drum. Somebody's gotta beat that drum!

NOAH: Beat it? What for?

STARBUCK: Don't ask questions!

JIM: (*He has caught on to the rules of the game*) And don't get sensible!

STARBUCK: That's right, Jimmy! Who's gonna beat that drum?

JIM: (*The stalwart*) Me—I'll beat it!

STARBUCK: Jim, you're gonna be my first lieutenant. Now you go on out there and every time you get the feelin' for it, you beat that drum—three times—boom—boom—boom—low, like thunder . . . Got it?

JIM: Got it! Every time I get the feelin'?

STARBUCK: That's it.

JIM: (*Eagerly*) When do I start?

STARBUCK: Mister, you've started!

(*Jim goes out quickly and Starbuck turns to H.C.*)

STARBUCK: Mister H.C., I want you to pay close attention. In that wagon I got a bucket of white paint. Now it ain't ordinary white paint—it's special—it's electro-magnetized, oxygenated, *de*chromated white. Now I want you to go out there and paint a great big white arrow pointin' away from the house. That's so the house don't get struck by lightnin'.

H.C.: (*With a wry smile*) That sounds reasonable.

STARBUCK: (*Pretending to talk to himself, but his eye on Noah*) Now . . . it's too bad you ain't got a mule on the place.

NOAH: (*Muttering*) We got a mule.

STARBUCK: You have? That's great—that's just dandy! Noah, get a length of strong rope and go out there and tie that mule's hind legs together.

NOAH: What? Tie the hind legs of a mule? What the hell for?

STARBUCK: (*Hurt*) Please—now, please—you gotta do like I ask you.

NOAH: I ain't gonna do it!

H.C.: Come on, Noah—you promised.

NOAH: I'll be damned! Tie the hind legs of a mule!

(*In a huff, Noah hurries outdoors. H.C. starts to follow him when Lizzie's voice stops him.*)

LIZZIE: Pop—wait! (*As H.C. stops, she turns to him, livid with rage*) Pop—I'm ashamed of you! I've been standing here—keeping my mouth shut—wondering how far you'd let this man go in making a fool out of you!

H.C.: (*Quietly*) He can't make me any more a fool than I make out of myself.

LIZZIE: You're making a big fool of yourself! Where's your common sense?

H.C.: Common sense? Why, that didn't do us no good—we're in trouble. Maybe we better throw our common sense away.

LIZZIE: For Pete sake, hang on to a little of it!

H.C.: You mean go along with this fella halfway, huh? Well, I can't do that. I gotta take a chance on him—the whole chance—without fear of gettin' hurt or gettin' cheated or gettin' laughed at. As far as he'll take me. (*To Starbuck—confronting him levelly*) A white arrow, did you say?

STARBUCK: (*A moment. Then, meeting his glance, his response to H.C. is serious, even respectful*) A white arrow, H.C.

H.C.: I'll paint it.

STARBUCK: (*With the faintest touch of desperation*) Dammit, Mister, you're gonna get your money's worth if it's the last thing I do!

H.C.: (*Quietly—almost gently*) Don't get nervous, Boy.

STARBUCK: I ain't—not a bit of it!

H.C.: That's fine. Confidence!
(*H.C. goes out. From outdoors, we hear the first deep, pompous sound of the bass drum—boom—boom—boom!*)

STARBUCK: (*Calling to Jim*) Attaboy, Jim—you beat that drum! Make it rumble!

JIM'S VOICE: (*In the spirit of things*) Make it rum-bullll!
(*The drum sounds off again. Lizzie, fuming with anger, whirls on Starbuck.*)

LIZZIE: Well! I'll bet you feel real proud of yourself!

STARBUCK: (*Smiling evenly*) Kinda proud, sure.

LIZZIE: (*Raging*) You're not satisfied to steal our money! You have to make jackasses out of us! Why'd you send them out on those fool errands? Why? What for?

STARBUCK: Maybe I thought it was necessary.

LIZZIE: You know good and well it wasn't necessary—you know it!

STARBUCK: Maybe I sent them out so's I could talk to you alone!

LIZZIE: (*Off balance*) What?

STARBUCK: You heard me.

LIZZIE: (*Her rage mounting*) Then why didn't you just say it straight out: Lizzie, I want to talk to you—alone—man to man!

STARBUCK: (*Quietly*) Man to man, Lizzie?

LIZZIE: (*Bitingly*) Excuse me—I made a mistake—you're not a man!
(*Starbuck tenses, then controls his anger.*)

STARBUCK: Lizzie, can I ask you a little question?

LIZZIE: No!

STARBUCK: I'll ask it anyway. Why are you fussin' at the buttons on your dress?

LIZZIE: Fussing at the . . .! I'm not!

(*And she stops doing it.*)

STARBUCK: (*Evenly, gently*) Let 'em alone. They're all buttoned up fine— as tight as they'll ever get. . . . And it's a nice dress too. Brand new, ain't it? You expectin' somebody?

LIZZIE: None of your business.

STARBUCK: A woman gets all decked out—she must be expectin' her beau. Where is he? It's gettin' kinda late.

LIZZIE: (*Breaking out*) I'm not expecting anybody!

STARBUCK: (*Quietly*) Oh, I see. You were—but now you ain't. Stand you up?

LIZZIE: Mr. Starbuck, you've got more gall . . .!

(*And she starts for the stairs. But he grabs her arm.*)

STARBUCK: Wait a minute!

LIZZIE: Let go of me!

STARBUCK: (*Tensely*) The question I really wanted to ask you before—it didn't have nothin' to do with buttons. It's this: The minute I walked into your house—before I hardly said a word—you didn't like me! Why?

LIZZIE: I said let go!

STARBUCK: (*Letting her go*) You didn't like me—why? Why'd you go up on your hind legs like a frightened mare?

LIZZIE: I wasn't frightened!

STARBUCK: Yes, you were!

LIZZIE: Of you? Of what?

STARBUCK: I don't know! Mares get scared by lots of things—fire—lightning—the smell of blood!

LIZZIE: I wasn't scared, Mr. Starbuck. You paraded yourself in here—and you took over the place. I don't like to be taken by a con man.

STARBUCK: (*Lashing out*) Wait a minute! I'm sick and tired of this! I'm tired of you queerin' my work, callin' me out of my name!

LIZZIE: I called you what you are—a big-mouthed liar and a fake!

STARBUCK: (*With mounting intensity*) How do you know I'm a liar? How do you know I'm a fake? Maybe I *can* bring rain! Maybe when I was born God whispered a special word in my ear! Maybe He said: "Bill Starbuck, you ain't gonna have much in this world—you ain't gonna have no money, no fancy spurs, no white horse with a golden saddle! You ain't gonna have no wife and no kids—no green little house to come home to! But Bill Starbuck—wherever you go—you'll bring rain!" Maybe that's my one and only blessing!

LIZZIE: There's no such blessing in the world!

STARBUCK: I seen even better blessings, Lizzie-girl! I got a brother who's a doctor. You don't have to tell him where you ache or where you pain. He just comes in and lays his hand on your heart and pretty soon you're breathin' sweet again. And I got another brother who can sing—and when he's singin', that song is there—and never leaves you! (*With an outcry*) I

used to think—why ain't *I* blessed like Fred or Arny? Why am I just a
nothin' man, with nothin' special to my name? And then one summer
comes the drought—and Fred can't heal it away and Arny can't sing it
away. But me—I go down to the hollow and I look up and I say: "Rain!
Dammit! *Please*—bring rain!" And the rain came! And I knew—I knew I
was one of the family! (*Suddenly quiet, angry with himself*) That's a story.
You don't have to believe it if you don't want to.

(*A moment. She is affected by the story—but she won't let herself be. She
pulls herself together with some effort.*)

LIZZIE: I don't believe it.

STARBUCK: You're like Noah. You don't believe in anything.

LIZZIE: That's not true.

STARBUCK: Yes, it is. You're scared to believe in anything. You put the fancy
dress on—and the beau don't come. So you're scared that nothin'll ever
come. You got no faith.

LIZZIE: (*Crying out*) I've got as much as anyone!

STARBUCK: You don't even know what faith is. And I'm gonna tell you. It's
believin' you see white when your eyes tell you black. It's knowin'—with
your heart!

LIZZIE: And I know you're a fake.

STARBUCK: (*In sudden commiseration*) Lizzie, I'm sad about you. You don't
believe in nothin'—not even in yourself! You don't even believe you're a
woman. And if you *don't*—you're *not*!

(*He turns on his heel and goes outdoors. Lizzie stands there, still hearing
his words. She is deeply perturbed by them. The heat seems unbearable.
From outdoors, the sound of the drum—boom—boom—boom.*)

LIZZIE: (*Upset—weakly*) Jimmy—please! Please—quit that!

(*But he doesn't hear her. The drum continues. She rushes upstairs as the
lights fade.*)

(*The lights come up inside the Sheriff's office. The room is dimly illuminated by the gooseneck lamp on File's desk and by the brilliant moonlight
streaming through the window. File is lying on his leather couch staring
unseeingly up at the ceiling. At last he gets up and stretches. He is unhappy and uncomfortable. He takes up a cardboard, fans himself once or
twice and throws down the cardboard. The door opens and the Sheriff
comes in.*)

FILE: Anything doin'?

SHERIFF: Not a thing—so I ran home for a while. . . . Any calls?

FILE: (*Looking at a paper on his desk*) The Gannoways had their baby . . .
Peak's Junction called and said that Tornado Johnson fella was seen ridin'
our way. Old lady Keeley called and said she heard thunder.

SHERIFF: How can she? She's deaf as a post.

FILE: I thought I heard it too. But it was too regular.

(*Far in the distance, the sound of Jim's drum.*)

SHERIFF: There it is! . . . Sure ain't thunder.

FILE: Lots of electricity in the air. My hair's full of it.

SHERIFF: Mine too. Even in my clothes. My wife says when she walks around, it sounds like she's walkin' in taffety. I says: "You been naggin' for a new silk dress—now I won't have to buy it for you!"

(*The Sheriff howls uproariously at his own joke. File doesn't smile—he is far away, preoccupied.*)

SHERIFF: What's the matter, File? Where'd you go off to?

FILE: What? Oh—I'm right here.

SHERIFF: (*Watching him closely*) Phil Mackie says the Curry boys came by.

FILE: Oh, yes—I forgot.

SHERIFF: Anything important?

FILE: No.

SHERIFF: Phil says he saw Jim Curry come out of here wearin' a black eye.

FILE: He did, huh?

SHERIFF: Yeah—and he wasn't wearin' it when he came in. . . . What happened?

FILE: (*With a flare of temper*) Tell Phil Mackie to mind his own damn business!

SHERIFF: (*Surprised—after a hurt instant*) And me to mind mine?

FILE: I'm sorry, Sheriff. (*A moody moment, then:*) Sheriff . . . I been thinkin' . . . I changed my mind.

SHERIFF: About what?

FILE: That dog you were talkin' about.

SHERIFF: You did, huh?

FILE: Yes. If the offer still holds, I'll take him off your hands.

SHERIFF: (*Embarrassed*) Well, I'll tell you, File—you said you didn't want him. And Little Bobby Easterfield come over . . .

FILE: (*Hiding his disappointment—interrupting*) Oh, I see. . . . Well, that's all right—it don't have to be that particular puppy.

SHERIFF: My wife gave the others away too—this mornin' . . . I'm sorry, File.

FILE: No—forget it.

SHERIFF: What made you change your mind about the dog, File?

FILE: (*Evasively*) Oh, I don't know. . . .

SHERIFF: Didn't have anything to do with the Currys, did it?

FILE: (*With an even greater flare of temper*) Now what the hell would my wantin' a dog have to do with the Currys, for God's sake!

SHERIFF: (*Equally angry*) File, what's the matter with you? What is it? What's the matter with you?

FILE: I don't know . . . Heat, I guess . . . Mind if I take an hour off?

SHERIFF: Take two hours—take three!

FILE: (*Trying to smile*) No—an hour'll do me fine. (*He starts for the door.*)

SHERIFF: If I need you where'll you be?

FILE: (*Evasively*) Oh—'round about. So long, Sheriff . . .

(*File goes out. The Sheriff's eyes follow him with a sober glance. The lights fade.*)

(*The lights come up inside the living room which is momentarily unoccupied. From outdoors we hear the sound of Jim's drum. H.C. comes in through the back door, carrying a whitewash brush and a pail of white paint. His face is daubed with whitewash as are his clothes. Bent nearly double from having been painting the arrow, he absent-mindedly sets the paint pail and the brush down on the floor. Abruptly he realizes that the paint bucket will leave a mark and he snatches up the bucket and sets it outdoors. Re-entering quickly he looks at the floor now marked with paint. He scurries guiltily into the kitchen, grabs a towel and rushes back to clean up the mess. About to apply the spotless towel to the floor he realizes one doesn't get paint on a clean towel. He tosses the towel away, pulls out his shirt tail and kneels, applying the shirt tail to the floor. Noah enters, unheard. Noah has had discourteous treatment by the recalcitrant mule; he is limping. He stops at the sight of his father and watches H.C. Then:*)

NOAH: He said paint the ground, not the floor.
H.C.: (*Startled*) I ain't paintin' the floor—I'm cleanin' it.
 (*He rises and Noah gets a good look at him.*)
NOAH: Your face is all over whitewash.
H.C.: Yep—I reckon it is.
NOAH: So's your shirt.
H.C.: Yep.
NOAH: To look at you, you'd think you never painted nothin' in your life.
H.C.: (*Sheepishly*) I didn't see the bush.
NOAH: What bush?
H.C.: (*Annoyed*) I was paintin' backward in the dark and suddenly there was that damn bush—and I bumped—and the paint slopped all over everything!
 (*Noah crosses the room away from his father. H.C. notices that Noah is limping.*)
H.C.: What you limpin' about?
NOAH: Mule.
H.C.: Kick you? (*As Noah grunts*) Bad?
NOAH: (*Annoyed*) Bad or good, a mule's kick is a mule's kick.
 (*Noah sits at the table, working at his ledgers. Suddenly, from outdoors, louder than ever: Boom—boom—boom! Noah goes to the window and calls cholerically.*)
NOAH: Jimmy, for Pete sake—come in here and quit beatin' that drum!
 (*The drumbeat stops. H.C. smiles.*)
H.C.: I think he enjoys it.
NOAH: Sure. He's got the easiest job of all of us.
H.C.: Well, he's the lieutenant.

(*Jim enters, carrying the biggest bass drum in the world. He just stands there in the doorway, grinning. They stare at him. He beats the drum once, with a flourish, just for the hell of it.*)

NOAH: Jimmy, you quit that!

JIM: He said for me to beat it every time I get the feelin'.

H.C.: (*Tolerantly*) Well, Jimmy, if you can try to resist the feelin' we'll all appreciate it.

JIM: Holy mackerel, Pop, your face is all over whitewash.

H.C.: (*Feigning surprise*) It is, is it?

JIM: Yeah—so's your shirt.

H.C.: Well, whattaya know?

JIM: Whyn't you wash up? You look foolish.

H.C.: You don't look so bright yourself, totin' that drum.

JIM: What am I gonna do with it?

NOAH: (*Exasperated*) For the love of Mike, don't be so dumb!

JIM: (*Hurt and angry*) Don't call me that, Noah!
(*Silence. He sets down the drum.*)

H.C.: I didn't notice—anybody see a cloud?

NOAH: Not a wisp of a one! And don't you expect it!

JIM: I wouldn't be so sure about that, Noah.

NOAH: You wouldn't—I would!

JIM: I think he *is* gonna bring rain! Because I been lookin' in his wagon. Boy, he's got all kinds of wheels and flags and a bugle and firecrackers . . .

NOAH: And all kinds of stuff that a con man would have—but nothin' that's got anything to do with rain!

JIM: You're wrong, Noah. Look at this book.
(*He pulls a small book out of his pocket.*)

H.C.: What's that, Jimmy?

JIM: I found this in his wagon. And I says to him, what's this? And he says: "You can have it—with my compliments!"

NOAH: Well, what is it?

JIM: (*Excitedly*) It's all about the weather! And you know what? I figure it's some kind of magic.
(*Noah groans.*)

H.C.: What's it say?

JIM: Listen! (*Reading with difficulty*) "Icy cirrus in the ascendant over aqueous cumulus. Prognostication fine if cirrus unchanged to rainy altostratus." (*Eagerly*) How's that?

NOAH: That's fine!

JIM: You know what that means?

NOAH: No. Do you?

JIM: I figure you don't have to know what it means—all you have to do is know how to say it!

NOAH: Like abracadabra.

JIM: What?

NOAH: Like . . . Never mind.

JIM: (*Resolutely*) I'm gonna study this book. Because I figure if this fella really knows how to bring rain, he knows it from this book. And after he goes—if *we* got the book—we won't never have to worry about rain no more.

H.C.: That's real foresight, Jimmy.

JIM: I'm sure glad he gave it to me. You know what he did? He wrote in it. (*Reading the flyleaf*) "To Jimmy Curry—who understands this book every bit as good as I do." (*Modestly*) Of course I *don't*—but I think it's real nice of him to write it.

(*Jim takes the cushion off a chest that is by the window. He opens the chest.*)

H.C.: What are you doin' in Lizzie's linen chest?

JIM: He asked me could he spend the night in the tack room and I said yes. So I figured I'd get him some bedding.

NOAH: You're stretchin' yourself to make him cozy, ain't you?

JIM: Why not? I like him!

H.C.: Funny—me too.

NOAH: (*Disgustedly*) Both of you! He's certainly pullin' the wool over *your* eyes!

JIM: I'm out there with the drum—waitin' for the feelin' to come—and he comes over and we had a great talk, the two of us!

NOAH: What'd he try to sell you *this* time?

JIM: (*In fervent defense of Starbuck*) Nothin'! He didn't try to sell me nothin'. He just come over—and I'm lookin' up at the sky—and he says: "What are you thinkin' about, Jim?" Real serious—like he gives a damn. "What are you thinkin' about, Jim?"

H.C.: And what'd you tell him?

JIM: (*Importantly*) I said: "Not much."

H.C.: Well, that's a good start to a conversation.

JIM: And then before I know it, I'm tellin' him everything about myself. I'm tellin' him how I never got good marks in school—I never could figure about the Revolution and the Silva War—but I could tell the goddamndest stories. And I'm tellin' him about Lizzie and about how Noah snores at night. And I even told him about Snookie.

NOAH: Yeah?

JIM: Yeah! I says to him: "What do you think of a girl that wears loud clothes and puts lip rouge on her mouth and always goes around in a little red hat? Is she fast?" And you know what he said? (*Triumphantly*) He said: "Never judge a heifer by the flick of her tail!"

H.C.: (*Suppressing a smile*) Sounds like sensible advice.

JIM: I think so! And then he says: "What do you think of the world?" And I say to him: "It's gonna get all *swole* up and bust right in our faces! And you know what he told me? (*This, to him, is the most wonderful part*) He said: "It's happened before—and it can happen again!"

NOAH: He's crazy!

JIM: No, he ain't! He said there's been stars that that happened to! They just went brrrroom! and blew up in the sky! And if it can happen to them, it can happen to us. Now I never knew that—I just made that up right outta my own head.

NOAH: There! I told you he'd sell you a bill of goods.

JIM: (*Angrily*) Noah, I understand that crack. You mean he was tryin' to make me feel smart—and I ain't.

NOAH: Oh, shut up!

JIM: No, I won't shut up.

NOAH: What the hell's got into you?

JIM: I just thought of somethin', Noah. You know the only time I feel real dumb?

NOAH: When?

JIM: When I'm talkin' to you! Now why the hell *is* that, Noah?
(*Lizzie comes down the stairs.*)

H.C.: Lizzie—I thought you went to bed.

LIZZIE: It's roasting up there.

H.C.: We oughta get one of those electric fans.
(*Starbuck appears at the open door. Lizzie sees him.*)

LIZZIE: It's not only the heat. Jimmy and his drum.
(*The telephone rings. Noah answers it.*)

NOAH: Hello . . . Who? . . . No—he's not here.
(*And summarily, he hangs up.*)

JIM: Who was that?

NOAH: Who else would have all that gall?

JIM: Snookie! Noah, that call was for me!

NOAH: Well?

JIM: (*Angry*) Why'd you hang up on her?

NOAH: Save you the trouble.

JIM: (*Raging to the point of tears*) You didn't even ask me.

NOAH: I didn't think it was necessary.

JIM: If she calls me on the phone, you don't have to tell her I ain't here. I can do it myself.

NOAH: How can you yourself tell her you ain't here? Talk sense!

JIM: Maybe it don't make sense but you damn well know what I mean.

NOAH: (*Incensed*) Listen, Jimmy! If you want to get yourself in hot water— if you want me to wash my hands of you—all you have to do is lift that phone and call her right back.

STARBUCK: (*With studied casualness*) He's right, Jimmy. That's all you have to do.

NOAH: Stay out of this!

STARBUCK: I'm just agreeing with you, Noah. (*To Jim*) You can call her right back.
(*A moment of painful indecision on Jim's part. He looks at Starbuck and at Noah who is standing squarely in front of the telephone.*)

STARBUCK: (*With quiet, urgent encouragement*) Go on, kid.

JIM: I—I don't have her telephone number.

STARBUCK: All you have to do is call the operator. I'm sure there ain't that many phones in Three Point.

JIM: (*Miserably—more plea than anger*) Let me alone, Starbuck!

STARBUCK: Go on!

(*Jim turns away. Starbuck wheels around to H.C.*)

STARBUCK: H.C., a word from you might be a lot of help.

H.C.: (*Quietly*) He'll work it out, Starbuck.

STARBUCK: (*Seeing that H.C. won't interfere, he moves quickly to Lizzie*) Lizzie! Tell Jimmy to make the call!

LIZZIE: (*With difficulty*) Starbuck, we'll all thank you not to interfere in our family.

STARBUCK: (*Squelched*) Sorry . . . Guess I'm a damn fool!

(*Quickly, he turns on his heel and goes out to the tack room. There is a heavy silence in the room. Lizzie notices the bedding.*)

LIZZIE: What are these sheets doing here?

H.C.: (*Indicating Starbuck*) For him. Jimmy was going to take them out to the tack room—if it's all right.

LIZZIE: It's all right. Go on, Jimmy.

JIM: I don't want to now!

(*And deeply upset, ashamed to face Starbuck, ashamed to stay with the others, he hurries upstairs.*)

LIZZIE: (*Quietly*) You shouldn't have done that, Noah.

NOAH: (*Guiltily—unhappily*) Somebody's gotta do it.

LIZZIE: I think you liked doing it.

NOAH: No, I didn't! (*In a hurt outburst*) For Pete sake—somebody take this family off my hands. I don't want to run it.

H.C.: You don't have to run the family, Noah—only the ranch.

NOAH: They're both tied up together. And if you don't like the way I do things . . .

H.C.: (*Interrupting*) That ain't so, Noah! There's some things you do real good!

NOAH: (*In a pained outburst*) Then why don't you give me a little credit once in a while? I'm tryin' to keep this family goin'. I'm tryin' to keep it from breakin' its heart on one foolishness after another. And what do I get for it? Nothin' but black looks and complaints! (*Passionately*) Why?

H.C.: Because you're tryin' to run the family the way you run the ranch.

NOAH: There's no other way.

H.C.: Noah, that's a terrible mistake. When I was your age I had my nose pressed to the grindstone—just like you—and I couldn't see what was goin' on around me. Your mother used to say: "Let up, Harry—stop and catch your breath." Well, after she died I *had* to take her advice—on account of you three kids. And I turned around to enjoy my family. (*Quietly, ur-*

gently) And I found out a good thing, Noah. If you let 'em live—people pay off better than cattle.

NOAH: (*In low anger*) Don't be so proud of the way you let us live, Pop. (*Pointing to Lizzie*) Just look at *her*—and don't be so damn proud of yourself.

H.C.: (*Angry and apprehensive*) What do you mean by that, Noah?

NOAH: Never mind! You think about it!

(*In cold fury, Noah goes out. Long silence. When H.C. speaks to Lizzie he doesn't look at her. There is heavy worry in his voice.*)

H.C.: What does he mean, Lizzie?

LIZZIE: (*Evasively*) I don't know. . . . Don't pay any attention to him, Pop. (*She is itchy, restless. Her mood is mercurial, changing quickly between her yearning to find something new to do with herself—and her need to hide this yearning . . . perhaps by laughing at herself, by laughing at the world, by laughing at nothing at all.*)

LIZZIE: I don't know whether I'm hungry or thirsty. You like something to eat?

H.C.: No, thanks. Noah's hinting that I made some big mistake with you, Lizzie. Did I?

LIZZIE: (*With surface laughter, with bravura*) Of course not. I'm perfect! Everybody knows I'm perfect! A very nice girl—good housekeeper, bright mind, very honest! So damn honest it kills me! How about a sandwich?

H.C.: (*Puzzled by her mood. More definitely than before*) No, thanks.

LIZZIE: "*You gotta get a man like a man gets got!*" That's what Noah said. (*Laughing*) Now isn't that stupid? Why, it's not even good English!

H.C.: (*Soberly*) Don't think about that, Lizzie.

LIZZIE: (*Protesting too much*) Think about it? Why, I wouldn't give it a second thought! (*Abruptly*) Pop, do you know what that Starbuck man said to me?

H.C.: (*Quietly*) What, Lizzie?

LIZZIE: No—why repeat it? A man like that—if you go repeating what people like that have to say. . . ! (*Abruptly*) Why doesn't it rain? What we need is a flood—(*With sudden false gaiety*)—a great big flood—end of the world—ta-ta—goo'-bye! (*Abruptly serious*) Pop, can a woman take lessons in being a woman?

H.C.: You don't have to take lessons. You are one.

LIZZIE: (*Here it is—the outcry*) Starbuck says I'm not!!

(*A split second of surprise on H.C.'s part.*)

H.C.: If Starbuck don't see the woman in you, he's blind.

LIZZIE: Is File blind? *Are they all blind?* (*Then, with deepening pain*) Pop, I'm sick and tired of *me*. I want to get out of *me* for a while—be somebody else.

H.C.: Go down to the Social Club and be Lily Ann Beasley—is that what you want to be?

LIZZIE: Lily Ann Beasley knows how to get along.

H.C.: Then you better call her on the telephone—ask her to let you join up.

LIZZIE: (*Defiantly*) I will! You see if I don't! And I'm going to buy myself a lot of new dresses—cut way down to here! And I'll get myself some bright lip rouge—and paint my mouth so it looks like I'm always whistling!

H.C.: Fine! Go ahead! Look like a silly little jackass!

LIZZIE: It won't be *me* looking silly—it'll be somebody else. You've got to hide what you are. You can't be honest.

H.C.: (*Angrily*) You wouldn't know how to be anything else.

LIZZIE: Oh, wouldn't I? Wouldn't I? You think it's hard? It's easy! Watch me—it's easy—look at this!

(*She crosses the room, swinging her hips voluptuously. When she speaks it is with a silly, giggling voice—imitating Lily Ann.*)

LIZZIE: (*To an imaginary man*) Why, hello, Gil Demby—how goodie-good-lookin' you are! Such curly blond hair, such pearly white teeth! C'n I count your teeth? One—two—three—four—nah-nah, mustn't bite! And all those muscle-ie muscles! Ooh, just hard as stone, that's what they are, hard as stone! Oh, dear, don't tickle—don't tickle—or little Lizzie's gonna roll right over and dee-I-die!

(*She is giggling uproariously. As she continues this makeshow, she carries herself into convulsions of laughter. And H.C., seeing that she has unintentionally satirized the very thing she proposes to emulate, joins her laughter. While this has been going on, they haven't noticed that File has appeared in the open doorway—and has witnessed most of Lizzie's improvisation.*)

FILE: Good evening.

(*The laughter in the room stops. Lizzie stands stock still in mortification.*)

H.C.: Hello, File. Come in.

FILE: Kinda late. I hope I'm not disturbin' you.

H.C.: No—no! We were just—well, I don't know *what* we were doin'—but come on in!

FILE: (*Entering. Quietly*) Hello, Lizzie.

LIZZIE: Hello, File.

FILE: No—uh—no let-up in the drought, is there?

LIZZIE: Nope. None—at all.

FILE: (*Uncomfortably—to H.C.*) H.C., I got to thinkin' about the little fuss I had with Jimmy and—about his eye and—well—I wanted to apologize. I'm sorry.

H.C.: (*With a hidden smile*) You said that this afternoon, File.

FILE: But I didn't say it to Jim.

H.C.: That's true—you didn't. (*With a quick look at Lizzie*) He's upstairs—I'll send him down.

(*And quickly H.C. starts up the stairs. But Lizzie, seeing it is her father's plan to leave her alone with File, takes a quick step toward the stairs and, all innocence, calls up to Jim.*)

LIZZIE: Oh, Jim—Jimmy—can you come down for a minute?

H.C.: (*With studied casualness*) That's all right, Lizzie—I was goin' up anyway.

(*And giving her no choice, he disappears from sight. Lizzie and File are both aware of H.C.'s maneuver. They are both painfully embarrassed, unable to meet one another's glance.*)

LIZZIE: (*Just to fill the silence*) Would you—do you care for a cup of coffee?

FILE: No, thank you—I already had my supper.

LIZZIE: (*Embarrassed at the mention of "supper"*) Yes—yes, of course.

FILE: I didn't mean to mention supper . . . sorry I said it.

LIZZIE: Lemonade?

FILE: No, thank you.

LIZZIE: (*In agony—talking compulsively*) I make lemonade with limes. I guess if you make it with limes you can't really call it *lemon*-ade, can you?

FILE: (*Generously—to put her at ease*) You can if you want to. No law against it.

LIZZIE: But it's really *lime*-ade, isn't it?

FILE: Yep—that's what it is. Limeade.

LIZZIE: (*Taking his mannish tone*) That's what it is, all right!

(*An impasse—nothing more to talk about. At last Jim appears. He comes down the steps quickly—and he is all grins that File is visiting.*)

JIM: You call me, Lizzie? . . . Hey, File.

FILE: Hello, Jim . . . My, that's a bad eye. I came around to say I'm sorry.

JIM: (*Delighted to have File here, he is all forgiveness. Expansively:*) Oh, don't think nothin' of it, File! Bygones is bygones!

FILE: Glad to hear you talk that way.

JIM: Sure—sure.

(*An awkward silence. Jim's grin fills the whole room. He looks from one to the other, not knowing what to say, not knowing how to get out.*)

JIM: (*Abruptly*) Well—well! File's here, huh? (*Silence. On a burst of enthusiasm*) Yessir—he certain'y is!

(*And, in sheer happy animal spirits, he gives one loud whack at the drum—and races outdoors. He leaves a vacuum behind him.*)

FILE: Was that Jim's drum I been hearin'?

LIZZIE: Yes.

FILE: (*With a dry smile*) Didn't know he was musical.

LIZZIE: (*Smiling at his tiny little joke*) Uh—wouldn't you like to sit down—or something?

FILE: No, thank you . . . (*Referring to the absent Jim and H.C.*) I guess they both knew I was lyin'.

LIZZIE: Lying? About what?

FILE: I didn't come around to apologize to Jim.

LIZZIE: What did you come for, File?

FILE: To get something off my chest. (*His difficulties increasing*) This afternoon—your father—he—uh—(*Diving in*) Well, there's a wrong impression goin' on in the town—that I'm a widower. Well, I'm not.

LIZZIE: (*Quietly—trying to ease things for him*) I know that, File.

FILE: I know you know it—but I gotta say it. (*Blurting it out*) I'm a divorced man.

LIZZIE: You don't have to talk about it if you don't . . .

FILE: (*Interrupting roughly*) Yes, I do! I came to tell the truth. To your father—and to the whole town. I've been denyin' that I'm a divorced man—well, now I admit it. That's all I want to say—(*Angrily*)—and that squares me with everybody.

LIZZIE: (*Soberly*) Does it?

FILE: Yes, it does! And from here on in—if I want to live alone—all by myself—it's nobody's business but my own!

(*He has said what he thinks he came to say. And having said it, he turns on his heel and starts to beat a hasty retreat. But Lizzie stops him:*)

LIZZIE: (*Sharply*) Wait a minute! (*As he turns*) You're dead wrong!

FILE: Wrong? How?

LIZZIE: (*Hotly*) It's everybody's business!

FILE: How do you figure that, Lizzie?

LIZZIE: Because you owe something to people.

FILE: I don't owe anything to anybody.

LIZZIE: Yes, you do!

FILE: What?

LIZZIE: (*Inarticulate—upset*) I don't know—friendship. If somebody holds out his hand toward you, you've got to reach—and take it.

FILE: What do you mean I've got to?

LIZZIE: (*In an outburst*) Got to! There are too many people alone . . .! And if you're lucky enough for somebody to want you—for a friend—(*With a cry*) It's an *obligation*!

(*Stillness. He is deeply disturbed by what she has said; even more disturbed by her impassioned manner.*)

FILE: This . . . this ain't somethin' the two of us can settle by just talkin' for a minute.

LIZZIE: (*Tremulously*) No, it isn't.

FILE: It'll take some time.

LIZZIE: Yes.

(*A spell has been woven between them. Suddenly it is broken by Noah's entrance. Coming in by way of the front door, he is surprised to see File.*)

NOAH: Oh, you here, File?

FILE: Yeah, I guess I'm here.

NOAH: (*Looking for an excuse to leave*) Uh—just comin' in for my feed book.

(*He gets one of his ledgers and goes out the front door. It looks as though the charmed moment is lost between them.*)

FILE: (*Going to the door*) Well . . .

LIZZIE: (*Afraid he will leave*) What were we saying?

FILE: What were *you* sayin'?

LIZZIE: (*Snatching for a subject that will keep him here*) I—you were telling me about your divorce.

FILE: No—I wasn't . . . (*Then, studying her, he changes his mind*) . . . but I will. (*As he moves a step back into the room*) She walked out on me.

LIZZIE: I'm sorry.

FILE: Yes—with a schoolteacher. He was from Louisville.

LIZZIE: (*Helping him get it said*) Kentucky? (*As he nods*) Was she—I guess she was beautiful . . . ?

FILE: Yes, she was.

LIZZIE: (*Her hopes dashed*) That's what I was afr—(*Catching herself*)—that's what I thought.

FILE: Black hair.

LIZZIE: (*Drearily, with an abortive little movement to her un-black hair*) Yes . . . black hair's pretty, all right.

FILE: I always used to think: If a woman's got pitch-black hair, she's already halfway to bein' a beauty.

LIZZIE: (*Agreeing—but without heart*) Oh, yes—at least halfway.

FILE: And she had black eyes too—and I guess that did the other half. (*Suddenly, intensely—like a dam bursting*) With a schoolteacher, dammit! Ran off with a schoolteacher!

LIZZIE: What was *he* like?

FILE: (*With angry intensity*) He had weak hands and nearsighted eyes! And he always looked like he was about ready to faint. And she ran off with *him*! And there *I* was . . . (*A cry of pain and rage*) I'll never understand it!

LIZZIE: (*Gently*) Maybe the teacher needed her and you didn't.

FILE: Sure I needed her!

LIZZIE: Did you tell her so?

FILE: (*Raging*) No, I didn't! Why should I?

LIZZIE: (*Astounded*) Why *should* you? Why *didn't* you?

FILE: Look here! There's one thing I learned. *Be independent!* If you don't *ask* for things—if you don't let on you *need* things—pretty soon you *don't* need 'em.

LIZZIE: (*Desperately*) There are some things you *always* need.

FILE: (*Doggedly*) I won't ask for anything.

LIZZIE: But if you *had* asked her, she might have stayed.

FILE: I know darn well she mighta stayed. The night she left she said to me: "File, tell me not to go! Tell me don't go!"

LIZZIE: (*In wild astonishment*) And you didn't?

FILE: I tried—I couldn't!

LIZZIE: Oh, pride . . . !

FILE: Look, if a woman wants to go, let her go! If you have to hold her back—*it's no good*!

LIZZIE: File, if you had to do it over again . . .

FILE: (*Interrupting, intensely*) I still wouldn't ask her to stay!

LIZZIE: (*In a rage against him*) Just two words—"don't go!"—you wouldn't say them?

FILE: It's not the words! It's beggin'—and I won't beg!

LIZZIE: You're a fool!

(*It's a slap in the face. A dreadful moment for an overly proud, stubborn man. A dreadful moment for Lizzie. It is a time for drastic measures—or he will go. Having failed with File on an honest, serious level, she seizes upon flighty falsity as a mode of behavior. Precipitously, she becomes Lily Ann Beasley, the flibbertigibbet.*)

LIZZIE: (*Chattering with false, desperate laughter*) Whatever am I doing? Getting so serious with you, File! I shoulda known better—because whenever I do, I put my foot in it. Because bein' serious—that's not my nature. I'm really a happy-go-lucky girl—just like any other girl and I—would you like some grapes?

FILE: (*Quietly*) No, thank you.

LIZZIE: (*Giddily*) They're very good. And so purply and pretty. We had some right after supper. Oh, I wish you'd been here to supper. I made such a nice supper. I'm a good cook—and I just love cookin'. I think there's only one thing I like better than cookin'. I'll bet you can't guess what that is! (*As he is silent*) Go on—guess!

FILE: (*Puzzled at her changed manner*) I don't know.

LIZZIE: Readin' a book! I love to read! Do you read very much?

FILE: (*Watching her as if she were a strange specimen*) No. Only legal circulars—from Washington.

LIZZIE: (*Seizing on any straw to engage him in the nonsensical chit-chat*) Oh, Washington! I just got through readin' a book about him! What a great man! Don't you think Washington was a great man?

FILE: (*Drily*) Father of our country.

LIZZIE: Yes—exactly! And when you think of all he went through! All that sufferin'! Valley Forge—and all those bleedin' feet! When you *think* of it!

FILE: I don't think about it much.

LIZZIE: And why should you? A busy man like you! (*More Lily Ann Beasley than ever*) Oh, my, what a nice tie! I just die for men in black silk bow ties!

FILE: (*Quietly—getting angry*) It ain't silk—it's celluloid!

LIZZIE: No! I can't believe it! It looks so real—it looks so real!

FILE: (*Significantly—like a blow*) It ain't real—it's fake!

LIZZIE: (*Unable to stop herself*) And when you smile you've got the strongest white teeth!

FILE: (*Angrily*) Quit that!

LIZZIE: (*Stunned*) What . . .?

FILE: (*Raging*) Quit it! Stop sashayin' around like a dumb little flirt!

LIZZIE: (*With a moan*) Oh, no . . .

FILE: Silk tie—strong white teeth! What do you take me for? And what do you take yourself for?

LIZZIE: (*In flight, in despair*) I was trying to—trying to . . .

FILE: Don't be so damn ridiculous! Be yourself!

(*Saying which, he leaves quickly. Alone, Lizzie is at her wits' end—humiliated, ready to take flight from everything, mostly from herself. H.C. enters.*)

H.C.: What happened, Lizzie?

(*Jim rushes in.*)

JIM: What'd he do—run out on you? What happened?

(*Noah comes hurrying in from outdoors.*)

NOAH: I never seen a man run so fast! Where'd he go?

LIZZIE: (*Berserk—to all of them*) My God, were you watching a show? Did you think it was lantern slides?

H.C.: I'm sorry, Lizzie—we couldn't help bein' interested.

JIM: What'd he say?

NOAH: What'd *you say?*

LIZZIE: I didn't say anything! Not one sensible thing. I couldn't even talk to him!

H.C.: But you were talkin'!

LIZZIE: No! I was sashaying around like Lily Ann Beasley! I was making a fool of myself! Why can't I ever *talk* to anybody?

H.C.: Lizzie, don't blame yourself! If *you* couldn't talk to *him*—I'm sure File couldn't talk to you either. It wasn't only your fault.

NOAH: (*Savagely*) No! It wasn't her fault—and it wasn't File's fault (*Squaring off at his father*) And you know damn well whose fault it was!

H.C.: You mean it was mine, Noah?

NOAH: You bet it was yours!

LIZZIE: (*Seeing a fight—trying to head it off*) Noah—Pop . . .

H.C.: No! He's got to explain that!

(*At this point Starbuck appears at the doorway. He leans against the door frame, silent, listening.*)

NOAH: (*Accepting H.C.'s challenge*) I'll explain it, all right. You been building up a rosy dream for her—and she's got no right to hope for it.

H.C.: She's got a right to hope for anything.

NOAH: No! She's gotta face the facts—and you gotta help her face them! Stop tellin' her lies!

H.C.: I never told her a lie in my life!

NOAH: You told her nothin' *but* lies. When she was a kid with eyeglasses you told her she's the smartest girl in the world. When she started growin' up you told her she was beautiful. And that's the worst lie of all. Because you know—deep down in your heart—you know—she's not beautiful. *She's plain!*

JIM: Noah, you quit that!

NOAH: (*Whirling on Jim*) And you go right along with him. Every time Lizzie admits she's plain you tell her she's a ravin' beauty. (*Whipping around to Lizzie*) But you better listen to me! I'm the only one around here that loves you enough to tell you the truth! You're plain!

JIM: (*Violently*) Goddamn it, Noah—you quit it!

NOAH: (*Brutally—to Lizzie*) Go look at yourself in the mirror—you're plain!

JIM: Noah!

(*Saying which, Jim hurls himself at his brother. But the instant he gets to him, Noah strikes out with a tough fist. It catches Jim hard and he goes reeling. He returns with murder in his eye but Noah slaps him across the face, grabs the boy and forces him back toward the table. Meanwhile, a frenetic outburst from H.C. and Lizzie:*)

H.C. AND LIZZIE: Noah—Jim—stop it! Stop it, both of you—stop it!

(*Simultaneously, Starbuck rushes forward and breaks the two men apart. Out of Noah's grip, Jim goes berserk, bent on killing Noah. But Starbuck holds him off.*)

JIM: (*Through tears and rage*) Let me go, Starbuck—let me go!

STARBUCK: Quit it, you damn fool—quit it!

JIM: (*With a cry*) Let go!

STARBUCK: Get outside! (*Letting him go*) Now go on—get outside!

JIM: (*Weeping*) Sure—I'll get outside! I'll get outside and never come back!

(*And in an outburst of tears, he rushes outdoors.*)

NOAH: The next time that kid goes at me, I'll—I'll . . .

STARBUCK: The next time he goes at you, I'll see he has fightin' lessons!

NOAH: Look, you—clear out of here!

STARBUCK: No, I won't clear out! And while I'm here, you're gonna quit callin' that kid a dumbbell—because he's not. He can take a lousy little bulletin that comes from the weather bureau—and he can see magic in it. He can hear thunder in a drum—and you wouldn't understand that—because it's not in your books!

NOAH: I said clear out!

STARBUCK: (*He cannot be stopped*) And while I'm here, don't you ever call her plain. Because you don't know what's plain and what's beautiful. You don't know what beautiful is.

NOAH: Starbuck, this is family—it's not your fight!

STARBUCK: Yes, it is! I been fightin' fellas like you all my life. And I always lose. But this time—by God, this time . . .!

(*He reins himself in, then hurries outdoors. We hear his voice calling "Jim!—Jim!" A long silence. Noah breaks the stillness with quiet deliberateness:*)

NOAH: (*To Lizzie and H.C.*) I'm sorry I hit Jim—and I'll tell him so. But I ain't sorry for a single word I said to her.

H.C.: (*Angry*) Noah, that's enough!

NOAH: (*Intensely*) No, it ain't enough! (*To Lizzie*) Lizzie, you better think about what I said. Nobody's gonna come ridin' up here on a white horse. Nobody's gonna snatch you up in his arms and marry you. *You're gonna be an old maid*! And the sooner you face it, the sooner you'll stop breakin' your heart.

(*He goes upstairs. Silence.*)

LIZZIE: (*Dully—half to herself*) Old maid . . .

H.C.: Lizzie, forget it. Forget everything he said.

LIZZIE: No . . . he's right.

H.C.: (*With a plea*) Lizzie . . .

LIZZIE: He's right, Pop. I've known it a long time. But it wasn't so bad until he put a name to it. Old maid. (*With a cry of despair*) Why is it so much worse when you put a name to it?

H.C.: Lizzie, you gotta believe me . . .

LIZZIE: I don't believe you, Pop. You've been lying to me—and I've been lying to myself!

H.C.: Lizzie, honey—please . . .

LIZZIE: Don't—don't! I've got to see things the way they are. And the way they will be. I've got to start thinking of myself as a spinster. Jim will get married. And one of these days, even Noah will get married. I'll be the visiting aunt. I'll bring presents to their children—to be sure I'm welcome. And Noah will say: "Junior, be kind to your Aunt Lizzie—her nerves aren't so good." And Jim's wife will say: "She's been visiting here a whole week now—when'll she ever go?" (*With an outcry*) Go where, for God's sake— go where?

H.C.: (*In pain for her*) Lizzie, you'll always have a home. This house'll be yours.

LIZZIE: (*Hysterically*) House—house—house!

H.C.: (*Trying to calm, to comfort her*) Lizzie, stop it!

LIZZIE: (*Inconsolable*) My skin's hot all over. When I touch it, it's cold.

H.C.: Lizzie . . .

LIZZIE: I'm all tied up! My clothes are tyin' me up! I can't move in my clothes!

H.C.: Lizzie . . .

LIZZIE: Help me, Pop—tell me what to do! Help me!

H.C.: Lizzie—Lizzie . . .!

(*Abruptly, without thinking—in a frantic movement—she snatches up the bed linens off the linen trunk—and races outdoors. The lights fade.*)

(*Brightest moonlight—moonlight alone—illuminates the inside of the tack room. It is a rough, picturesque room—a junk room really—at the rear of the house. A slanting ceiling with huge hand-hewn beams; large casement windows which give such a vast expanse of bluest night sky that we feel we are more outdoors than in; a wagon wheel against a wall; leather goods—saddles, horse traces and the like; a wagon seat made into a bench, with faded homemade pillows to fit it; an old castaway cot against the wall. It is a room altogether accidental, yet altogether romantic. . . . Starbuck is preparing to go to bed. He takes off his boots and his neckerchief, then he stands in the center of the room, not moving, thinking intently. He hurries to the door, closes it and barricades it with the wagonseat bench. He moves to the windows and tries to open them but they are nailed shut.*)

It's stifling in here. He takes his shirt off and sits on the edge of the cot, suffering the heat. He waves his shirt around to make a breeze. Then he decides to forgo caution—and removes the barricade, opening the door. He lies down on the cot. The stillness is a palpable thing, and the heat. As he relaxes, as he slips back into his solitude, a lonely little humming comes from him. It grows in volume and occasionally we hear the words of the song. Suddenly he hears a sound and sits bolt upright.)

STARBUCK: Who's that? (*He rises tautly*) Who's there?

(*Lizzie stands in the doorway, trying not to look into the room. She is carrying the bed linens. She knocks on the door frame.*)

LIZZIE: (*Trying to sound calm*) It's me—Lizzie.

(*Starbuck starts to put on his shirt. An awkward moment. Then Lizzie, without entering the room, hands the bedding across the threshold.*)

LIZZIE: Here.

STARBUCK: What's that?

LIZZIE: Bed linens—take them.

STARBUCK: Is that what you came out for?

LIZZIE: (*After a painful moment*) No . . . I came out because . . .

(*She finds it too difficult to continue.*)

STARBUCK: (*Gently*) Go on, Lizzie.

LIZZIE: I came out to thank you for what you said to Noah.

STARBUCK: I meant every word of it.

LIZZIE: What you said about Jim—I'm sure you meant that.

STARBUCK: What I said about you.

LIZZIE: I don't believe you.

STARBUCK: Then what are you thankin' me for? What's the matter, Lizzie? You afraid that if you stop bein' sore at me you'll like me a little?

LIZZIE: No . . .   (*And she starts to go.*)

STARBUCK: (*Stopping her*) Then stay and talk to me! (*As she hesitates*) It's lonely out here and I don't think I'll sleep much—not in a strange place.

LIZZIE: Then I guess you never sleep. Running from one strange place to another.

STARBUCK: (*With a smile*) Not runnin'—travelin'.

LIZZIE: Well, if that's the kind of life you like . . .

STARBUCK: Oh, it's not what a man likes—it's what he's got to do. Now what would a fella in my business be doin' stayin' in the same place? Rain's nice—but it ain't nice all the time.

LIZZIE: (*Relaxing a bit*) No, I guess not.

STARBUCK: People got no use for me—except maybe once in a lifetime. And when my work's done, they're glad to see me go.

LIZZIE: (*Caught by the loneliness in his voice*), I never thought of it that way.

STARBUCK: Why would you? You never thought of me as a real rainmaker—not until just now.

LIZZIE: I still don't think it!

(*Now she starts to go more determinedly than before. Starbuck stops her physically this time.*)

STARBUCK: Lizzie—wait! Why don't you let yourself think of me the way you *want* to?

LIZZIE: (*Unnerved*) What do you mean?

STARBUCK: Think like Lizzie, not like Noah.

LIZZIE: I don't know what you're talking about.

STARBUCK: What are you scared of?

LIZZIE: You! I don't trust you!

STARBUCK: Why? What don't you trust about me?

LIZZIE: Everything! The way you talk, the way you brag—why, even your name.

STARBUCK: What's wrong with my name?

LIZZIE: It sounds fake! It sounds like you made it up!

STARBUCK: You're darn right! I did make it up.

LIZZIE: There! Of course!

STARBUCK: Why not? You know what name I was born with? Smith! Smith, for the love of Mike, *Smith*! Now what kind of a handle is that for a fella like me? I needed a name that had the whole sky in it! And the power of a man! Star-buck! Now there's a name—and it's mine.

LIZZIE: No, it's not. You were born Smith—and that's your name.

STARBUCK: You're wrong, Lizzie. The name you choose for yourself is more your own than the name you were born with. And if I was you I'd sure choose another name than Lizzie.

LIZZIE: Thank you—I'm very pleased with it.

STARBUCK: Oh, no you ain't. You ain't pleased with anything about yourself. And I'm sure you ain't pleased with "Lizzie."

LIZZIE: I don't ask *you* to be pleased with it, Starbuck. I am.

STARBUCK: Lizzie? Why, it don't *stand* for anything.

LIZZIE: It stands for me! *Me*! I'm not the Queen of Sheba—I'm not Lady Godiva—I'm not Cinderella at the Ball.

STARBUCK: Would you like to be?

LIZZIE: Starbuck, you're ridiculous!

STARBUCK: What's ridiculous about it? Dream you're somebody—*be* somebody! But Lizzie? That's nobody! So many millions of wonderful women with wonderful names! (*In an orgy of delight*) Leonora, Desdemona, Carolina, Pauline! Annabella, Florinda, Natasha, Diane! (*Then, with a pathetic little lift of his shoulders*) Lizzie.

LIZZIE: Good night, Starbuck!

STARBUCK: (*With a sudden inspiration*) Just a minute, Lizzie—just one little half of a minute. I got the greatest name for you—the greatest name— just listen. (*Then, like a love lyric*) Melisande.

LIZZIE: (*Flatly*) I don't like it.

STARBUCK: That's because you don't know anything about her. But when I tell you who she was—lady, when I tell you who she was!

LIZZIE: Who?

STARBUCK: (*Improvising*) She was the most beautiful . . .! She was the beautiful wife of King Hamlet! Ever hear of him?

LIZZIE: (*Giving him rope*) Go on! Go on!

STARBUCK: He was the fella who sailed across the ocean and brought back the Golden Fleece! And you know why he did that? Because Melisande begged him for it! I tell you, that Melisande—she was so beautiful and her hair was so long and curly—every time he looked at her he just fell right down and died. And this King Hamlet, he'd do anything for her—anything she wanted. So when she said: "Hamlet, I got a terrible hankerin' for a soft Golden Fleece," he just naturally sailed right off to find it. And when he came back—all bleedin' and torn—he went and laid that Fleece of Gold right down at her pretty white feet. And she took that fur piece and she wrapped it around her pink naked shoulders and she said: "I got the Golden Fleece—and I'll never be cold no more." . . . Melisande! What a woman! What a *name*!

LIZZIE: (*Quietly*) Starbuck, you silly jackass. You take a lot of stories—that I've read in a hundred different places—and you roll them up into one big fat ridiculous lie!

STARBUCK: (*Angry, hurt*) I wasn't lyin'—I was dreamin'!

LIZZIE: It's the same thing!

STARBUCK: (*With growing anger*) If you think it's the same thing then I take it back about your name! Lizzie—it's just right for you. I'll tell you another name that would suit you—Noah! Because you and your brother—you've got no dream.

LIZZIE: (*With an outcry*) You think all dreams have to be your kind! Golden Fleece and thunder on the mountain! But there are other dreams, Starbuck! Little quiet ones that come to a woman when she's shining the silverware and putting moth flakes in the closet.

STARBUCK: Like what?

LIZZIE: (*Crying*) Like a man's voice saying: "Lizzie, is my blue suit pressed?" And the same man saying: "Scratch between my shoulder blades." And kids laughing and teasing and setting up a racket. And how it feels to say the word "Husband!" . . . There are all kinds of dreams, Mr. Starbuck. Mine are small ones—like my name—Lizzie. But they're *real* like my name—real! So you can have yours—and I'll have mine!

(*Unable to control her tears, she starts to run away. This time he grabs her fully, holding her close.*)

STARBUCK: Lizzie . . .

LIZZIE: Please . . .

STARBUCK: I'm sorry, Lizzie! I'm sorry!

LIZZIE: It's all right—let me go!

STARBUCK: I hope your dreams come true, Lizzie—I hope they do!

LIZZIE: They won't—they never will!

STARBUCK: Believe in yourself and they will!

LIZZIE: I've got nothing to believe in.

STARBUCK: You're a woman! Believe in that!

LIZZIE: How can I when nobody else will?

STARBUCK: *You* gotta believe it first! (*Quickly*) Let me ask you, Lizzie—are you pretty?

LIZZIE: (*With a wail*) No—I'm plain!

STARBUCK: There! You see? You don't know you're a woman!

LIZZIE: I am a woman! A plain one!

STARBUCK: There's no such thing as a plain woman! Every real woman is pretty! They're all pretty in a different way—but they're all pretty!

LIZZIE: Not me! When I look in the looking glass . . .

STARBUCK: Don't let Noah be your lookin' glass!

LIZZIE: He's not. My looking glass is right on the wall.

STARBUCK: It's in the wrong place. It's gotta be inside you.

LIZZIE: No . . .

STARBUCK: Don't be afraid—*look*! You'll see a pretty woman, Lizzie. Lizzie, you gotta be your own lookin' glass. And then one day the lookin' glass will be the man who loves you. It'll be his eyes, maybe. And you'll look in that mirror and you'll be more than pretty—you'll be beautiful!

LIZZIE: (*Crying out*) It'll never happen!

STARBUCK: Make it happen! Lizzie, why don't you think "pretty" and take down your hair?

(*He reaches for her hair.*)

LIZZIE: (*In panic*) No!

STARBUCK: Please, Lizzie!

(*He is taking the pins out of her hair.*)

LIZZIE: No—no . . .

STARBUCK: Nobody sees you, Lizzie—nobody but me! (*Taking her in his arms*) Now close your eyes, Lizzie—close them! (*As she obeys*) Now—say: "I'm pretty!"

LIZZIE: (*Trying*) I'm—I'm—I can't!

STARBUCK: Say it! Say it, Lizzie!

LIZZIE: I'm . . . pretty.

STARBUCK: Say it again!

LIZZIE: (*With a little cry*) Pretty!

STARBUCK: Say it—mean it!

LIZZIE: (*Exalted*) I'm pretty! I'm pretty! I'm pretty!

(*He kisses her. A long kiss and she clings to him, passionately, the bonds of her spinsterhood breaking away. The kiss over, she collapses on the cot, sobbing.*)

LIZZIE: (*Through the sobs*) Why did you do that?

STARBUCK: (*Going beside her on the cot*) Because when you said you were pretty, it was true!

(*Her sobs are louder, more heartrending because, for the first time, she is happy.*)

STARBUCK: Lizzie—look at me!

LIZZIE: I can't!

STARBUCK: (*Turning her to him*) Stop cryin' and look at me! Look at my eyes! What do you see?

LIZZIE: (*Gazing through her tears*) I can't *believe* what I see!

STARBUCK: Tell me what you see!

LIZZIE: (*With a sob of happiness*) Oh, is it me? Is it really me? (*Now she goes to him with all her giving.*)

END OF ACT TWO

Act Three

THE LIGHTS COME UP inside the house to reveal H.C. at the telephone.

H.C.: *(Into phone)* Thank you, Howard—I'm sorry I woke you up. . . . Well, if you hear from Jimmy, you call me right away, will you? No, nothin's wrong. . . . Thank you.

(He hangs up and paces worriedly. Noah comes down the stairs wearing his bathrobe. He has been unable to sleep a wink.)

NOAH: *(Grumpily)* Jimmy get home yet?

H.C.: Nope.

NOAH: That dopey kid. It's near two o'clock.

H.C.: Go back to sleep, Noah. Don't worry about him.

NOAH: I ain't worryin' about him. I don't give a damn what happens to him.

H.C.: Okay—fine.

NOAH: Maybe he's at the Hopkinsons. . . . I'll call them.

H.C.: I called them all. Nobody seen him.

NOAH: If you'da seen my side of this, it wouldn't of happened.

H.C.: I see your side, Noah—I just ain't on your side.

NOAH: *(Angrily)* Nobody is!

H.C.: Cheer up, Noah. For a fella who's got nobody on his side you sure have twisted those kids around your little finger. If you tell Jim he's a puppy dog, he starts to bark. If you call Lizzie a monkey, she scratches.

(At this instant, Jim stands in the doorway. He looks very cocky, very self-satisfied, ten feet taller than before. He is smoking an enormous cigar with an air of aloof grandeur. He struts majestically into the room.)

JIM: Good e-ve-ning!

NOAH: Where the hell you been?

JIM: *(With a lordly gesture)* Out—out—out!

NOAH: What's wrong with you? Are you drunk?

JIM: *(With an air of superiority)* No, Big Brother, I ain't drunk. But if I cared to be drunk, I'd be google-eyed!

H.C.: *(Secretly amused)* Where'd you get the stogie, Jim?

JIM: It ain't a stogie. It's a Havana Panatela. Eighty-fi' cents. And it's a present.

NOAH: Who the hell gave it to you?

JIM: I-the-hell gave it to me! For bein' a big boy. Write it on the books, Noah. In big red numbers.

NOAH: You didn't tell us where you been.

JIM: I don't have to—but I will. I been out with my favorite girl—*(He takes a little red hat out of his pocket, unfolds it and slaps it on his head)—Snookie!*

NOAH: You crazy, dumb little . . .

JIM: *(Warningly—with an even smile)* Uh-uh-uh-uh! Don't say dumb no more, Noah. Or I shall take this eighty-fi' cent Havana Panatela and I shall squash it right in your mean old face.

H.C.: What happened, Jimmy?

NOAH: Can't you see what happened? He went ridin' with Snookie Maguire and she got him all hot up and then, by God, she trapped him. And she gave him her little red hat for a consolation prize.

JIM: Big Brother, you got it all wrong.

NOAH: Don't lie to me, Jimmy Curry! The minute I stopped lookin' after you, you got yourself in trouble.

JIM: Noah, when I tell you what *really* happened, you're gonna split your britches! We went ridin'—yep, that's right. We opened that Essex up and we went forty million miles an hour. And then we stopped that car and we got out and we sat down under a great big tree. And we could look through the branches and see the sky all full of stars—*damn*, it was full of stars. And I turned around and I kissed her. I kissed her once, I kissed her a hundred times, I kissed her *real!* And while I was doin' that, I knew I could carry her anywhere—right straight to the moon. But all the time, I kept thinkin': "Noah's gonna come along and he's gonna say 'Whoa!' He's gonna say: 'Jim, you're dumb! You're so dumb you ain't got sense enough to say whoa to yourself—so I'm sayin' it for you—Whoa!' " But Noah didn't show up—and I kept right on kissin'. And then somethin' happened. *She* was cryin' and I was cryin' and I thought any minute now we'll be right up there on the moon. And then—then!—without Noah bein' there—all by my smart little self—*I said whoa!*

H.C.: Yippeeeeee!

JIM: *(Formally)* Thank you, Pop—your yippee is accepted.

NOAH: I don't believe a word of it. Why'd she give you the hat?

JIM: For the same reason I give her my elk's tooth! We're engaged!

NOAH: So I was right. She did trap you.

JIM: *(Warningly)* Noah, I see I'm gonna have to give you this Havana Panatela.

H.C.: Don't listen to him, Jimmy. Congratulations.

JIM: *(Touched)* Thanks, Pop—thank you very kindly. *(Suddenly elated)* I gotta tell Lizzie! Where's Lizzie?

NOAH: Where the Sam Hill do you think she is? She's asleep.

JIM: *(Hurrying to the stairs)* Well, then, I'll wake her up!

H.C.: Wait, Jimmy . . . Lizzie's not up there.

JIM: Where is she?

(A moment.)

NOAH: Where is she, Pop?

H.C.: She's out in the tack room.

NOAH: You mean with Starbuck?

H.C.: Yes.

JIM: Man, that's great! *(Pulling another cigar out of his pocket)* I got another cigar for Lizzie.

NOAH: *(Quietly to H.C.)* Wait a minute. You mean you let her walk in on that fella when he's sleepin'?

H.C.: I don't think she just walked in on him, Noah. I'm sure she knocked on the door first.

JIM: Sure—Lizzie's real polite.

NOAH: Pop! You didn't even try to stop her?

H.C.: No, I didn't! You called her an old maid. You took away the last little bit of hope she ever had. And when you left, she lifted up those bed linens and ran out. I didn't ask her where she was goin'—but I'm glad she went. Because if she lost her hope in here—maybe she'll find it out there.

NOAH: That was in your mind the minute you laid eyes on that fella.

H.C.: If it was in my mind, I didn't know it.

NOAH: That's why you let him stay.

JIM: We let him stay because he's a rainmaker.

NOAH: It's got nothin' to do with him bein' a rainmaker! *(To H.C.)* You knew he was a fake the minute he opened his mouth. But you gave him a hundred bucks—you let him order us around—you gave him the run of the whole ranch. Why? Was it for rain? No! It was for Lizzie!

H.C.: You put it awful cut and dried, Noah.

NOAH: It's the truth! *(Deeply affected)* And I don't see how you could do that, Pop!

H.C.: Noah, you got a sound in your voice makes me feel I oughta be ashamed. Well, I'm not.

NOAH: If you're not ashamed of sellin' your daughter short, then you lost your self-respect.

JIM: What the hell is self-respect anyway?

NOAH: You shut up!

JIM: I'll never shut up no more! I think it's great them bein' out there together. They might get real serious about each other. And before you know it, I got me a new brother. Boy, I'd swap him for you any day!

NOAH: You won't have to swap him for anybody. Because he ain't the marryin' kind—not that faker.

JIM: I bet he is the marryin' kind—I bet he is! Hey, Pop, what do you figure a rainmaker makes?

NOAH: *(Exploding)* Rain!

JIM: No—I mean money! I guess there ain't no scale of wages to go by. A hundred here—a hundred there. Pop, you reckon a fella can support a wife makin' rain around the country?

H.C.: *(Soberly)* Don't let's be beforehand, Jimmy.
(Suddenly there, on the threshold, File and the Sheriff. File knocks on the door frame.)

FILE: Mind if we come in, H.C.?

H.C.: Hello, File . . . Hey, Sheriff—come on in.

NOAH AND JIM: Hey, File . . . Hey, Sheriff.

H.C.: Kinda late to be visitin', ain't it, Sheriff?

SHERIFF: Well, we're not exactly visitin', H.C.

FILE: How's Lizzie?

H.C.: Fine, boy, fine. *(With a trace of puzzled amusement)* You just seen her a little while ago.

FILE: *(With a little embarrassment)* Yeah—I know.

H.C.: You and the Sheriff come callin' on Lizzie?

FILE: *(Quickly)* No—no.

H.C.: What can I do for you?

FILE: I'll tell you, H.C. We been gettin' a lot of phone calls from Pedleyville and Peak's Junction and all down the state line. They been lookin' for a fella—well, he's a kinda con man. Name of Tornado Johnson. . . . *(But he can't get his mind off Lizzie)* She asleep?

H.C.: *(Baiting him goodnaturedly)* Who—Lizzie?

FILE: Well, I reckon she is . . . You get any wind of him?

H.C.: Who?

FILE: *(Irritably)* Tornado Johnson.

H.C.: Nope.

FILE: *(Referring to a "wanted" circular he has brought with him)* Tornado Johnson—alias Bill Harmony— alias Bill Smith.

H.C.: I never met anybody called himself by any of those names.

FILE: Well, a fella that's got three aliases can easy have four. Anybody else come around here?

H.C.: *(Smiling)* Only you, File.

FILE: (*Looking toward the stairs*) Kind of a hot night to be asleep, ain't it?

H.C.: Lizzie's a good sleeper.

FILE: Yeah ... must be.

SHERIFF: No Tornado Johnson, huh?

H.C.: Nope.

SHERIFF: Seems a little fishy.

JIM: How do you mean fishy?

SHERIFF: Well, Pedleyville and the Junction and Three Point—we all kinda figured this together and—uh . . .

(*Embarrassed, he looks at File*)

FILE: Look, H.C., we know it ain't like you to protect a criminal.

NOAH: (*Quickly*) Really a criminal, huh?

FILE: (*Uncomfortably*) Well, he's wanted!

H.C.: What's he wanted for, File?

FILE: (*Referring to his "wanted" bulletin again*)
He's wanted in the state of Kansas. He sold four hundred tickets to a great big Rain Festival. Well, there wasn't no rain—so there couldn't be no festival. In a small town in Nebraska he drummed up a lot of excitement about what he called a Spectacular Eclipse of the Sun—and he peddled a thousand pair of smoked eyeglasses to see it with. No eclipse. In the month of February he sold six hundred wooden poles—fifteen dollars apiece. He called them Tornado Rods. Claimed that if that town ever got hit by a tornado the wind would just blow through there like a gentle spring breeze— and not hurt a thing. Well, when he left, the town got hit by every blow you can imagine—windstorm, hailstorm, cyclone and hurricane! Blew the Tornado Rods off the roof and blew the town off the map!

JIM: How about a tornado? Did it ever get hit by a tornado?

FILE: No, it didn't.

JIM: Well, that's all he guaranteed—that it wouldn't get hit by a tornado. And it didn't!

H.C.: Don't sound like a criminal to me, File.

FILE: (*As H.C. shakes his head*) Does sound like a con man, don't he, H.C.?

H.C.: Maybe.

SHERIFF: Anyway, we got orders to lock him up—and we'd sure appreciate some help.

H.C.: Sorry I can't help you, Sheriff.

FILE: I got a feelin' you can. They say this fella carries a great big bass drum wherever he goes. Whose drum is that?

JIM: It's mine. I'm figurin' to be a drummer.

FILE: What do you figure to be, H.C.—a whitewash painter?

H.C.: Maybe.

FILE: Must be some reason you painted that big white arrow on the ground.

H.C.: It's my ground, File.

FILE: (*Taking a step toward the window*) Yeah—it's your ground all right. But whose wagon is that?

(Silence.)

SHERIFF: Let's go have a look at that wagon, File.

(File and the Sheriff quickly go out.)

NOAH: *(In an outburst, to H.C.)* Why'd you do that? Why the hell did you do that?

H.C.: *(Upset)* I don't know.

NOAH: I heard it said that the dry heat makes some people go crazy in their heads!

H.C.: You think I'm crazy, Noah?

NOAH: I think somethin's wrong with you, Pop! Why didn't you tell them— straight out: "The fella you're lookin' for is in the tack room with my daughter"?

H.C.: Because he's with my daughter!

NOAH: *(With angry resolve)* All right! I didn't tell them you were lyin'. I kept my mouth shut—I stood by you. But I ain't standin' by you any more! *(He starts for the door.)*

H.C.: Where you goin', Noah?

NOAH: I'm goin' out to the tack room and bring her in.

H.C.: Noah, wait!

NOAH: And I'm gonna bring him in too!

H.C.: He's a quick fella, Noah—and you're a little slow on your feet! *(Noah rushes to the sideboard, opens a drawer and brings out a gun.)*

NOAH: I'll be quicker with this!

H.C.: *(Angry)* Put that down!

NOAH: You want Lizzie out there with him? You heard what they said about him. He's a swindler and a crook and a fourflusher and I don't know what else.

H.C.: I'll tell you what else, Noah—he's a man!

JIM: Pop's right! Gettin' married is gettin' married!

H.C.: Jimmy, you always say the smart thing at a dumb time!

JIM: Well, I'm all for her gettin' married—I don't care who the fella is.

NOAH: Is that the way you think, Pop?

H.C.: You know it's not the way I think.

NOAH: Then I'm goin'.

H.C.: I said stay here.

NOAH: *(Raging)* It ain't right, Pop—it ain't right!

H.C.: *(Exploding)* Noah, you're so full of what's right you can't see what's good! It's good for a girl to get married, sure—but maybe you were right when you said she won't ever have that! Well, she's gotta have somethin'! *(With desperate resolution)* Lizzie has got to have somethin'! Even if it's only one minute—with a man talkin' quiet and his hand touchin' her face.

JIM: Sure—let's give her a minute.

H.C.: Shut up! *(To Noah)* And if you go out there and shorten the time they have together—if you put one little dark shadow over the brightest time of Lizzie's life—I swear I'll come out after you with a whip! *(Quietly)* Now you give me that gun!

(A taut moment during which Noah and H.C. confront each other in open hostility. Noah is too righteously proud to give the gun to his father, yet not strong enough to defy him. At last, to give in without entirely losing face, he puts the gun back in the drawer. H.C. turns away; so does Noah. The lights fade.)

(The lights come up inside the tack room. Starbuck and Lizzie are sitting on the floor, leaning against the back of the wagonseat bench. They are quite intimately close, looking out through the open door at the bright expanse of sky. Lizzie has the shine of moonlight over her face and this glow, meeting her inner radiance, makes her almost beautiful.)

STARBUCK: And I always walk so fast and ride so far I never have time to stop and ask myself no question.

LIZZIE: If you did stop, what question would you ask?

STARBUCK: Well . . . I guess I'd say: "Big Man, where you goin'?"

LIZZIE: *(Quietly)* Big Man, where are you going?

STARBUCK: *(After an indecisive moment)* I don't know.

LIZZIE: Where do you want to *get* to?

STARBUCK: *(Inarticulate for the first time)* I—I want to touch somethin'. Somethin' big—to send shivers down my spine!

LIZZIE: Yes . . . I get shivers just thinking about it.

STARBUCK: But every time I get near anything big like that, I blink my eyes and it's gone. *(With a little revolt)* Why is that? Why is it the things you want are only there for the blinkin' of an eye? Why don't nothin' stay?

LIZZIE: *(Quietly)* Some things stay forever.

STARBUCK: Like what?

LIZZIE: *(A little abashed)* Never mind.

STARBUCK: You gotta tell me! Please!

LIZZIE: You fall in love with somebody—not *me*, I don't expect it'll be me— just *somebody*. And get married and have kids. And if you do, you'll live forever.

STARBUCK: *(Yearning)* I'd sure like to live forever. *(As they look at each other intently)* I reckon I better kiss you again. *(He kisses her and they are close for a moment)* Didn't anybody ever kiss you before I did, Lizzie?

LIZZIE: *(With a wan smile)* Yes—once.

STARBUCK: When was that?

LIZZIE: I was about twelve, I guess. I didn't know then whether I was pretty or plain—I just didn't think about it. There was a boy with freckles and red hair—and I thought he was the beginning of the world. But he never paid me any mind. Then one day he was standing around with a lot of other boys and they were whispering and cutting up. And suddenly, he shot over to me and kissed me hard, right on the mouth! And for a minute I was so stirred up and so happy . . .! But then he ran back to the other kids and I heard him say: "I'll kiss anything on a dare—even your old man's pig!" So I ran home and up the back stairs and I locked my door and looked at myself in the mirror—and from that day on I knew I was plain.

STARBUCK: Are you plain, Lizzie?

LIZZIE: *(Looking at him, smiling)* No—I'm beautiful.

STARBUCK: You are—and don't you ever forget it!

LIZZIE: *(A little sadly; reconciled to his ultimate going)* I'll try to remember—everything—you ever said.

(Starbuck rises restively. Somehow he is deeply disturbed, lonely. He walks to the door, his back to Lizzie, and looks out at the night. There is searching in his face, and yearning. At last it comes out in a little outcry:)

STARBUCK: Lizzie, I want to live forever!

LIZZIE: *(Full of compassion)* I hope you do—wherever you are—I hope you do!

STARBUCK: You don't say that as if you think I'll ever get what I'm after.

LIZZIE: *(Gently)* I don't really *know* what you're after.

STARBUCK: I'm after a clap of lightnin'! I want things to be as pretty when I get them as they are when I'm thinkin' about them!

LIZZIE: *(Hurt. He seems to disparage the moment of realization they've had together)* I think they're prettier when you get them. I think when you get something you've been dreaming about—oh, it's so beautiful!

STARBUCK: I wasn't talkin' about us, Lizzie.

LIZZIE: Weren't you?

STARBUCK: No—I'm talkin' about everything. Nothin's as pretty in your hands as it was in your head. There ain't no world near as good as the world I got up here. *(Angrily tapping his forehead)* Why?

LIZZIE: I don't know. Maybe it's because you don't take time to see it. Always on the go—here, there, nowhere. Running away . . . keeping your own company. Maybe if you'd keep company with the world . . .

STARBUCK: *(Doubtfully)* I'd learn to love it?

LIZZIE: You might—if you saw it real. Some nights I'm in the kitchen washing the dishes. And Pop's playing poker with the boys. Well, I'll watch him real close. And at first I'll just see an ordinary middle-aged man—not very interesting to look at. And then, minute by minute, I'll see little things I never saw in him before. Good things and bad things—queer little habits I never noticed he had—and ways of talking I never paid any mind to. And suddenly I know who he is—and I love him so much I could cry! And I want to thank God I took the time to see him real.

STARBUCK: *(Breaking out)* Well, I ain't got the time.

LIZZIE: Then you ain't got no world—except the one you make up in your head. So you better just be satisfied with that.

STARBUCK: No!

LIZZIE: I'm sorry. I didn't mean to hurt you.

(*A long moment. When at last he speaks, it is with painful difficulty.*)

STARBUCK: Lizzie . . . I got somethin' to tell you . . . You were right . . . I'm a liar and a con man and a fake. (*A moment. The words tear out of him*) I never made rain in my life! Not a single raindrop! Nowhere! Not anywhere at all!

LIZZIE: (*In a compassionate whisper*) I know. . . .

STARBUCK: All my life—wantin' to make a miracle! . . . Nothin'! . . . I'm a great big blowhard!

LIZZIE: (*Gently*) No . . . You're all dreams. And it's no good to live in your dreams.

STARBUCK: (*With desperation*) It's no good to live outside them either!

LIZZIE: Somewhere between the two . . .!

STARBUCK: Yes! (*After a moment*) The two of us maybe. . . .

LIZZIE: (*Forcing herself to believe it might work*) . . . Yes!

STARBUCK: Lizzie! Lizzie, would you like me to stick around for a while?

LIZZIE: (*Unable to stand the joy of it*) Did I hear you right?

STARBUCK: Not for good, understand—just for a few days!

LIZZIE: You're—you're not fooling me, are you, Starbuck?

STARBUCK: No—I mean it!

LIZZIE: (*Crying*) Would you stay? Would you?

STARBUCK: A few days—yes!

LIZZIE: (*Her happiness bursting*) Oh! Oh, my goodness! Oh!

STARBUCK: Lizzie . . .

LIZZIE: I can't stand it—I just can't stand it!

STARBUCK: (*Taking her in his arms*) Lizzie . . .

LIZZIE: You look up at the sky and you cry for a star. You know you'll never get it. And then one night you look down—and there it is—shining in your hand!

(*Half laughing, half crying, she goes into his arms again as the lights fade.*)

(*The lights come up inside the house where H.C., Noah and Jim are waiting for things to come to pass. Noah is at work at his books. Jim is looking out the window. A restless tension in the room.*)

H.C.: (*To Jim*) Any sign of rain?

JIM: No—nothin'.

NOAH: You may as well stop lookin' for it.

JIM: Reckon I ought to beat the drum again?

NOAH: What for?

JIM: (*Abashedly*) Oh, I forgot. (*With sudden anger*) Look at them—look at what that Sheriff's doin'!

H.C.: What?

JIM: They're ransackin' his wagon—gettin' it all messed up.

NOAH: Well, they got a right.

JIM: No, they ain't! Why, he had everything so neat in there—big wheels and books . . . Why, he's been collectin' those things for years! I ain't gonna let them hurt none of that stuff!
(Unhappily—anxious for action, anxious to come to Starbuck's rescue in some nameless way—he rushes out the front door.)

NOAH: Damn fool. *(Writing in his ledger)* How much did he say that Panatela cost?

H.C.: Eighty-five cents.

NOAH: He coulda had a whole box of Sweet Caporals for a dime!
(Lizzie enters through the rear door. The moonlight still glows on her. Noah and H.C. turn, their eyes fixed on the girl. Lizzie looks from one to another, trying to contain the rhapsody in her.)

NOAH: Where's Starbuck?

LIZZIE: In the tack room. *(To H.C.)* He wanted to come in and talk to you, Pop—but I said let me do it first.

NOAH: What's he want to talk about?

LIZZIE: Well—I—we . . . *(Unable to speak in front of Noah, she shifts nervously to:)* You know—I think I saw a wisp of a cloud.

NOAH: You're seein' things!

LIZZIE: *(Her happiness bursting forth)* No! The smallest wisp of a cloud—floating across the moon—no bigger than a mare's tail.

NOAH: You're talkin' like him.

LIZZIE: Yes—I am—yes!

NOAH: Whyn't you comb your hair?

LIZZIE: *(With an excited laugh)* I like it this way! I'm going to wear it this way all my life! I'm going to throw away my pins! *(Taking a handful of pins out of her pocket she tosses them high in the air)* There! I've got no more pins! *(Then, in a rush to her father)* But I've got something else!

H.C.: *(Quietly)* What, Lizzie?

LIZZIE: Pop . . . Oh, Pop, I've got me a beau!

H.C.: *(Heavily, trying to smile)* Have you, honey?

LIZZIE: Not an always beau—but a beau for meanwhile! Until he goes! He says he'll go in a few days—but anything can happen in a few days—anything can happen, can't it, Pop?

H.C.: Yes . . . it sure can.

LIZZIE: *(Ecstatically)* Oh, Pop, the world's turned clear around!

NOAH: Why don't you tell her, Pop?

LIZZIE: Tell me what?

H.C.: *(With difficulty)* Lizzie, you were right about that fella. He's a liar and a con man.

LIZZIE: *(With a cry)* But there's nothing bad about him, Pop! He's so good—and so alone—he's so terribly alone!

NOAH: That's what he deserves to be.

LIZZIE: No—nobody ought to be that. And I'll see that he's not any more. I'll be with him every minute he wants me.

NOAH: *(Going to the window—not unkindly)* Lizzie—come here.

LIZZIE: *(Instantly apprehensive)* What?

NOAH: I'm sorry, but you better look out this window.

(She crosses to the window and looks out. A moment of bewilderment and dread.)

LIZZIE: What are they here for? What are they doing on his wagon? *(As Noah turns away)* Pop!

H.C.: They're gettin' evidence against him, Lizzie. The Sheriff's here to lock him up.

LIZZIE: No!

(Suddenly she starts for the back door but Noah stops her.)

NOAH: Stay here, Lizzie!

LIZZIE: Let me go, Noah! *(In a panic, to H.C.)* They've got no right to arrest him!

H.C.: I'm afraid they have.

NOAH: He cheated and swindled everywhere he went.

LIZZIE: Pop, we've got to help him!

H.C.: *(Painfully)* Lizzie, quit it! There's nothin' we can do for him!

LIZZIE: Not for him—for me! I love him!

NOAH: You're out of your mind! He'll be gone in a day or two. He'll never even remember he saw you.

LIZZIE: No—that's not true!

H.C.: *(Quietly)* You think he'd marry you, Lizzie?

LIZZIE: I don't know . . .

NOAH: Well, you won't marry him, I'll tell you that! You're as different as mornin' and night. He's opposite to everything you are.

LIZZIE: Opposites go to each other.

NOAH: And they wind up apart.

LIZZIE: *(Desperately)* I'll pull him to me! I'll change him—I'll make him settle down! I'll make him see the world like the world is!

NOAH: Will you make him see *you* like *you* are?

LIZZIE: He does see me like I am!

NOAH: What'd he do? Tell you you're beautiful? Tell you you're a princess—straight out of a fairy tale?

LIZZIE: *(With an outcry of fright—because he has struck home)* Let me alone!

NOAH: He did, didn't he?

H.C.: *(With a violent shout)* Stop it, Noah! *(A moment. He goes to Lizzie and talks to her quietly)* Lizzie—listen to me. There's some truth in what Noah says . . .

LIZZIE: No—

H.C.: Not all truth—but some. Noah's right when he says you two ain't matched.

LIZZIE: But we are!

H.C.: No, you're not! You're only matched if you see life the same way. Take Noah. He sees life the way it is—but he sees it small and he sees it mean.

You see life the way it is—but you see it big and beautiful!

LIZZIE: So does Starbuck!

H.C.: No. He don't see life at all. He only sees somethin' he made up in his mind. And I'm sure you ain't Lizzie to him—I'm sure he just dreamed you up in his head.

LIZZIE: No! He sees me as real as you do!

H.C.: Do you believe that, Lizzie? *(As she doesn't answer)* Do you think he sees you real, Lizzie? Answer me!

LIZZIE: *(With great difficulty)* Yes . . . he does.

H.C.: *(With an effort—pulling himself together)* All right—then you better help him get away. Go out the back door and . . .

NOAH: You're not gonna let her do that, Pop!

H.C.: Yes, I am!

NOAH: Pop, it's a terrible mistake!

H.C.: *(Exploding)* Don't you think I know that? But if she don't make this mistake, she'll make a bigger one. She'll stay at home and turn sensible the way you want her to be. She'll follow your rules and jump through your hoop—and pretty soon we'll have another Noah in this house. And then she won't be plain—she'll be downright ugly! *(Whirling to her)* Now go on, Lizzie!

(She starts for the door but Noah grabs her as she tries to get by.)

NOAH: No! I won't let you!

LIZZIE: Noah, please!

H.C.: Let her go, Noah!

NOAH: You're not goin'—no!

(H.C. rushes between them and violently tears them apart. But Noah stands there, barring the door. Lizzie, in a wild flight, starts for the other door. But just as she reaches it, File and Jim enter, blocking the doorway. A taut moment.)

FILE: Well . . . you awake?

LIZZIE: Hello, File.

FILE: They said you were asleep.

LIZZIE: Did they? *(Trying to get past him)* Excuse me.

FILE: *(Blocking her path)* Where you goin', Lizzie?

LIZZIE: *(Afraid of giving Starbuck away)* Nowhere. Outside.

FILE: *(Suspiciously)* Wait a minute, Lizzie! What are you in such a rush for?

LIZZIE: *(Confused)* I—I just wanted to see what you were doing out there—on that wagon!

FILE: Well, I came in now. So you don't have to go out.

(Shrewdly—quickly) Unless there's some other reason for you goin'?

LIZZIE: No—no.

FILE: *(To the others—his eye on Lizzie)* I guess we got what we came for. He's got a half-dozen Tornado Rods out there and a boxful of smoked eyeglasses like this. *(He holds up a pair of glasses)* All right, H.C.—where is he?

H.C.: Do your own work, File.

FILE: H.C., I don't want this family mixed up in trouble. Tell us where he is—please!

JIM: He left about an hour ago.

FILE: Where'd he go?

JIM: Pedleyville.

FILE: How'd he go? His wagon's still here.

H.C.: He took Jim's roan.

JIM: Yeah—he took my roan.

FILE: I think you're lyin'—all of you! *(With sudden enraged exasperation)* What the hell's goin' on here anyway? I ask you questions and you tell me a pack of lies! And for what? A stranger! A man who don't mean anything to you! *(Abruptly he goes still as the thought assails him:)* Or does he? *(As he feels the tautness of the silence, his attention slowly, slowly turns to Lizzie. Slowly, slowly he crosses the room and places himself squarely facing her)* Maybe you better answer that question, Lizzie.

(It is too much for her. She takes a quick step away, in flight—but File grabs her.)

FILE: No—wait a minute! They said you were asleep—but you weren't! Why did they lie about that? Where were you, Lizzie?

LIZZIE: *(Painfully)* It has nothing to do with you!

FILE: *(Impulsively—with deep feeling)* It's got a lot to do with me! Tell me!

LIZZIE: Let me go!

FILE: *(Angry—pleading)* Lizzie . . .!

(Suddenly we hear the voice of Starbuck. He is outdoors, approaching, singing at the top of his voice. A quick, sharp stir in the room.)

LIZZIE: *(Shouting desperately)* Starbuck—go away!—run!

(His singing continues.)

LIZZIE: *(Wildly as the singing gets closer)* Starbuck—run!

(Starbuck enters through the open door. His pace is so rapid that he comes full into the room, still singing. File slams the door shut behind him. The instant Starbuck takes in the room, his song stops. His body goes tense, alert.)

LIZZIE: *(With a wail)* I told you to run!

STARBUCK: What's goin' on?

FILE: Smith? Johnson? Starbuck?

STARBUCK: What do you want?

FILE: Sheriff. You're under arrest.

(Starbuck makes one move toward the door but File steps in his way, gun in hand.)

FILE: Don't go for that door!

(Starbuck holds his position. Lizzie rushes to him with a cry.)

LIZZIE: If you hadn't been singing, you'd have heard me!

STARBUCK: *(With an attempt at bravura)* I never regret singin'! *(Then, turning away from her)* All right, Sheriff—let's go!

LIZZIE: *(In an outcry)* File, wait a minute! Let him go!

FILE: What?!

LIZZIE: Let him get away!!

FILE: I can't do that, Lizzie. *(Showing her his "wanted" circular)* Look at this bulletin.

H.C.: We don't have to look at that! We've been looking at *him*!

FILE: This is all I have to go by, H.C.

JIM: You've got us to go by, File! We spent the whole evenin' with this fella!

H.C.: We gave him a hundred dollars, and we'll never regret a nickel of it!

JIM: He's not a criminal!

H.C.: He don't belong in jail!

FILE: *(With a sense of being stampeded)* Now wait a minute!

LIZZIE: *(To File)* We took a chance with *him*, File. Now *you* take a chance with *us*!

STARBUCK: Give up, folks. A sheriff's a sheriff, and he can't see any further than his badge!

(File flinches and Lizzie hurries to him.)

LIZZIE: *(Confronting him squarely)* Is that true, File?

FILE: You know damn well it's not true.

LIZZIE: Then let him go!

JIM: Please! Let him go!

FILE: *(The smallest instant. He looks at Noah)* Haven't heard a word from you, Noah. There'd be a lot of people around here who'd say I was breakin' the law. Right?

NOAH: *(After a struggle with himself)* Nobody I know of.

FILE: *(To Starbuck)* All right, get goin'! Get out of here!

STARBUCK: Well, I'm a son of a gun!

(He rushes to the door and stops on the threshold.)

FILE: Hurry up before I change my mind!

STARBUCK: *(Desperately)* Lizzie! It's as lonely as dyin' out there! Will you come with me?

LIZZIE: *(Dumbfounded—unable to handle the sudden offer)* Starbuck . . .

STARBUCK: I'm talkin' to you, Lizzie! And there's no time! Come on!

(She takes a step toward him—tentative, frightened. Suddenly, out of the tense stillness—File's voice! The words he was never able to say tear out of him in a tortured cry:)

FILE: Lizzie—don't go!!

(She turns and looks at him, stunned, unable to believe it is File's voice.)

LIZZIE: What's . . . that . . .?

FILE: I said don't go!

LIZZIE: Oh, what'll I do?

STARBUCK: Hurry up, Lizzie—please!

(Caught between the two men, Lizzie glances wildly around the room.)

LIZZIE: Pop, what am I going to do?

H.C.: Whatever you do, remember you been asked! You don't never have to go through life a woman who ain't been asked!

STARBUCK: I'm sure askin'! Lizzie, listen! You're beautiful now, but you come with me and you'll be so beautiful, you'll light up the world!

LIZZIE: *(Frightened)* No—don't say that!

STARBUCK: *(He cannot be stopped)* You'll never be Lizzie no more—you'll be—you'll be Melisande!

LIZZIE: *(With a cry that is part lament, part relief)* Oh, Starbuck, you said the wrong thing! I've got to be Lizzie! Melisande's a name for one night—but Lizzie can do me my whole life long!

STARBUCK: Come on!

LIZZIE: I can't!

(She turns away from him.)

STARBUCK: Lizzie!

(Too late. Her decision has been made. Starbuck tries to hide the deep desperation. He tries to smile, to be the braggart again. He addresses the Curry men with a bravura shout.)

STARBUCK: Well, boys! I'm sorry about the rain—but then I didn't stay my full time. So there's your hundred dollars! (He tosses the bundle of money on the table) Another day maybe—in a dry season! So long, folks!*

(And he's out in a streak of dust.)

LIZZIE: Thank you, File, thank you.

FILE: *(Admiringly)* Well! Somethin' about you—you sure have changed.

JIM: She's got her hair down.

FILE: It's more than her hair, I'd say. But whatever it is . . .

(He takes a few steps toward her. They look at each other closely. He smiles—the first full, radiant smile we've seen on his face. And the warmth of it shines on Lizzie—and she starts to smile too . . . Suddenly a sound in the distance—a quick, low rumble.)

NOAH: *(Hearing the sound; not watching Jim)* Jimmy, for Pete sake, stop beatin' that drum!

JIM: I ain't beatin' no drum!

(They all look at Jim. He is yards away from Starbuck's drum. Another rumble is heard.)

H.C.: *(Unable to believe what he hears)* That sounds like . . . (With a shout) It's thunder!

(A streak of lightning flashes the lights, dimming the room and electrifying it at the same time.)

JIM: Lightning!

H.C.: Light—ning!

FILE: Look at it! It's gonna rain!

JIM: He said twenty-four hours—he said twenty-four hours!

(More lightning, more thunder.)

LIZZIE: *(In highest exaltation)* It's going to rain! Rain!

(Suddenly the door bursts open and Starbuck stands on the threshold—with a look of glory on his face.)

STARBUCK: Rain, folks—it's gonna rain! Rain, Lizzie—for the first time in my life—rain! *(Hurrying to the table)* Gimme my hundred dollars! *(He takes his money and hurtles to the door. In the doorway, he pauses only long enough to wave to Lizzie)* So long—beautiful!
(And he races out.)

END OF THE PLAY

EVERYBODY, SMILE!

A Play in Two Acts

CHARACTERS

(In the order of their appearance)

Dennis Ryan
Rebecca Ryan
Becky Ryan
Julia Ryan
Simon Sperry
Patrick Ryan

PLACE

Dennis Ryan's country house in New England and Patrick Ryan's apartment in Manhattan

TIME

In the late forties

FOREWORD

The two main characters of this play will, inescapably, be associated with Eugene O'Neill and Charlie Chaplin. Oona O'Neill Chaplin was the daughter of the dramatist and the wife of the comedian. It is commonly believed that O'Neill was so enraged by their marriage that he refused to meet his son-in-law, and they never met. In the play, of course, they do meet. This, then, is a work of fiction.

Act One

SINCE THE TALE IS TOLD in the imagination of Dennis Ryan, the scenery is as free-floating as his images. We do not see "sets," but only a single environment, and lights. Right now we are in Dennis's study. It is mid-morning of an autumn day. This workplace—like the mind—of a writer approaching seventy, is a jumble of worn things and memories and unanswered questions. No light in the room except for the October colors, pouring in through illusory windows. Dennis is gazing into this light, when suddenly he turns from it; he has witnessed a catastrophe. He starts shouting at the vision:

DENNIS: Dennis! Dennis—no! Don't do that! Dennis—please—don't do it! Dennis!
(*He comes straight downstage and speaks to us*) I'm calling to my son. Sometimes I forget that he is dead—and I keep calling for him—but he never appears. Other visions do appear, but not him, not my older son. He isn't there anymore—he just isn't there. Dennis!
(*He halts, he listens*) My name is also Dennis, and that might be causing the confusion. Sometimes I think that since we have the same name, I may be calling myself! As I get older, I have other confusions—but I don't want to give the impression that there's anything wrong with my mind. Except that I'm a playwright, and that means, I suppose, that *everything* can be

wrong with it. And I admit it, my mind is always going on strange errands, I make crazy little bargains with myself. For example, I'd give a year of my life to have written The Song of Solomon. I'd give my Nobel Prize for an hour of real conversation with my dead son. My daughter says I make these ridiculous offers because I don't know what's available and what's not. But she knows—oh yes, Becky's very good at distinguishing the fiction from the fact. And she insists on the distinction. "We're living in the late forties, Father, and today is Tuesday—write that down!—Tuesday!—don't you forget it!" Becky knows the difference between a horse and a unicorn, by God—and if I see a horse with a horn, one of us is mighty peculiar. (*He laughs a little*) I'm nuts about Becky—I'd like you to meet her. (*He calls off*) Becky!

(*Back to us*) You'll be surprised when you see my daughter—she's only nine years old. You'll say, perhaps, how are we to perceive reality through the eyes of a nine-year-old child who has a seventy-year-old father? Isn't there some discrepancy . . .?

(*Rebecca enters. Although she is not yet eighteen, she is a mature woman, lean of body and mind, beautiful only on second glance, but then—heart stopping.*)

REBECCA: There certainly is. I'm not nine years old, I'm seventeen.

DENNIS: You're quibbling, Becky.

REBECCA: My name is not Becky, it's Rebecca. And I'm seventeen, Father.

DENNIS: What's a decade on two? You're nine.

REBECCA: I haven't seen you for a while—how are you?

DENNIS: Oh, I'm fine. This new doctor is a wonder. He's made me young again. I'm as steady as a post.

(*He makes a fist and a single strong gesture of pounding a post into the ground.*)

REBECCA: You're lying, aren't you?

DENNIS: Not at all. I feel wonderful. I've got these new hormones I'm taking. Pee well and be well. It's the precept of my life. And I'm as spry as a cat. Shall I touch my toes for you?

REBECCA: No, unless it's to tie your shoelaces.

DENNIS: Oh, did somebody untie them? (*As she starts to laugh*) No, don't laugh. Some sneaky little bastard comes in every morning and unties my shoelaces.

REBECCA: When you used to say things like that I used to believe them. Every single one. Hard fact.

DENNIS: Hard fact—Jesus! Is that what they do to women at Cambridge—turn them into fact freaks? How can you be devoting your life to Aeschylus and Euripides, and be a statistician? Your mind should be filled with meaningful metaphors.

REBECCA: Goodbye, metaphor—hello, fact.

DENNIS: What's a fact, what's a metaphor?

REBECCA: Love is a metaphor, fucking is a fact.

DENNIS: I retract the question. (*He smiles; he dotes on her*) If you're about to regale me with your English sexual adventures, I'll have a nap. Or have I had it?

REBECCA: (*Grinning*) I love you—you're adorable.

DENNIS: So are you . . . . What are you doing home? You're not pregnant, are you?

REBECCA: No. Funny, it was the first question Paddy asked.

DENNIS: (*Alert*) Patrick?—you've seen Patrick? When?

REBECCA: This afternoon. Went straight from the airport.

DENNIS: I'm green with jealousy. You went to see your brother first?

REBECCA: Don't be jealous, Dad. He was so down when I arrived and so up when I left. And guess what—he's working!

DENNIS: (*With quick pleasure*) Really? What's he doing?

REBECCA: He wouldn't tell me. But he read me something.

DENNIS: He did?—what?

REBECCA: Well, I don't really know. It wasn't words exactly. Just syllables, kind of. Blunkee-frabbee, beeble-ruck-beeble, mungo-flug-mungo. Flug-flug!

DENNIS: Flug-flug, huh? There's profundity in that.

REBECCA: He said it wasn't meant for comprehension.

DENNIS: Then it must be a poem. Anyway, I'm glad he's working again.

REBECCA: Why don't you tell him so?

DENNIS: The subject's over, I think.

REBECCA: He's dying to see you.

DENNIS: He knows where I live.

REBECCA: You know damn well he hasn't left that dingy little apartment in over three years.

DENNIS: If he wants to see me badly enough—

REBECCA: What do you mean, "badly enough." When he mentions your name, he closes his eyes.

DENNIS: It's rage.

REBECCA: It's not rage—he loves you!

DENNIS: Loves me? The last time I saw him, he almost beat the hell out of me.

REBECCA: He says you started it.

DENNIS: (*Wounded*) It's not true. I didn't start it—I didn't raise a hand to him! Even when he was hitting me, I didn't hit him back!
(*An angry outburst*) Christ, do we have to talk about Patrick every time we meet?

REBECCA: (*Mostly to herself*) Yes, because we never know what you're thinking about us. Maybe if we're all in your next play . . .

DENNIS: You're not—it's a comedy.

REBECCA: (*Pleased*) A comedy?—really?

DENNIS: I thought I was writing a comedy. A pretty little fluffery—happy—cheery—light as a feather! And suddenly the feather began to bleed.

REBECCA: Got caught in a family fight.

DENNIS: Battling against this monster!

REBECCA: What monster?

DENNIS: Well, in the background of the play there's a ferocious monster that's brutalizing this sweet, harmless, helpless little lizard.

REBECCA: (*Smiling*) Your play's about a lizard?

DENNIS: (*Laughing*) No, not really. It's about a man who's a painter. And he's having trouble with his work. One day he sees a pretty little lizard with a curled-up tail, and big eyes that blink with curiosity. And it changes color—very easily, no trouble at all, no artist's block of any kind. All those lovely shades of gold and green and bright blue azure—and nothing muddy on the palette. Well, the painter is so envious—he tries to capture the little varmint in a butterfly net, and at last he does capture it. So he gets a sharp-pointed safety pin, and he pokes the pin through the lizard's tail, and hangs the little creature around his neck.

REBECCA: God, what a bastard! Around his neck?—what a creep!

DENNIS: Yes, but don't be too rough on him. Aside from that initial cruelty, he's very kind to the little beastie. He feeds it, waters it, speaks to it as if it's an infant child. And in return the chameleon performs its brilliant magic—changing its hues to match his colors—any shade, any tint at all!—quick!—willing!—like an old vaudeville performer, it'll do anything to please—anything! And the tiny chameleon takes on the color of whatever shirt is on the painter's back. It's as if the little crawling thing wants to be a part of its captor's costume—it wants to be absorbed into the *life* of its master! And one day the painter needs to know how far the creature can go, he needs to push the limits of the chameleon's art! So he puts on a plaid shirt—many colors—a mayhem of color! And he sets the lizard on his shoulder. And the little creature tries with all its heart to take the complicated color pattern upon itself. It twists and turns and strains desperately to be what the artist wants it to be—it writhes, it glows, it screams in scarlet! But it can't make it—torturing its heart out—it simply can't make it. So it gives up all its colors and goes to gray. Dark and dismal gray. And the thing is dead, and will never glow again.

REBECCA: What a heartless story.

DENNIS: That's not the end of it. The painter looks closely at the countenance of the dead chameleon. And it starts to seem very human to him. It is someone he remembers, someone he recognizes. But who is it? Then suddenly he knows! He is looking at the face of his dead son.

REBECCA: (*Pause. Then, with a pained smile*). You do that very well. I think I'm weeping about a lizard, and suddenly it's you.

DENNIS: (*Urgently*) Don't weep—I don't want you to weep! I want you to laugh! It's ridiculous—laugh! I'm trying to turn it into a comedy! I need to write a comedy, Becky, a comedy!

REBECCA: We're all home for Christmas—tinsel and mistletoe—jelly beans and candy canes—jingle bells, jingle bells!

DENNIS: What's wrong with that? That's what I want to write—a joyous, mindless, pleasure-giving entertainment! Cheers!—what a happy family—cheers!—*everybody, smile*! And what happens? I get all tangled up in the torments of this one and the agony of that one, and the misery we all put ourselves to, and suddenly I'm not writing a happy idyll by the fireplace, but a massacre in hell!

REBECCA: You don't have to write about us.

DENNIS: What else can I write about? I start with these wonderful, kindly strangers—their mouths clean and their eyes clear—lovable personalities—not a bile duct in the lot of them. And suddenly they're ripping at each other and there's blood in the gutter, and they're no different from my own family. And what are they?—they're lizards, and I'm sticking pins in them!

REBECCA: Immortalizing them.

DENNIS: Don't be a press agent.

(*His hand trembles; she notes it, and tries to sound casual.*)

REBECCA: Have your hands been shaking very much?

DENNIS: (*Quickly*) No, not at all.

REBECCA: Then why are they doing it now?—just for show?

DENNIS: For show?—why the hell would I do that?

REBECCA: Because you want me to stay home.

DENNIS: Who the devil wants you to stay home? Why would I need you here? I've got Julia—she's very good to me, very considerate. She's certainly the best of my three wives, I can tell you that—and she's all I ask for.

REBECCA: And you never see her.

DENNIS: Of course I see her!

REBECCA: No you don't. You've got a house full of rooms—sixteen rooms. You live in the north wing and she lives in the south. You pass each other in the hallway once in a while and you raise your hat—"How do you do, Mrs. Ryan?" How does she *do*?—she does lousy! And so do you. I've never seen such a lonely pair in all my life!

DENNIS: I am not lonely!

REBECCA: Yes you are!

DENNIS: I'm not! I've got my work—I've got my people! And good or bad, they're as real to me as you are! They make me think, they make me wonder, they make me *feel something*!

REBECCA: And you hate them!

DENNIS: I never start that way!

REBECCA: Sooner or later, you hate them! You make them cruel to one another, you make them sick, you put them through every kind of tribulation, and then when you can't stand them any longer, you bump them off!

(*Silence. He is somewhat unbalanced by this. But he is honest.*)

DENNIS: You're quite right. They cause me pain. But I don't complain about that—pain is the necessary condition. It's my address—it's where I live.

Without it my work is dead, it's a graveyard. Pain is what keeps it alive. . . . And maybe me too.

REBECCA: (*Silence. Then, muted*) I'll come home any time you ask me to.

DENNIS: (*Trying to lighten the moment*) Who's asking?—who wants you?

REBECCA: You do.

DENNIS: Holy Moses, you think I'd interfere with your work? You think I'd screw up your getting your degree?

REBECCA: (*Also smiling*) Yes, I think you might—if you could convince yourself you're not a bastard.

DENNIS: I am not a bastard!

REBECCA: I know you're not! But you don't know it! And you're not, Father—you're not a bastard!

DENNIS: (*Dryly*) Thank you, my dear—that's intoxicating praise.

REBECCA: You should say that to yourself a hundred times a day. "I'm not a bastard. I'm the kindest, the most loyal, the most conscientious character I've ever written."

DENNIS: *Written*?!

REBECCA: Yes.

DENNIS: I have not been *written*! I have been born, I have worked, I have brought children into the world, I have scrambled for a buck, I have lied in the confessional, I have bled, I have sent flowers, I have wept. *I have not been written—I am not a fantasy*!

REBECCA: The jury is still out, Father.

DENNIS: I wish you wouldn't call me Father. When in God's name did you stop calling me Dad?

REBECCA: When I stopped calling myself Becky.

DENNIS: Why the hell did you toss Becky away?

REBECCA: Because I outgrew it.

DENNIS: Outgrew it, my ass. Why should you ever outgrow it?—it's perfectly serviceable for the rest of your life. Becky's a sweet name, it's endearing. It makes me feel warm to say it. Like tea and Oreo cookies. I like Becky a hell of a lot better than Re-becc-aaa.

REBECCA: Yes. I know you do.

DENNIS: I wasn't referring to the person, I was referring to the name.

REBECCA: Let's not make an event of it, Father—I know you like Becky more than you do me.

DENNIS: You're two different people—I love you in different ways. And I want you to know, Becky: no matter how much I love you both, I am making no bid to bring you home.

REBECCA: Are you sure?

DENNIS: Have I ever sent you an SOS, have I ever called you in the middle of the night?

REBECCA: Rock of independence.

DENNIS: Damn right!

REBECCA: Well ... if you're sure about that ... it makes it easier to say what I came home for.

DENNIS: Sounds ominous. Should I gird my loins? How exactly does one gird one's loins? Is rope required?

REBECCA: I'm going to get married.

DENNIS: Really?

(*He is smiling and seemingly at ease, hiding quite well how off-balance he is.*)

REBECCA: Yes, really.

DENNIS: Before I ask you who the man is—so that you won't think I'm prejudiced against some particular person—I have to say I think you're too young to be married.

REBECCA: I'm seventeen.

DENNIS: Dear baby, your gills are still wet!

REBECCA: I'm years and years ahead of myself—you've always said that.

DENNIS: You're nine years old.

REBECCA: Please, Father, don't do that.

DENNIS: And your name is Becky. Not Rebecca—Becky!

REBECCA: It's Rebecca—and you can't call me a child just by using a childhood name!

DENNIS: (*Calling with a note of desperation*) Becky! Becky!

REBECCA: Please—no—stop it!

DENNIS: Becky!

(*Becky appears—the child Becky, nine years old. She is a serious, attractive person who has learned how to summon merriment as an ally. Dennis's manner with her is totally different from his manner with Rebecca—it is easy, felicitous, playfully teasing, but tender.*)

BECKY: Why do people change their names?

DENNIS: Guess.

BECKY: They don't like what people are calling them.

DENNIS: Yes, I think that's one reason. Any other?

BECKY: They don't like who they are.

DENNIS: Well, well, well!—very good.

BECKY: I like what I am, and the heck with it.

DENNIS: Good—what's your name?

BECKY: What's yours?

DENNIS: Ishkabibble.

BECKY: That's too cute—I don't like it.

DENNIS: Nebuchadnezzar.

BECKY: No, it's not—it's Dad.

DENNIS: Daddy Ishkabibble.

BECKY: My name's Becky, and I'm not going to change it. Not even for cuteness.

DENNIS: Promise?

BECKY: You're supposed to ask for a promise to a hard thing. That's easy. Sure I promise.

DENNIS: Good. I'll buy you a doughnut.

BECKY: You don't have to—I sell them.

(*It's the start of a game.*)

DENNIS: Got any left?

BECKY: Oh, yeah—lots.

DENNIS: How much?

BECKY: Doughnuts are a dollar.

DENNIS: That's very expensive. Do you sell on credit?

BECKY: No—cash.

DENNIS: Hm—doughnuts are really out of sight these days. How about holes?

BECKY: Ten cents.

DENNIS: I'll have two holes.

BECKY: Sorry, sir, we don't sell the holes without the doughnuts.

DENNIS: If I buy a doughnut with its hole, can I eat the doughnut and you take back the hole?

BECKY: Yes, sir—five cent refund.

DENNIS: But you sold it to me for ten.

BECKY: We're buying back a second-hand hole.

DENNIS: Do you *sell* second-hand holes?

BECKY: Only with second-hand doughnuts.

DENNIS: I'll have two second-hand doughnuts with second-hand holes.

BECKY: Sorry, sir, the second-hand doughnuts are still in the oven.

DENNIS: (*Laughing*) Do you play that game with your mother?

BECKY: I don't want to go back there anymore.

DENNIS: I didn't ask if you wanted to go back, I asked if you played that game with your mother.

BECKY: I started to once, but Wesley said not to.

DENNIS: Not to?—why?

BECKY: He said "hole" was a dirty word.

DENNIS: Hoity toity. A man of fastidious morals. What's he say about Swiss cheese?

BECKY: He pinches my titties.

DENNIS: What?

BECKY: My stepfather pinches my titties, even if I don't have any.

DENNIS: (*He is as disturbed as she is*) Did you tell your mother?

BECKY: Yes.

DENNIS: What'd she say?

BECKY: (*Imitating her mother*) Luck-eeee.

DENNIS: Next time he does that to you, I'll tell you what you do.

BECKY: Not going to be any next time—I'm not going back.

DENNIS: Yes you are. It's in the agreement—Visitation Rights. The contract says you've got to spend the summers with your mother.

BECKY: Nobody made a contract with *me*.

DENNIS: True enough, but still—

BECKY: But still nothing! If you send me back to that titty-pincher—

DENNIS: *Will you listen to me?* If he pinches you again, you slug him!

BECKY: Easy for you to say.

DENNIS: Easy for you too! Just pick something up—a baseball bat, a frying pan—and crack him one on the nose. And if you've got nothing to hit him with, kick him in the balls. And start screaming—do you still know how to scream? (*As she lets out a blood-chilling scream*) Good—that's very good! (*Pow! She slams her elbow into his stomach. He doubles over, but shouts in encouragement:*)

DENNIS: Attagirl—now the kick—the punch—good girl—give 'im the old one-two—

(*They are mock-fighting with one another. He is letting her get the better of the battle. She is shouting, screaming, while he cheers her on, keep punching, that's great, get him, get him! Hi-jinks, laughter, athletics, hilarity. It winds up with Becky the victor. She is lying on top of him, her legs astride his chest, her hands holding his arms down on the ground, above his head. Silence. A latent moment, strange, joyous, complicated. The stillness holds. Then:*)

BECKY: How come we can get rough with each other and it's fun, and if he even touches me with a finger, it makes me vomit?

DENNIS: (*Evading*) Just stay away from him.

BECKY: (*With quiet resolve*) That's right, that's what I'm going to do. I'm going to stay away. I'm not going back.

DENNIS: I didn't mean that. You've got to go back—it's the law.

BECKY: You can break the law!

DENNIS: No, honey, I can't.

BECKY: Yes you can! You're my father and you're brave! You can fight the law and you can break it!

DENNIS: I'm not brave enough—you have to go back.

BECKY: Why can't I live with someone who loves me instead of someone who hates me?

DENNIS: Your mother doesn't hate you! You've just got yourself thinking that she hates you!

BECKY: Is there any difference?

DENNIS: . . . That's a hard question.

BECKY: *I'm not going back! And if you force me to, it means you don't love me enough to keep me here, you don't love me enough to keep me!*

DENNIS: I do love you—and so does your mother!

BECKY: No!—she hates me! And I hate her! And if you don't let me live with you, I'll hate you as well! I'll hate you, I'll hate you! (*She runs away. The grown up Rebecca stands in Becky's stead. She speaks quietly:*)

REBECCA: I'm not going back.

DENNIS: I want you to tell Wesley—and I want you to tell your mother at the same time—

REBECCA: Stop it! We're not talking about mother and Wesley! They died six years ago. We're talking about Becky—I'm not going back to her. She's gone too.

DENNIS: She'll never be gone.

REBECCA: She grew up. She's old enough to get married.

DENNIS: (*Silence. Then:*) . . . To whom?

REBECCA: Simon Sperry.

DENNIS: His son?

REBECCA: No—him.

DENNIS: Simon Sperry, the comic?

REBECCA: He hates to be called a comic. He's an actor—at worst, a comedian.

DENNIS: Are you serious?

REBECCA: Yes.

DENNIS: Are we speaking about the same man? My God, he must be fifty years old.

REBECCA: Fifty-eight.

DENNIS: But the man is old enough to be—

REBECCA: My father.

DENNIS: —your grandfather!

REBECCA: Any minute now you'll start counting. When I'm thirty he'll be seventy—when I'm fifty he'll be ninety—

DENNIS: When you're a hundred he'll be a hundred and fifty.

REBECCA: Hundred and forty. (*Trying to lighten things*) When I'm a hundred and he's a hundred and forty, the difference won't seem so big. That's a pleasant thought—don't you think that's a pleasant thought?

DENNIS: (*Not smiling*) For somebody who's awful in arithmetic, you've got the figures down pat.

REBECCA: (*Hotly*) Of course I have—you think I'm an idiot? You think I haven't added and subtracted and multiplied and done everything to the goddamn figures that they'd let me do to them?!

DENNIS: And the result?

REBECCA: The arithmetic is unimportant.

DENNIS: You think if you trivialize the arithmetic, you can trivialize the truth?

REBECCA: I'm not trivializing anything. Every day the problem gets bigger and bigger—and I don't know what to do—(*She starts to cry*)—and the only way I can handle it—

DENNIS: —is by marrying him?

REBECCA: Yes.

(*He sees how afflicted she is and he hurts for her. He wants to touch and comfort her, but keeps his distance. His voice is gentle.*)

DENNIS: Becky . . . baby . . . I know how you feel. As though you're locked in—no choices. Well, being in love *does* that, and if you're in love with a man who's pushing sixty it's even worse. Well, you've got to fight that kind of imprisonment. You're so young, you've got a right to a lot of trial-and-error before you settle down to a big binding commitment. You've got things to do—places to go—a thousand *earthshaking* love affairs with boys your own age! My God, you're seventeen!—the world should be getting bigger, not smaller. And if you give yourself some time, it *will* get bigger—and you'll be able to *breathe*! Give yourself time, Becky—it's precious—give yourself *time*!

REBECCA: (*Recovered, she says with quiet resolve*) I love him—I want to marry him.

DENNIS: Please—try not to talk with your gonads.

REBECCA: (*In a temper*) Do you have to be flippant about this?

DENNIS: (*Helpless, frustrated*) How shall I *be*? What ponderous tone of voice shall I use to make you listen?

REBECCA: I'm trying *not* to listen! Your experience with love and marriage hasn't made you a very good adviser!

DENNIS: You're quite right. My experience with love and marriage is that they have very little to do with one another.

REBECCA: I think you're wrong.

DENNIS: You'll see. Love and marriage are crummy companions.

REBECCA: You use the word "love" all the time, and you don't know anything about it.

DENNIS: (*Trying not to wince*) I'd like for you not to say that anymore.

REBECCA: You don't. Love has to be something pleasant and manageable to you—that's why you like Becky better than you do Rebecca. But when it's too difficult—when it upsets you too much—you turn your back on it! The point is, you can't really love anything but your work, can you?

DENNIS: That was true until you came along, Becky.

REBECCA: It hasn't anything to do with my coming along. Dennis came along before me—and you treated him rottenly.

DENNIS: (*Losing his temper*) You don't know anything about Dennis—you were an infant when he left home.

REBECCA: Patrick, then. You've treated him like a leper.

DENNIS: (*More and more distressed*) How I've treated Patrick has nothing to do with you. I was a failure in those days. Everything I touched turned to shit. But when you were born, I had had two successes in a row. And for once in my life something was more important to me than my writing had been. And I watched you grow—healthy—without disfigurement—joyous!—all your parts in place!—no second-act problem! And from that time on, what I've wanted most out of life was for you to grow and be happy. (*A moment*) I think it's unfeeling of you to suggest that I don't love you.

REBECCA: I'm sorry. . . . That's the way Simon loves me.

DENNIS: You're special to me—are you special to him? Don't you take your place in a long line of women?

REBECCA: (*Impatient*) I'm not writing his biography, I'm just contributing to it!

DENNIS: (*Irascibly*) Can you talk together—can you fight without getting ugly? When you cry, does he cry with you—or is he just watching you, taking notes? Are you ever the same age? That's the most vital question—*are you ever the same age?*

REBECCA: Yes.

DENNIS: When?

REBECCA: When he makes me laugh.

DENNIS: He makes everybody laugh. Everybody in the world. He's the most famous comic that ever was.

REBECCA: Actor.

DENNIS: (*Pouncing*) Yes, actor—don't you forget that! (*Playing the conceited actor*) How do I look? Do you think I'm romantic? Do you like me better when I'm sad or when I'm funny. Do you love me, do you love, love, love me? Do you love my new haircut, do you love my new diet, my new religion, my new *teeth*?!

(*He shows a wide mouthful of teeth.*)

REBECCA: (*With quiet composure*) He's not at all like that. (*A moment*) He came to Cambridge in the spring . . . and talked to a small group of students. He didn't posture, he didn't make a speech, he simply told us who he was. And the way he spoke—it was quiet, it was inspiring—as if he had no censor telling him what he couldn't say. He could reveal anything—and it seemed to come from as far back as the day he was born. And I thought: I'm joined to this great man, I'm joined to him in every way—in my thoughts, in my feelings—I'm tuned to his heartbeat! . . . And when he touched me, it was the most natural touch I have ever felt.

DENNIS: (*Quietly*) Yes, he has a very natural technique.

REBECCA: (*In a rage*) *It's not a technique*! He's real—he's certainly more real than you are!

(*Silence. Dennis speaks quietly, trying to hide that she has wounded him.*)

DENNIS: What do I have to do to make myself real to you, Becky?

REBECCA: See *me* as real! I'm not a character in one of your plays. *I am very ordinary*! And when you get down to it, so is Simon!

DENNIS: He's not ordinary—I wish he were! He's a star, he's in the spotlight. His films are applauded in every corner of the world. Everybody googles over him. America adores him, England offers him the crown. Even the French who love nobody, love him. My dentist—with the electric drill in his hand—begins to giggle when he talks about him. My podiatrist loves him better than he loves bunions. So does his wife and his sisters and his daughters. Simon Sperry is a letch.

REBECCA: You have that on good authority.

DENNIS: I hear his name on the evening news—I read the papers. A while back there was a photograph of him with a slightly dressed floozy. Very rich, very glittery. She was a whole head taller than he was. His eyes were on a level with her boobs. I wondered if he ever raised his head.

REBECCA: Please try not to be a crumb.

DENNIS: (*Pleading*) Becky, this is all wrong! I want you to marry an ordinary man, not a spectacular one. I want you to marry someone to whom you will be the most special person he can ever imagine! I want you to have a life of wonder, a life of The First Time!—not a worn-out existence with a dissipated old man!

REBECCA: You want me to be a virgin again.

DENNIS: Oh, Jesus.

(*Frustrated, in distress because he cannot make her comprehend him, he turns away.*)

REBECCA: (*Silence. Then, carefully*) In a few months I'll be eighteen. Then I can legally marry him without your consent.

DENNIS: (*He turns back to face her; his voice is uneven*) Then I will have nothing further to say, will I?

REBECCA: (*Urgently*) Yes, you will, Father! I don't want to marry him without your approval—I don't want to do that!

DENNIS: I don't know what to say to you—I want you to be happy—you can't be serious, can you?—you'll be miserable, Becky—a man that age—with that reputation—

REBECCA: God*damn* his reputation!

DENNIS: No—*you* damn it! He's heavy cake, Becky! He's what we used to call a gash hound. He goes for women, all kinds of women—especially those that blaze in the camera—film stars, face-lifted jet setters, high-priced prostitutes—cruel, calculating killers with blood on their hands. As he himself must be!

REBECCA: (*A moment. Then:*) I want you to meet him.

DENNIS: Meet him?! Do you think I would agree to meet him?

REBECCA: I don't see how you can avoid it.

DENNIS: By simply saying no! I'm not going to consent to this marriage, Becky. I'm not going to be talked into it, and I'm not going to be charmed into it!

REBECCA: (*Quietly*) When shall I ask him to come here?

DENNIS: Never!—don't you dare!—never!

REBECCA: When you meet him—

DENNIS: I'll never meet him!—you're out of your mind!

REBECCA: You've got to meet him, Father. You can't go raging against a man you've never seen, a man you've never spoken to!

DENNIS: I will not meet him, Becky! I will not meet him!

(*In a rage, he has lost control of himself. Silence. They confront one another. She does not give an inch. Firmly, with natural dignity, she departs. He remains, shaken. He rubs his palm across his mouth, the reminiscent gesture of a man who, long ago, needed a drink.*

The lights fade and come up in a pinpoint of illumination on Dennis's desk. He is sitting there, deeply preoccupied, trying to work. It is not going well. He addresses us.)

DENNIS: I need a drink. Sometimes I wish I had never quit. Give up the rotgut or rot your gut—that's what they said. Drink and die, they said. If I don't have a drink, then I should be rewarded, shouldn't I? Something should be going well for me. *Something!* My new play—shouldn't that be going well?—if I don't hit the bottle, can't I hit the right note?—sound the right echo? I'm trying to write a play about my family, and I want to write it as a comedy, I *yearn* to write it as a comedy. Isn't it possible to write a family play with a happy ending? Is there a discrepancy in that expectation? If one of the classic criteria of comedy is a happy ending, is there a contradiction between my two wishes? Is happiness a sophistry we've made up in the course of a passing conversation? Dennis!—what do *you* think? Dennis! Why is it I can summon the others, but not the one I need most to talk to! You used to sing so sweetly—sing a song for me, Dennis! Help me write the comedy! Dennis—*please*—help me write the comedy! *Dennis!* (*Dennis Junior appears. That is, in Dennis Senior's mind, this is his older son. Actually, it is his younger son, Patrick. Lean, in his thirties, not too well, Patrick is the image of his father. Seeing his son, the father is frantic with joy.*) Dennis!—oh, I'm so glad! Dennis, where have you been—where've you been hiding—I've been calling and calling—why don't you answer me!? Dennis—I'm talking to you!

PATRICK: (*Muted*) I'm not Dennis.

DENNIS: Please don't play this hide and seek with me—I've been going nearly crazy—how are you—where've you been? Why don't you answer me? Dennis!

PATRICK: (*Under quiet restraint*) Look at me, Father—I'm not Dennis.

DENNIS: I *am* looking at you—don't talk nonsense! Where've you been? Where've you been hiding? Talk to me! Dennis—please!

PATRICK: I'm not Dennis—I'm Patrick. You have trouble with our names.

DENNIS: (*Angry*) I don't have trouble with your names, goddamn it! You're Dennis!

PATRICK: (*Quietly*) Dennis was your older son. He's dead. I am Patrick, your younger son—I'm alive.

DENNIS: (*Shaken—almost ill with disappointment*) You're . . . not Dennis?

PATRICK: No. I'm sorry to disappoint you, Father.

DENNIS: (*To mend the damage*) No—no!—you don't disappoint me—no!

PATRICK: (*Mostly to himself*) I'm sure I do. I'm sorry—I'm very sorry.

(*To keep from crying, he departs. Dennis watches him go. His regret is painful.*

Julia enters. She is younger than Dennis, still beautiful with a fine face and eyes that tell a trouble. Her presence gives Dennis something difficult to deal with, but he is glad to see her. They talk with the careful kindness of people who still love each other but have become estranged. Of late, to hide her anxieties, Julia has become a chatterer; her pretended good cheer is almost persuasive. She is carrying a bag the contents of which she identifies:)

JULIA: I brought you some fruit.

DENNIS: Thank you, Julia. But you didn't have to. Agnes brought me some pears and apples yesterday.

JULIA: A wife's fruit is sweeter than a servant's. I think that's in the Bible: "A wife's fruit is sweeter than a servant's." Isn't that in the Bible?

DENNIS: If it's not it should be. Because a wife's fruit *is* sweeter than a servant's. And juicier—don't you think?—juicier? Hallelujah!

JULIA: Don't overplay it.

(*Making a singsong of the dull routine*) I bring you fruit, you don't eat it, it gets rotten, I take it away, I bring you fresh fruit.

DENNIS: (*Smiling wryly*) There it is—the whole life cycle. Man's destiny as seen in the rottening banana.

(*Julia takes the spoiled fruit out of the basket on his desk, takes the fresh fruit out of the bag she has brought, and puts the fresh fruit in the basket. Then she puts the spoiled fruit into the empty bag. As she is doing this, she murmurs:*)

JULIA: I really should put the fruit in your refrigerator—that's where it should be, in the refrigerator. But if it's not in front of your eyes where you can stare at it, you're *sure* to forget it's there.

DENNIS: I try not to, Julia. A few days ago I set the alarm, and told myself: when it rings, I will eat an apple. When the alarm went off I couldn't remember what I had set it for. So I took a bath. If it weren't for uneaten apples, I would never get clean.

(*They laugh slightly. Silence. He watches her with affection, but with guilt.*)

DENNIS: Julia . . . you don't have to bring me fruit as a pretext for visiting. You can come anytime, fruitless.

JULIA: I have to have a reason. (*She goes to his desk and picks up some letters and yellow scribbled pages*) Letters to answer?

DENNIS: Yes, please.

JULIA: (*Looking at the yellow pages*) Your handwriting's getting smaller.

DENNIS: Well, they're always telling me I overwrite. (*Then more seriously*) Sorry about the handwriting. Is it really important?

JULIA: No, it's not—if you don't mind that I can't read it.

DENNIS: I'll write big next time—*big*. Buy me some wallpaper.

JULIA: Please—it *is* important, Dennis.

DENNIS: All right, Julia—all *right*!

JULIA: It's just that I can't help you if you—

DENNIS: I know that—now don't nag!

(*She tries not to show she is hurt; he tries not to show how vexed he is. Silence.*)

JULIA: You were awake last night.

DENNIS: Yes, mostly. I wish you wouldn't notice.

JULIA: Your shades were up. I could see your light across the courtyard. I worry about you, Dennis—so far away—alone in this end of the house.

DENNIS: I'm not alone. There's Agnes.

JULIA: But you've cut her down to two afternoons a week.

DENNIS: She talks about ingrown toenails. Even if she's fervently against them, I figure twice a week should exhaust the subject.

JULIA: Still, if there's some sort of emergency—

DENNIS: That's why you had the phone installed, isn't it?

JULIA: But you never use it.

DENNIS: Because there's no emergency—that's *good*, isn't it?—wouldn't you say that's good?

JULIA: But you *could* use it for other things.

DENNIS: Oh, I do!—it's great for cracking nuts. Sometimes I do it when somebody's talking on the other end. It doesn't seem to make any difference. . . . But I do use it, Julia, really I do. I often call about the time—or the weather.

JULIA: It used to be that you would ring your bell when you wanted me. I don't even hear your bell anymore.

(*He picks up the little brass bell she is referring to. Smiling, he rings it vigorously.*)

DENNIS: There! I've rung it! I want you!

JULIA: (*A wry smile*) You don't want anybody. You're getting to be like your son.

DENNIS: (*Trying to sound cheery*) No, that's not true. Patrick's locked himself up in his apartment—but I'm not locked up anywhere. I go out whenever I want to. I trot down for the paper in the morning, I take long hikes in the woods. On Tuesday I went over to the post office, I bought some stamps, I had a long chat with Emily Brewster—about septic tanks. I didn't mean to have an in-depth discussion about septic tanks, but she said God preferred them to be flushed out every year or two. She's very cozy with God—He comes to her Reading Club every Thursday and tidies up the bawdy books. Like septic tanks, God prefers them to be cleaned out. How about you?

JULIA: I don't need cleaning out, Dennis, and I'm not Emily Brewster.

DENNIS: No, what I mean—are you cozy with God—did you go to church today?

JULIA: Yes.

DENNIS: Confession?

JULIA: Yes.

DENNIS: What did you confess?

JULIA: (*Lightly*) None of your business.

DENNIS: Why do you go to confession when you do nothing wrong?

JULIA: I don't know how many hundreds of times you've said that, and it never occurs to you that the question comes out: "Why do you go to confession when you do nothing?"

DENNIS: I didn't say that.

JULIA: It's what you meant.

DENNIS: Don't put unkind words in my mouth, Julia—it's not at all what I meant.

JULIA: Yes, it is. Because you pay no attention to what I do! Yesterday, I stood with a cannon and broadsword in front of your door and I prevented a rabble of invaders from interfering with your work. There was a man about the roof, a woman from the Boston Globe, an old stage manager who was just dropping by to say hello, and two girls from Yale who wanted your picture and your autograph. And I put them all to rout!

DENNIS: I appreciate it, Julia—and I think it's sad you had to spend the whole day saying no.

JULIA: (*Passionately*) I *want* to say no to anyone who interferes with your work, Dennis! It's the most important thing in the world to me. It's as sacred as going to church!

DENNIS: (*A slight outburst*) Then why don't you let me do it!

JULIA: I try not to interfere.

DENNIS: I don't think you try at all. I think you want me aware of your presence all the time.

JULIA: That's not true, Dennis!

DENNIS: Yes it is! I feel you outside my door—listening—waiting!—hungry for pages you can type! "Have you got anything for me today?—have you done any work? Have you got anything?" No! I've got nothing!—nothing!

JULIA: I've never asked you for pages!—never!—never in my life!

DENNIS: You don't have to ask for them! Your presence asks for them! It demands them! It gets me by the throat!

(*He is holding a book which he slams down on the desk. Their outbursts cease. She is shocked by his violence. She speaks quietly:*)

JULIA: Do you want me not to come at all?

DENNIS: (*Conscience-stricken, filled with remorse*) No—I'm sorry, Julia—please forgive me—I'm sorry.

JULIA: I could stay away for a while.

DENNIS: No—please—*beloved*!—please—I'm sorry.

JULIA: . . . It's lonely here. . . . I miss you, Dennis.

DENNIS: . . . Yes . . . I know.

JULIA: You used to come to lunch every once in a while—like a visitor. It was nice.

DENNIS: Yes. I wonder what happened to that. We . . . lose things.

JULIA: We used to have at least one meal together every day.

DENNIS: Dinner, mostly.

JULIA: Yes—in front of the fire. Whatever happened? Ever since you started writing this new play . . .

DENNIS: It's harder than the others.

JULIA: You always say that.

DENNIS: It's always true.

JULIA: But you used to have time. . . . I long for those days again . . . It's so . . . isolated.

DENNIS: I know. Bear with me until I finish—at least a first draft—bear with me.

JULIA: It's a such a big house . . . and hundreds of acres . . . far from anywhere. No wonder we can't hold on to the servants—they feel so far from everything. The place always seems so empty—just a trail of temporary people. They leave nothing behind but their footprints on the carpets. And even those are temporary . . .

DENNIS: If there were any way to provide permanence . . .

JULIA: Oh, I know there isn't. But when we were together—loving one another—we had the illusion of permanence, didn't we? (*With muted desperation*) And that's very important, Dennis, isn't it?—clinging to the illusion?

DENNIS: But it *is* only an illusion.

JULIA: And you say the hell with it.

DENNIS: No—really—I don't.

JULIA: Patrick says you do! He says you feel that way about all your real relationships. You don't care what happens to them. He says you much prefer living with phantoms.

DENNIS: (*Annoyed*) So that's where Becky hears it.

JULIA: And he said you'd better get into the real world with real people if you want to save yourself.

DENNIS: (*Losing his temper*) Real world, real people, real, real, real! God, what a vicious word! We use it like a truncheon on each other! Our children get their revenge by bashing us with it! (*Raging—on a rampage*) Not real?! Who the fuck is Patrick that he can say that about me! I live a damn sight closer to people than he does! I haven't shut myself away from them as he has! How dare he say that?

JULIA: Don't yell at me—I didn't say it.

DENNIS: But you gave it lip service—you agree with him—you talk behind my back—you scheme with him—

JULIA: I do not scheme with him! He's your son, not mine! And if he happens to be closer to me than he is to you, it's your own damn fault!

DENNIS: (*An instant. He studies it*) Yes . . . it is. (*Another pause*) I've thrown out the new play.

JULIA: (*With immediate sympathy*) You have? Oh, poor Dennis! . . . Why?

DENNIS: No good.

JULIA: But it sounded so promising. What happened?

DENNIS: I suddenly realized I couldn't write it with only one son in the family, I had to put the other son in as well. And overnight it stopped being a comedy, and wouldn't write itself.

JULIA: Of course not.

DENNIS: (*Upset*) Don't say "of course not" as if I'm denying that my older son is dead! That shouldn't have mattered in this play. I wasn't writing about Denny's death.

JULIA: You're always writing about his death. He's been gone for three years.

When will you stop grieving?

DENNIS: I was not writing about his death—I was writing about a happy summer in Cape Cod. He was still alive, and as cheerful as the rest of us. His death happened years after that—years! My God, we say the past informs the future—why should the future inform the past?

JULIA: Who says life has to be chronological?

DENNIS: (*An outbreak*) I just want to know what I'm writing for—what does it mean? How long can I go on sitting at that goddamn desk without knowing what I'm there for? How long can I tear at my own skin—

JULIA: (*Trying to comfort him*) You don't have to, you know—you're a famous man—you've done your share of work.

DENNIS: (*Getting unnerved*) My share—what's my share?

JULIA: Many happy people have lived and died without ever writing a single play. Yet, their children are born with the right number of hands and feet, and they brush their teeth and go to school—

DENNIS: —and even to heaven!

JULIA: (*Anxious for him, and needing to help him*) Dennis—dearheart— aren't you entitled to some peace? Do you have to go on digging and digging at yourself? Is it imperative, is it worth it?

DENNIS: (*Passionately, and with a touch of desperation*) Is it worth it?—who the hell knows? What if I should come upon some meaning—what if I could make all the pieces fit together—what if the puzzle could come alight in a great bright illumination—would all the pain be worth it? What if I could get some glimmer of Justice or Beauty or God, would it be worth it? What if I could scribble my way to some clear and abiding peace not only for myself but for you and my children and others—would it be worth it? Oh yes!— even if every page is soiled with bloodstains—oh yes!—worth it, worth it! (*An ecstasy, a frenzy. Then, silence. At last, quietly:*) But how do I get there? What do I write about?

JULIA: (*Quietly*) Write about me, Dennis.

DENNIS: You wouldn't want that.

JULIA: (*A plea*) Oh yes I would. I'm not the subject of an epic, I know that. But you love me, Dennis, and I'm as good a starting point as any if you don't know where you're going.

DENNIS: Julia—

JULIA: Maybe—if you *really* want to write a comedy—it would be good for you to start with somebody you love who also loves *you*!

DENNIS: If you think I could just sit down with the deliberate purpose of *using* you—

JULIA: But I want to be used! If you only knew how I long to get into a part of your life from which I'm absent. I hate being absent, Dennis, I hate it! Write about *me*!

DENNIS: You think I could consider reducing you to something on a page?

JULIA: But you won't reduce me!

DENNIS: You think I can love you as I do—and subject you to the kind of venom I write with?—the anger, the malice? My God, haven't I hurt you enough?

JULIA: But you don't seem to *know* what hurts me! Maybe if you write about me, you *will* know! Maybe you will, Dennis—and stop being as tortured as you are! Just let me be in your thoughts—let me *matter* to you! *Write about me*!

DENNIS: I couldn't do that to you.

JULIA: (*She is still. Then:*) It's strange . . . You can do it to your children.

DENNIS: They'll hardly notice.

JULIA: You're wrong.

DENNIS: By the time I'm finished, they won't see the faintest resemblance.

JULIA: Rebecca will know the genesis of every line.

DENNIS: You overestimate her.

JULIA: I know her better than you do. She's on the phone to me all the time.

DENNIS: (*Somewhat surprised*) Is she?

JULIA: Lately, yes. I wish she wouldn't call me so often. I'm sure she never called her mother as much as she does me.

DENNIS: She likes you better.

JULIA: That's a responsibility I don't think I need. She makes me feel guilty.

DENNIS: About what?

JULIA: She thinks I haven't done my best to change your mind?

DENNIS: Stay out of it. You have nothing to do with whether they get married or not.

JULIA: Maybe you haven't either.

DENNIS: Julia—I beg you—please—don't get mixed up in it.

JULIA: I will never say another word if you simply agree to meet him.

DENNIS: (*Angry*) No! Stay out of it!

JULIA: (*An instant*) I've invited him to come here.

DENNIS: You—*what*?

JULIA: This afternoon.

DENNIS: You're making this up, aren't you?

JULIA: For tea—or cocktails—or whatever.

DENNIS: Jesus! "For tea or cocktails or whatever." A nice, friendly little social gathering. (*With fake airiness*) Tell me about your dreams, Mr. Sperry, about your ideals, your appraisal of the model family and the exemplary society. (*Hard*) Tell me how you screwed my daughter!

JULIA: Well, I wouldn't put it in those words.

DENNIS: Call him on the phone and tell him it's canceled.

JULIA: No. I don't even know his number.

DENNIS: Tell Becky to tell him.

JULIA: I won't do it, Dennis.

DENNIS: (*Between command and pleading*) Julia—I need you to *help* me!

JULIA: Please don't ask me to call this off. (*Pleading*) Let's both take a step toward making a bigger family, Dennis. We're so small—and so far apart. Oh, please, let's come in closer, Dennis! Let's welcome new love and new children. Let's be kind to one another.

DENNIS: You think I don't want her to get married? Of course I do—but not to him!

JULIA: Take a chance on him!

DENNIS: No! Now call her on the phone—and call it off.

JULIA: No.

DENNIS: You say my work's sacred to you, and you protect me from the roofer and the stage manager, but when something happens that hurts me to the guts, you don't help me one damn bit!

JULIA: It's *living*, Dennis—I can't protect you from being *alive*!

DENNIS: I beg you, Julia!

JULIA: I can't do it.

DENNIS: Then I'll have to do it myself. I'll get her on the phone and we'll quarrel. It may be the worst quarrel of our lives—and never remedied. And until my dying day, I'll hold you responsible for it! (*An instant. His anger changes to pleading:*) Now I beg you one last time—call her—please—call her. (*Silence. A difficult moment for her. She goes to the phone and starts to dial Rebecca's number. The lights fade.*)

There is a faint glow on Dennis's desk. He sits at it, not really working—not writing, that is—merely engaged in busy work—rearranging, neatening, putting things into things. It wards off pain. Almost unheard at first, there is a distant outcry, eerie and unidentifiable. He pauses to listen: is he imagining? The cry comes closer. Suddenly it is there—in the room with him, and it comes from Becky—the shriek of the nine-year-old child being molested—struggling with an unseen assailant. Her arms flail, she tries to wrest herself away from the attacker.)

BECKY: No!—let me go!—help me!—somebody, help me! Oh, let me go—help me—he's hurting me—help me!

(*Dennis, terrified for her, has leapt from his chair. He strikes out at the invisible enemy, grapples with him, shouts, struggles.*)

DENNIS: No! Let her go—let her alone!

BECKY: He's hurting me—he's hurting me—!

(*Rebecca appears.*)

REBECCA: No he's not, you little idiot—he's making love to you!

DENNIS: Stop it—let her alone—stop it!

(*Now all the voices are raised together. Dennis is shouting, "Let her alone, you bastard, get your hands off her!" Becky is shrieking in pain, "He's hurting me—he's hurting me! Help me—help me!" Rebecca is pulling at Becky, trying to get her to stop her outcries. "Be quiet, you damn fool—shut your mouth—be quiet!" "She's only a child—let her go!" "Help me! Somebody help me!" Now, Dennis seems to be fighting all of them—Rebecca, Becky, the invisible molester.*)

DENNIS: Please—please—let her go, let her go!

(*Dennis thrashes about, fighting desperately to rescue his daughter from the unseen assailant. He keeps shouting and struggling until they all dis-*

*appear and only the attacker is visible. It is Simon Sperry. As Dennis
continues to rail at him, Simon becomes more and more illuminated.)*

SIMON: Let me go, you lunatic!

DENNIS: You're molesting my daughter!

SIMON: No I'm not—I'm making love to your daughter!

DENNIS: A man your age—she's nine years old!

SIMON: She's not nine—she's nearly double that.

DENNIS: (*Out of control*) Double double, toil and trouble! Get out of here,
   get out!

SIMON: No I won't! You called me!

DENNIS: Called you?—you're out of your head!—called you?!

SIMON: Yes you did—clearly! I'm Simon Sperry—you asked me to come.

DENNIS: My wife called and said I would have nothing to do with you! Get
   out of here!

SIMON: No, I won't! You've stopped writing about your family and have
   started to write my name! You've been thinking nothing but my name,
   every one of your characters has my name. You've been begging me to arrive!

DENNIS: No! I warned you to stay away from me—and from my daughter.

SIMON: All right, *all right*! The point is, I won't go away as long as you keep
   calling me to mind. And it's a good thing too—because we have to know
   one another, you and I—you're going to be my father-in-law.

DENNIS: (*Trembling, inarticulate*) What is this?—are we really talking about
   Becky? And marriage?

SIMON: Yes—exactly!

DENNIS: No! That marriage won't take place—you won't get my consent!
   I'll see one of us dead first!

SIMON: For a dramatist as distinguished as you are, Mr. Ryan, melodrama
   comes too easily to you. You realize you're making your daughter very
   unhappy.

DENNIS: Who's doing that to her? Who started this insanity?

SIMON: She loves you—she doesn't want to hurt you.

DENNIS: (*Another outbreak*) Why do people say that to their families? We
   do want to hurt one another! If she hurts herself, she *does* want to hurt
   me!

SIMON: No, I swear to you—she doesn't—she's trying her best to avoid it.
   I begged her to marry me without your blessing, and she said, "I can't—
   he loves me too much. I can't bear for him to feel I've betrayed him."

DENNIS: There!—she said "betrayed," didn't she? And it is betrayal! That's
   in her mind, isn't it?—marrying someone like you—betrayal!

SIMON: "Someone like me"? You don't even know who I am!

DENNIS: Nobody knows who you are! In the three weeks since she said your
   name to me, I've read everything about you I could lay my hands on—
   and in all that publicity garbage, there aren't two stories about you that
   match. Was your father really a coffee millionaire or was he a drunken

drifter who died in a Mexican jail? Did you play Vivaldi on the harpsi-chord when you were only three years old? Did your mother smear her body with goosefat and swim the English Channel?

SIMON: Those were all—uh—improvisations. I played some of those parts in films. Newspapers get mixed up about what is fact and what is celluloid.

DENNIS: Who gets mixed up?—who?

SIMON: I am not mixed up about who I am—and if you give me half a chance, you won't be mixed up either.

DENNIS: Half a chance?—what the hell does that mean? Half a chance to do what?

SIMON: (*A moment. Then, quietly*) To be your friend.

DENNIS: My friend?—are you senseless?

SIMON: Don't be so surprised—I have friends. And some of them really like me. And why not? I'm kind, I'm understanding, I'm generous. Sometimes I even say something that strikes them as being true. It's an accident, of course, but I do have these felicitous accidents—and I'd like to share them with you.

DENNIS: I wouldn't share anything with you.

SIMON: Not even your daughter's happiness?

DENNIS: Happiness?—my God!

SIMON: Yes, happiness!—let me convince you I can make her happy. (*Genuinely*) Let me start by telling you why I love her.

DENNIS: I know the obvious reason: she has youth and beauty.

SIMON: Yes, but that's not the only reason. She makes me feel safe—that's the big one. She forgives me everything. She absolves me of the sin of van-ity, she pardons my failures, she lets herself forget that there was ever any other woman in my life. I can sit in a room with her—in light or in dark-ness—and not need to make a conversation. I can go walking in the street with her, and not see the debris on the sidewalk, and not hear the heartaching whimpers of people who know very well that there's no place to go. I can feel her touch me on the cheek, and know that this will not be the last time—she will touch me tomorrow. Oh, safety!—how can I tell you what a bliss of safety she has brought into my life! It is something I thought I would never have—and here I am, with my bifocals and my touch of arthritis and my pills in my little brass pillbox, and at last I have come to safety! I have found it, I have found it!

DENNIS: (*Drily*) Very good reading—quite impressive.
(*Dennis has disdained a deep-felt confidence, and Simon is wounded; he feels belittled. His words are subdued, mostly to himself.*)

SIMON: I'm sorry I've wasted an intimacy on you.
(*But Simon is no moper. He looks around and finds something that will lift his spirits—a framed photograph on Dennis's desk.*)

SIMON: What's that?

DENNIS: Clearly, it's a photograph.

SIMON: I can see it's a photograph, but of what?

(*He picks it up*) Good heavens, it's your family. That's you and your former wife, I take it—and—don't tell me! Is that Rebecca?

DENNIS: Yes.

SIMON: (*Her image buoys him*) Oh, how beautiful, how dear! How old was she then?

DENNIS: Nine, I think.

SIMON: Look!—look at her! What a lovely face! How appealing she is, how innocent! And the two boys—that's Patrick, of course. And Dennis—isn't that Dennis? I thought he had left home.

DENNIS: (*Grudging the information*) He came back on a visit.

SIMON: Ah, then, it was a happy occasion, wasn't it?

DENNIS: (*Inwardly*) Yes it was.

SIMON: (*The enthusiast*) Oh yes indeed—I can see that! How close and loving you all look! And laughing—heads up—eyes shining—all that glowing good will in your faces! Even you, Mr. Ryan, grinning like a cat! You see?—that's the kind of family we hope to have—smiling, Ryan, smiling, rejoicing in the fact of life!

DENNIS: Most families never rejoice excepts in photographs.

SIMON: I think you're wrong!—do you have any statistics on the subject? My family will rejoice—more often than in photographs, I can tell you that!

DENNIS: Smile, goddamn it.

SIMON: You're damn right! (*In a transport*) I'll give lessons in happiness! In our house there'll be a full curriculum of Smiles and Games and Dances! Baccalaureates and doctorates and summa cum laudes in joy ascendant! And when our first child is born, it will be merrier than all of us, and— (*More quietly serious*)—if it's a boy, we'll name him Dennis, after you.

DENNIS: (*Muted*) I've already had a son named after me.

SIMON: (*Looking at the photograph*) Yes, of course. But he has—regrettably—passed away. And I'm sure you would like his name remembered. And yours as well.

DENNIS: What makes you think I want his name remembered? Or mine, for that matter?

SIMON: You're a man with an eye on posterity.

DENNIS: One eye on posterity and the other on the grave.

SIMON: (*In a gust of sympathy*) Oh, dear man, you think the grave is final?

DENNIS: (*Wondering at him*) What a jughead.

SIMON: I'd rather be a jughead than a crepehanger. My God, Ryan, I came here not a minute too soon! You've got an urgent need of me!

DENNIS: To do what?

SIMON: To restore the mood of this photograph. To sweep some of the gloom out of your life. To make you smile.

DENNIS: I don't get you, Sperry. I don't know whether you're dead serious or setting me up for a practical joke.

SIMON: A practical joke?—oh no!—that would be mean! My God, you think making people laugh is an act of hostility?

DENNIS: Much of the time, yes.

SIMON: Ah! That's why your plays are so humorless!

DENNIS: You think they're humorless?

SIMON: Oh, solemn as the Bible.

DENNIS: Do you think the Bible would have been improved by a few gags and an occasional pratfall?

SIMON: No, but your *plays* might be.

DENNIS: (*Dryly*) It grieves me that you think so.

SIMON: There's no merriment, Ryan—no *gaiety*! When you see a foible, you go at it with a blackjack, you beat it bloody, you pound it with a bludgeon of righteousness! There's no affection for human frailty in your plays, there's no forgiveness.

DENNIS: Have you ever seen one of my plays?

SIMON: Uh . . . no.

DENNIS: Good, then you're qualified to criticize.

SIMON: (*Quickly*) But I've read them.

DENNIS: You must put on your bulletproof vest and go and see one sometime.

SIMON: God forbid. The subject matter scares the hell out of me. Sons and daughters killing their parents—incest—beautiful young men with consumption, coughing their lungs out—sick whores and rotted-out dope fiends. Jumpin' Jupiter, is there no enjoyment in the world?—doesn't anybody eat an ice cream cone?

DENNIS: (*A wry smile*) The ice cream cone being the zenith of human fulfillment.

SIMON: The pinnacle!

(*As Dennis smiles more fully*) Are you really laughing?

DENNIS: Not really. . . . Make me laugh.

SIMON: (*The challenge is clear*) Oh, I can—easily.

DENNIS: What does she see in you? You don't look very prepossessing. You're not handsome, and I can't imagine that you're very sexy. What's more, you look even older than I think you are. She says you make her laugh. Well, go on—make me laugh.

(*Simon debates whether to accept the challenge.*)

SIMON: Have you ever seen me juggle oranges?

DENNIS: No.

SIMON: I did it in a two-reeler, once, many years ago.

DENNIS: I didn't see it.

SIMON: I don't see your stuff, you don't see mine.

DENNIS: It keeps us free of prejudice.

SIMON: (*Smiling*) Yes . . . Five of them.

DENNIS: Five what?

SIMON: Oranges. I juggle five at a time.

DENNIS: I regret I have no oranges.

(*Pointing to his desk*) A couple of apples, a pear, a banana.

SIMON: That's all right—I always carry lots of oranges.

(*He tosses an "orange" into the air. It is an imaginary orange, and he catches it*) There!—there's one! And here's number two.

(*Another orange, and another*) Three—four—now, where's number five?

DENNIS: You just dropped it.

SIMON: No, I didn't—it's in your ear.

(*A quick dart of his arm, and he snatches the imaginary fifth orange out of Dennis's ear. He starts his spiel:*) Now watch them—watch them—keep an eye on them! Look how they chase one another—look how they try to escape—fly away—fly somewhere else—catch up with one another—fly away, come back, come home! They're a family—they try to stay together, they try to separate. They can't stay together and they can't stay apart! How silly they are, how sad, how funny! Fly, fly, you beauties—fly—fly—!

(*Suddenly it is as though one of the oranges turns renegade and out of reach. Simon pursues it toward the space that Dennis occupies. The juggler's purpose is to move his audience, physically unbalance him in some way. But as Simon advances toward Dennis, to catch the imaginary orange, Dennis doesn't budge. Simon, foiled, has to run around Dennis to catch the orange on the other side of him. Simon carries his act back to where he started. He is now juggling in a more casual way, his attention not on the oranges but on Dennis. At last he stops juggling.*)

DENNIS: Is that it?

SIMON: Yes, that's it.

DENNIS: You didn't make me laugh.

SIMON: (*Chagrined*) I don't blame you. I did it very badly.

DENNIS: Do you generally do it better?

SIMON: Oh yes. You froze me up.

DENNIS: That's right—blame the audience. I do it all the time.

SIMON: But I'm not giving up. Before I'm through, I'm going to make you laugh.

DENNIS: I'll make you cry first.

SIMON: I make 'em laugh, you make 'em cry—it's what we do for a living. Which will happen—a smile or a tear? You wanna bet?

DENNIS: Do you make everything into a game?

SIMON: It's not a game! You're in trouble—I'm trying to help you—it's a simple act of humanity!

(*Quietly, genuinely*) Why do you object?—why don't you let me do this for you?—why don't you let me help you laugh?

DENNIS: (*Breaking out*) Because you and Becky are not a laughing matter! This is not a comedy, Sperry, it's a potential tragedy—and anybody who says otherwise is either a fool or a liar!

SIMON: (*Desperately*) We can't cry our lives away, man!—we can't!

DENNIS: It's the way it happens!

SIMON: I hate that, I hate it! I hate that more than you hate *me*!

DENNIS: Don't underestimate how much I hate you.

SIMON: (*Genuinely troubled*) But why?—tell me why.

DENNIS: Because you're Hollywood—you're a fake. You may be one of the most celebrated men in the world, but to me you're nothing but a cheap comedian.

SIMON: Cheap comedian—in your mind those words were born together, weren't they?

DENNIS: In a way, yes.

SIMON: Comedy is cheap and tragedy is noble.

DENNIS: Much to be said for that.

SIMON: (*Squaring off, in deep, righteous rage*) All right then. What makes you think you've got a corner on tragedy? You think because you've won a Pulitzer Prize and a Nobel award that you've got a monopoly on tears? All of us are crying!—all of us! Every man in the street feels he's less than he should be, or his daughter is on drugs or his wife has a disease that has withered her body and her hopes. We're all going to die—and, worst of all, we know it! My God, you've lost one son, and I've lost two of them— and neither of my sons called for me when he was dying. You had TB when you were a kid—and at the age of fourteen I weighed seventy-nine pounds because I was starving! I am not fifty-eight years young, I am fifty-eight years closer to my death. My heavenly dreams will get buried with my casket! Death, man!—decay and heartache and death! Tragedy, Ryan— yes—all of us! And I'm as true a tragedian as you are—except that I won't cry! The only way to beat it—or pretend to beat it—is to laugh! Well, you may not hear me at the moment, but I'm laughing!

(*Silence. Absolute silence. Then, quietly:*)

DENNIS: What a charlatan you are.

SIMON: (*Flinching*) I am not a charlatan!

DENNIS: What a fake!

SIMON: (*Enraged*) Don't you dare to use that word again! Never!

DENNIS: Did you really have two sons who didn't call you when they were dying? Did you really almost starve to death? Are those the stories you tell to the press—and to your women? What other lies have you been telling!

SIMON: *I am not a liar*!

DENNIS: Mr. Sperry, you're a liar in everything you say and do! Even in your work!

SIMON: You've never seen my work!

DENNIS: I have a confession! I *have* seen your work—three of your most successful films. I ran them a few days ago. And I was dumbfounded at what a fraud you are. As an actor, Mr. Sperry—even as an actor—you're a fake. You try to manipulate me into feeling things you yourself have no feeling for. Sentimental little droopings of the head—cloudings of the eye. And that artificial smile—so precisely painted on your mouth—with a hundred teeth gleaming white—and not a glimmer of respondence in your eyes. And oh how coy you are—how sweet, how tender—(*Pointing to the fruit on his desk*)—like rotting fruit.

SIMON: That looks pretty fresh to me.

DENNIS: It's rotting—it's *always* rotting—and if you tell yourself it's not, that's a lie. And that's what's at the heart of your work, a big sentimental lie. And you know you're telling a lie, but you keep right on telling it!

SIMON: And you don't believe me for a moment.

DENNIS: No! Because you don't believe it yourself. It's the worst kind of corruption.

SIMON: (*With a hoot*) Corruption? Good cheer is corruption?

DENNIS: (*Passionately*) Yes, it's a falsehood! You try to make life appear less disastrous than it really is. Is that art? Is it honest, is it decent? Is it worth the time of a talented man? Aren't you ashamed to draw a laughing picture of a crying breed? Isn't that a cruel mockery? Isn't it the role of the cowardly clown—to hide behind the painted grin?

SIMON: It's not cowardly—it's brave! Can you think of a braver way of fighting than to smile!?

DENNIS: Yes—shriek! Scream! Rail against a cruel existence we never asked for, against a death we never chose! Not like you, you craven bastard—smiling the fake forgiving smile—smothering back your tears and your heartache! Why don't you scream, you hypocrite!—why don't you cry out in the streets?—why don't you shriek your guts out?!

(*Silence. Then:*)

SIMON: I will think about what you've said. In the spirit of noblesse oblige, will you also think about what I've said?

DENNIS: I have no spirit of noblesse oblige. If I can, I will kill you.

(*Simon reacts as Simon would: he smiles.*)

SIMON: Then I'd better get out of here.

(*He starts to go. At the door, he turns*) You really think I'm such a bad actor?

DENNIS: Execrable.

SIMON: Can't convince you I'm not?

DENNIS: Never.

SIMON: I'm sorry. Very genuinely—I am sorry.

(*Simon gets to the door. He is not as cocky as he has been. In fact, he's a bit unsteady. At the door, he stops. His hand starts toward his head, then halts, mid-gesture, as though he has forgotten something. He suddenly looks frail and disoriented. Somewhat dizzy, he turns.*)

SIMON: Could I—would you please give me a glass of water—I'm not feeling well.

DENNIS: Yes—of course.

(*Dennis hastens to the water carafe on his desk, pours a glass half-full and hurries back to to Simon. Too late. Simon has fainted. Stunned, Dennis goes down on his knees beside him.*)

DENNIS: Sperry—Sperry—!

(*He raises Simon's head off the floor, puts an arm around the man's shoulder, keeps calling his name*) Sperry, can you hear me? Take deep breaths—breathe—can you hear me?—Sperry—Sperry!

(*Suddenly, like an athlete, Simon leaps up off the floor. His arms are out in the gesture of an actor taking a curtain call—his face is an expansive, ingratiating smile.*)

SIMON: There! You believed me, didn't you?

DENNIS: You son of a bitch.

SIMON: (*Crowing*) You believed me! There was nothing in that performance that you could call a fake! I falsified nothing! I'm a better actor than you said I am! And a true one! So true that it made you go down on your knees to help me! It turned you from a mean-tempered miserable old monster into a decent, considerate human being!

DENNIS: It had nothing to do with you—it was a reflex.

SIMON: You want to kill me, but you didn't let me die! In fact, you tried to revive me! It was an act of kindness—and it was a sign!

DENNIS: A sign of what, you maniac?

SIMON: A sign that somewhere—buried inside you—you could have a kindly feeling for me. Person to person, we might be charitable, we might think twice before we inflict a wound, we—my God, we're civilized men—we're basically *good* men—we might try to be part of the same family—we might even be friends.

DENNIS: I don't see how that could ever happen. And I can't see how it would be important either way.

SIMON: (*Passionately*) It's important to *me*! And I think it's important to you too, Ryan! We've got a lot in common, you and I. We're both chasing a dream in much the same way. We're both artists, we both see our work come alive and we watch it die! I've been married three times—and so have you. We've had six wives between us—six—count 'em—six! My God, what hope and what disillusionment! What are we crying for, you and I? What do we want, what do we need, what are we begging for? A few more dollars in the bank? Another flare in the theater, another triumph? We've had all that—why do we need more of it? Well, you know what we need, you know what we're crying for! It's the look of kindness, Ryan, it's the touch of the tender hand—it's the solace against the cruelty of dying—*it's love, Ryan*—it's the unfulfilled passion of our lives! That's what we all need of one another.

DENNIS: Not I! I have no such passion!

SIMON: You're a liar, Ryan!

DENNIS: None!—no such passion—none! I am not a love-slobbering idiot—my brain hasn't softened to a pulp! If life is a stone, I'll beat my head against it, and I won't go to mush. Love, you say?—love, for Chrissake!? I have no such passion—none!

SIMON: What do you have in its place, Ryan? What do you do to escape? Do you sneak off to a secret little bar around the corner?—are you still taking a little nip out of the old bottle? Are you, man? Let me smell your breath! Are you back to drinking, Ryan?

DENNIS: Shut up!—stop that!

SIMON: *Are you a drunk?*

(*Dennis slaps him. For the first time, Simon loses his control. Enraged, he lashes out:*)

SIMON: If you ever do that again, I'll cripple you, I'll cut your old balls off.

DENNIS: I'm going to get you first, you bastard! I'm going to dig up every corpse in your life, I'm going to line up every woman you've ever misused, I'm going to drag you through every latrine you've ever dumped in! Now, get out of here! Go on—get out!

SIMON: Put some clothes on.

DENNIS: What?

SIMON: You're naked. All your wounds are showing. What an agony you have—to be loved! And you don't know where to look or where to turn! (*As he starts to leave, Dennis calls after him.*)

DENNIS: I have no agony to be loved—don't you say that! I am perfectly content to live my life the way I have been living it! I don't need you and I don't need anybody! I don't need my dead son to come back—and I don't need my living son to love me! I need nobody! I need only to be left alone! That's all—let me alone—let me alone! (*The light fades.*)

END OF ACT ONE

Act Two

THE LIGHTS HAVE PICKED UP another area of Dennis's consciousness: Patrick's studio apartment. It is a cramped, inexpensive room, jammed with books, manuscripts, junk, knickknackery; the abode of a man whose total life is in this enclosure; he is a recluse. There is one narrow table which serves as Patrick's desk, dining surface and general dumping ground. A single desk lamp illuminates what he is now doing—building a house of cards. He is skilled at it; already his structure is quite high. He works with anxiety, coming to the end of the challenge. In his thirties, Patrick is unkempt, restless. But, despite his isolation, he is wry without being embittered, and not too patently unhappy. There is a knock on the door; it startles him. His first thought is for the safety of his house of cards. He puts his arms around it without touching it, to catch the structure if it tumbles. Another knock. He calls out:

PATRICK: Slowly! Open the door slowly—don't make a draft—come in slowly!
  (*The door opens and Dennis enters. As he closes the door, the draft does it: the house of cards collapses.*)
PATRICK: Damn it!—look what you've done—five hours of housebuilding and look at it!—shot to hell! Look what you've done! I told you to come in slowly.

DENNIS: I took three years and three months.
(*Silence, long silence. They try not to stare at one another, but their awareness of their presence together is like a musical vibration.*)
PATRICK: How are you, Father?
DENNIS: I'm pretty much as you see.
PATRICK: If I seem very calm, I'm not.
DENNIS: Me either.
PATRICK: What made you come?
DENNIS: I missed you.
PATRICK: (*He smiles to hide how much this means to him*) I'm trying to believe that.
DENNIS: Give it a good try.
(*A silence.*)
PATRICK: You're looking thin.
DENNIS: So are you.
PATRICK: It's the way I stand in the light—sometimes fat, sometimes thin.
DENNIS: Thin is supposed to be better.
PATRICK: So I'm told.
DENNIS: I try to stay impartial.
PATRICK: Do you?—you've changed. You used to say it was important to be partial about everything—never be neutral—hate, love, get angry over causes, have a fervor for the moon!
DENNIS: (*Embarrassed*) A fervor for the moon—did I actually say that? What an airbag!
PATRICK: Oh no—I used to subscribe to it. Sometimes I still do.
DENNIS: Do you? What can you do with it?
PATRICK: Nothing in particular. I build houses.
DENNIS: Nice. No maintenance, no mortgage. I'm sorry I wrecked it.
PATRICK: It's okay—it's a house that gets built rapidly.
(*Dennis has picked up one of the cards. He studies it closely.*)
DENNIS: What's this gooey stuff?
PATRICK: A little Scotch tape. Sometimes, when the cards won't stay in place, I cheat.
DENNIS: Doesn't that—uh—diminish the accomplishment?
PATRICK: Not very much. It connects me with reality. That's how real houses are built.
DENNIS: Does Scotch tape attach you to reality?
PATRICK: I don't need much, Father. Do you?
(*Silence. Difficult.*)
DENNIS: It's very stuffy in here. Don't you need more air?
PATRICK: Is the air out there any better than in here?
DENNIS: Please—let's not start that again.
PATRICK: Start what?
DENNIS: You're trying to make me feel smug, and you're succeeding.

PATRICK: I'm just trying to suggest, Father, that you're no more in the world than I am.

DENNIS: Well, I feel that I *am* in it, and that takes a bit more courage than I thought I had.

PATRICK: How are you in it?

DENNIS: I don't know. I bump into people—inadvertently, I must say—I quarrel, I take issue with things. When an election comes up, I sometimes vote. Last week I sent a letter to the *Times*. Jesus, you've got me sounding like a jackass. I guess there's no way I can really prove I'm in the human race. No membership card. Except . . . maybe . . . work.

PATRICK: Still at it, huh?

DENNIS: (*He lies orotundly*) Oh yes, always at it. Doing a new play, you know.

PATRICK: Good. (*An instant. Tentatively*) I'm at it too.

DENNIS: (*With genuine pleasure*) Yes! Becky told me you're writing again. I'm delighted, Patrick. Is it something you can talk about?

PATRICK: A book.

DENNIS: What subject?

PATRICK: It's called *32 Ways to Kill Yourself.*

DENNIS: (*Grim as the jest may be, he not unpleasantly falls in with it*) Hm— are there only thirty-two?

PATRICK: Thirty-one that are sure-fire. Holding your breath is unreliable.

DENNIS: (*Trying to be cheery*) The others are guaranteed?

PATRICK: Or your money back. Especially if you double up on the methods: say, eat bad oysters and hang yourself.

DENNIS: You've got to do it in the right order—oysters first, right?

PATRICK: Yes, if you hang yourself first, you don't get to eat the oysters.

DENNIS: (*The jest is over. Soberly*) So Becky was wrong—you're not writing, are you?

PATRICK: I can't find what it's for.

DENNIS: The glib answer is that it's for itself.

PATRICK: You know quite well it has to be more than that. But what? Is it a search, is it a confession?

DENNIS: Whatever it's for, I wish you'd go back to it.

PATRICK: Why?

DENNIS: I've said it for years and years, Patrick—you're the most talented of all of us.

PATRICK: Please.

DENNIS: You know I mean it. And I had hoped . . .

(*He lets the wish linger*)

PATRICK: I know you hoped . . . Sorry.

(*A moment*) But I *have* been writing a little.

DENNIS: (*A ray of optimism*) Have you?

PATRICK: I started a new poem a few days ago. I've only got a first draft. Would you like to read it?

DENNIS: (*Eagerly*) Oh yes, I would!—very much, very much.

(*He is rooting through his pockets*) But—no reading glasses. Would you read it to me?

PATRICK: Are you sure?

DENNIS: (*Keyed up, full of anticipation*) Yes, yes—please. Oh, I'm so delighted. Go on—please go on.

(*Patrick roots through the papers on his table, finds the one he wants. He reads:*)

PATRICK: God guard me from those thoughts men think
In the mind alone;
He that sings a lasting song
Thinks in a marrow-bone;

From all that makes a wise old man
That can be praised of all;
O what am I that I should not seem
For the song's sake a fool?

I pray—for fashion's word is out
And prayer comes round again—
That I may seem, though I die old,
A foolish, passionate man.

(*Silence. He puts the paper down. The silence holds.*)

DENNIS: It's beautiful.

PATRICK: You mean it?

DENNIS: Oh yes—a lovely poem, lovely.

(*A moment*) It's called "The Presence," isn't it?

(*Patrick is caught. He takes a moment.*)

PATRICK: No . . . "Presences."

DENNIS: That's right—"Presences." I've always loved that poem. It's Yeats, isn't it?

PATRICK: Yes.

DENNIS: William Butler Yeats.

PATRICK: Don't rub it in—"Yeats" is enough.

DENNIS: Why did you say you had written it?

PATRICK: I wanted to watch you tear it apart. I thought, for once, it would be amusing to see you do that to William Butler Yeats.

DENNIS: I never tore your stuff apart.

PATRICK: Every time.

DENNIS: That's not true, Patrick.

PATRICK: Oh, you'd always start exactly the way you did this time. "It's beautiful—it's a lovely poem, lovely." And you'd pick out your choice phrases, the lines you particularly favored—and you'd make me feel so blessed—so *chosen*—as though I'd been touched by a wand. And then you'd say "Except." And those little tiny exceptions would pull little threads out of the fabric—little tiny threads, one at a time—and the whole weaving would fall apart, as if the rats had been at it.

DENNIS: You can't imagine that I was trying to be helpful, can you?

PATRICK: Yes, I think that's true.

DENNIS: I was—I swear to you I was. I wanted to help you improve your work, I wanted to share in it, I wanted to be part of the world you were creating.

PATRICK: As you allowed us to be part of yours.

DENNIS: You couldn't very well come to my rehearsals when you were away at school.

PATRICK: Nor could I get you to the school.

DENNIS: Don't bring that up again, Patrick. It happened twenty years ago.

PATRICK: It goes on happening all the time.

DENNIS: (*Not blaming Patrick, he is pleading*) That's morbid, son—it's just morbid. If you hadn't cheated, I would have come up to the school and defended you. But you admitted cheating in the exam, so you had to take your punishment and forget about it. And it wasn't such a cruel punishment—two weeks suspension—my God, he would have expelled you if I hadn't talked to him!

PATRICK: On the phone.

DENNIS: It's all that was required.

PATRICK: *You weren't there*!

DENNIS: (*Hot, agitated*) No, I wasn't—I was in rehearsal! It was my most important play. I'd never have gotten the Nobel if that play had been a failure—never!

PATRICK: You never come when I need you—never! You don't even come to my funerals!

DENNIS: (*Finally losing his temper*) Stop that! Don't knife me in the back with your fake poetry!

PATRICK: I'll knife you every way you deserve!

DENNIS: You miserable bastard—!

PATRICK: Go on—hit me! Then tell Rebecca that I beat you up—that I'm sick and violent and uncontrollable—go on—hit me!
(*Dennis might do it, but he forbears. Silence. There is nothing to mitigate their misery. At last, almost to himself:*)

DENNIS: You always wanted more from me than I was able to give.

PATRICK: I would have said the same about you.

DENNIS: I tried, Patrick—I swear to you I tried.

PATRICK: So did I. I tried my heart out for you. I'd go off into dark corners and weep over the way I was disappointing you. Sometimes I thought of killing myself. It might be the only perfect act I could perform for you. . . . Maybe that's what Dennis thought.

DENNIS: No!—don't say that!

PATRICK: It could be true—it could be true.

DENNIS: Please—*please*!

(*He twists his head. He is suddenly weeping—silently, secretly. A quiet. Then:*)

DENNIS: Why don't you open a window? You need some air in here. It's not healthy . . .

(*They both smile wanly at how inconsequential it is.*)

PATRICK: Why did you come? Really—why?

DENNIS: I told you—I missed you. The last few months I've been thinking about you a great deal. And I dream. I've been having these guilty dreams about a lizard.

(*He smiles in embarrassment*) Did I ever put a pin in your tail?

PATRICK: (*Smiling*) Let me see now . . . I don't think so.

DENNIS: Damn dumb dream. But lizards aren't all of it. I've had pleasant dreams about you, too. We go on trips together. We find useless things to take home.

PATRICK: I'm very touched by that, Father.

DENNIS: (*He pauses. Then:*) I wish you would try.

PATRICK: Try what?

DENNIS: Try to go out again.

PATRICK: If I go out . . . and get drunk . . . and fall down in the street . . . will you come and pick me up?

DENNIS: Yes, I will, Patrick—I will! I won't fail you this time—I promise—I won't! I want to start doing things for you, Patrick—real things—just let me do something *real* for you.

(*Silence*) How are you managing about money? You need any?

PATRICK: No, thanks. Mother's money is still holding out.

DENNIS: Which reminds me—Julia sends her best.

PATRICK: Tell her thanks. She's still sending me those awful food packages. Stuff I hate. Glazed fruit. Marzipan. Mince pie. I throw it all in the garbage! I asked Rebecca to tell her to stop, but I guess she didn't tell her, did she?

DENNIS: I don't know—I guess not—she probably didn't have the heart.

PATRICK: (*With a wry smile*) How kindheartedly we torment one another.

DENNIS: For Christ sake, nobody's tormenting you, Patrick. If you want Julia to quit sending you packages, you tell her so yourself. Write her a letter or send her a postcard. Just lift the telephone, for Pete sake!

PATRICK: I don't have any telephone.

DENNIS: Then go and see her! Keep in touch with us, Patrick, keep in touch with the family. Especially Rebecca—she's going through a tough time.

PATRICK: What's so tough about it?

DENNIS: That guy she thinks she's in love with. Talk to her about that.

PATRICK: I have talked to her about it.

DENNIS: Well, help her to change her mind. She loves you, she listens to you. This is urgent, Patrick. Write her a note. Tell her to come and see you—tell her it's an emergency.

PATRICK: What sort of emergency?

DENNIS: Patrick, she can't marry that guy! Please tell her that!

PATRICK: (*Quietly*) But I think she should.

DENNIS: (*Stunned*) You're not serious.

PATRICK: I think she should and I think she shouldn't. That's what I think about everything. Don't move in any direction.

DENNIS: You have to move. She's your sister—she's going to destroy herself.

PATRICK: I don't think so.

DENNIS: Patrick—I ask you, I beg you—

PATRICK: That's what you came for, isn't it?

DENNIS: What?

PATRICK: You didn't come here for my sake. "I miss you, Patrick—I love you, Patrick!" That's a load of crap, isn't it? You didn't come here for me—you came for Rebecca!

DENNIS: I came for both of you!

PATRICK: For her!—not for me!—for her!

(*Painfully he starts to laugh*) It's funny about us. We send one another on errands. I send her to stop the marzipan, and you send me to stop the marriage. And no matter how we beg one another for help, nobody runs the errand!

(*Silence. They are both in distress. Patrick controls himself, then says quietly:*)

PATRICK: You want to stop the marriage, do it yourself.

DENNIS: I don't know how.

PATRICK: Yes you do.

DENNIS: How?

PATRICK: Ask Diana Green.

DENNIS: Who's Diana Green?

PATRICK: You don't know who she is?

DENNIS: No, I don't.

PATRICK: Read the papers.

DENNIS: I do read the papers.

PATRICK: No, you glance through them as if they refer to somebody else's world! Nothing in them is personal to you. And you certainly don't read the gossip columns, do you?

DENNIS: No, and I don't look at other people's shit.

PATRICK: It's your shit, Father, and it's mine! And now it refers to your own daughter and the man she wants to marry! And if you think that's a cesspool, don't ask me to get into it. Do it yourself! Stop running away!

DENNIS: (*Wounded, angry*) Running away?! My God, you can say that to me?—you?! Why, you goddamn quitter—!

(*He stops himself. A hurtful pause. Patrick speaks quietly.*)

PATRICK: Quitter . . . All those times when you got cut to pieces by the critics, you were never a quitter. Because you knew you had the talent to prevail. If I had as much talent as you have, I might not be a quitter either.

DENNIS: If I had it in my power to give you a great present, I wouldn't give you more talent, I'd give you more guts.

PATRICK: I'd accept with thanks.

(Silence. Aware how much he has wounded Patrick, Dennis wants to make amends, wants to ask for forgiveness. They are in pain and need their meeting to be over, but don't want it to end this way.)

DENNIS: Come and see me, Patrick.

PATRICK: *(After a moment)* Last winter—when you had pneumonia—I was about to leave for the hospital, when Rebecca called and said you were no longer there—you had recovered.

DENNIS: I'm sorry I jumped the gun on you.

PATRICK: That's rougher than it needs to be.

DENNIS: *(A hurt outbreak)* What should I do?—ask you to forgive me for recovering before you could pull yourself together to come and see me? Well, stuff it—I don't ask you to forgive me for anything!

PATRICK: *(With a quiet and awesome sense of discovery)* O-ho-ho-ho— *that's* what you came here for, isn't it?

DENNIS: What?

PATRICK: Forgiveness.

DENNIS: *(Hurt and angry, he loses control)* For what, for Christ sake? What have I done to you that I still need forgiveness for? Something twenty years ago? What have I done to you as a father that you wouldn't have forgiven years ago if I were a stranger? Does being a father make me eternally guilty and unforgivable? *What am I to be forgiven for?*

PATRICK: *(Quietly)* That's what you've been asking all of us, isn't it?—"what am I to be forgiven for?" All of us—Mom—Julia—Rebecca—me—

DENNIS: Dennis.

PATRICK: Yes—him too—even though he's dead.

DENNIS: *(A muffled outcry)* He won't talk to me!

PATRICK: *(With a wry smile)* It's one of the privileges of mortality.

DENNIS: Don't make a joke of it! All the others in my life—if I summon them in my memory—they speak to me! They do! But not Dennis.

PATRICK: *(Pitying him)* I'm sorry, Father.

DENNIS: His voice—if I could hear his voice—! He used to sing a lot—do you remember how he used to sing? . . .

(Patrick doesn't answer. They gaze at one another for a painful moment, then Dennis leaves. Patrick is more solitary than before. He takes up the Scotch tape and starts to rebuild his house of cards. The light fades on Patrick and comes up on Dennis. He is trying to bring into focus a dimness in his memory.)

DENNIS: Diana Green. Wasn't that the name he mentioned? How do I know that name? How can I find it?

(He calls) Diana! Diana Green!

(To himself) No—nothing. Perhaps I need to put a detective to work up here.

(He points to his forehead. He calls as loudly as he can) Diana Green!

(Becky appears.)

BECKY: Diana Who?

DENNIS: Nobody, honey—nobody you would know.

BECKY: Maybe I would.

DENNIS: No, sweetheart, she was long after your time.

BECKY: Is she bothering you?

DENNIS: (*Lying*) No, not really.

BECKY: She giving you trouble, Dad?

DENNIS: No, no, I'm just trying to find her in my mind—and I can't.

BECKY: Don't worry, Dad—you'll find her. You always find *me* easy enough.
   (*Rebecca appears.*)

REBECCA: And me. (*To Becky*) Even if he does confuse the two of us.

DENNIS: (*Defensively*) I do not confuse you—I know you are the same.

REBECCA: He doesn't really know the difference.

DENNIS: Difference?—what difference?

BECKY: Between the doughnut and the hole.

REBECCA: Between Becky and Rebecca.

BECKY: So you have to keep me a child, don't you? Isn't that right, Dad—
   you have to keep me a child.

REBECCA: You won't let her grow up.

BECKY: Why don't you let me grow up?

REBECCA: Because you're one of his dearest memories—and you're comforting. No trouble to him at all. If your stepfather's molesting you, it's in
   another house, in another country—childhood. He doesn't have to deal
   with it. So why should he let you grow up?

DENNIS: I did let you grow up! You're not nine years old anymore—you're
   a woman!

REBECCA: Then why don't you let me *be* a woman?! Why don't you let me
   have a life of my own, a love of my own!? Why can't I choose my own
   husband?!

BECKY: I think he's afraid.

DENNIS: No! I know she thinks that, but I'm not!

REBECCA: Yes!—that's it!—he's afraid!

DENNIS: Afraid of what, for God's sake?

REBECCA: Of me! You love her and you're afraid of *me*!

DENNIS: *That's not true!*

REBECCA: Yes—afraid of me. Because I can hurt you more than Becky could.

BECKY: Is that why?

REBECCA: Yes. Go away, Becky. He's got to love *me* now! Go away.

DENNIS: No! Don't go away—stay here, Becky—stay here!

REBECCA: Go, Becky! We'll never get anywhere if he hangs on to you. Go—
   please go!

BECKY: Dad . . .?
   (*Her voice makes a mournful sound. Then Becky disappears. Rebecca
   remains.*)

DENNIS: Is she gone?

REBECCA: I suppose so, yes.

DENNIS: Really gone?

REBECCA: You tell me.

DENNIS: Where did she go? Is she gone forever? I don't think I can stand that. Where did she go?

REBECCA: Wherever phantoms go.

DENNIS: Why didn't you go with her?

REBECCA: Because I'm not a phantom. Though I think you'd rather have me be one.

DENNIS: That's not so.

REBECCA: Yes, I think it is. I think you get on better with phantoms than you do with real people.

DENNIS: They're more believable.

REBECCA: Because they do what you want. They tell you what you need to hear. They lie to you.

DENNIS: No, they don't—they never do—I count on them!

REBECCA: They lie to you, Father. From beginning to end, they're liars!

DENNIS: No—you're wrong! I'm not the only one who believes in them! Crowds of ticket-buyers believe in them! My God, I've built my whole existence on the believability of my phantoms! Large audiences!—standing room only!—full houses!

REBECCA: How about us? No full houses here!

DENNIS: Is that totally my fault? I do the best I can with my family—I do my best! What more can I do for you?

REBECCA: I want you to see him!

DENNIS: I've *been* seeing him. In the past few weeks, he's been with me more than I can stand!

REBECCA: I mean *really* see him, Father. In the flesh—no phantoms! Touch him—shake hands with him—have a drink together—sit down and be sensible with him.

DENNIS: Holy God, what is there about flesh that is more persuasive to you than images?!

REBECCA: I don't know what that means.

DENNIS: *Why is flesh more persuasive than the figment?*
(*She sees how irrational, how possessed he is becoming, and goes more slowly.*)

REBECCA: It has to do with what things *are*, Father—how people can recognize one another. If you ask me what I know about Simon, I can't talk about a famous comedian or a big star. He's a person, he's an intimate person.
(*An instant*) I told you once that he makes me laugh. It's not altogether true. I've never laughed at a single one of his pictures, never. But I can laugh at him. He puts earplugs in his ears at night, then he complains because he can't hear the alarm in the morning. If he neglects to give a beggar a handout, he worries about it miles away, and he trudges back. He refuses to read a newspaper that someone else has read—he says the print's

been worn off the page. In the movies he embarrasses me by screaming with laughter when people are crying. He's very real, Father, and I *understand* him.

(*A moment*) As I think I understand you. Not you, the great dramatist, the Nobel prize winner, but you, my father, the man who hides fruit he hasn't eaten so that his wife's feelings won't be hurt, who still sends me toy animals on my birthday, who awakens in the night and calls Denny, Denny, as if his son were still alive and out there, shooting baskets in the yard. And I can't stand how unendurable it is for you to have lost your favorite child—and I know how your heart is breaking, and I cry over you, I cry and I love you because you're my real father, and your pain is real, and everything about you is real, is real!

(*She is weeping softly. She pulls herself together and moves toward him*) *I am in love with reality, Father.* I believe you and Simon can be two real human beings together, and that you can really come close to one another. On Saturday we're going to get married. Please come to our wedding.

(*He suffers the deepest anxiety. Then:*)

DENNIS: I can't, Becky.

(*He turns away. Rebecca is as afflicted as he is.*)

REBECCA: Yesterday was my birthday.

DENNIS: Yes.

REBECCA: You didn't send me a present, you didn't call, you didn't even drop me a note. Did you forget about it?

DENNIS: You know I didn't.

REBECCA: Yes, I was sure you didn't.

(*A moment*) I'm eighteen years old.

DENNIS: Yes.

REBECCA: I don't need your consent.

DENNIS: That's right—you don't need me for anything.

REBECCA: Please—please—come to our wedding.

DENNIS: Thank you for the invitation.

REBECCA: Will you come?

DENNIS: No.

(*They are both hurting. Quietly, she leaves. Dennis is alone with a single light upon him. Then there's another light, and Simon is in it.*)

SIMON: Who's Diana Green?

DENNIS: Are you telling me that you don't know anybody by the name of Diana Green?

SIMON: Let me see now. Diana Green, Diana Green.

(*Turning quickly*) Is that the name?—Diana Green?

DENNIS: Yes, that's the name.

SIMON: (*As if it's a guessing game*) Give me a minute, now. I used to know a woman by the name of *Bertalily* Green. She was a good old-fashioned midwife—but by the time we knew her, she was out of fashion—who was using midwives anymore? So, unfortunately, she had to give up the prac-

tice. Now, that's sad, isn't it?—you know, when a person becomes obso-
lete—it's *very sad*. But it's also funny. I know I shouldn't laugh at that poor
unfulfilled old midwife, but fate is funny—don't you think fate is funny?

DENNIS: Laugh riot.

SIMON: Did you say Bertalily Green?

DENNIS: *Diana* Green.

SIMON: Diana Green, Diana Green. I had a gaffer on a picture, once—his
name was *Waldo* Green. Very good electrician—he could light the world
with a candleflame. But he got his real kicks out of selling porno stuff.
Dirty films, dirty books, dirty gadgets. Isn't it amazing what a sleazy,
brutish business we've made of the act of love? Love is a gift we don't deserve—we fuck it up.

DENNIS: It's like a mail-order disappointment—we should send it back.

SIMON: Waldo Green, did you say?

DENNIS: I said Diana Green.

SIMON: Never heard of her.

DENNIS: She heard of you.

SIMON: Who hasn't?

DENNIS: Diana says nobody knows you as well as she does.

SIMON: How does she know me?

DENNIS: Let me count the ways.

SIMON: I've never met a Diana Green.

DENNIS: You met her with her agent, Jay Meltzer, at the William Morris office.

SIMON: I've met lots of people at the William Morris office. The William
Morris office is constituted for me to meet lots of people. That's its solitary function.

DENNIS: You said to her, "You're too beautiful—you don't need to be a
good actress."

SIMON: I can't begin to tell you how many times I've spoken that line.

DENNIS: I'm sure it's most effective when spoken in bed.

SIMON: Everything is.

DENNIS: But that line—especially that line . . .

SIMON: Oh yes, very good. Actor-proof.

DENNIS: And actress-proof, of course.

SIMON: Goes without saying.

DENNIS: It's rather a cheesy line, actually, and I'm surprised you have to resort to it.

SIMON: If you're using the line as a sex ploy, I agree it's a touch on the crummy
side. But if the line suggests that the art of acting attracts people who are
far less beautiful than they yearn to be, there's an empathic ache in it.

DENNIS: Even comedians go for the—uh—empathic ache?

SIMON: Oh especially comedians. Laugh till it hurts.

DENNIS: When you told Diana Green that she was so beautiful she didn't
have to be a good actress, did she laugh till it hurt?

SIMON: (*Losing his temper*) I never said that line to any Diana Green or Bertalily Green or Waldo Green or any Green person I've ever met!

DENNIS: You met her on January third, over a year ago. On the seventeenth of January, she read for you in the conference room of the William Morris office. She read for you again—in the presence of Jay Meltzer and your casting director, Mindy Rowbeck—in the rehearsal room of a studio on Gower Street. She started to be a visitor at your house the beginning of February. In the early spring, she stopped being a visitor at your house, and you started being a visitor at hers—a sublet apartment overlooking the ocean in Trancas Beach. You have been going there, staying for two or three days at a time—approximately once a month—for over a year. You still go there from time to time. Even now, while you're ostensibly about to marry my daughter, you are intimately involved with Diana Green.

SIMON: I don't buy tickets to your plays, but I have to believe you're a better playwright than this.

DENNIS: It's not playwrighting.

SIMON: You could invent a better scenario with your brains tied behind your back.

DENNIS: Not one word of it is invention.

SIMON: It's a lie. The whole damn thing is a lie.

DENNIS: There are witnesses—Jay Meltzer—Mindy Rowbeck—your house-keeper—the parking attendant at the apartment house in Trancas Beach—

SIMON: It's a lie!

DENNIS: You've written her letters—you gave her an opal ring—

SIMON: For God's sake, can't you write it more ingeniously than that?

DENNIS: Of course I can! But time after time, you become a cliché. Have you noticed that the most richly creative people fall into clichés the instant they fall in love? In one of your letters you call her Bunny Wabbit! Bunny Wabbit, for Chrissake!

SIMON: (*Angry*) I have never in my life called anybody Bunny Wabbit! I have never *met* a Bunny Wabbit! I don't even call a bunny rabbit a Bunny Wabbit!

DENNIS: In your letters, you didn't dot your *i*'s with ordinary dots, you dotted them with little circles. You signed *x*'s for kisses and you drew little cupids under your signature, with their adorable smiling little faces and their cutesy little behinds. Little cupids mooning for love!

SIMON: It's untrue. I never wrote *x*'s for kisses—I didn't dot my *i*'s with circles—and no cupids, no cupids, no cupids!

DENNIS: Bunny Wabbit!

SIMON: I see what you're doing. You're trying to turn me into a simpleton, you're pulling my pants down! Well, that's not your game, Dennis Ryan! That's *my* game! I'm the comedian, I'm the one who does the ridiculing! You're not supposed to make fun of me—I'm supposed to make fun of you!

DENNIS: I thought you said you don't use ridicule in your comedy.

SIMON: I stretched a point—as you are doing now.

DENNIS: Not at all. Whenever you went to visit her in Trancas, you instantly got out of your clothes and into a gaudy bathrobe. It was actually a kimono that you bought in Tokyo. It had huge reddish chrysanthemums all over it, and rot-green parrots.

SIMON: That's plain bullshit! I never wore a kimono in my life—never!—with parrots or without parrots!—never!

DENNIS: Green parrots, red chrysanthemums. And you always played the same song on the piano—and she sang the words!
(*Singing, dancing, lampooning*) Who's my little whosits?
Who's my turtledove?
Who's my little whosits?
Who do I love?

SIMON: Stop that! It's all a lie! A dirty and mean-spirited lie—and I won't listen to any more of it!
(*Dennis picks up a Polaroid camera.*)

DENNIS: Good!—stay angry!—I want to take your picture!

SIMON: (*Enraged*) What the hell for?!

DENNIS: Rebecca says you're very real—I want to see how real you are! Hold it!
(*He snaps the picture. A flash.*)

SIMON: The camera won't tell you a bloody thing! Because I'm not flesh and blood. I'm something you're making up in your mind! You can't photograph that, you goddamn fool!

DENNIS: Who knows what palpable object can emanate from an impalpable dream?

SIMON: That's hogwash.

DENNIS: Look at that.
(*Pointing to the family picture on his desk*) Study that picture. It's a snapshot of my family. Nobody posed happiness into that photograph, but that is what it's a picture of—happiness! It's *there*—look at it—it's as real as the people are. It's so real you can touch it. Spirit made substance.
(*More intently*) Who knows where the boundaries are? If you are as real as you are to me, is it not possible that some emanation of you might appear on the film?

SIMON: No!—it's not possible!
(*Dennis holds the framed picture in one hand and the camera in the other. He speaks passionately:*)

DENNIS: *Why not*!? If happiness can appear on this picture, why can't torment appear on this one!

SIMON: (*Pointing to the camera*) Well, let's see.
(*Dennis takes the picture out of the camera.*)

SIMON: Well? Well? What did you get?

DENNIS: (*Quietly*) Nothing.

SIMON: What the hell did you expect?

DENNIS: *(An outburst of anger and frustration)* But why?! If I break my heart to create something, why can't it appear on the film?! Why can't it appear on the page!?

SIMON: *(With real sympathy for him)* Stop tormenting yourself, Ryan. Make do with reality. Come to our wedding.

(Dennis has put the framed photo back on the table, but still holds the Polaroid one.)

DENNIS: *(Quietly)* I *do* see someone in this photograph.

SIMON: Who?

DENNIS: Diana Green.

SIMON: She's as real as the other phantoms. She does not exist.

DENNIS: Yes she does—and so does her child.

SIMON: She has no child.

DENNIS: She's pregnant.

SIMON: That's what she says.

DENNIS: That's what her doctor says.

SIMON: There will be a second opinion.

DENNIS: Yours?

SIMON: The calendar's. The months will pass and there will be no child.

DENNIS: She intends to have it. She says you're the father.

SIMON: I am the Father, the Son and the Holy Ghost. Take a picture of *that!*

DENNIS: Will you say that in court?

SIMON: *(With increased urgency)* Come to our wedding—please!

DENNIS: No.

SIMON: Look, Ryan, the battle can only get nastier all the time, nastier, more vicious. And I must confess, I'm scared. So I want to suggest a truce.

DENNIS: *(Warily)* What sort of truce?

SIMON: A complete cessation of hostilities. We lay down our arms. We bury the dead and go to a quiet place and sign a historic treaty! *The war's over!* Let's have a drink on it!

DENNIS: I don't drink.

SIMON: *(An instant. Then, quickly)* We'll try something else—a ritual. Let's nick our fingers and mix our blood. I offered to be your friend—now I'll do better—I'll be your son. I need a father and you need a son who will love you without all those memories of cruelty and pain. Father and son, Dennis, father and son! And I promise you—I will love you without reproach—and you can love me without guilt! Is it a truce, Dennis, is it a truce?

DENNIS: I'm not your father, Sperry—I'm your enemy.

SIMON: Jesus, what's the size of your hatred? How enormous can it get?

DENNIS: Did you expect a petty little disaffection from a man like me? I've lived with passions so terrible that every breath was a torture—would you be satisfied with a feeble little antipathy? You think I would demean myself with that?—or demean you, for that matter? I loathe you, Sperry—I hate you with all my guts and heart and soul! I hate you as I hate—

SIMON: Life itself.

DENNIS: . . . Yes, life itself.

SIMON: *(With sudden realization)* My God! I know why I've been failing with you!

DENNIS: Why?

SIMON: Because for all your disparagement of comedy, you are secretly in love with it. And I failed you—I never made you laugh.

DENNIS: I told you you wouldn't.

SIMON: Laugh, Ryan—please—for your own sake—please laugh. It'll hurt you at first—but pretty soon the muscles will take over and then—presto!—you'll be enjoying it! Everybody, come and watch! He's going to laugh! Everybody, come! Join the fun!

(He picks up the bell and starts ringing it) Laugh! There are jugglers in town and a dancing bear and tumblers and conjurors! There are clowns on the avenue, and they're screaming with hilarity! Everybody, laugh! Laugh, Ryan!

DENNIS: Stop that bedlam—stop that noise!

SIMON: I'm inviting everybody to the circus—the carnival—the laugh parade! Come one, come all! There's enough laughter to go around. I'm inviting the family!

DENNIS: There's no family here, you idiot. Stop ringing that goddamn bell—stop it! There's no family!

(Simon stops ringing the bell. Tense pause. Simon is off balance, full of regret.)

SIMON: I thought—if I could make a happy family—

DENNIS: *(Pointing to the framed photograph)* It's only in the picture.

SIMON: *(Forlornly)* Everybody, smile.

DENNIS: . . . Yes.

(Dennis picks up the picture off his desk, and he smashes it, glass, frame and all. Quietly, Simon puts the bell down. He is unsteady, lost.)

SIMON: And now where are we?

DENNIS: We are in a courtroom, and I am Diana Green. I look across the room, I see you, I point my finger at you. "That is the father of my child!"

SIMON: There's no child as yet, and I am not its father.

DENNIS: You came to my apartment on Trancas Beach. You stayed there with me often. You wore a Japanese kimono—

SIMON: Never!

DENNIS: Who's my little whosits?

SIMON: Never, never!

DENNIS: Who's my turtledove?

SIMON: Never, never, never, never, never!

DENNIS: We made love on countless occasions!

SIMON: Over a year ago! It stopped in April of last year.

DENNIS: It's still going on!

SIMON: That's not true!

DENNIS: Even now—even while you're seeing Becky.

SIMON: I swear it's not true!

DENNIS: The pregnancy is only four months old. And you are the child's father!

SIMON: Not true, not true!

DENNIS: I am Diana Green's attorney. Will you allow a blood test?

SIMON: Yes—anything—I *will* allow a blood test, yes!

DENNIS: I am the medical examiner—hold out your arm. Why do you wince?—what a coward you are!

SIMON: I didn't wince and I am not a coward!

DENNIS: Too cowardly to acknowledge the child!

SIMON: It's not my child! Look at that paper—look what it says—look at my blood type! The child's type is B, and the mother's type is O, and my type is A—and there is no possible way that I could be that child's father! It is medically impossible! I am not the father, not the father, not the father!

DENNIS: You're under arrest!

SIMON: But I'm not guilty—you've made the test—I'm not the father.

DENNIS: You're under arrest for having committed a federal crime.

SIMON: I committed no crime—not ever—no crime!

DENNIS: You violated the Mann Act. You transported a woman across state lines for the purposes of prostitution!

SIMON: It's a fake, it's a set-up, it's not true!

DENNIS: Arrest him!

SIMON: No!

DENNIS: Arrest him!

SIMON: *(As if fighting his captors)* No—take your hands off me—no!
(He struggles with them, he breaks away. Picking up one of the shards of glass, he goes toward Dennis threateningly:)

SIMON: I'll kill you, I'm going to kill you!
(As he crosses the room, there is the sound of a police siren, and the light on Simon fades. Dennis listens to the din of the receding siren. He is very still. He goes to the desk, opens a drawer, and brings out an unopened fifth of bourbon. He tears the cap label away, opening the bottle. The light lowers. When it comes up again, it shines on Julia who is entering with a bag of fruit. As she speaks, the light broadens to include Dennis. He is a bit less steady than before, but not even on the edge of being drunk. As to Julia, she is tied tight, more tense than usual, hence more genial and more garrulous.)

JULIA: I brought you some fruit. Oranges. The man says I shouldn't call them oranges, they're a new kind of tangerine, so I guess I should call them tangerines, shouldn't I? Whatever I call them, they're so sweet they make the mouth happy. Would you like one?

DENNIS: No, thank you.

JULIA: I'll be glad to peel it for you.

DENNIS: No—really—thank you, Julia.

(She points to the shards of glass on the desk and on the floor.)

JULIA: What's that?

DENNIS: I thought you mightn't notice.

JULIA: I didn't want to. What happened?

DENNIS: It broke.

JULIA: How did it break?

DENNIS: It just exploded.

JULIA: All by itself?

DENNIS: All by itself. It said "I've had enough of all this smiling and scratching and phony good cheer," and it exploded.

(An instant. She goes down on her knees to start gathering the shards.)

DENNIS: What the devil are you doing?

JULIA: *(Annoyed, tighter and tighter)* What does it look like I'm doing?

DENNIS: Leave it alone. Julia—please—Agnes will be here today—she'll clear it away—stop it, Julia.

(He reaches for her arm to help her up. Julia lashes out in a fury.)

JULIA: Let go of me!

DENNIS: *(Arrested)* Julia . . .?

JULIA: Let go of me—take your hands off me—let go!

DENNIS: Julia, what's the matter?

JULIA: You never notice anything!

DENNIS: *(Trying to calm her)* No—I'm sorry—tell me—

JULIA: You haven't noticed that for the last five days I haven't brought you your letters to sign! You didn't notice that, did you?

DENNIS: No, I confess I didn't.

JULIA: *(Accusing)* Aren't you curious?

DENNIS: If you'd like me to be curious—I'm curious.

JULIA: *(A fierce outbreak)* I didn't *do* them! I didn't type a single one of them! You want to know why? Because I can't read your notes—I can't read what you've written for me to say! I can't read your handwriting! And you never intended for me to read it!

DENNIS: Julia, this is pure nonsense.

JULIA: Your handwriting has been getting smaller and smaller, and the words are getting so illegible that I can't make them out—and you don't *want* me to make them out! You want to hide more and more of yourself from everybody, so that ultimately we won't know what you're writing or what you're saying or who you are! That's what you want, isn't it?

DENNIS: That's the most outlandish notion I've ever heard.

JULIA: You want to run away from all of us!

DENNIS: *(At last, losing his temper, fighting back)* If I do, you've encouraged it!

JULIA: Me?—*me*?!

DENNIS: Yes! You've helped to shield me and hide me and keep the world away from me! And I admit it's what I've wanted, but it's what you've wanted as well! You said my work was sacred to you—that's the word you used, sacred—and I took you to mean it!

(The truth of it strikes her, gives her pause. Her words are quiet, almost to herself.)

JULIA: Yes, I did mean it.

(They have made a momentary truce. He gets the wastebasket, carries it near her, gets down on his knees and starts helping her to clear up the shards. He speaks kindly; he is concerned for her:)

DENNIS: Please don't be so upset. . . . You don't have to do this, you know.

JULIA: *(Compulsive)* Yes, I have to.

DENNIS: *(He touches her gently)* You don't, Julia—you don't have to hold yourself accountable for every goddamn thing that goes wrong in the world.

(It's something else for her to cogitate. They finish the chore in silence. He puts the wastebasket back.)

JULIA: Why did you break it?

DENNIS: Forget it—it's over.

JULIA: *(Her tension starting to return)* You couldn't stand it anymore, could you?

DENNIS: Stand what?

JULIA: The smiling family.

DENNIS: *(Defensive)* Most of the time, I like the look of the smiling family.

JULIA: But the smiles were phony, weren't they? And you can't stand the censure, can you?

DENNIS: Censure of what?

JULIA: Of a man who holds precious the idea of a happy family, but who does nothing to preserve it.

DENNIS: We preserve it in our own way.

JULIA: Why did you break the picture, and why did you break out the bottle?

DENNIS: If you're implying that I'm drunk—look—

(He holds up the bottle)—I've had two small drinks.

JULIA: I think you're ill, Dennis.

DENNIS: Of course I'm ill. I've been ill every day of my life. I've had hardly an organ that hasn't malfunctioned at one time or another. Nowadays my hands are a little unsteady.

JULIA: So is your mind.

DENNIS: Don't let's frighten one another, Julia.

JULIA: I hear you talking in the middle of the night.

DENNIS: What's new about that?

JULIA: Quarreling—weeping—

DENNIS: It's the nature of the scene.

JULIA: It's not a scene—you're not writing anything. You're talking to Simon, aren't you?

DENNIS: Please! Stop it!

JULIA: Quarreling with him—fighting—

DENNIS: I told Rebecca I wouldn't meet him, I haven't met him, and I don't intend to.

JULIA: You're meeting him all the time.

DENNIS: (*With quiet deliberateness*) I am not crazy, Julia.

JULIA: Looking back, it seems to me there was never a time when you weren't crazy. You've been talking to some Simon or other as long as I've known you—

DENNIS: That's gibberish!

JULIA: —some enemy—invader—sickness—

DENNIS: Stop it!

JULIA: —addiction—threat of dying—

DENNIS: I have no fear of death.

JULIA: You think you haven't. You try to think of death as a sort of literary device—something you can use or not use—revise—transpose—cut. Writer's choice! Deep down, you're afraid that if you confront death as it is—something real—you won't be able to stand your terror of it. And the irony is, that if you confronted the real thing, it might not be terrifying at all . . . Certainly Simon isn't.

DENNIS: Not terrifying?

JULIA: No, he isn't. Rather wonderful, in fact.

DENNIS: You've met him?

JULIA: Yes, I have.

DENNIS: In the flesh?

JULIA: It's how I meet everybody.

DENNIS: Don't you think that's a bit disloyal of you, Julia?

JULIA: No, I don't. I think they should get married. And I told them so.

DENNIS: (*Appalled; quietly*) You didn't. I don't believe you would betray me like that.

JULIA: But I did. I even offered to go with them—in whatever capacity—as a witness—matron of honor—give the bride away—

DENNIS: She's not yours to give!

JULIA: But I am *mine* to give!

(*An instant. It is her clearest declaration of independence. Then, more lovely:*)

JULIA: And if we're talking about people *giving* people, she's not *yours* to give either. The naked fact is nobody belongs to anybody.

DENNIS: My characters belong to me.

JULIA: I hate your characters!

(*Savagely, it is torn out of her. Stunned, he takes a moment to adjust.*)

DENNIS: They're not meant to be lovable.

JULIA: *I hate them!* I hate every single one of them, Dennis—and I hate your writing nowadays! I used to be excited by it! I used to be inflamed by the sheer passion in it, the anger, the energy, the rage! But then I saw that your people are inhuman to one another, they despise everybody, they despise the world,

they despise themselves. Cruel—monstrous! And I can't stand it anymore—because every one of them is you—and I just can't stand it, I can't stand it!
(*Silence. He is too appalled, too wounded to talk. She speaks quietly.*)

JULIA: I hoped I'd never have to confess it, but I can't hold it back anymore . . . I can't . . . I know how much it will hurt you . . . I know it, and I've been trying to keep everyone from hurting you . . . everyone . . . and now it's me . . .
(*Her pain is deep, and his is an agony. He says nothing.*)

JULIA: (*As gently as she can*) I'm leaving you, Dennis.

DENNIS: For a long time, I've been afraid you would say that.

JULIA: Not very afraid. You left me years ago.

DENNIS: No, that's not true.

JULIA: Let's put it casually: you haven't been around for a while.
(*He suffers a moment of deep difficulty.*)

DENNIS: (*Scarcely a whisper*) Don't leave me, Julia.

JULIA: I have to, Dennis

DENNIS: I won't be able to stand it without you.

JULIA: Stand what?

DENNIS: Whatever it is we endure together . . . I don't think I can do it alone.

JULIA: You'll do it. You've *been* doing it.

DENNIS: I don't think I'll be able to get up in the morning.

JULIA: You'll get up. Sooner or later, you'll write yourself another woman.
(*She goes out. He doesn't know what to do with himself. His heartache is inconsolable. He starts toward his desk, and the bottle. The lights fade.*

In the dark, we hear the ringing of the bell. It continues in one area of Dennis's study after another. The lights come up. Dennis is stalking about the room, ringing the bell. Lonely, abandoned, there is desperation in him; he is drunk but not, even for an instant, maudlin. Desperate to bring back someone he loves, someone to mitigate his aloneness, he calls to the void:)

DENNIS: Julia? Julia? Did you go, Julia? Are you there? Julia? . . .
(*He is confused*) Becky . . . Becky, can you hear me? . . . Patrick? Will you ever come to see me, Patrick? . . . Denny? . . . Denny? . . .
(*The outcry for Denny is the most desolate. He can't endure the loneliness. Out of the darkness, Simon emerges. He behaves staidly, the parody of the movie butler, complete with English accent.*)

SIMON: You rang, sir?

DENNIS: Yes, but not for you.

SIMON: There's only me, sir—Simon the Butler, sir—to look after you, sir. Your wife's gone, sir, so have the children. Cook's left, sir, and so's the upstairs maid. You are—as you always wanted to be—alone. Sir.

DENNIS: Drop it.
(*Simon drops it. Quite seriously:*)

SIMON: You're a very bad sport. You've lost and I've won, and you haven't congratulated me.

DENNIS: You have not won.

(*Rebecca enters.*)

REBECCA: Yes he has—on all counts. He was declared innocent in the paternity suit, totally innocent.

SIMON: And the criminal case, with that faked-up Mann Act charge, has been quashed. I am a man without a blemish!

DENNIS: You lost the civil suit.

SIMON: It's one of the idiocies of the law.

REBECCA: If he's not the child's parent, why should he pay for its support?

DENNIS: He said that in the courtroom—many times, as I understand.

SIMON: I say it again!

(*Then, more relaxed*) But it really doesn't matter, does it? It's only a small amount I'll be paying every year, and I really don't begrudge it to the child.

DENNIS: How kind you are to an infant you disowned.

SIMON: I disowned it but I've got nothing against it.

REBECCA: He's a human being, Father.

SIMON: Which you also might try to be.

DENNIS: In any special way?

SIMON: Common decency will do.

DENNIS: Specifically?

SIMON: We'll be married tomorrow morning. We still want you to come. Don't throw stones . . . throw rice.

DENNIS: I will not throw rice.

SIMON: Then you will be the only one who doesn't. You will be left with nobody. You'll be a sick, sad old man.

REBECCA: And alone, Father.

DENNIS: I am told that I've always been alone. Well, then, nothing has changed.

(*To Simon*) Nor have you. In my eyes, you are still a bastard.

SIMON: In your eyes, *you* are.

(*Silence. Dennis turns to face him squarely. Simon continues to speak quietly:*)

SIMON: You can't stand the idea of me marrying her because you think— as Rebecca sometimes thinks—that I am you.

DENNIS: Not a hair of resemblance.

SIMON: But you believe there is! You believe my life is strewn with tragedies—just like yours! You think I'm a drunkard—

DENNIS: I am not a drunkard.

SIMON: —and a whorefucker—

DENNIS: I am not, and I never was!

SIMON: You are a sickness, Dennis! You are rotten lungs and the clap—

REBECCA: Stop it, Simon, stop it!

SIMON: —and syphilis and a blighted mind—

REBECCA AND DENNIS: (*Together*) Stop—stop! . . . I'm as healthy as you are!

SIMON: You think I'll desert her or beat her and abuse her as you've done to your wives!

DENNIS: Never! I never harmed them—not any one of them!

SIMON: You disowned your eldest son on the day of his birth and you denied him for twelve years!—and yet you thought of him as your favorite. You condemn me for not recognizing a child I never made with a woman I never married. But you actually married the boy's mother a year before he was born, you professed to love her, you were *actually* the child's father—but when he came to life, you were in another drama, drinking, gambling, whoring—

REBECCA: Simon—no—Simon—please—

SIMON: (*Not heeding her, he continues*) For twelve years, Dennis—you didn't see your first son for twelve years! And then when he was in his teens and bright and talented, you took him in, you cherished him, you made him believe you loved him! Because he looked like you, he was going to be a young man of some accomplishment—he bore your name, he was *your son*! But when he *became* like you and took to drinking, you turned away from him, you drove him out! And at last, when he was sick, when he was a wreck, he came back to you, he needed you, he came begging to your door, he cried for a loving word, for a handout—and you didn't help him, you didn't give him a dollar or an embrace, you left him there to die! You killed him!

DENNIS: That's not true! That's not how it happened! He killed himself!

SIMON: You killed him!

REBECCA AND DENNIS: (*Together*) Simon—please—Simon! . . . No—no!

SIMON: Confess it, man—you're in confession—confess it, you killed him!

DENNIS: (*In despair, weeping*) No! I can't stand it! Help me to forget it! Help me, Becky!

REBECCA: I can't help you. I was never any part of your life with your older son. And right now I wish I were no part of *your* life either.

DENNIS: Becky—

REBECCA: No! I don't want this. I can't stand it anymore. I don't want to be the theoretical proposition that you both quarrel over. I am not an abstraction. I am not a figment of an artist's imagination. Nor will I let myself be. I am a person. *I am my own person*—and I will no longer battle with phantoms or phantom-makers! If one of you kills the other, I will be nobody's accomplice!

(*She departs. The men are silent. Then Simon starts to laugh, a muted, private sort of laugh.*)

DENNIS: What the devil can you find so funny?

SIMON: You—me—especially you.

DENNIS: In what way am I funny?

SIMON: You are very good at *seeing* your characters, but you can't see *through* them.

DENNIS: What does that mean?

SIMON: You should have known that all that stuff about your son—I didn't tell it to you—you were telling it to yourself.

DENNIS: No, that's not true! Oh God!

SIMON: Laugh, Dennis! It's funny!—laugh!

DENNIS: (*At the edge of agonized laughter*) Yes—funny!

SIMON: It'll roll you in the aisles! Kill you! Murder you!

DENNIS: (*Tormentedly, he is laughing*) Yes—funny—funny—!

SIMON: And you're telling it yourself!

DENNIS: (*Hilarious*) Yes—myself—myself—

SIMON: Life's a joke you tell upon yourself!

DENNIS: Yes—a joke—a joke—

(*They both rock with painful laughter. The lights fade and their sounds fade with them. When they come up again, Dennis is wearing a bathrobe and sitting in his wing chair. His health has deteriorated. His right arm is unsteady. From time to time it jerks in a spasm, and the right side of his face twitches. He cannot move his head too well. But he is in full command of his senses. The door behind him opens and Julia is there. She is wearing a winter coat, and gloves. She simply stands on the threshold for an instant, not announcing herself, not moving. Dennis feels her presence.*)

DENNIS: Who's there?

JULIA: It's me, Dennis.

DENNIS: Julia?

JULIA: Yes.

DENNIS: You've . . . come back?

JULIA: Well . . . I'm here . . . for the moment.

DENNIS: (*Gratified*) Yes, so you are. Thank you, Julia.

JULIA: How do you feel?

DENNIS: Oh, good enough. I'm not in any pain. And I can pretty much do for myself—

(*His right arm trembles. He holds it down with his left. He tries to smile*)

—if I time my activity between shakes.

JULIA: Can you work?

DENNIS: I . . . haven't tried.

JULIA: You must try, Dennis, you must try.

DENNIS: You're looking well, Julia. Beautiful, in fact.

JULIA: Thank you.

DENNIS: Why did you come?

JULIA: It's your birthday.

DENNIS: Is it? Is it really?

JULIA: Yes, really.

DENNIS: How old am I?

JULIA: You're seventy years old.

DENNIS: Hm. Am I as old as that?

JULIA: Threescore years and ten. It's a milestone.

DENNIS: Is it? What do we celebrate?

JULIA: Forgiveness.

DENNIS: Did you say forgiveness?

JULIA: Yes.

DENNIS: Who forgives whom?

JULIA: We forgive each other. It's our present to one another.

DENNIS: Is that what you're giving me for my birthday?
(*Touched*) I do appreciate it.

JULIA: (*More lightly*) I wanted badly to bring you something tangible. I thought of fruit, of course, and decided against it. And then champagne—but it occurred to me, why should I?—he can create his own and get drunk on it.

DENNIS: If I could get drunk on imaginary wine, you think I'd ever have drunk rotgut?

JULIA: I racked my brains, but I couldn't think of anything that would please you. Can you think of anything you'd want? Seventy years old—I should have made you a party.

DENNIS: I'm not very good at parties. Somehow I don't get there. There was a birthday party years ago. It was for Becky—she was nine years old. I didn't attend it—I was in Chicago, I think—trying out a new play. You told me about it on the phone. All the kids were there. Patrick made crepe paper hats for everybody—he made you a golden coronet. Dennis sang old sea chanties. And you had quite a little wine. Everybody had a lovely time, and everybody missed me. I was sick with guilt over it. I dreamed of lizards.
(*He tries to laugh, but he can't make it; he is weeping quietly. He takes out his handkerchief and tries to hide the signs of his indisposition. But it becomes worse: his hand trembles more violently than before. Reflexively, with a murmur of pity, she takes his quaking hand.*)

JULIA: Oh, Dennis!

DENNIS: It's nothing—don't pay any attention to it. I can make my hand do that, and I can make it stop. It's really nothing.
(*She sees that her pity bothers him, and she releases his hand. Another pause.*)

DENNIS: Did they go through with it?

JULIA: Yes.

DENNIS: When?

JULIA: On the day they planned.

DENNIS: Did you go to the wedding?

JULIA: No.

DENNIS: Really? Why not?

JULIA: (*Troubled*) I don't know . . . a certain sadness . . . A lingering loyalty to you, perhaps.
(*Then, more lightly*) I can't stay—I just dropped in—I have things to do—or pretend to do.

DENNIS: (*With a gentle smile*) Yes, I know. Thank you for coming. Seventy, did you say?

JULIA: Yes, seventy.

(*Then with sympathetic urgency*) Go back to work, Dennis—you must.

DENNIS: (*Airily—not meaning it*) Oh, I will! I promise you I will!

(*She kisses him on the forehead; she departs. Dennis deals with his solitude.*)

DENNIS: Seventy. What do I want for my birthday? Only one thing I dare to ask for. I want . . .

(*He is having difficulty*) I want to write a comedy! Once more—before I die—I want to write a play *with a happy ending*! I want to do it—I must—oh God, I *must*!

(*An instant*) A party, did she say? Oh, Patrick, how kind of you to come! And looking so well too! Teaching, are you?—in that little college in New England? And your wife—a marine biologist, is she?—collecting lovely seashells and little shining pebbles. She's pregnant, isn't she?—how pretty she is! And Becky—glowing—and her husband doing hi-jinks with non-existent oranges, and their twin daughters screaming deliriously over mice that aren't there. Oh, Becky, you don't mean it—you'll have twelve children more? Go on, girl, have a baker's dozen—your belly's full of wonders, and you're the most wondrous one of all! And Julia—everywhere—beloved Julia—giving hugs and affirmations and being decorated at last—for what?—for marzipan! And—who's that?

(*Stillness. A special image*) Is that you, Dennis? Oh no!—is it you, my son? Oh Dennis, oh Dennis, is it you? Oh Denny, oh Denny! Oh, sweet heaven, a time for forgiveness! Let's not lose it—let's take a picture of it—let's secure it safely in our memory! A family portrait—a photograph of happiness! Come, Julia, come sit by me. And Rebecca on the other side, with Becky right behind you! Patrick standing, and Dennis right behind me. Put your hand on my shoulder, Patrick, and Dennis on my right! And children squatting on the floor—how beautiful they are! All of us—how beautiful, how beautiful! And everybody home again! Smile for the picture, everybody! Be happy—you're home now—smile! Everybody, smile!

(*He sits there posing with the invisible absent ones and he smiles for the camera. He holds it—smiling—waiting for the picture to be taken. There is no flash. The lights fade.*)

END OF THE PLAY

BREAKING THE TIE

A Play in Two Acts

CHARACTERS

(In the order of their appearance)

Nora Bailey
Jesse Weaver
Robbie Weaver
Frank Weaver
Henrietta Weaver
Carrie McIlvaine
Hugo Lockman
Mr. McIlvaine

*THE PLAY TAKES PLACE IN PHILADELPHIA DURING
THE THIRTIES.*

FOREWORD

Although the play does not resort to the use of a narrator, it is in fact a memory play. In that regard, the scenery, the costumes, the physical ambiance should be simple and abstract, like fragments of remembrance, with frequently a suggestion that there has been a lapse in recall, and properties should be summoned vaguely, mistily, as in a haze of unresolved recollection.

For example, when we go to the bedroom of the twins, we need not be presented with the factuality of beds, nor need the bedrooms be a full story above the living room; a slight elevation will create the illusion. Also, the churchyard can be summoned with little more than a distant and indistinct crucifix, as seen through a dream-vision of a trellis; a blackboard, with a mathematical equation on it, or the parsing of a sentence, can evoke a classroom; a door with a grilled peephole can become a speakeasy.

And the movements from scene to scene should be as swift and fluid as possible, hardly more than a shifting of the lights, with as little recourse to costume change as the imagination can substantiate.

Nothing realistic.

Nothing realistic, that is, except for the relationships among the people of the play, which should be informed by the richest naturalism the actors can bring to the family they pretend to be. What the characters need from one another, the faith with which they believe in their daily existence, what they feel about their life and time—these, rather than the literal details of particularized scenery, are the basic fidelities to realism that should make the play seem true.

Act One

A LIGHT PICKS UP a blackboard on which the parts of speech are listed: Noun, pronoun, verb, etc. In front of the blackboard stands Nora Bailey, a schoolteacher, speaking to her English class (the audience). Nora is young and trying to appear older; she's attractive, sensitive, not a hint of stuffiness. She holds a stack of composition papers in her hands.

NORA: The best paper in the class was actually a tie. As usual—the Weaver brothers. Robbie Weaver—A-minus. Jesse Weaver—the same. Would you come for your papers, please.
(*Out of the darkness, Jesse Weaver appears. He is bright, generous, animated.*)
JESSE: Not me—you're going to ask us to read 'em.
NORA: Not both of you—whichever one volunteers. Robert, how about you?
(*The light picks up Robert. Although he is Jesse's twin, they are not identical. In fact, one would hardly suspect they are brothers, except for the familial decencies they share. Robbie is more tautly drawn, more reflective. The boys are deeply attached to each other; their affection is genuine.*)
ROBBIE: I volunteer to stay right here.
JESSE: Go on, knucklehead—yours is better than mine.

ROBBIE: It's a tie—didn't you hear her?—it's a tie.

NORA: Come on. Up here. Both of you—to the front, to the front!

(*Robbie doesn't move, but Jesse goes to the blackboard.*)

NORA: Jesse read his the last time—it's your turn, Robert.

ROBBIE: No—I can't.

JESSE: Go on, birdbrain—read it.

(*Robbie is about to demur again, but Nora hands him his paper.*)

NORA: Go on.

(*He goes through the high school shenanigans of preparing to read. He clears his throat with a monumental cough, reaches into his outside breast pocket for his glasses, puts them on upside down, and finally perches them on the tip of his nose like an elderly professor. Then he snuffles and wheezes a few times as his brother howls in appreciation. Nora also enjoys him but pretends not to.*)

NORA: Come on, clown—start reading.

(*He shoves his glasses into their more dignified position. Abashed because the composition is a serious one, he looks at the paper and can't make it. A final plea—earnestly:*)

ROBBIE: It's very private, Miss Bailey.

NORA: Start reading, please.

ROBBIE: It—it's called "On the Way to the Library." (*He starts to read, falteringly at first, then more confidently*) "One day my twin brother and I got into a really dumb argument. We were on the way to the library. He had a load of six books that he was returning, and I had only two. Everything was fine and we were mooching along, when suddenly we were in this dopey discussion about whether it was better to read a lot of books and read them fast, or to read slowly and in depth. Jesse was in favor of reading fast—he does everything fast. And I like to take my time and stop every once in a while, to see what I think about what the author is saying. Jesse made some smart aleck crack like, 'What's the matter, clunkhead, can't you think while you're reading?' and I said he reads sloppily like a greedy eater who's afraid somebody will snatch the food away. And when I said that, Jesse lost his temper and said books were more important than food, and all at once we were both angry and quarreling, and by the time we got to the library, we weren't talking to each other."

(*As Robbie reads, his diffidence vanishes, and he starts to walk from the sidelines to the position of prominence in front of the blackboard. As he moves, we observe that he limps; he has a clubfoot and wears a heavy-soled orthopedic shoe.*)

ROBBIE: (*He continues reading*) "And that night, at dinner time, I put a toy cockroach in Jesse's rice pudding, and he thought it was a raisin and almost ate it, and both of us got laughing so hard and making such a racket that my father got mad and my mother got very dignified—and everybody was getting really hysterical—"

(*A shrieking sound—a fire alarm bell.*)

NORA: It's all right, class—it's only a drill. Fire drill! Fire drill, and you know what to do. Boys in twos to the right, girls in twos to the rear door. Quietly now. No talking. Roger—no talking, please. Marilyn, not threes—twos. (*If it's only a drill, the alarm should have stopped by now. But it goes on, continuing through Nora's speech. She is upset. Abruptly the lights go out and start flashing crazily—white, red, white, red. Someone is shouting "Fire!" In the darkness—with the havoc of lights—we hear the voices of students and teachers, in panic.*)

VOICES: Open the door—open the door! Fire!—it's a fire! Not that way— go down the fire escape! Miss Bailey—Mr. Galloway—where are you? Quiet, everybody! Shut that door! Girls—this way, this way! Get her— don't let her go down there! Quickly, please—quickly! Open that door! No, keep it closed! Why don't you open the door? Mr. Watkins—stand against it—stand against the door! The other way! Open the door, open it! (*Rush, terror, chaos. People running, colliding, yanking and striking at one another. Lights continue to flash, white, red, white, red. The emergency bell keeps clanging and—at a distance—the sirens of fire engines.*

Finally, the lights stop flashing and the stage goes quiet, except for the wail of a distant siren and, occasionally, the blast of a police whistle. We are now in almost complete blackness, when Jesse stumbles onstage carrying his unconscious brother. Out of the smoky area, he kneels and sets Robbie on the ground. He starts to bring his brother to consciousness.)

JESSE: Robbie! Robbie, wake up! Robbie!
(*Jesse lifts Robbie's torso so the boy can breathe. He shakes him, he slaps him.*)

JESSE: Robbie! Robbie, get up! Oh God, get up! Robbie—please! Robbie! (*He shakes him some more, he hugs him as if to squeeze some of his own breath into him, then he goes back to slapping him.*)

JESSE: Robbie! Robbie!
(*Robbie starts coming to. Jesse continues to agitate him. At last, being roughed up, Robbie struggles to his feet and groggily puts his fists up in the mocking stance of a prizefighter.*)

ROBBIE: Put 'em up, fathead.
(*He starts to cough*)

JESSE: (*Concerned*) Take a few deep breaths. Deep, deep!

ROBBIE: I'm all right. (*Trying to laugh*) You wanna fight? (*Another cough*)

JESSE: Breathe, you turtlehead—*breathe!*

ROBBIE: I'm *okay!* Want me to prove it? Want me to prove it?—put your dukes up, put 'em up, put 'em up.
(*Sparring and laughing, they run off.*

Toward the end of the foregoing scene, another area has been lighting up to reveal the dinner table of the Weavers. The mother of the twins, Henrietta Weaver, is bringing in the Thanksgiving dinner. Frank Weaver,

their father, is already seated. Frank is an electrical engineer, now work-
ing as a pick-and-shovel laborer. He is a wry man, skeptical but not cyn-
ical, with a kindly and seamy face, lean, craggy. Henrietta is gentler than
her husband; yet, possibly, a bit stronger; strong enough to have no need
to show it. Jesse and Robbie enter and take their places at the table. As
Henrietta sets down the small casserole.)

HENRIETTA: Happy Thanksgiving, everybody.

FRANK, ROBBIE, JESSE: Happy Thanksgiving, honey . . . Happy days, Mom
. . . Happy Thanksgiving, everybody.

FRANK: (*Taking the lid off the casserole*) Mmm—smells wonderful,
Henrietta—but what is it?

HENRIETTA: Don't ask what it is—it's Thanksgiving dinner. But if you need
a fancy name for it, call it Turkey Ravigotte or Gobbler a la Charlemagne.

JESSE: Or stew—what's wrong with stew?

ROBBIE: (*In a loud singsong*) Stew, stew, what's wrong with stew?

JESSE: (*Also loud singsong*) Nothin's wrong, and the sky is blue!

JESSE & ROBBIE: (*Singsong together*) You're all hungry, and we are too!
And guess what's in the stew! It's *you*!
(*Everybody laughs.*)

HENRIETTA: Say the prayer, Frank.

FRANK: (*Surprised*) What?

HENRIETTA: I said say the prayer.

FRANK: Me?

HENRIETTA: Yes, you. I decided that one day of the year, you're going to
take a vacation from being a very busy atheist and say a prayer of
Thanksgiving.

FRANK: Now, hold on, Henrietta.

ROBBIE & JESSE: Go on, Pop, say the prayer. . . . Just once, Pop—just
Thanksgiving.

FRANK: Now wait a minute. If I say it, I wouldn't want anybody to think
I'm being hypocritical.

JESSE: We won't think that, Pop.

ROBBIE: We'll just think you're a good guy.

JESSE: And while you're saying it, we wouldn't want anybody up there to
think you were lying, so you can keep your fingers crossed.
(*They laugh again, and Frank clears his throat and says the prayer.*)

FRANK: Dear God in heaven—whom we don't all believe in—we thank you
for many things. We thank you that one son was brought home safely by
another. We thank you for the love of our children. We thank you that the
school was not damaged beyond repair. We thank you for this Turkey
Ravigotte. And we thank you for health and Franklin Delano Roosevelt
and the WPA which makes an engineer happy to be working as a ditch
digger. Amen.

HENRIETTA: (*Laughing, to her sons*) You notice he had to get in that one
cynical dig about being a ditch digger.

FRANK: It was not cynical. Nothing in that prayer was cynical.

HENRIETTA: Oh come on, Frank.

FRANK: (*Needing them to believe him*) It wasn't! Every word I said was absolutely sincere. You think I wasn't grateful that Robbie got saved from the fire?

ROBBIE: You don't have to thank God for that. Thank Jesse.

FRANK: Thank you, Jesse—and my fingers aren't crossed.

HENRIETTA: (*To Jesse*) You think they'll put that on your scholarship record?

JESSE: (*A bit annoyed*) Hey, Mom—what's that got to do with the scholarship?

HENRIETTA: Well, if I were giving out a free scholarship to the university, I would certainly take into consideration that a young man performed an act of remarkable bravery.

ROBBIE: (*Enjoying the flare*) She's right. If we were living in the days of chivalry, you'd be called a fearless knight errant who went storming through the flames with your clothes all ablaze like a banner, with your sword in one hand—and a free scholarship in the other.

HENRIETTA: Never mind the sword. Maybe he'll be carrying *two* free scholarships, one for himself and one for you.

ROBBIE: Mom, we both looked into that, and the rumor about two scholarships is wrong. There's only going to be one.

JESSE: And Robbie's going to get it.

ROBBIE: You know darn well you've got a better chance than I have.

JESSE: (*Quietly, realistically*) Well, neither of us is going to get it.

FRANK: Don't you say that—don't either of you say that!

JESSE: Pop—we all know who's going to get it.

HENRIETTA: Here we go on the Carrie McIlvaine excuse.

ROBBIE: It's not an excuse—Carrie's just going to get it, that's all.

JESSE: Yeah, she's the smartest one in the class.

ROBBIE: She's smart all right. She doesn't even wear a brassiere.

HENRIETTA: (*Shocked*) Robbie!

JESSE: Well, she doesn't. And those things poke out of her blouse like two pistols pointing right at you. Bang, bang.

(*He and Robbie burst into laughter.*)

ROBBIE: Maybe she's going to shoot her way to a scholarship.

HENRIETTA: Now stop that kind of talk! The two of you—go out into the hallway, and when you've got that vulgar joke out of your system, you can come back!

(*It's all very goodnatured. The twins are hysterical with laughter, pummeling one another as they go out. Henrietta tries not to laugh, but she catches the twins' merriment, as does Frank. The lights fade on the dining room.*

Lights come up in the bedroom of the twins. The boys are undressing. Both are lost in thought.)

ROBBIE: Jesse . . .

JESSE: Hm?

ROBBIE: You know something? We *say* we're not going to make it. But in our hearts we think we *are* going to make it. And the truth of it is, we're *not* going to make it.

JESSE: That's very well thought out—except I don't know what you're talking about.

ROBBIE: You know damn well what I'm talking about. College.

JESSE: Robbie—tell me the truth—do you really mind—not going?

ROBBIE: Yes. I mind.

JESSE: Very much?

ROBBIE: I mind so much I could die. . . . How about you?

JESSE: You know who I mind about most? Pop. I think it's killing him that he went through college—and he can't send his kids.

ROBBIE: It's a funny thing. Every time I ask you how much it really means to you, you avoid the question. You tell me how much it means to Pop or to Mom or to me—never how much it means to yourself? Why the hell don't you answer my question? What'll it do to you if you don't make it?

JESSE: (*Still evading, with a laugh*) I'll just stay poor and ignorant, that's all.

ROBBIE: Answer me, you creep!

JESSE: (*Inarticulate with yearning and confusion*) I don't know the *answer,* Robbie—I don't *know*! I want to go to college so badly that if I don't—! Oh murder, I want to go so much that if I don't I'll go a little crazy and get mad at the world—and go out and kill somebody!

(*He laughs to hide that he is on the edge of being frantic. Deeply upset, he turns away from Robbie. Silence.*)

ROBBIE: We've got to stop caring so much.

JESSE: Yes. We're making that goddamn scholarship a matter of life and death!

ROBBIE: Well, it is! We've only got one little hope to hang on to—and it's tied to college. What else have we got? Money in the bank? A family business we can step into? A set of parents who are proud of their place in the world? Nothing! . . . You, at least, have got a good pair of feet.

JESSE: (*A flare of temper*) Why does the conversation always come around to my good feet?!

ROBBIE: I'm sorry.

JESSE: What do you want me to do—give you my feet? How the hell can I?!

ROBBIE: (*Angry*) I said I'm sorry!

(*Silence.*)

JESSE: . . . The worst part is that we act as if we've already lost the damn thing!

ROBBIE: (*A quick return of spirit*) And we haven't! We've got to remember that! We've still got a chance!

JESSE: That's right! We're still in there!

ROBBIE: You bet we are! In my dreams, I've already made it! It's the first day of college—and it's a bright beautiful morning—and I'm crossing the bridge to the University—

JESSE: (*He has heard versions of this before*) Oh, shit, here we go.

ROBBIE: (*Undeterred, on a high*)—and I'm wearing a brand new suit with a vest—with a vest—with a *vest*! And I'm carrying a brand new genuine leather briefcase with my initials in gold letters. And I come to the end of the bridge and there I am—me—Robbie Weaver!—sauntering along on my college campus—proud—like a major in Advanced Self-Confidence . . .
(*Shivering*) Boy, it gives me goosebumps.

JESSE: (*Caught by it*) Yeah, me too.
(*With the joy of discovery*) You know what happened to me at dinner tonight? When Pop was saying grace, I felt sad that we don't believe in God—or in anything.
(*With quiet fervor*) And suddenly I realized we *do* believe in something.

ROBBIE: In what?

JESSE: Education.

ROBBIE: . . . Yes.
(*They smile. A moment of closeness, communion. But the dream is shattered by reality.*)

ROBBIE: Oh, goddamn it.

JESSE: (*With quiet resolve*) You're going to go to college, Robbie.

ROBBIE: (*Bitterly*) Sure.

JESSE: I swear to you—some way or other, you're going to go!

ROBBIE: Yes *sir*!

JESSE: I mean it, you jerk!

ROBBIE: (*Soberly*) I know you mean it, Jess.

JESSE: Oh, damn Carrie McIlvaine and her two big tits!

ROBBIE: Amen.
(*They laugh wryly. They get in bed.*)

JESSE: Goodnight, Rob.

ROBBIE: Goodnight, Jess.
(*The light brightens on the blackboard again, except that this time it's a biology class, and the blackboard shows a labeled sectional drawing of a frog. The light broadens to include Carrie McIlvaine. It is more difficult to identify her as the smartest girl in the class than as the one who doesn't wear a brassiere. It's a distorted jest to have to identify her that way, for Carrie is more complex: beautiful without taking pleasure in her beauty; brainy in a way that distresses her; and starting to get the suspicion she may wind up not loving anyone. Tangentially, she is a girl born a half century too soon. If she were growing up today instead of the nineteen-thirties, she might, in these more liberative times, come in out of the cold. A racy girl, older than her years, certainly older than Jesse and Robbie; restless, self-deprecating, lonely.*)

Over the Public Address system, as if in a dream, we hear the voice of the biology teacher. We never see this character. This hearing-but-not-seeing some of the minor characters will be, like the schematized scenery, one of the conventions of the play.)

BIOLOGY TEACHER'S VOICE: The nervous system is in yellow chalk. The urino-genital system is in blue chalk. The vascular system is in red. In doing your drawings, please be sure to use these color codes.

(*As the teacher finishes speaking, Jesse enters and advances toward his seat alongside Carrie.*)

CARRIE: Okay, we're through with the nervous system.

JESSE: Wait, Carrie. I haven't got it all labeled.

CARRIE: I labeled it. We're up to the conclusion. What do we say about the nervous system of the frog?

JESSE: He's nervous.

CARRIE: That doesn't make him particularly froggish. You're nervous too.

JESSE: No, I'm not. Look. (*He extends his arm*) My hand doesn't shake.

CARRIE: (*Quietly*) *Something* shakes.

(*An instant. She is clearly making an overture. He realizes it. It throws him off balance.*)

JESSE: What's left to do?

CARRIE: Vascular and reproductive systems.

JESSE: Which one shall we do?

CARRIE: You choose.

JESSE: Vascular.

CARRIE: Wouldn't you rather do the reproductive?

JESSE: I have to admit I would. I started to dissect it out last night. I quit when I got to these little things.

CARRIE: (*Mocking*) Don't say "little things." Call them by their right name.

JESSE: (*Defensive*) I didn't *not* call them by their right name.

CARRIE: Testicles.

(*Girls didn't talk that way in those days. It unnerves him. He tries not to show it. With a bit of bravura:*)

JESSE: Yes—testicles.

CARRIE: (*Enjoying herself*) You're shocked.

JESSE: (*His defensiveness increasing; his bravura also*) No, I'm not—testicles are testicles.

CARRIE: Yep, there's no denying that. But you're still shocked.

JESSE: (*Angry*) You *said* it to shock me—but I'm not!

(*With an irrelevant flare of temper*) The truth is, we're making all this up, because frogs don't even *have* testicles!

CARRIE: Does anybody?

(*It's so oblique a question that it stops him. He can't collect himself enough to deal with this. Then he does.*)

JESSE: Hands off, Carrie.

CARRIE: I'm nowhere near you.

JESSE: You've got your hands all over me.

CARRIE: You *are* nervous, aren't you?

JESSE: . . . Yes.

CARRIE: Why?

JESSE: I don't know.

(*Disturbed*) Because you're—I don't know what it is—you're too strange.

CARRIE: (*Wryly*) You mean I'm too smart.

(*He has to face this. He does, with honesty.*)

JESSE: Yes.

CARRIE: (*With a laugh*) Well, I don't have to be—I can be stupid. If I'm smart enough to be smart, I'm smart enough to be an idiot.

(*She puts her fingers to her mouth and goes bblllbbbllbbb. He only half smiles. More disturbed by her than he wants her to know, he goes back to dissecting the frog. But his hand does shake. They each work in silence. She is the first to look up—and at the dissection.*)

CARRIE: Boy, that frog's a bloody little bastard, isn't he?

JESSE: It's not him. It's me.

CARRIE: What is?

JESSE: I cut my finger.

CARRIE: (*Solicitously*) Oh, let me see—where?

(*She takes his hand. She holds up the finger, and wipes it with a paper towel.*)

CARRIE: Gee, that's quite a cut.

(*She wipes it again. Then deliberately, but without warning, she puts his finger in her mouth. It is so sudden, so unexpected, that he is immobilized; then perturbed—enjoying it—excited. Slowly he takes his finger out of her mouth. They stare at each other.*)

The light comes up in the twins' bedroom. We see only Robbie at first, addressing Jesse who has not as yet entered.)

ROBBIE: Everybody in the world knows you've got a good imagination—everybody knows that! But when you go one step too far, you turn a very good story into a very stupid pile of shit!

JESSE: (*Coming into the light*) I swear it's true. Honest to God—I swear it's true!

ROBBIE: What do you *mean* she sucked your finger?

JESSE: I mean she sucked my finger.

ROBBIE: Don't just say that. How do you mean? What for? What way? What'd she do?

JESSE: (*With deliberateness*) She took my dumb finger and she stuck it in her mouth.

ROBBIE: And then what?

JESSE: She sucked it.

ROBBIE: (*To himself, in wonderment*) Son of a gun.

JESSE: Yeah.

ROBBIE: You know what that means, don't you? You know what that's a symbol of?

JESSE: (*With pleasure*) Yes I do. But tell me.

ROBBIE: (*Again, in wonderment*) Son of a gun . . . Did you make a date with her?

JESSE: No.

ROBBIE: Oh God! Oh God almighty, why *didn't* you?

JESSE: I . . . don't know.

ROBBIE: (*Agog*) Well, you're going to, aren't you?

JESSE: I don't know.

ROBBIE: What do you mean, you don't know? You can't just let a sucked finger dangle in the air that way.

JESSE: (*Soberly*) Yeah, you've got a point there.

ROBBIE: What did you do to drive her crazy like that?

JESSE: Do? I didn't do anything.

ROBBIE: Yes, you did. You must've *looked* at her in some way, or smiled at her in some way. A girl doesn't just purse up her lips and suck your finger unless you made something buzz. What'd you buzz?

JESSE: (*Exasperated*) I didn't buzz anything! I just cut my finger! Maybe she likes the taste of blood, maybe she's a vampire, maybe she's a leech! *I didn't DO anything*!

ROBBIE: (*Quietly, mostly to himself*) That's what's so damn unfair. You don't do anything, and suddenly you got a girl suckin' on your finger. Because you know some secret about girls and they know some secret about you. And me—I could be standing on my head—stark naked—and they wouldn't notice *anything*!

JESSE: A big toe, maybe—she could suck your big toe.

ROBBIE: Never!—because I don't know how to behave with a girl. I don't know how to get into a conversation with her, I don't know how to get into the same *city* with a girl! One day, Carrie was across the table from me in Art Class, and I was looking at her—looking at her *face*, honest to God, her *face*—and she saw me staring, and she buttoned the top button of her blouse. I don't even know how to *look* at a girl!

JESSE: (*With a note of discovery*) Hey, Robbie!—maybe if you made her button her blouse, then that's the way to look at her!

ROBBIE: But I don't remember how I *looked* at her. Geez, now I'll stay awake all night trying to remember how to look at a girl so that she'll button her blouse.

JESSE: You'll fall asleep in five minutes.

ROBBIE: If I do, I'll have a wet dream.
(*With admiring amazement*) Hey . . . really sucked your finger?

JESSE: (*Happily, dreamily*) . . . Yeah.

ROBBIE: It's perverted.

JESSE: (*Enjoying it*) Yeah, it is, isn't it?
(*He is smiling. The light fades on them and comes up on Carrie sitting on a park bench, mid-winter. As she talks, Jesse comes into the light.*)

CARRIE: I thought—that day in the lab—"He's going to ask me for a date. Any minute he'll ask me." But you didn't. It was very strange to me that you didn't. And suddenly—! What made you decide? And why didn't you do it sooner?

JESSE: I don't know. I didn't have the nerve.

CARRIE: Nerve? What'd you need all that nerve *for*? It wasn't as though you were going to rape me or something.

JESSE: I wish you wouldn't say words like that.

CARRIE: Why not? You say them among the boys, don't you?

JESSE: Yes.

CARRIE: Then you can say them to me. Go on—say "rape."

JESSE: (*Starting to ease up, even to smile*) Well, I don't really have any deep *need* to say it right now. I haven't raped anybody since last Tuesday.

CARRIE: (*Going with it*) Was it fun?

JESSE: (*Relaxing, he pretends to be blasé*) Nah—not for me. After a while, I get bored with stuff like that.

CARRIE: I hope *she* enjoyed it.

JESSE: No complaints.

CARRIE: Do you feel as shitty as I do, joking about a thing like that?

JESSE: Come to think of it . . . I do. Why did we do it?
(*A somewhat troubled silence. Then, quietly:*)

CARRIE: You're a virgin, aren't you?

JESSE: . . . Yes.

CARRIE: Most fellas lie about that.

JESSE: I would too—if I thought I could get away with it . . . Are you?

CARRIE: Well, you know what that little bastard Howard Macklin says about me.

JESSE: No, what?

CARRIE: I'll take anything that holds its shape.

JESSE: Well . . . will you?

CARRIE: No.

JESSE: I didn't think you would. . . . Why don't you wear a brassiere?

CARRIE: (*With the voice of a duchess*) Oh, that! What an odd, ungentlemanly question! What*ever* made you inquire?

JESSE: Doesn't everybody inquire?

CARRIE: Why the hell should they?

JESSE: Why *should* they?—you encourage it.

CARRIE: No I don't!

JESSE: You walk around like that—bouncing all over the place—you expect nobody to notice?

CARRIE: Yes! That's exactly what I do expect!

JESSE: You'd be damned disappointed if they didn't notice.

CARRIE: (*Angry*) That's not true! I wear my breasts this way because I like them this way! I like to feel free—not trussed up like a dead chicken! I'm a human being—and I've become a woman! And if I *am* a woman, these are a sign that I am! Why should I hide them? I'm not doing anything obscene! I'm not drawing dirty pictures on my bosom! *Am I?*

JESSE: Others do.

CARRIE: Well, that's their dirty pictures, not mine!

JESSE: (*Silence. Then . . . gently . . .*) I don't draw dirty pictures, Carrie.

CARRIE: (*Hesitantly*) Don't you?

JESSE: No . . . only beautiful ones.

(*She doesn't reply, feeling more embarrassed by Jesse's tribute than by the insults of others. Slowly, with a surprising accession of modesty, she folds her hands across her bosom.*)

CARRIE: You're making me feel naked.

JESSE: Do you mind?

CARRIE: I . . . yes . . . no . . . I don't know.

(*Slowly, not sure of himself, he reaches to touch her hand. It is the most innocent of contacts but, confused, she cannot stand it. She gets up and moves away. Shaken somehow, she instinctively feels the need to change the subject.*)

CARRIE: What do you want to be when—as the saying goes—you grow up?

JESSE: I don't know. Something to do with books—I've gotta have books. It's as if I'm starving—I can't get enough of them.

CARRIE: You like books better than people, don't you?

JESSE: (*It's a new speculation for him*) Hey—do I? Gee, that's a new question for me—and I'm not sure I like the answer. Yes . . . I have to admit it. . . . I think I do like books better than people. And I'm . . . I don't know—sad about that. . . . How about you?

CARRIE: I like books a lot, but I don't like people very much.

JESSE: (*With genuine sympathy*) I would've guessed that . . . I'm sorry. . . . What do *you* want to be when you grow up?

CARRIE: (*With self-certainty, but without assertiveness*) I *am* grown up.

JESSE: (*A bit regretfully*) Yes, you are, aren't you? We're the same age, and you're about ten years older than I am.

CARRIE: Don't sound so sad.

JESSE: I am sad. I don't think I'll ever catch up with you.

(*Shaking the mood*) Well—later—what do you want to do with yourself?

CARRIE: (*With false bravura*) Conquer the world!

JESSE: That's just in your leisure time. What do you want to *work* at?

CARRIE: You're not taking me seriously.

JESSE: (*A moment. Does she mean it?*) You think you're going to conquer the world?

CARRIE: (*Simply*) Yes.

JESSE: What makes you so sure?

CARRIE: I've always been the first in everything. First in my class. First to get kissed. First to grow up. Carrie McIlvaine—Winner of the World!

JESSE: (*Ruefully*) Well, there's no question—you *have* been winning.

CARRIE: You mean that lousy scholarship? You don't think I was talking about *that*, do you?

JESSE: College is one of the steps, isn't it?

CARRIE: You think I give a damn about going to college?

JESSE: You're certainly trying hard enough to win the scholarship.

CARRIE: No, I'm not! If I happen to get the highest grades in the class, that's only because I'm quick, that's all. I don't *try* to get the grades. They just happen.

JESSE: (*Sharply*) And if you *happen* to get the scholarship, you'll turn it down.

CARRIE: I didn't say that.

JESSE: You said you didn't want to go to college. Well, I do want to go. I want to very much. And if you don't, you ought to turn it down!

CARRIE: I didn't say I don't want to go! I said I didn't care!

JESSE: (*Angry*) It's the same thing, isn't it?

CARRIE: (*In a fury*) No, it's not! I don't care about anything—not a god-damn thing!

JESSE: (*An instant. He is confused by this*) You say you want to be the Winner of the World. If that's what you want, then you do care about something.

CARRIE: You stupid jerk! If a person says she wants to be the Winner of the World, she knows she can't be the winner of *anything*! *Of anything*!

JESSE: (*Quietly, sympathetically*) That's a terrible thing to say.

CARRIE: (*A bit wild*) It's only terrible if I care!

JESSE: (*Urgently*) You do care—you do!

CARRIE: What if I don't! What am I supposed to care about? And what if I don't care about anything? What am I supposed to do—kill myself?
(*Her unexpected outbreak, her pain, her confusion are too much for him to handle, to understand. They are still. She sees she has unnerved him and, by main force, pulls herself together.*)

CARRIE: I'm sorry if I upset you. . . . Sometimes I come apart, but I can always put myself together again. . . . I kind of challenge myself to go batty . . . It's a kind of game.

JESSE: If you . . . when you . . . go to college . . . I hope you find something to care about.

CARRIE: (*She is under complete self-control now, facing the reality of despair.*) I won't.

JESSE: Don't say that.

CARRIE: I'll settle for something to *do*.

JESSE: Like what?

CARRIE: (*In an outburst of resentment, she strikes her forehead with her fist*) Something to do with *this*!
(*She grabs her breast*) Something to do with *these*!

JESSE: Why are you pretending to be trash? Don't you want me to like you? I can't help it—I *do* like you. Because you're a good person!

CARRIE: (*An outbreak*) Don't *say* that! I'm not a good person! I don't want to have to live up to any of that stuff! I don't want to *be* a good person!

JESSE: (*With warm sympathy*) That's tough, Carrie—because that's what you are.

CARRIE: No, I'm not! Come on—come on!

JESSE: Where?

CARRIE: I'm going to take you to a new place! Come on!

(*She rushes off as if in panic. He hastens after her. The light comes up on the indoor side of a a door with a peephole in its panel. We are in a speakeasy. A dark, vignetted hideaway, with music in the background. Hugo Lockman, a part-owner of the establishment, is at a bar, wiping glasses. He's about forty, wearing sharp clothes that were tidier a while ago. A bitter and unhappy leftover from prohibition, Hugo is handsome in an unsafe way. He moves quickly—he's been a boxer—his body has cunning in it. He's a bit drunk, and his current trouble has made him combative. There is a knock on the door.*)

HUGO: Who's there? We're closed—who the hell is it?

CARRIE'S: It's me, Hugo—it's Carrie.

(*Surprised, Hugo goes to the door, opens the peephole to make sure it is really Carrie. Satisfied that it is, his manner changes, he assumes a false gaiety. He unlocks the door, lets her in, and marginally notes her companion. Jesse is puzzled and uncomfortable.*)

HUGO: Well, if it ain't Milky McIlvaine. How are you, Milky?

CARRIE: (*Embarrassed*) Please don't call me that. How are you, Hugo?

HUGO: I been better.

CARRIE: Closing up for good, huh?

HUGO: For good, for bad, for somethin'. I shoulda done it a year ago. But I figure, Roosevelt or no Roosevelt, people will still want speakeasies.

CARRIE: Well, now that they can get the stuff legally—

HUGO: (*A heartfelt outburst*) Legally? Who wants to get drunk legally? The whole trick is doin' something *illegal*—and gettin' away wit' it! Like— I never saw a whore that was prettier than my wife. But the t'rill about bangin' a whore is you can get locked up for it. I can't get that t'rill from my wife, but I can get it from a whore!

CARRIE: Yes—and other things.

(*Hugo howls with laughter far beyond the wit of the joke. Jesse laughs too, but he is getting more and more uneasy.*)

HUGO: I'm laughin', but it ain't funny. If it's true, it ain't funny, right? Who's your friend?

CARRIE: Oh, I'm sorry. This is Hugo Lockman. And this is Jesse—he's my— uh—cousin.

(*Jesse laughs nervously. Hugo looks from Jesse to Carrie. He suspects that they have a private joke, they're making a fool of him. He tightens.*)

HUGO: What's the joke, kid?

JESSE: If it's true, it ain't funny.

HUGO: (*Distrustfully*) What ain't true?

JESSE: I'm not her cousin.

(*Again Jesse laughs nervously. Hugo is certain he's being mocked. His wariness puts something threatening in the air. Hugo smiles as if to join them; the threat is not mitigated, it worsens.*)

HUGO: What'll you have to drink?

CARRIE: I'll have applejack. Jesse doesn't drink.

HUGO: (*Ignoring her*) What'll you have to drink, Jesse?

JESSE: I'll have a daiquiri.

HUGO: Same rules as always—kids pay in advance.

JESSE: I—uh—I don't have enough money, I'm afraid.

HUGO: It's okay—we do it fair-exchange-no-robbery. A smooch for a daiquiri and a feel for an applejack. But I don't like to smooch wit' boys, so I'll collect from your "cousin."

(*He reaches for Carrie, pulls her into an embrace and forcibly kisses her, meanwhile groping for her breast. She tries to break away.*)

CARRIE: Let me go! Goddamn it, let me go!

JESSE: Stop it—let her go!

(*Jesse tries to pull Hugo away. A scuffle.*)

CARRIE: Take your hands off—let me go!

JESSE: You bastard, let her go!

(*Jesse gets off a punch; it misses. Hugo grabs him, doesn't hit him. But Jesse is unstoppable. He breaks away and punches again, landing it this time. Hugo strikes back—a smashing blow.*)

CARRIE: Quit it—both of you—quit it!

(*The fight is on, but only briefly. Jesse is bleeding.*)

CARRIE: *Stop! Goddamn you, stop it!*

(*She succeeds at last in breaking them apart. Hugo does not view this as a victory—it merely adds to his frustration.*)

HUGO: (*To Jesse*) Get the hell out of here, you dumb little shit.

(*Turning to Carrie*) Take him out of here, Milky! In all the time I'm a speakeasy, I got a nice quiet little place! No fights!—no blood on the floor! As soon as the country goes legal, the place turns into a fuckin' slaughterhouse! Get outta here, you little snotnose! You too, Carrie—get the hell out of here!

(*No need to expel them—they're on their way. Carrie, humiliated; Jesse, bleeding. They hurry to disappear.*

Light fades on the speakeasy and comes up on doorsteps. Carrie and Jesse enter. She sits him down on the stair so she can continue ministering to his bloody nose. Now she wipes his face with her handkerchief. There is a stubborn spot of blood on his cheek. She wets the handkerchief with her tongue and wipes it off. She does a final cleanup with the handkerchief, and inspects him.)

CARRIE: Are you sure it stopped?

JESSE: Yes.

CARRIE: Then you can spit out that piece of paper.

(*He pokes his finger under his upper lip and pulls out a tiny wadded up piece of paper. He looks at it.*)

JESSE: It worked.

CARRIE: I told you it would.

(*He pitches it away. She sees some blood on his hand. She wipes it with her handkerchief.*)

CARRIE: Boy, you sure go in for bleeding. Strike one with a frog—strike two with a goon. You better watch it—one more and you're out.

JESSE: (*Quietly*) Who *was* that goon?

CARRIE: I introduced him—Hugo Lockman.

JESSE: That doesn't tell me anything. Who is he?

CARRIE: He's one of the owners of the speakeasy.

JESSE: And you're one of his customers.

CARRIE: . . . No.

JESSE: You must have been a regular customer. He certainly knows you well enough. He even called you by a nickname, Milky. Why'd he call you that?

CARRIE: (*Disturbed*) Why do you think? Tits.

JESSE: And you allowed him to call you that?

CARRIE: (*More and more discomfited*) I told him not to. There was nothing I could do about it.

JESSE: Well, a guy doesn't insult one of his customers—

CARRIE: (*An outbreak*) I was not one of his customers!

JESSE: Don't lie to me.

CARRIE: He was one of mine!

JESSE: (*Confused*) One of your what?

CARRIE: What the hell word are we using? *Customer*!

(*Silence. He half understands, and half refuses to understand. He has an intuitive dread.*)

JESSE: I don't know what you mean by that.

CARRIE: (*She knows that he does understand.*) My first.

JESSE: . . . You're lying.

CARRIE: My first and only.

JESSE: (*He can't handle this. A violent outburst:*) You shut up—shut up!

CARRIE: For ten dollars.

JESSE: I don't believe it! I won't believe it! You didn't do it for money!

CARRIE: Well, money wasn't the only reason—though God knows I had use for the ten bucks.

JESSE: Why? What did you do it for? Why?

CARRIE: For the same reason you're asking—to find out.

JESSE: Find out what?

CARRIE: What it's about. Christ knows it's not about love. At least it hasn't been for me. So it must be about something. Maybe it's about money. Maybe ten bucks won't do it. Maybe a thousand bucks, and it'll mean something. Some way, it's got to mean something!

(*It has been an outcry—desperate, inarticulate, chaotic. Now, looking at Jesse, and seeing his frustrated expression, she realizes she hasn't said anything she means to say; certainly nothing that would be explicable to him.*)

CARRIE: Oh, Christ!

(*Then, suddenly, unaccountably*) You want to touch me? You want to touch me the way Hugo did? Here—put your hand on my breast—you want to touch me?

(*She reaches for his hand, grabs at it. He pulls it away angrily.*)

JESSE: No!

CARRIE: Why not? Because I'm a whore?

JESSE: I didn't say that.

CARRIE: (*Not listening to him*) Once doesn't make a whore, does it? Does once make a whore?

JESSE: No! I didn't say that! No!

(*Now she grabs his hand forcefully and, with sheer rage, puts his hand on her breast.*)

CARRIE: Here—put your hand here! Put it where he had it! Let me see if it feels any different. Let me see!

(*He pulls his hand away and is abruptly filled with painful compassion for her.*)

JESSE: Carrie, don't! Don't do that to yourself!

CARRIE: (*On the verge of hysteria*) It wasn't any different! It wasn't any different!

(*She rushes away.*)

JESSE: Carrie—come back! Carrie!

(*He is stricken for her. As the light fades on Jesse, it comes up on Robbie, at home, studying. On the desk in the bedroom, a disarray of books, a teapot, a bottle of milk, nearly empty, a teacup, the remains of crackers. Also, a number of soiled handkerchiefs—Robbie has a cold. He is studying definitions, committing them to memory, aloud.*)

ROBBIE: Calculus is a method of mathematical analysis that uses special symbols and notations. It is a study of quantitude and magnitude in terms of their—(*He has forgotten*)—shit! (*He remembers*)—in terms of their integral and differential relationships. The word "calculus" is derived from the Latin, and signifies a small stone used in reckoning. (*He coughs, and takes a sip of tea to boost his flagging energy. Groggy, he doesn't know what he's saying, so he repeats it:*) Calculus is a method of mathematical analysis—

(*He's stuck again. Jesse has entered. He prompts:*)

JESSE: —that uses special symbols and notations.

(*Robbie coughs.*)

JESSE: That cough sounds worse.

ROBBIE: It's not better and it's not worse. It's just a pain in the ass.

JESSE: Why don't you go to bed?

ROBBIE: What time is it?

JESSE: Three o'clock.

(*As Robbie coughs again*) Go to bed, for Pete sake.

ROBBIE: I can't—I'm not finished.

JESSE: Finished what?

ROBBIE: You know damn well "what." You just defined it.

JESSE: Oh, Christ! The test isn't tomorrow, is it?

ROBBIE: (*Irritably*) I reminded you of it this afternoon.

JESSE: You didn't.

ROBBIE: I did, damn it.

JESSE: (*Hitting himself on the head*) Oh God, I forgot! I forgot, I forgot!
(*A moment of real worry on Jesse's part: what to do? Robbie watches him. An odd silence. Then:*)

ROBBIE: (*Quietly*) Boy, I envy you.

JESSE: (*Annoyed*) Why? Because I'm going to flunk?

ROBBIE: That's just it—you *won't* flunk. I envy that you can totally forget that you've got a test tomorrow, and go into that class and come out with an A-plus—and I sit here chewing my guts!
(*Robbie coughs again.*)

JESSE: Why the hell don't you got to bed?

ROBBIE: I'm only half through. . . . Aren't you going to study at all?

JESSE: What's the use? It's too late.

ROBBIE: (*He shivers*) I wish Pop wouldn't turn the heat off at night.

JESSE: It costs.

ROBBIE: So does pneumonia.

JESSE: Then don't catch pneumonia—unless you can afford it.
(*Another cough*) Get your ass in bed, for Chrissake!

ROBBIE: (*Angry, dogged*) No! I'm going to get a better grade than she does if I have to spend Christmas in the hospital!

JESSE: Don't worry about Carrie. She didn't study any more than I did.

ROBBIE: You were with her?

JESSE: Yes.
(*Putting an arm around Robbie's shoulder, he starts to guide him away from the desk*) Now go on, Rob—I'll get your stuff together—and I'll turn out the lights.

ROBBIE: (*Suddenly wrenching away*) Why the hell are you so insistent that I go to bed? Because you don't want me to study any more? Because it's busting your balls that I might come in first tomorrow?
(*Stillness. Stunned by the outburst, Jesse slowly turns away from Robbie. The latter is mortified by what he has said.*)

ROBBIE: I'm sorry.
(*Jesse still does not speak. He busies himself with his own books at the other end of the desk. Robbie is on the verge of tears.*)

ROBBIE: I said I'm sorry.
(*An instant. Jesse still does not look at him. He touches the teapot.*)

JESSE: This tea is cold. If you're going to stay up I'll get you some hot.

ROBBIE: (*Another outbreak of anger*) I've just been a shit—now don't you be kind to me!
(*Teapot in hand, Jesse silently starts for the kitchen. Robbie can't stand it.*)

ROBBIE: Now wait a minute! You just wait a minute! I don't want you to be kind to me! It's tough enough as it is, and if you're going to be the good goddamn Samaritan, it'll be unbearable! Now you listen to me! Pop makes eighteen dollars and fifty cents a week. That's not going to get either of us to college. And I've got to go!

(*Feverishly*) I—have—got—to—go!

(*In a passion*) So I'm going to do everything I can to get that scholarship, Jesse. Everything! I'm going to beat Carrie out! And I'm going to beat you too, Jesse! Any way I can. On the level if possible—but if not on the level—any way I can!

(*A moment. Then, more controlledly*) I thought it only fair to warn you of that. So you could watch out for yourself. And I'm going to ask—please—don't be kind to me. Don't feel responsible for me. Don't save my life anymore. I've got to walk out of the burning schoolhouse all by myself—even if I hobble out. So stop carrying me around as your burden, Jesse. Don't make me feel grateful. . . . *and don't make me feel guilty*.

(*A short, motionless, wordless moment.*)

JESSE: I'm going to make you some tea. For a cup of tea you don't have to feel grateful—and you don't have to feel guilty. But i'm going to make it so hot I hope it burns your stupid tongue out.

(*They both try to smile, try to find their way back to some communion. Jesse goes out of the light, presumably to the kitchen. Robbie is still trying to smile, even trying to laugh. But it looks more like crying. The lights fade.*

The class bell is ringing as the light comes up on the blackboard again. Chalked on it this time, a neatly written calculus diagram, also a list:

    Calculus, integral
    Calculus, differential
    Geometric theorems
    Probability
    Variations

Over the P.A. system, we hear the voice of the Mathematics Teacher.)

VOICE OF MATH TEACHER: And don't forget to review the section on the relationship between calculus and geometry—up to the end of Chapter Nine—we'll go over it on Thursday. . . . Your graded exam papers are on the desk. Some of them are good and some are terrible—a bell-shaped curve. Please take your paper with you as you go.

(*Carrie, Jesse and Robbie walk in out of the darkness, make their way to the desk, pick up their papers and depart. Jesse and Carrie are preoccupied with their graded exams as they move through one light and into another, presumably into a corridor. Robbie, hanging back, holds his paper but is scared to look at the grade. Jesse speaks to Carrie.*)

JESSE: What'd you get?

CARRIE: (*With a casual shrug*) Ninety-seven.

ROBBIE: (*With a groan*) Ninety-seven?—oh, brother!

CARRIE: (*To Robbie*) How about you?

ROBBIE: I'm scared to look.

CARRIE: (*Teasing*) Don't be scared. Maybe you got a hundred.
(*She laughs and departs.*)

ROBBIE: Why are the winners always so damn smug?

JESSE: (*Quietly*) She's not smug.
(*Pointing to Robbie's paper*) What'd you get?

ROBBIE: (*Looking at his paper*) Shit. . . . Eighty-three.

JESSE: (*Forcing himself to say it*) That's *good*, you dope.

ROBBIE: How about you?

JESSE: Seventy-eight.

ROBBIE: Did you? . . . You're a liar.

JESSE: (*Stunned*) What?

ROBBIE: You got better than a seventy-eight.

JESSE: I said seventy-eight.

ROBBIE: Let me see.

JESSE: If you don't believe me—

ROBBIE: No, I don't. Let me see!
(*He snatches the paper out of Jesse's hand. He looks at it.*)

ROBBIE: Ninety.

JESSE: It was only luck, Rob. And *I* didn't beat her either.

ROBBIE: Ninety—without studying.
(*He hands back the piece of paper*) Congratulations.

JESSE: It was a fluke, that's all. He happened to ask what I happened to remember. Robbie!—it was only a fluke!

ROBBIE: Congratulations, you goddamn liar.
(*He hurries away. Jesse, ashamed and frustrated, tears the paper into bits. The lights fade.*

Light comes up on a crucifix in the background. We are in a churchyard. Where the path ends, there's a bench. Carrie enters, walking backward, speaking to someone offstage. She is calling directions:)

CARRIE: No—to your left! To your *left*, dummy—or you'll bump into the wall. Now you're coming to the steps. Not too fast—slow down. One—two—three. Now come forward. Follow your nose.
(*Jesse enters. He is wearing a blindfold, obeying Carrie's directions, in a sort of intimate variation of blindman's buff.*)

JESSE: Are we there yet?

CARRIE: Yes, but don't take the blindfold off.

JESSE: The last time you took me to a place, it was a speakeasy and I got beat up.

CARRIE: You won't get beat up here.
(*As she guides him to the bench*) Now we've come to a place where you can sit down.
(*She helps him to sit; she sits beside him.*)

JESSE: (*Reaching for the blindfold*) Do I take it off now?

CARRIE: Almost. Not yet.

JESSE: What are we waiting for?

CARRIE: A sound. Ah, there it is! . . . Listen.

(*It is the pealing of the church bell—deep, sonorous, sad, full of old mysteries. The tolling captures her, like hypnosis. For a moment she says nothing, enrapt. Now slowly, like a ritual, she takes the handkerchief off his eyes. She watches him closely, with happy expectancy.*)

JESSE: Where are we? Where did you bring me?

CARRIE: Don't you recognize it?

JESSE: I've never been here. Yes, I have! It's the churchyard behind St. Martin's.

CARRIE: (*Smiling*) Yes.

JESSE: I forgot it ever existed. You mean it's been here all the time?

CARRIE: Yes. And hardly anybody ever comes here.

JESSE: Holy—!

CARRIE: (*Laughing*) Yes, that's right. . . . Do you like it?

JESSE: It's beautiful. (*An instant*) But how did you find it?—you're not a Catholic.

CARRIE: (*Unsettled at having to explain*) I . . . made a try at it. But it didn't take.

JESSE: Didn't anything?

CARRIE: No. My father's a Methodist. My mother wasn't anything until a few days before she died. She asked for the Methodist minister to come and give her some religion, but there was a snowstorm, and he was late in getting there. My father said it was my mother who was late. I guess if you're going to get religion, you have to be punctual.

(*They both smile wryly.*)

JESSE: Then you're a Methodist really, huh?

CARRIE: No. I couldn't be anything that my father is.

(*She laughs*) I had a girl friend in grammar school—she was Jewish—she was the only real friend I ever had. When she died, I missed her so much that I wanted to be Jewish. So I went to a rabbi. But I asked too many questions and he said I was fiddling around with faith. But I wasn't fiddling with anything—*I meant it*!

JESSE: Did you really?

CARRIE: Well, I didn't *know*!

(*Quietly, with longing*) I wish I *could* know about something. Here I am—the smartest girl in the whole damn universe—and I don't know anything. Do you suppose anybody knows?

JESSE: My father says he knows.

CARRIE: What religion?

JESSE: He's an atheist.

CARRIE: Is he so sure that no is an answer? . . . Are you?

JESSE: Sometimes I think that no is not the answer to anything.

CARRIE: Really? Sometimes it's the only word that comes to my mind.

JESSE: (*Quickly: he doesn't want to be different*) But just because I don't say no all the time doesn't mean I say yes all the time. I guess I'm a—what do you call it?—an agnostic.

CARRIE: Well, *that's* no trick, knowing that you don't *know*. I've known *that* all my life.

JESSE: (*With a quiet yearning*) Except, I think I *will* know one of these days.

CARRIE: (*Gently*) I hope you do. I sincerely hope you do.
(*They have reached, and have touched. They are fleetingly aware that the moment is precious. He points off, toward the church.*)

JESSE: Have you ever been inside?

CARRIE: (*Tightening*) No.

JESSE: You mean you come here—a few feet from the door—and you've never been inside?

CARRIE: A few feet can be another world.

JESSE: Or just within reach. You want to go inside?

CARRIE: No.

JESSE: Why not?

CARRIE: I'm . . . afraid.

JESSE: Afraid of what?

CARRIE: (*Confused*) I don't know—I can't keep going inside all the time, and then just come *out* again!
(*A moment. Inarticulate as she is, he understands. He touches her gently.*)

JESSE: Come on—I'll go with you.

CARRIE: No—please!

JESSE: (*Urging too strongly, trying to give her his own impulse, he grabs her arm*) Come on, Carrie—come *on*!

CARRIE: Let me go, goddamn it!
(*Silence. Then, wryly*) It's hardly the place to say goddamn it.
(*In some inchoate way, he is sorry for her, and wants to reach out. She has moved away from him; he takes a step or two toward her.*)

JESSE: I—Carrie—I don't know what to say—I think I'm in love with you.

CARRIE: (*Gently*) I think you are.

JESSE: Can you . . . can you say something to me?

CARRIE: (*Regretfully*) No.

JESSE: Try.

CARRIE: (*She tries, but it's too difficult, and she is too honest to lie. She is in pain.*) I can't.

JESSE: Then I'll say it to you until you can! I love you, Carrie—I love you—
(*She is getting unaccountably frightened, starting to panic.*)

CARRIE: Stop that! Stop saying that!

JESSE: I love you—I love you—

CARRIE: (*Suddenly out of control*) You think you're saying something nice to me—but you're only trying to hurt me—to hurt me—
(*Silence. He is stunned by her outburst. He speaks very quietly.*)

JESSE: I'm not trying to hurt you, Carrie. I don't know what *is* hurting you—but I'm trying to help.

(*She pulls herself together. In order not to detonate again, she speaks with intense control.*)

CARRIE: My father is a teacher. He teaches history and civics. He's a slave to his students—and to books. Everybody in his school loves him—the faculty—the kids—everybody. When he comes home from school, he tells me how much he loves me—he would do anything for me—and then he finds some excuse to beat the hell out of me.

JESSE: . . . I think you're making it up.

(*She rolls up the sleeve of her dress and reveals a bruise on her upper arm.*)

CARRIE: Look.

JESSE: Oh God. . . . Does anybody know?

CARRIE: No.

JESSE: You've got to tell somebody—the police—somebody—you've got to do something about it.

CARRIE: I tried to, once. I found a fenceboard with nails sticking out of it. And one night when he started to beat me, I went at him and I beat him with it. And you know what?—he just allowed me to do it. He stood there—his face and his arms were bleeding—and he didn't try to take the board away from me, he didn't raise a hand. He hardly moved—his mouth was open and his eyes were shut, and he didn't even seem to be breathing. I stopped hitting him and I began to cry. He walked away, then. He didn't pay any attention to his cuts, he didn't bandage them, he didn't wash, he didn't eat. He just went back into his room and sat at his desk with his books, reading all night . . . just reading . . .

JESSE: (*Pointing to her arm*) That thing—on your arm—someway, you've got to defend yourself, Carrie.

CARRIE: I can't. I've still got that fenceboard. It's standing in a corner of my closet and I can't bear to look at it. But I'm afraid to throw it away—(*Shivering*)—and I can't touch it.

JESSE: Well, some way or other, you've got to fight back.

CARRIE: You think I don't know that? If you don't fight back, it's no longer a war, it's a partnership. . . . I guess I deserve what I get.

JESSE: Don't say that. You don't have to take the blame because your father's a bastard!

CARRIE: But he's not. He's sick. He's just a lonely sick man with his head in his books.

(*An instant. With quiet intensity*) I told you that I love books—the way you do—but I think I really hate them.

JESSE: No, you don't. If you did, you wouldn't be at the head of the class.

CARRIE: I hate them! They're the Great Big Lie!

JESSE: The big lie?—what does that mean?

CARRIE: They promise to tell you everything you need to know! The answer to all the big secrets! How the world works—how to make life a great adventure—what God's all about! They promise you everything and they give you lies! And the worst lie of all is the great big whopping one about love! How it heals your heart and eases your soul! Bullshit! All it does is hurt!—it's a board with nails in it! So don't write me any more books on the subject of human devotion! I don't want to have anything to do with it! You understand me?—*you understand me?*

(*Verging on hysteria—frightened—she flees. Jesse starts to follow, but doesn't know how to help her. At a loss, he is momentarily unable to move in any direction. The lights fade.*)

The light comes up on the blackboard again—Nora Bailey's classroom. After school. Only Nora and Robbie are present. She sits behind her desk; he, in the seat closest to her. She is angry.)

NORA: So what it means is you're throwing in the sponge.

ROBBIE: (*Also angry*) I'm not throwing in the sponge. I just don't know how to climb back into the ring.

NORA: High grades aren't everything.

ROBBIE: Aw, come on. You think I don't know better than that?

NORA: They're not everything! Lots of other things are taken into consideration.

ROBBIE: (*Biting*) Like what? Charm?

NORA: What sort of *person* you are—what potential you have—how you work with people.

ROBBIE: I work by myself.

NORA: Well, don't be so proud of that. What do you say when they ask how you fit into the social life of the school? What do we tell them?

ROBBIE: Tell them that I fit in zero—goose egg! You want to know something? I never had a date in my life!

NORA: Well, what do we put on your record? He never had a date in his life—he doesn't go out for anything—no school clubs, no student council, no sports—

ROBBIE: (*Seizing on her faux pas*) Ah, sports! Well, you tell 'em I'm captain of the football team, but I fell just a little short in track.

(*With studied nonchalance he puts his lame foot on her desk. She stares at it with silent reproach. Her wordless rebuke makes him self-conscious and he removes his foot.*)

NORA: Now you stop playing the defeated warrior, Robert. There are other things you can try out for. The debating team. The drama club. Where were you last night when we started auditions for "The Mikado"?

ROBBIE: I can't sing a note.

NORA: How do you know? I bet you've never *tried* to sing a song in your whole life!

ROBBIE: Listen, what chance would I have of getting a part as a performer on the stage? None—just absolutely none!

NORA: Who says? Last night—at the first audition, fifty-two girls showed up. And do you know how many boys? Four. You'll get a part just by eenie meenie miney mo!

ROBBIE: I don't exactly see myself as a musical comedy star, Miss Bailey.

NORA: (*Lashing*) What do you see yourself as—a cripple?
(*He is hit hard, more than he can take. Quickly he departs. The lights fade.*

The light comes up on the Weaver living room. Henrietta is mending a lampshade with adhesive tape. The main occurrence in the room is: A Sound. It is the sound of Robbie upstairs, in his bedroom, singing. He doesn't have a good voice, but a shatteringly loud one. There's an angry challenge in his singing, a howl of brass. We hear Jesse's voice as the front door opens and slams shut.)

JESSE: I'm home!
(*He enters and stands still, galvanized by the racket of Robbie. He listens. He shivers.*)

JESSE: What the hell is that?

HENRIETTA: You know darn well what it is. It's your brother.

JESSE: For God's sake, what's he doing?

HENRIETTA: Don't you recognize the activity? It's called singing.

JESSE: Holy mackerel, do we allow it?

HENRIETTA: Oh come on, it's not so terrible.

JESSE: He sounds like he's killing a pig.

HENRIETTA: Now, don't get smart.

JESSE: (*Turning serious*) Well, he doesn't sound like he's singing, Mom, he sounds like he's angry.

HENRIETTA: Not angry—challenged. He's going to try out for "The Mikado."

JESSE: He's what?

HENRIETTA: Yes, on Friday.

JESSE: Geez, it makes my blood run cold.

HENRIETTA: Now, I want you to quit it! His voice isn't at all bad. Anyway, he's got to *think* it's all right or he won't be able to get up on the stage.
(*With a threat in her voice*) And if you make him feel self-conscious—

JESSE: Mom—*Mom!*—it's got nothing to do with self-conscious. He doesn't have to prove he's a singer, for Pete sake! He's got enough on the ball without that!

HENRIETTA: *He* doesn't think so. And if he doesn't, it doesn't matter what we think— he's got to change his own mind.

JESSE: But, Mom—he'll feel worse if he fails! He'll make himself ridiculous!

HENRIETTA: (*Not too sure*) I hope he won't.

JESSE: Is that all you're going to say? You mean you'll just sit there and let him do it? You won't help him protect himself?

HENRIETTA: He'll have to do that on his own.

JESSE: Isn't that a pretty callous thing to say, Mom?

HENRIETTA: No! And don't you protect him!

JESSE: Yes I will. I'm going to talk to him.

HENRIETTA: Don't you dare! Don't you dare to say a word to him!

JESSE: If you won't, somebody's got to do it!

(*He starts off.*)

HENRIETTA: Now you wait a minute. He's building himself up to perform an act of courage, and if you pull the pins out from under him, he's going to collapse—and I won't have you doing that!

JESSE: Mom, I see this the other way around! He's about to perform an act of desperation. Not courage—desperation! And he doesn't have to do that. He's smart and he's hard-working and he's got the stuff—and there's nothing he has to get desperate about. And we've got to help him to *know* that—and that's what I'm going to do!

(*He starts off again. Henrietta goes after him, calling.*)

HENRIETTA: Don't you say a word to him, Jesse—don't say a word!

(*He is already out of the room, enroute to the bedroom. Henrietta hurries after him.*

The lights fade on the living room and come up on the twins' bedroom. Robbie, full of daring and defiance, stands on his own bed and sings. He doesn't sing with any great joy, he sings as a remonstrance, a denunciation, with pugnacious gestures. His face is flushed, his hair disorderly; he is a lion rampant. He doesn't notice that Jesse has appeared. The latter's concern for his brother is now tempered by amusement. Robbie makes a grand and sweeping gesture to include his entire audience, and sees Jesse watching him. Robbie is embarrassed. He stops, mid-note.)

ROBBIE: Shut up.

JESSE: I didn't say a word.

ROBBIE: No smart-ass cracks!—understand?

JESSE: I understand. I won't say anything. Not a word.

ROBBIE: (*Belligerent, ready for battle*) Why shouldn't I be in the show?

JESSE: (*With false innocence*) Who said you shouldn't be? Did I say that? Who said it?

ROBBIE: Why shouldn't I surprise everybody and be a goddamn good singer?

JESSE: That's a real valid question, Robbie—why *shouldn't* you surprise everybody?

ROBBIE: And be a musical comedy star!

JESSE: That's *right*! Why *shouldn't* you be a musical comedy star? I betcha nobody's got an answer to that. *I* certainly don't have an answer. Why shouldn't you be?—why not?

ROBBIE: Yes, why not? Being a cripple doesn't mean a goddamn thing!

JESSE: Nothing—nothing at all! It certainly doesn't have a damn thing to do with how well you sing.

ROBBIE: Or with anything! Julius Caesar had epilepsy!—he was the greatest general Rome ever had!

JESSE: And he became the Emperor!

ROBBIE: Right! And could he sing?

JESSE: Not a note. He'd certainly be lousy in an audition.

ROBBIE: He'd never even make the Glee Club!

JESSE: (*Seeing an opening*) No, he wouldn't! But did anybody kill him for having a lousy voice? No. Matter of fact, there have been geniuses who couldn't even *speak*. Take Demosthenes. He was a stammerer!

ROBBIE: Yeah, a *stammerer*, for God's sake!

JESSE: Couldn't talk to his mother, couldn't even call his cat.

ROBBIE: So he put pebbles in his mouth and he screamed at the ocean, and, son of a bitch, he became the greatest orator of Greece!

JESSE: (*Exhilarated because he's making his way by an oblique route—without hurting Robbie*) Attaboy, Robbie—put pebbles in your mouth! Want some pebbles? I'll go out and get you some pebbles!

(*Silence. The fake euphoria has come to an end. Robbie looks quietly and soberly at his brother.*)

ROBBIE: That's not what you started to say, is it?

JESSE: (*Trying to sustain the euphoria*) Yes, it is! Put pebbles in your mouth. Sing, Robbie!

ROBBIE: (*Subdued, with gravity, he comes down from the bed*) No. You were going to tell me not to try for the show.

JESSE: No, Robbie.

ROBBIE: To hide in a corner.

JESSE: No.

ROBBIE: To run scared. Or not to run at all—because I'll fall down.

JESSE: No! Sing, Robbie—and I'll sing with you—

(*On a note of bravura, Jesse jumps up on the bed and starts to sing. But as Robbie watches him with sad, appraising eyes, Jesse stops singing. Stillness. Then:*)

ROBBIE: You've got a good voice, Jesse. And I haven't. And you've got nerve enough to get up on that stage—just to test how good you are. And I haven't got the nerve to find out.

(*He has given up, and leaves the bedroom. Jesse slowly gets off the bed.*

The lights cross-fade to Nora's classroom again. This time her altercation is with Jesse. Unlike Robbie, he is not slouched in a seat, but pacing.)

NORA: If he's not going to audition, he's not going to audition. But I think it's rotten of you to discourage him!

JESSE: I didn't discourage him. He saw the light all by himself!

NORA: Saw the light?! If he doesn't get up on stage and try to win a part for himself, it'll be the most idiotic decision he's ever made. And I'm not thinking only about his being an actor in a musical or winning a scholarship! I think it's important for him to take a chance, and quit locking himself up all alone the way he does! And this'll give him an opportunity to make something with others, and maybe even make a friend or two!

JESSE: Maybe he doesn't want to make friends! All he wants is to go to college—and you're giving him a false hope that he will!

NORA: What is so false about the hope he'll get a part in a play, for God's sake?!

JESSE: He can't *sing*!

NORA: What's that got to do with a high school production of "The Mikado"?

JESSE: It's not whether he can sing, it's that he knows he can't sing—and he'll be too scared to audition. And why the hell should he go through that agony? It won't give him any points toward a scholarship!

NORA: I am sick to death of this obsession with a scholarship!

JESSE: Then stop making it worse! Stop telling Robbie that he's got a chance to win!

NORA: What shall I do?—tell him that he *hasn't* got a chance? Do you tell him that?

JESSE: (*Giving way a little*) . . . No. . . . But it's the truth.

NORA: Maybe in this case the truth is not so almighty important!

JESSE: (*Confused, wretched*) It's got to be important.

NORA: Then why don't *you* tell him the truth? Tell him you don't *want* him to win the scholarship—you want it for yourself.

JESSE: (*With quiet, angry deliberation*) Miss Bailey, you have certainly got it all wrong.

NORA: Then tell him what's right! Tell him whose side you're on! Which one are you rooting for, Jesse? Your brother or yourself? Or is it your friend, Carrie McIlvaine?

JESSE: (*An outburst*) No! That's not true!

NORA: Which one, Jesse?—which one?

JESSE: (*An outcry*) I want all of us to win!—all of us! Why can't we all win?!

NORA: You know you can't all win—so you have to take sides. Whose side are you on?

JESSE: (*Losing control, he lashes out at her*) I'm on Robbie's side! This scholarship is the only dream he's got—and I want him to win! I want Robbie to win! Robbie! Only Robbie! *Robbie!*

(*The lights fade on the classroom and come up on a large pyramidal sign, two-sided, lettered in red, white and blue and draped with an American flag. The sign reads: JOIN THE C.C.C.—ALL EXPENSES PAID— GOOD SALARY—A REAL FUTURE. Over the Public Address system, as we read the sign, we hear the strains of "Happy Days Are Here Again." The music cuts off and the voice of a C.C.C. worker is heard on the P.A.*)

C.C.C. WORKER'S VOICE: (*Singing*) Don't be idle, don't be poor, Get a job that's yours for sure, Drain a swamp and plant a tree, Come and join the C.C.C.

(*The light fades on the sign and comes up on the Weaver dinner table.*

The family is seated. Dinner is nearly over. Henrietta has just cleared away the dishes. Robbie is holding a picture pamphlet on the C.C.C., reading some of the literature; Frank is studying the blue application card. Jesse is very still.)

HENRIETTA: But I don't understand it. What *is* the C.C.C.?

JESSE: (*Trying to show how calm he is*) I told you what it is, Mom. It's the Civilian Conservation Corps.

HENRIETTA: But what is it *about*?

JESSE: (*Annoyed*) Mom, you're trying *not* to understand it. It's about helping the government to drain swamps and mend roads and plant trees and build bridges.

ROBBIE: Look at these pictures. These guys are working their tail off.

JESSE: (*Trying to lift the gloom*) As Hercules said in the stable, I'm not afraid of hard work.

ROBBIE: He was shoveling horse manure, Jesse.

HENRIETTA: Robert, please.

ROBBIE: Well, it's all sweat, Mom—
(*To Jesse*)—and very little reward. It's like being in a chain gang.

JESSE: (*Quietly, with dignity*) No it's not—and please stay out of it.

FRANK: (*Coolly*) It says here you have to be eighteen to join.

JESSE: I'll be eighteen in July.

(*Frank hands the blue card to Jesse.*)

FRANK: Here. I'm giving this back to you. When you're eighteen we'll discuss it.

JESSE: (*Not taking the card*) It says there that I can join before I'm eighteen—with my parents' permission.

FRANK: You don't have my permission.

JESSE: Please sign the card, Pop.

(*Pause. Frank speaks as gently as he can.*)

FRANK: Jesse . . . I know what it's like to lose all your good choices, and have to look around for substitutes. But this is dumb. I can't see one single logical sensible reason for signing this.

JESSE: What kind of logical sensible reason do you need? I want to go.

HENRIETTA: (*Trying to sound equitable*) What we're trying to say to you, Jesse, is that we don't think you do want to go.

JESSE: You think I'd give myself all this trouble—blood tests and letters of recommendation and birth certificates—if I didn't want to go? What do you think I'm doing—playing around?

ROBBIE: What about college?

JESSE: Well, what about college? How do you think we can manage it? Do we have a rich uncle somewhere? Is Momma going to pawn all the diamonds and emeralds she hasn't got? Has Poppa got a fortune stashed away somewhere?

HENRIETTA: But you can get a job—for the summer—for after school.

FRANK: And work your way through. I did it—and you're smarter than I was.

JESSE: (*Getting cornered, he starts to lose control*) I'll be glad to work my way through! But how do I get a job?
(*Picking up a newsaper, he waves it with angry frustration*) Look—read the want ads! Not a single ad for a boy or a young man—not one! Last week—Tuesday and Wednesday—I didn't go to school. I went job hunting. I wasted shoe leather. Nothing! Tell them, Robbie—nothing, nothing!

ROBBIE: Things are going to change, Jesse.

JESSE: That's what they tell us, Rob—things are going to change. But not for us!

FRANK: For everybody! Believe me, Jess—they will! Since Roosevelt came in, things are already changing. You wait and see. No jobs today, but lots of them tomorrow. And if you can work and help yourself to a college education—and if Robbie should win a free scholarship—both of my boys—

JESSE: (*At last he explodes*) Both of your boys, my foot! *Stop dreaming*! Robbie and I are tied for second place! *Not first, Pop*! Robbie's not going to win a scholarship any more than he'll win a part in "The Mikado"! He's going to wind up carrying props—and I'm going to wind up selling newspapers—if I'm lucky, *if I'm lucky*!
(*His explosion leaves a vacuum. A troubled silence. Jesse fills it. He is conciliatory, pleading. His plea is directed to his mother.*)

JESSE: Now, look—Momma—please tell him to be reasonable. This is the most sensible thing I can think of. I'll get my board and lodging totally free—I won't have a nickel's worth of personal expenses—the government pays for all of it. At the end of the month, I'll get my salary—and I won't have any use for it. I'll send it right home—I'll put my check in the mail—every month—check in the mail!

FRANK: (*Hurt*) Thank you, but we've done without your "check in the mail"—all through the depression. We won't need your money.

JESSE: Robbie will.
(*The words have escaped him; he didn't mean to say them. Robbie rises.*)

ROBBIE: You're doing this for me?

JESSE: (*Quickly*) No! I'm doing it for myself—I'm doing it for the family!

ROBBIE: (*An accusation*) You're doing it for me!

JESSE: You're part of the family, aren't you?

ROBBIE: You're doing it for me so I can go to college!

JESSE: Wouldn't you do it for me? If you didn't have a game leg—and if the government would take you—wouldn't you join up to help me get through? Wouldn't you?

ROBBIE: No! I want to go to college so badly that I wouldn't do anything that got in the way of it! Nothing!

JESSE: (*With bitter triumph*) There! I trapped you into admitting that's all you've ever wanted! And why shouldn't you get it? And why shouldn't I help you to get it? I'm your brother, for God's sake! If that's what you want so badly—

ROBBIE: How about what *you* want?!

JESSE: I don't want it!

FRANK: (*Quietly*) That's not the truth.

JESSE: Yes, it is, Pop. I don't care whether I go to college. I really don't care.

FRANK: Since when don't you care?

JESSE: A long time, Pop. I just haven't said anything about it. I'm bored with school. I've had it.

HENRIETTA: Being a martyr doesn't become you, Jesse.

JESSE: (*A flare of anger*) I'm not being a martyr! Jesus Christ, what a lousy thing to say! You and Poppa do things for us all our lives, and nobody calls you martyr! My God, can't I do something for somebody I love without being called a martyr?!

HENRIETTA: Don't do it for him—do something for yourself!

JESSE: I am doing it for myself! He's my twin! I'm half of him, he's half of me!

FRANK: (*Letting out his pent-up rage*) No! *There aren't any half people!* You're *one* and he's another *one! No more half people!* Even if the depression made us think we *were* half people, it's over! There will never be half people again! Never! None of us! And not you, Jesse! You're a full human being—and you're entitled to a full life!

JESSE: I can have a full life without a college education!

HENRIETTA: Some people can—but not you!

FRANK: She's right. You need it! You need it in your heart and soul—*you need it!*

JESSE: No I don't!

FRANK: You're crying for it! Look at that! Look at these!

(*From the sideboard he picks up a stack of college publications*) Look! Catalogs—bulletins from colleges and universities! Letters! Applications! Amherst, Bates College, Brown, Dartmouth, Penn, Haverford! You've been reading these things as if they're adventure stories! And they *are!*—they *are* adventure stories!

JESSE: Stories—yes! Fairy tales! I don't want any more fairy tales! I want to face the facts—and I want you to face them! I'm not going to college, Pop—you want to know why? Because I don't give a damn about books anymore!

FRANK: That is the most asinine, the wildest—

JESSE: But it's true! I'm not like you and I'm not like Robbie! I'm bored with studying and exams and aptitude tests and application blanks! *And—I—am—bored—with—books!*

HENRIETTA: He's lying to us!

FRANK: You are!—you're lying!

JESSE: No I'm not! You want to know something? I go to the library with Robbie—and I sneak away and he doesn't even notice! I haven't read a book in two months! Because I don't think that books are worth a good goddamn!

FRANK: You're putting on a big act!

JESSE: No! I mean it!

(*Grabbing a book, he starts to tear it. As he rips out the pages, the words tear out of him.*)

JESSE: They're worthless—they're useless—they're senseless. And they're a big bag of wind! They're full of promises they never keep! They're the Great Big Lie—they're full of lies, *full of lies!*

(*Only marginally aware that he is echoing Carrie's words, he starts tearing the college catalogs, ripping one after another to pieces. Robbie tries to stop him.*)

ROBBIE: Stop that! Stop it! Jesse—please—*please*—stop it! Stop it, stop it!

(*They are fighting, struggling over the destruction of the books. Henrietta and Frank try to put an end to the conflict.*)

HENRIETTA & FRANK: Stop it—Jesse—Robbie! Frank, stop them, stop them! . . . Quit it, both of you—quit it, I say!

(*The struggle is over. Silence.*)

FRANK: Go to bed, both of you.

(*An instant. Robbie slowly leaves the room. Jesse remains.*)

FRANK: (*More gently*) I said go to bed.

HENRIETTA: Let him alone, Frank.

(*She goes upstairs. A moment, then Frank follows. Jesse is alone. He remains very still. Slowly he starts gathering the torn books and catalogs. He rearranges them on the sideboard as neatly as possible, trying to make a little order out of the chaos. He is quietly, almost imperceptibly, crying. The lights begin to fade.*)

END OF ACT ONE

Act Two

SHORTLY FOLLOWING THE END of Act One, the light comes up on the bedroom of Frank and Henrietta. In troubled silence, they are undressing for the night. Frank is distressed.

FRANK: I don't understand it. I don't know how to *begin* to understand it . . . Tearing up those books . . . Saying all those things . . . I don't believe him. I don't believe a word he says.

HENRIETTA: Maybe *he* believes it, Frank.

FRANK: You know as well as I do that he doesn't.

HENRIETTA: (*Worriedly trying to figure it out*) What if he does? What if books aren't the magical ticket to happiness that everybody promised. Maybe he's getting old enough to be . . . disillusioned.

FRANK: Because he's getting older doesn't mean he *has* to get disillusioned, you know.

HENRIETTA: Doesn't it?

FRANK: No. I'm forty-six—I'm not.

HENRIETTA: (*Slowly, aridly*) I'm forty-three.

FRANK: And you are?

(*The implication that Henrietta has become disenchanted with life is too troubling for Frank to face. Silence.*)

HENRIETTA: I don't know how to make sense of anything, Frank. I think we were—somehow—deceived. Not only about books, but in other ways. We were led to believe—when we were growing up—if we do certain things, other things were certain to happen. If you Work Hard, you'll Prosper. If you're Loyal to the Company, you'll get Promoted. If you Put Your Money in a Nice Safe Honest Bank—they'll take Care of it for you and keep it Secure. Well, you worked hard—and we're poor. You were loyal to the company, and you got fired. We put our money in an honest bank—and we lost everything.

FRANK: Not everything.

HENRIETTA: We lost our security, Frank.

FRANK: No we didn't. It's just that it's changed. Security used to be all the things we *had*—now security is all the things we can do without.

HENRIETTA: Can we do without faith, Frank?

FRANK: Depends what kind of faith you're talking about.

HENRIETTA: Every kind. In the government—in tomorrow—in God.

(*An instant. It troubles him not to be able to deal with this. A statement, not a question:*)

FRANK: You haven't lost your faith in God, Henrietta.

HENRIETTA: I'm not sure. I go to church. But I'm the only one in the family who does. I understand your reason for *not* going, and I'm not blaming you for being an atheist. But I'm beginning to wonder why *I'm* going. Just to keep the door open, I suppose. For my family. But they're certainly not there *with* me. And I certainly don't want to-force them. And it isn't only *our* kids who are missing from the congregation. All the young people are missing. I'm generally the youngest one there. So what do the kids believe in? And how in the world can we ask them to believe in us?

FRANK: I'm not asking them to believe in us.

HENRIETTA: *They're* asking.

FRANK: (*An outcry*) I can't help that! I didn't give them any reason to lose faith in me. I never promised them any fabulous futures. And I never demanded impossible things from them. They won't disappoint me if none of them becomes a captain of industry or the head of our government. They don't owe me that, any more than I owe them a God they can believe in. But I do owe them a decent start—which means an education. And if I can give it to them, it's not earthshaking if they don't believe what I believe. Let them believe in themselves! Let them believe in their teachers!

HENRIETTA: Who are their teachers? What do *they* believe in?

(*They are silent. As the night lights fade in the bedroom, they come up on library shelves. On the wall, a large sign: SILENCE. THIS IS A LIBRARY, NOT A PLAYGROUND. Jesse sits at a library table, the light shining on his face and on the open books. He is totally lost in what he is reading. His face has the rapt expression of a young man transported into a mystical, wonder-making world. Now, for a moment, he stops reading, sim-*)

ply to live more deeply a thought he has just come upon; a thought perhaps too magical to lose. His head tilted upward so that he seems to be looking at the ceiling, he turns slowly back and forth in the swivel chair, a slow arc at a time, left, right, back, forth, easily, dreamily. Then abruptly a thought strikes him—an exciting flare of a thought, a light breaking—and he laughs in delight, swinging his swivel chair around in a wider arc—whee!
Then he sees him!
Far across the stage, a pinspot bursts alight. In it, Jesse's father. The two spots of light—Jesse's and Frank's—at diagonally opposite corners of the stage—have, as yet, no relation to each other. Frank, returning a book to the library, holds it open to its back, where a book-card is inserted in the envelope. He lifts the book-card out of its sleeve, and is about to present the two objects to, presumably, a librarian—when he sees Jesse.

FRANK: Jesse!

(Jesse looks up, sees his father. Frantic, in a rout, he must escape. He starts gathering his things—books, papers, his cap, his jacket—and is frustrated at how long it takes. At last he is collected enough to run.)

FRANK: Jesse—wait!

(A wild scurry back and forth across the stage, a scramble, flight, pursuit. Just as he is about to elude his father—Jesse's books burst out of his arms. He muddles to collect them, and his father catches up. Out of breath, filled with anger, Frank vents his rage.)

FRANK: You don't go to the library anymore, do you? You don't read books anymore, do you?
(He kicks one of the books that has fallen) You don't read books, do you? Do you?
(He snatches the books Jesse has managed to collect and throws them down) They're full of lies, aren't they? Books are full of lies! Full of lies!
(He slaps at the rest of the books in Jesse's arms, slaps them out of his arms.)

FRANK: You're full of lies, Jesse—you!

JESSE: *(In pain, he cries out)* All right—I lied to you! You think I wanted to lie? You want to know why I lied? Not only to do something for Robbie, but to do something for you! To save *you*!

FRANK: Me? *Me?*

JESSE: Yes!—to save your face! I *do* want to go to college! You're right—I *do* want to go! I'm dying to go!
(Then, the blow) Why don't you send me?!

FRANK: *(Stunned)* What?

FRANK: Why don't you send me to college? Why don't you have enough money to do that? Why aren't you rich? Why are we so poor—so poor!

FRANK: *(Desperate for an answer)* Everybody's poor nowadays!

JESSE: No, not everybody! But we are! Why are we? Whose fault is it? Is it mine? Is it Robbie's? Is it Mom's? No, it's yours! Because you're a failure!

FRANK: *Everybody's a failure nowadays!*

JESSE: A failure!

(He suddenly realizes the enormity of pain he has inflicted) Oh God, oh God!

(Weeping, he rushes away. Frank remains. For a long time he is still, too anguished to move. At last he becomes aware of Jesse's books on the ground. He gets down and starts to reassemble them. Severely wounded, he stops, too dispirited to finish the task; he must leave the books where they are, unreclaimed. But at last he does get them together, rises with them, and slowly departs.

The stage is black for a moment, then brightens to a glow on the church-yard bench. Jesse is turned away from Carrie. He is weeping; she is trying to console him.)

JESSE: I could kill myself for saying it—I could kill myself.

CARRIE: Well, he *is* a failure isn't he?

JESSE: *(In passionate defense)* But he's not—he's not!

CARRIE: *(Grimly humoring him)* Okay, he's a big roaring success.

JESSE: No, he's not a big roaring success. He's a quiet success—the only way a quiet man can get to *be* a success.

CARRIE: Well, tell him so. Tell him you've changed your mind.

JESSE: I can't! He wouldn't believe me. Oh Christ, how could I hurt him like that?

CARRIE: Who says you shouldn't hurt him?

JESSE: . . . What?

CARRIE: That's what we're here for, isn't it?

JESSE: No, it's not.

CARRIE: What, then, to spread happiness all around? Christmas presents? Joy to the world? All that Sunday school crap?

JESSE: I hate it when you talk like that.

CARRIE: *(With a sad smile)* Okay, I'm sorry I said it.

(With compassionate affection) Maybe you *are* here to give out Christmas presents. . . . Dumb jerk.

(A moment) I wish I could make you less unhappy.

JESSE: *(Miserably)* It's impossible—just let me alone.

CARRIE: Maybe that's not the right answer. *(She touches him gently. She tries to caress away the hurt)* Kiss me, Jesse.

JESSE: *(Too troubled)* No, not when I'm like this.

(He covers his face with his hands)

CARRIE: *(Taking his hands away—smiling in order to make him do so)* Come on—you can't hide from me.

(She kisses each of his hands) Touch me. . . . You can touch me anywhere.

JESSE: *(Miserably unhappy)* Don't tease me, Carrie.

CARRIE: I'm not teasing. You can't hide from me—I'm going to make love to you.

JESSE: No—please—don't.

(*She has started to undress him.*)

CARRIE: I didn't hide from you—and you can't hide from me.

JESSE: I want to hide from everybody.

CARRIE: (*She laughs gently*) In a little while, you won't feel that way.

(*She continues undressing him. He turns away from her.*)

CARRIE: (*Gently, tenderly*) Come on, now—don't turn away—don't turn away—

JESSE: You're making fun of me.

CARRIE: Is that what it looks like?

(*With sad irony*) God, we don't even know it when we *see* it. Believe me, I *am* making love you. But you've got to help me.

JESSE: I can't. I'm too sick of myself.

CARRIE: Only for a while. But it'll pass. Believe me, it'll pass. Now come on, Jesse—help me get this thing off.

(*He is not resisting as much as before, but he is filled with misgiving. His voice has a plea in it.*)

JESSE: Please . . . You're trying to make a fool of me, aren't you?

CARRIE: Oh, no. You'll soon see that I'm not.

(*As she continues to undress him*) You'll be very proud of yourself before you know it. I promise you—take my word—I promise you. I'll give you a Christmas present even if it's not Christmas. A present that'll make you very proud. Before long, the whole world will be looking different to you. Christmas presents, honey, it's time for Christmas presents—

(*She is fondling him now, kissing him, as she continues to undress him. The lights fade.*

A glimmer illuminates Robbie's bed in the twins' room. He is having a dream, thrashing about, making strange noises. In a while, Jesse appears. Concerned that Robbie may be having a nightmare, he starts to awaken the sleeper.)

JESSE: Robbie. Robbie—what's the matter? Robbie—wake up—what's the matter?

ROBBIE: (*Disgusted at having been tricked by the dream*) Oh . . . dammit.

JESSE: What's the matter? Did you have a nightmare?

ROBBIE: No . . . a dream.

JESSE: (*Understanding*) Oh, another one?

ROBBIE: Yeah.

(*Jesse laughs softly*)

ROBBIE: What's so funny? You think I'll ever be old enough to get over these damn things.

JESSE: (*Amused*) Yeah. When you get a girl.

ROBBIE: Boy, I'll sure be glad when I don't get passionate over a canteloupe.

JESSE: A what?

ROBBIE: A canteloupe named Mildred.

JESSE: A canteloupe named Mildred?

ROBBIE: Yes, I was dreaming about this beautiful canteloupe named Mildred, and suddenly I was kissing it and hugging it and one thing was leading to another.

JESSE: (*Trying to contain his laughter*) A canteloupe, huh?

ROBBIE: Yeah—I'm disgusted with myself—holy mackerel, a *canteloupe*! Where are my values, where are my *standards*?
(*Jesse's laughter bursts out of him.*)

ROBBIE: Stop laughing, it's not funny.
(*Muttering and rustling around in the bed clothes*) Damn it. . . . messing up the goddamn bed. . . . What do you think Mom thinks?

JESSE: Nothing. You're always washing your own sheets.

ROBBIE: Yeah, but what do you think she thinks of *that*?

JESSE: She thinks you're a good laundress.
(*Jesse laughs but Robbie doesn't. Instead, he throws a pillow at Jesse's head. A moment, then Jesse says quietly:*)

JESSE: I'm not going to have to wash my sheets anymore.

ROBBIE: Why not? (*The truth starts getting to him*) Why not, why not?
(*Silence*) What happened, for God's sake?

JESSE: (*With a smile*) . . . Yep.

ROBBIE: No!

JESSE: Yep, yep, yep.

ROBBIE: (*Excited, elated*) No!

JESSE: Yes, *sir*!

ROBBIE: With Carrie?

JESSE: Who else?

ROBBIE: (*Dithering with happiness for him*) Oh, congratulations! Many happy returns of the day—many happy returns of the night! Lemme look at you—are you any different? Does it show anywhere? Is your hair more curly—they say it makes your hair curly! Lemme look at your eyes—did they change color? *Are you a new man, Jesse?*

JESSE: Well, I guess maybe I'm a man.

ROBBIE: That's right—you're a *man*! Stand up straight like a man, Jesse—*you're a man*!
(*Suddenly they are a bit shy with one another, self-conscious. Robbie is full of wonderment.*)

ROBBIE: You mean the whole thing—the whole damn thing?

JESSE: Well—kind of.

ROBBIE: What do you mean, kind of?

JESSE: (*Slightly chagrined*) Well . . . just as I was about to—uh—just that one second before I was about to—uh—

ROBBIE: (*Helping him*) You mean you didn't make it?

JESSE: Well, I did and I didn't.

ROBBIE: What does that mean, you did and you didn't? Are there two ways of looking at this?

JESSE: There are a thousand ways! What I mean is, I *did*—but too soon!

ROBBIE: You mean . . . phphffft?

JESSE: Well, slightly phphffft. Uh . . . on the grass.

ROBBIE: Geez—what a waste!

JESSE: Yeah. Well, what the hell.

ROBBIE: That's right—what the hell! There's more where that came from.

JESSE: (*Laughing proudly*) Yeah, lots more, lots more!

ROBBIE: And it isn't as if you didn't *do* it! Right?

JESSE: Right! I did it, dammit, I did it! (*He thinks about this*) But—you know something—*she* did it.

ROBBIE: She did? What do you mean?

JESSE: I don't know, but she just took things into her own hands.

ROBBIE: Well, maybe that's the way it's supposed to be.

JESSE: I'll tell you next time.

ROBBIE: Yeah—you do that.

(*It occurs to him:*) I bet you didn't think about the scholarship at all—while it was happening.

JESSE: What scholarship?

(*They both laugh. Jesse's laugh is free and complete in itself, but Robbie's has reservation in it.*)

JESSE: You want to know something? I don't feel as bad about her as I did—I mean as a competitor.

ROBBIE: (*With some misgiving*) You don't, huh?

JESSE: No. I figure—if you can't beat 'em, join 'em!

(*Jesse laughs and expects his brother to laugh with him. But instead, Robbie asks gravely:*)

ROBBIE: Join 'em to do what, Jess? Share a scholarship?

JESSE: (*Sobering*) There's no way to share a scholarship—you think I don't know that?

ROBBIE: It's a good thing you do know it. And don't you forget it.

(*They are extremely quiet. Jesse gravely starts undressing to go to bed.*)

A pinspot of light comes up on Carrie. She is talking to someone in quite reasonable tones. Although she is angry she is at great pains to hide her resentment.)

CARRIE: I wonder why you feel you've got the right to say that to me. What've I ever done to you—or to anybody—that gives you the privilege to take that high-and-mighty tone. Why should I stop seeing Jesse? Who says so? What goddamn right do you have?

(*The light has widened to reveal that we are in a corridor at school. Robbie is now included in the broader circle of illumination. He is mortified at the position he has placed himself in, but driven by the prospect of Jesse in peril.*)

ROBBIE: I have no right except he's my brother—and he's wrecking his chances to go to college.

CARRIE: I don't think he is. But even if that's true, is it my fault?

ROBBIE: Yes—his thoughts are only on you nowadays.

CARRIE: They're *his* thoughts, not mine! Jesus, when do I stop being responsible for what people think about me?!

ROBBIE: Never. We're all responsible for one another.

CARRIE: You self-righteous little shit! You're not responsible for him and he's not responsible for you!

ROBBIE: He's my brother and I love him!

CARRIE: And you're jealous of me for having him for a while, is that it?

ROBBIE: I didn't say that—and it's not true!

CARRIE: Isn't it? Is that what's eating you—that I've got your brother for a little while? Or are you jealous of *him* for having *me*?

ROBBIE: No I'm not! *That* I'm sure of!

CARRIE: Are you? I see you staring at me in the hallways. In the art room, you pretend to be looking at what I'm working on, but what *you're* working on is how I look without my clothes on.

ROBBIE: That's not true! You think the whole world is undressing you! You think everybody's trying to *get* you in one way or another! That's the way your mind works!

CARRIE: How does *your* mind work?

ROBBIE: Not like that!

CARRIE: No, not like that! I'll tell you how it works! Scared! Scared to imagine a girl undressed, scared to speak up in class, scared to try out for the school show! *Scared of everything!*
(*Robbie can't endure it. Quietly he turns and departs. Carrie remains. She is guilt-stricken at having attacked him. Slowly she departs in the opposite direction. The light fades.*

We are now in the school auditorium, identified by the school flag—brown and gold—and the American flag. Auditions for "The Mikado" are going on. Offstage, a pianist provides the accompaniment. Nora, conducting the auditions, has a clipboard to which she refers from time to time. Somewhere in the wings, a student is singing badly. She comes to the end of the song.)

NORA: Thank you, Evelyn. That was very nice. Don't go away—we'll be announcing parts this afternoon. Who's next?
(*An assistant's voice is heard from offstage.*)

ASSISTANT'S VOICE: Bill Eberly—but he didn't show up.
(*Nora crosses him off her list, then calls:*)

NORA: Okay, Peggy—who's next?

ROBBIE'S VOICE: I think I am, Miss Bailey.
(*He enters. As Carrie described him, he is scared. He approaches diffidently. Nora is surprised and pleased.*)

NORA: Well, what do you know! I'm glad to see you, Robbie.

ROBBIE: (*With an abashed smile*) I'm not so sure how I feel about seeing *you.*

(*They both laugh reservedly.*)

NORA: I'm sorry I pushed you so hard, Robert. And I've been thinking that if you showed up for the tryouts, I would make it easy for you. So if you'll be content with a walk-on part or one of the extras, there will be no need for you to go up onstage and audition.

ROBBIE: I—uh—I appreciate that, Miss Bailey. But I won't be satisfied with being an extra.

NORA: (*Surprised*) You won't?

ROBBIE: No. If I'm going to be in the show, I want a real part.

NORA: Good, Robbie—good—I'm glad!

ROBBIE: Don't be glad 'til you've heard me sing. It's real scary.

NORA: (*Laughing*) I'm sure it's not so bad.

ROBBIE: Yes it is, it's awful. When I open my mouth, terrible things happen. Water freezes and dogs start foaming at the mouth.

NORA: Onstage, please.

(*Turning offstage*) Play the intro, Peggy, and play it loud!

(*The introduction is heard with a clamor. Then a more deafening clamor— Robbie's voice bellows like a gored bull. Miss Bailey cringes as if assaulted. She gets smaller and smaller.*

The lights fade on the auditorium and come up on the Weaver dinner table. Neither Frank nor Robbie has arrived. Jesse and Henrietta are arguing.)

JESSE: It's up to him, it's not up to me.

HENRIETTA: Yes, it *is* up to you—he's your father.

JESSE: Well, I'm his son—and I apologized to him. What more do you want?

HENRIETTA: You apologized in a note. I want you to *talk* to him.

JESSE: I did try to talk to him—he wouldn't talk to *me*. So I quit talking. If he's so damn proud—I've got a right to a little pride too!

HENRIETTA: There's an old proverb that says: Only a man with a mind like a chicken is as proud as a peacock.

JESSE: My mind's all right, Mom.

HENRIETTA: But you're not using it very sensibly, are you? You're great with books, but you haven't shown any real judgment where people are concerned, have you?

JESSE: "People?" You mean Pop, don't you—just Pop.

HENRIETTA: (*Quietly*) No, I don't.

(*A moment. Their glances meet. Jesse is the first to look elsewhere. Then, quietly.*)

JESSE: I don't want to talk about Carrie, Mom.

HENRIETTA: That's the first time you've said her name since you started seeing her. Do you have any idea what you're doing?

JESSE: No. . . . I'm all mixed up, Mom. I think I'm in love with her.

HENRIETTA: She's a difficult girl, Jess. Miss Bailey says she may be a sick girl.

JESSE: But she's not a bad person—honest she isn't.

HENRIETTA: (*An outburst*) She's a mess!

JESSE: (*Shocked*) Mom, for God's sake!

HENRIETTA: (*Ashamed, and deeply distressed*) I'm sorry—it was a terrible
thing to say—I am very sorry.
(*A moment, then:*) But what really worries me is I don't think you'd be
attracted to her if she weren't a mess.

JESSE: (*Shocked*) What? You don't mean that, do you?

HENRIETTA: (*Quietly*) Yes, I do.

JESSE: Why in the world would you say a terrible thing like that?

HENRIETTA: Because you feel guilty about cripples. It's one of the kindest
things about you—and one of the scariest.

JESSE: I don't want to get into a fight about that, Mom—I don't know
what we would be fighting *about*. All I see is a girl who's been hurt—
and I hurt *for* her. She needs a friend. She needs someone to take care of
her.

HENRIETTA: So do we all. But there's a sickness of the spirit, Jesse—it's very
catching.

JESSE: I won't get caught by it.

HENRIETTA: Don't be so sure. I'm afraid you will.

JESSE: (*Unhappily*) You're not helping me, Mom. You're making me even
more confused than I was. What can I do about it? What do you want me
to do?

HENRIETTA: Quit seeing Carrie—and make up with your father.

JESSE: Do those two things go together? What are they—a package?

HENRIETTA: Well, in a way, they are. The hardest thing in the world is to
draw the line between hurting someone and getting hurt yourself. It's, as
you say, a package. It's called Growing Up.

JESSE: Is that all that's in it?

HENRIETTA: There are other things, but you can start with that.

JESSE: I don't know that I can, Mom. Pop won't let me make up with him.
And Carrie—I can't bear the thought of not seeing her again. I just can't
bear it.
(*Frank enters.*)

FRANK: Good evening.

HENRIETTA: Good evening, Frank.
(*Pointedly, Jesse doesn't greet his father.*)

FRANK: Where's Robbie?

HENRIETTA: Goodness, I don't know.
(*To Jesse*) Your father asked where your brother is.

JESSE: (*Narrowly to his mother*) Tell him he's at the auditions.

HENRIETTA: (*To Frank*) He's at the auditions.

FRANK: (*To Henrietta*) Is he really going to sing?

HENRIETTA: (*To Jesse*) Is he really going to sing?

JESSE: (*To Henrietta*) Tell him if he's there, he's going to sing.

HENRIETTA: He says if he's there, he's going to sing.

FRANK: I heard him. I don't think I'll be able to stand it when he comes in and says they turned him down.

JESSE: Tell him there's always a chance they won't turn him down.

HENRIETTA: (*Again she lets her anger out*) Tell him yourself! Both of you— talk to each other—talk to each other! What are you both doing to this family—what are you doing? And why do I have to be the interpreter of your bad feelings and bad faith and bad manners!

FRANK: (*Also losing his temper*) You don't have to be the interpreter for me!

JESSE: For me either!

(*The three of them are in the midst of a fully-armed battle when, unheard, Robbie appears. His eyes are bright and his face is flushed—with victory! He takes a dramatic position, throws his arms wide with a matinee idol's gesture of glory and, as if there were a fanfare of drums and brass, he sings out:*)

ROBBIE: Ta-RAAAH!

(*The family all turn to him—alarmed at first, then wild-eyed with hope.*)

JESSE: Robbie—what happened?

ROBBIE: (*Exultant*) I made it! I made it! I sang—and nobody threw a tomato! I read a whole scene—and no rotten eggs! And I got the part, I got the part!

JESSE, FRANK, HENRIETTA: Oh God, he made it—he made it! ... Congratulations, Robbie ... I'm proud of you! ... Oh Robbie—did you— did you? ...

(*They surround Robbie, hugging, kissing, congratulating him.*)

JESSE: What's the part, Rob—what part is it?

ROBBIE: (*With a flourish*) Ko-Ko! The Lord High Executioner of Titipu!

(*Ornate histrionics—his big speech!*) "Katisha! For years I have loved you with a white-hot passion that is slowly but surely consuming my very vitals! Ah, shrink not from me! If there is aught of woman's mercy in your heart, turn not away from the love-sick suppliant whose every fibre thrills at your tiniest touch!"

JESSE: Now, *that's* great acting! That is *vibrant* acting!

ROBBIE: And I get to sing too! And dance—and *dance*, do you hear me?— *dance*!

(*Overcome with happiness*) Oh God, I love Miss Bailey!

JESSE: Everybody loves Miss Bailey!

ROBBIE: But I *love* her—I'm in *love* with her! She said I could act—and I can! She said I could sing—and I can! If she says I can dance—oh, I can, I can! I can dance for Miss Bailey—oh, I can, I can, I can!

(*In a transport, he is indeed dancing—around and around the room— freely, happily—as if his clubfoot were a thing of the past, as if dancing were the most special, the most singular talent of clubfooted people. The lights fade.*)

We are once again in the churchyard. A dark night; the bench is dimly lighted. Jesse is waiting for Carrie. He has been waiting a long time. He *rises, starts to leave, thinks better of it, returns and sits down once more. The church bell begins to toll. He gives up and departs.*

The light fades on the churchyard and comes up on a door in a run-down neighborhood. Jesse appears. He rings the bell. No answer. Another ring, longer, more insistent this time. The door opens scantily. Mr. McIlvaine appears. He is in his late forties, with a thin, puritanically rigid face, his eyes deep-sunk and unhappy. He tries to be as civil as possible, but after a while his civility runs thin and his rage breaks through.)

McILVAINE: Yes?

JESSE: Hello—Mr. McIlvaine. I'm Jesse Weaver, and I . . .

(He stops. McIlvaine is not hostile, but also not hospitable.)

McILVAINE: What do you want?

JESSE: I was supposed to meet Carrie tonight, but she didn't show up. And she wasn't in school today—in fact, she wasn't for quite a few days—so I wondered if she was sick.

McILVAINE: *(Caught between gratitude and annoyance)* No, she's not sick.

JESSE: *(Getting more and more uncomfortable)* I—well—is she here?

McILVAINE: No. She'll be back after Easter.

JESSE: *(Inarticulate, and with difficulty)* Well, you told Miss Bailey that she'd be back in a week or two, and you tell me she'll be back after Easter and—I've gone to the place where we usually meet—I've gone a number of times—and she hasn't shown up. And I—*(His difficulties increasing)* Is there anywhere I can call her?

McILVAINE: No. No telephone.

JESSE: If you could give me her address—

(Taking a letter out of his pocket)—I wrote this letter to her.

McILVAINE: *(Hardening)* Then send it.

JESSE: *(On a note of desperation)* I *can't* send it if I don't know where she *is!*

McILVAINE: She doesn't want anyone to know. And I don't either.

JESSE: Mr. McIlvaine, I don't mean to be a pest, but if you won't give me Carrie's address, would you mind sending this letter to her?

(He holds out the envelope, hopefully. For an instant McIlvaine wavers.)

McILVAINE: No. Go away.

JESSE: Please, Mr. McIlvaine—I've been waiting and waiting for her—and I—it's only a note—

McILVAINE: I said go away!

JESSE: You can read it if you want to. See?—the flap is open—I left it open and I—

McILVAINE: *(An explosion of rage)* If you don't go away, I'll call the police—now go away!

(He shuts the door. Silence. Jesse starts to depart, stops, turns back, slips the letter under the door and departs.

The light comes up on the churchyard. Jesse enters, sits down—worried, confused. He is restless and cannot remain seated. Rising, he paces, with mounting anxiety. Suddenly, in the darkness an unidentifiable shadow stirs. His heart leaps with hope.)

JESSE: Carrie?—is that you? Carrie!

(Without warning, the figure invades the light. It is Hugo Lockman.)

HUGO: Where is she?

JESSE: I don't know.

HUGO: *(Going toward him)* I said where is she?

JESSE: I don't know. I wait for her—I always wait for her but I don't know.

HUGO: You're a liar!

(Hugo slaps him. Jesse reaches up to hit him but Hugo pulls him into a vicious embrace. He punches him.)

JESSE: Ow—let me go!

HUGO: Yeah, when you stop lyin'. Where is she?

JESSE: I swear—

HUGO: You wrote her a letter. Where'd you write it to?

JESSE: No place!

(As Hugo wrenches him) Ow—please! I didn't send the letter to any address—I just stuck it under the door. You think I'd give it to her father if I knew where she was?

HUGO: Yeah—I think you and her are up to some trick. You're trickin' me, you're trickin' her old man, you're trickin' everybody! Now where the hell is she?

(He slugs him once more.)

JESSE: I don't know! I swear, I swear!

(Useless. Hugo is now beating him. With a moan, the boy slumps to the ground, in pain, like a tortured animal.)

HUGO: You stay away from my girl, you understand?—stay away from my girl!

(Hugo departs. Jesse tries to get up, but he cannot. An almost inaudible sound comes from him, a forlorn entreaty.

The lights come upon Robbie who holds a book in his hand from which he is reading aloud; more accurately, coaching.)

ROBBIE: Come on, now, it's not that hard. Just *visualize* it, Jess, try to *visualize* it. C is at a distance of two feet six inches from B-sub-one. Now if both triangles are equilateral, and each side measures five feet, what is the distance from A to A sub-one?

(The light has broadened to include Jesse in a hospital wheelchair. His head is bandaged, but he is almost ready to go home.)

JESSE: Five million miles, four feet, two inches.

ROBBIE: Come on, Jess, quit the horseplay. Figure it out.

JESSE: I told you I can't. I hate calculus.

ROBBIE: It's not calculus—it's simple geometry—you had it two years ago, and you got an A-plus.

JESSE: (*Losing his temper*) I forgot it, I forgot it!

(*An instant*) I'm tired. Holy murder, Rob, I got every other question right—why don't you let up on me?

ROBBIE: You're right—I'm sorry.

(*An instant*) You know, you don't *have* to take the test the first day you get back to school.

JESSE: (*Laughing*) You crack the whip and tell me to keep trying, and then you tell me I don't *have* to take the test. Make your mind up.

(*He points to the book*) Now, these two lousy triangles—how far apart are they?

ROBBIE: (*Grinning*) Three feet.

(*Something in Robbie's glance has caught Jesse. The latter turns to follow the glance. Out of the shadows, Frank appears. He carries a paper bag the contents of which are indeterminate.*)

ROBBIE: Hi, Pop.

FRANK: Hello, Rob—how's he doing?

ROBBIE: Fine. He's a stubborn bastard, but he's doing great.

(*To Jesse*) I've got to study. I'll leave you the last two assignments—there's a worksheet in the folder.

JESSE: (*His inner attention is on his father*) Yes . . . thanks.

(*Robbie goes. Frank slowly moves to where Robbie was sitting. Jesse is deeply gratified by his father's presence, but somewhat nervous.*)

FRANK: Hello, Jesse.

JESSE: Hello, Pop. I'm glad to see you.

FRANK: I was around the first day—when they brought you in.

JESSE: I know. I wasn't seeing anybody then.

FRANK: Then twice again—both times you were asleep.

(*An embarrassed silence.*)

FRANK: They—uh—they say you're well enough to come home.

JESSE: Yes—the day after tomorrow maybe.

FRANK: Good . . . We've missed you. . . .

(*Handing him the bag*) I bought you some books. Two of them are second-hand, but "The Tale of Two Cities" is new.

JESSE: (*Deeply moved*) Thank you, Pop.

(*Their hands reach out awkwardly to each other. Jesse takes the bag and puts it in his lap.*)

JESSE: Pop—what I said to you—about being a failure—I—

(*Having difficulty, he looks down at the books in his lap. Frank sees his distress.*)

FRANK: We don't have to talk about it, Jesse, if you don't want to.

JESSE: But I do! Pop—listen—that day—the words just said themselves—I didn't have anything to do with them! I never thought of you as a failure—never, Pop—not once in my whole life!

FRANK: You must have, Jesse—deep down. And you had to let it out. And believe me—I'm not blaming you anymore—I'm not!

JESSE: (*Desperately*) But you're not a failure, Pop! The times have failed *you*, but you never failed any of *us*! You didn't stop loving me when I called you that terrible name—and I didn't stop loving you! And where did all that love come from? Somebody had to make it *happen* in our lives—and it was you and Mom. And it's the best thing that happened to all of us! It kept us all together—it saved us through the depression! And you did it, Pop—and anybody who can do that is not a failure!

FRANK: Thank you, Jesse. I appreciate what you're saying—I do, I'm very grateful. But we can't expect love to do *everything* for us. Feed us—pay the bills—send the kids to college. And I've been saddling it with all my burdens. "It's okay," I kept saying, "as long as we all love one another." But love *doesn't* make everything okay. It does a great deal, but it doesn't do the whole job. And somehow—someway—I've got to give it a little more help.

JESSE: How, Pop?

FRANK: I don't know the answer.

(*He laughs wryly*) I don't even know how to formulate the question. But at least I'm asking it.

(*They smile with each other, warmly. Frank's voice moves a key higher in his effort to restore life to a lighter tone.*)

FRANK: I told you that "The Tale of Two Cities" was bought new. But it's not exactly new—I read it before giving it to you. It's a hell of a good book.

(*They both smile, and, in a moment, are laughing quietly.*

The lights fade, then come up once more upon the classroom of Nora Bailey. She is writing on the blackboard which already reads:)

REVIEW FOR FINAL EXAM:

GRAMMAR

Gerund and Gerundive

Personal and Impersonal Pronouns

LITERATURE

Julius Caesar

The Prince and the Pauper

The House of Seven Gables

NORA: —and "The Prince and the Pauper" and "The House of Seven Gables."

(*As she writes, there is the sound of the wall telephone ringing. She answers it.*)

NORA: (*Into phone*) Hello. Yes. He's here. Yes, Mr. Prentiss.

(*She hangs up*) Jesse.

JESSE: (*Appearing out of the darkness*) Yes, Miss Bailey.

NORA: The principal's office called—you're wanted at home. Right away.

JESSE: (*Alarmed*) At home? What's wrong?

NORA: I don't know. Go at once.

ROBBIE: (*Appearing*) What's wrong, what's wrong?
(*To Nora*) They want us at home?

NORA: Not you. Just him. Hurry, Jesse.
(*He races out. Robbie starts after him.*)

NORA: I said not you, Robert.
(*He stops, deeply worried.*

The lights cross-fade to the Weaver living room. Henrietta and Frank are there. So are Mr. McIlvaine and Carrie. She looks terrible—worn, thin, slightly untidy—and deeply unhappy. There is an anxiety in the room, an armed silence. As Jesse comes rushing in, he sees Carrie.)

JESSE: Carrie—!

CARRIE: (*Numbly*) Hello, Jesse.

JESSE: You—I—where've you been?

FRANK: Jesse, if you can hold the question for a moment—

JESSE: (*Pointing to the McIlvaines*) What are they doing here?

HENRIETTA: (*Troubled*) Jesse—wait—

JESSE: (*To Carrie*) Where did you go?—where've you been?

FRANK: Wherever Carrie's been, the police found her last night and brought her home.

JESSE: Police?

FRANK: (*With difficulty*) Mr. McIlvaine tells us she's pregnant. He has a doctor's report to that effect. And Carrie claims that you are the child's father.

JESSE: . . . Me?

HENRIETTA: That's what she tells us, Jesse. And we're trying to find out if it's true.

JESSE: Carrie—! Did you say that?
(*Silence.*)

McILVAINE: She may not say it to you, but she said it to me!

JESSE: But it's—it can't—it's not true!

McILVAINE: He's lying.

HENRIETTA: (*Angry*) Now you stop that!

McILVAINE: He's lying—you can see it in his face.

FRANK: (*Quickly, at his son's side*) Jesse, we're not listening to him. We're only interested in what *you* have to say.

JESSE: (*Confused; too unsettled to find the right words*) But if she said that—I—I've never—it's—I've never—

HENRIETTA: (*Prompting him hopefully*) Do you mean you never had—relations—with Carrie?

JESSE: Well, yes I have in a way—but—! Carrie, tell them!

McILVAINE: She's already told us—there's no sense putting her through it again. And you yourself admitted—

FRANK: He admitted nothing!

McILVAINE: Yes he did! He just admitted having relations with her—we all heard him say that!

JESSE: (*An outburst*) You heard me wrong! It happened only once—and even that once—it couldn't—! Carrie, please, you know as well as I do— on the grass—you know as well as I do! (*His voice is breaking*) Carrie, tell them! Goddamn it, Carrie—*talk!*

(*She cannot answer, and she cannot endure it. With a stifled sound of distress, she gets up and flees from the house.*)

JESSE: Carrie—!

(*He starts to run after her, but his father stands in his way, and grabs him*).

FRANK: Jesse, stay here!

JESSE: Let me go, Pop!

HENRIETTA: No, Jesse—don't go! Jesse!

JESSE: *Let me go!*

(*He wrests himself away from Frank and runs in pursuit of Carrie, calling her name. The room remains still as we hear Jesse's outcry receding in the distance. As it fades, so do the lights.*)

We are once again in the churchyard, at night. Carrie sits alone on a bench. She is wretched and she is cold. Her eyes focus on someone offstage. Jesse appears. He moves toward her slowly, irresolutely. He does not, finally, get too close to her. There is an uncertainty, a deep hurt in both of them.)

JESSE: I was here twice tonight—and you weren't here.

CARRIE: (*With a wry smile*) And now I am.

JESSE: Where did you go?

CARRIE: I started to go away again. And then I decided to come back—to talk to you.

JESSE: I'm glad.

(*Silence. For something to say:*) Have you been here long?

CARRIE: Since . . . the bells.

(*She trembles with the chill and he moves closer, but does not sit down.*)

JESSE: You're cold.

CARRIE: Yes. (*As if betrayed*) It's not really spring after all.

JESSE: (*Tentatively*) You want my jacket?

CARRIE: (*With odd formality*) No . . . thank you.

JESSE: You don't look well, Carrie.

CARRIE: I'm just cold, that's all.

JESSE: You're thin.

CARRIE: (*Trying to smile*) At the beginning, some get fat and some get thin. (*Long silence. He sits beside her, but not intimately. At last he is able to ask:*)

JESSE: Whose baby is it, Carrie?

CARRIE: (*Unable to face him*) I . . . don't know. There've been other men . . . I think it's Hugo's.

JESSE: Why did you say it's mine?

CARRIE: Because if I had a choice . . .

JESSE: You really mean that?

CARRIE: (*Not looking at him*) Yes.

JESSE: (*Deeply touched*) Thank you.

CARRIE: But we don't really *have* a choice, do we?

JESSE: (*Quietly*) Yes we do, Carrie.

CARRIE: (*Grimly*) I don't believe that.

JESSE: Carrie—honey—

(*He reaches toward her but she pulls away.*)

CARRIE: No—don't touch me, please.

(*Suddenly weeping*) Oh God, I'm so miserable!

JESSE: Carrie—honey—I love you—Carrie, I love you—

CARRIE: Don't say that! I can't stand all that talk about love! It doesn't mean anything! It's just a word for getting into bed together! Why don't we just admit that we're no better than animals, and let it go at that?!

JESSE: Because it's not true!

CARRIE: Yes it is true! And if I had any sense, I'd tear this baby out of my guts and get rid of it!

(*An instant*)

JESSE: You mean you *are* going to have it?

CARRIE: . . . Yes.

JESSE: Why?

CARRIE: I don't know why!

(*Struggling with confusion, and trying not to cry*) Maybe it's what I have to do. I'm eighteen years old and it feels like I've tried everything! And nothing works for me—nothing! Maybe this'll work! Maybe it'll do something for me! Maybe it's my only chance!

JESSE: (*Quietly*) Are you sure, are you absolutely sure you want to go through with it?

CARRIE: Yes—I've got to—yes!

JESSE: (*Getting up*) All right, then, come on.

CARRIE: Where?

JESSE: We're going to see your father.

CARRIE: (*Alarmed*) What for?

JESSE: If you're going to have this baby, I'm going to be its father.

CARRIE: Oh, Jesus.

JESSE: Come on, Carrie.

CARRIE: Are you out of your mind? You're a high school boy, for God's sake! It's bad enough that this whole goddamn thing is rotten—does it have to be ridiculous?

JESSE: (*Confused, unhappy*) Then why did you tell them it's mine?

CARRIE: Because I didn't know what else to say! What should I have said? Hugo? And have to marry *him*? Or have him and my father kill each other? There isn't a hell of a lot of choice after all, is there?

JESSE: (*With gathering strength*) Now you listen to me. You chose me to be this baby's father. The reason you did it is because you love me.

CARRIE: No!

JESSE: You may not know it, but you love me!

CARRIE: (*She cannot, at last, control the tears*) No! I don't love anybody! No matter how I try—no matter how I go from man to man, I don't love anybody! Maybe if I have this child, maybe I will love it! Oh God, how I'm going to try! And I *will* love it—I *will*! Because it'll be mine—it'll be my own—and I'll give it everything I am!—everything! I swear to God, I will love this baby with my life!

(*It has been a convulsion of pain. Now, the final desperation:*) God help me if I don't.

JESSE: (*Quietly*) God help the child.

CARRIE: . . . Yes.

JESSE: (*Quietly*) I've decided. I'm coming with you.

CARRIE: You think I'd let you do that?

JESSE: You've already let me. You chose me as the child's father. That's all the love you need to give. I'll supply the rest.

CARRIE: You think I'd let you? You think I'd let you leave your family— give up your hope of college—wreck your whole life? You think I want you on my conscience? Don't I have enough to feel guilty about? How can I bear any more of it? *How can I bear it?*

(*Her outcry is followed by an aching silence.*)

JESSE: What will you do? Where will you go?

CARRIE: I don't know. I'll get a job somewhere.

JESSE: There aren't any jobs, Carrie.

CARRIE: I'll go on relief, then. I don't know. I'll work it out. I'm very smart, remember that?

(*Her irony is her courage, but it does not hide her havoc*) I am! The smartest in the class! I'll work it out!

(*Ruefully brave*) Carrie McIlvaine—the Winner of the World!

(*Unhappily*) I'll work it out.

(*Another silence. She pats him tenderly on the cheek, as though it is he who needs the help and the comfort.*)

CARRIE: Don't worry about me, Jesse.

(*A moment*) Do you have any money?

(*Heartsick for her, he reaches into his pocket. He pulls out a half dollar and a penny.*)

JESSE: Fifty-one cents.

(*They both smile, without merriment.*)

JESSE: Here—take it.

CARRIE: No—it's all right—I have a few dollars. My father must have put them in my pocketbook.

(*Wryly*) He would never give them to me in person.

JESSE: (*Handing her the money*) I want to give you something—please take it.

CARRIE: I'll take the penny . . .

(*With a smile that belies her bitterness*) . . . for my thoughts.

JESSE: I hope your thoughts become happier, Carrie.

CARRIE: Well, that has to be, doesn't it?

(*A hesitation*) Goodbye, Jesse.

JESSE: No, don't say goodbye—I love you, Carrie.

CARRIE: I know. That's the thought I'll try to hold on to.

(*As she turns to go, she calls back:*) Thanks for the penny!

(*She departs. His gaze follows her. He is about to cry. He raises his hand to his eyes, as if to blot out the sight of her departure, and perhaps to hide his tears.*

The lights cross-fade to Nora's "home room." She is concluding a series of announcements.)

NORA: Also—please finish your book reports. You only have a week to turn them in. And another announcement: There are still a few seats left for the performance of "The Mikado" which will happen on Friday night—so if you haven't bought your ticket, you'd better hurry. And—finally—the day has come, I guess—you're supposed to elect your class valedictorian.

(*Looking at her watch*) We don't have much time—we'll have to beat the bell.

(*Robbie has appeared in the light.*)

ROBBIE: We don't need much time, Miss Bailey. We all got together—and we talked it over—and we'd like to elect Jesse Weaver—by acclamation.

(*There is a chorus of approval, a burst of applause.*)

NORA: Well! Jesse, that's a special honor. Before we vote, would you like to respond to it?

JESSE: (*Appearing in the light*) Thank you—thanks to everybody—but I decline.

(*There is a murmur of shock in the class.*)

NORA: Why, Jesse?

JESSE: Well, I don't have to give my reasons, and I—I'm very grateful—but I decline.

(*The class bell rings.*)

NORA: It doesn't look as though we'll be able to do this as quickly as I thought. So—let's leave it for our next meeting in home room. Dismissed.

(*The murmur of the class departing.*)

NORA: Jesse, would you stay, please?

(*Disturbed at having to stay, Jesse is relieved at not having to meet his friends in the corridor. He doesn't approach Nora who is awaiting him. So she approaches him. He makes an elaborate point of not looking at her. When the sound of the others has died away, she says softly:*)

NORA: Why did you do that?

JESSE: It's my own business, Miss Bailey.

NORA: Because you didn't want another honor to be written on your record?

JESSE: I don't think it's such an honor.

NORA: Because you don't want to be singled out—

JESSE: That's right!

NORA: —above your brother!

JESSE: It's got nothing to do with my brother!

NORA: Now that Carrie's gone, you're first in line for that scholarship. Why are you trying to throw it away?

JESSE: I'm not throwing it away!

NORA: Yes you are! Why? You want to get out of the competition? You want to forfeit the game? You want to forfeit your life away?

JESSE: (*Angry*) I am not forfeiting anything!

NORA: (*Equally angry*) You're letting your brother move into first place, and he's moving in.

JESSE: If he is, he deserves it.

NORA: He does if he wins—in an honest competition. But not if you simply default.

JESSE: If *I* default, it's not *his* fault, is it?

NORA: (*Angered*) *But why should you default?!*

JESSE: (*An outbreak*) Because he needs it more than I do! Can't you and my family get it into your heads? I'm going to get along! Even if I don't go to college, somehow I'll get along—I'll make it! But unless we give Robbie a break, his life will be a wreck!

(*She doesn't respond immediately. Then, quietly*:)

NORA: I think you're wrong. But even if that is so, he can't be your first responsibility. And I still want you to be the class valedictorian.

(*He responds with profound emotion, but he is controlled, biting, strong.*)

JESSE: All right, let's pretend I'm the valedictorian. Well, I get up on the platform and what do I say? I'll tell you what you expect me to say:

(*With mock histrionics*) Farewell to the glories of the William Jennings Bryan Public High School—and hail to the glories of the new world, the world of opportunity we're all going out to! And all this happiness, all this prosperity, all this hope of the future is made possible through only one thing—the wonderful miracle of education!

(*Now, lashing out*) It's a fake, Miss Bailey! I don't think education is such a wonderful miracle! We're just coming through a lousy, dirty, miserable, cruel Depression! There are as many educated people selling apples on the street as there are uneducated! And it serves them right! Because who's to blame for the Depression? The poor dopes who never went through high school? No, all those guys with college degrees, those educated bastards who screwed up the banks and manipulated the stock market and ran the factories into the ground! My father's got a college education and my mother never went through high school—and she solves her problems a hell of lot better than my father ever solved his! And if I'm entitled to a scholarship, then Carrie McIlvaine is more entitled to it—because she's smarter than I am! And where's the glorious school that asks me to be valedictorian and lets her get lost?! *Why does she get lost*? !

NORA: (*Outraged*) Don't blame it on the school! Carrie McIlvaine is a flawed person! There's something deeply wrong with her!

JESSE: There's something wrong with all of us!

NORA: Not you! You're one of the *whole* people in the world! You're strong, you're decent! You couldn't do anything deeply wrong if your life depended on it!

JESSE: I don't *want* you to say that to me! I don't want to be locked into being so goddamn good!

NORA: You can't help it! You're one of the good ones—one of the leaders— one of the people we thank God for! And if that's going to be a burden to you—there's not a damn thing you can do about it!

JESSE: Yes, there is! I'll get the burden off my back!

NORA: How? By killing somebody? By stealing?

JESSE: (*Frenzied*) Yes! I'll get caught cheating in a final examination! I'll vandalize the faculty room! I'll get caught! I'll get expelled!

NORA: That's just words, Jesse! It isn't *in* you to do such things!

(*He has stopped being rational. His manner is even wilder than his words— he has momentarily gone berserk.*)

JESSE: I'll get expelled—I'll get expelled—!

NORA: (*Suddenly frightened for him*) Now, stop that! Stop it, Jesse! Jesse! (*She starts toward him and puts a hand on his arm. The instant she touches him, his action explodes. Violent, he reaches toward the neckline of her dress. He tears at it, ripping the dress down, exposing her brassiere, the curve of her bosom. The instant he has done it, he is wrenched back to reality. In shame and remorse:*)

JESSE: Oh Christ, oh Christ . . .

(*Silence. Nora is steady. She carefully pulls her torn dress up to conceal herself again. Then, quietly:*)

NORA: I will never tell anyone you did that to me.

(*Unhurriedly, she departs. Jesse stands there, shaken, unable to comprehend what has happened to him, abject with guilt and sick with confusion. As the lights fade—*

There is a loud burst of music. It is a section of "The Mikado." The lights come up on a tall flight of steps, on the top landing of which we see the figure of Ko-Ko. The costume is gaudy and long-skirted. As the character comes walking down the steps—declaiming and limping—we recognize the voice, the orthopedic shoe, the hobbled gait of Robbie.)

ROBBIE: (*Declaiming flamboyantly*) "Katisha! For years I have loved you with a white-hot passion that is slowly but surely consuming my very vitals! Ah, shrink not from me! If there is aught of woman's mercy—"

(*When he gets halfway down the steps, his lame foot gets caught in his long Oriental skirt. The foot pulls the skirt loose from the waist. Entangled, Robbie falls down the steps. The audience gasps. There is a low hubbub of murmurs, and a sprinkling of nervous laughter. Humiliated, Robbie rises, doesn't know what to do with himself, starts offstage in one direction, then turns and runs—lamely—the other way. The music swells and the lights fade.*

A red EXIT sign lights up to reveal the back side of the flight of stairs— we are now on a fire stairway. Robbie comes rushing in, tearing the top of his costume off, and he is revealed in an ordinary undershirt and the silky costume trousers. The boy has been devastated by his failure and what seems to him the mockery of the audience. From offstage we hear Jesse's voice calling:)

JESSE'S VOICE: Robbie! Robbie, where are you? Robbie!

(Robbie doesn't answer. He sits in the darkest corner he can find.)

JESSE'S VOICE: Robbie!

(The door to the fire escape bursts open and Jesse hurries in.)

JESSE: Robbie—

ROBBIE: Let me alone.

JESSE: Don't sit up here by yourself. Come on—let's go.

ROBBIE: No. I ruined the show.

JESSE: No, you didn't. It was nearly over anyway, and Willie Cooper is finishing it for you. Come on—we'll join the others.

ROBBIE: (*Quietly*) I said no, Jesse.

JESSE: (*Pleading*) Robbie—please—we'll go down together. We'll pretend nothing happened.

ROBBIE: Something did happen.

JESSE: It's not *important*!

ROBBIE: They laughed at me. It may not be important to you, but it is to me.

JESSE: They did not laugh at you!

ROBBIE: Don't tell me! I heard them laugh!

JESSE: They were not laughing, dammit! They were worried about you— they thought you hurt yourself!

ROBBIE: Jesus, I thought the laughing days were over. I thought people had stopped calling me Gimpy.

JESSE: (*Urgently*) Will you listen to me?! They didn't call you Gimpy— nobody's calling you Gimpy! They cared about you—they thought you got hurt—they felt sorry for you!

ROBBIE: You think pity is better?

JESSE: *Will you please stop it*!

(Pleading again. Gently:) Now, come on—Robbie—please—come on down.

ROBBIE: Let me alone.

JESSE: What the hell are you going to do? Just sit up here on the fire escape?

ROBBIE: There's a fire—but no escape.

JESSE: What the hell does that mean?

ROBBIE: Remember the fire? You carried me out of it. But I didn't escape. Neither of us escaped.

JESSE: Escape from what, for God's sake?

ROBBIE: Each other.

JESSE: (*Gently: his brother is irrational. Pleading*) Robbie—please—I know how upset you are—but it'll pass. I promise you, it'll pass. Now, come on, Rob—we'll go downstairs.

ROBBIE: For what? Applause? That's not for me—it's always for you!

JESSE: Now, quit that! I don't get any more applause than you do!

ROBBIE: Yes you do! You were elected valedictorian even when you declined. Twice you declined and yet you were elected! And I'd have given my eye teeth for it! But do you know why you got it? Not because you're smarter than I am, but because you're a winner! Even when you try to lose, you can't! And me—no matter how much I try—no matter how I work, how I slave—no matter how I kill myself—!

JESSE: (*Very quietly*) Don't kill yourself. You're going to college and I'm not.

ROBBIE: How am I going to do that? You got a miracle in your pocket?

JESSE: (*Reaching inside his jacket*) No, I've got this in my pocket.

(*He brings out the C.C.C. blue card*) I'm going to join the C.C.C.

ROBBIE: No, you're not. Nobody's going to let you. Pop won't let you. He'll never sign that!

JESSE: He doesn't have to. In two weeks I'll be eighteen years old. I won't need his signature!

ROBBIE: (*An outcry*) I won't let you do it!

(*He reaches for the card, captures it and tears it a number of times. Jesse responds quietly:*)

JESSE: It's okay. I'll get another one.

ROBBIE: (*A rage and a lamentation*) Who the fuck do you think you are— Jesus Christ? You think I want your charity? You think I could live with myself if I took your handout?

JESSE: It's not a handout!

ROBBIE: Brother, can you spare a dime!

JESSE: *It is not a handout*!

ROBBIE: Throw a nickle to a cripple!

JESSE: *Robbie—listen—*

ROBBIE: (*Pointing to the ground*) Did you have to flash that card at me? *Did you have to do that to me?!*

(*Abruptly all Jesse's forbearance for his brother vanishes. He blasts out in a fury.*)

JESSE: You selfish bastard!—is everything in terms of you? Do you know what I had to go through to make this decision? *Do you know what's been happening to me?—do you know, do you know?!*

ROBBIE: No, I don't—tell me!

JESSE: You go to hell, you bastard—go to hell!

ROBBIE: (*Quietly*) No, thanks—this'll do.

(*Then, the merciless blow*) Every day of your life you tell me I've got a handicap.

JESSE: (*A gasp!*) *Me?! I tell you?! Me?!*

ROBBIE: Yes—by your help—by your pity! Handicap, handicap!

JESSE: You son of a bitch, you think you're the only one with a handicap? Everybody's got one!

ROBBIE: What's yours, Brother?

JESSE: (*The kill!*) YOU!

(*Having gone this far, he has to administer the coup de grace*) You—you're my handicap! Whenever I look at you, I feel guilty for not having a club-foot! I feel guilty for having come into the world ten minutes ahead of you! As if you're my leftovers!

ROBBIE: No! Don't you call me that!

JESSE: You're my afterbirth! You're my also-ran! You're my lame leg!

ROBBIE: You bastard! You dirty bastard! You bastard, you bastard, you bastard!

(*He hits Jesse wildly, awkwardly, in the body, in the face, hurting him, not hurting him, sobbing, weeping convulsively. Jesse, in self-defense, strikes back, once, twice—and Robbie is on the floor. Instantly Jesse is filled with remorse.*)

JESSE: I'm sorry—I'm sorry, Robbie—I'm sorry—I'm sorry!

(*He starts to help Robbie up, but the latter shakes him off and quickly flees. Jesse, bereft, keeps crying:*)

JESSE: I'm sorry—I'm sorry—I'm sorry—

(*The lights fade on Jesse. In the darkness we hear the pleasant and elderly voice of Mr. Prentiss, the high school principal. As he makes his address to the commencement audience, a glow gradually lightens the figures of Jesse and Robbie, sitting side by side, at the graduation ceremony, both wearing cap and gown.*)

PRINCIPAL'S VOICE: And so, on this eighty-fourth commencement exercise of the William Jennings Bryan Public High School, I am pleased to make the presentation of the Board of Education Scholarship. This year, more than ever, I'm sorry there aren't at least six free scholarships instead of one. For in this fine class there are at least six students who are worthy of this signal honor and opportunity. But since there's only one scholarship to be given, I am happy to say that this year's scholarship goes to a student who has distinguished himself far above all others. It gives me pleasure to award this honor and distinction to Jesse W. Weaver . . . Jesse.

(*The boys' faces are inscrutable. Jesse rises and crosses from the pinpoint of light, through the valley of stage darkness, to another glow where he stops and stands. He stands alone—the singularity of the winner. There is a weird echo of applause, like a ringing in Jesse's ears. He does not revel in his victory; he scarcely smiles. The lights fade.*)

We are again in the Weaver house. Frank and Henrietta are putting the finishing touches on a large gift package. He is tying it; she is doing the gift card.)

HENRIETTA: Wait—wait—you forgot the card.

FRANK: I thought you said you'd put it on the outside.

HENRIETTA: No, I changed my mind—it should go on the inside.

FRANK: Doesn't it read the same no matter when he reads it? What difference does it make?

HENRIETTA: (*Reluctantly*) I'll put it on the outside, but it does make a difference.

JESSE: (*Entering*) No, it doesn't, Mom. I know it's from you and Pop.

(*They turn and smile. He is wearing a new suit—with a vest. It makes him look older. She hands him the package.*)

HENRIETTA: And you know what the card says.

JESSE: (*Gratefully, as he opens the package.*) Yes, Mom, I know.

FRANK: But you don't know what's inside.

JESSE: It's heavy.

FRANK: (*Proudly*) Well, it's a thing of substance.

(*Jesse discloses it—a gleaming dark brown briefcase. He is happy over it.*)

JESSE: Holy—! A briefcase!

HENRIETTA: Do you like it?

JESSE: Do I like it?—it's beautiful!—it's my first briefcase!

HENRIETTA: It's your first day of college.

FRANK: A college man has to have a briefcase.

JESSE: Oh, thanks! Thank you, Mom—thanks, Poppa!

HENRIETTA: We love you, boy.

(*As they embrace, the lights fade on them and come up in the twins' bedroom. Robbie is dressing. His mood is quiet and contained; his face has taken on the set of a man. A man who has had strength thrust upon him.*

Carrying his briefcase, Jesse appears. The brothers do not speak for an instant. They share a secret without knowing that the secret is their enveloping maturity.)

JESSE: I was hoping you'd be awake.

ROBBIE: I was awake when you went downstairs.

JESSE: (*With a smile*) I wondered if you were.

(*Pause. Their conversation has been shy, self-conscious; they've been avoiding a full meeting with each other. Now, finally, it is Robbie who takes the first step toward intimacy.*)

ROBBIE: Your new suit fits great.

JESSE: Thanks. I don't know if I'll ever get used to wearing a vest.

ROBBIE: Sure you will. . . . Do you like the briefcase?

JESSE: Very much. (*It suddenly occurs to him*) Did you pick it out?

ROBBIE: (*With a modest smile*) Yes.

JESSE: Thanks. I like it even better now.

(*He runs his hand over the leather*)

ROBBIE: Will you get me one when I go to college?

JESSE: Damn right I will!

ROBBIE: But I don't want a dark brown one. I'll want bright yellow cowhide—so everybody sees it.

JESSE: And your initials in great big letters.

ROBBIE: You bet—the biggest!

(*More soberly*) You're not sure you'll ever have to buy it, are you?

JESSE: If you're sure, I am.

(*A new note comes into Robbie's voice. The self-pity is gone, a banished enemy. In its place a grim determination, prematurely tough for a boy so sensitive . . . maybe even a bit hard.*)

ROBBIE: I'm so sure I'll get there that I can feel my feet walking across that bridge right now. And I can see every part of the bridge, the way the railing has spikes on it, and the tall curved lamps with the three globes on every one. And I see myself walking on the bridge, and some way—somehow— I'll get to the other side . . . on my own.

JESSE: You will, Robbie. I know you will.

ROBBIE: Good luck to you, Jess.

JESSE: Thank you.

ROBBIE: (*With a smile*) You know something? I bet you need it more than I will.

JESSE: (*Smiling, he nods*) You could be right.

ROBBIE: Now go on—over the bridge!

JESSE: Yes—over the bridge.

(*A pause. They do not know how to part. Jesse turns away. Then quickly he turns back. They move to each other, they embrace, holding one another a long time. Then Jesse leaves. Robbie goes to the window and looks out on the street, to watch his brother's departure for college. The light fades.*)

The light comes up on The Bridge. It is as Robbie described it. The railing rises in a curve, with a spiked decoration on top of the scallop. The bridge is deserted as Jesse arrives, carrying his briefcase and his high hopes. As he starts across, a young girl appears out of the darkness. She is nicely dressed. We do not see her face because she is upstage, on the shadow side. But when she comes abreast of him, Jesse stops as if stricken.)

JESSE: Carrie?

(*An instant. She stops but does not speak.*)

JESSE: Oh, I'm sorry—I thought you were someone else.

CARRIE: I *am* someone else.

(*It is indeed Carrie, so different as to be almost unrecognizable. She is well dressed, albeit somewhat cheaply. Her hair is well coiffed, her makeup skillful but a bit overmuch.*)

JESSE: Carrie! My God, it *is* Carrie. You look so different.

CARRIE: I'm different and I'm the same.

JESSE: What are you doing here?

CARRIE: I heard about the scholarship, and I thought: today's his first day. And I—well—I felt partially responsible for you being here—and so I—I wanted to see you crossing the bridge.

JESSE: You might have done it yourself.

CARRIE: (*A bit forlorn*) Yes . . . But if it's not me—I'm glad it's you.

JESSE: Thank you. Very much.

(*A strained pause. They study one another*) What are you doing these days, Carrie?

CARRIE: I—uh—I work in the financial district.

JESSE: Doing what?

CARRIE: (*With a wry smile*) Ask me no questions, I'll tell you no lies.

JESSE: How is . . . the baby?

CARRIE: . . . I didn't have it.

JESSE: (*Surprised*) You didn't? Why?

(*As she doesn't answer*) Did you change your mind?

CARRIE: No. (*Pause*) I never changed my mind about that. I wanted it— yes—I wanted it very much. And one day—Wharton Street—I was walking along—a bright summer afternoon—everything was going to be fine—I was going to have the most wonderful baby! And suddenly—this sharp pain, and I fell on the sidewalk—and they took me to the hospital, and . . . I lost it.

JESSE: I'm sorry. Oh God, I'm sorry.

CARRIE: (*With a laugh*) It was as though somebody played a trick on me. It was the first time in my life that I really wanted anything.

JESSE: Well, you're bound to have children in your life. After all, you're not even nineteen. We're only kids.

CARRIE: I don't feel like a kid anymore. . . . Do you?

JESSE: No.

CARRIE: I wonder how we know that about ourselves—that we're not kids anymore.

JESSE: I don't know. (*With a sad smile*) But there isn't any doubt about it when we find out.

(*Her smile is like Jesse's; there's melancholy in it. She tries to lift the mood.*)

CARRIE: I like this old bridge. I walk by here a lot nowadays. I thought— well—if you wanted to—we might see each other from time to time.

(*A difficult moment*)

JESSE: I . . . think not, Carrie.

CARRIE: Too late, huh?

(*His nod is barely perceptible. As she speaks, she makes a brave fight against her sorrows.*)

CARRIE: That's one of the ways I know I'm not a kid anymore. When I was younger, I couldn't wait for things to happen. And now . . . the better things have already happened . . . and it's too late.

(*He is silent, just gazing at her, trying to see her as a meaning in his life.*)

CARRIE: Before I go, would you mind kissing me? I mean before we say goodbye.

(*Slowly, delicately he goes to her and kisses her with the utmost tenderness—on the cheek.*)

JESSE: . . . Goodbye, Carrie.

CARRIE: Goodbye, Jess.

(*She departs and he remains there, watching her as she retraces her footsteps across the bridge. He raises his arm to wave.*)

JESSE: Goodbye . . .

(*At last, when she is at a far distance and, presumably, no longer watching him, he brings his arm down and covers his eyes with his forearm. He may be doing it to block her out of his sight, he may be doing it to keep from crying . . . for many other reasons. Not the least of which is that he is saying farewell to his childhood, and he can scarcely bear it. Finally, he pulls himself together, turns, and resumes his journey across the bridge. The lights fade.*)

END OF THE PLAY

ALCHEMY

A Play in Two Acts

CHARACTERS

(In the order of their speaking)

Giacomo Levanto
Nicolo Tafi
Vitale Galbaio
Antonio Celsi
Pasquale Ziani
Giovanna di Savoia di Participazio
Alcestor
Zeno
Lieutenant of Police
Policeman
Fabio da Gritti Selvo
Carla Murano
Orfeo
Marco
Orso Tadeo
Colignari
Miniore

ABOUT THE SCENERY

Where the devil cites gospel to his purpose, and the white angel cites the canon of hell; where logic can be magical and magic logical; where the mind rages against the blood; where God and Lucifer play the game of musical chairs; where the infinite can be the absolute; where reason and ravish are two faces of the same—what meets the eye had better not be altogether real.

Nor altogether magical, either. Part fact, part dream; part astronomy, part astrology; part chemistry, part alchemistry; as literal as lust, as illusory as love.

PLACE

Venice

TIME

Early Eighteenth Century

A NOTE ON THE BLACK MAGIC OF VENICE
AT THE DAWN OF REASON

On the Grand Canal, they are fire-baiting a bull adrift on a gondola. . . . On the Rialto Bridge a street vendor sells hashish and aphrodisiacs. . . . In the cobwebbed crypt the young man weeps over Aristotle. . . . In the guttering torchlight a masked lady in emerald velvet and a tricorne hat slips in and out among the Baroque colonnades. . . . A rat scurries in the scullery of the Palazzo Pesaro and the white confection is carried high to the glittering hall. . . . In the dark basement of the basilica, under the lofty altar, the young priest perspires and rubs the philosopher's stone. . . . The dice boxes clack in the Lido. . . . A pikeman tortures a shaven-headed cat, and urinates on its nearly-dead body. . . . The young boy whispers the secret of the geometric theorem: all parallel lines. . . . The guano floats on the water. . . . A harpsichord plays the passion of Jesus. . . . The old alchemist makes false gold and fondles the white dove he stole from the Merceria: be still, be still. . . . The gladioli are heaped high on the funeral barge. . . . The bloody lips of the man left for dead in the culvert move, the mouth murmurs: fata morgana. . . . On the parapet of the Palazzo Ducale the astronomer does cube root, focuses his telescope and behold, the Chair of Cassiopeia. . . . A peacock screams on a gilded barge and the artist with wet brush gilds the soft thigh of the Contessa's beating woman. . . . The carnival revelers fly across the Piazetta like a scare of birds. . . . Ave Maria purissima, conceived without sin. . . .

Act One

MANY TINY RIVERS that used to flow through the underground of Venice have been drained, earth-filled and paved. Others have been re-routed and their water beds abandoned. The drainage pipes that lead to them thereupon have become haunt and hideaway for the riff raff of the city. The sewage culvert we now see is a choice lair. It has two outlets. One is an overhead grating; the other, an opening that gives onto a wayside along the canal. We cannot see this culvert mouth; we know of the presence of water because of the light that shimmers, like the beating of wings. The light through the grating is less wondrous, murky but steady, augmented by a brazier flame which presently heats a crucible and retort. Nico Tafi, dressed in clerical habit, stirs the contents of the crucible. He is elderly, quick-witted but scatterbrained, unkempt and nearly always drunk. He hears Giaco's voice and guiltily stops working at the crucible.

GIACO'S VOICE: Nico! Put up the ladder! Nico!
(Nico doesn't know what to hide first, the forbidden wine or the forbidden crucible. He throws a cover on the brazier. It smokes and, with his hands, his skirt, the wine bottle, he dispels the fumes. He takes a swig out of the bottle and hides it. Giaco's voice is still shouting for the ladder. Nico pushes the ladder to the opening.)
NICO: Here it is! Give an old man a little time!

GIACO'S VOICE: Here—catch!

(*Now, like a cornucopia being emptied down the opening, foodstuffs drop on the elated old man. A capon, bread, vegetables. Nico scurries in ecstasy.*)

NICO: Oh, a capon! (*Giacomo Levanto comes down the ladder carrying a bottle of wine. Giaco's attractiveness: vitality, flash of mind, readiness to laughter. And the inchoate sense that he lives alone. With fondness, he watches Nico's delight.*) Oh, Giaco, where did you get all the food, the money? . . . You sold the beauty extract!

GIACO: Not a jar. Why would they need our beauty extract? Every woman in Venice is beautiful.

NICO: You said that in Genoa.

GIACO: Not like here. How this city glows and glimmers! This is where we stay, Nico. And nobody drives us out. No police clanking behind us—no! And we won't live in this dirty sewer drain—we'll have a little palazzo on an old canal. We'll watch the gondolas go by and we'll. . . What stinks here? (*He starts toward the crucible. Nico intercepts him.*)

NICO: It's nothing—what was left of the rabbit stew.

GIACO: Throw it away. Cook the capon.

NICO: Where did you get the money, Giaco?

GIACO: I . . . sold the ring you made for me.

NICO: Oh, no—the dear little golden ring with the rubies?—that I made with my own hands?

GIACO: The dear little golden ring that you made with your own hands turned black on my finger.

NICO: It couldn't—it was gold!

GIACO: Gold? Where's the brass button that was here on my coat?

NICO: I didn't make it out of your brass button. I swear!

GIACO: You promised—no more brass into gold.

NICO: It was your birthday, Giaco. Could I give you a brass ring? I didn't know it would turn black so soon.

GIACO: Turn black? It started to pull at my finger like a boil.

(*Nico finds this funny and starts to cackle. Giaco laughs too.*)

NICO: But how did you get all this for a dirty little black ring?

GIACO: (*Happily*) Today, Nico, today I was bathed in radiance! I walked in a gloriole of light!

NICO: What happened? Tell me—how?

GIACO: The Rialto Bridge! Casually, easily—with inconspicuous grace—I wedged the ring between two boards of the bridge. I walked a few innocent steps away. Then—suddenly! (*He shrieks*) And then again! (*Another shriek*) From all directions they came running "What? Is the man ill? Is he bereft?" (*He alternately plays his own part and the parts in the crowd*) "Ill, signore? Bereft? No—I am mad! Lock me in the ducal dungeon! Tie me, bind me against my own stiletto or I'll slash myself to pieces! I've lost the ring of my father! Lost the solid gold ring with the the three red rubies of India! Lost! Swept down the black waters of the Adriatic! Oh, do not let me live—kill me!" (*Jumping onto the table*) I leap up on the railing of the bridge! I am ready to jump! All around me, hands reach out! Strangers lay hold of me! They snatch me from the railing. I lie on the bridge—a mad thing, screaming, beating my head on the wooden planks. At last, I sob quietly, I break everybody's heart—I break my own! And then I see—oh, miracle!—oh, blessed vision of heavenly fortune! There!—between the boards of the bridge!—little boy, what shines there?

NICO: (*Becoming the little boy*) Where, signore—where?

GIACO: There, boy—there, little street urchin—go see!

NICO: (*Reaching down for the imaginary ring*) I think, signore—your ring—it is your lost ring!

GIACO: Oh, blessed ring! Oh, blessed boy! (*He kisses the boy and the ring many times*) Oh, blessed bridge! (*He kisses the bridge*) Dear vault of heaven, you've been kind to me today! (*Suddenly enraged at himself*) But no—I do not deserve this jewel! So heedless—to have lost the precious memento of my honored sire! I don't deserve it! And if anyone will take it from me, free me from it, *I will give this ring away*!

NICO: (*Now playing one of the suckers*) Give it away?—for nothing?

GIACO: For nothing! For a mere good-faith-fraction of its worth!
(*They have come to the nub of it. They smile to one another.*)

NICO: . . . Ten ducats?

GIACO: Ten ducats. To a roundish man. (*He sniffs*) What's that?—the smell gets worse. (*Going to the crucible*) Rabbit stew, did you say? What rabbit smells of sulphur?

NICO: (*Elaborately innocent*) Sulphur? You smell sulphur?

GIACO: Sulphur, damn you. What magical mess is that?

NICO: No magic. Rabbit stew.

GIACO: What? Changing an old rabbit to a young one? A dead one into a live one? What magical stew?
(*Giaco throws the pottery crucible on the ground. It breaks and the contents spill. Nico cries out—heartbreak and anger.*)

NICO: Giaco!—it was a youth elixir—and I almost had the secret of it!

GIACO: You foolish old fart. I begged you. The last time you made a stew like that—you remember?—you tried it on your old mongrel dog. Did he get younger? No, he stretched out with a sick tongue, he made a green vomit and he died. And for three days you lay in a corner with your face to the wall. You want to break your heart again?

NICO: (*Enraged*) It's for my sake, is it? For me?

GIACO: Why, you ungrateful old—

NICO: Not for my sake you forbid it—no! It scares you!

GIACO: Scares me?—what?

NICO: I might *find* something in that crucible! Something magical! Eternal youth! Gold from lead! Some secret deeper than the mind, deeper than the heart—*it scares you*!

GIACO: You lunatic old fool! If there were a hope in your idiocy, you think I'd waste my time selling black rings and beauty notions made of pig fat? Little stinks to scare away bad tidings? Love powders for impotent old men? Why, if I believed in your shitty little magics, I'd—! (*Controlling himself, he speaks more quietly*) No . . . This is dreaming, Nico. It breaks the heart, and I forbid it.

NICO: Go scratch your ass and forbid. I go on.

GIACO: Without me.

NICO: You don't frighten me. What will you do without me? I leave you alone and you'll catch the plague the way you did two winters ago.

GIACO: Go back to the cloister, Nico. You were better off there. Go back.

NICO: (*Angry*) You think it's any different there? It's all hypocrisy! "We don't believe in magic here," the bishop says to me—and he's diddling the beads in his silly little rosary. Don't believe in it, do you? You all believe in it— all, all! Only it daren't be done in that! (*He points to the spilled crucible*) It's got to be done in your own damn crucible!

(*Raging and weeping, Nico is on his knees to retrieve the pieces of the broken crucible. Giaco's love and pity for the old man assert themselves.*)

GIACO: Get up, you misery. I'm sorry.

NICO: Let me alone. (*There is a commotion above. Giaco rushes to the ladder.*) What's the noise?

GIACO: It's the man! The one I sold the ring to! Police! Come—through the culvert!

(*Nico starts toward the fondamenta.*)

NICO: Look! In the gondola! Carabiniere!

(*Noises at the grating overhead, an Officer coming down the ladder. Noise from the opposite direction.*)

GIACO: Light the sulphur! Open the phosphorous boxes!

NICO: Smoke and the devil! Fire and brimstone!

(*They set up a racket. False fire and yellow smoke. The culvert teems with police and the roundish, near-eyed Orio Zeno, the victim of Giaco's swindle. Bedlam. Now, no one is visible in it.*)

VOICES: Here he is! Who's this? I've got him! No, it's me, you idiot! Through the culvert! To the Rialto!

(*The culvert is empty. Now, out of the shadows behind the smoke, comes Giaco. He doffs his coat to wave the smoke away, looks to see if he's safe, and hurries off . . . From darkness, we come up on the brilliant light of the racy commerce of Rialto Bridge. Vendors of all sorts. Among the pedestrians, three merchants. They are not street vendors but the middle class tradesmen now starting to be felt in the surging political life of Venice. One has already succeeded to high estate—a merchant elected to the Black Tribunal. His name is Vitale Galbaio, a falcon of a man, wearing the scarlet costume of the Black Tribunal with bloody pride. With him, two toadying merchants—Antonio Celsi and Pasquale Ziani. . . . Celsi is buying aphrodisiacs. Ziani is purchasing spices.*)

VENDORS: Lanterns, gondola lanterns . . . Gladioli, gladioli for the living, for the dead . . . Sweet herbs, nutmeg and incense, balsam, sandalwood . . . Love philters, aphrodisiacs, unguents for the elderly . . . Herbs, camphor of borneo, aloes wood, rose water . . . Passion potions, spirit of musk, stag water . . . Tonics, tantalizers, tormentors, titillators . . . Hashish-sh-sh-sh . . .

(As the soft shush of the hashish fades, enter the Contessa Giovanna di Savoia di Participazio. A restless unhappy woman, beautiful and too proud. She carries a jeweled mask at the end of a stick. Her retainer, Alcestor, carries a scepter almost as tall as himself. The Vendors turn to her. So does Galbaio. He gives her his most formal bow.)

GALBAIO: Ah—the Contessa Giovanna di Savoia di Participazio!

(She pretends he does not exist and continues past him, her head high—the total snub. Ziani and Celsi are shocked. Galbaio goes white.)

CELSI & ZIANI: As if she didn't know he was there! . . . As if she didn't see him, didn't see him!

GALBAIO: Perhaps she did not see me. I am too short, too low for our eyes to meet. Just the right height for a bitch-in-heat to piss on!

(He speaks loudly so she can hear them. She pretends not to. He leads Ziani and Celsi off. . . . Nico, in flight from the police, rushes across the scene, his friar's skirts high—and he's gone. Giaco hurries in. Walking backward, he bumps into a Radish Vendor. She drops her tray.)

GIACO: Ah, signora, forgive me! But do not grieve. Where I stepped on a radish, a lily will grow.

(He reaches for the radish, closes his fist over it, waves his hand, and, in it—a lily! The woman twitteringly takes it from him to the appreciation of the crowd. In his haste he flies past the beautiful Giovanna, seeing her but not really taking her in. He is gone. An instant, he's back, as if Giovanna's face has belatedly registered on his perception: wonder-struck.)

GIACO: Ah, pardon, lady. What an insult to hurry past this Eighth Wonder of the World which is your face! However—*however*—when I reach the other side of this bridge I shall kneel down and scoop up two handfuls of the cool water of this canal and I shall hope—humbly I shall pray—that in my hands I'll hold forever the shimmering memory of—*your countenance*! I drink you, lady!

GIOVANNA: *(Amused, but aloof)* Ah, too bad—you stayed for one drink too many.

(She indicates. Giaco turns. The police, with Zeno. Giaco starts off. Too late. Another Policeman.)

ZENO: There! There he is! There's the worm!

GIOVANNA: Ah, sad. The worm is snagged.

(The police start for Giaco. She loses interest and gestures for Alcestor to follow her away. But Giaco's voice, challenging:)

GIACO: Worm, is it? Watch me wriggle out of this, madonna mia, and come crawling into my lady's lap. *(As the police seize him)* What's this?—let go! Do you dare lay hands on me?

(An instant. His lordly manner momentarily works. He shakes them off. They do not immediately seize him again. Giovanna's interest is reawakened.)

GIOVANNA: Just a moment, Alcestor.

ZENO: Don't let him go! Poliziotto, don't let him go!

GIACO: *(As they start for him again)* Wait! You! Is this how you repay kindness? My father's ring—his gold ring which I gave you—

ZENO: Gold? You heard him—he claimed gold! Look, thief, look how black it is!

GIACO: This? You call this my father's ring? Where's the gold one?

ZENO: What is he saying? This is it—this is the very one!

GIACO: *(Snatching the ring from Zeno)* Lead! Black lead. You call this the ring? Black lead!

(With loathing, he casts the ring into the canal. Zeno is apoplectic.)

ZENO: No! Get it! It's my only evidence! Fetch it!

(Commotion. The crowd hurries to the rail. Enjoying himself, Giaco turns to Giovanna.)

GIACO: We rally a little, do we not?

GIOVANNA: I wouldn't be too certain.

GIACO: Watch. I'll make a casual decampment in that direction. I regret to leave you, but I must. Arrivederci, lady.

(Sauntering, he starts to depart.)

ZENO & OTHERS: No—stop him! Don't let him get away! Police!

(More commotion. Giaco is seized.)

GIACO: No!—let me go!—you have no evidence against me!

POLICE OFFICER: You're under arrest.

GIACO: On what—the word of this liar? Oh, how I'm slandered and vilified and—and—

GIOVANNA: Calumniated.

GIACO: —calumniated! You have no evidence against me! I'll charge you all with false arrest!

OFFICER: That will be a serious charge, Zeno. Will you stand to it?

ZENO: *(Wavering)* But there were witnesses! Oh dear—oh heavens!

OFFICER: If you have no stomach for this, Zeno, we better let him go.

(As Zeno continues mumbling, another Policeman enters with Nico.)

POLICEMAN: Tenente! I have the other one.

NICO: Let go! Do you dare lay hands on Mother Church?

POLICEMAN: Quiet, Mother. *(To Officer)* Here's his crucible.

OFFICER: *(Receiving the bits of pottery)* What's left of it. Zeno, new evidence. *(To Giaco and Nico)* The charge against you is alchemy. Perhaps false coinage. Come.

(A hushed murmur in the crowd. The police take Giaco past Giovanna.)

GIACO: One moment. Please—one moment.

GIOVANNA: Please, Tenente. Give him leave. *(As they comply. To Giaco)* Yes?

GIACO: Nothing. Only to gaze an instant longer. You are enchantment, lady. Not arrivederci, I'm afraid—addio.

GIOVANNA: (*Still that mockingly amused smile*) Catastrophe!

GIACO: (*Ruefully*) Indeed . . . Would it have been a silken lap to crawl upon?

GIOVANNA: Velvet. Emerald velvet and vermilion satin.

GIACO: Vivid, vivid. And, oh dear heaven—soft! Catastrophe indeed! Addio, lady.

(*The police take him. The crowds drift after him. Giovanna's eyes follow him narrowly. Not turning to Alcestor:*)

GIOVANNA: That is the man.

ALCESTOR: Him? Are you sure, signora?

GIOVANNA: Go and get him off.

ALCESTOR: Surely, you cannot mean it?

GIOVANNA: Him. Do as I say.

(*She departs. Alcestor bows and hurries after Giaco. The lights fade. They come up on the figure of the Marchese Fabio da Gritti Selvo. He is elderly, patrician, cunning with cruelty. Now he is officiating over the chastisement of Alcestor. Orfeo, a brute servant, holds Alcestor while Marco, another brute, strikes him. As the light focus broadens, we see the Marchese's chamber, austerely aristocratic.*)

FABIO: Again. (*Marco strikes Alcestor*) Again . . . That will do. I said that will do. (*He gestures. Marco and Orfeo go.*) Now . . . In whose employ are you, imbecile?

ALCESTOR: In yours, Marchese.

FABIO: You're sure of that, imbecile? You're quite sure the Contessa does not pay your wages, imbecile—you're sure I do?

ALCESTOR: Yes, signore, yes!

FABIO: Then why did you not come to *me*, imbecile?—to me first? Why did you go to the police without asking my permission?

GIOVANNA: (*Entering*) There wasn't time.

FABIO: (*To Alcestor*) Get out. (*In a rage, to Giovanna*) You strain my affection, Giovanna.

GIOVANNA: You're perturbed too soon.

FABIO: Does it serve a good purpose to link my name with an alley thief?

GIOVANNA: You'll suffer nothing, Fabio. We got the man off before they could put him in the register. They didn't even charge him.

FABIO: You think those near-eyed shopkeepers on the Tribunal need a charge? All they need is a rumor, a whisper. And you *did* whisper my name, didn't you?

GIOVANNA: Fabio—

FABIO: Didn't you, Giovanna?

GIOVANNA: Yes. I'm sorry. I didn't know that the few ducats I handed over would have done it well enough, *without* mentioning your name. I had no idea corruption came so easily.

FABIO: The law—it's become a merchandise.

GIOVANNA: It's always been a merchandise. What provokes you is that the merchandise is now being sold by the merchants, and they're better at it than we were.

FABIO: We never sold the law so cheap.

GIOVANNA: Well, they can afford to lower the prices—they do a larger trade.

FABIO: Tradesmen, I loathe them!

GIOVANNA: Better learn to love them, Fabio.

FABIO: And this man you got out of prison today—am I to love him next? A common thief?

GIOVANNA: Uncommon, Fabio . . . This is the man we've been looking for.

FABIO: A gutter man, without one shred of quality—?

GIOVANNA: No quality, but all the qualifications. A stranger—nobody knows him in Venice. A dabbler in alchemy—he can talk the jargon of it. And a beguiling fake.

FABIO: Giovanna, I am not going through with this enterprise.

GIOVANNA: Do I understand you've miraculously come into a large fortune?

FABIO: I cannot go through with it.

GIOVANNA: Cannot? Can you give up your palazzo?

FABIO: I will not give it up.

GIOVANNA: You'll have to. You may as well send for Tadeo and sell it to him now.

FABIO: No—I'm not selling my palazzo to a greasy-fingered pawnbroker—no!

GIOVANNA: You've already sold him a good portion of it.

FABIO: Who said that?

GIOVANNA: I did. The Tintoretto, the three crusader's cups, the ruby tapestry—

FABIO: They're stored away somewhere.

GIOVANNA: Come, don't lie to me. I saw Tadeo here last month—sneaking up the gondoliers' stairway. And not the first time he was here, either. Soon there'll be nothing left to sell—a trinket maybe, a few silver spoons. Who'll do the sneaking then? You!—down the same stairway—with a brass goblet under your cloak, and your heart pounding for fear no pawnbroker will give you a ducat for it!

FABIO: If you knew . . . You shouldn't have told me.

GIOVANNA: I'm sorry if it pains you . . . I *am* sorry, Fabio.

FABIO: (*He turns away from her, too unhappy to speak. At last:*) My great grandfather owned a fleet of the most beautiful, beautiful ships. The canals used to be so clogged with them that hardly a gondola could move. At night, when they were still, people walked from deck to deck, carrying torches . . . Before he died, he paid Titian to paint him a new picture and Galileo to find him a new star. Yesterday I sold the Titian to the pawnbroker.

GIOVANNA: You might get a bit more for the star.

FABIO: Oh, I would sell it! (*More cheerfully*) You know, if I sold everything—a little at a time—I could live my life out, and be content. If you married me, I'd be content to live poor.

GIOVANNA: I would not.

FABIO: What? Marry me? Or be content to be poor?

GIOVANNA: No need to be poor. I'm on the verge of making us a fortune. There never was a city so ready to be swindled! Greedy. False. Selling itself as a floating paradise when it's built on puddles of muck. Loud and sick and cynical. And because it believes in nothing, it will believe anything. What a duping it will take! . . . And I'll be glad to give it.

FABIO: But I won't. Giovanna, I'll make a terrible partner for you. Go down to the Rialto. Find a merchant—someone expert in bargaining and theft—

GIOVANNA: Stop it! I'm sick of your patrician ironies. I'm as highborn as you are. But it's too late to cry nobility, too damn late! We'll have to dig around in the alleys, and find a slimy ducat somewhere. Because the way the world's going, we have nothing to count on.

FABIO: Not each other, Giovanna?

GIOVANNA: (*An outburst*) To do what? Cry in one another's arms?

FABIO: (*With a wry smile*) Well, if you can't cry in my arms, I must count that as another of my failures.

GIOVANNA: The failure's not totally yours.

FABIO: (*Bowing derisively*) Thank you. That's generous of you.

GIOVANNA: (*Angry*) What do you want me to say? That I don't like either of us? Need it be said?

(*Carla Murano enters. She is a lady's maid whose good looks and raffishness almost hide her wild flight, her terror. Right now she is enraged, and alarmed.*)

CARLA: Excuse me, Contessa. They have brought a man to see you. His name is Levanto.

GIOVANNA: Bring him here.

CARLA: I . . . May I have Orfeo or Marco do it, signora?

GIOVANNA: Why?

CARLA: He's a dirty-quick one, signora—with his hands. But I gave him one of mine—across his mouth! (*Blurting*) How did he know? Did you tell him?

GIOVANNA: Tell him what, Carla?

CARLA: About my father.

GIOVANNA: (*Puzzled*) No, I didn't.

CARLA: (*Her fright showing*) He said—right after I slapped him—he said, "Whom have you lost, my dear?"

GIOVANNA: (*Annoyed*) So? It doesn't mean a thing.

FABIO: We're always losing something . . .

CARLA: Not some *thing*, Signore—he said whom! As if he knew my father had died. How did he know?

GIOVANNA: (*Pause. Then, to start the legend:*) He is . . . a very special man, Carla. . . . Send him here. (*As Carla departs*) You see? He turned that girl into a most intriguing calling card. He's shrewd.

FABIO: Giovanna, you're inching me into this.

GIOVANNA: Yes, I am. If you're content to let all you have go sliding into the water—! Please, Fabio—I'm trying to help you—accept it with good grace.

FABIO: (*With an arid smile*) Good grace . . . that's sliding too. Some men, as they get older, mellow and turn sweet. Not I. More and more, each morning, I wake up tasting gall. I search for ways to venge myself. Oh, if I could find an object! You know, it's not easy, days like this, to be a judge at the trials, and stay benevolent. The mind runs cruel. It runs to mutilations. . . . Good grace, you say? I'll try.

(*A disturbance somewhere. Orfeo and Marco bring in Levanto.*)

GIACO: No—gently! I wasn't trying to escape, you lummoxes! Let go!

GIOVANNA: Let him go.

(*They release him. He sees Giovanna.*)

GIACO: Ah, me! The Lap—The Velvet Lap! Have I been thrown upon The Velvet Lap?

GIOVANNA: (*Ignoring him. To the servants*) You may leave now.

ORFEO: Leave him here, Contessa?

(*She gestures Orfeo and Marco away. They go.*)

GIACO: Contessa, did he say? If it's to you, Contessa, that I owe my present liberty . . . (*He makes an expansive gesture.*)

GIOVANNA: Yes?—then what?

GIACO: Then everything. Everything—all yours—my soul and service— all—they're yours!

GIOVANNA: (*Dryly to Fabio*) Stand back a little. He makes large gestures.

GIACO: And what gesture I extend to you I equally extend, signora, to your lover. No, no—don't bridle, lady. I say lover only in the sense that all men must surely love you.

GIOVANNA: (*To Fabio*) There's a shoddy little greasiness about him, but if we keep rubbing away at it, we may clean him off.

GIACO: (*With a smile*) I am right here, signora. Please do not talk about me as if I were in another room. (*To Fabio*) Who is she?

GIOVANNA: The Contessa Giovanna di Savoia di Participazio. This is the Marchese Fabio da Gritti Selvo.

GIACO: Da Gritti—? She did say da Gritti Selvo, did she not? (*As Fabio nods*) The judge? On the Black Tribunal? (*Another nod*) You bastards! So this is the way your law works in Venice! You bring a prisoner to a fine palazzo, you encourage him to think he's free—and before he can belch, he has confessed himself to a member of your snake-blooded Tribunal. Send me back to prison, you jackals—the hell with you!

FABIO: (*Good-humoredly*) I thought you said he was a stranger in Venice. (*To Giaco*) How did you know I was a member of the Tribunal? . . . Come now, man, it's not an incriminating question. How did you know me?

GIACO: I make a point! The instant I enter a strange city, I learn all I can about the judges of the law.

FABIO: You have answered an innocent question in an incriminating way. If you're honest, why so sedulous about the law?

GIACO: So that I won't break it. Your honest man, signore—he's always breaking the law. And always paying a penalty for it. For what?—for throwing a chicken bone into the street. Didn't he know it's against the law to throw a chicken bone into the street? No, poor boobyhead, he didn't. But me—I know about chicken bones. I respect the laws of chicken bones. I warrant, I respect them more than you do!

GIOVANNA: As a consequence, you're never arrested.

GIACO: (*He laughs at her quickness*) Well, this arrest—you embarrass me to mention it. But—! A soldier is more likely to sustain a wound than is a bookseller, no? And considering the hazards of the business . . .

FABIO: What *is* your business?

GIACO: (*With a cunning smile*) The tribune cannot resist asking questions, can he?

FABIO: Since you're so sure-footed in the law, why resist answering them?

GIACO: The Marchese challenges me. Your question again, signore?

FABIO: Your business.

GIACO: I've had many businesses. I've sold potions that misbegotten ladies thought would make them beautiful, I've sold elixirs that old gentlemen thought would make them young.

FABIO: They *thought* so. You did not claim them to be so?

GIACO: Oh, no, signore. I never claim anything. Maybe I wink a little. Maybe I ask: "I wonder if this will make you young?" But answer it? No need to. The idiotic fools are only too eager to answer it themselves.

FABIO: You're charged with alchemy. False coinage. Is that your business?

GIACO: Oh no! No, no, no, no, no!

GIOVANNA: (*After an instant, casually*) Why, then, you're free.

GIACO: Your pardon, signora? . . What did you say?

FABIO: You heard her—free.

(*Fabio smiles. Giaco doesn't believe it. He crosses to the window, looks out.*)

GIACO: Truly free?

GIOVANNA: Go.

(*Giaco is full of wonder—and suspicion. He studies them, then relaxes, smiles.*)

GIACO: Well, then. If I am truly free to go, I some way suspect it will be more profitable to stay. . . . What do you want of me?

GIOVANNA: We want you to accept our gift of one hundred thousand ducats.

GIACO: (*With a silly flourish*) Oh, how kind of you. I accept.

GIOVANNA: You do not believe me?

GIACO: It's a lot of money on an empty stomach, Contessa.

GIOVANNA: You're hungry?

(*She gestures to the fruit bowl. He goes to it and admires a peach.*)

GIACO: So perfect!—is it not marble? Ah, no! You folk, you make the *marble* ones with minor imperfections. The *perfect* ones you eat. (*He bites into it ravenously.*) Now! A number was mentioned, one hundred thousand, I recall. What did it refer to? Pebbles, buttons, chickpeas?

GIOVANNA: Ducats. Gold.

GIACO: What do I do for it?

GIOVANNA: Nothing, immediately. We're not certain you're the man.

GIACO: A hundred thousand ducats makes *me* certain that I am.

GIOVANNA: Would you eat more slowly, please?

GIACO: I'm sorry. I'll toy daintily with food when I no longer need it. Oh, forgive me—I should share it. (*He carries the bowl to her.*)

GIOVANNA: No, thank you. Would you mind standing away a little?

GIACO: Why? This is no weapon. A fruit bowl is not a—(*He stops smiling as he sees her meaning. Trying to hide his humiliation:*) I see. I smell bad. (*He puts down the bowl.*) Yes, I do. I've crawled through a drainage culvert and lain three hours in a filthy cell. The stench is in my clothing, lady, not in me.

GIOVANNA: Could we start by learning something—perhaps your name? Giacomo Levanto—is that your real name?

GIACO: Real?—who knows? Between the sprinkling of holy water and the sprinkling of dust, a man's identity changes many times.

GIOVANNA: That is an idiocy, signore. Now, answer me. What is the first name you responded to?

GIACO: Sweet-Ass.

FABIO: I beg your pardon?

GIACO: Sweet-Ass. I responded to no other name until I was five years old.

GIOVANNA: Do you mean for us to call you that?

GIACO: It would be friendly . . . But would it suit the purpose?

FABIO: Do you have a name for every purpose?

GIACO: Of course. Forgive me, you do not understand. To be a marchese— that's a splendid purpose to begin with, no need for modification. So the name that goes with it is quite satisfactory—why change? But me—!

GIOVANNA: How old are you?

GIACO: Whatever I tell you, add ten years.

FABIO: What age do you tell?

GIOVANNA: Never mind. (*To Giaco*) Where were you born?

GIACO: Some say Madrid, some say Mecca. There is merit in all claims.

GIOVANNA: (*In a temper*) Will we not get a direct answer from you? On anything?

GIACO: (*Smoothly, enjoying her annoyance*) No, Contessa. Only impressions. But please do not fret. It has advantages.

GIOVANNA: I fail to see any.

FABIO: (*Starting to enjoy Giaco*) I think I do. One advantage is that when he gives us unlimited choices, we can think of him as we will—and cut him to our own requirements.

GIACO: The thought is right, Marchese—even if the image is somewhat alarming.

(*He and Fabio smile. This irritates Giovanna even further.*)

GIOVANNA: If you set so low a store on one hundred thousand ducats that you'll tell us no more about yourself—

GIACO: Why need you know any more, Contessa?

GIOVANNA: This is no easy enterprise. If you're to be one of us, we must know everything about you.

GIACO: Everything? Contessa, who knows everything? And even if I did, what use would it be if I told it? None. Clutter! . . . So you will forgive me, signora, if I suggest that your curiosity—flattering as it is—has nothing to do with the business at hand. It is very likely . . . personal. And so, I promise to let you know more and more about me as we become more and more . . . intimate.

GIOVANNA: This man will not do.

FABIO: Why, Giovanna? He's exactly as you described him to me.

GIOVANNA: Not a single direct answer from him. Only subterfuge and lies!

GIACO: (*A flare of vexation*) Of course I lie! When you plucked me out of a crowd, what recommended me to you? My childlike honesty? My innocence? The clerical cut of my collar? No! You brought me here because you took me for a liar! And whatever your enterprise is, a liar is apparently what it needs. What you did not bargain for is that I'm a more artful liar than you may require—one who can *make* a lie without *saying* one. My superiority to the function you have in mind for me—is that what nettles you?

FABIO: Is it, Giovanna?

GIOVANNA: (*Hotly*) No! What "nettles" me is that the man is equivocal. Is he this or is he that? (*To Giaco*) Speak plainly, signore. What are you?

GIACO: What am I? My dear Contessa, I am nothing!

GIOVANNA: I asked you a serious question.

GIACO: Because I laughed did it mean I was not serious? I am nothing. I have no knowledge what you have in mind for me—but will I not serve your purpose better if I am nothing?

GIOVANNA: If you have no intention to make yourself known to us—

(*His upraised hand interrupts her outbreak. He explains, now, with an air of playfulness. But what comes out is not playful—it is a more serious self-revelation than he had intended. This inadvertence, in the end, angers him.*)

GIACO: I will be—whatever you require. Always I have been whatever the moment required. Which is to say: nothing. If you are more comfortable putting a name to it, call me a charlatan. Which I am. I have swindled the best of men and unctuously flattered the worst of them. I have lain abed with women I did not cherish so that they would recommend me as a man of unblemished character to their husbands. I have promised my return to people who have loved me—and have left them, forever gazing through their empty windows. I am a coward. I lie sluggish in the sunlight and I dart about at night. I am a glutton for the small and crummy pleasures of living, without the appetite for life. I can trick anyone, milady—I can make

an illusion of anything! Shall I then be tricked by the worst illusion of all—
that I am something? Not I, milady! Nothing! I do not exist!

GIOVANNA: (*Caught. Alarmed. Trying to smile*) Shall I take you literally and
see if you are there?

GIACO: Try, signora. Touch me.

GIOVANNA: . . . No.

GIACO: Why? Are you afraid to find me insubstantial? Try.
(*Slowly, very slowly she crosses, smiling to cast off his hypnotic hold on
her. When she reaches and touches him, she tries to hide her relief:*)

GIOVANNA: I touched you, and you *are.*

GIACO: An illusion, my dear. I have tricked your mind into believing what
is not.

GIOVANNA: Oh, come.

GIACO: Shall I prove it to you? A moment ago, you warned me away from
you because I stank. And now—look at you—you've crossed the room to
me, of your own free will. And you've forgotten my ill-favored aroma.
Why? Has my odor changed? No. An illusion.
(*The spell is broken by Carla's entrance.*)

GIOVANNA: What is it?

CARLA: You rang, Contessa?

GIOVANNA: No—no one rang—go away.

FABIO: I rang . . . Take the signore to the chamber at the end of the gallery.
See that he is bathed. I'm sure his head's vermiculated. Have it scoured.
As to new clothes—the Contessa will see to it.

GIOVANNA: Not yet, Fabio—I am too unsure of him—!

FABIO: You asked me to accept with good grace. I do.
(*She turns away. Fabio takes this as agreement. To Giaco:*)
You are agreeable to join us?—without asking questions?

GIACO: Oh, I do not need to ask questions. If you want *me,* then there's a
fraud afoot. Well, signore, if a velvety countess and a marchese member
of the Tribunal are the patrons of it—bless us all, the day is promising!

GIOVANNA: (*Warningly, to Fabio*) Tell him—tell him we're not yet committed to him!

GIACO: (*With a smile*) I am committed to you, my dear. To your . . . skin.

GIOVANNA: I beg your pardon?

GIACO: Your skin! Dear God, the silk of it! Why, if I knew your magic
recipe—! Your wash water—sell me your wash water! I'll put it up in red
Venetian glass, and sell it, fifty ducats for the ounce! (*To Carla*) Come,
girl, show the way!
(*He goes out with Carla. Giovanna watches him go. Fabio watches
Giovanna. The lights fade. They come up again on a sumptuous bedchamber. Carla, carrying a lighted candelabra, shows Giaco in. He is impressed by the room.*)

CARLA: This will be your chamber. And do not dirty it. No—don't sit down—
not till you're clean . . . Your bath will be here soon.

GIACO: Thank you, my dear. I'll kiss your hand. (*He extends his hand; she rears.*)

CARLA: You reach for me, I'll pull your fingers off! Or any other part that gives offense.

GIACO: Do girl—sheer pleasure.

CARLA: And while you're here, you mind: I struck you once and I will again.

GIACO: Will you make the wager of a ducat on that?

CARLA: (*Arrogantly*) How did you know my father?

GIACO: Your what?

CARLA: My father—how did you know my father?

GIACO: Girl, I didn't know you *had* a father. (*She slaps him, hard.*) Had you laid a ducat, girl, you'd now have two. (*Again he reaches for her*)

CARLA: Beware, I say! . . . My father . . . how did you know?

GIACO: I didn't know. I still don't know. Begone.

(*The fact that he denies any previous knowledge now convinces her to the contrary.*)

CARLA: You *did* know him, didn't you? Or *about* him. Now, don't deny it! You said: "My dear, whom have you lost?" What did that signify?

GIACO: (*Annoyed*) Signify? It signified nothing, girl. It's simply one of the more cuddly overtures to a lady. "Whom have you lost, my dear?" Or another one: "Your eyes are dry, but I do think you weep?" Or "If I tell you one word, will you promise not to beg me to explain it?"

CARLA: What word?

GIACO: Oh, dear God—*no* word! Tell a woman any word, ask her not to beg you to explain, and suddenly her hands are folded: "I beg you, what did you mean, what did you mean?" With you the word is—

CARLA: Father.

GIACO: Yes.

CARLA: What did you mean?

GIACO: Nothing.

CARLA: (*Folding her hands in entreaty*) Please.

GIACO: (*Genuinely irritated*) Stop it.

CARLA: I *know* somebody told you about him! You won't make me believe you simply guessed—that you're one of those traveling magicians who can divine something from a leaf that falls from a tree. I don't believe in such magical nonsense!

GIACO: Good girl—nor do I.

CARLA: (*Whirling on him, in a fury*) You liar! How did you change hickory nuts into pearls?

GIACO: What?

CARLA: How did you change wet straw into China silk?

GIACO: Who told you I did that?

CARLA: Your friend the friar.

GIACO: (*Excited*) Nico?—where is he?—Nico—where?

CARLA: In the scullery. Alcestor got him off, the same as you.

GIACO: And he is well—is he well? Has he been fed?

CARLA: All that he can drink.

GIACO: Ah, you're a dear good thing and I shall kiss your—! Oh, I forgot. I'll forgo the pleasure this time.

CARLA: You may . . . kiss my hand. (*He does. An instant*) Some men kiss a girl's hand, she feels it on the lips.

GIACO: And other men?

CARLA: (*Reaching to her breast*) I felt it here.

GIACO: (*An instant. Gently*) Dear child . . . go away.

CARLA: (*Quietly, very soberly*) You are . . . a tease.

GIACO: . . . Yes . . . I am a tease.

CARLA: And a mountebank to boot. I heard you—potions to make ugly women beautiful.

GIACO: I didn't claim any such thing—you heard me wrong! That's what happens to words when they get squeezed through a keyhole.

CARLA: I wasn't listening at the keyhole! Everybody in the corridor could hear you. You talk so loud—as if trying to drown out the sound of your own voice!

GIACO: Drown out the sound of my . . . ? What a strange thing to say.

CARLA: (*Unexpectedly, she starts to tremble*) It doesn't make sense, does it? I don't know why I said it. Sometimes what I say . . .

GIACO: (*Concerned*) Is there something wrong with you, my dear?

CARLA: (*Shaking and angry*) Wrong? Is that another of your "cuddly overtures"?

GIACO: (*Quietly*) No, it isn't, Carla—is that your name? . . . I'm sorry if you thought it was. (*Turning away, to dismiss her*) You said something about a bath?

CARLA: (*Very, very quietly. And apprehensive*) . . . Can you make a seance, signore?

GIACO: A what?

CARLA: Your friend Nico said . . . I don't believe him, understand, but I ask you—can you make a seance?

GIACO: . . . No.

CARLA: I don't know which of you is lying now.

GIACO: (*Angry*) You said you don't believe in magic! A seance is magic!

CARLA: Can you make a seance?

GIACO: No!

CARLA: You lie. Nico says you can.

GIACO: God, how perverse you all are! The one thing you will *not* believe is the truth! Why are you all so eager to be cheated?

CARLA: (*Blurting*) I cannot sleep, signore!

GIACO: . . . Cannot sleep?

CARLA: Since my father died . . . He comes to me. He stands there, by my bed. With a look so full of pain. I say to him, "Speak—tell me how to help you!" Each night he tries to say something—and cannot. Last night . . .

last night, he opened his mouth and . . . Oh, Jesus . . . a gush of blood . . . oh, Jesus. (*She is quaking. At last, she pulls herself together, and tries to smile*) There used to be an old lady from the Giudecca . . . she is gone now . . . she used to bring back the dead . . . make them speak.

GIACO: (*Gently*) She didn't. It was a trick, girl.

CARLA: No, signore.

GIACO: A trick! I can show you hundreds of them. Look. (*He flicks his thumbnails together—a flash of flame! Carla cries out.*) You want to see how it is done?

CARLA: No.

GIACO: You *must* see. (*Twisting her around. Angry*) I told you: look! You see my thumb?—I stick it in this pocket. I have a bit of white powder here. And I have other tricks. Look!

(*He whisks his cloak off and reveals, strapped around his waist, a belt which holds a number of tiny bottles, flasks, jars.*)

My tricks—my bag of tricks! Bottles, flasks, vials. This bottle here—this changes wine to water, and this one, water to wine. It's my Jesus-the-Vintner trick. This little vial—I take a few drops and—mirabile dictu!—no pulse, no heartbeat, no breath to cloud a looking glass—sometimes it's useful to be dead! Levanto Lazarus! Beauty waters for sad, ill-favored girls who weep in chimney corners! Potions, drafts, elixirs to inflame the passions! All sorts of milks to suck from the tit of Mother Miracle! For whom? For fools, so they can snatch a moment of false hope from the long-sufferance of their miseries! But best of all—would you like to see what's best of all? Look! (*He holds up a small bottle*)

CARLA: What . . . is it, sir?

GIACO: My homunculus.

CARLA: Homunculus? What is that?

GIACO: A man. A little man—of my own creation. A tiny man in a tiny bottle. *A living man!*

CARLA: (*Alternately dreading and disbelieving*) Alive, sir? A real man—alive? Oh no, sir.

GIACO: Come and see.

CARLA: No. You . . . made him?

GIACO: Yes. Come and look at him.

CARLA: No.

GIACO: Come, girl, he won't get out, he won't hurt you. Come.

(*Slowly she crosses and looks. A terrified outcry*)

CARLA: He moves! He is alive!

GIACO: No! No, girl—a trick! A trick, Carla—like all the others—only a trick. Don't shake—please—don't tremble, child. It's only a tiny doll, my dear, suspended in a gas. When my hand warms the gas, the little man dances. A trick, my dear, a fake!

CARLA: He . . . seems . . . alive.

GIACO: He's *meant* to seem alive. He's not.

(*Alcestor enters with Marco and Orfeo, who wheel in a bathtub on casters. It is built like a gondola, ornately ornamented. Marco lifts birch heather brushes out of the tub; Orfeo brings an urn of steaming water.*)

ALCESTOR: Your bath, signore.

GIACO: Is this a bathtub—or will it sail?

ALCESTOR: Would you please to undress, sir? . . Carla.

(*Carla goes. Giaco undresses. Marco flicks a birch branch like a whip.*)

GIACO: What's that?

ALCESTOR: Birch and heather whips, signore. They make a healthy reddening of the skin.

GIACO: Whose skin?—do I do it to you, or you to me?

(*A Tailor, Cobbler and Haberdasher enter.*) Who are all these people? Am I to give audience while I am beaten in my bath? Who *are* these powder faces?

ALCESTOR: Your tailor, cobbler and haberdasher. Please to get in, signore.

GIACO: (*Getting into the tub, he yells.*) This is scalding oil! (*Noise. Hubbub*) No—no more hot water—no!

(*Giovanna enters.*)

GIOVANNA: For shame, such noise! Stop making such a madhouse!

GIACO: Oh, excellent! Now the ladies come to ogle me in my tub! Would you like to wash my appendages, Contessa?

GIOVANNA: I have no such interest. Tailor—get his measurements.

GIACO: Stop! Come at me with that measuring rod while I'm stark and I'll impale you on the figurehead of my craft!

GIOVANNA: You—take his cloak. You—his linens—get his dimensions. Signor Vendiero, can you arrange for a scepter? Something like Alcestor's— longer, I think. (*To Giaco*) How tall are you?

GIACO: Shall I stand so you can take my measure, signora?

GIOVANNA: (*Dryly*) I have already taken your measure . . . Guess him at what you will. The rest of you, begone.

(*They go. Giovanna appraisingly stares at Giaco. For the first time, he is embarrassed. But, a smiling recovery:*)

GIACO: Would you care to scrub my back?

GIOVANNA: (*She has come to a resolution*) If we are to go on together you must accept . . . conditions. First: Recognize and accept—without cavil or complaint—

GIACO: Cavil or complaint—a tidy phrase.

GIOVANNA: —that all authority is mine.

GIACO: I accept.

GIOVANNA: You accepted too easily. You may rue it.

GIACO: Did I have an alternative?

GIOVANNA: No.

GIACO: (*With a complacent smile*) Then I'll not rue it.

GIOVANNA: Damn! If only once you'd not try to be brighter than I!

GIACO: If that's the second condition, it's more difficult. But why does it bother you, since you are convinced that you're the brighter one?

GIOVANNA: Shall we proceed? As we do not want it noised about that you have been a petty quack, we must get rid of this. (*She indicates his bottles and boxes.*) No more tricksy-trancy bottles, sleight-of-hand, no more hocus pocus. If you accept, I'll throw this rubbish into the canal.

GIACO: It's not rubbish. I've worked long hours on those things.

GIOVANNA: Do you accept?

GIACO: (*With difficulty*) I accept.

(*She throws things out the window, into the canal. He is pained. When she gets to the homunculus bottle:*)

GIACO: Wait! Not that one!

GIOVANNA: . . . What is it?

GIACO: It's my little man.

GIOVANNA: Why, it's a homunculus! How disgusting!

GIACO: Not at all—he's beautiful! He has all his parts, that's more than most of us can say. No—please—don't throw him away!

(*She tosses it to him. It falls in the tub. He pulls it out, wipes it dry.*)

GIOVANNA: Now, about your name. You are no longer Giacomo Levanto.

GIACO: Who am I, then?

GIOVANNA: Domenico di Mastromare.

GIACO: Hm. The Count Domenico di Mastromare. How it rolls!

GIOVANNA: I did not say Count.

GIACO: Please . . . Count?

GIOVANNA: (*A reserved smile*) Count. You are the son of the Marchese's best friend. And you have recently arrived from Tuscany.

GIACO: Where I was rich, I hope.

GIOVANNA: You are still rich.

GIACO: Excellent. By the way, does such a count really exist?

GIOVANNA: No.

GIACO: From now on, he will.

GIOVANNA: I must tell you one little idiosyncrasy of Count Mastromare. He dabbles in alchemy.

GIACO: What? Back to that again?

GIOVANNA: With a difference.

GIACO: You mean Count Mastromare—? No! He's found the way to turn cheap metal into gold?

GIOVANNA: Exactly.

GIACO: Oh, bravo for me! Oh, I do thank you—what a part you've given me to play! (*Caught in it*) I—Count Mastromare—I have found the secret! What the world is made of—the prima materia—I've found it! The water and fire of life—I have held them in my hand—*and I have made them one*!

GIOVANNA: What a strange phenomenon you are. You've scarcely been introduced to this new role and already you're lost in it.

GIACO: Lost?—not at all. Found, perhaps.

GIOVANNA: I'll arrange a meeting with Signor Orso Tadeo. And if he approves of you—

GIACO: Someone else to approve of me? Why? Who is he?

GIOVANNA: He is a pawnbroker. He will be our partner in this. And if Tadeo approves of you, you will then hear the entire plan . . . Which brings me to my last condition.

GIACO: Yes?

GIOVANNA: The plan you will hear is mine. I have been at work on it a long time. Mine! You're not to tamper with it. No criticism, no advice. You're not to derogate it in any way.

GIACO: May I admire it?

GIOVANNA: Without comment, yes.

GIACO: Perhaps I should pretend Count Mastromare is a mute.

GIOVANNA: I'm deadly serious.

GIACO: So am I. If you don't avail yourself of what talents I have, it makes more sense that I be altogether dumb.

GIOVANNA: I told you not to accept my conditions too quickly. If you would care to retreat—

GIACO: No. I merely ask why you make this foolish demand. I'll not be good to you silent. I'm not sure I can even *be* silent. I'm not accustomed— (*Maddened by his immobility in the tub*) Please—would you hand me something to wrap around myself—I must get out of this damnable ship! (*As she doesn't move*) Look here, Giovanna—I won't talk to you at this disadvantage! If you don't hand me a towel, I'll stand up as I am—and we'll see who *then* has the advantage!

GIOVANNA: (*With a smile*) Do you think you will have it?

GIACO: If you doubt it—I stand! Now I count to three. One— (*She hands him the towel. He drapes it around himself and stands with as much dignity as he can.*) I'm aware I'm still at a disadvantage. A man caparisoned in a towel—! You're not serious, are you? You don't intend me to be silent when I meet Tadeo, do you?

GIOVANNA: Yes, I do.

GIACO: Why? Why do this to me? Talking, as you must realize, is what I *do.* I don't carve a statue, I don't build a bridge—I *talk!* It's how I live. Why, with words I don't need a gun to shoot a bird—I can *talk* it down! But if you tie my tongue—! (*Silence. He has gotten nowhere*) Why do you want to do it? Is it a test? Why?

GIOVANNA: Do you accept the condition?

GIACO: Why are you apprehensive of me, Giovanna? I've done nothing to hurt you. On the contrary, I've only told you how beautiful you are. Why are you alarmed?

GIOVANNA: I am not.

GIACO: (*He studies her. Then:*) What is this ice-blue-blooded affair you're having with this white-browed Marchese?

GIOVANNA: You're making it easy for me to send you packing.

GIACO: Why should it be difficult?—it's entirely within your choice. What's that gold wedding ring?

GIOVANNA: Real gold.

GIACO: Real wedding?

GIOVANNA: Yes.

GIACO: I think not. You turned it around. It has a stone in it. (*He goes to her and grabs her hand*)

GIOVANNA: Stop it—let me go.

GIACO: A stone, I said. A bright emerald—a fine one, I'm sure. Why were you at such pains to lie about being married?

GIOVANNA: I did not lie! I *have* been married! My husband is dead!

GIACO: Then why at such pains to tell the *truth* about being married? To show you're a woman? I know you are! A woman?—my God, you're a queen! Must you be a king?

(*The insult flicks her raw. She tries to hide it, to maintain a smiling calm. She's not successful.*)

GIOVANNA: You mean to cut deeply with your insults, but I must tell you: you only chafe my skin. If you are shameless in saying you are nothing, I'm shameless too: I mean to be everything. I've been nothing and seen the loss of two duchies. My father was a rank romantic. My brothers were embroiderers of dreams, fritterers and peepers. Bit by bit, they sold everything. And when they had nothing left to sell—

GIACO: They sold you.

GIOVANNA: On the marriage block—hail, all bidders! My husband was the Count Felice di Participazio. He was six years older than my father. But rich. And when my foul-smelling diseased old husband died—when my *rich* husband died . . .

GIACO: He was not rich at all.

GIOVANNA: His palazzo, not his own—his furnishings, left in trust to his grown children. Never—mark it, never in the lifetime of my father or my husband was I told anything! My advice was never solicited. I was held accountable for nothing—except their funerals, of which I was in complete charge . . . And the wind never carries the scent of gladiolus that I do not recall the thick sweet odor of dying old men.

GIACO: What is the odor of the Marchese? (*As she turns angrily to him*) Ah, did I chafe your skin again?

GIOVANNA: There's a difference here.

GIACO: You're in complete charge.

GIOVANNA: While he is alive.

GIACO: And is he?

GIOVANNA: He's as alive as you are!

GIACO: Not if he lets you call all the turns.

GIOVANNA: *He lets me because he knows I need to do it! I would die if I couldn't!*

(*There is such desperation in it that it quickens his curiosity and his sympathy. He capitulates to her need.*)

GIACO: When I meet Tadeo, I will do my best to hold my tongue.

GIOVANNA: (*All defenses momentarily down*) Thank you, oh thank you! I'll make it up to you! (*Pulling herself to dignity*) Thank you, Count di Mastromare.

(*She goes. He is still. The lights fade. When they come up again, we are in the Marchese's library. The Marchese is with Orso Tadeo, a nervous, choleric middle-aged man, always paranoiacally certain he is being cheated.*)

TADEO: She promised! I distinctly recall the Contessa promised to choose a man of some nobility.

FABIO: No, Signor Tadeo. Only a man that *seemed* of the nobility.

TADEO: Seemed? Wouldn't you, a Marchese, be the first to say that people will not be deceived by *false* nobility?

(*Giovanna enters.*)

GIOVANNA: What people, Signor Tadeo?

TADEO: (*Angrily*) I catch your drift, Contessa. You mean tradesmen like myself—we can be deceived, but you nobles—never! Well, let me remind you I'm as good a judge of the real article as you are. I've bought your art works cheap and sold them dear. So if you think you can deceive me—

GIOVANNA: (*Mollifyingly*) It is not *you* we want to deceive, Signor Tadeo—you are our partner. It is everybody else.

TADEO: But a rat out of a sewer, a thief—!

GIOVANNA: If we weren't sure of him, do you imagine we would risk our names—

TADEO: (*With elaborate sarcasm*) I have a name too, Contessa. And the name of a well-known tradesman has *nearly* the value of a dusty Marchese.

FABIO: (*Wryly*) Oh, more. In these days, more.

TADEO: In addition to which I risk my money.

GIOVANNA: Then you will not even see him?

TADEO: Yes, I will—but I tell you, I've lost my partiality to this affair! (*Giovanna opens the door and gestures*)

GIOVANNA: Signor Tadeo . . . the Count Domenico di Mastromare.

(*Giaco enters. He is the quintessence of Venetian elegance. Silk, satin, the powdered peruke, the mouche on whitened cheek, the jeweled staff. And on his face, the mask of bored disaffection. He enters one step and poses. Silence. Tadeo is puzzled by his splendiferous presence.*)

TADEO: Won't you step further into the room . . . signore.

GIACO: (*So delicate, so fatigued!*) You will forgive me. A headache. A dismal disaffection in the eyebrow.

TADEO: Nothing serious, I trust.

GIACO: Truly, I don't know. Brought on, I think by the—uh—overpopulation of the planet. Too many people—they press—they press in upon me. So if I may keep distance, sir . . . ?

TADEO: By all means. (*What to make of him?*) What name do they call you, sir?

GIACO: (*Too tired to say it*) Oh, dear. Do tell him my name.

GIOVANNA: We've already announced it. The Count Domenico di Mastromare.

TADEO: (*To Giaco*) You mean you have not learned to say your new name?

GIACO: Bedeviled heaven, will this small fellow badger me? Must I address myself to him?

(*An impasse. Tadeo is bewildered. To Giovanna:*)

TADEO: You say this man came from a . . . culvert? I—uh—?

GIOVANNA: (*Starting to enjoy it*) What is it you do not understand, Tadeo?

TADEO: I confess he's not what I expected. But I certainly will not go a step further if he doesn't answer questions.

GIACO: (*To Fabio, wearily*) What does the creature want?

TADEO: The Contessa and the Marchese—they tell me, being an alchemist, you are a judge of gold. Would you mind a test, signore?

(*Giaco makes a wide, lazy gesture. Frustrated, Tadeo turns to Giovanna.*)

When he makes that gesture, does he mean yes or no?

GIOVANNA: I think yes.

TADEO: I hand you my snuff box. Would you appraise it, please? Only roughly, of course. How much alloy, sir, and how much gold?

(*Giaco takes an indolent step into the room. Then he stops, forcing the pawnbroker to go the rest of the distance. Tadeo hands him the snuff box. Giaco wearily opens it, helps himself to a pinch of Tadeo's snuff. As he brings it half way to his nose—a painful grimace—the snuff is not exquisite. He sets down Tadeo's snuff box, wipes his hand and finds his own box. His own snuff is poignantly to his liking. One nostril, followed by the daintiest sneeze; the other nostril, again the kittenish sneeze. With a minor flourish he snaps his own box shut and pockets it. Kerchief from sleeve, preciously brought to nose; then he wipes sleeve and jabot. Now ready for the appraisal of Tadeo's snuff box, he picks it up, studies it at arm's length, slowly bringing it to his squinting eye. No judgment yet. With lorgnette, he studies the box. He snaps at it with fingernail, ticks it lightly against his teeth, carries it to the light, haws his breath against it, shines it on his cuff, studies the glow of it. At last he breaks his concentration on the object by looking at the others with a beguiling smile. He holds the box in the air as if to say: behold! Then, with a lazily contemptuous flick of the wrist, he tosses the box out the window. Junk!*)

FABIO & GIOVANNA: Oh no! . . . Count Mastromare!

(*Only Tadeo is not shocked; he admires*)

TADEO: No, no—he is quite right. Gilded brass—worthless! You're an excellent judge of gold. But not of snuff.

GIACO: Oh, but I am, sir! I did not misjudge your snuff. An exquisite blend. But it was tainted, sir, by being in a brazen box. Fine snuff, sir, wants fine gold.

TADEO: (*With a loud, fatuous laugh*) Magnificent! Oh, Contessa, what a delicious joke! An alley thief indeed—you think I can't identify nobility when I'm in the presence of it? This is the true nobility—just as you promised—and I congratulate you—I congratulate us all! (*With a deep* *deferential bow*) Count di Mastromare, sir—your servant, sir. Now, sir—our plan—it is most diabolically sweet, don't you think?

GIACO: Your plan? I have not heard it, signore.

GIOVANNA: I promised secrecy, Tadeo.

TADEO: Tell him! Tell the count everything!

GIOVANNA: Very well—the plan . . . It will be given out to Venice that the Marchese da Gritti Selvo is entertaining as a guest the son of his dear friend, the Count Domenico di Mastromare. You are a man of bountiful good fortune. You will publicly demonstrate this by the most extravagant largesse. Sumptuous entertainments, music and lanterns on the water, lavish gifts to servants, tradesmen, gondoliers.

TADEO: Excuse me. The money will be advanced by me. So if you can make it *appear* to be lavish without being preposterous about it—

GIOVANNA: Signor Tadeo, please.

TADEO: Oh, do not think I will stint! . . . Please go on.

GIOVANNA: The question will inevitably go up: In these days when nobility is pigeon-poor, where did Mastromare get his money?

TADEO: Conflicting stories. He trades in spices of the Orient—

GIOVANNA: —emerald mines in Asia Minor—

FABIO: —the opium trade—

TADEO: Mystery—all mystery!

GIOVANNA: At last—when the mystification is the itch of everyone—I give the signal. Thereupon, in a public place, you and the Marchese engage in a clamorous quarrel. He violently accuses you of cheating him.

TADEO: (*Giggling*) This is the most devilishly ingenious part! (*To Giovanna*) Tell him—tell him how!

GIOVANNA: You cheated him, he says, by buying one of his paintings—and paying him with false gold! . . . You're arrested as a counterfeiter, and thrown into the ducal prison. At the trial, the Marchese testifies. You are an alchemist, he says. The gold you gave him is false—and of your own making. You are called to your own defense and—! You confess! Everything he has said of you is true. You are *indeed* an alchemist. You did make the gold. All true—*except*—

TADEO: Ah—*except*! Listen to this!

GIOVANNA: Except that the metal he calls false—is true gold!

TADEO: True gold! *And you yourself made it*!

GIOVANNA: The metal is brought forth as evidence. Is it true gold or false? The experts come thronging in. Goldsmiths, jewelers, minters. And since the evidence was in the first place the very reputable twenty-four karat gold of our own Signor Tadeo, the testimony is unanimous. Gold!

TADEO: True gold! Pure gold!

FABIO: And you—ostensibly—made it.

GIOVANNA: You are acquitted . . . *And you leave the courtroom a man whom the very Tribunal of Venice has approved as an alchemist who makes pure gold*!

TADEO: Imagine the hue and cry! *You make gold*! The Tribunal has said so! Every merchant, every Rialto tradesman wants to buy it from you—cheap!

GIOVANNA: You thereupon announce you'll sell a limited supply—ten million ducats worth of gold—

TADEO: —at the bargain price of *five*!

GIOVANNA: And these five million are to be paid to you in gems and precious stones. Your so-called gold is sealed in boxes that no tradesman is permitted to open. He either buys or not. They turn over their gems to you—and you, to us. That same night we pay you one hundred thousand ducats—and you depart.

TADEO: Brilliant! Isn't it brilliant?

FABIO: The aspect I like most—! Tell him, Giovanna.

GIOVANNA: After your flight, the Rialto will scream with the agony of a wounded purse. And the Marchese will have been the man who cried warning against the thief. Cried warning—and went unheeded. Was not even vindicated by his own Tribunal!

FABIO: What a revenge!

TADEO: Magnificent? Don't you think it's magnificent?

(*Giaco, under orders to be silent, is silent.*)

GIOVANNA: Quite clearly, he's impressed. Let's proceed.

TADEO: No, not so fast. If the Count has reservations—

GIOVANNA: He would have mentioned them.

TADEO: Is there some reason we should not hear from him?

GIOVANNA: (*Cornered*) . . . Go ahead, Count Mastromare.

GIACO: Go ahead and what, Contessa?

GIOVANNA: . . . Speak.

GIACO: Speak? (*Silence*) Do you insist?

GIOVANNA: . . . Yes.

TADEO: (*Impatiently*) Well—well? What do you think of it?

GIACO: . . . I am shocked.

GIOVANNA, FABIO & TADEO: What? . . . What does he mean? . . . What do you say, sir?

GIACO: I said I am shocked! This scheme is quite against the law!

GIOVANNA: This is not a time for jest, signore.

GIACO: Shocked at all of you—to plot such an unlawful hoax as this! . . . Besides, it will not work.

GIOVANNA: You will let us worry about that.

GIACO: You? You're amateurs! A great hoax is great art! And you are bungling dilettantes!

GIOVANNA: You promised not to interfere!

TADEO: (*To Giaco*) No—speak! I liked what you said—great hoax, great art!

GIACO: Greatest art of all, my friend. For it deals with what men believe in. And if you want them to *believe*, you do not perpetrate a hoax with lies, but with the truth!

FABIO: A hoax with truth?

GIACO: How, then—with a boxful of falsehood? Who will give his gems and precious stones for it? I ask you, signori, is there a single jeweler in Venice who will surrender the measliest trinket for gold in a box he is not allowed to open?

FABIO: I think it was the Contessa's hope that the merchants would be so bedazzled by your court trial—

GIACO: What will dazzle a jeweler? Only what he sees in the loup he puts in his eye! And if I can detect false gold *without* a glass, what can he do *with* one?

TADEO: (*Starting to depart*) Too bad . . . The plan is worthless.

GIACO: (*Quietly at first; then, warming to it*) My dear friends, if we are to perpetrate a superb swindle, it dare not lack—integrity. It must be simple and virtuous, like a love lyric. If there are fools in it, *we* must seem to be the fools. If there are scoundrels, they—whoever they may be—*they* must be the scoundrels! *They* must swindle *us*! (*An instant. Then, quietly:*) We do not sell the gold . . . we buy it!

TADEO: I'm afraid I do not understand. Buy brass, buy lead?

GIACO: No. Buy real gold. Cheap. Listen now. The trial is over. I, the alchemist, am free. Free to turn lead into real gold. And I can do it—the court has said so! Now that I have been vindicated, what will I do? Everybody is dying to know the answer: Will I make vast quantities of gold? Will I flood the Rialto with it? The goldsmiths begin to tremble, the minterers cannot sleep. What will the alchemist do? At last—in a rage because I cannot make my gold in secret anymore—I announce myself. "To hell with you! I am going to make illimitable quantities of the precious stuff!" The instant I say this—

TADEO: —the price of gold goes down!

GIACO: Precisely!

TADEO: And we buy!

GIACO: Buy, yes, buy! For practically nothing! Buy!

TADEO: Buy all that we can carry!

GIACO: Without breaking a single law!

TADEO: Dear sir, I kiss your hand—I kiss your most astonishing head! We will go forward with this—forward! Yes, Marchese?

FABIO: I am willing.

TADEO: Oh, indeed, willing! There's only one thing. I will advance all the moneys, provided you—you, Count Mastromare—are in full charge of the entire enterprise.

(*There is a taut silence.*)

GIACO: (*Hiding the mixed pleasure*) You do me too much honor, sir. But you must ask—them.

TADEO: But I insist. Have you an objection, Marchese?

FABIO: (*Smiling obliquely*) It is her plan. You must consult the Contessa.

TADEO: Have you an objection, Contessa?

GIOVANNA: (*Tight-lipped*) . . . None.

TADEO: Splendid, splendid! We are happily begun! (*To Giaco*) Your credits with me begin whenever you say. When, Contessa? Or should I ask Count Mastromare? When, sir?

GIACO: May I attend you tomorrow morning, then?

TADEO: Fine—most excellent. Good day, Contessa. Your servant, sirs. Happily begun!

FABIO: I will see you to the balcony, signore.

(*Fabio goes with Tadeo. Stillness between Giovanna and Giaco. They do not look at one another. He knows she's in a rage. He tries to lighten the mood.*)

GIACO: Well, as our friend Tadeo says, we are happily begun. (*Silences, one after another*) Ah, yes, you do agree. I was afraid you mightn't . . . I wasn't pretending about the headache—this wig's too tight. We'll have it eased a little, yes? Please see to it.

(*He takes off his wig and carries it to her. She ignores it icily. He bows a little and places the wig on a chair.*) Come now, you're not going to be peevish because I ventured an opinion. I resisted saying a word—remember that—I did resist. And you finally did give your permission. You did, you know . . . Giovanna . . . You're not going to be tedious on a small point, are you?

(*With slow deliberation she goes to the bell and rings. She speaks quietly.*)

GIOVANNA: You come from Sicily, do you not?

GIACO: Sicily? Why? Is it apropos?

GIOVANNA: I hear—in Sicily—when one is betrayed—

GIACO: I did not betray you, Giovanna.

GIOVANNA: —one goes to vengeance. Vendetta. Strangulations. Knives.

GIACO: What betrayal? Does authority mean so much you can't stand it being taken away from you for even one instant? I give it back!

GIOVANNA: (*Still icily pursuing her course*) If you Sicilians think you know something of vengeance, let me show you the Venetian kind.

(*The door opens and Carla appears*) Send Orfeo and Marco to me, please. (*To Giaco*) Now, what were we saying? Ah yes, Venetian vengeance. Take the Marchese. A mildly mannered man. And yet . . . the first night I spent in his bedchamber he caught a footman gazing across the balcony. Next day, the man was quietly spirited back to his home in Campalto, his eyes gouged out.

GIACO: Perhaps the footman didn't mind. A fair exchange for what he saw.

GIOVANNA: In Venice, eavesdroppers have their ears cut off. A prostitute is tied in bed with a poisonous snake. Pickpockets, we hack off their fingers, joint by joint.

GIACO: (*With an expansive smile*) So, then!—since it was my tongue that offended you . . .

(*Orfeo and Marco enter. Giovanna addresses them quietly.*)

GIOVANNA: Cut out his tongue.

GIACO: (*An instant. He laughs*) Oh, Giovanna, your humor is beyond compare! (*To Orfeo and Marco*) You hear what your mistress says—come, cut my tongue out.

(*He sees the men impassively unsheathe their stilettos. Giaco's laugh turns hollower.*)

GIACO: Giovanna, these baboons—they're taking you in earnest. (*As he sees them advancing*) Stay away, you monsters! Giovanna, they lack your playfulness—tell them you're joking—call them off! (*As they grab him*) They'll muss my satin coat! Let me go, you lizard heads! Giovanna, please! Giovanna, you cannot mean—?! Giovanna, I promise—never again—never against your wishes! On my knees, Giovanna!

GIOVANNA: On your knees, then! Let him down! *Your knees!*

(*They release him, and he kneels. She gestures the men away. They are alone. Giaco is trying as always to turn this into jest, but he is unnerved. Giovanna speaks low:*) Get up.

(*He continues to smile, but does not move. Suddenly all trace of the smile disappears. In a spasm, he twists his head away from her.*) I said get up!

GIACO: (*Almost to himself*) No, not yet. Let me first try to . . . understand . . . a little. Surely, you did not intend such violence. Surely, I did not *believe* you intended it . . . Or did you, Giovanna? . . . No, not even in Venice . . . Then, if I didn't believe it, what brought me to my knees? What was the cruel emanation from you . . . ? (*He recovers his smile, but it is bitter.*) Well, Giovanna, you have really humbled me! You couldn't have done it better had you indeed cut out my tongue!

GIOVANNA: (*Suddenly alarmed by what she has done, her tone becomes even sharper*) It was a jest—get up. You did not think—? It was a jest!

GIACO: . . . Was it?

GIOVANNA: Get up! (*Raging*) In future, whatever your position with Tadeo, you'll know what your position is with me!

GIACO: Yes, Giovanna—my position with you is in genuflection.

GIOVANNA: I said get up! (*He gets up slowly. She eases.*) I'm sorry to have brought you so low in your own esteem.

GIACO: I'm sorry too, milady.

GIOVANNA: Don't call me milady. It's a foreign affectation. I don't like it.

GIACO: I am sorry.

GIOVANNA: (*Trying to laugh*) You braggarts, you deflate so easily! There you are—flags flying on your proud pavilions! But take one stake away, and all the fancy colors come flopping around your ears! Nothing left to be proud of!

GIACO: At the moment, not much left.

GIOVANNA: Then let me tell you a number of things you have a right to be proud of. Not to puff you up again, but fair is fair. You were excellent with Tadeo—until you broke your promise to me—excellent! The way you walked, the way you simpered with a frozen lip—quite the magnifico! Superb!

GIACO: (*The compliments distress him*) Thank you.

GIOVANNA: And larger, I think, in your new clothes. More breadth of shoulder. You could stand high, it seems, to anyone! Especially to a woman.

GIACO: Is knee high tall enough, milady?

GIOVANNA: (*Stung*) Will you sulk and bear grudges?

GIACO: Forgive me, milady.

GIOVANNA: Forgive? Yes—each other. Come . . . kiss my hand.
(*He bends over her hand; doesn't kiss it*) You did not kiss my hand, Mastromare . . . Forget the hand. You may kiss me.

GIACO: No, milady.

GIOVANNA: You said I was beautiful. Did you not mean it?

GIACO: I did, milady.

GIOVANNA: And yet you do not want me?

GIACO: You could be a kitchen hag and I might want you. Or beautiful, and I might not.

GIOVANNA: Come here.

GIACO: You bitch!

GIOVANNA: I asked you to come here.

GIACO: Why now? You bitch, why now, when I'm still down there—when I'm a most degraded half man on my knees—*why now*?

GIOVANNA: Very well. I'll choose another time.

GIACO: (*Enraged*) You'll choose? Will it not occur to you to let it happen as it will—between us—so that we can both imagine we have come an equal distance to each other?

GIOVANNA: Come, now. In my station, there's a protocol.

GIACO: Protocol? Are you so desperate that you fall back on protocol?

GIOVANNA: How dare you!

GIACO: Are you so unhappy?

GIOVANNA: How dare you pity me!

GIACO: Did I cut you? Here, Giovanna!
(*He reaches into his sleeve and tosses her his handkerchief. She lets it fall to the floor, and lashes at him in rage.*)

GIOVANNA: I will not be pitied, do you understand? Not by you! You!—look beneath the clothes I gave you and sniff behind the scent I sprayed on you, and remember your rags and your culvert stench—and do not pity me!
(*A noise in the corridor. Giovanna is so unnerved this enrages her further. Giaco retrieves his handkerchief as she rushes to the door.*) What is that noise? Carla! Alcestor!
(*We hear Nico's voice singing drunkenly.*)

CARLA'S VOICE: No—please, sir—you cannot go in there!
(*Carla enters, closes door quickly*)

GIOVANNA: What is the disturbance?

CARLA: His friend, Contessa—the friar. He's been storming the corridors—looking for the signore.

(*Giaco makes a movement to the door. Giovanna's voice stops him.*)

GIOVANNA: Wait! Carla, send him here.

(*Carla goes out. Giovanna faces Giaco squarely. She is now in command again, challenging:*) Now—you and I—we shall see.

GIACO: See what, Giovanna?

GIOVANNA: When the old man comes in, you are to send him away.

GIACO: Send him away? Where?

GIOVANNA: Anywhere—so he'll no longer be a bother to you.

GIACO: He's no bother to me, Giovanna.

GIOVANNA: If a drunken, loose-mouthed old man is a bother to our enterprise, I should think you'd consider him a bother to *you*.

GIACO: I'll answer for him.

GIOVANNA: You're to send the man away.

GIACO: Giovanna—please—I am attached to him. And he to me. He thinks he looks after me. Giovanna, it would be too unkind—the old man loves me!

(*She is absolutely still*) I will not do it, Giovanna!

(*The drunken voice of Nico, singing. Carla appears, lets the friar in and departs. Nico is happy drunk and calling Giaco's name. He sees Giovanna and the elegantly dressed Giaco, and does not recognize his friend.*)

NICO: Oh, nobility! The pretty little girl made a mistake. She said I'd find my friend Giaco Levanto here. Ho, girl—nobody here but nobility! Arrivederci, nobility!

(*Giaco and Giovanna are still. Nico stumbles to the door. As he fumbles with a knob, a gold cup falls out of his capacious clothes. He giggles to hide his embarrassment.*) This thing—I was—it looked so beautiful—I thought I'd borrow it for my friend to look at. Well—here—maybe you'll see him before I do.

(*He crosses back to the table and sets the cup on it as Giovanna stares at the stone-still Giaco. The look on her face says I-told-you-so. Nico glances sheepishly from one to the other.*) If you see him—(*To Giaco*) Why, he has something of your glance. But not your fashion. Would you like to hear a song? (*Singing loudly*) There were two maidens in a wood, one was pretty and one was good. Which one couldn't and which one could? The good one wouldn't, but when she would—

GIACO: (*Blurting. Rough, not hurtful*) That's enough.

NICO: That voice—! Is it—? *Giaco*! (*Laughing, crying with drunken joy*) Oh, my friend! Oh, my friend Giaco! All frilled and fancied! Oh Giaco, what good luck are you dressed in? Oh, my dear Giaco!

GIOVANNA: He is not Giaco.

NICO: (*In a cascade of laughter*) Not Giaco? I'd know him anywhere!

GIOVANNA: (*To Giaco*) Tell him.

NICO: Giaco—?

GIACO: (*Gently*) Take your hands off, old man. I'm not Giaco. I am the Count di Mastromare.

(*It is as if Nico has sobered. He understands that this is Giaco, and he is not wanted.*)

NICO: Not Giaco . . . ? Excuse me . . . Count . . . signore . . . (*With drunken self-respect*) Addio, signora. (*To Giaco*) You, signore, if you see my friend Giaco . . . Excuse me.

(*He goes. Silence. Giaco is in pain.*)

GIOVANNA: That was well done . . . Please—don't twist your face like that. It can't have been so painful. In the kind of life you've led, I'm certain you've been called upon to do things far worse than that.

GIACO: (*A murmur*) Yes . . . far worse . . . yes.

GIOVANNA: (*Trying to lighten the moment*) By the way, I noticed a moment ago that your left hand . . . I'm sure you thought you had cleansed it well. But underneath the nails—I still see a little grime.

(*Reflexively he closes his fingers in a fist. He cries out in self-loathing:*)

GIACO: Oh, God! (*Under control again*) I'm sorry, milady. (*Correcting himself*) Signora.

GIOVANNA: See you scrub yourself.

GIACO: Indeed, yes. Your servant, signora.

(*Slowly, watching her with deliberation, he goes down on his knees again. She starts violently.*)

GIOVANNA: Levanto—get up! You will not do that again! Get up! You will not mock me on your knees again!—you hear me?—not again!

GIACO: (*Quietly, mordantly*) No, signora—this is the last time. Nico says a man must take to his knees only three times in his life. Once to his lady, once to his liege, and once to his God. You have now used up two of my three genuflections. I have none left for you—unless you should demand the one for God. But perhaps, since I have never knelt to Him, I'll give it to you—

GIOVANNA: (*Violently*) Get up! You were right about yourself! Nothing! All you can do is talk! Deprive you of your tongue and you are nothing!

(*Quickly, almost in rout, she leaves. He still does not arise. His head falls on his breast in self-revulsion. When he lifts his head again, his eyes are filled with tears of pain and shame.*)

GIACO: Nothing! I am nothing!

(*The lights fade. In the darkness, we hear a voice that is Giovanna's, yet not Giovanna's. As the light comes up we see Signor Colignari, a pompous ventriloquist.*)

COLIGNARI: I may look like Colignari, but I am actually the Contessa di Savoia di Participazio.

(*There is laughter as the lights come up, a little at a time, to reveal that we are at a reception in the palazzo. Most of the guests have departed; the festivity is drawing to a close. Galbaio remains. So do Ziani and Celsi, with their overdressed wives. Each of the ladies carries a jeweled bird mask at the end of a stick. Tadeo is nervous and tipsy. Giaco is absent. Giovanna and Fabio try to hold the reception together with the diversions of Colignari.*)

CELSI: (*To the ventriloquist*) You do her voice precisely.

GIOVANNA: Yes—it is my voice to the natural.

COLIGNARI: (*In her voice*) Yes, it is my voice to the natural.

ZIANI: Miraculous, sir! How can you do such a likeness?

TADEO: It's nothing. Called ventriloquism. Nothing but a trick.

COLIGNARI: (*In dudgeon*) A trick, sir? Nothing but a trick?

TADEO: Well, if it's not, then what the devil is it?

COLIGNARI: (*Imitating Tadeo, his voice in the air*) Well, if it's not, then what the devil is it?

(*More laughter, to Tadeo's discomfiture. Galbaio, in his blood red Tribunal robe, steps forward. The austerity of his smile, his dark certitude cast a pall on the gaiety.*)

GALBAIO: Well done, Signor Colignari. Now, sir, can you do the voice of the Count di Mastromare?

COLIGNARI: I have just arrived in Venice, signore—I have not yet had the pleasure to meet him.

GALBAIO: (*Narrowly*) Nor are you likely, this afternoon. I was hoping, since we cannot have *him* at his own reception, we might have some other— uh—doubtful emanation of him.

GIOVANNA: Did you say doubtful, signore?

GALBAIO: (*Has he trapped her?*) A doubtful *voice*, Contessa. Did you think I meant a doubtful man?

GIOVANNA: We've all been witnesses to his charms, haven't we, ladies? Can there be a doubt he is a man?

(*She laughs; the others join her. She has won the point. But Galbaio is not put down.*)

GALBAIO: Mightn't there be some other uncertainties?

FABIO: (*With seeming good humor*) Signor Galbaio is constantly beset with uncertainty.

GALBAIO: True. Nothing is ever what it seems. Someone asked me, "Why do members of the Black Tribunal wear red instead of black?"

FABIO: And your answer, sir?

GALBAIO: It's all blood, signore. Some red, some black. What color is Mastromare's? Blue, did you say?

FABIO: You seem in doubt. Would you like to see for yourself?

GALBAIO: (*Pretending to laugh*) Oh, no indeed! I would not tap him for a drop of it!

TADEO: You have tapped him for other things.

GALBAIO: I beg your pardon.

TADEO: He is your best customer. He pays you any prices you ask.

GALBAIO: You think my prices are too high?

GIOVANNA: (*Trying to head off a confrontation*) No, not at all.

TADEO: They're exorbitant! You sold him a garnet and emerald ring—

GALBAIO: (*With a tight smile*)—which seems worth far more than he paid for it, now that the Contessa's finger graces it.

TADEO: All of you—extortionate! Ziani—three thousand for a mantle that doesn't even fit him!

ZIANI: Why does this upset *you*, Tadeo?

GALBAIO: Yes, why? The way you shriek every time he spends a ducat, one would think it issues from your own pocket.

TADEO: (*Alarmed*) Oh no, it doesn't!

GIOVANNA: (*Raising her voice to cover for Tadeo*) Signore, signori—ladies of Venice—worthies of the Rialto—a token—a small golden token from the Count Domenico di Mastromare! "If I should be delayed," he said, "give each one my regrets and add this inconsequential portrait of myself!"

(*She holds up a gold ducat. As she distributes them from a jewel box, the guests laugh and dither with delight.*)

GUESTS: Yes, his face! . . . A minted portrait of him . . . It's the Count himself—look, look!

ZIANI: Is money the best portrait of him?

GIOVANNA: (*A dig at Galbaio*) Yes, the only certainty. True, Signor Galbaio?

GALBAIO: Where did he have them minted, may I ask?

FABIO: Who knows? Somewhere privately, I suppose.

WOMEN: (*Excited*) And is it gold? . . . Is it truly gold?

FABIO: (*Studiedly casual*) Oh, I would not think so.

GALBAIO: (*Watching him closely*) You think not, Marchese?
(*Galbaio moves to a table. He bounces the ducat on it. They watch him alertly.*) The ring is true. Marchese, you said this wasn't gold. Why, signore?

FABIO: (*Carefully*) Well, I can't imagine such largesse.

GALBAIO: Nor can I. In fact, I miss entirely the point of this occasion.

GIOVANNA: The point, signore?

GALBAIO: Yes. Since when do you invite tradesmen to this house? I could pass you ten times on the Rialto Bridge, and carry my head on a walking staff—and you would not notice me. And suddenly—here I am—your guest.

GIOVANNA: Not my guest—Mastromare's.

GALBAIO: Why? What do I want of him, or he of me? And what does this ducat mean? That he can fling his money away?—we know that. Where does it come from? And if we are his guests, where is he?

GIOVANNA: You ask prickly questions, signore.

FABIO: Signor Galbaio is a new member of the Tribunal. He is practicing the art of interrogation.

GALBAIO: I hadn't thought of it as a matter for the Tribunal. But you may be right—where there's mystery there may be misdemeanor . . . Well, anyway, it has been pleasant.

GIOVANNA: You must come again.

GALBAIO: Must I, do you think? If I do, it will lose its uniqueness—the nobility receiving tradespeople. . . . Good day, Contessa—Marchese. I beg you—for me—thank your friend for this.

(Galbaio holds up the ducat and departs. The others leave with chattery farewells. When they have gone, Giovanna's composure cracks.)

GIOVANNA: That miserable man! That near-eyed miserable man!

FABIO: Why? He's mystified. That's what you wanted—to mystify them. Why are you angry at him? Or is it not Galbaio you are angry at? *(As Carla enters)* The Count—has he come in yet?

CARLA: No, Marchese.

(Carla lifts a small table and takes it away)

TADEO: That Galbaio—he frightens me. We'd better do it—now!

GIOVANNA: Do what, Tadeo?

TADEO: As we planned. The Marchese has an altercation with Mastromare in a public place and then—arrest him!

GIOVANNA: Too soon—too hasty.

TADEO: Why? You don't need any more mystery than you've got.

FABIO: Quite right. The air is thick with questions. If we wait any longer, someone like Galbaio will find answers.

TADEO: And I don't want to risk any more money. Oh, the cost! The way that man scatters the ducats—!

FABIO: He overflows with the milk of human kindness.

TADEO: My milk.

GIOVANNA: *(Annoyed)* Which you were at no great pain to hide from Galbaio.

TADEO: *(Near tears)* I *was* at great pain. Do you know how much Mastromare got from me this morning? We could live on it for years! If he were to take that money and run—
(He stops, realizing this calamity might now be happening. Fabio and Giovanna too are struck by its possibility. Tadeo lets out a wail.) No! You don't think he ran off with my money, do you? Oh no, he's not a thief, not a swindler. But what else is he? A filthy pickpurse, that's what he is!

GIACO: *(At the door, smiling sardonically)* Did someone call my name?

TADEO: *(Weeping with relief)* Count Mastromare! Oh, will you ever forgive my thinking—! Oh, my friend! I'm so happy to—! Welcome, sir, and welcome and welcome!

GIACO: Three welcomes. Was one from each of you? *(To Giovanna, ironically)* Or do you prefer to say a more cordial one for yourself?

TADEO: *(Tipsy and delirious with relief)* What a droll man! What a dear, endearing droll man!

GIACO: Wine makes you too kind. *(To Giovanna)* I hope you also had a cup.

GIOVANNA: A reception was given in your honor. Where were you?

GIACO: I saw the guests departing. Oh, the fat wives and the poor boats, listing. How can anyone look dreary in a gondola?
(Tadeo laughs. Giaco says, not unkindly:) Try to restrain yourself. I'll tell you when to laugh. *(To Giovanna)* I'm sorry about your reception.

GIOVANNA: You're not sorry. You told me this morning your absence would add a fillip of mystery, and when I disagreed, you disappeared. You do such a thing again—!

GIACO: Don't threaten me, Giovanna. Everything you've bade me do, I've done. Forsworn all pleasures—fortune telling, hocus pocus, sleight of hand. Now if you think you can force upon me your dreary turnip-headed friends—and oh, their pig-faced wives—! If you want to show off the silk purse you've made out of a sow's ear, for heaven's sake, don't show me off to the sows! (*To Tadeo, quietly*) You may laugh now.

TADEO: What a fellow! Oh, Mastromare, what a man you are!

GIACO: (*Depressed; with weary sarcasm*) Thank you. Your testimonial that I am a man is most conclusive. Now, if you'll excuse me . . . (*He starts out of the room*)

TADEO: Count Mastromare. May I see you in private, signore?

GIACO: No.

TADEO: Why not, sir?

GIACO: Because when we're alone, I feel sorry for you, and I forget that you are as contemptible as all of us. So now—in public—what do you want?

TADEO: (*Embarrassed*) I—what I want—it's a favor—(*A flash of inspiration*)—for a friend of mine.

GIACO: I doubt it. Well?

TADEO: He's a man of my age, sir—just married to a lady younger than himself.

GIACO: As young as your lady, Tadeo?

TADEO: Please—do not think I want it for myself.

GIACO: What is it you want?

TADEO: Well, a man like you—I imagine you have wonders at your fingertips.

GIACO: What sort of wonders?

TADEO: (*Perspiring*) Dear heaven, you're not making it easy. Love wonders, Mastromare. Please—he's wretchedly unhappy. When he looks at his young and beautiful wife, his heart leaps up.

GIACO: But nothing else.

TADEO: Precisely. He's tried everything, poor devil. Tonics, elixirs—all the cantharides to excite the skin and shoot hot torrents through the blood. Blister beetle, the oils of musk, the wines of Egypt! Nothing—it avails him nothing! Mastromare, I beg you—give him something magical!

GIACO: (*Sorry for the pathetic fool*) Unhappily, Tadeo, I've been forbidden the practice of the black arts.

TADEO: I'm sure, sir, in this case the Contessa will grant an exception. Dear Contessa, if you knew how deep the need—! Please, Mastromare, there must be some little aphrodisiac—!

GIACO: I have only one, sir.

TADEO: Yes—yes?

GIACO: There.

(*He points to Giovanna. She and Fabio go tense. Fabio recovers. With a smile.*)

FABIO: But how do you dispense it?

GIACO: (*To Tadeo*) It is the Marchese's opinion it is not dispensable.

TADEO: (*Humiliated, on the point of tears*) Well, you've succeeded in making sport of me.

GIACO: I'm sorry, Tadeo.

TADEO: You treat me abominably, sir!

GIACO: (*Ashamed*) No worse than I treat others and myself.

TADEO: And considering the sums of money I've entrusted you with—

GIACO: Quite right, Tadeo. And you certainly should call a halt. I think we've now finished our preliminary work. I for one am ready to proceed.

FABIO: You are so eager to be arrested?

GIACO: That *is* the next step, is it not?

TADEO: Good. Where will you have your altercation, you and he? When?

GIOVANNA: (*In scarcely a whisper*) When I say so.

TADEO: But we're all of like mind, Contessa. And remember, we agreed that whatever Mastromare says—

GIACO: (*Quietly*) Mastromare says we await the decisions of the Contessa. Your servant, signora. Signori.
(*He goes.*)

TADEO: No—come back! This is monstrous! Before I paid out my money, everybody listened to me! But now, the only attention paid to me is insult!

GIOVANNA: I regret that. But when you engaged yourself with us I guaranteed you'd be treated fairly in the matter of money. I did not promise we'd oblige you with any of the social graces.

TADEO: (*He controls his whining. With dignity:*) Your noble station promised it, Contessa.

FABIO: (*Muted*) Indeed it did, sir.

TADEO: Arrivederla, signora—Marchese. (*He goes out. After a heavy silence:*)

FABIO: How soiled we've become!

GIOVANNA: Did you think five million could be conceived immaculately?

FABIO: So be it—let's move onward. We're invited tonight to gamble at the Conte Gramani's table. As we leave the casino I shall quarrel with Mastromare, as prearranged. By midnight he'll be arrested.

GIOVANNA: Tonight? I said no.

FABIO: Giovanna, I've had my fill. Enough of Galbaio's prying nose and Tadeo's drunken drooling—

GIOVANNA: I need more time!

FABIO: —and enough of *him*! Boasting that he lays abed with you!

GIOVANNA: He does not!

FABIO: His aphrodisiac, he called you.

GIOVANNA: He has not touched me! (*She is so vehement that it stops him.*)

FABIO: Has he not indeed? . . . I see. It is for this you need more time.

(*Perturbed, she starts to leave.*)

FABIO: Stay, Giovanna . . . He attracts you, doesn't he?

GIOVANNA: I despise him!

FABIO: (*Goading*) Attracts you, attracts you.

GIOVANNA: I hate him—he torments me. He doesn't come near me unless I summon him. And then he is civility itself! His manners—this guttersnipe—his manners are more elegant than mine! He talks politely down to me as if I were a scullery girl! To shame him I send him on errands that should mortify him! But he performs them with such self-certainty—! I think I dispatch a popinjay—and he returns a man! Yesterday I sent him out—no boat, no carriage—in the rain. He returned without stain or wrinkle, completely dry! Social drudgeries that would boggle any gallant of Venice—he emerges smiling, leaving a trail of titillation behind him! He plagues me—knows precisely what will flick me raw! And what is worse, each day I know less and less of him!

FABIO: You've blown this smoke of mystery around him yourself, Giovanna. Don't complain if you cough in it.

GIOVANNA: Not my smoke—his! Fabio, sometimes when I hear him tell one of his fanciful lies—my solemn word—I start to believe him!

FABIO: (*An instant*) Yes . . . because he is not really trying to delude. He is himself deluded . . . But by what?

GIOVANNA: By . . . God, I think.

FABIO: I beg your pardon?

GIOVANNA: Shall I beg yours? Is it not a polite word?

FABIO: I thought you said God. It's hardly *any* word in this day of blinding enlightenment . . . You really think he's a . . . religious?

GIOVANNA: Oh, he would deny it.

FABIO: He's a more dangerous mountebank than I thought . . . We'll arrest him tonight.

GIOVANNA: Please, not yet—bear with me a while—he plagues me.

FABIO: Then be rid of him.

GIOVANNA: Keep him, be rid of him—I can't move in any direction. Please wait.

FABIO: (*Angry*) Wait until when? Until you've gone to bed with him?—consumed him?—used him up?

GIOVANNA: No! You, with that judge's brain of yours, you try to make me confess to what I'm not guilty of!

FABIO: (*Quietly*) . . . What a praying mantis you are, Giovanna.

GIOVANNA: Not guilty, not guilty!

(*She is unstrung. Carla comes in. Giovanna turns away so that the girl will not see her upset.*)

CARLA: The porter says he has arrived. He came in by—

FABIO: Yes, we've seen him. No, stay. Look to your mistress. (*To Giovanna*) It need not be tonight. I agree to wait for a sign from you. I will wait.

(*He goes out. Carla notes Giovanna.*)

CARLA: Are you not well, signora?

GIOVANNA: Where has he been? Come—answer! Where's he been all afternoon?

CARLA: I do not know, Contessa.

GIOVANNA: (*With mounting fury*) You little trull! I'll ask you once again, and this time—

CARLA: Why me? Why ask me?

GIOVANNA: You think I don't hear? Whenever he's alone, he's not alone— he's with you! I'm sure you're privy to every secret of his mind! Where does he go?

CARLA: I don't know, signora.

GIOVANNA: (*She slaps her. Then, penitent*) I'm sorry, Carla—please—I'm sorry—forgive me. (*Wounded, crying out*) But why do you lie to me? Have I not loved you? This man's a stranger and when he's gone you'll have only me to console you, as I've done before! Why do you lie? Do I lose you to him so easily? (*Suddenly stopping herself, ashamed*) No, I will not throw myself on your mercy—get out!

CARLA: (*Compassionately*) Signora, if I could help you—!

GIOVANNA: Damn you, if you could help me!—of course you can help me! Who is she? Where does he spend his afternoons?

CARLA: She, signora? There is no she.

GIOVANNA: If you pile one lie upon another—

CARLA: No! I'd lay my soul he goes to no other woman.

GIOVANNA: How can you be sure? Oh, of course, you're sure of *him*!

CARLA: No, Contessa—no!

GIOVANNA: (*Lashing*) But don't you be so certain of him! Just because he nibbled and nippled you—

CARLA: He has *not* made love to me!

GIOVANNA: If you persist in lying—

CARLA: No! It's you he loves!

(*This halts Giovanna. It affects her strangely. Then she realizes she's been victimizing the girl. She puts a gentle hand on Carla's face.*)

GIOVANNA: You need not say this to comfort me. I am not interested in whether he loves me or not.

CARLA: But he *does* love you, signora.

GIOVANNA: Please . . . go away.

CARLA: Signora, he told me so.

GIOVANNA: (*Held*) . . . He told you what?

CARLA: When he speaks of you, he is so . . . violent.

GIOVANNA: Don't improvise. What did he actually say?

CARLA: Last night—I can remember exactly—he said: "For all her beauty and her shine, she's a black witch and I despise her."

GIOVANNA: (*With a dry laugh*) I'm not convinced this is a love lyric to the woman of his dreams. Still . . . Carla, will you do me a service?

CARLA: Of course, signora, you are my mistress.

GIOVANNA: Find out where he goes of an afternoon—and tell me.

CARLA: Oh no—I couldn't!

GIOVANNA: (*Mimicking Carla*) "Of course, signora, you are my mistress."

CARLA: Please . . . I can't give you confidences not mine to give!

GIOVANNA: You haven't always been so scrupulous. I've known you—

CARLA: Contessa—

GIOVANNA: —to lie and cheat and fornicate with another woman's man! Not always been so scrupulous!

CARLA: Signora, he and I—we have a pact—we'll both keep trust. I'm sure he'd never betray me and I—(*As Giovanna laughs*) Oh, I know you think he's all lies! But he's not—there is a clean truth in the man! And whatever I confide in him—

(*Carla stops herself. Sensing a means of reaching the girl, Giovanna says, carefully:*)

GIOVANNA: Have you confided something, Carla? What?

CARLA: I . . . would rather not say.

GIOVANNA: You trust *him*—and suddenly not *me*!

CARLA: It's not that! Please, signora—

GIOVANNA: Is it something about your father?

CARLA: Please! If you will excuse me, Contessa—

(*She starts to go. Giovanna rages.*)

GIOVANNA: I'll not excuse you! You ungrateful tart—after the nights I've spent mothering and consoling you! *Where does he go in the afternoons?*

CARLA: No! You'll not make me betray him—no! (*On the outcry, she runs away*)

GIOVANNA: Carla!

(*She quiets her rage, thinks, leaves the room. The lights fade and come up on Giaco in his chamber, still wearing his capacious mantle. He holds his homunculus bottle and is lost in wry speculation of it. About to remove his cloak, he hears a noise. Guiltily, he draws his mantle tighter. Carla breaks in, distraught.*)

CARLA: Oh, sir—Count Mastromare!

GIACO: My dear, if you burst in—you catch me just this side of nudity.

CARLA: She's been questioning me!

GIACO: Gently, my dear—gently, child.

CARLA: I didn't tell her where you go the afternoons! I vow I didn't!

GIACO: Of course not, Carla.

CARLA: And I swear I didn't tell her about the seance.

GIACO: (*Alerted*) You—? What didn't you tell her about the seance?

CARLA: That you're going to make one for me.

GIACO: (*Vexed*) Carla, stop that! I'm not making any seance and you—

CARLA: You promised, you promised!

GIACO: I promised no such thing.

CARLA: Yes! You said if you could make my father speak to me—

GIACO: *If* I could. I cannot. My God, girl, you've got to stop this!

CARLA: Oh, Mastromare—please—

GIACO: You make yourself believe I said I would—you make yourself believe anything!

CARLA: (*Shaking convulsively*) Oh, please—oh, Mastromare—last night—he came again—oh, signore, I can't endure—oh, blood—oh, Mastromare—! And this morning—in the church—I knelt to take communion—and as I raised my mouth to take the wafer—no priest, no wafer—my father—and from his hand—blood! I can't endure—blood dripping from his fingers into my mouth—I can't endure, I can't endure! (*As if in seizure, she falls to her knees, weeping and quaking. To console her, he kneels beside her.*)

GIACO: Carla—my dear child—stop it—I beg of you! I'll do what I can—Carla—I'll help you whatever way I know—Carla!
(*To restore her to her senses he lifts her into a tight embrace. He gentles and consoles her:*) Poor child—poor night-afflicted child! Hold still—be still, girl—hush, my dear, hush. (*As her fit subsides*) Come—no trembling now—and no such staring. No—don't turn away—look at me—*see me!*
(*Quite slowly, she brings her eyes, her being into focus upon the world and upon him.*)

CARLA: . . . Yes . . . yes.

GIACO: Do you know me?

CARLA: You are . . . Mastromare.

GIACO: And you know that you are dear to me? And I will do for you whatever I can?

CARLA: Yes . . . I know you are . . . good . . . to me.

GIACO: (*Trying to smile*) As we deserve of one another.

CARLA: Oh, how fortunate I am that you came here when you did! What will I do when you go away?

GIACO: (*Troubled, he pretends to joke*) Go away?—not me—I'm in the world forever—part of the furnishings.

CARLA: (*With a sad smile*) When you go away, may I go with you?

GIACO: My dear, you wouldn't like it with me.

CARLA: I would. Anywhere. Please take me somewhere.

GIACO: (*Insisting on the lighter mood*) But where I go is nowhere. It's hard to find.

CARLA: (*Starting to smile*) I'll find it with you.

GIACO: It's tricky. When you think you have arrived, you've just departed. (*They laugh. But suddenly she shivers again. He holds her tighter*) No, don't wilt—or the flower in your hair will do the same.

CARLA: I have no flower in my hair.

GIACO: What's this?
(*He reaches to her hair; a flower materializes. As she takes it, Giaco sees Giovanna at the door. He "makes" another flower for Giovanna.*) And a red rose for signora.

GIOVANNA: (*Without taking it. With a smile*) It was my understanding you would resist the temptation to this petty hocus pocus.

GIACO: Forgive me, lady: the flower blooms without permission. Ah, winter—and the rose has withered.

(*A pass of his hand and the rose disappears. Giavanna to Carla, not unkindly:*)

GIOVANNA: Now that you've reported I've been quizzing you about his wanderings—(*She notes Carla's drawn face. With concern:*) What is it, girl?—your face is deathly.

CARLA: Nothing, signora—I'll look to it.

(*She hurries away. Puzzlement adds botheration to Giovanna as her eyes follow Carla. Then:*)

GIOVANNA: She breathes the worst in here. You must air your chambers. There's an odor of—what is it—brimstone?

GIACO: I don't smell it. They say that Satan carries the odor with her. (*Reaching into his cloak*) Forgive me, I must get rid of this rose—a thorn in my arm. You're sure you wouldn't like it? (*He hands it to her; she doesn't take it*) Ah, look—a drop of blood on the thorn. Mine, signora. Doesn't that endear it to you?

GIOVANNA: Where do you spend your afternoons, Mastromare?

GIACO: Does madame have complaint of me?

GIOVANNA: Where do you go?

GIACO: Do I not comport myself as you've ordered me to do? Am I not the fine gentleman you've made me, exciting admiration of my style, my wit, my bountiful wealth? Have I not worn the mantle of mystery according to your plan? What, Giovanna?—do I play the mystery too well?

GIOVANNA: I asked you where?

GIACO: (*Turning in anger*) Go ask your footpads! Ask those turtleheaded idiots you've hired to dog my footsteps!

GIOVANNA: Not I—Galbaio and the merchants.

GIACO: You too! You send ferret-faces after me, to spy up my breeches! You count my cunning too little, Giovanna! Them—I could give them the slip by walking on my *hands*, signora—for I am coated with fine Persian oils and the unguents of Arabia—not with muttonfat!

GIOVANNA: (*Dryly*) Splendid. Where do you spend your afternoons?

GIACO: Go to hell!

GIOVANNA: Is that where? Then I did smell brimstone. You are much preoccupied with hell. But I still demand to know—

GIACO: Demand? Have you no other resources than the whip?

GIOVANNA: (*Shaken a little*) You will please to lower your voice.

GIACO: (*More quietly and gently*) Giovanna . . . on Tuesday evening, Carla came to me—her face all open and her words all kindly—as one might ask a friend, "Where do you go, Mastromare?" Can you not ask that way? Softly, gently, without the lash?

GIOVANNA: (*Unsteadily*) You think I'd like it better to be refused that way?

GIACO: Is that where the hornet stings? What makes you think I'd refuse you? I didn't refuse Carla.

GIOVANNA: (*More and more forsaking her pride*) You . . . love Carla. No, I'm sorry I said love.

GIACO: Why? Why is it so much easier to speak of hatred than of love?

GIOVANNA: Because the word is more precise.

GIACO: Imprecisely, then: I love her, yes. I've kissed her once—on the forehead, which seemed the needful place to kiss a troubled child. I hurt for her. And so, whatever she wants to know of me, I tell.

GIOVANNA: (*She is unnerved*) You try to shame me.

GIACO: No, Giovanna.

GIOVANNA: You try to shame me—and you don't! But please—I beg you— tell me where you go the afternoons!

GIACO: Giovanna—

GIOVANNA: No—please—don't touch me!

GIACO: Must you go from one extreme to the other? Imperious queen one moment, and beseeching servant girl the next?

GIOVANNA: That is it! It frightens me that if I'm not one I must surely become the other!

GIACO: Giovanna—no!

GIOVANNA: Please tell me! I hate not knowing where you are and what you're doing! It terrifies me something's in you I don't know—you won't *let* me know!

GIACO: (*Touched, he gently touches her*) Very well, Giovanna . . .
(*He moves away. Slowly he takes his mantle off. Under his magnificent cloak he wears his old culvert rags. She is dumbfounded.*)

GIOVANNA: Your . . . old clothes? And the smell of sulphur in them? Why? . . . Where do you go?

GIACO: Nico and I—we used to have a culvert. We still do.

GIOVANNA: You go there? With Nico?

GIACO: I'm sorry, Giovanna. I've kept faith in all but this. I couldn't send him off— alone—to cadge a crust wherever he could find it. He's an old one and his world has dwindled down to—me. I couldn't disappear. I love the man.

GIOVANNA: There it is again—love. You're not chary of it.

GIACO: Why should I be? I've such a plentitude—enough for everyone!

GIOVANNA: For Nico even.

GIACO: Don't say even. Oh, I know he's dirty, drunken, steals the unattended silver, but he's kindly and his jests are loud.

GIOVANNA: His jests are loud. For this—?

GIACO: There are less cogent reasons to love a man than that he makes you laugh.

GIOVANNA: But that is not your reason.

GIACO: (*More and more defensive*) What reason do I need? We're much alike—both liars—and yet I'll wager there's more truth between us—! (*Halting himself*) Never mind!

GIOVANNA: No, tell me! Why do you love him? You were about to tell me something truer than the rest! Why?

GIACO: *He believes!*

(*A passionate outburst which he regrets.*)

GIOVANNA: (*Pressing him*) Believes in what, Giaco?

GIACO: In the magic, whatever the devil it may be! You smell the brimstone on me? It's Nico's brimstone. Now that I can spare a ducat, he buys ingredients and makes a stinking stew. And in this stench he some day will find gold.

GIOVANNA: You think he will?

GIACO: *Me* think it? Come, Giovanna!

GIOVANNA: If you don't, why spend money on it—and your time?

GIACO: (*Feverishly*) Because he's not fooling me—it's not gold he's looking for! What he seeks is *alteration*! What is the secret behind *change*? How can the common metal become the precious one? How can good turn to evil? If life can become death, can it then be life again? Change, change, change and alteration! Is the Devil another name for God? God and the Devil, God and the Devil!

(*The ecstasy of his outcry stuns her. Long stillness.*)

GIOVANNA: (*Quietly*) Bring him back.

GIACO: What did you say?

GIOVANNA: I said bring Nico back. We'll find chambers for him. Perhaps, somewhere, a place for his magical pursuits.

GIACO: (*Overjoyed*) I can't believe it! Nico—you mean Nico?

GIOVANNA: (*Smiling*) As long as I do not have to hear his ditties when he's drunk.

GIACO: (*Inarticulate with joy*) Oh, I promise you! I can't believe—Giovanna, you do mean it, do you not?

GIOVANNA: (*In a burst*) Please! Don't run away from me again!

GIACO: I didn't! I won't! Oh, Giovanna!

(*He takes her in his arms. She starts to break away, then clutches to him desperately.*)

GIOVANNA: Tell me everything, Giaco! Don't hide from me! It frightens me when you hide! I'm not like you, in love with mystery—it scares me! Tell me everything!

GIACO: (*With a laugh*) Everything! But I know so little!

GIOVANNA: (*Wildly*) Everything! Promise! Every thought—every slight imagining—keep nothing from me—tell me everything!

GIACO: I will! I promise! I will!

GIOVANA: Oh, ridiculous to ask such things of you!

GIACO: No—no!

(*They kiss passionately*)

GIOVANNA: I don't want to need you—and I won't! I can't let you win at that!

GIACO: Win at what, for God's sake! Why do you make it such a combat? I want to make love to you! Why can't we play at it?

GIOVANNA: (*Snatching at the word*) Yes—*play* at it! Hold me—hold me close!

GIACO: How warm you are!

GIOVANNA: Closer—don't let me breathe!

GIACO: You have a fever!

GIOVANNA: Yes, the rages! Need you, hate you! Oh, why do I need you?

GIACO: Because I'm true and honest and steady as a clerk! And I sing madrigals under your window!

GIOVANNA: You are mischief! Kiss me! (*After he does*) Turmoil and mischief!

GIACO: Mischief—me? I am a choir boy!

GIOVANNA: Mischief! Why did you say to poor Tadeo that I was your aphrodisiac? With Fabio listening!

GIACO: Because that's what you are.

GIOVANNA: It suggested we had slept together.

GIACO: It was not meant as history, Giovanna, but as hope.

GIOVANNA: No! I don't like it—cheap Rialto talk!

GIACO: But it's true! You're the elixir that awakens me, the powder that excites my skin—

GIOVANNA: Don't speak that way—it sounds as if you're mocking me—as if you're tricking me into buying a potion—it all sounds false!

GIACO: It's not! You're the essence quickening my blood—

GIOVANNA: Stop it!

GIACO: —the wines of Egypt—
(*He reaches for her and she wrests herself away.*)

GIOVANNA: No, let me go!

GIACO: (*Trying to restrain her*) Giovanna, come back!

GIOVANNA: No, I don't want you to make love to me! Let me go!

GIACO: Stay, I said!

GIOVANNA: *Let me go!*
(*She strikes him. Instantly, in remorse, she puts her hands to her face.*) Oh, why did I do that?
(*Pulling her hands away, she cries out:*) Strike me back!
(*He strikes her once and again and again, as she cries:*) No! I don't want to need you—no—
(*Roughly he takes her in his arms*) No, do not make love to me—kill me! Hate me—hold me—kill me—

GIACO: Giovanna—Giovanna—

GIOVANNA: (*Berserk*) Mischief—hold me—hold me—wines of Egypt—kill me if I go away—
(*She falls back on his bed*)

GIACO: Giovanna—

GIOVANNA: Oh, mischief—hold me—wines of Egypt—kill me—

END OF ACT ONE

Act Two

T HE RIALTO. It is night, the market place deserted. Under a dim street lamp, Galbaio has just heard a report from Celsi and a footpad, Brescia. Galbaio is fractious.

GALBAIO: I didn't ask about the old man, I asked about him.

CELSI: They are together every afternoon.

GALBAIO: (*Impatiently*) And—and?

BRESCIA: They work at alchemy, signore.

GALBAIO: Don't prattle about alchemy. (*He holds up Mastromare's present, the ducat*) This isn't alchemy. It's hard Venetian gold.

CELSI: No, but listen to him, Galbaio. He has followed the man down to the culvert, and the fumes that issue forth—

GALBAIO: What fumes?

CELSI: Tell him, Brescia.

BRESCIA: Hell fumes, signore! Of the devil!

GALBAIO: Take him away—I cannot stand this quaking idiot! The only dev-iltry in this—(*Waving the coin*)—is not heaven or hell, only the Rialto! Dismiss this fool if he brings talk of witchcraft!

CELSI: But it *is* witchcraft, sir. There's to be a seance!

GALBAIO: . . . A seance, did you say?

BRESCIA: Yes, signore—tonight.

GALBAIO: Where? By whom?

BRESCIA: By him, signore.

GALBAIO: Come.

(*They depart. Light comes up on Fabio and Alcestor.*)

FABIO: You're sure? How do you know?

ALCESTOR: The old man, Marchese—he mentioned it while drunk.

FABIO: The Contessa—does she know?

ALCESTOR: Oh, no, sir. I came to you first, signore.

FABIO: Ask the Contessa if . . . No, I'll do it myself.

(*They hurry out. The light comes up in Giaco's room. Carla is helping Giaco on with his waistcoat. She points to his dirty culvert clothes on a tailor's dummy.*)

CARLA: And these, sir, may I not clean them?

(*Giovanna storms in, white with fury.*)

GIOVANNA: You liar!

GIACO: I beg your—? Carla, please.

(*Carla departs quickly.*)

GIOVANNA: You miserable liar! You miscreant misery of a liar!

GIACO: Once more, dear love.

GIOVANNA: Don't call me that. You promised—you gave your promise in the truest truth we've had between us—that you would not keep secrets from me!

GIACO: (*Teasing*) What secret, love? What secret, oh my heart?

GIOVANNA: You will laugh once too often.

GIACO: (*More seriously*) Perhaps. Come, love—what secret?

GIOVANNA: A seance!

GIACO: (*Troubled*) Yes . . . that.

GIOVANNA: In how many ways—tell me—in how many ways will you break faith with me? You promised no more cheap little sleights-of-hand.

GIACO: This is no cheap little sleight-of-hand. (*Unhappily, on a note of plea*) Giovanna, turn away. Pretend you never heard of this.

GIOVANNA: I *have* heard. And thanks to your loose-lipped friar, all Venice will hear. And what will that do to our enterprise?

GIACO: Perhaps only good, Giovanna.

GIOVANNA: No! Sorcery and witchcraft—we don't toy with them in Venice! (*Resolved, at the bell pull*) I'm sorry, Giaco. I'll call Carla and tell her— there will be no seance here.

GIACO: (*Quietly*) Then I'll make it somewhere else.

(*She does not pull the bell cord. She is stunned.*)

GIOVANNA: Are you so intent on this?

GIACO: I promised her.

GIOVANNA: You have made promises to me.

GIACO: But her need—

GIOVANNA: —*my* need!

GIACO: Her need is sickness!

GIOVANNA: So is mine! My dependence upon you is a sickness! (*Then, with all the deliberateness she can gather in her agitated state:*) I'll find some cure for it. Tonight—no seance! We go to the gaming room of the Lido. At ten o'clock Fabio will strike you. . . . So starts the conclusion of our enterprise . . .

GIACO: We've waited so long, we can wait another night.

GIOVANNA: Tonight.

GIACO: Why do you spite yourself, Giovanna?

GIOVANNA: (*With a little outcry*) Yes, spite myself! I had hoped to prolong the time we have together—and not lock everything away. But it's no good. And when you leave—

GIACO: Why talk of leaving? Come, kiss me. Let the seance be tonight, and kiss me.

GIOVANNA: No.

GIACO: Please! The girl's in torment. If I can comfort her—

GIOVANNA: With chicanery—

GIACO: Any way I know! She gets no peace—each night a bloody nightmare.

GIOVANNA: She's an hysteric! If reason does not help her—

GIACO: *Reason?*

GIOVANNA: In a day of reason, *reason!*

GIACO: Reason *what*? What words? What proven physic? What persuasive letting of the blood? What syllogism to save her soul?

GIOVANNA: (*Taken aback by his intensity*) Her soul? You think you'll succeed where ministers and doctors have failed? Indeed, all of us—! I've listened to her by the hour, held her hand, put compresses on her heartache. You think you'll do better than all of us?

GIACO: It's not a contest, Giovanna. The girl's in terror. I'll try to deliver her from it.

GIOVANNA: Exorcise her devil?

GIACO: Yes!

GIOVANNA: Or will you exorcise your own?

GIACO: *You bait me, Giovanna!*

(*A constrained moment in which neither of them can speak.*)

GIOVANNA: (*Quietly*) I have to know. Is this seance for the child or for yourself?

GIACO: Let it be, Giovanna, let it be.

GIOVANNA: (*Attempting a smile*) Are you a friar or a fake?

GIACO: (*Also trying to smile*) May I think about it?

GIOVANNA: Which are you?

GIACO: Are there only two choices? . . . I've been so many people in my life, I don't know what I am. This? (*He indicates the silk clothes he wears, then the rags on the dummy*) Or that? Or something else? How can I tell? I've never worn a suit of clothes that didn't scratch my soul.

GIOVANNA: Soul!—there it is again!—the same damn word!

(*Suddenly, irrationally, she goes to the dummy and rips at the clothes, tearing them off.*) These clothes! I told you—I begged you, get rid of these stinking sulphurous clothes!

GIACO: Don't, Giovanna! Gently! A few rags!

GIOVANNA: You love them better than you love anyone!

GIACO: No—Giovanna—please—

(*He grabs her, holds her in his arms, and she allows him to calm her a little. But when he tries to kiss her, she turns her face away. At last, under her own control once more, she moves away from him. She speaks quietly.*)

GIOVANNA: What would you do at this seance? (*No answer*) Make it seem that her father appears to her?

GIACO: Something like that.

GIOVANNA: But her father appears every night. What would you add?

GIACO: Giovanna, please.

GIOVANNA: No, tell me. Can you make her father touch her, make him speak? Ah, that's it? You'd make him *seem* to speak. Is that it? . . . What nonsense.

GIACO: Do you doubt that I can make the voice seem real to her?

GIOVANNA: (*Ironically*) Perhaps even to me.

GIACO: Yes, perhaps even to you. You're invited to attend.

GIOVANNA: Thank you . . . You've never heard her father's voice. How would you imitate it?

GIACO: No one will imitate it.

GIOVANNA: You mean it would be *altogether imaginary*? Oh, come!

GIACO: (*Off balance, he turns away*) I'll not pursue this with you, Giovanna.

GIOVANNA: No—please—tell me. You mean you can make her hear a totally imaginary voice?

GIACO: Yes! Because she needs so desperately to hear it!

GIOVANNA: And what would it say?

GIACO: What she needs to hear! That she's to sleep again! That he loves her! That if she carries some cross of guilt about him, she's to lay it down!

GIOVANNA: (*With a mocking laugh*) Is it so easy? Could you do the same for me, sir—please, sir—thank you, sir? Will you do it with a soft voice or a loud one?

GIACO: A loud one!

GIOVANNA: Loud, you say? Loud?

GIACO: (*Lashing*) A shrieking voice—*inside her*!

GIOVANNA: And you think she'd then be delivered of her devils? What a sense of power! How you'll enjoy to make life easy—gentle—kind!

GIACO: Why do you make it cruel?

GIOVANNA: *I* do not make it cruel—it *is*! In everything—in birth, in death, even in love! And if you do this seance, you'll make it crueler for her! If you rid her of her terrors, you'll bring her worse ones!

GIACO: She's not afraid!

GIOVANNA: *But I am!*

(*So reflexive was it that Giovanna herself is surprised by her confession. Silence.*)

GIACO: (*Quietly*) Of what, Giovanna?

GIOVANNA: (*Routed; anxious to retract her confession*) If you break faith with me for that girl—

GIACO: That's not what frightens you, is it?

GIOVANNA: (*Avoiding confrontation*) If the city hears of it—if you're put down as a quack—

GIACO: Nor that either. What frightens you, Giovanna?

GIOVANNA: (*Tense and muted*) That *you* are frightened.

GIACO: By what?

GIOVANNA: (*In quiet dread*) I don't know. Some devil terrifies you. Some horror in yourself that you must exorcise . . . and yet are afraid to meet.

GIACO: What devil is it, do you suppose?

GIOVANNA: Have your seance—and find out. I hope you meet him.

GIACO: Is that a blessing or a curse?

GIOVANNA: Let us see.

(*As she leaves, the lights fade. In the darkness we hear Fabio's voice calling "Signor Colignari!" Fabio enters his drawing room carrying a lighted candelabra. His irritation mounts. He would like to call the name more loudly, but secrecy is urgent.*)

FABIO: Colignari! Signor Colignari!

(*Colignari, the ventriloquist, appears.*)

FABIO: Where the devil have you been?

COLIGNARI: Right behind you, sir.

FABIO: I told you we didn't want anyone to know you're here—

COLIGNARI: I followed your candles and all at once they were gone.

FABIO: (*Nervously*) I certainly hope—

COLIGNARI: Be secure. Nobody saw me, nobody . . . Is this the room?

FABIO: Yes.

COLIGNARI: (*He raises his voice; makes an echo*) Ha-ha-ho-o-o . . . I must tell you, signore, that this is a very difficult room for a maker of voices.

(*Giovanna enters. She is tense.*)

COLIGNARI: Contessa—again—a second delight.

GIOVANNA: You've told him, Fabio—what I want?

COLIGNARI: Only in the most preliminary way, Contessa.

GIOVANNA: (*Nervous, irritable*) The Count di Mastromare—if he were perchance to see you—would he know you?

COLIGNARI: Why should he, signora?—we have never met. Almost—once— at a reception given here. But alas, he never—

GIOVANNA: —never appeared, that's right. If he sees you, who are you, then?

COLIGNARI: (*With a glance at Fabio*) Her old teacher of music, did you say? Harmony, solfeggio—?

GIOVANNA: Exactly. Did I hear you complain about the room?

COLIGNARI: Signora, if I'm expected to re-create the voice of a dead man, I must point out it's difficult in a room deficient in echo.

GIOVANNA: Deficient in what?

COLIGNARI: Echo, dear lady. A dead man's voice must throb and quaver. Listen. Ho, ho, ho, ha, ho. You hear? The room refuses to resonate. No tremolo. A dead man wants a tremolo.

GIOVANNA: A dead man wants nothing. What do *you* want? More money?

COLIGNARI: (*Put off by her directness*) Would an extra hundred be too much?

FABIO: Tremolos come high.

COLIGNARI: The Contessa wanted the best. I am the best. A master of sounds and voices. Clamors and clangs. Glissandos and tremolandos. And hushes! Signora, I can make a hush that drifts down upon the world like snow. I am an artist!

FABIO: Everybody's an artist. The bootmakers, cravat makers, gondoliers— all artists. Who are the ordinary men?

COLIGNARI: Those who pay, Marchese.

FABIO: (*Laughing*) Very well—a hundred more.

COLIGNARI: Good. Now, then. Tone and timbre. The girl's father—was there some special characteristic of his voice?

GIOVANNA: A pompous man. A voice through metal.

COLIGNARI: It sounded so to you, signora. But will the girl remember it that way?

GIOVANNA: Quite right—I valued you too cheap. A baritone, I think.

COLIGNARI: (*He takes a paper out of his pocket*) Excellent, dear lady. And the words? These words that the Marchese gave me—I'm not to improvise?

GIOVANNA: No. Except as the situation demands.

COLIGNARI: I am most challenged. Now—with permission—I'd like a moment with my part.

FABIO: You know where to wait. We'll send Alcestor for you.

COLIGNARI: Your servant, signora—signore.

(*He withdraws. She is edgy.*)

GIOVANNA: He'll do well, don't you think?

FABIO: He'll do as he is told. Now, if you'll excuse me, I'll not be present.

GIOVANNA: Not? Why?

FABIO: I do not attend bear baiting or cock fighting.

GIOVANNA: Come, Fabio, it's a joke. Mastromare will be the first to laugh. Nothing more than a practical joke.

FABIO: I don't think so. You have no taste for practical jokes except as they are really practical. To the purpose.

GIOVANNA: And my purpose tonight—?

FABIO: —is deadly serious. To cripple a little. Giovanna, why must you mangle what you take into your arms?

GIOVANNA: This is too far! Of a sudden, you're his partisan! Why?

FABIO: Because he does for me what I've not been able to do for myself. He hurts and humbles you. When I see him do it, something in me cheers him on. "Wound her once for me!" And when you wince, it's as if I myself have struck the blow. It's most gratifying.

GIOVANNA: You—to become his ally—against me!

FABIO: (*Mockingly*) Poor helpless Giovanna! You need no allies. With both hands tied, you can slaughter him.

GIOVANNA: Stop it! If you have such a devoted feeling for him, why don't you stay for the seance—protect him?

FABIO: Oh, I'd not go *that* far. His partisan, yes. But I'm also corrosively jealous of him. Go on—destroy him!

(*With a faint smile, he starts out.*)

GIOVANNA: No, wait. Please stay, Fabio.

FABIO: Why? Are you queasy about what may happen, Giovanna?

GIOVANNA: No, I'm not.

FABIO: You should be. How will he respond to this? And why do you want to do it to him?

GIOVANNA: He behaves like a visionary boy. He needs some of the moonlight beaten out of him.

FABIO: He's not a moonstruck boy, Giovanna. He's a bedeviled man, you said as much yourself. In search of God, you said. If that's so—beware! The terrifying thing about a mystic is that if he cannot find God, the devil will do just as well.

(*Giaco's voice is heard. There is a clamor of anxiety in it.*)

GIACO'S VOICE: Giovanna! Giovanna! Where is she?

FABIO: Here he comes. Good luck to both of you.

(*Giaco enters, dressed in stunning brilliance. He is deeply unnerved. Fabio pretends to admire his clothes.*) Well, what a wonderful costume—what a shine you make! I've changed my mind, Giovanna. I *will* be a spectator and come back for the performance.

(*He goes out.*)

GIACO: Giovanna, what in hell have you done? Turned this seance into a soiree? Have you invited half of Venice?

GIOVANNA: I've invited the Marchese. It's his palazzo, bear in mind.

GIACO: Tadeo's carriage—what's it doing here? And the man in the alcove?

GIOVANNA: Colignari?—my old music master? Come now—quibble over a singing teacher?

GIACO: (*Disarmed*) I thought—the way I planned it—only Carla, Nico, you and I—in a smallish room.

GIOVANNA: Is that why you're dressed in all that jeweled brilliance?—for the four of us in a smallish room?

GIACO: (*Ruffled*) I—don't know why. The humbug in me. Popinjay—I'm a popinjay!

GIOVANNA: Were you secretly hoping for an audience perhaps?

GIACO: I—don't—I wish I knew. I'm nervous, Giovanna. My hands—feel how cold I am.

GIOVANNA: You—nervous? No—look at you—ignited!

GIACO: No—please.

GIOVANNA: Dressed in fireworks! Roman candles, Catherine wheels!

GIACO: Fireworks can fizzle. Why is it so deathly urgent to me, this seance? And why so suddenly impossible? I've made seances before. I've—(*Trying to pull himself together*) You're right—I'm frightened, Giovanna.

GIOVANNA: (*Gently*) Come here, my moonstruck boy.

GIACO: (*In her arms*) I love you, Giovanna.

GIOVANNA: Please don't . . . But if you could always love me just this way . . .

GIACO: Suddenly I know nothing, I'm sure of nothing. Tell me something I can know.

GIOVANNA: Remember this moment, Giaco. This moment is very dear to me. Some time when you're angry with me . . .

GIACO: Never—I'll never be angry with you again. It's you who may be angry.

GIOVANNA: If ever you feel I am, come to me this way—as a boy—

GIACO: You're so beautiful to me. (*Slowly he moves away*) Has it made you happy that you're beautiful?

GIOVANNA: You know it hasn't. Has it made you happy that you're cunning?

GIACO: Will we be happy when we've cheated half the gold of Venice into our pockets?

GIOVANNA: I doubt it, Giaco.

GIACO: (*Restless. Namelessly angry*) Well then, well then, well then?

GIOVANNA: Well then what, my dear?

GIACO: (*Distressed and irrational*) Well then something, nothing! Oh, Giovanna—if you could only love me as I love you—

GIOVANNA: (*Tenderly*) Poor lad, poor lad. You put too much store in love—as if it cures all maladies. You think that when two people drivel their devotion to one another, it makes them less alone?

GIACO: It should! It pledges that it will!

GIOVANNA: Pledges. In the end it's separation—always—loving or weeping or raging—but alone. Then . . . that last separation all the others have been hinting at.

GIACO: Dying has nothing to do with me. I'm not afraid of the dark of night, it's the *daily* dark—

GIOVANNA: (*Wryly*) What can we do about it? Carry lamps to one another?

GIACO: Yes! If I can't lighten the world for someone—for you or Carla—someone—! If we can't hold a candle's worth of light for each other—why have we been put together? Why not beyond sight or shadow of one another, beyond the sound of another voice?

GIOVANNA: But we *are* beyond, my dear—beyond!

GIACO: (*Mostly to himself*) Oh, murder—whose revenge is this?

GIOVANNA: You see what you do to yourself? Why are you so unhappy tonight? Because you know this seance will bring no good to anyone! (*Tenderly, entreatingly*) Oh, my dear, we are all in the dark, beyond one another's candlelight! How can I teach you this? If you expect too much of love and life—and me—you will forsake us all! And I can't bear the thought of it!

GIACO: (*Taking her in his arms*) Nor I, nor I!
(*As they cling to one another, Nico enters. He is not quite sober.*)

NICO: The men are here. They have been waiting.

GIACO: Tell them to come in. (*He separates himself from Giovanna, then gently indicates for her to go*) Please.

GIOVANNA: You mean I may not watch the preparations?

GIACO: No. My tricks—you will only laugh at them.

GIOVANNA: If I promise not to—

GIACO: No, please. We'll call you when we're ready. Look to Carla. Ease her mind. When I left her she was close to frenzy.

GIOVANNA: Isn't that how you want her to be?
(*Her change in tone distresses him. She goes out. Orfeo and Marco enter carrying a brazier, two music boxes, a hamper full of paraphernalia. Giaco impatiently dismisses them.*)

GIACO: Leave it. Go. Thank you. No, never mind, I'll do it. Nico, you stay.

NICO: What is it, Giaco? Are you distressed with me?

GIACO: No. Help me. The music boxes—hide them. Get the brazier started.
(*They move things. Nico stumbles noisily. Giaco looks up, annoyed.*)

NICO: I'm sorry. Stumbled. This music box—a hundred ducats, sure. (*He inadvertently starts it playing*)

GIACO: Quiet! Close the lid! Are you drunk?

NICO: No, Giaco—surely not.

GIACO: Let me see. Stand straight.

NICO: I'm not built to stand straight, Giaco.

GIACO: You reek of wine. (*Losing his temper, he shakes Nico*) I told you— sober!

NICO: Giaco—please—!
(*Giaco lets him go; is filled with remorse*)

GIACO: Forgive me.

NICO: My fault, mine. I shouldn't have. But I looked up at the sky and—all confusion there, Giaco. So I took a drop, to put the moon in focus . . . You have never been rough with me.

GIACO: (*Snapping*) I said that I was sorry.

NICO: What is it, Giaco—are you ill?

GIACO: Perhaps, perhaps. There's nothing steady. (*Suddenly*) I can't go through with this tonight.

NICO: Oh, dear friend—so bad?

GIACO: Why should I? What's this girl to me?—a child who touched me for a moment—! There's no pride or profit in this—! Why do it?—because the girl's possessed?—we're all possessed!—who's to deliver us?

NICO: (*Frightened, murmuring*) . . . from evil . . . deliver us from evil . . .

GIACO: Don't.

NICO: You frighten me. If you start looking for deliverance—

GIACO: Why not? You're a believer, aren't you? Why not?

NICO: I'm a little drunk for this kind of talk.

GIACO: Don't put me off—talk to me! Say a good, believing word! Say hope, say heaven, say grace, salvation! Say a word to me! . . . Say faith.

NICO: Don't tinker, Giaco. Faith's a full day's work.

GIACO: (*Grabbing him*) But you believe!

NICO: I did! In the cloister—before I went away.

GIACO: Now! You believe now!

NICO: Let me go!

GIACO: *Now!*

NICO: (*With a desperate cry*) I am a tinkerer! It's too hard to believe all the time! When things go well, I believe! When they go badly, I get drunk!

GIACO: You too?

(*He lets Nico go. The old man weeps softly.*)

NICO: It's not right to force this out of anyone. I don't even tell these things to myself. It only hurts me . . . It hurts you too . . . You will have the seance, won't you?

GIACO: (*In control of himself once more, he speaks grimly*) Yes, we'll have the seance. Why not? It's only hocus pocus after all. Why not? (*With precision*) Put the lamp there. The mist will come from here—as if through the window—at the height of the confusion. Will you remember?

NICO: Yes. Then I start the tolling of the bells.

GIACO: I hear a man's voice sobbing—

NICO: —I cross myself—

GIACO: —then I repeat your first words of the ceremony—"By bell, book and candle"—

NICO: —that's when I pretend to hear the voice speaking to us—

GIACO: Correct. Now—everything ready? Very well, then. Darkness!

(*Nico extinguishes the lamp. As he starts to extinguish the candles:*)

GIACO: No, give me that. (*Nico gives him the lighted candelabra*) Go and fetch Carla. (*Nico leaves. Giaco takes one lighted candle and blows out the others. He sets down the candelabra. He starts to the brazier, to light it with the flame of his candle. He trembles. As if physically ill, he doubles up. Slowly he straightens. His eyes are filled with pain. He looks for some nameless help.*)

GIACO: Let me serve the child! Let me not harm her! Oh, peace to her, poor benighted believer, poor benighted fool! Peace to all of us!

(*Nico enters, unheard. He sees Giaco in this beseeching attitude and stops short, alarmed. Giaco lights the brazier. The fire makes a glow. He sees Nico; realizing the latter has seen him so naked, Giaco speaks with gruff efficiency.*)

GIACO: Well—to it—get ready! (*Nico opens a music box. A soft harpsichord melody. He lights a candle which he carries to an urn. He takes the lid off; a mist emanates from it. He opens the hamper and brings out a variety of objects. An amphora which he lights; prayer book and a bell; a cruet of wine. Giaco sits beside the brazier. For a long while he will remain there, in trancelike stillness. Nico sees him take up his position and opens the door. He speaks gently, without trace of formality or pomp.*)

NICO: Come. Enter here. Simply and in silence. Come as your believing bids you.

(*Tadeo enters with his young wife. She is vacuously pretty. She giggles nervously. Nico gently shushes her.*)

NICO: Please . . . in silence.

(*Nico gestures them to go ritually to their places. Colignari enters and Nico seats him. Giovanna enters, dressed in black. She is playing to the moment and walks austerely, as if in religious premises. Dutifully she sits where Nico directs her. She whispers in Nico's ear. It disturbs him. He whispers something in return.*)

GIOVANNA: Could we please wait for the Marchese?

FABIO: (*At the doorway*) No need to wait. I'm here.

(*Fabio, also in black, finds a seat. Silence. Nico addresses the doorway.*)

NICO: Carla di Murano . . . Come here now, child.

(*Silence. Carla does not enter.*)

NICO: Carla . . . come . . . Come, child. Do not be afraid.

FABIO: She's not there. There was no one in the hallway.

NICO: Carla—?

(*Nico rises, calls her name once more. No response. A chill settles over everyone. Nico looks apprehensively to Giaco, who raises his head. Giaco's glance does not go to the corridor door where the others look; he points to the French windows. An instant, then we see Carla's silhouette. Nico opens the windows and Carla enters. She is dressed in white and has a look of ecstasy on her face. She points to Giaco.*)

CARLA: He knew where I was, didn't he? He was the only one who knew me to be there!

NICO: (*Affecting sadness*) Were you testing the master, child?

CARLA: No—oh no! You did not think I was testing you!

(*Giaco doesn't answer. His face is filled with ineffable sadness. He lays a comforting hand on her cheek.*)

NICO: He wants you to be seated . . . and be still.

(*Meekly, she sits. All eyes go to Giaco. He does not speak, does not make a movement. In the distance, the crowing of the cock.*)

NICO: When there is crowing in moonlight, there will be new morning in the world. Let it not be devil's morning.

(*A distant churchbell, profound in tone. Nico sounds his own smaller bell.*)

NICO: By bell, book and candle, we abjure you, Satan. Begone from the night, begone from the day—and let us be cleansed of temptation.

(*He sets down bell and prayer book. He takes up the single lighted candle.*)

NICO: Burn sin from your hands.

(*He puts the candle snuffer over the candle. The only light in the room now comes from moonlight and the burning brazier which glows on Giaco's face. Slowly Giaco holds his hands over the brazier, then puts both hands into the burning flame. Someone gasps.*)

TADEO: He's burning his hands!

NICO'S VOICE: Be still.

(*Giaco takes his burning hands out of the brazier and covers his face with his hands. He inclines his whole torso forward, in prayer or shame. Now he straightens up. He removes his hands from his face. Transfigured, he speaks:*)

GIACO: Hear us. Whatsoever is in darkness and hidden, let our hope shine upon it. Whatsoever is beyond this place and cold, let our fire warm it and give it welcome. Do not mock us with shadows. Do not afflict us. Whatever you are, know that our ignorance besets us. Know that in our not knowing, we pain and perish. Have mercy upon us for we are alone, we are alone, we are all of us alone! Have pity on us—gentle us and give us a sign! Speak to us! Tell us, we beg you, a signifying word! If it be blessedly of good, let it be good. If evil, evil. *But let it signify!* (*As if exorcising evil, softly*) By bell, book and candle—

NICO: (*In a tight whisper*) Oh, master!

GIACO: Silence and let us listen.

NICO: But I heard, master!

GIACO: (*As if he too is hearing*) By bell, book and candle!—the voice!

OTHERS: What? . . . I hear nothing! . . . Did you hear? . . . Silence! . . . Was there a voice?

CARLA: Please! Please be quiet—please—I must hear him!

GIACO: *Silence!*

(*Stillness. Suddenly out of the distance, a voice—Colignari's ventriloquizing voice—lets out a moan. In alarm:*)

GIACO: That sound! What was it?

COLIGNARI'S VOICE: (*As Carla's father*) Car-la-a!

CARLA: (*Hysterically*) I hear him!

(*Giaco rises, transfixed*)

COLIGNARI'S VOICE: Car-la-aaaa!

CARLA: (*Running to center of room*) Father! Where are you? Father!

COLIGNARI'S VOICE: I am here, child! Carla! I am here!

CARLA: (*Distraught*) Where? Oh, tell me—where?

NICO: Oh, dear heaven!

(*Slowly, Giaco moves away from the brazier. He looks to heaven. Ever so slowly, he raises his hand above him, as if to shield his eyes from light, or to ward off a blow.*)

CARLA: Father, speak! Don't go away—speak!

GIACO: (*Trembling*) Stay—stay!

COLIGNARI'S VOICE: Do not grieve! Rest! Rest in the quiet night! Sleep!

CARLA: Father!

COLIGNARI'S VOICE: Carla! Carla!

OTHERS: (*In terror-stricken voices*) He's here! . . . No, there! . . . I saw him at the window! . . . Where? . . His voice, his shadow! . . . Here! . . . He's gone!

(*Carla shrieks in terror, and collapses. Giaco rushes to her. As he starts to lift her:*)

GIACO: Lights! Let us have lights! More candles! Light the way!

GIOVANNA: No! The women will see to her, Mastromare! (*To Signora Tadeo*) Signora, help me! Tadeo—ring! Alcestor!

GIACO: Gently! Be gentle with her!

(*As he is about to follow after those who carry Carla, Giovanna's commanding voice stops him:*)

GIOVANNA: Stay, Mastromare!

(*As if seeing Giovanna for the first time since the seance began, he turns to her, needing her strength. He is quaking.*)

GIACO: Giovanna, I heard it! Her father's voice—I heard! (*Getting only stillness as response, he turns to Nico*) Nico—I *heard* it! I *did* hear it! Believe me—I *did*!

NICO: (*Trembling*) Yes, master. I heard it too!

GIACO: (*Wonderstruck*) And Carla too! It was there, Nico, was it not?— oh, tell me it was there!—not in our minds!—*it was there*!

NICO: It was there, master!

GIACO: (*Suddenly suspicious*) No! What did it say? If you heard the same words—what did it say?

NICO: "Do not grieve!"

GIACO: (*Nodding*) "Rest! Rest in the—

NICO: —quiet night! Sleep!"

GIACO: (*In terror, in ecstasy*) Oh yes!—oh dear heaven, yes!

(*In a transport, he goes down on his knees. Giovanna and Fabio step forward, watching tensely.*) Oh, sweet beloved God—tell me what it means!

FABIO: (*Whispering tensely to Giovanna*) You see? I told you!

(*He goes to the bell cord and pulls it.*)

GIACO: Oh, dear God, tell me what it means! I meant no harm! I meant the poor child only good and kindness! I lied, but do not lay a blame upon her! Oh, tell me, was it your voice I heard? Was it in anger, was it in love? I lied—oh mea culpa, mea culpa! Do you speak gently to me? Oh, can it be true? Can truth come out of falsehood like a flower out of dung? Tell me! Oh, dear beloved, tell me! Dear God, tell me! *Tell me what it means*!

(*His eyes flooded with tears, his body quaking, he is in violent entrancement. As he sobs convulsively, Alcestor comes in answer to Fabio's ring. The latter whispers to him. We do not hear it but Giovanna does.*)

GIOVANNA: No—wait—wait!

FABIO: (*To Alcestor*) I said go.

(*Alcestor departs. Giovanna starts after him.*)

GIOVANNA: Wait!

FABIO: No—stay here! If we don't do it now, the man will never be responsible to us—not even to himself!

GIOVANNA: No—not yet! Let me talk to him!

(*She breaks away and crosses to Giaco who is still on his knees. Nico stands in a dark corner, terrified. Giaco's sobbing has subsided. Giovanna speaks firmly but not unkindly.*) You have knelt for the third time. Now, my friend, get up.

GIACO: (*In a state of wonder*) We heard it, Giovanna! Nico and I—and Carla!—we heard the voice!

GIOVANNA: Yes . . . I heard it too.

GIACO: (*His wonder increasing. With joy*) You, Giovanna?

GIOVANNA: Why not me? Are you the select ones of God?

GIACO: God, Giovanna? You said the word—and you didn't smile!

(*Abruptly she starts to laugh. It is as if she has struck him.*) Don't, Giovanna! . . . Giovanna, stop!

GIOVANNA: Oh, you charlatans! You think because you can gull others, you can't be gulled yourselves!

GIACO: . . . Gulled?

GIOVANNA: But you're the easiest!

GIACO: Gulled?

GIOVANNA: I warned you—I begged you—! No more sleight-of-hand—no more trickery and incense! But you had to play your magic!

GIACO: *I was not playing*!

GIOVANNA: (*Heedless, headlong*) Maybe this will bring you to your senses! Maybe you'll stop hearing voices—maybe you'll hear *me* when I speak! Maybe you'll stop your fakeries—

GIACO: No fakery, Giovanna! The voice spoke! Of *itself*! It wasn't *my* voice, Giovanna!

GIOVANNA: No! It was mine!

GIACO: . . . What?

GIOVANNA: (*Calling*) Colignari! Colignari, are you there?

GIACO: What, Giovanna? What?

(*Colignari enters. Giovanna lashes*)

GIOVANNA: You want to hear the voice again, Giaco? Where would you like to hear it? There?

GIACO: Giovanna—

COLIGNARI'S VOICE: (*Parroting Giaco's words*) Giovanna!

GIACO: Who is that? That sound—who made it?

COLIGNARI'S VOICE: Who is that? That sound—who made it?

GIACO: Stop—please—stop!

COLIGNARI'S VOICE: Stop—please—stop!

GIACO: (*With an agonizing outcry*) Stop it! Nico! Help me!

(*He rushes into Nico's arms. Stillness. Giovanna gestures Colignari to go. She looks at Fabio, then to Giaco. Slowly Giaco comes out of Nico's embrace. His jaw is set with pain and loathing—of himself, of her, of heaven.*)

GIACO: This was the meaning, then? Lies. All of it? (*With a sob*) Oh dear heaven, was this your meaning—lies? This the answer I went down on my knees to hear? *Lies?* (*He weeps with rage and heartbreak.*)

GIOVANNA: (*Gentler now*) I'm sorry to have to have gone to this extremity, Giaco. But it'll be to the good. From now on, I think you'll be a man of considerably more reason.

GIACO: (*Maddened*) *Reason?*

GIOVANNA: Yes. And reason *is* important in the matter before us. A matter of considerable gold—

GIACO: No! Our bargain's over!

GIOVANNA: Not yet, Mastromare!

GIACO: (*In demented rage*) Over—I said over! And my name's Levanto! (*He rushes to the window, throws it open, shouts wildly to the city*) Levanto, the liar! A liar among liars! Ho, Venice—awaken! We are liars here—all liars here—and cheats! We will cheat you of your gold! We are all liars here! Liars and frauds!

GIOVANNA: Stop him! Fabio, stop him! Stop him! Take him *now*!

(*Fabio opens the door. Marco and Orfeo come in with two policemen. Giaco is still shouting:*)

GIACO: We will cheat you! As we cheat each other! As we cheat God!

FABIO: (*To the police*) Take him.

GIACO: (*Seeing them*) Ah, so soon—so soon?

POLICEMAN: What is the charge!

GIACO: (*Crazed*) The charge, the charge! A minor offense against a lady!

GIOVANNA: Not a minor offense—and not against a lady. But against almighty heaven!

FABIO: Giovanna—

GIOVANNA: He has brought spirits here—and devils!

GIACO: The charge! What is the charge?

GIOVANNA: Sorcery!

NICO: (*With an outcry*) No—not sorcery—no!

GIOVANNA: Take him!

(*As they take Giaco toward and door*)

NICO: No, let him go! I beg you, let him go! Giaco—Giaco—!

(*The men push him away and take Giaco off. Fabio goes after them. Giovanna and Nico are alone onstage. He sobs brokenly. She cannot bear to hear him. She goes to him: compassionate, strangely tender.*)

GIOVANNA: Be still, old man.

NICO: Please—I beg you—let him go! Not sorcery . . . let him go!

GIOVANNA: (*Gently caressing his head*) Old man, be still . . .

NICO: Giaco—Giaco—

GIOVANNA: Be still . . . be still . . .

(*The lights fade. The lights come up again, a few days later, in Fabio's waiting room. He is questioning Alcestor.*)

FABIO: Has she gone to visit him?

ALCESTOR: No, signore, she has not.

FABIO: Are you sure of it?

ALCESTOR: Yes indeed, signore. Di Falco has watched the south gate of the prison and Marco, the north. She has not entered either one. Not even once.

GIOVANNA: (*At the door*) Nor do I intend to go there.

(*Giovanna is much altered. Her body has lost its mettle, and her spirit is desolate, gray. Fabio gestures for Alcestor to leave.*)

FABIO: You will have to go and see him, Giovanna.

GIOVANNA: I cannot.

FABIO: You must. Don't let another day go by—make your peace with him.

GIOVANNA: I wouldn't know how.

FABIO: Find a way. Galbaio has questioned him three days in a row. So far, he has not betrayed us. He claims his shouting was the madness of the instant, and I suppose it was. But how long will he keep faith with us?

GIOVANNA: (*Guiltily*) And why should he?

FABIO: Unless his love for you, and yours for him . . .

GIOVANNA: I can't ask him to keep faith with us against himself. The charge against him is sorcery. Sorcery! (*In a torment of self-blame*) My God, I was demented!

FABIO: (*With cool detachment, withholding his belief*) Were you indeed, my dear?

GIOVANNA: When he called us liars and cheats—at the window—shouting, shouting—my head was a storm—rage and terror—! There was witchcraft in the air and I clutched at it . . . Demented.

FABIO: I don't think you were demented, Giovanna. You wanted to divert attention from our guilt to his. It was a desperate remedy—but not at all deranged. In fact, it may be the only one we have. And you must use it.

GIOVANNA: I will not betray him further. You think I want him tortured—killed?

FABIO: You might be saving him.

GIOVANNA: How?

FABIO: Strike a lover's bargain with him—and I will strike one with you. If he keeps his silence, I will help him.

GIOVANNA: In what way?

FABIO: If Galbaio is a tribune, so am I. He's the only tradesman on the court, and the most detested. The balance weighs with us.

GIOVANNA: If I go to Giaco . . .

FABIO: Go.

GIOVANNA: No matter what I say, he won't believe me.

FABIO: He will because he must.

GIOVANNA: No. I've been a vandal. Whatever idols he yearned to pray to— I smashed them. How can I make him believe me now?

FABIO: By convincing him that he'll go free.

GIOVANNA: Free to do what?

FABIO: To leave. To go anywhere he wants. He won't mind leaving, we can be sure of that. He has no need of Venice, as we do. His self-esteem does not rely on good-will and old confidences. He will not pine for holidays at home or birthdays he can't celebrate. He can ride out of here richer than he crawled in—shiny carriage, new wardrobe, a ring or two that won't turn black. The jackanapes goes forth a jackadandy. And good riddance.

GIOVANNA: And everybody heaves a sigh of relief.

FABIO: Won't you?

GIOVANNA: No . . . I love him.

FABIO: (*With level voice. Mordantly*) I do not believe you are capable of it.

GIOVANNA: (*Desperately*) I am, I am!

FABIO: Could you love him and try to hew him so rigidly to your will? Could you love and betray him as you did?

GIOVANNA: Yes! I can love him and kill him and love him!

FABIO: That's a vivid answer, but it says nothing. (*Quietly*) Can you love him and—when he goes—go with him? (*As she does not answer*) Can you?

GIOVANNA: (*She is starting to weep*) No. Then why do I ache when I think of him gone? Why do I wish to die when my mind sees him in prison, why do I wish that I were in his place? How can I feel that my whole life has changed since I met him, and that I am half the woman that I was, yet more of the woman that I yearn to be? How can I be so wretchedly happy and unhappy, how can I wish to live every moment that I wish to die, to die!
(*As she weeps, he starts to go to her, but there is no consolation he can offer. He departs. With an effort, she begins to pull herself together. There is the sound of altercation in the corridor, and Carla bursts in, followed by Alcestor.*)

GIOVANNA: I told you I would see no one.

ALCESTOR: I tried to stop her, signore—

CARLA: I have to talk to you! Twice I tried today—and they said you would not allow me—

GIOVANNA: That hasn't changed. Please go.

CARLA: There's a rumor about Giaco—
(*Giovanna has a moment of indecision. She nods to Alcestor, and he leaves.*)

GIOVANNA: Rumor? What rumor?

CARLA: (*With inordinate control*) They say the court will burn him.

GIOVANNA: There's always that rumor. Matches are cheap and words are cheaper. Go away.

CARLA: No.

GIOVANNA: (*Threatening with her fan*) I said go away!

CARLA: (*With quiet firmness*) If you must hit me, do it. But I'll not skulk out of this room. I won't do that anymore, Signora. I have changed.

GIOVANNA: Yes? How so?

CARLA: I stand straight in the daytime, I sleep at night, and I do not have nightmares of my father anymore. All this is thanks to Mastromare.

GIOVANNA: (*Pitying her*) Dear fool, do you still believe you heard your father's voice?

CARLA: Oh, I know about the man you hired to make false voices. But there are truths within falsehood, signora. And somewhere in the inmost quiet of us all, there is some voice we must believe in. And Mastromare made it speak to me.

GIOVANNA: But this is the most irrational—! The nightmares of your father appeared irrationally and irrationally they disappeared. You cannot credit Mastromare for their departure any more than you can blame him for their arrival!

CARLA: Then why did I have them until the seance, and not thereafter?

GIOVANNA: (*Angry*) Because you did it—you! You are your own irrationality!

CARLA: (*Very quietly*) No, you are wrong. Giaco did it. And if there's a danger he may suffer because of what he has done for me, I mean to help him.

GIOVANNA: You cannot!

CARLA: Because you cannot—or will not—will you let no one else try?

GIOVANNA: (*Losing her temper*) No! You've caused damage enough! I'll not let a wild girl get her hands in this!

CARLA: (*Calmly*) Wild girl? Which of us is wild, signora? My bedroom faces yours across the court. Have you noticed that these nights my room is dark? I sleep, signora! Could I sleep if I were not sure that I can help him? . . . Is *your* room dark these nights?

GIOVANNA: (*Somewhat stilled*) How do you think you can help him?

CARLA: The charge is sorcery, is it not?

GIOVANNA: Yes.

CARLA: What is sorcery, signora?

GIOVANNA: What is it?—it's magic—black magic.

CARLA: Why do you call it black?

GIOVANNA: It's what the court calls it. Witchery. The aid of evil spirits.

CARLA: Why evil, signora? If Mastromare had helped me with the aid of evil spirits, would I be as you see me now? No, signora, I would still run screaming on the balconies, I would still dig my nails into my breast. But I do not, signora. I am at peace. So if there was sorcery, he used it for the good and not for the evil.

GIOVANNA: (*With alarm*) How did he use it? What will you say if they ask you that?

CARLA: He made a seance for me and—however it happened—I felt my father's presence.

GIOVANNA: You will say that? You don't see how dangerous that would be for him? You would say that in the court?

CARLA: Yes, I would!

GIOVANNA: You lunatic! You and your babble of voices—you'll convict him of sorcery! You'll be doing exactly as Galbaio wants you to do! Have you heard the rumors that the monster spreads? Last night Galbaio's boatman said he approached the prison where they keep Mastromare. No matter how heavily he plied his oar, he says, his gondola refused to go under the Bridge of Sighs. When he withdrew his oar, it was dripping blood. Another tale: One of the prisoners touched Mastromare's sleeve—and his hand was burned. On the palm—the mark of a cloven hoof. Stupid lies—calumnies—in every wineshop—they're the tipple of Venice! Black magic—and Mastromare behind every evil!

CARLA: If they say evil, then someone must say good! He has brought me only good!

GIOVANNA: With sorcery!

CARLA: Can the court not tell the difference between good and evil?

GIOVANNA: (*In a rage*) No! Good and evil are not the business of the court! (*Reining herself in, she goes to the bell cord and pulls it. Quietly now:*) I forbid you to testify.

CARLA: But if I can save him—

GIOVANNA: If you speak, they will kill him. Or worse, torture him. Have you ever seen a man with burning coals in his mouth? Do you know what the bastinado is?

CARLA: A man who seeks God as Giaco does—he has had the bastinado all his life.

GIOVANNA: (*In dread quiet*) I cannot allow you to speak for him.
(*Marco and Orfeo appear at the doorway.*)

GIOVANNA: (*Gently*) Carla . . . you will be taken back to your home in Murano.

CARLA: No, signora.

GIOVANNA: No harm will come to you.

CARLA: Please, signora—no one is there. My family are all gone!

GIOVANNA: Marco and Orfeo will look to you. Until the trial is over.

CARLA: No! I will testify for him!

GIOVANNA: (*To the men*) Take her to Murano. See that she does not leave her room until a boat has been arranged.

CARLA: I will testify for him! I will, I will!
(*She is about to revert to her one-time hysteria. But, by main force, she brings herself under control. With quiet dignity, she leaves the room with Marco and Orfeo. Giovanna remains, unhappy, anxious, still. The lights fade. In the darkness we hear a Jailer's voice:*)

JAILER'S VOICE: Don't stumble. Wait until I light the lamp.
(*The flicker of a match, a lamp is lighted to reveal a Jailer. Giovanna enters. We are in an anteroom in the prison.*)

GIOVANNA: You say he has asked to see no one?

JAILER: No one has been allowed to see him.

GIOVANNA: That was not my question. I'll not continue to pay you ten ducats a day to hear evasions. Has he asked to see anyone?

JAILER: Last night he asked me would I—for a favor—find out about the girl—whatever is her name—does she rest well, does she sleep? I told him I couldn't.

GIOVANNA: That is all?

(He nods. We hear the opening of another door, then footsteps. Giaco appears, followed by a Second Jailer. The prisoner is unkempt, hollow-eyed. The Jailers step back in the shadows. Giovanna looks at Giaco, hoping he will speak. He stares into distances. Her voice is unsure.)

GIOVANNA: It has been reported that you . . . sit in silence . . . gazing at your hands.

GIACO: *(He looks at hands; his smiles, far away)* And that daily I depart further from my senses.

GIOVANNA: You've grown frailer. I . . . send you food and you return it.

GIACO: It is too dark here to eat.

GIOVANNA: They say you nightmare.

GIACO: It is not dark enough to sleep.

GIOVANNA: *(A lament)* Why did you not send for me?

GIACO: I did not know you were at my beck and call.

GIOVANNA: I come here every night, up to the Bridge of Sighs. In the darkness I tell the boatman to stop. I look up at the guard and he shakes his head. You've never asked for me—not once.

GIACO: *(Quietly)* Time enough to see you at the trial.

GIOVANNA: No—too late. We have to speak—before the trial.

GIACO: Why? Are you to defend me?

GIOVANNA: You think I would not?

GIACO: Perhaps you would. Then you'd be everything. The prosecutor to charge me, the advocate to defend me, and, I'm sure, the Tribunal too. How do you find me, Giovanna—guilty of witchcraft?

GIOVANNA: The charge can be changed.

GIACO: To what?

GIOVANNA: To a minor charge.

GIACO: Like what? The man was urinating in the Grand Canal? Come now, Giovanna, a bit more glory, please . . . What did you come for?

GIOVANNA: *(At pains not to weep)* I . . . when we first met, you genuflected to me. I've come to do the same to you.

GIACO: Don't, please. The floor will soil your dress.

GIOVANNA: I planned to weep and ask forgiveness and make you quite a show. But I find that I mean it too much to pretend it even a little.

GIACO: Will you excuse me, please. I am a busy man.

(As he turns as if to go she reaches toward him)

GIOVANNA: No—please—you must believe me!

GIACO: I cannot believe you any more than you would me.

GIOVANNA: Were you to tell me that you love me, I'd want to hear it so badly I would put trust in every word.

GIACO: . . . I love you, Giovanna.

GIOVANNA: You lie.

GIACO: There—you see?

GIOVANNA: You always lie that way. So that you will trip over your own falsehoods.

GIACO: (*Wryly*) Why do you suppose that is?

GIOVANNA: Because you need to believe in them yourself. You have to make seances and hear your own fake voices.

GIACO: You think that I play Barabbas and want to be crucified as Christ?

GIOVANNA: Yes! (*Pleading with him to change*) This little touch of Jesus in you doesn't give you heaven, Giaco, it gives you hell!

GIACO: Perhaps for the burnings of hell, I get a glimpse of heaven.

GIOVANNA: When have you had a glimpse—when?

GIACO: When I heard the voice of Carla's father and was deluded into thinking I had summoned it—oh, it was like the voice of God! (*With an ironic smile*) You know, if I had really accomplished such a thing, it might be worth standing trial for sorcery.

GIOVANNA: (*Alarmed*) I can't believe you mean it.

GIACO: If I only had the courage.

GIOVANNA: Courage? Why don't you have the courage to stand trial for what you have been, not what you dream yourself to be?

GIACO: What have I been, Giovanna?

GIOVANNA: A charlatan.

GIACO: I stand trial for being a charlatan every day of my life. That takes no courage—that is what I *am*. But to stand trial for the discrepancy between what I am and what I might have been—! (*He laughs*) Oh, for that I might have the courage to go to the stake!

GIOVANNA: (*Chilled*) That's mystical nonsense. Out of the Middle Ages.

GIACO: Yes, I'm a leftover, I suppose—and refuse should be burned. But I'm not beguiled by this Age of so-called Reason.

GIOVANNA: You're beguiled by madness.

GIACO?: Yes, I confess it. I can love every wild imagining of the human mind—and believe them all! Small wonders, large wonders! A man can write a poem to stanch a wound! Alchemy can take dregs and dross and turn them into something golden—golden, Giovanna! (*His brief rhapsody ends in dreariness.*) But the age is brass—and I am made of it. And I suppose if I can save my greasy neck by standing to a smaller charge—why, lady, I'll stand smaller. (*Then, with an ache*) But oh, my dear—if I had the fortitude—! (*An instant. He smiles wanly*) You want to hear a foolish dream I had? . . . That Carla was at peace again.

GIOVANNA: (*Startled*) . . . What?

GIACO: Yes—at peace. That the seance did not fail, that her father's voice was truly heard, that she still believes in wonders . . . and sleeps her nights in peace.

GIOVANNA: Oh, why—why do you need to believe in this?

GIACO: Because if we can exorcise each other's ghosts—oh, sweet alchemy—! If I could do it, I'd stand to any charge!

(*She feels he is bent on havoc and it terrifies her. At last she says quietly:*)

GIOVANNA: No need to stand to serious charges . . . Not on Carla's account.

GIACO: (*Alerted*) Why? How is she?

GIOVANNA: . . . She is worse.

GIACO: Oh, poor child. Does it go so badly for her? Her terrors . . . ?

GIOVANNA: Have never left her.

GIACO: Poor girl . . . Send her to me.

GIOVANNA: I can't. She's not in Venice.

GIACO: Where, then?

GIOVANNA: No one knows. She has disappeared. From sight . . . and mind.

GIACO: And mind, you say?

GIOVANNA: (*Slowly, with difficulty*) She is demented, Giaco.

GIACO: Demented?—no! (*An outcry*) Oh God, I did this to her!

GIOVANNA: No! She was bent on madness!

GIACO: No! I did it!

GIOVANNA: It was not your fault!

GIACO: It was, it was! My spirit was too small to help her! I have diminished what I could have been! I have said lies and I've played tricks with God, and whittled at myself until there is very little of me left. I have shrunken into a little man inside a bottle. Ecce homo, ecce homunculus! (*For an instant, he goes berserk. As if to destroy himself, he tears at his clothes, then stops and yells:*) Guards! Guards!

(*The Guards rush forward and lead him away. Trembling, Giovanna too departs. The lights fade and come up again, in single focus, upon the Marchese, dressed in the blood red robes of the Tribunal. As he speaks, the light includes Galbaio and Signor Miniore, who is also in red robes and sits as capo of the court. He and Galbaio, the prosecutor, are listening to Fabio, the defender. As the light broadens, we see the remaining seven judges of the Black Tribunal. Giovanna barely takes her gaze off Giaco. His eyes are empty, in despair.*)

FABIO: I do not understand Signor Galbaio's bitter resistance. If we commute the charge against the prisoner to a lesser offense, in the end even Signor Galbaio will be gratified. If he persists in charging the prisoner with sorcery—without a single witness—patently the prisoner will go free. On the other hand, since the prisoner has confessed himself a quack and is willing to plead guilty to a lesser charge than witchcraft, I should think Signor Galbaio would be gratified to see the prisoner—in *some* way—punished.

GALBAIO: Signor Miniore, the Marchese has been a friend of the prisoner—a devoted friend. The Marchese has been host to the prisoner—a cordial host. (*Turning to Fabio*) Devoted friend, cordial host, steadfast defender—if you're so certain the prisoner will be acquitted of sorcery, why not let the charge stand?—and get him altogether free? Why do you insist on punishing him, even if it be for a minor charge?

FABIO: You've delayed enough! Each day it becomes more difficult to shut out the voices of the crowd. You've incited them to whisper witchcraft against the prisoner!

GALBAIO: They whisper more than witchcraft, signore! Look to this! (*A high gesture: He holds up the ducat—the coined souvenir of Mastromare.*)

JUDGES: What is that? . . . Let me see, Galbaio . . . A ducat!

MINIORE: A ducat, sir—is that a ducat?

GALBAIO: Yes—a golden ducat! Gold it is, oh yes, but whose is the mintage? And why the prisoner's face? Some say vanity—but some say swindle! Some say that he has friends in this!

FABIO: (*In a rage*) You say swindle and look at me! Then make an open charge, signore—face the consequence, and make a charge. (*Silence. Turning to the others*) You see? Why do we have a tribune's chair for a wriggling thing like that?—can we not find him a slimy rock?

GALBAIO: (*Pointing at Fabio*) A rock for a thief—a swindling thief!

OTHERS: (*In an uproar*) Silence! . . . Call the charge! . . . Thief! . . . Call order, order! . . . Disgraceful!

MINIORE: Silence! Silence!

FABIO: If he has a charge against me, let it take precedence.

MINIORE: Signor Galbaio, do you withdraw your insinuations?

GALBAIO: No! The Marchese knows how difficult it is to prove sorcery without witnesses. But there were witnesses! To a certain seance! (*To Fabio*) Where are they now?

FABIO: Here, sir—in the room! And I am one of them! But which of us will testify to sorcery? Which? (*He points to Giovanna, himself and Giaco.*) Her?—myself?—him? Go on—question us!

GALBAIO: Where are the two servants Orfeo and Marco? Why did they take leave of Venice? Where is the pawnbroker Tadeo and his wife? Why did they depart Venice on the very night of the seance? Why? Ask him, Signor Capo.

FABIO: Am I expected to know the whereabouts of discharged servants?

GALBAIO: How about the whereabouts of a special servant, one Carla di Murano. (*Silence. Then:*)

MINIORE: Where is she, Marchese?

FABIO: It seems that, after all, I *am* on trial!

MINIORE: (*Annoyed*) Come, Marchese, it was you who asked for a commutation of the charge. The whereabouts of an important witness is moot to the point. Where is she?

FABIO: The girl was unhappy in her position, signore. One night she disappeared. (*Galbaio passes Miniore a sheet of paper. The capo reads it. They exchange glances. To Fabio:*)

MINIORE: Marchese, there is an opinion that it was you who sent the girl away.

FABIO: That is not true.

MINIORE: To save her the pain of testifying against the prisoner.

FABIO: Not true!

GALBAIO: (*Jumping up*) There is an opinion that you sent her to the town of Murano—

FABIO: No!

GALBAIO: —and that is where we found her! . . . Send her in.

(*The door opens and Carla is ushered in. She is quietly dressed and has a quiet manner. For the first time, Giaco speaks. He rises above the confusion.*)

GIACO: No! Let her alone! Let her go!

MINIORE: Order! Silence! . . . Please be seated, Signorina di Murano. We must now address ourselves to the prisoner. (*To the other judges*) Will you allow me, masters?

JUDGES: Yes . . . Yes, go on! . . . Question him, capo.

MINIORE: (*To Giaco*) Signore . . . your case is a dark one. And you cast no light. To each one who has come to question you in your cell you have given different answers. Even to your name. What is your true name?

GIACO: I do not know my true name. I am a bastard . . . Does the girl have to stay?

MINIORE: You will stand trial as Giacomo Levanto. The charge against you is sorcery. If you are found guilty, you are punishable in severe measure. By the rack, by the scourge, ordeal by fire, ordeal by water . . .

GIACO: This child can tell you nothing! Her presence here can only bring her pain and shed light on nothing! Let her go!

MINIORE: She is here to testify.

GIACO: Why do you need her? I have offered to plead guilty to any reasonable charge!

GALBAIO: Do you plead guilty to sorcery?

MINIORE: Signor Galbaio!

GALBAIO: Ask him!

MINIORE: Signor Levanto, do you plead guilty to the charge of sorcery?

GIOVANNA: He does not! Fabio, tell them he does not!

MINIORE: Contessa, please. I ask you, Signor Levanto—do you plead guilty to the charge of sorcery?

(*Giovanna and Carla are staring fixedly at him. He does not meet their eyes.*)

GIACO: No.

MINIORE: You are not a sorcerer?

GIACO: No.

MINIORE: Are you a witchman, a wizard?

GIACO: No.

MINIORE: A necromancer, a conjuror, a dealer with devils?

GIACO: No.

MINIORE: Are you yourself a devil of any kind? . . . You will answer the question, please. Are you yourself a devil of any kind?

GIACO: (*With a rueful smile*) "Of any kind?" The question is ambiguous.

MINIORE: Do you believe in sorcery? Witchcraft, necromancy—do you believe in any of these?

GIACO: Am I on trial for what I believe?

MINIORE: Signor Levanto, the practice of sorcery is occult and cunning, hence quite difficult to prove. Unlike other states, the republic of Venice will not find you guilty of sorcery if it cannot be justly proved upon you. However, if you confess to a *belief* in sorcery, it will be sufficient against you to warrant a charge of sorcery . . . Now—what do you believe?

(*Giaco tightens. Carla cries out:*)

CARLA: Tell them—please! Tell them!

GIACO: Send her away. Will you please send her away!

MINIORE: What do you believe?

(*In order to bring himself under control, Giaco turns away from Carla. He pauses and looks at Fabio who nods to him. Then, still looking at Fabio—and at no one else—Giaco speaks, measuring every word.*)

GIACO: Masters, I am told by my advocate that if I say I believe in any other God than the one worshipped in Venice, I will be held culpable under the laws of this republic. Signori, I am innocent—I do *not* believe in any other God . . . I believe in nothing.

(*A shocked outcry in the court. Galbaio exults:*)

GALBAIO: Heresy! We will add the charge of heresy!

MINIORE: Silence! Galbaio, you will be held for disorder!

GALBAIO: The man is a self-confessed heretic!

(*Commotion. Miniore holds up the fasces, the bound bundle of rods and ax, symbol of law and authority. He threatens with them high in the air and does not lower them. A hush.*)

MINIORE: Signor Galbaio, I raise the fasces. Must I single you out with them?

(*Galbaio subsides. Fabio rises. Miniore recognizes him.*)

FABIO: Signor Galbaio is not only disorderly, he is ignorant. This is not an ecclesiastical court. Heresy is not a crime against the state. The prisoner says he believes in nothing. It is no crime to believe in nothing. But if he confesses that he does believe in sorcery or magic . . . (*He pauses. To Miniore, tactfully*) Lest he inculpate himself, you must advise him, Signor Capo.

MINIORE: (*To Giaco*) I advise you again. If you confess you believe in any of the black magics, the charge of sorcery will stand. Now what do you believe in?

GIACO: I've said it. Nothing.

MINIORE: (*With a remote smile*) That suggests a vacuum of the spirit, inimical to nature. What is more, it suggests perjury—since we have been told there is someone in the court to whom you did claim to believe in something. Will you face the witness Carla di Murano, if you please. (*As Giaco complies*) Now then, signore: do you believe that you can exorcise a devil?

GIACO: No, I cannot. Send the girl away!

MINIORE: How about ghosts, Signor Levanto? Can you exorcise a ghost? Do you believe you can?

GIOVANNA: (*Breaking in*) He has told me no! He does not believe such things!

CARLA: Let him answer!

GIOVANNA: You—be quiet! You want them to torture him!

CARLA: Better than that he torture himself! (*Running to Giaco*) Tell them! Tell them what you believe! Do not torment yourself over me!

GIACO: Send her away!

CARLA: You have not betrayed me! You have given me back my courage and my peace! Let me give you a little in return!

(*A taut instant. Giaco has been looking beseechingly to Miniore, begging the capo to remove Carla. Hearing the word "peace" he slowly turns to her. He speaks softly.*)

GIACO: Peace . . .? Did you say peace?

CARLA: Quiet in my heart! And sleep—and peace!

GIACO: (*In an uplifted voice*) Peace! (*He turns to Giovanna in a rage*) You lied to me! She said peace! She said sleep—and peace!

GIOVANNA: (*Wild*) Tear her away from him! Fabio—tear her away!

GIACO: No—let her stay! (*Exalted*) Masters—I believe! I believe in magic! I believe in all magic! I believe in the magic of God and the magic of Christ Jesus! I believe in the magic of Moses smiting the rock! I believe in the fiery magic of truth and the bloody magic of birth! White magic and black magic—all!—I believe in all, in all!

GALBAIO: A crime—a crime!

GIACO: But no crime to believe in nothing, is it? No crime to believe we live in a void, in a godforsaken emptiness! Well, I would sooner be mad and believe in everything! In the angels of heaven and the devils of hell—for I have lived with all of them! And you—you devils that I live with now— you lean men of reason, you skeletons of judgment—you who believe in nothing—you terrify me most! So go on—scourge me!—drive me to sanity! In the end I will exorcise you all!

GALBAIO: Sorcery!

VOICES: Sorcery! . . . By his own mouth! . . . Sorcery! . . . Call the charge!

(*Miniore stands. The court goes quiet. He raises the fasces and points them at Giaco.*)

MINIORE: Culpus stet. Sorcery. The charge stands.

(*The lights fade. When they come on again, we have returned to the prison. Nico, in the company of a Jailer, huddles in a corner. On his lap are Giaco's culvert clothes. As the old man waits, suddenly: an animal cry of pain from the passageway. Nico cannot stand it. In agony, he makes himself as small as he can. The Second Jailer leads Giovanna in. She is under self-bridle, hiding terror and heartbreak. Nico, full of fury at her, does not rise. She tries not to note it.*)

GIOVANNA: Is he alive? (*As Nico does not answer*) I asked you a question, old man.

NICO: (*Hard*) He might as well be dead, thanks to you. What do you want here?

GIOVANNA: I've come for him.

NICO: If you've come for his body, you're premature, signora. But if he should die, no need to trouble—I will claim him.

GIOVANNA: (*Quietly, indicating Nico's bundle*) He might not want to be buried in those clothes. They smell of sulphur.

NICO: He has no reason to fear hell, signora.

GIOVANNA: (*Indicating her own bundle—with a forlorn smile*) Not that these smell of paradise.

NICO: Why don't you let him alone? You'll hurt him worse than the bastinado. (*As he catches her quick glance*) Ah, you didn't know that's what they do to him? Well, let me describe it.

GIOVANNA: If you're trying to pain me—

NICO: Is that possible, signora?—let us see. All kinds of bastinado! This one—it's the walking kind. They give him "measures." He has had two of them. First, they hang him by the heels, to drain the devil out of him. Do I pain you, signora? Then they stretch his body on the rack, to break the devil's grasp. Now they scourge him. Do I pain you, do I pain you?

(*She remains seemingly impassive. It is Nico who is falling apart.*) The walking bastinado! They promenade him down the passageway so all the prisoners can see. When he walks, only one man belabors him with whips. But when he falls or faints—! Do I pain you, Contessa? If he survives the fifth measure—ah, then they know the devil in him has been routed—and he is free! It is reasonable, is it not? Do I pain you?

(*He breaks down and sobs. Giovanna quietly goes to him and takes him in her arms. Silently she comforts him.*)

GIOVANNA: No more, Nico.

NICO: (*Weeping*) These are good times, signora—a reasonable age.

(*At last he grows quiet. From the corridor, another outcry. A moan, a stillness, another outcry. Then, an ominous stillness.*)

GIOVANNA: What has happened?

NICO: Jailer!

GIOVANNA: *Giaco!*

NICO: Oh no, oh no!

(*Giovanna runs to the door leading to the inside corridor. The Second Jailer stands in her way. Now a light is seen advancing toward us, outside the corridor door. Carrying the lantern, the Third Jailer enters. He is the scourger, with a bloody flail. They watch him in agonized stillness. He talks low:*)

THIRD JAILER: He has walked five times . . . and lives.

GIOVANNA: He lives?

NICO: Thank God, thank God!

THIRD JAILER: Who will receive him?

GIOVANNA: I will.

NICO: No, he's mine! I'm his friend!

(*The Third Jailer goes to the door. He talks to those in the passageway.*)

THIRD JAILER: Do not help him. Let him come in .. Can you rise?

NICO: Let me help him!

THIRD JAILER: No—stand back. (*To the unseen Giaco*) Come . . . the left knee now. Raise the left knee, man. Now—up. Come forward. Come. Come forward.

(*He steps aside, vacating the doorway. Giaco appears—bloody, stumbling, shuffling, but upright.*)

THIRD JAILER: Whichever wishes to claim him—he is yours.

(*The Third Jailer goes. Giaco collapses. Giovanna and Nico rush to him.*)

GIOVANNA: Oh, my dear—oh, my dear—!)
) TOGETHER

NICO: Oh, beloved friend—poor friend!)

(*Giovanna hurries to the bundle she has brought and finds a flacon which she takes to Giaco. He drinks a little.*)

GIOVANNA: More—more, if you can—

NICO: Oh, beloved friend—

GIACO: (*Like a child*) They beat me, Nico—and they beat me—but—I—have beaten them!

NICO: Yes, Giaco—yes!

GIOVANNA: He trembles—he is cold.

(*Again she goes to the bundle. Nico unfolds a robe.*)

GIACO: Help me up, Nico.

NICO: Rest, Giaco—rest.

GIACO: No—I want—not stay here—want to go—

NICO: Please—(*To Giovanna*) He means to rise.

GIOVANNA: We'll help him up.

(*They support him as he stands. Gently he pushes them away. The fact that he can now stand alone brings a ray of pride to his face, illuminating it. He tries to walk again. But abruptly he shivers, as if with cold. They support him again. Giovanna puts the robe around his shoulders.*)

GIACO: Thank you . . . but . . . too heavy.

(*Nico lets it fall to the floor and covers him with the lighter robe he has brought. Nico is muttering under his breath, and weeping.*) What sound is that?

GIOVANNA: (*To Nico*) Can you not be quiet?

NICO: (*Half weeping, half laughing*) Forgive me, I am saying thanks to God—and blubbering a little.

GIACO: No need to cry. I'm restored. I am much restored.

GIOVANNA: Come, then. Can you walk? Stand close. I'll help you.

NICO: He goes with me.

GIOVANNA: Nonsense. He'll need tending. I have a boat below there. Come.

GIACO: I go with him, Giovanna.

GIOVANNA: Please. I must look after you. And you must let me. (*Entreating*) Giaco . . .

GIACO: No, I say.

GIOVANNA: Giaco—please—I beg you—come!

(*She reaches out to his arm. She touches a wounded place. He cries out in pain.*)

GIACO: No! You have no way of touching me that will not pain me!

GIOVANNA: It will pass—I promise you, it will. You will heal—and I will help to heal you!

(*From the outer corridor, a bloody shriek. A commotion of voices:*)

VOICES: No! I must see him! . . . Stop her! . . . I have a present for him! . . . Wait, girl! . . . No—let me!

GIOVANNA: Who is it?

NICO: (*At the door*) Oh, dear heaven!   )

)   TOGETHER

GIACO: Who is coming?   )

GIOVANNA: Oh no! Jailer—please—don't harm her—

NICO: No—no!

GIOVANNA: Let her in, let her in!

(*The Jailer opens the door. Carla enters. Her clothes are filthy and disarrayed, her hair wild. She is demented.*)

CARLA: Ah, Mastromare—ah, dear signore! They told me you were dead. The writhing things, the lizards—the lizards came to me last night and said, "Dying, dying, dead," they told me, "All dead and gone to heaven!" . . . I see it is not so.

GIACO: (*Gently*) No, child.

CARLA: "Not so," I said to them. "It cannot be the truth! And if it is, I have the means to bring him back again!" And oh, I do, sir! A kind word and a light! Why, I can strike a light from nothing—see? (*She pretends to strike a light as Giaco did, without a match. There is, of course, no light.*) See it shine? And I have other things. I have a warm red nipple to suck and I can summon voices! And this—I've brought you this! (*She holds out her hand. In it, Giaco's homunculus.*)

GIACO: (*Gently*) What is it, my dear?

CARLA: Your little man, your dear homunculus. (*To the others*) Have you seen his little man? Look how dear he is! And small! Why, he's no bigger than the penis of a pig! (*She giggles*) I kiss you, little man! (*She kisses the homunculus. Her face goes grave as she sees Giovanna.*) Oh, signora, how sad you look! May I kiss you, my beautiful lady?

GIOVANNA: Yes, my dear.

(*Carla gently takes Giovanna's hand, kisses it, holds it lovingly to her own cheek, rocks it like a child, kisses it once more and hands it back to Giovanna as if it were a gift.*)

CARLA: (*To Giaco*) And you, signore?

GIACO: Yes, dear child.

(*She goes to him. He kisses her gently. She then puts her head very sadly on his breast. She sighs and starts to weep softly.*)

CARLA: Why did the lizards tell me that you died?

GIACO: Hush. Hush, my dear.

CARLA: I have nothing precious to bring to you. I have nothing to bring to you that I have ever made. I will go and make something for you . . . make something. . .

(*Murmuring, she departs. An instant. Giaco turns to Giovanna.*)

GIACO: You knew this about her.

GIOVANNA: I was told of it, yes. But when I looked for her, I could not find her.

GIACO: (*Desolately*) You were right, weren't you, Giovanna? She made your lie come true. And I thought she was in peace.

NICO: She *was* in peace . . . a little while.

GIACO: Why did it not last? (*Starting to recover his ironic humor*) There's nothing wrong with magic . . . except it does not last. Like being in love with a fickle mistress. (*He looks down at the homunculus in his hand.*) Ah, little man, little man! (*Slowly he goes to the barred window. He throws the homunculus through it.*) Farewell.

NICO: Oh, no!

GIACO: Magic, farewell. Come, Nico. (*Again he starts to tremble.*) Help me! (*As Nico and Giovanna rush to him.*) Not you, Giovanna . . . Nico, which way?

GIOVANNA: Wait! Where will you go?

GIACO: Go? Somewhere, I suppose.

GIOVANNA: But where?

GIACO: (*Wryly*) I don't know, Giovanna. I have never had . . . an itinerary.

GIOVANNA: Wait! Giaco, wait! (*Begging*) Take me with you!

GIACO: . . . What, Giovanna?

GIOVANNA: Let me go with you!

GIACO: No, Giovanna.

GIOVANNA: Please—I beg you—

GIACO: My dear—

GIOVANNA: I can help you! Where will you go—what will you do? You have no clothes, no money! Why, this ring—(*Trying to smile*)—remember, you bought it for me! Or this brooch—we can all live for a year on what it will bring! Let me come with you—let me help you!

NICO: No—no help—we don't need your help!

GIOVANNA: Stay out of it, old man!

GIACO: But he is right, my dear. We do not need your—

GIOVANNA: *But I need yours!* Oh, help me, Giaco!

GIACO: Help *you*? Oh, Giovanna!

GIOVANNA: Help me to love you and not hate myself for loving someone! For the first time I think I might—with you I might!

GIACO: (*Quietly*) How am I to help you do that?

GIOVANNA: Help me to become as you are! I don't want to be Giovanna anymore! Teach me to hope—and to believe—and not cry mercy when they beat me! Teach me to believe in something, Giaco!

GIACO: In what?

GIOVANNA: What you believe in!

GIACO: Magic?—out that window.

GIOVANNA: But you will search—

GIACO: (*A despairing cry*) For what? A scourge of pain? A number? A confluence of stars? The prima materia—what is it? Fire and brimstone?—a crumb of bread?—a ring, a brooch? Is it fact, is it spirit? Is it earth, water, dung and worms? Is it death? Is it a dream of God?

GIOVANNA: Whatever you find—

GIACO: Find? Ah, there it is! Suppose it is all searching and no finding—never any finding! Suppose, Giovanna—suppose all we have—all we'll ever get—is the search itself?

GIOVANNA: Oh no—that's endless!

GIACO: (*Relentlessly*) Does it terrify you?

GIOVANNA: If I'm terrified, I'll share your courage!

GIACO: My courage—mine?

GIOVANNA: I love you, Giaco—take me with you—

GIACO: No—let me go—

GIOVANNA: (*Bereft*) I must go with you! Oh, please—oh, Giaco—please—!

GIACO: Let me go, Giovanna—

GIOVANNA: (*She sinks to her knees*) Oh, Giaco—oh, please—oh, please! Without you, Giaco—! If you don't take me with you, I will die! I'll die! *I'll die of nothing, die of nothing!*

GIACO: (*With an agonized cry*) Enough—oh, enough! I've had the bastinado long enough!
(*It is his first cry for mercy. Hearing it, Giovanna has compassion, and she importunes him no further.*) Come . . . Get up, my dear . . . Get up.
(*She slowly brings herself under control. She takes off her ring and hands it to him.*)

GIOVANNA: Here. May I give you this?

GIACO: No. I thank you. No.

GIOVANNA: Let me give you something.

GIACO: (*Deeply, gently*) You have, my dear. Once—for a moment—a golden doublet. I loved that doublet, Giovanna . . . and I loved you.

GIOVANNA: Yes, I think you did . . . I love you still . . . Goodbye, my dear.

GIACO: Goodbye, Giovanna.

GIOVANNA: Look to him, Nico. Wash him where he bleeds.

NICO: Yes, signora.
(*Giovanna goes. Silence. Nico, seeing Giaco's suffering, goes to him. He notes the blood on Giaco's shoulder. He starts to help Giaco off with his shirt but Giaco cries out. Nico grieves:*) Oh, Giaco—why? You were only trying to do a kindness to a frightened child. Why need they have hurt you?

GIACO: The scales are inexact, my friend. (*As Nico tries to help him again*) No—please. No—let me down for just a moment. (*Now, letting himself* *down to the kneeling position*) I was getting a bit tired. (*With the saddest of smiles*) Oh, how fatiguing is the upright position!

NICO: Yes, Giaco, yes.

GIACO: Let me stay here on my knees a moment . . . It's strange. I have not found anything to pray to. But how comforting it is down here.

NICO: I will get down with you, if you like.

GIACO: No, Nico—help me up.

(*Nico helps him to stand again. Giaco straightens and takes a breath.*)
Now. Where shall we go, Nico? Rome? Padua? I hear that Florence was once beautiful in the blaze of the sun. Perhaps it still is. Where shall we go? Where shall we . . . look for it?

NICO: Look for what, Giaco?

GIACO: For . . . whatever it is.

NICO: I shall continue with my work. I've heard of a new thing, Giaco. I'd very much like for us to work on it.

GIACO: What is it?

NICO: Something new—a new secret! It's a way—a wonderful way—to turn grass into emeralds!

GIACO: (*With the most rueful smile*) Yes . . . it would fetch a fine ducat. But do you suppose . . . can we turn emeralds into grass?

(*Nico looks at him, puzzled. Giaco smiles gently. They go out together. The lights fade.*)

END OF THE PLAY

YES, TOM, YES!

A Musical

Based on "Tom Jones" by
Henry Fielding

Book and Lyrics by

N. RICHARD NASH

Music by

JOHN MORRIS

CHARACTERS

(In the order of their appearance)

Wilkins	Sophia
Allworthy	Thwackum
Bridget	Square
Jenny Jones	Molly
Mrs. Partridge	Mrs. Waters
Mr. Partridge	Northerton
Western	Florizelda
Tom Jones	Innkeeper
Philomenia	Mr. Waters
Blifil	Mrs. Bellaston

Travelers, villagers, beggars
jailkeepers, police

PLACE

Somerset and London

TIME

Eighteenth Century

MUSICAL NUMBERS

ACT ONE

What's Happening? . . . . Everyone
Young Tom Jones . . . . Squire Western & Others
I Like Everything I See . . . . Sophia
Two Faces . . . . Western, Allworthy, Tom, Sophia
Blifil, Thwackum & Square . . . . Blifil, Thwackum & Square
Farewell, My Home . . . . Tom
Tom is on His Travels . . . . Everyone
Make a Noise . . . . Partridge, Tom
Begone . . . . Tom

ACT TWO

Tom is on His Travels (Reprise) . . . . Everyone
Say Yes to the World . . . . Tom, Partridge, Others
Learn to Love Me . . . . Western, Bellaston
Dance to a Slower Dance . . . . Bellaston
Follow the Fashion . . . . Tom, Sophia
Hang Him . . . . Western, Blifil, Thwackum,
                                                                       Square, Others
Where Do I Find My Love? . . . . Tom
Young Tom Jones (Reprise) . . . . Everyone
Say Yes to the World (Reprise) . . . . Everyone

Act One

IN THE DARKNESS we hear stately music, pompously manorial, as befits the dignity of Squire Allworthy's estate. Somewhere, a clock strikes ten. Someone screams. We hear excited voices. As the shadows lighten, servants and retainers appear. They run through imaginary corridors, they flap their nightclothes, bandy their candles and rushlights from one to the other. One of them brandishes a poker; another, a quarterstaff; a third, a drawn sword. Then they sing and dance the following:

WHAT'S HAPPENING?

VOICES: WHAT'S HAPPENING?
WHAT'S HAPPENING?
I HEARD SOMEBODY SCREAM.
SHATTERING AND PIERCING
LIKE A DEVIL IN A DREAM.
I'M FRIGHTENED THAT SOMEONE
WAS MURDERED IN HIS BED.
OR MAYBE A MONSTER HAS RISEN FROM THE DEAD.

I HEARD RUNNING DOWN THE HALL,
AND THEN A CRASH,
BUT THERE'S NO ONE THERE AT ALL.
SOMEONE WAS CALLING

FOR THE SQUIRE TO COME.
BRANDY OR WHISKY
OR A SPOT OF RUM.

I HEARD A SHRIEK
AND THEN I HEARD A THUD.
I WONDER IF SOME CREATURE
IS LYING IN HIS BLOOD.
WHERE IS THE SQUIRE?
PERHAPS HE'S BEEN SHOT.
OH SQUIRE, PLEASE TELL US:
ARE YOU DEAD OR NOT?

SQUIRE! SQUIRE!
DID YOU CROAK IN YOUR GORE?
WHAT SHALL WE DO NOW?
LET'S OPEN HIS DOOR!
YOU! GET YOUR SWORD OUT!
MY SWORD IS DRAWN!
SQUIRE! OH, SQUIRE!
OH, LOOK! HE'S GONE!

SQUIRE! OH, SQUIRE,
WHERE DID YOU GO?
OH, WHAT HAPPENED AFTER
YOUR FATAL BLOW?
SQUIRE, OH, SQUIRE . . .

(*The music stops, for they have heard the cry of an infant. Utter silence. The cry is heard again. The lights go out, except for a small spotlight in which Mrs. Wilkins, an elderly servant, holds an infant in swaddling clothes. The lady is upset.*)

WILKINS: Squire! Squire Allworthy!

(*Squire Allworthy enters, a kindly man in middle age*)

ALLWORTHY: What? What is it, Mrs. Wilkins?

WILKINS: Oh, Squire, it's a baby!

ALLWORTHY: A baby? Where did you ever find it?

WILKINS: In your bed, sir!

ALLWORTHY: In my bed? Mine?!

WILKINS: Oh yes, sir!

ALLWORTHY: Surely you must be mistaken!

WILKINS: Mistaken in what, sir? Whether it's your bed or it's a baby?

ALLWORTHY: Where's my sister? Bridget! Call my sister! Bridget!

(*Bridget Allworthy enters. She is considerably younger than her brother.*)

BRIDGET: In the name of heaven, what's the racket?

ALLWORTHY: See for yourself. It looks very much like a baby!

BRIDGET: Why, it looks like a baby!

ALLWORTHY: I suspect you are correct, Bridget.

BRIDGET: But whose is it?

WILKINS: I have the strongest suspicion whose it is.

BRIDGET: Jenny Jones?

WILKINS: Yes, Jenny Jones!

(*A pin spot picks up Jenny Jones. She is a voluptuous serving girl.*)

JENNY: (*Too innocently*) Me?

ALLWORTHY: (*Entering Jenny's spotlight*) Yes—you! And you're to take yourself out of this house, Jenny Jones—and leave my service! But not before telling me who is the father of this misbegotten foundling!

JENNY: The father, sir?

(*The spot on Jenny and Allworthy goes out. Another spot illuminates Mrs. Partridge. She is a shrew. Beside her stands her cowed husband.*)

MRS. PARTRIDGE: The father? You say my husband is the father of Jenny Jones's bastard? I can't believe it! He's not man enough! He doesn't have it in him!

ALLSWORTHY: (*Entering her spotlight*) It's true, Mrs. Partridge. He is the father of Jenny Jones's bastard.

MRS. PARTRIDGE: But it can't be true—he's a schoolmaster!

ALLSWORTHY: Spare the rod and spawn the child.

MRS. PARTRIDGE: (*Turning to her quailing husband*) Spare the rod and spawn the child, would you? What a miserable miscreant you are! Out of this house, you weasel—and out of the village too! And whatever enabled you to beget a bastard—take it with you!

(*As she beats him with a stick, the light goes out. It comes on again, center stage, where Bridget now holds the child as Mrs. Wilkins admires it.*)

WILKINS: How sweet it is! How dear it is!

BRIDGET: Don't say *it*, Mrs. Wilkins. Does it not have any sex?

WILKINS: Oh yes, madam, quite a lot.

BRIDGET: Which, Mrs. Wilkins, which?

(*Squire Allworthy appears*)

ALLWORTHY: Yes—which?

(*Mrs. Wilkins has been unswaddling the child. She giggles with embarrassment.*)

WILKINS: Look, Miss Bridget, it's a boy.

BRIDGET: (*Looking*) Oh my! . . . Yes, a boy.

ALLWORTHY: (*Gazing admiringly*) He certainly is. No question about it.

(*The lights go to black. In the darkness we hear a roisterous, boisterous noise—a fistfight is in progress. Two young men—Tom Jones and Blifil—are going at it, fists and feet, gouging, biting, ripping, tearing—while a crowd of men and women watch the battle and make wagers on it. The betting is loud, uproarious—it is a great sport, watching the two young*) *men killing each other. And the loudest of all is Squire Western—middle-aged, hearty, good-natured, shrewd, vulgar, and often in his cups.*)

WESTERN: Go get him, Tom! Get him, Tom Jones—get him!

A DANDY: Smash him, Blifil! Smash that blighter Jones—smash him!

WESTERN: Five quid on Jones!

DANDY: Five quid on Blifil!

WESTERN: Kick him in the belly, boot him in the bollocks! Denature him, Tommy!

DANDY: Smash his crown in, Blifil! Ten sovereigns on Blifil!

A CLOD: Ten sovereigns on Jones!

THE CROWD: Beat him, Tom, kill him, make a mince pie outen him! . . . Here's a quid on Tommy! . . . Here's a fiver on Blifil! . . . Murder the blighter—blighten the bloke! . . . Here's a tenner on Tommy!

(*The fight has been progressing—an even match. Then suddenly—POW! —Tom lifts Blifil, slams him on the ground and stands on him! The victor!*)

WESTERN: Tommy! Tommy wins! Tom Jones wins!

(*Blifil throws one last, defeated unfair kick at Tom who catches his leg and drags him offstage as the crowd roars with hilarity and appreciation.*)

WESTERN: Tommy, you're a hero! I won a hundred quid on you, boy—a hundred quid! You're a bloody bunghole hero!

(*Laughing, shouting, the crowd fusses over Tom—and sings:*)

YOUNG TOM JONES

WESTERN: WAS THERE EVER A BOY LIKE YOUNG TOM JONES? WAS THERE EVER?

ALL: THERE WAS NEVER!

WESTERN: ALL THE WORLD IS A JOY WITH YOUNG TOM JONES, AND HE'S CLEVER!

ALL: IS HE EVER!

WESTERN: DESPITE HIS BIRTH, HE'S HELD AS UPPER CLASS, HE'S HELD THE VOGUE LIKE FASHION'S LOOKING GLASS, AND HOW HE'D BE HELD BY ANY LOVELY LASS!

ALL: YOUNG TOM JONES!

TOM: PLEASE DON'T FLATTER THE BOY CALLED YOUNG TOM JONES, YOU AMAZE HIM WHEN YOU PRAISE HIM.

SIMPLY SCATTER THE CLOUDS AND SMILE AT JONES,
THAT'S HIS PLEASURE
IN FULL MEASURE.
AN UGLY DUCKLING?—IS IT THEN A SWAN?
IF YOU SAY PRO, I HAVE TO ANSWER CON.
BUT IF YOU MUST—DO SAY IT!—PLEASE GO ON!
AND LOVE TOM JONES!

WOMEN: WAS THERE EVER A LAD LIKE YOUNG TOM JONES?
HE'S SO DASHING,
OH, HOW SMASHING!

ALL: AND THE WORLD'S NOT SO BAD WITH YOUNG TOM
JONES,
ALWAYS SMILING,
SO BEGUILING!

WE LIKE TO THINK THAT HE IS WHAT WE ARE,
FOREVER YOUNG AND GUIDED BY A STAR,
HE MAKES US FEEL THAT HEAVEN'S NOT SO FAR,
WE LOVE TOM JONES!

TOM: I'M NOT SO GREAT, I'M SIMPLY FOND,
EXPRESSING ALL MY WARMEST FEELING,
IT'S VERY KIND THAT YOU RESPOND.

A WOMAN: OH GOD! THE BOY IS SO APPEALING!

ALL: LIFE'S A GAME THAT IS FREE WITH YOUNG TOM
JONES,
AND WE'RE PLAYING
WITHOUT PAYING,
AS IF LIFE WERE A SPREE WITH YOUNG TOM JONES,
GONE A-MAYING,
HOLIDAYING.

OLDER   TO HELL WITH TIME AND EVERY RIGID RULE,
PEOPLE: WE'RE TOTS AGAIN AND TOTTING OFF TO
SCHOOL,
AND OLD NOVEMBER IS AN APRIL FOOL—

ALL: WITH YOUNG TOM JONES!

WESTERN: A HUNTING LAD OF PLUCK AND LUCK,
A NIMROD WHO IS QUICK AND FOXY,
HE'LL RUN A RABBIT, THROW A BUCK—
WHILE HE'S PURSUED BY EVERY DOXY.

ALL: WE ALL BELIEVE THAT THE JOY OF YOUNG TOM
            JONES,
         EVER SPLENDID,
         WON'T BE ENDED.
         WE PRETEND WE'RE THE BOY NAMED YOUNG TOM
            JONES,
         NOW AND EVER,
         YOUNG FOREVER.

TOM: YOUR FLATTERY IS JUST A BIT ABSURD.
         I'M OLD ENOUGH TO WISH I HADN'T HEARD,
         BUT YOUNG ENOUGH TO TAKE YOU AT YOUR WORD.

ALL: WE LOVE TOM JONES!

TOM: I thank you.

ALL: WE LOVE TOM JONES!

(*Everybody leaves the stage with the exception of Tom and Sophia Western. She is as bright as she is beautiful. Her brightness consists of a shrewd evaluation of spirit versus substance. As Tom is the idealist/romantic, she is the pragmatist/realist. At the moment Sophia is in a rage.*)

SOPHIA: There was no reason to fight with him—no reason!

TOM: There was every reason—the best damn reason in the world!

SOPHIA: Name it!

TOM: You!

SOPHIA: You think you flatter me by fighting over me? Why did you do it?—why?

TOM: Because he was bragging about how he was going to marry you—and your two properties would be joined—and he would be the richest squire in the county!

SOPHIA: Well, it's true, isn't it?—it's true!

TOM: How can you say that with one breath and say that you love me with another?

SOPHIA: (*Angry*) Because I have more than one breath! And it's been true ever since Blifil and I were infants! And there's nothing any of us can do about it!

TOM: (*Enraged*) If something's unfair, you don't say there's nothing you can do about it!

SOPHIA: (*Biting*) No!—you just whomp Blifil on the head with a hot leg of mutton!

TOM: It wasn't a hot leg, it was cold. And he had it coming to him.

SOPHIA: And so do I?—is that what you think, so do I?

TOM: Yes! If you don't love that wormhead, how can you marry him? Why don't you tell your father that *properties* can't be in love and get married and have children, but *people can*! Why don't you tell him?

SOPHIA: You've told him a dozen times—has it done any good?

TOM: (*Frustrated*) How can you do it, Sophia, how can you go through with it?

SOPHIA: Because I don't fight life the way you do, Tommy! I don't whomp life on the head with a leg of mutton! I take things as they are, and I make the best of them!

TOM: Even stupidities?—injustices?

SOPHIA: I try not to look at them—I try not to see them! You think I don't know how mean and cruel and miserable the world can be? You think I could stand it if I didn't pretend it's better than it is?

TOM: But how can you make yourself *believe* it? You're the brightest person I know, Sophia—how can you make yourself believe such an idiocy?

SOPHIA: Oh, I can!—and I must!—and I do!

(*She sings:*)

I LIKE EVERYTHING I SEE

I LIKE EVERYTHING I SEE,
PRETENDING NOTHING HAS TO CHANGE,
THE BOUNDING BROOK
AND THE WAY I LOOK,
AND WHAT SOME DAY I MAY BE.

I LIKE GAZING NEAR AND FAR
AND SEEING LIFE WITHIN MY RANGE,
TO SET A GOAL
AND TO PAY MY TOLL
ON THIS NEARLY PERFECT STAR!
AND IN ALL THIS BLISS,
THE QUESTION IS THIS:
WHY NOT LEAVE THINGS AS THEY ARE?

TOM: If you keep spouting absurdities like that, nobody's going to believe a word you ever say.

SOPHIA: Oh yes they will—because the wise ones need the fools to tell them the world's a good place to live in.

I LIKE RIDING TO HOUNDS
ON A SUNDAY MORNING.
I LIKE WALKING THE GROUNDS
EVERY DAY.

I LIKE TAKING A ROAST
TO THE SERVANTS' QUARTERS,
I LIKE DRINKING A TOAST
WHEN I MAY.
I LIKE EVERYTHING I SEE,
IGNORING ALL VEXATIOUS VIEWS.
IN MY HAPPY ROOM
THERE WILL BE NO GLOOM,
NO REGRETS, NO WEEPING-TREE.

I LIKE EVERYTHING I SEE,
AS IF I LIVE THE LIFE I CHOOSE.
GOOD FORTUNES FLY
IN MY MADE-UP SKY,
MY LIFE SUITS ME TO A T,
AND THE WORLD I MAKE
WON'T LOOK LIKE A FAKE
IF YOU SEE THE WORLD WITH ME.

TOM: No! I can't see the world your way. But I'm not giving up on you, Sophia. I'm going to your father once again. And this time—by, God, this time—!
(*He rushes off. Sophia, left alone, faces her realities. Pensively, she sings:*)

IF I LIKE EVERYTHING I SEE,
HOW CAN THE DOUBTING WORLD SEE ME?
IF THEY THINK I'M INANE
OR GONE QUITE INSANE,
I MUST SAY THAT I AGREE.

(*The light fades on her, then brightens to pick up an important meeting. Present are: Squire Western and his sister, Philomenia—and Squire Allworthy. Philomenia is a spinster. She knits. Her pince nez, ribbon trailing, is perched low on her nose. Western, only slightly tipsy this time, bellows.*)

WESTERN: A dilemma, Squire Allworthy, a dilemma! Your ward, Tom Jones, has come to me again, and this time I must say, I weakened. Which puts me into a sizable dilemma. So now I put *you* into it!
ALLWORTHY: What is it, Squire Western?
WESTERN: It's this: You have two wards and I have one daughter. Is that correct?
ALLWORTHY: It has been correct for quite a while.
WESTERN: Good. Then—so far—we're agreed. Now let us proceed. Both of your daredevil young men love my girl, and both want to marry her. And she can be satisfied—in a polite manner of speaking—by either one of them. So the choice is up to you.

ALLWORTHY: Up to me, Squire Western? Why to me? I am not marrying your daughter.

WESTERN: Well, in a sense, you are. Let us look closely at the situation. Here is my daughter Sophia.

(*A spotlight picks up Sophia.*)

WESTERN: (*Continuing*) She's a bright-thinking, fine-speaking, sensible girl—in that respect she resembles my sister Philomenia. And she is pretty—in that sense she does not. Ah, look at the girl—she shines like a shilling.

> A VERY QUICK MIND AND A VERY FINE FIGGER,
> SHE'S SMALL IN THE REAR, BUT HER FRONT IS MUCH
>   BIGGER.

Now here is your first ward—your true nephew, Blifil.

(*A spotlight picks up Blifil.*)

He's handsome enough, Lud knows, but not to my taste. Yet, beauty, they say, is in the arse of the beholder. Love, however, is in the heart—which, in the body of Blifil, has not as yet been discovered.

> A RIGHTEOUS YOUNG MAN, AND AS SHREWD AS A
>   WIZARD,
> THE BRAIN OF A FOX, AND THE HEART OF A LIZARD.

Now—here is your other ward—Tom Jones.

(*A spotlight picks up Tom Jones.*)

Now, this is quite a boy, this young Tom Jones. I have taken him a-hunting many's the time. I have drunk a pint with him and caught a fish or two. Truth to relate, I am very fond of Tom Jones. He has about him, however, two inconveniences. First, he is illegitimate. Second, he is afflicted with what may turn out to be an incurable ailment—honesty. But ah, what a dear, sweet, adorable character! He loves everybody—and everyone loves him. Especially the ladies—he is still an innocent who scarcely knows how he awakens their languishing lusts.

> I WISH THAT TOM JONES COULD BE JUST A BIT
>   SHREWDER,
> BUT AH ME, HIS LADIES GET NUDER AND NUDER.

(*The lights go out on the three young people*)

Now, then, affections and prejudices being discounted, who will marry whom?

ALLWORTHY: It is difficult. Have you a suggestion?

WESTERN: (*Sing-song*) Ah, Squire, Squire, delighted you inquire. Yes, I have a suggestion. But I must be forthright. I myself prefer Tom Jones. And I will make a gift to him of my daughter—if you will make a gift as well.

ALLWORTHY: What gift, sir?

WESTERN: Your estate.

ALLWORTHY: But I am still alive, sir.

WESTERN: Oh, you are, sir, you are—all signs point to it. In fact, if I were asked to give you a testimonial, I would say: *The man is still ALIVE.* But I was thinking of what you will write in your will, sir—and whether you might leave your estate to Tom Jones.

ALLWORTHY: Instead of bequeathing it to Blifil?

WESTERN: Precisely, sir.

ALLWORTHY: But, my dear Squire, I cannot leave my estate to a man without a legitimate name. Tom Jones is a bastard.

WESTERN: Blifil is a snake.

ALLWORTHY: Let us say, sir, that in varying nuances of the term, each of them is a bastard. But Blifil has the advantage. He is the son of my sister Bridget—my true nephew—flesh and blood.

WESTERN: Then your decision is . . .?

ALLWORTHY: Regrettably . . . she marries Blifil.

TOM: *Oh no!* (*He rushes in and approaches Allworthy*) You can't do that to me, Father!

ALLWORTHY: Do not call me Father.

TOM: I've called you that on a number of occasions when you said you loved me.

ALLWORTHY: This is not such an occasion.

TOM: How can you explain the difference? How can you explain that you loved me once and will cut me off now? How can you explain it?

WESTERN: Hypocrisy.

ALLWORTHY: Sir! You slander me!

(*Western sings:*)

TWO FACES

WESTERN: HYPOCRISY, HYPOCRISY,
        THE ART OF THE ARISTOCRACY,
        AND YOU PLY THE PRACTICE TOO!

ALLWORTHY: NOT TRUE! NOT TRUE!

WESTERN: YOU DO, YOU DO,
        YOU CERTAINLY, CERTAINLY DO!

TOM: Squire Western, you have known me all my life. You have taken me with you as if I were your son. You have taught me how to ride and fish and drink my ale. You have shown me how to hold a gun and a girl. And I am sure that, whether I inherit the squire's estate or not, you will finally give me your daughter's hand in marriage. I am certain you will give it!

WESTERN: (*He belches*) Do not be so certain.

TOM: Sir, if I do not understand that you love me, what must I understand this to be?

ALLWORTHY: Hypocrisy.

WESTERN: Sir! You are asking for my whip!

ALLWORTHY: THE HYPOCRITE, THE HYPOCRITE,
THERE'S NOT A FRAUD HE WON'T COMMIT,
NO DECEIT HE WOULDN'T TRY.

WESTERN: NOT I! NOT I!

ALLWORTHY: YOU LIE, YOU LIE,
YOU CERTAINLY, CERTAINLY LIE!

WESTERN: TWO FACES, TWO FACES,
A WARM SMILE WITH ONE
WHILE THE OTHER ONE CHILLS.
TWO FACES, TWO FACES,
CARESSING WITH ONE
WHILE THE OTHER ONE KILLS.

ALLWORTHY: TWO FACES, TWO FACES,
A NEIGHBOR WHO CALLS
WITH A NEIGHBORLY SOUND.
TWO FACES, TWO FACES,
HE'S DRINKING MY ALE
WHILE HE POISONS MY HOUND.

TOM: TWO STORIES, TWO STORIES,
THEIR SWEET TALES OF LOVE,
HOW THEY FILL THE HEART FULL!
BUT LISTEN, JUST LISTEN,
THE FABLES THEY TELL
ARE JUST PLAIN COCK-AND-BULL!

HOW CAN YOU DANCE IN TWO DIRECTIONS,
ONE STEP NORTH AND THE OTHER ONE SOUTH?
HOW CAN YOU SPEAK WITH TWO INFLECTIONS,
OUT OF BOTH SIDES OF YOUR MOUTH?

ALL: FAKE FRIENDSHIP, FAKE FRIENDSHIP,
YOU OFFER A DRINK
AND A SPOT OF GOOD CHEER,
FAKE FRIENDSHIP, FAKE FRIENDSHIP,

I PAY FOR THE TAB,
WHILE YOU SPIT IN MY BEER.

TOM: LIP SERVICE, LIP SERVICE,
THE SWEET MILK THAT SOURS
INTO WHEY AND TO CURDS.
FALSE KINDNESS, CHEAP PRESENTS,
THE RIBBONS AND BOWS
THAT ARE TIED AROUND TURDS.

TOM: (*Continuing*) To hell with you—to hell with both of you! Sophia and I don't need your consent! We'll run away without it!—and we'll get married! Sophia! Sophia!
(*Allworthy and Western disappear as the lights come up on Sophia whom Tom has confronted. She is in a panic.*)

SOPHIA: No! I can't do it! No!

TOM: But you say you love me!

SOPHIA: What has love to do with marriage?

TOM: Dear God in heaven!

SOPHIA: Don't call upon God—he's not an authority on marriage. Call upon a woman!—she'll tell you what marriage is! It's not love—it's practicality! It's wiping children's noses and keeping the drains clear and pretending you want marigolds when what you need is money. Marriage is Blifil!

TOM: One side of you loves me and the other side marries Blifil!

SOPHIA: Yes! That's right!

TOM: TWO FACES, TWO FACES,
CONFESSING YOUR HEART
WITH THE BLESSING OF BLISS,
TWO FACES, TWO FACES,
EMBRACING YOUR LOVE
WITH A JUDAS'S KISS.

SOPHIA: It's you who are Judas! You say you love me, but it's a conventional love that sees no further than a marriage contract!

FALSE FEELINGS, FALSE FEELINGS,
THE BLINKING OF EYES
AND THE ROSY-PINK FLUSH.
FALSE GESTURES, FALSE TEARDROPS,
THE CRY OF THE HEART
THAT IS NOTHING BUT MUSH!

TOM: HOW CAN YOU DANCE IN TWO DIRECTIONS,
ONE STEP NORTH AND THE OTHER STEP SOUTH?

SOPHIA: HOW CAN YOU SPEAK WITH TWO INFLECTIONS,
OUT OF BOTH SIDES OF YOUR MOUTH?

BOTH: TWO FACES, TWO FACES,
A WARM SMILE WITH ONE
WHILE THE OTHER ONE CHILLS.
TWO FACES, TWO FACES,
CARESSING WITH ONE
WHILE THE OTHER ONE—KILLS!

(They disappear as the lights go to black. Blifil comes out of the darkness, in the company of Reverend Thwackum and Constable Square. Thwackum is a thin hypocrite; Square is a fat one.)

BLIFIL: I need your help, Constable Square.

SQUARE: Oh, please, Master Blifil—do not call me Constable. I am a schoolmaster.

BLIFIL: Blight me, it is not shameful to be an officer of the law. Is it, Reverend Thwackum?

THWACKUM: No, no, he should be proud. Officer of the law, officer of the Lord—they are much alike.

BLIFIL: Well said, well said! You are sworn to maintain order in society, and you, the order of God. And Mr. Thomas Jones will bring disorder to both of them. When I marry Sophia Western, Tom Jones will be a threat to my marriage and my appurtenances. Can either of you suggest a remedy?

SQUARE: Well, the boy has not infracted any law, sir.

BLIFIL: Not yet, not yet, sir.

THWACKUM: Nor has he blasphemed God, sir.

BLIFIL: But he will. Let us be patient, sir.
(To Square, as he hands him money:)

YOUR SCHOOL IS IN NEED OF SOME PENS, CHALK AND
SLATE, SIR.

(To Thwackum, as he hands him money:)

AND MAY I DONATE TO YOUR CHARITY PLATE, SIR?

SQUARE: I'VE HEARD THAT THE BOY'S GONE FROM WANTON
TO WORSE, SIR.

THWACKUM: I'VE HEARD HE BLASPHEMES AND HE'S QUITE A BAD
CURSER.

(Almost entirely losing them, another light focuses upon Tom and Molly Seagrim. She is the daughter of a gamekeeper. Roughly dressed, the girl is as sensually delicious as ripe fruit, and no more moral than necessary. Watching them, Blifil, Thwackum and Square hide.)

MOLLY: But why can you not *pretend* to love me?

TOM: Because I love Sophia Western.

MOLLY: But she has turned you down.

TOM: That's why I've turned up.

MOLLY: They say that women make you as hot as a teapot ever since Sophia spurned you.

TOM: (*He smiles sheepishly*) After the spurning, the burning.

MOLLY: Does every woman set you afire?

TOM: No, only the combustible ones. Come, Molly, you beautiful slattern, let us make a warm day of a chilly one.

MOLLY: Not until you forget Sophia.

TOM: I will never forget Sophia. Kiss me, Molly.

MOLLY: Never! Not on a chilly day, not in the heat of hell—never! What foolery is this, that you love Sophia and want to bed with me?

TOM: What is it?—it's what she has taught me. Hypocrisy.

MOLLY: Well, you're not a very good student. You'll never make a top-hole hypocrite.

TOM: But you will. You pretend you do not itch for me, but you stand there scratching.

MOLLY: Scratch me, Tom. (*He kisses her*) Do you find it pleasurable, Master Thomas?

TOM: (*Shifting his weight*) Yes, and discomfiting too.

MOLLY: Men's garments are an unfortunate geography, I think. The britches are never made with sufficient latitude for the longitude.

TOM: Would you mind settling your hemispheres on the terra firma?

MOLLY: I would gladly lie aground for you, Tommy, if you would forget Sophia Western.

TOM: How can I do that? How can I promise such a thing?

MOLLY: Then promise something else.

TOM: What?

MOLLY: Will you ask Sophia to give me a position? I want to be her maid.

TOM: Do you really want to be her maid? Why so?

MOLLY: (*Coyly*) So that if anyone asks me if I am still a virgin, I can say, "Oh, indeed, sir, I am a maid."

TOM: You shall be Sophia's maid tomorrow and mine today. Come.

MOLLY: Wait. Will you give me a little something?

TOM: A little something?

MOLLY: A few shillings to remember you by.

TOM: You want to be paid, Molly?

MOLLY: Oh, perish, no! Just a little present, sir.

TOM: But in money? (*Smiling, enjoying her*) Have you no pride?

MOLLY: Oh, no sir. A woman's pride is dependent on her price. Only the expensive woman can be proud. I have to be satisfied with prudence. A few shillings is a matter of prudential wisdom, sir. And even moral rectitude. I'm sure even The Good Book would praise me for it.

TOM: (*Nodding*) A prudent economy is praised by Deuteronomy.

(*They both laugh and kiss again. His clothes are getting tighter*)

TOM: Do you want it now?—the coin, I mean.

MOLLY: Ah yes! I love a warm coin that has been heated in a gentleman's pocket. I put it in my bosom, here, and you would be amazed how it raises my temperature. Sometimes I can barely remain in an upright position for fainting of the heat.

TOM: Ah, poor thing, then you should lie down, shouldn't you?

MOLLY: The coin, did you say?

TOM: I don't know which to open first—my purse or my pantaloons.

MOLLY: Well, sir, there is coin of the realm in both places!

(*They disappear behind the shrubbery. Now, to musical accompaniment, a number of people pass along the forestage. First, Mrs. Wilkins. Even though the shrubbery moves a bit, she doesn't notice. As she is about to disappear, Thwackum re-enters. She makes him a casual curtsey and he gives her a perfunctory bow. He remains still an instant, not certain in which direction Tom and Molly have gone. As he passes the shrubbery that conceals them, the greenery moves. Thwackum doesn't notice—until he's offstage. Quickly now, a delayed registry, he hurries back to look at the shrubbery, then behind it. He is aghast and delighted. He scurries off—for reinforcements. Now Mrs. Partridge enters. She sees the energetic shrubbery at once. She looks, is shocked, starts to depart, cannot overcome the temptation to look again. Now she stands there unashamedly watching, enjoying the spectacle, making a variety of noises and grimaces that signify surprise, outrage, pleasure and awe. She hears sounds offstage and scrambles away. The sound she has heard was the approach of Blifil, Thwackum and Square. They dither with excitement, but try to keep their voices down. As silently as possible, Thwackum points to the shrubbery. Blifil and Square look. They're ecstatic: they've run their prey to earth!*)

BLIFIL: Excellent! Excellent! (*To Thwackum*) Have you told everybody?

THWACKUM: Oh yes, sir—everybody within earshot!

SQUARE: (*Pointing to the shrubbery*) Shall we flush 'em out?

BLIFIL: Oh no—not yet—let's wait for a crowd to gather!

THWACKUM: Ah yes—what a humiliation!

SQUARE: Serves him right too—fornicating bastard!

BLIFIL: We've got him this time! We've certainly got him!

(*They sing:*)

BLIFIL, THWACKUM AND SQUARE

BLIFIL: I'M BLIFIL—

THWACKUM: I'M THWACKUM—

SQUARE: I'M SQUARE.

ALL: WHERE MORALS ARE MURKY, WE'RE THERE.

THWACKUM: OUR TASK IS POLICING
THE VICE THAT'S INCREASING,

SQUARE: THE LUST THAT IS FOULING THE AIR.

BLIFIL: WE'RE BLIFIL—

THWACKUM: AND THWACKUM—

SQUARE: AND SQUARE.

BLIFIL: I do not hold with evil. Depravity and degeneracy are detestable to me. Fraud and swindling are disgusting. Still—if deception has to be, why not deceive with subtlety?—make an art of it!

I'M AN ARTIST AT DECEIT,
HOW CRAFTILY I CHEAT!
THE CROCODILE HAS TAUGHT ME HOW TO CRY.
IF I HAVE TO TELL A TRUTH
WHICH IS SOCIALLY UNCOUTH,
I TELL THE TRUTH AS IF IT WERE A LIE.

SINCE LYING IS MY FORTE,
I DO IT FOR THE SPORT,
BUT ALSO FOR THE SUBSTANCE AND THE PELF.
AND IF I CANNOT MEET
SOME FELLOW I CAN CHEAT,
I OFTEN END UP STEALING FROM MYSELF.

ALL: WE'RE BLIFIL AND THWACKUM AND SQUARE.
WHERE LICENSE IS LOOSEST WE'RE THERE.

BLIFIL: WHEN VIRTUE'S INFRACTED
WE GET QUITE DISTRACTED,

T. & S: IT DRIVES US TO UTTER DESPAIR!

BLIFIL: WE'RE BLIFIL—

THWACKUM: AND THWACKUM—

SQUARE: AND SQUARE.

THWACKUM: THERE ARE MEN WHO TRY TO SMIRCH
THE GOOD NAME OF THE CHURCH.

I WISH THEM DEAD AND BURIED IN THE SOD.
BUT THE ONES WHO MIND THEIR WAYS
I GIVE A WORD OF PRAISE,
AND WHEN YOU'VE HEARD FROM ME, YOU'VE
   HEARD FROM GOD.

THE SCRIPTURE AND THE BOOK,
THAT'S WHERE I ALWAYS LOOK
TO FIND THE MOST COMPLETE DETAILS OF SIN.
BUT THE GOOD BOOK DOESN'T TELL
THE ENTIRE TALE OF HELL,
SO WHAT I DON'T FIND WRITTEN, I WRITE IN.

ALL: WE'RE BLIFIL AND THWACKUM AND SQUARE.

BLIFIL: I'M SINGLE—

T. & S.: AND WE ARE A PAIR.

SQUARE: ALL BASENESS AND BADNESS
CAN PUSH US TO MADNESS
CAN DRIVE US TO CLAWING THE AIR.

BLIFIL: WE'RE BLIFIL—

THWACKUM AND THWACKUM—

SQUARE: AND SQUARE.

I DON'T MEAN TO IMPEACH
THOSE MODERN MEN WHO TEACH
THAT LOVE'S A BETTER MASTER THAN IS FEAR.
BUT THE HEADS OF BOYS ARE THICK
SO I ALWAYS USE A STICK,
I DO NOT TEACH THE HEAD, I TEACH THE REAR.

BUT I HOPE THAT YOU DISCERN
I WANT MY BOYS TO LEARN
AND I ANSWER EVERY QUESTION WITH A FACT.
YET I THINK IT ONLY FAIR
TO SHOW A LAD I CARE,
AND IF I DON'T KNOW THE ANSWER, HE GETS
   WHACKED.

BLIFIL: WE'RE BLIFIL—

THWACKUM: AND THWACKUM—

SQUARE: AND SQUARE.

ALL: WHERE SIN IS BEFOULING THE AIR,
OUR NOSES ARE TELLING
THE STENCH WE ARE SMELLING,
WHEREVER IT STINKS, WE ARE THERE!
WE'RE BLIFIL AND THWACKUM AND SQUARE!

(*Squire Western and a group of hunters, men and women, enter in a flurry.*)

WESTERN: What—what? What is this, Thwackum—this summons—interrupting a hunt just as it's about to begin! Don't you know that nothing—by God, nothing is as important as a hunt?!

THWACKUM: Oh, this is a hunt too, sir!

WESTERN: Is it now?—what?—where?

SQUARE: In the undergrowth—look there!

WESTERN: (*Agog*) What?—what is it?—fox?—deer?—snipe?

SQUARE: Cock, sir!

WESTERN: Cock? What kind of cock?—woodcock?—peacock?—turkey cock?

SQUARE: A Tom turkey, sir!—see for yourself!

(*Silently—his gun raised—the squire approaches the shrubbery. As he peers into it*)

WESTERN: (*With a loud hoot*) Well, by God, it's Tom-cock! Everybody, come and look! Look at the boy go! Go it, Tommy, go it! Cock-a-doodle do!

ALL: (*Cheering*) Well done—well done! . . . Hip, hip, hooray! . . . Cheers, boy—all cheers! . . . Well done—well done!

(*Tom and Molly come out, adjusting their clothing. Abruptly, the Jailers appear with handcuffs and irons. Blifil and Thwackum go to greet them. Constable Square steps forward.*)

SQUARE: Master Jones, you are under arrest.

TOM: Arrest? What for, sir?

SQUARE: Fornication.

TOM: You mean loving? Love is not a crime, sir!

SQUARE: Fornication! Arrest him!

(*As they start to do so, Tom fights. At first, it looks like a contained match, but suddenly it includes everybody, a raucous free-for-all. At last the minions of the law overpower the boy, and the stage goes empty as the light picks up the relative quiet of Squire Allworthy. He is wringing out a poultice which he applies to Tom's bruised face.*)

ALLWORTHY: Hold still. Fornication, Thomas. Do you know what that means?

TOM: Ow. Yes, it's a nasty word for loving.

ALLWORTHY: Loving? Do you love Molly Seagrim?

TOM: When I was *making* love, I loved her.

ALLWORTHY: And do you love all of them?

TOM: Not all—each. Each one—while it is happening—is beautiful to me. And I am beautiful to myself.

ALLWORTHY: You are learning to equivocate.

TOM: Isn't that what you teach me, sir?

ALLWORTHY: (*Upset*) No, it is not! When I was your age, I did not lie to myself!

TOM: Ah, then, I am getting older.

ALLWORTHY: You will get older in jail.

TOM: Surely not, sir. You will pay for my acquittal, will you not?

ALLWORTHY: (*Quietly*) No, I will not, Thomas.

TOM: You will let me go to jail?

ALLWORTHY: No. You won't be here.

TOM: Where will I be, Squire?

ALLWORTHY: Away. You are going to leave Somerset.

TOM: Leave here? But it is my home.

ALLWORTHY: No longer.

TOM: (*Wincing*) Ow!

ALLWORTHY: Sorry. Did that hurt?

TOM: Yes, it did. . . . Where will I go?

ALLWORTHY: To some place where they do not know you as a bastard.

TOM: You are really sending me away?

ALLWORTHY: (*With difficulty*) Yes . . . sending you away. Sorry if this hurts a little. (*Meaning the handkerchief*)

TOM: (*Breaking away from him in a rage of heartbreak*) It hurts more than a little, sir!

ALLWORTHY: I'm sorry, Thomas, but it will mend.

TOM: No, it will never mend! If you send me away—! But this is my home! You—I have looked upon you as my father!

ALLWORTHY: (*Angry and in distress*) I have repeatedly told you not to call me your father. I have never implied that I am—and you must stop thinking of me in that way. You must stop looking for love in every closed-up closet of your life! Love is a forlorn dream for you, Thomas! You're a bastard and you have no father!

TOM: (*An outcry*) Yes I do—I do! Somewhere in the world I do have a father! And I'll find him! And he'll be a better father than you ever were! He'll never turn me out—never! He'll take me to himself—and he will love me, he will love me, love me!

(*Too moved to stay here, Allworthy hurries away. Tom weeps with rage and loneliness. He calls after the departed Allworthy:*)

TOM: I hate you, Squire Allworthy—I hate you—I'll never love you again! I am cursed with loving too much—and I will never love anyone again!

(*He weeps. After a while, he looks up to gaze at the world he loves, the world he must leave. He sings:*)

FAREWELL, MY HOME

FAREWELL, MY HOME,
FAREWELL TO SPRING,
FAREWELL TO EVERY FRIENDLY THING
I ALWAYS HELD TOO DEARLY.
THE LOVE I THOUGHT I'D ALWAYS OWN
WAS ONLY MINE TO BORROW.

FAREWELL, MY HOME.
THE HAPPY DAY
I ALWAYS THOUGHT WAS HERE TO STAY
IS GONE—FORGOTTEN—NEARLY.
EACH HOPEFUL DAY I'VE EVER KNOWN
WAS THREATENED BY TOMORROW.

AND NOW IT'S HERE AT LAST,
TOMORROW'S HERE TOO SOON,
THE FUTURE COMES TOO FAST,
THE EVENING CHASES NOON.
WHY IS THE PRESENT PAST?
WHY DO I HAVE TO GO AWAY?
WHY CAN'T I STAY?

FAREWELL, MY HOME,
FAREWELL, MY HEART,
FAREWELL IS QUITE THE CRUELEST PART OF LOVING.
FAREWELL, MY HOME,
FAREWELL, MY HEART,
FAREWELL, MY HOME,
FAREWELL, MY HOME,
FAREWELL, MY HOME!

(*As Tom starts to go, an Elderly Gardener, enters*)
GARDENER: I hear you're goin', Master Tom. I wanted you to know I will
miss you . . . and . . .
(*He tries to keep from crying*)
TOM: Goodbye, Joris.
(*Two other Servants enter*)
SERVANTS: Goodbye, Thomas. . . . Goodbye—and bless you, sir!
TOM: Goodbye, Philip. Maria, I will think of you.
(*Mrs. Wilkins enters*)
WILKINS: Master Tom—Tommy—!
(*She does not restrain her weeping. Tom embraces her*)
TOM: Goodbye, dear Mrs. Wilkins—and thank you . . . thank you . . .

(Other servants enter. They murmur "Farewell, sir . . . God speed you, Thomas . . . Goodbye, Tommy." The lights dim as they disappear. Tom reprises:)

FAREWELL, MY HOME,
FAREWELL, MY HEART,
FAREWELL IS QUITE THE CRUELEST PART OF LOVING.
FAREWELL, MY HOME,
FAREWELL, MY HEART,
FAREWELL, MY HOME,
FAREWELL, MY HOME,
FAREWELL, MY HEART!

(Darkness. The sadness settles. A bright change of tone: briskness, even gaiety, as the Chorus sings about Tom's travels. Against this musical background we see porters, soldiers, beggars, pickpockets, chambermaids, postchaise drivers, dramatizing the start of Tom's quest. They scurry about, performing their occupations against the musical obbligato of galloping horses, rolling wagon wheels, the hubbub of quick encounters and sudden departures.)

TOM IS ON HIS TRAVELS

CHORUS: TOM IS ON HIS TRAVELS,
HIS TRAVELS, HIS TRAVELS,
OUR TOM'S A NAMELESS OUTCAST
IN SEARCH OF HIS NAME.

TOM IS ON HIS TRAVELS
TO FIND HOME AND FATHER,
TO CLAIM HIS PROPER BIRTHRIGHT,
HIS FORTUNE, HIS FAME.

THE SEARCH IS AN ADVENTURE,
A HUNTING, A TESTING,
PURSUING LOVE AND QUESTING,
A CAUSE TO DEFEND,
A HEIGHT TO ASCEND,
A FATHER, A FRIEND,
BUT WILL HIS QUEST REWARD HIM?
AND WHERE IS RAINBOW'S END?

TOM IS ON HIS TRAVELS,
TOM IS ON HIS TRAVELS,
TOM IS ON HIS TRAVELS . . .

(Precipitately, without seeming cause, the music stops. The stage is suddenly bare except for Tom. Absolute silence. He stands there nonplussed, not knowing why the sound has ceased and the people, vanished. A woman's scream is heard, then another, bloodcurdling. As a bright light picks up the opposite side of the stage, Mrs. Waters comes rushing in. Actually, she is Jenny Jones whom we saw in the opening scene, but she is maturer now, in the full bloom of womanhood. She might be considered well dressed if she were dressed at all, but there is little left of her clothes. Stripped practically nude, she is in full flight, screaming:)

WATERS: Help! Robber! I've been robbed—help—help!

(Her pursuer enters. He is Mr. Northerton, an ensign deserter from the army, a great mountain of a man, a brutish animal. He brandishes a bullwhip which he cracks and slashes in the air. As Mrs. Waters screams, he shouts:)

NORTHERTON: Come back, you soft-bellied bitch! Tell the world I robbed you—go on, tell 'em! I'll give you the bull-thwacking, blacksnaking, cat-o-nine-tailing of your life! Ha!—got you!

(He grabs her and she fights, bites, scratches)

WATERS: No—let me go! Help! Robber!—cutthroat!—whoreson murderer! Let me go! Help!

NORTHERTON: I'll string you up on an oak tree, that's what I'll do!

(He starts tying the bullwhip around her neck)

WATERS: No—help! Murder! Help! Murder!

TOM: Leave off! Let her go! Leave off!

(As Tom attacks, Northerton turns and hits him)

NORTHERTON: Go, boy! You want a noose of your own?

(He twists to Mrs. Waters and resumes tying her up)

WATERS: No—no!—don't hang me!—no!

TOM: Stop—stop, I say—stop!

(Tom sails in again, hits the man. Northerton strikes back, and the two men go at it. It is a violent knockabout fistfight, much rougher than Tom's fight with Blifil. In the melee, Mrs. Waters flees.)

NORTHERTON: *(As they fight)* Enough, boy—enough, or I'll skin you!

(The fight goes on, and suddenly Tom is on the ground. Northerton falls on top of Tom and starts to strangle him. Abruptly, another man enters the scene—it is Partridge, the erstwhile schoolmaster.)

PARTRIDGE: Off, man! Let him up—let him up!

(He pulls two guns and shoots into the air—once, twice. Northerton jumps up and runs. Tom is practically unconscious. Partridge hurries to him.)

PARTRIDGE: Are you dead, lad—are you dying?

(Tom strikes out weakly, still fighting, not realizing Partridge is an ally.)

TOM: Let her go, let her go!

PARTRIDGE: She's gone, boy—whoever she is—and I'm your friend, whoever I am!

TOM: (*Reviving a little*) Who—what?

PARTRIDGE: Who-what! indeed!—you tell *me* who-what.

TOM: He was trying to rob her, I think—whoever he was.

PARTRIDGE: Whoever *she* was.

TOM: Whoever *you* are.

PARTRIDGE: Partridge is the name. One of the birds—of the quail family— good to shoot at and good to eat—partridge! One-time schoolmaster, one- time ostler, one-time pickpocket—and now a barber. Would you like me to put my razor to your skin, sir? I can give you a very close shave.

TOM: No, thank you, I've had one today.

PARTRIDGE: (*Howling with pleasure*) Well said—that's jolly well said! I could dine in the palace on that one! Did you make it up?

TOM: It's as old as my grandfather, whoever *he* is.

PARTRIDGE: Let's not start that up again, that he is, she is, we is. What's your name, lad?

TOM: Jones, Mr. Partridge. Tom Jones.

PARTRIDGE: Oh, the good Lord hold me! I will perish of shock!

TOM: Why, sir—what, sir?

PARTRIDGE: Oh, what an ass I am! Why should I perish of shock?—there are a multitude of Tom Joneses in the world.

TOM: Did you know another one?

PARTRIDGE: In a manner, yes. There was a girl—her name was Jenny Jones. Oh, I had a large wet appetite for that juicy wench. I'd have given her any- thing—my left arm or my right leg—or any other appendage she had a mind to. Oh, by my belly and balls, how I loved that girl! And suddenly she was with child—and they said I was the father—and they drove me out of the county! And it was told, after I was gone, that they named the little bastard Tom.

TOM: Oh, I will perish of shock, sir!

PARTRIDGE: I advise against it.

TOM: (*Arms wide*) Father!

PARTRIDGE: Oh, heaven help me, are you the one?

TOM: Father—oh, Father, embrace me!

PARTRIDGE: Tom—oh my dear *dear* Tom!

(*They embrace. They both laugh, they both cry—extravagantly. Partridge, bellowing with guffaws and happiness, cannot remain still.*)

TOM: Stand still, Father—let me look at you.

PARTRIDGE: (*Hopping about*) Oh no, boy—don't look at me—you'll be ashamed to find a father so dirty and impecunious as I am!

TOM: I don't care! Father—oh my Father!

(*He starts to embrace Partridge again, but the barber extends his arm, hold- ing Tom off*)

PARTRIDGE: No—wait! You're a good lad and if you ask me to put a dag- ger in my heart for you. you had better stand back for my heart's blood

will spurt out and soil your waistcoat! . . . But . . . I am not your
father.

TOM: Not? But you said . . .

PARTRIDGE: I said I had an appetite for Jenny Jones, but I never sat to a
meal with her. . . . And I have to ask your pardon, lad—for, much though
I loved your warm embrace, I accepted it under false pretenses.

TOM: Then give it back.

PARTRIDGE: What, sir?

TOM: My embrace, you thief!—give it back!

(*For an instant, Partridge does not understand. But as Tom opens his arms
wide to take the man into an embrace, Partridge almost swoons with joy.*)

PARTRIDGE: Oh, Tom Jones, I could be your slave!

(*They embrace even more warmly than before.*)

TOM: The trouble with your *not* being my father is that there is still a father to find. Where will I look for him?

PARTRIDGE: Go to the city, Tom, to the city. London is full of bastards and
the fathers of bastards.

TOM: Yes, that's what I thought. Meanwhile, Partridge, is there a place to
dine and spend the night?

PARTRIDGE: Two miles—that way. The name of the inn is Upton. It is said
to be a friendly place.

TOM: Let us go, then.

PARTRIDGE: Us? Oh no, sir. You should not be seen in my company.

TOM: Why not?

PARTRIDGE: There's hardly a constabulary where I am not wanted. A bit of
petty thievery, a touch of trespass—poaching, pickpocketry. Besides which,
I am none too clean. For I moisten my innards, but rarely my skin. You
would not dare to stand windward of me, sir.

TOM: Then I will stand leeward. Come.

PARTRIDGE: Oh, Tom, what can I give you for the kindness of your good
heart? Here—take this!

(*He hands Tom one of his pistols.*)

TOM: No, thank you. Hunting was for the fields and brakes of Somerset.
There is no game on the highway.

PARTRIDGE: The game is men, Thomas—men! There are highwaymen and
brigands!

TOM: I could not kill a man, Partridge.

PARTRIDGE: Kill?—who says kill? (*Conspiratorially whispering*) This is not
for killing—it's for frightening. There are no bullets here.

TOM: But I heard you shoot them.

PARTRIDGE: Firecrackers!

TOM: What?

PARTRIDGE: Noise, lad—noise!

(*He sings:*)

MAKE A NOISE

THE POWER OF MY PISTOL
IS THE NOISE IT MAKES.
IT'S THE WIND IT BREAKS,
IT'S HOW STRONG IT MAKES YOU FEEL.
THE POWER OF MY PISTOL
IS THE SIZE OF IT,
NOT WHO DIES OF IT,
IT'S THE PRETENSE, NOT THE REAL.

MAKE A NOISE, BANG, BANG!
MAKE A NOISE!
AND YOU'LL HAVE THE GREAT ILLUSION
YOU ARE ONE OF THE BOYS!
MAKE A NOISE, BANG, BANG!
MAKE A NOISE!
AND YOU'LL MAKE THE GREAT CONFUSION
THAT A BULLY ENJOYS!
MAKE A NOISE, MAKE A NOISE, MAKE A NOISE!

TOM: If all it does is make a noise—if I never have to kill a man with it—
by God, there's nothing wrong with just *having* it!
(*He takes the pistol*)

THE POWER OF MY PISTOL'S
NOT THE STEEL OF IT,
IT'S THE FEEL OF IT,
IT'S THE FEEL THAT MAKES ME STRONG.
THE POWER OF MY PISTOL'S
NOT THE STRENGTH OF IT,
IT'S THE LENGTH OF IT,
FOR THE BIG ONE CAN'T BE WRONG!

MAKE A NOISE, BANG, BANG!
MAKE A NOISE!
AND CREATE A MINOR TERROR
WITH THE TERRIBLE TOYS!
MAKE A NOISE, BANG, BANG!
MAKE A NOISE!
WE'LL BE PARDONED EVERY ERROR
IF WE SAY WE'RE JUST BOYS!
MAKE A NOISE, MAKE A NOISE, MAKE A NOISE!

BOTH: THE POWER OF MY PISTOL'S
NOT THE DRAW OF IT,
IT'S THE AWE OF IT,
IT'S AN AWFUL DARLING THING.
THE POWER OF MY PISTOL'S
NOT THE GRIEF OF IT,
IT'S BELIEF IN IT,
IT ASSURES ME I'M THE KING!

MAKE A NOISE, BANG, BANG!
MAKE A NOISE!
SINCE WE'RE ALL OF US CONFRONTED
BY THESE DEVILISH TOYS!
MAKE A NOISE, BANG, BANG!
MAKE A NOISE!
IF WE ALL FEEL LIKE WE'RE HUNTED,
IT IS ONE OF LIFE'S JOYS.
MAKE A NOISE, MAKE A NOISE, MAKE A NOISE!

MAKE A RACKET, RAISE A SHOUT,
THAT'S WHAT PISTOLS ARE ABOUT.
DON'T DISCOUNT THE VOICE OF ARMS,
THERE'S A LOVELY CHOICE OF HARMS
IN THE BELLICOSE ALARMS.

MAKE A NOISE, BANG, BANG!
MAKE A NOISE!
NO ONE MINDS A LITTLE KILLING
IF IT'S DONE BY NICE BOYS!
MAKE A NOISE, MAKE A NOISE, MAKE A NOISE!

(*As they conclude the song, they shoot off their pistols, cavorting noisily, the orchestra at its loudest. The light changes to pick up the portico of the Inn. Florizelda, a lush looking maid is sweeping the doorstep. Tom and Partridge appear.*)

PARTRIDGE: Holla! Is there accommodation at the inn?

FLORIZELDA: Nothing to accommodate *you*, Old Stinkbody.

PARTRIDGE: Call me Stinkbody, do you?—as if I never bathe myself?

FLORIZELDA: When was the last occasion?

PARTRIDGE: I walked in the rain last Whitsuntide.

FLORIZELDA: Between raindrops?

PARTRIDGE: I got spattered by a few.

FLORIZELDA: Well, there's no room for you, Old Stink and Stench, unless you sleep in the stable. (*Provocatively*) But there's a nice one for your friend, I'd say.

PARTRIDGE: I'll go and have a look at it.

(*He goes indoors.*)

FLORIZELDA: (*Seductively to Tom*) There's fresh water in the cistern if you want to put something wet in your mouth.

(*Tom bends over to drink out of the cistern. His rump is to Florizelda. She studies it with pleasurable contemplation. As he drinks, as she looks, Mrs. Waters comes out of the inn. She is fully clothed now, in enticing near-splendor. She too studies Tom's rear, then, with a peremptory gesture, dismisses the maid. Tom, after his long drink, comes to his full height. He and Mrs. Waters face each other—without a word. He is struck by her.*)

WATERS: Well, my brave cockerel, I am happy to see you're alive.

TOM: (*With as much charm as he can muster*) You have the advantage, madam.

WATERS: What?—don't remember me?—without a noose around my neck—and with my clothes on?

TOM: (*Delighted to remember*) Ah, it's *you*, madam—and looking well too— that brute didn't hang you—and you're in good spirit.

WATERS: To the devil with my spirit—it was my neck I was worried about. That whoreson dog almost separated my head from my body.

TOM: I am glad to see you are one piece.

WATERS: (*Warming to him*) Ah, do you think so? Call me Mrs. Waters. Do you really think so?

TOM: (*Studying her*) There is little doubt of it, Mrs. Waters.

WATERS: Then I owe the one piece entirely to you, sir. You saved my neck from being stretched, my eyes from popping out of my head and my tongue from hanging out like a dead sausage. In fact, you have saved my body from a most damnable obliteration. Now, what do you intend to do with it?

TOM: Your body, madam?

WATERS: My body, sir.

TOM: I . . . I will have to think what use I can put it to, madam.

WATERS: Are there so many alternatives? Can you not settle upon one?

TOM: I am giving it much thought, madam.

WATERS: Does nothing come readily to mind? Is your imagination not lively, lad?

TOM: (*Quickly*) Oh yes, madam, very lively!

WATERS: Then what about you is not?

TOM: (*Annoyed at himself*) Nothing is not! All of me is lively—that is my undoing!

WATERS: Ah—too much roodle-doodle, eh?

TOM: Too much lovemaking—that's what my guardian told me.

WATERS: And so you have come to distrust it.

TOM: Yes—damme—yes!

WATERS: Do not upbraid yourself, lad—your guardian is wrong. We have little we can trust in the world, beautiful boy, very little we can trust. Not the schoolmaster, not the judge. We must stop laying store in what men

say is right and wrong. Yes, even in the church! For the preacher's rectitude in the pulpit is his erection in the pub.

TOM: Surely there must be something we can trust!—something in the
church!

WATERS: Trust the organ.

TOM: (*With a wry smile*) It is a meretricious pun, madam—but I get the
point. Howsoever, I cannot trust the object we are discussing for it is always getting me in trouble.

WATERS: But that's life, isn't it? In trouble, out of trouble—in, out, in, out.

TOM: I would rather be out than in.

WATERS: Would you indeed? Let us see about that. I'm going into the hostelry
again. When I am ready for you I will make a barking-howling sound, like
a dog. It will reverberate like no other dog you have ever heard—the
warmest bitch in the hottest season. When you hear me—come.

(*She goes indoors. Tom, his resolve starting to fail him, talks to his weaker,
stronger member.*)

TOM: Trust the organ, indeed! I'd sooner trust a serpent in the grass than
trust you! (*Pointing to the inn*) You will not lead me this way—no!—for
I will lead you that way! I must learn to put you under restraint, you
monster!

(*He sings:*)

BEGONE

SELF-RESTRAINT IS BARELY WON
WHEN TROUBLE IS A-BREWING.
IF MY BRITCHES COME UNDONE
YOU WILL BE MY UNDOING.

YOU'RE A BEAST, YOU'RE A TRAITOR,
YOU WILL CHEAT AND BETRAY ME,
AND THEN SOONER OR LATER
YOU ARE BOUND TO BELAY ME.

YOU DEMAND MY ATTENTION
BY THE SIZE OF YOUR GROWING,
A CONFUSING DIMENSION:
ARE YOU COMING OR GOING?
BEGONE! BEGONE!
GO BACK WHERE YOU CAME FROM,
AND DON'T COME AGAIN
EXCEPT WHEN I CALL YOU
AND I'LL TELL YOU WHEN.
BEGONE, MY GOOD ENEMY,
BEGONE, MY BAD FRIEND,

BEGONE, OR YOU'LL COME TO A VERY BAD END,
BEGONE! BEGONE!

YOU WRECK MANY A GOOD MAN BY BEING HIS
    MASTER,
THE CRIMINAL COURT IS A PENAL DISASTER.
YOU HAVE NO DISCRETION. WHEN YOU'RE HIGH AND
    MIGHTY,
THE PLAINEST OF MILK MAIDS BECOMES APHRODITE.
I THINK I CAN TELL HOW I GOT TO THIS STATUS:
I SOLVE EVERY PROBLEM WITH THE SAME APPARATUS.
YOU'LL MAKE ME WIND UP WITH A ROPE FOR A
    NECKLACE,
WHY WASN'T I BORN WITH A PECKER THAT'S
    PECKLESS?

ARE YOU STILL THERE?
YES, YOU'RE STILL THERE!

YOU'RE A GUN THAT WILL KILL ME,
YOU'LL GO OFF BOOMERANGING,
OR A TEMPTER TO THRILL ME
AND WE'LL BOTH END UP HANGING.

OH, YOU DON'T EVER MIND ME,
YOU'RE A CAUSE OF DISSENSION,
I WILL LEAVE YOU BEHIND ME,
YOU'RE A BONE OF CONTENTION.

BEGONE! BEGONE!
WHY CAN'T YOU LISTEN TO REASON?
HOW CAN I PUT YOU TO ROUT?
WHY ARE YOU ALWAYS IN SEASON?
WHY DON'T YOU JUST PETER OUT?

BEGONE! BEGONE! BEGONE!

(He looks in the direction of the hostelry, tempted by the thought of Mrs.
Waters. He resists the temptation and hurries away. An instant. The stage
is empty. Now we hear the loud barking and baying wail of the dog in heat.
Tom comes rushing back, sprints across the whole width of the stage and
pell mells into the inn.

From the other side of the stage, Sophia and Molly come hurrying in.
They are both dressed alike, in great scarlet mantles ornamented in gold.
The mantles are hooded so that they can be thrown over the head, with a

half-mask arrangement that conceals the wearer's face. The young women are in a panic.)

SOPHIA: Are they following—are they following?

MOLLY: Please you, mistress, if I am to continue being your maidservant, we must stop from time to time or I will die of exhaustion.

SOPHIA: Nonsense, Molly—look sharp! Are they following, are they following?

MOLLY: No, mistress—I am certain they are not.

SOPHIA: It was a carriage like my father's!

MOLLY: There are many such. Besides which, he has never laid eyes on your red mantle and he could not possibly recognize it. And it would be doubly misleading for him to see *two* of them.

SOPHIA: (*Relaxing only a little*) Yes—yes, it would, would it not? (*Giggling*) Oh, how clever I am!

MOLLY: Let *you* call yourself clever—I would not. Jilting a man on the eve of a money-fat marriage, and giving up two estates—two of them! And for what? A foolishness!

SOPHIA: For love!

MOLLY: As I said, a foolishness.

SOPHIA: (*On the edge of tears*) I didn't know I believed in it until I lost it!

MOLLY: What if you've lost it forever? What if you never find Tom in London, what if he's not there?

SOPHIA: Not in London? Nonsense. When a person leaves home he's either dead or alive. If he's dead, they bury him. If he can so much as breathe, he goes to London. And there are many there who can scarcely do *that*.

MOLLY: But what if your aunt's friend—whatever her name is—

SOPHIA: Mrs. Bellaston.

MOLLY: What if Mrs. Bellaston doesn't take us in?

SOPHIA: She will take us in. She loves me.

MOLLY: What if she gives you away to your father?

SOPHIA: She won't give me away—she hates him. Now go on, Molly, go inside and see if there is room at the inn.

MOLLY: It's getting warm—I'll leave my cloak.

(*She throws her mantle on the well-coping and hurries indoors. Suddenly, offstage, a commotion. Sophia is alarmed.*)

SOPHIA: Oh heavens, what is it? God save me—it's my father!

(*She starts to run indoors, thinks better of it, runs off in another direction. Squire Western and Philomenia enter. He is in a bother of annoyance.*)

WESTERN: The devil burn my hide, I tell you I saw her! She was wearing a red mantle.

PHILOMENIA: She does not *possess* a red mantle.

WESTERN: And I saw her companion—also wearing a red mantle.

PHILOMENIA: You saw two of them?

WESTERN: Two—two!

PHILOMENIA: (*Steadily*) You saw two Sophias in red mantles?

WESTERN: I didn't say I saw two Sophias—I said I saw two women in red mantles.

PHILOMENIA: You know what seeing double comes from, don't you?

WESTERN: (*Outraged*) I am not drunk! I saw two red mantles with two golden hoods!

PHILOMENIA: Now I am certain of it. Red mantle, golden hood—what a vulgar fashion! No lady of quality would wear it!

WESTERN: (*He catches sight of Molly's mantle*) There—look! (*He grabs it and waves it at her*) Oh, scruff and scrofula, I'll get that lying, cheating bitch daughter of mine! I'll have her flogged in the marketplace, I will! Landlord! Publican! Hostelkeeper!

(*The Innkeeper comes out.*)

INNKEEPER: Sir?—what noise?—sir?

WESTERN: Are you the innkeeper?

INNKEEPER: I am, sir—what can I do for you?

WESTERN: You can do my daughter for me—where is she?

INNKEEPER: I do not have your daughter, sir—I have only my own. And such a daughter do I have that, if you are lacking a girl child, I would gladly give you mine.

WESTERN: Two red cloaks—another one like this—you did not see her?

INNKEEPER: No, on my honor, sir. But perhaps my daughter did. Go inside and call for her—her name is Florizelda.

WESTERN: (*Shouting as he goes inside*) Florizelda! Florizelda, damn your bed and body, where are you? Florizelda!

PHILOMENIA: (*Following him, calling*) Florizelda! Florizelda!

(*As they disappear, there is a playful scream from the opposite side of the stage. Florizelda runs across the courtyard, ruttishly pursued by Partridge.*)

INNKEEPER: (*Angry*) Florizelda! Florizelda, come back! Florizelda!

(*An instant, then Partridge comes back, puffing and panting. Florizelda is nowhere in sight; she has given him the slip.*)

PARTRIDGE: Where is she—where did she go—which way?

INNKEEPER: (*Burning*) I think you've lost her, sir.

PARTRIDGE: Ah, what a pity. Innkeeper, I must congratulate you on the chambermaids you hire. That one is so soft, with not a bone in her body, I swear she is all bosom and buttock. Have you ever had her?

INNKEEPER: Yes, sir, I had her by her mother.

PARTRIDGE: (*Swallowing*) I see. You are—as luck would have it—her father?

INNKEEPER: As bad luck would have it.

(*Bang! He hits Partridge who goes down in a heap. The innkeeper departs and Florizelda enters. She laughs at Partridge's plight*)

PARTRIDGE: Oh, is it Miss Velvet Skin again?

(*He gets up and starts toward her when Mr. Waters enters. Waters is a man of size, strength and substance. Right now he is angry and on the hunt.*)

MR. WATERS: *(Shouting)* Innkeeper! Innkeeper!

FLORIZELDA: I am his daughter, sir. Is there some way I can please you.

MR. WATERS: I'm sure there are many ways, but I am not for the moment seeking pleasure. On the contrary, I am seeking my wife. Have you seen her?

FLORIZELDA: Who is your wife?

MR. waters: Her name is Mrs. Waters.

FLORIZELDA: There is no Mrs. Waters here, sir.

MR. WATERS: No Waters?

FLORIZELDA: None, sir.

WATERS: I think you lie, girl. I will see for myself.

(He hurries indoors)

FLORIZELDA: *(Titillated, giggling)* Oh, what beatings and thrashings there's going to be!

PARTRIDGE: Why—where is she?

FLORIZELDA: In heaven, I think—stark naked.

PARTRIDGE: Naked?—with one of the angels?

FLORIZELDA: Yes—an angel named Jones.

PARTRIDGE: Oh no! Tommy—run! Run, Tommy—a husband's after you—run, Tom, run!

(He rushes off. Florizelda laughs in delight.)

FLORIZELDA: Oh, there'll be blood before nightfall! *(She sees the red mantle)* Ah, how lovely! *(Putting it on)* And how becoming it is to me! Not that I can see myself—but I do feel myself—and feeling is what pushes the daisies up!

(She hears a noise offstage and pulls the hood over her face. Western storms in, shouting:)

WESTERN: Sophia! Sophia! God snatch your soul, girl, where are you? *(Seeing Florizelda in the mantle, her face concealed, he thinks it's Sophia)* Ah, Sophia!—you red bedizened bitch—you take that off! Run away from home, would you? Run to London to be with your bastard, would you? *Sophia, take that off!*

(He tears the cloak off.)

FLORIZELDA: *(Pretending shock)* Oh, sir, you have quite dismantled me!

WESTERN: *(An instant, then perceiving her charms)* Well, my dear! Unless I am most chowderheadedly mistaken, you are not my Sophia.

FLORIZELDA: *(Coy)* I am your Florizelda, sir.

WESTERN: Are you, indeed? Yes, I suspect that you are. My daughter is not so well accoutered as you are.

FLORIZELDA: Do you have an inclination to my accoutrements?

WESTERN: Yes, and to your paraphernalia. Such accoutrements and paraphernalia have caused men to duel with one another—weapons up! Parry and thrust, parry and thrust, parry and thrust!

PHILOMENIA: *(Entering in a fuss)* Sophia! Sophia!

WESTERN: This is not Sophia, you old Guernsey. This is the innkeeper's daughter.

PHILOMENIA: (*Pointing offstage*) There!—out there, you numskull—Sophia's running out there in another red cloak!

(*They both rush off screaming "Sophia, Sophia!" At this instant, from the other side, Mr. Waters comes hurrying in.*)

(*NOTE: FROM HERE TO THE END OF THE ACT, THE DIA-LOG AND ACTION ARE MUSICALLY UNDERSCORED. IT IS THE FARCE BALLET OF MISTAKEN IDENTITIES, WRONG PEO-PLE IN THE WRONG PLACE AT THE WRONG TIME.*)

MR. WATERS: Where is she?—where's my wife? I saw her—I just saw her—she was climbing out of a bedroom window—and a young man after her! Where is she? Mrs. Waters! Mrs. Waters!

(*He rushes off, left. Partridge runs on, right.*)

PARTRIDGE: Tommy! Tommy! A husband's after you! Tommy! Where are you—where are you?

(*Florizelda, laughing, throws the red cloak over Partridge, and runs. As he is extricating himself, Squire Western and Philomenia thunder in again. The Squire sees the red cloak.*)

WESTERN: There she is!—there's my Sophia! Go on, hide! Think I don't know my own daughter?

(*He pulls the cloak off Partridge.*)

PHILOMENIA: It's a man, you muttonhead! (*She sees Sophia offstage*) Sophia!

(*She runs off, followed by the Squire yelling for Sophia. The Innkeeper races in and grabs Partridge.*)

INNKEEPER: Where's my daughter, you knave!—where is she?—what have you been doing?

PARTRIDGE: Running!

(*He sprints off, pursued by the Innkeeper. Sophia rushes on.*)

SOPHIA: Oh, heaven help me!

(*Molly comes rushing out of the inn.*)

MOLLY: All the rooms are occupied.

SOPHIA: In the middle of the day? Here, take my cloak—my father has seen me in this. Hurry—put it on!

(*Molly takes the cloak from her and starts putting it on as Sophia runs offstage again. We hear the Innkeeper's voice, shouting:*)

INNKEEPER: (*Offstage*) Florizelda! Florizelda, I'll beat you as bloody as a beefsteak—where are you?

(*Florizelda runs onstage and puts on the other mantle. Now she and Molly are both wearing mantles, the hoods concealing their faces. The innkeeper hurries in from the left side.*)

INNKEEPER: Florizelda! *Which of you is Florizelda?!*

(*Mr. Waters storms on from the right side.*)

MR. WATERS: *Mrs. Waters! Which of you is Mrs. Waters?!*

(*Western and Philomenia race in, center stage.*)

WESTERN: *Sophia! Which of you is Sophia?!*

(*Florizelda drops her mantle and runs; Molly drops her mantle and runs. Almost instantly there is a world-shaking scream offstage. The innkeeper, Mr. Waters, the squire and Philomenia yell simultaneously and respectively: "Florizelda, come back here!" "Sophia! Sophia!," "Mrs. Waters! Mrs. Waters!" Shrieking which, they all race off, they disappear. Partridge, the last one, yells "Thomas! Tom Jones!" The stage is bare for a fraction of a second. Then Tom rushes across the stage, stark naked. Another instant and Mrs. Waters rushes across the stage, also naked. Another fraction of an instant and they both run on again—and each dons a red mantle. Tom doesn't raise the hood to hide his face, but Mrs. Waters does. Now, everybody enters—all together. Bedlam! Out of it emerges:*)

WESTERN: (*To Mrs. Waters*) Sophia! I know you—take that off!

INNKEEPER: (*Also to the hooded Mrs. Waters*) Florizelda! I know you— take that off!

MR. WATERS: (*Also to Mrs. Waters*) Mrs. Waters! I know you—take that off!

(*Tense silence. In the stillness, Sophia enters.*)

SOPHIA: (*Pointing to Mrs. Waters*) Oh, who *is she*, who is *she*?

(*Mrs. Waters drops the hood, revealing her face.*)

PARTRIDGE: Good God! It's Jenny Jones!

TOM: Oh no! No, it cannot be!

PARTRIDGE: Yes, you poor bastard!

TOM: *My mother?!*

SOPHIA: You incestuous monster!

TOM: Oh, woeful day!

PARTRIDGE: Oh poor boy, poor boy! You were brought to bed of your mother, and now you have brought *her* to bed!

WESTERN: Turn about is fair play!

(*Sophia faints. The music which has been running wild during the ballet of mistaken identities now rises to a climax.*)

END OF ACT ONE

Act Two

WE ARE IN ONE of the rougher sections of London—Billingsgate or Cheapside, where a man takes his life into his hands. The Chorus is drawn from the street vendors, alley criminals, harlots, beggars.
(*The song is a reprise of TOM IS ON HIS TRAVELS.*)

CHORUS: TOM IS NOW IN LONDON
           TO SEEK OUT HIS BIRTHRIGHT,
           OUR TOM IS NOW IN LONDON
           TO SEARCH FOR HIS DAD.

           TOM IS NOW IN LONDON,
           STILL ASKING, STILL HOPING
           FOR REASONABLE ANSWERS
           FROM A WORLD THAT'S GONE MAD.

           THE SEARCH IS AN ADVENTURE,
           A HUNTING, A TESTING,
           PURSUING LOVE AND QUESTING
           A CAUSE TO DEFEND,
           A HEIGHT TO ASCEND,
           A FATHER, A FRIEND.
           BUT WILL HIS QUEST REWARD HIM?
           AND WHERE IS RAINBOW'S END?

TOM IS NOW IN LONDON,
TOM IS NOW IN LONDON,
TOM IS NOW IN LONDON . . .

(Tom and Partridge enter. They are dressed raggedly. Tom has lost his clothes and money at the Upton Inn, but his spirits do not flag.)

PARTRIDGE: Give it up, Tommy, give it up! This damn London town is no place for any man who wants to live to a healthy old age.

TOM: But you said London's the place to find my father.

PARTRIDGE: Full of bastards, I said—and cutthroats, too! They'll slit your throat for a ha'penny.

TOM: *(Laughing)* Pecker up, Partridge. Nobody would *pay* ha'penny for my neck.

PARTRIDGE: Tommy, please—let's change the geography. To anywhere! Back to the hedgerows or the highways—any place but London.

TOM: Not until I find my father.

PARTRIDGE: But how will you ever go *about* it?

TOM: By asking, by searching. And then someday somebody will point him out to me, and say, *(With a formal bow)* "Tom Jones, I have the extreme pleasure of presenting you to—your father!"

PARTRIDGE: Who in the name of the devil's arse will ever say such a thing?

TOM: Jenny Jones! She will likewise confess that she is my real mother—to my unending shame.

PARTRIDGE: Don't worry about your shame. She'll never confess to anything—because you'll never find Jenny Jones again. Slithered out of sight like a little snake, she did. She's much better at getting lost than you are. So you better give up, Tommy—give up!

TOM: I will not give up—I'll never give up.

PARTRIDGE: *(Exasperated)* But you won't *find* her, Tom. You've asked everybody and his uncle—and all you ever got was crusty answers.

TOM: My luck will change. It's a lesson I've got to learn from Sophia: *I like everything I see*! My luck has got to change!

PARTRIDGE: It's *been* changing, Tom—always for the worse. And now it's hanging as low as a cow's tits. You've been run out of your home by a man you looked to as your father. You've been beaten on the highway, you've been robbed of your money and had your clothes snatched away by an angry husband. You haven't had a good meal in three days—and you've lost your girl. Your luck is low, boy, low!

TOM: Very true! Nowhere to go but upward!

(He sings:)

SAY YES TO THE WORLD

IT'S TIME TO SAY I'M LUCKY,
EVEN IF I'M NOT.

SO I'LL PRETEND I'M DINING
FROM A BRIMMING POT.

IT'S TIME TO SAY I'M HAPPY
WHEN I FEEL FORLORN.
SO I WILL SAY I'M JOYFUL
I WAS EVER BORN.

WHEN I DON'T HAVE AN ANSWER,
NOT A SINGLE GUESS,
IT'S TIME TO SAY THE ANSWER
IS INDUBITABLY YES!

SAY YES TO THE WORLD, SAY YES!
ALWAYS TELL IT—YES!
IT MAY SEEM A FOOLISH RULE
WHEN YOUR LUCK HAS DAMNED YOUR EYES,
BUT AT TIMES WHEN YOU'RE THE FOOL
YOU'RE THE WISEST OF THE WISE.
SAY YES TO THE WORLD, SAY YES!
ALWAYS TELL IT—YES!
IT'S THE TRUEST OF THE LIES
THAT OUR HEAVEN'S GONE TO HELL.
WE CAN'T LIVE UP IN THE SKIES
ON THE EARTH AS WELL.

BOTH: SAY YES TO THE WORLD, SAY YES!
YES, WORLD, YES, YES, YES!

PARTRIDGE: SAY YES TO THE WORLD, SAY YES!
ALWAYS TELL IT—YES!
WHEN THE IDIOTS CAN SMILE
AND THE WISE MEN ONLY FROWN,
MAYBE FOR A LITTLE WHILE
LET'S TRY STANDING UPSIDE DOWN.

BOTH: SAY YES TO THE WORLD, SAY YES!
ALWAYS SAY IT—YES!

TOM: SINCE WE'RE NEVER BRIGHT ENOUGH
AND OUR IGNORANCE IS STARK,
LET'S STOP PLAYING BLINDMAN'S BUFF
AND LIGHT CANDLES IN THE DARK.

BOTH: SAY YES TO THE WORLD, SAY YES!
YES, WORLD, YES, YES, YES!

TOM: Thank you for joining me, Partridge. Thank you for saying yes.

PARTRIDGE: Oh, I'll say it for a *moment*, lad. The world always gives you a moment of it, now and then—just to throw you off guard. But all the rest of the time it's no, no, no!

TOM: To hell with you, then. I'll find others who'll be as optimistic as I am—I'll find a whole world of optimists.

(*He approaches an unprepossessing looking beggar.*)

Sir!

BEGGAR: (*Suspicious, surly*) You callin' me by the name of "sir"?

TOM: Yes, I am. Have you ever heard of a woman named Jenny Jones?

BEGGAR: If she's a decent woman, 'ow would I know 'er? Is she decent?

TOM: Let's leave that question open. She goes by the name of Waters.

BEGGAR: Waters? I don't even drink 'em.

TOM: Well, anyway, the weather's beautiful, isn't it? Now don't say no too quickly, will you, my friend? Try to say yes, the day is beautiful—will you please try it?

BEGGAR: (*To Partridge*) What kind of barmy bloke is 'e?

TOM: Try it—please try it—just say yes.

BEGGAR: Well—maybe—

TOM: Go on, go on!

BEGGAR: —yes!

TOM: Yes! Yes!
ALWAYS SAY IT, YES!
SAY YES, WORLD—YES, YES, YES!

(*Tom approaches a blacksmith—huge, mean-looking.*)

TOM: Sir—a moment, sir!

BLACKSMITH: Don't bristle me, boy.

TOM: Only a moment. Are you happy?

BLACKSMITH: Mind your dirty tongue!

TOM: I said are you happy?

BLACKSMITH: (*Suspiciously*) What the 'ell kind of incriminatin' question is that?

TOM: Just a simple question—are you happy? Just say yes!

BLACKSMITH: Like shit I will! You don't catch me on that one. I know me rights. I'm not 'appy and nobody in me family was ever 'appy. And we all come to our un'appiness in a decent, honorable way. My mother was the un'appiest, most miserable dog bitch that ever lived.

TOM: But she's dead now, is she?

(*An instant. The blacksmith studies the implication. He suddenly grins.*)

BLACKSMITH: Well, come to think of it, I ain't exactly *Un*-'appy!

TOM: Happy, then—say yes!

BLACKSMITH: Well—yes.

TOM: ALWAYS SAY IT—YES!
SAY YES TO THE WORLD—YES, YES, YES!

(*He approaches a man who is crippled on one leg, the other leg hale. The cripple carries a homemade crutch.*)

TOM: Good morning, sir. How's your leg?

CRIPPLE: It's crippled, you blasted idiot!

TOM: No, the other one—how's the other one?

CRIPPLE: What other one?

TOM: Didn't you know you had another one?

CRIPPLE: (*A burst of discovery*) By juniper—yes!

TOM: ALWAYS SAY IT—YES!
      SAY YES, WORLD—YES, YES, YES!

BEGGAR & BLACKSMITH: SAY YES, WORLD—YES, YES, YES!

(*The cripple joins them. Now, the song reprises as the stage fills with street people, and all join:*)

CHORUS: SAY YES TO THE WORLD, SAY YES!
      ALWAYS TELL IT—YES!
      IT'S THE WORLD'S MOST FOOLISH RULE
      WHEN YOUR LUCK HAS DAMNED YOUR EYES,
      BUT AT TIMES WHEN YOU'RE THE FOOL
      YOU'RE THE WISEST OF THE WISE.
      AND THE TRUEST OF THE LIES
      ARE THE LIES THAT TELL
      THAT THE WORLD'S NOT HELL!
      SAY YES TO THE WORLD, SAY YES!
      ALWAYS TELL IT—YES!
      SAY YES, WORLD—YES, YES, YES!

(*As the song carries everybody offstage, the lights change to reveal we are in the home of Mrs. Bellaston. She is a handsome woman in her forties, who lives in a handsome town house in London. Squire Western, slightly lubricated as usual, comes roaring in, bellowing in his customary manner.*)

WESTERN: Mrs. Bellaston! Mrs. Bellaston! I know you're there, you harpy Mrs. Bellaston—and you've got my beldam daughter with you! MRS. BELLASTON!!

(*Mrs. Bellaston enters.*)

BELLASTON: Stop your noise, you stupid hippopotamus! What are you doing in my house? I told you you're never invited here—and I mean for you never to put in your ugly appearance!

WESTERN: (*With elaborate sarcasm*) I'll put in as pretty an appearance as I can, dear Mrs. Bellaston. And if you don't want me here, don't hide my daughter.

BELLASTON: Who's hiding your daughter, you jug-bitten jackanapes! I have not seen your daughter for so long I would not recognize her if I were to collide with her in The Strand.

WESTERN: (*Seeing her charms through his annoyance*) But you would recognize me, would you not?

BELLASTON: Only by smell.

WESTERN: (*Warming to her*) Still the same snake's tongue as always—and not a day older.

BELLASTON: *You* look seventy-five.

WESTERN: No, I do not. I look just the right age to reach under your farthingale.

BELLASTON: Hands off, you rumpot! If you so much as stretch your arm toward me, your reach will be shortened at the elbow.

WESTERN: (*He laughs, enjoying her*) Oh, lady-my-girl—if you were only to smile at me—by heaven, if you'd smile at me in the morning, I'd be the Prince of Wales by nightfall—and we'd be married in the palace!

BELLASTON: I shall take care not to smile at you.

WESTERN: Tell me, dear darling woman, why do you dislike me? I don't dislike myself. When I look in my mirror, you know what I see?

BELLASTON: Let me guess. A bibulous baboon.

WESTERN: On the contrary, I see a sweet and lovable young fellow. However can you dislike me?

BELLASTON: I do it with very little strain.

WESTERN: A man of my magnetism—a man of my money.

BELLASTON: Oh, I do like your money. I am devoted to anyone's money. I find it a dear companion and a cherishable friend. I could fall hopelessly in love with your money—it is only you I detest.

WESTERN: What reason, did you say?

BELLASTON: You are vulgar, sir.

WESTERN: A quibbling detail. I can mend my vulgarity and be as delicate as a popinjay. And I will do that for you, Mrs. Bellaston! I will learn to talk to you with the most exquisite finesse, with the most finical refinement—yes, by my britches and bowels, I will do that!

BELLASTON: (*Dryly*) Thank you—you are dissolving my stony heart.

WESTERN: I will dissolve everything that is stony about you—your bones, your teeth, your fingernails! And you will be soft with me, soft as a pillow, and you will learn—

(*He sings:*)

LEARN TO LOVE ME

YOU WILL LEARN TO LOVE ME!
BECAUSE I AM ADORABLE!
I AM KNIGHTHOOD IN FLOWER,
THE MAN OF THE HOUR!
I'M SO GREAT, SO GRAND,
SO SUPERB I CAN'T STAND IT!
HOW ADORABLE CAN A MAN BE?
YOU WILL LEARN, YOU WILL LEARN TO LOVE ME!

BELLASTON: How asinine you are!

WESTERN: Me?—asinine?—me?

BELLASTON: You are as stupid as a table leg.

WESTERN: That is a triviality—a very small matter.

BELLASTON: Your brain, did you say?

WESTERN: (*Laughing, enjoying her*) There! I knew we would start getting on with each other. I am very smitten by you—and I'm wondering what it is you're starting to like about me. Is it my good humor? Wouldn't you say that my good humor is beginning to overpower you a little?

BELLASTON: No, sir—your modesty. (*As he howls with laughter*) Oh, dear God, I cannot stand how boorishly you laugh. How obscene you are!

WESTERN: *There!—I knew it*! I knew that sooner or later my wit and whimsicality would win you!

> YOU WILL LEARN TO LOVE ME!
> BECAUSE I'M IRRESISTIBLE!
> I'M THE SAGEST OF SAGES,
> THE ROCK OF AGES.
> I'M SO STRONG, SO SPRY,
> CAN I EVER DENY IT?
> HOW ADORABLE CAN A MAN BE?
> YOU WILL LEARN, YOU WILL LEARN TO LOVE ME.

> LEARN, LEARN, PLEASE LEARN TO LOVE ME, AND
> TURN, TURN, PLEASE TURN YOUR HEART ABOUT.
> LEARN, LEARN, PLEASE LEARN TO LOVE ME
> OR I'LL TOSS MYSELF INTO THE SEA.

BELLASTON: Ah, that would be a pity. You're a good-humored fool with a heart of gold plate. You're a mercenary opportunist who would sell his affection like a cheap little strumpet.

WESTERN: No, madam, it is only that I want you so desperately that I am hopefully trusting while mannishly lusting.

BELLASTON: Disgusting.

WESTERN: Oh, madam, don't deal so sternly with me.

> STERN, STERN, STERNLY YOU SPEAK TO ME,
> LEARN, LEARN, PLEASE LEARN TO SMILE AT ME,
> LEARN, LEARN, PLEASE LEARN TO LOVE ME
> OR I'LL HANG MYSELF UP ON A TREE.

BELLASTON: What a tragedy that would be! What a noble mind would be laid waste!

WESTERN: YOU WILL LEARN TO LOVE ME!
BECAUSE I'M SO PROVOCATIVE!
I'M KIND AS A SHEPHERD,
AS FIERCE AS A LEOPARD,
I'M A FOND MAIDEN'S PRAYER,
I'M AMAZED I CAN BEAR IT!
HOW ADORABLE CAN A MAN BE?
YOU WILL LEARN, YOU WILL LEARN TO LOVE ME!

(*A young woman enters, masked and costumed. It is Sophia, unrecognizable. She does not immediately see her father.*)

SOPHIA: Mrs. Bellaston.

BELLASTON: Not now—not now, dear girl.

SOPHIA: Only a moment. Is this costume becoming to me? (*Seeing her father, she halts*) Oh, dear!

WESTERN: (*His temper in check*) It does indeed become you. And if I'm not mistaken, it becomes my daughter as well.

SOPHIA: Oh, heavens!

WESTERN: (*Witheringly to Bellaston*) You haven't seen her in so long you would not recognize her in The Strand.

BELLASTON: (*Not losing face*) Indeed I wouldn't—if she were decently silent and wearing a mask, which is what I recommend to all vulnerable young women.

WESTERN: (*Indicating the costume*) What is the significance of this frippery nonsense? One damn bloody disguise after another! Why?!

SOPHIA: (*Equal to the fight*) This one is for the masked ball—and I tell you once and for all, I mean to stay here for it.

WESTERN: You will not. You will come home and marry Blifil!

SOPHIA: I would sooner choke.

WESTERN: You can do that later. Egad, girl, what made you change your mind?

SOPHIA: I didn't change my mind, I changed my feelings! On the evening of the wedding, I simply could not go through with it.

WESTERN: If you're still in love with that bastard Tom Jones, I tell you he's after every woman who'll pull her skirt up.

SOPHIA: Hearsay! I do not *know* such a thing!

WESTERN: You do not choose to know!

SOPHIA: Hearsay—rumors—gossip!

WESTERN: (*Frustrated, to Bellaston*) Talk to her, madam. You are a woman of the world—please talk to her.

SOPHIA: (*To Bellaston*) Don't you, of all people, dare to talk to me of Tom Jones's promiscuity.

BELLASTON: Heavenly morning, I would not talk about *anyone's* promiscuity. Unless you look at life through a keyhole, promiscuity does not exist—for which we women must be eternally grateful. However, there are things that do exist. Money, for example. Jones is penniless. And because Blifil will come into a very lucrative estate—

WESTERN: YOU WILL LEARN TO LOVE HIM!
HIS MONEY IS ADORABLE!

SOPHIA: But he is deplorable!

BELLASTON: We're not talking about Blifil, we're talking about his character—which is sterling. Pounds and pounds of it!

WESTERN: YOU'LL START TO ADMIRE IT
AND GET TO DESIRE IT.
IT WILL BRING SUCH BLISS
YOU'LL BE YEARNING TO KISS IT!
WHEN YOU GIVE UP ROMANCES
YOU'LL ADORE HIS FINANCES.
FOR THEY'RE NOT A SMALL TRIFLE OR PIFFLE,
YOU WILL LEARN, YOU WILL LEARN TO LOVE BLIFIL!

BELLASTON: For once, your father is telling the truth. Money *is* adorable!

SOPHIA: You are both abhorrable—abhorrable!

(*She rushes away. The stage goes to blackness. In the dark two masks are
spotlighted. The beams broaden to reveal two masked and costumed
figures. They are Partridge and Tom. The former is wearing a monkey
costume too large for him. Tom's costume, a domino, is too small*)

PARTRIDGE: What an egregious insult—to send me a monkey costume.

TOM: It could be worse. You could be an animal down on all fours.

PARTRIDGE: Or a snake, dear God. It's nice to be up in the world.

TOM: Who do you suppose sent them to us?

PARTRIDGE: Only one person—Jenny Jones Waters. (*As Tom moves his
arms and legs uncomfortably*) Too tight, is it? Looks like you're strangling.

TOM: (*Hand to his neck*) Yes—got me by the throat.

PARTRIDGE: And elsewhere. . . . I'm surprised Mrs. Waters doesn't remember your dimensions.

TOM: Careful, man, you're speaking of my mother.

PARTRIDGE: Ah, dear Jenny. Just think—she's somewhere right here in our
midst.

TOM: And we'll find her! You go this way—I'll go that way.

(*They put on their masks. Partridge leaves first. As Tom crosses the stage
to go in the other direction, Mrs. Bellaston stands there, blocking his exit.
She wears the costume of a country girl, and the mask of a pretty young
thing.*)

BELLASTON: Mr. Jones, I think. Mr. Thomas Jones?

TOM: Madam, you have the advantage.

BELLASTON: I am Mrs. Bellaston.

TOM: The advantage is still yours, Mrs. Bellaston. How did you know me—
especially behind a mask?

BELLASTON: I sent you the mask. In fact, I sent you the entire costume.

TOM: You did? For what reason?

BELLASTON: For someone else's reason.

TOM: (*Agog*) Someone else? Who asked you to do it? Who?

BELLASTON: It's supposed to be a surprise. I am not permitted to tell you.

TOM: Oh, do please tell me! Was it Mrs. Waters? Jenny Jones? Did she ask you to send it to me?

BELLASTON: Sir, I told you—it is a confidence. Please be patient.

TOM: But I cannot! Please—I beg you—tell me!

BELLASTON: Stop! If there's anything I dislike, it's impatience—either in the ballroom or the bedroom. Now do please try to control yourself.
(*Guests—all costumed and masked—cross the stage, coming from many directions. Despite their masks and disguises, they all recognize one another. Mrs. Bellaston, their hostess, greets them.*)

BELLASTON & GUESTS: Good evening, Mrs. Welloughby ... Ah, Mrs. Bellaston, how beautiful, as always ... Captain Otisfield, how are you? ... Lovely April, Lady Dill ... Sir Otto, glad to see you about again. ... Splendid party, Mrs. Bellaston—smashing. .... Ah, Millicent, how good of you to come from Bath. .... Lady Vera, Mr. Cooperthwaite.
(*Tom watches as the masked people greet one another as if unmasked. When they thin away—*)

TOM: With their masks on, how did you recognize them? Did you send costumes to all of them?

BELLASTON: (*Laughing*) Oh no, indeed not. Dear boy, we wear the same disguises every year. What is more to the point, we are all experienced at seeing who is behind the mask—every day of the year we wear false faces. The mask and the face become one. We're all identifiable and ridiculous.

TOM: I would not call you ridiculous, Mrs. Bellaston.

BELLASTON: Ah, but I am! When I put my mask on, what do you see? A young girl in the first flush of her youth—how silly she is! Now I take my mask off—and what do you see? An older woman anxious for you to see her as a young girl. How silly *she* is! Silly in the pretense, silly in the real.

TOM: Then—in this costume—I must appear silly too.

BELLASTON: No. At your age, you do not appear silly in or out of anything.

TOM: You still will not tell me who sent this to me?

BELLASTON: No, only that I regret its small size. I did not imagine you were so ... considerable.

TOM: Please do not flatter me, Mrs. Bellaston—I am most susceptible. I love all women.

BELLASTON: Love—who speaks of love? I do not approve of it. Love is an affliction of adolescence—like acne. But I can understand how a mature woman in your presence can think of herself as a schoolgirl.

TOM: Do not think of me as a schoolboy, madam. In some chambers I am as mature as you are. And yet, there are people who—no matter how mature—are young forever. I am one of them. And so, madam, are you.

BELLASTON: How good you are with the ladies! Young forever, did you say? Poor boy, if you imagine your youth will run on and on forever, you will run into the heartaching fact that it has already run out.
(*She sings:*)

DANCE TO A SLOWER DANCE

DANCE, DANCE TO A SLOWER DANCE,
WALK AT A SLOWER PACE.
WHILE THE YOUNG ONES RACE,
TURN AND SMILE, ENJOY THE JOKE
AT THE EXPENSE OF THE SILLY FOLK
WHO DANCE AS IF THEY'LL DANCE FOREVER,
BUT WE KNOW THE TRUTH, IT'S NOW OR NEVER.

DANCE WITH ME,
ONE, TWO, THREE,
THAT IS AS HIGH AS THE NUMBERS MOUNT,
AFTER YOU'RE FORTY YOU DON'T DARE COUNT.
ONE, TWO, THREE,
DANCE WITH ME.
TRY TO FORGET IT'S A PASSING THING,
NEVER REGRET IT'S THE END OF SPRING.

SEPTEMBER IS ALWAYS THE LOVELIEST TIME,
AND TALES TOLD AT TWILIGHT ARE OH, SO TENDER,
A KISS IN THE DUSK IS A KISS IN ITS PRIME,
ENDEARMENTS ARE HEEDED,
SOLICITUDE NEEDED,
AND LETTERS OF LOVE DON'T GO BACK TO THE SENDER.

THREE, TWO, ONE,
SPRING IS DONE,
AND IT IS TRUE THAT THE SUMMER'S GONE,
STILL, IN THE AUTUMN, THE DANCE GOES ON.
DANCE WITH ME,
WON'T YOU DANCE WITH ME?
ONLY DANCE TO A SLOWER DANCE.

(*The guests join and soon everyone is dancing. During the festivity, Mrs. Bellaston and Tom are lost to view. But as the dancing concludes, and the guests evanesce into the shadows, only Tom and Mrs. Bellaston are left—dancing romantically. The music stops—and they are kissing. At which juncture, Sophia enters. She watches from behind the quasi-anonymity of her mask, then slowly lowers it. As she does, Mrs.*

Bellaston sees her, emits a small sound, laughs suppressedly, and quickly departs. Tom and Sophia hold their moment. Then:)

TOM: Sophia! I cannot believe it is really Sophia. You are a woman wearing the mask of Sophia Western, are you not?

SOPHIA: (*Coolly*) I am as you see me, Thomas.

TOM: As I see you, what are you doing here?

SOPHIA: I've come to London to find you, Tom. I cannot marry that disgusting Blifil, for all the lands of England. I have . . . as I say . . . (*Losing her aplomb a little*) . . . come to find you.

TOM: Come to find me kissing another woman. (*As she turns away*) No, don't run away, Sophia.

SOPHIA: (*Her composure returning*) I was not *running* away—merely *looking* away.

TOM: Forgive me—will you ever forgive me? I had given you up in my mind, surrendering a dream. And suddenly you find me in that most compromising circumstance.

SOPHIA: (*With effort, she preserves her equanimity*) In what compromising circumstance?

TOM: Sophia—please—don't punish me any more than you need to! I tell you I'm sorry—I am most distressfully sorry!

SOPHIA: Sorry for what?

TOM: (*Getting exasperated*) For what you saw!

SOPHIA: But I saw nothing!

TOM: (*Losing control*) Dammit, Sophia, you *can't* like everything you see! This is a spiteful pretense! You clearly saw me kissing Mrs. Bellaston!

SOPHIA: Did I? I don't recall it.

TOM: This is a mean, malicious, revengeful joke! Now, stop it!

SOPHIA: (*An outburst*) And you stop being a fool! If you force me to admit I saw you kissing Mrs. Bellaston, I will have to stand up to you as a jealous woman! And then you will defend your own jealousy by reminding me that I did in fact consider marrying Blifil. To which I will say it was a madness I could not possibly go through with. And you will answer that if I have my madness, you are entitled to a number of insanities of your own, and that they all have names like Mary So-and-So and Nellie Such-and-Such and Molly Seagrim and Mrs. Waters—and that you have made love to all of them! And it will all be very cruel and foolish!

TOM: Call it what you will, it's the truth! I *have* made love to a number of women—and we both know it!

SOPHIA: *You* know it—I do not! I have not been privy to any of your bedroom adventures! I know only what you tell me—and until this day you have told me nothing!

TOM: But if I do tell you something, what should it be—lies?

SOPHIA: I don't want you to tell me *anything*! (*In a fury*) My God, have you no *manners*?

TOM: Manners? You mean I'm to tell you lies in silence?

SOPHIA: I want you to tell me nothing! I want you to observe the amenities!

TOM: Be courteous, you mean—and play the hypocrite!

SOPHIA: Hypocrite—I am sick to death of that word! Do you think, Thomas, that you can make a better case for promiscuity than you can make for hypocrisy?

TOM: You are baiting me!

SOPHIA: I asked a forthright question! Can you make a better case for promiscuity than for hypocrisy?

TOM: (*Losing his temper*) I don't make *any* case for promiscuity! I apologize for it because the flesh is weak—and I'm ashamed that it is! But you are apparently not ashamed of hypocrisy!

SOPHIA: I do not call it hypocrisy. I call it—

TOM: Courtesy.

SOPHIA: Yes!

TOM: Good manners!

SOPHIA: Yes!

(*They both sing:*)

FOLLOW THE FASHION

BOTH: PLEASE MIND YOUR MANNERS,
BE SUAVE AND WORLDLY WISE,
PRESERVE YOUR DECORUM—

TOM: —AND TELL A PACK OF LIES!

BE KIND TO THE LADIES,
BE HONEST EVERY WAY,
BUT YOU MUST LAY THE RULES DOWN—

SOPHIA: —AND LAY THEM IN THE HAY!

BOTH: LET'S FOLLOW THE FASHION,
LET'S FOLLOW THE CODE,
AND LET'S CORRUPT EACH OTHER, A LA MODE.
LET'S FOLLOW THE FASHION,
A FINE SOCIAL TRUCE,
THE GOOSE GETS THE GANDER
AND THE GANDER GETS THE GOOSE,
AND WE ALL HANG TOGETHER
IN THE SAME OLD NOOSE.
THE FASHION, THE FASHION,
FOLLOW THE FASHION,
FOLLOW, FOLLOW THE STYLE.

SOPHIA: POLITE PEOPLE ALL SAY PLEASE AT THE TABLE—

TOM: "DO PASS THE KNIFE, PLEASE," SAID CAIN TO ABEL.

SOPHIA: BE KIND WHEN SOCIAL CUSTOM IS IN A KINDLY STAGE—

TOM: BUT CRUCIFY YOUR DEAREST FRIEND WHEN RAGE IS
         ALL THE RAGE.

BOTH: LET'S FOLLOW THE FASHION
         IN GOOD SOCIAL FORM,
         LET'S NOT DISPARAGE CORPSES WHILE THEY'RE WARM.
         LET'S FOLLOW THE FASHION,
         THE PURE PROTOCOL,
         THE SNAKE LOVES THE RABBIT
         AND POLITELY EATS HIM WHOLE.
         WE DO NOT DAMN OUR NEIGHBOR,
         WE PRAY GOD TO DAMN HIS SOUL!
         THE FASHION, THE FASHION,
         THE MASQUERADE SMILE.
         FOLLOW, FOLLOW THE STYLE.

SOPHIA: Goodbye, Tommy.
TOM: Goodbye again, is it?
SOPHIA: You may live in your fashion and I will live in mine.
   (*Tom, graver now, is stricken by her departure. As he goes off in the opposite direction, the lights dim. Then a single spot on another area picks up Squire Western. As the scene progresses, the light broadens and brightens until the stage is in full brilliant light. Squire Western is speaking to Blifil.*)
WESTERN: (*Heatedly*) No, by God, no! No, Blifil, I won't have it, I won't have it!
BLIFIL: Hear me out, Squire—listen to reason!
WESTERN: I say I won't permit it—never!—no! I don't approve of Tom Jones any more than you do, but I will not allow you to have him arrested!—no!
   (*Thwackum enters left, with two constables. Square enters, right, with two more constables. Seeing them, Western is apoplectic.*)
WESTERN: What is this, Blifil—you've already summoned the constables? Now, man, you send them away! You hear me?—send them away! (*To Thwackum, Square and the constables*) Go away!—all of you!—scat!— shoo, shoo—scat! There'll be no arrest today! Go away—away, I said!
   (*Blifil moves between him and the others. As the constables start to depart, Blifil's voice stops them.*)
BLIFIL: No—wait!—everybody, wait!
WESTERN: Blifil, there's no need to lay hands on the man! Once you're married to Sophia, Tom Jones will not be a threat to anybody. There's no *reason* to arrest him!

BLIFIL: There is a reason, Squire. It has nothing to do with marriage. The charge against Tom Jones is theft.

WESTERN: (*Dithering*) Theft?—what kind of theft? What'd he steal?—what?

BLIFIL: A locket.

WESTERN: A locket? What the devil do you mean, a locket?

BLIFIL: My mother—in her will—mentioned that she was leaving me a locket. It was a large golden locket inlaid with enamel of Chinese red. I remember it very well. And when she died I went to look for it—and it was gone.

WESTERN: Well, Tom couldn't have taken it. He wasn't even in Somerset when your mother died.

BLIFIL: It was stolen before she died—and someone saw the locket in Tom's possession.

WESTERN: Someone?—who? I don't believe it! Who?

SQUARE: I saw him with it.

WESTERN: Well, you're a liar, Constable Square. Everybody knows you're a liar. You'd lie to your own asshole about where the chamber pot is!

THWACKUM: Mr. Square is not lying. I also saw the locket in Tom's possession.

WESTERN: You did?

THWACKUM: Yes, I did.

WESTERN: (*Pointing to Thwackum's clerical collar*) You wouldn't be turning your collar to tell a thing like that, would you?

THWACKUM: (*With dignity*) My collar is in its customary position.

WESTERN: I can't believe Tom Jones is a thief.

BLIFIL: Why not, Squire? You yourself have seen him attempting thievery.

WESTERN: No, not I!—never! When?

BLIFIL: He is trying to steal your daughter.

WESTERN: Oh, well, what's that? She's only a woman—not a fine golden locket.

SQUARE: But if a man steals one thing, he is prone to steal another.

WESTERN: (*Wavering*) Well, there *is* a morsel of truth in that, but . . .

BLIFIL: And if he should succeed in stealing your daughter, the next thing you know he'll be stealing something else that's precious to you. If you have a special brace of hounds or a favorite horse—

WESTERN: What? Not my hounds—not my horse! No, by jumpin' Jupiter, he won't get away with *that*!

BLIFIL: And of course—married to your daughter—it would be very easy for him to have your estate entailed to a bastard—now, wouldn't it?

WESTERN: (*Losing control*) No, it wouldn't, by God! I won't allow it! Steal my hounds, steal my horses—and entail my estate?! No, by God—arrest the bastard!

BLIFIL: Arrest him!

THWACKUM: Arrest him—arrest him!

WESTERN: Hang him!—hang the bastard!

BLIFIL: Now, Squire—let us not go too far!

WESTERN: (*Carried away*) Hang him, hang him!

BLIFIL: Not without a trial, sir, not without a trial!

(*As they sing, the Chorus appears and joins them. Developing rapidly, the crowd becomes more and more excited, more blood-lusty. Whipped up by Western, Blifil, Thwackum and Square, it becomes a loud, raucous, disorderly mob.*)

HANG HIM

WESTERN:

HANG HIM FIRST, TRY HIM LATER!
DOWN WITH REASON, RAISE A SHOUT!
HANG HIM FIRST, TRY HIM LATER!
THAT'S WHAT LAW IS ALL ABOUT!
HANG HIM HIGH! HANG HIM HIGH!
HANG THE BASTARD AND WATCH HIM DIE!
HANG-A-LOO, HANG-A-LIE,
HANG HIM, HANG HIM HIGH!

THEY CUT THE CONVICT'S HEAD OFF,
THEY CHARGED CONTEMPT OF COURT,
THE ARMY THEN REJECTED HIM
BECAUSE HE WAS TOO SHORT!

BLIFIL:

THE ROPES THAT BRITISH HANGMEN USE
ARE PUREST HEMP AND WAXEN,
FOR WE ARE FINICAL AND CHOOSE
FINE FIBERS THAT ARE FLAXEN,
FOR HOW CAN BRITISHERS ABUSE
THE NECK OF AN ANGLO-SAXON?

SQUARE:

A BRITISH SOLDIER WENT TO WAR
AND KILLED SOME FRENCHMEN, TEN OR MORE.
WHEN HE CAME BACK TO LONDON TOWN
HE STOLE SOME MUFFINS WORTH A CROWN.
THEY GAVE HIM A MEDAL FOR KILLING THE TROOPS,
AND FOR STEALING THE BREAD, THEY STRUNG
HIM UP. OOPS!

THWACKUM: WE MUST EMPTY THE JAILS, THE DUNGEONS, THE
TOWERS,
DON'T SEND LAWYERS, JUST SEND FLOWERS!

ALL:

HANG HIM FIRST! TRY HIM LATER!
DON'T TAKE CHANCES, WISE MEN FEEL!
HANG HIM FIRST! TRY HIM LATER!
THAT SAFEGUARDS THE COMMON WEAL!

HANG HIM HIGH! HANG THE BLOKE!
HANG THE BASTARD AND WATCH HIM CHOKE!
HANG-A-LOO, HANG-A-LIE,
HANG HIM, HANG HIM HIGH!

THWACKUM: A MAN SAID THE KING WAS AS FAT AS A PORPOISE,
THE KING TURNED THE MAN INTO HABEAS
CORPUS.

WESTERN: A STRUMPET NAMED GLORIA ONE DAY
WALKED OVER THE BRIDGE ON A SUNDAY.
SHE SOLD ALL HER RAPTURE,
BUT THEN CAME HER CAPTURE.
SIC TRANSIT GLORIA MONDAY.

ALL: HANG HIM FIRST! TRY HIM LATER!
WRITE MORE LAWS AND LET THEM PASS.
HANG HIM FIRST! TRY HIM LATER!
LET'S KICK JUSTICE IN THE ASS!
HANG HIM HIGH! HANG HIM HIGH!
HANG THE BASTARD AND WATCH HIM DIE,
   HANG-A-LOO, HANG-A-LIE,
HANG HIM, HANG HIM, HANG HIM, HANG HIM,
HANG HIM, HANG HIM HIGH!

ALL: (*Shouting*) Hang him! Hang him! Hang him!

(*When the song has concluded and the crowd dispersed, Partridge comes running on to the empty stage. He is followed by Tom.*)

TOM: Wait a minute!—catch your breath!—why are you in such a bloody panic?

PARTRIDGE: Because they're constables!

TOM: Hold on!—what makes you think they're constables?

PARTRIDGE: I saw their uniforms!

TOM: It was dark—you couldn't see a thing!

PARTRIDGE: And I saw their billies! Every damn one of them had a billy in his hand!

TOM: It could have been a walking stick.

PARTRIDGE: You don't walk when you get hit by one of *them* sticks!

TOM: But why should we be hit, you fool?—we've done nothing!

CONSTABLE'S VOICE: Tom Jones!

PARTRIDGE: Oh, merciful God!

TOM: Look! It's Blifil!

PARTRIDGE: I told you—constables!

(*All at once, the stage is overrun with Blifil, Thwackum, Square and the constables.*)

CONSTABLE: Which one?

BLIFIL: The younger one.

CONSTABLE: Tom Jones, you are under arrest.

TOM: Under arrest?—for what?

PARTRIDGE: Tom—run!

TOM: I will not run! Blifil—why?—what's the charge?

BLIFIL: Take him, Constable.

PARTRIDGE: Tommy—don't ask questions—run! That way, that way!

CONSTABLE: (*As they move in*) Now don't make a fuss, boy!

PARTRIDGE: Tommy—run—run! (*Partridge raises his gun in the air*) Don't anybody come closer!

CONSTABLE: Drop that pistol!

PARTRIDGE: Run, Tom—they won't give you a fair chance—run!

TOM: Don't, Partridge!—put the gun down!

CONSTABLE: (*Pointing to Partridge*) Get him!

(*Partridge shoots in the air—once, twice. From somewhere, another gun-shot. Billy clubs are swung at Partridge. A fight—noise—melee—confusion.*)

TOM: Let him alone—let him alone!

VOICES: Run, Tommy—run! . . . Let him alone—he didn't do anything—let him go! . . . Grab him—grab the bastard! . . . Hit him—grab the other one! . . . This way—this way!

(*Abruptly the battle is over. Tom is hustled off, irons around his wrists. Partridge lies on the floor, moaning—as the music takes up a forlorn version of MAKE A NOISE.*)

PARTRIDGE: (*Out of his wits now*) Run, Tommy, run. . . . I won't let them get you, Tom . . . the power of my pistol is the noise it makes . . . the noise . . . make a noise, bang, bang . . .

(*As the music and lights fade, we come up again on a prison guard. He is reading out a list of names. As he does, the prisoners appear and file past him.*)

GUARD: The following will present themselves in due and proper order for visitors. Friends and family are permitted five minutes, barristers ten, King's Counsel unlimited. Lathrop, John—Eggleston, Simon—Russell, William and Robert—and Sheridan, Harold.

(*The men whose names have been called come out of the shadows and disappear. Behind them, trailing, is Tom. The guard sees him.*)

GUARD: Not you, Jones. I did not call your name.

TOM: But there must be *some* visitors for me, sir.

GUARD: If there was somebody, I'd say somebody, wouldn't I?

TOM: Yes, sir.

(*The guard disappears. Tom smiles mirthlessly and, to himself, ironi-cally sings WAS THERE EVER A BOY LIKE YOUNG TOM JONES. It is in a disconsolate mode, and soon dwindles lamely to silence. The guard returns.*)

GUARD: Tom Jones! A lady to see you, boy.

TOM: (*Jumping up. Reflexively*) Sophia!
(*An instant and Mrs. Bellaston appears. She hands the guard a few coins and the latter disappears.*)

TOM: Oh, it's you, Mrs. Bellaston.

BELLASTON: Yes, and I can see you're disappointed I'm not someone else. But be of good cheer, boy, for I have brought you excellent news.

TOM: From her?

BELLASTON: (*Annoyed*) No, not from her.

TOM: From whom, then?

BELLASTON: From King's Counsel and from Blifil.

TOM: (*Wryly*) That must be cheery news indeed.

BELLASTON: But it is! They tell me they will advocate clemency on the murder of Mr. Partridge if you will confess to the theft of the locket.

TOM: (*Angry*) Tell them to go to hell! Tell them there was no murder since nobody has even found Partridge's body. And if he *was* murdered, I certainly did not do it. I had no billy in my hand—and the bullets in the gun I carried were firecrackers—they wouldn't scratch a mouse. Besides which . . . I loved the man.

BELLASTON: Did you also love the locket?

TOM: I did not *steal* the locket, I never saw the locket, I do not believe there ever *was* a locket! I think Blifil concocted the whole damn thing!

BELLASTON: Is that what you want me to tell Blifil?

TOM: I don't care what you tell him!

BELLASTON: What you have told me—that is your whole defense?

TOM: Yes!

BELLASTON: Then you will hang, Thomas.

TOM: No! I don't believe that!

BELLASTON: If you believe otherwise, then you must secretly have *another* defense. Tell me what it is.

TOM: I have no other defense than the truth, madam.

BELLASTON: But the truth is always the worst of defenses! Now, come on, boy, tell me your secret.

TOM: (*Exasperated*) But I haven't any secret!

BELLASTON: Please, Tommy. I know we are hardly more than acquaintances, but that is all to the good. Never entrust a secret to your friends and family, for sooner or later they use it against you. Confide only in strangers. Confide in me, Tom. What is your secret defense?

TOM: Only to be honest.

BELLASTON: (*Appalled*) Only to be honest?! I can see that Sophia was right. My dear boy, you make a vice of honesty—and perhaps that is the vice you have been arrested for.

TOM: I can't help it, madam. When I've been stripped of nearly everything I have, the only thing I can fall back on is honesty.

BELLASTON: You idiot!—don't love yourself for being honest, love yourself

for being *alive*! You think we love one another for being good or kind or
true? If that were so, where are all those who supposedly love you? Squire
Allworthy—where is he? And Squire Western—and Mrs. Waters—and
even Sophia—where are all the people to whom you gave your sweetest,
your kindest, your truest affection? Where are they all? I tell you, Thomas,
they loved you when it was safe to do so—when you were young, when
you were innocent!

TOM: I am still innocent.

BELLASTON: Well, that is your undoing! In a world of the guilty, the innocent are the guiltiest of all! So you had better come in and be one of us.
Compromise! Confess that you stole the locket even if you never laid eyes
on it! *Compromise*! Give up all those childhood pacifiers—truth!—honesty!—love! Give them up!

TOM: What does that mean, madam—to give up love!

BELLASTON: Give up the search for it. Stop running about—looking for your
father, for your home, for Sophia, for your own legitimacy. None of us is
legitimate! *We are all bastards*! And as for love, don't look for it anymore.
It's gone—you'll never find it again. It's the last lingering illusion of childhood—give up the search for it! Give it up, Tommy, give it up!
(*Having to say this to him, she is almost as moved to tears as he is—and
she departs quickly. Tom is alone now. He sings:*)

WHERE DO I FIND MY LOVE?

TOM: GIVE IT UP!
        GIVE IT UP!
        THE LAST LINGERING ILLUSION,
        THE FIGMENT OF THE MIND,
        THE LOVE YOU'LL NEVER FIND,
        THE CHAOS OF THE HEART, THE DESPERATE CONFUSION,
        GIVE IT UP!

        WHERE DO I FIND MY LOVE
        WHO ONCE LOVED ME?
        WHERE DO I FIND THE LOVE
        THAT USED TO BE?
        CAN I FORGET
        THE CHILDHOOD MAGIC OF THE BYGONE YEARS?
        AND NOT REGRET
        THE LOSS WHEN LOVE'S ILLUSION DISAPPEARS?

        WHERE DO I FIND THE WORLD,
        SO YOUNG AND FAIR?
        WHERE DO I FIND THE WORLD

THAT WASN'T THERE?
WHY DO I SEARCH AN ANGRY EARTH AND EMPTY SKY?
WHY CAN'T I LET LOVE GO? GO, WILD BIRD, FLY!
NO! I WILL SEARCH FOR LOVE UNTIL I DIE!

(*As the orchestra re-plays part of the song, Tom remains very still—as if retracing his life from the day he said farewell to Somerset, to home. Slowly he walks to the bars of his cell. He holds the bars in his hands and puts his head against the cold, metallic, unremitting rods of reality. He shuts his eyes and tries to remember the felicities of childhood. But they are unrecallable. He raises his head, he opens his tear-clouded eyes.*)

WHERE DO I FIND THE WORLD,
SO YOUNG AND FAIR?
WHERE DO I FIND THE WORLD
THAT WASN'T THERE?
WHY DO I SEARCH AN ANGRY EARTH AND EMPTY SKY?
WHY CAN'T I LET LOVE GO? GO, WILD BIRD, FLY!
NO! I WILL SEARCH FOR LOVE UNTIL I DIE!

(*When the song concludes, the lights go to black and, in the darkness, we hear the commotion of a crowd, the banging of a gavel. The lights come up to reveal a courtroom. The Judge pounds his gavel and shouts:*)

JUDGE: Order! Order! There will be order in this courtroom! . . . Will the prisoner please rise to the bar, and face his sentence.

(*Tom rises, steps forward and faces the judge.*)

JUDGE: Thomas Jones, all the evidence having been heard and pondered, you are sentenced by this court for the charge of robbery. You are to be incarcerated for ten years. And, all the evidence having been heard and pondered, you are sentenced for the charge of murder. You are to be hanged by the neck until you are dead. . . . Thomas Jones, do you have a final statement?

TOM: (Wryly) Only a request, Your Lordship. Since there are ten years on the first charge, and hanging on the second, could I serve my first charge first?

JUDGE: I'm afraid not, Mr. Jones. Hanging always takes precedence.

(*Tom smiles grimly and sings mutedly.*)

TOM: HANGING FIRST AND PRISON LATER, THAT'S WHAT THE LAW IS ALL ABOUT. . .

JUDGE: Take the prisoner away!

(*Two constables start to hustle Tom off when, suddenly, a commotion. Partridge, his head bandaged, comes rushing in.*)

PARTRIDGE: Hold your blasted horses!

JUDGE: Order! Order! What's the noise?

PARTRIDGE: I'm the noise, Your Lordship! The dead man—Partridge—that's me! The man he murdered! Here I am!

TOM: Partridge!—alive!—oh my dear Partridge!

PARTRIDGE: (*Exulting*) I'll be dearer yet—when you see what I brought you! Bring her in, Squire!

(*Squire Allworthy appears.*)

TOM: Squire Allworthy! Squire!

ALLWORTHY: (*Calling to someone as yet unseen*) Come in, come in, woman—come in!

(*Mrs. Waters, nee Jenny Jones, enters. She is magnificently dressed in shining black—with a huge red locket hanging around her neck.*)

TOM: Mrs. Waters! Jenny Jones!

ALLWORTHY: May it please your Lordship—I would like to present—in evidence—Jenny Jones!

JENNY: And a *locket*!

(*Noise in the courtroom.*)

JUDGE: Order! Order! Jenny Jones—come forward—what is that locket? Is it the stolen one?

ALLWORTHY: It appears now that it was never stolen, Your Lordship. It was given by my sister Bridget to Jenny Jones—for safekeeping—until Bridget's son should be of marriageable age.

BLIFIL: Bridget's son—that's me—the locket's mine!

ALLWORTHY: No—not yours, Blifil. Open it, Jenny—read it!

JENNY: (*Opening the locket, she reads*) To my son, Tom Jones, with the love of his mother, Bridget Allworthy.

TOM: Your sister was my mother?!

ALLWORTHY: Yes, she was.

TOM: Uncle!

ALLWORTHY: Nephew!

(*Loud commotion in the court. The orchestra takes up YOUNG TOM JONES. The crowd disappears—all except Tom, Allworthy, Western and Partridge.*)

ALLWORTHY: Will you forgive me, Thomas? I drove you off and now I beg you to come home.

TOM: I . . . I'm still not sure I know where home is, sir.

ALLWORTHY: But everything has worked out for you, Tommy.

TOM: But it hasn't as yet, sir. I still haven't found what I was looking for. Not Sophia—and not my father.

PARTRIDGE: Tom, by God, *I'm* going to be your father! After all, I was the first one you truly acknowledged by that name!

ALLWORTHY: Then let me be the last. If there's to be a surrogate, I would like to be the one.

WESTERN: To the devil with both of you! If there's going to be *any* father, I'll be the one! He's going to marry my daughter and be my son-in-law— and that brings him closer to being *my* son than yours!

TOM: I don't think I'm going to be marrying your daughter, Squire.

WESTERN: Why not?—all the obstacles are gone!—why not?

TOM: She has discovered a terrible fault in me, sir. I am too honest.

WESTERN: Well, by the devil's bollocks, man, that's not difficult to remedy. I'll teach you how to be a first class liar! I'll be your father that way too! And who has a better right? Who loves you as much as I do? Who quarreled with Blifil when he wanted to have you arrested? Me! Who stuck to you through thick and thin? Me! Who loves you—I ask you, Tommy—who loves you as much as I do?

(*Sophia and Mrs. Bellaston enter quietly.*)

SOPHIA: Well?—what do you say to that, Tom?

TOM: What would you have me say, Sophia?

SOPHIA: Tell the truth, Thomas.

TOM: (*Surprised and pleased*) You mean it?—the truth?

BELLASTON: No—don't listen to her. Don't ever tell the whole truth, Tom. Compromise, Tom, compromise!

SOPHIA: Don't listen to either of us, Tommy. Tell your own truth—and help me to endure it.

TOM: If you do mean it. . .

SOPHIA: I do. (*Indicating her father*) Tell him.

WESTERN: Well, it is the truth, isn't it? By God, you do know I love you better than anybody else does! You do know that, Tommy, don't you?

BELLASTON: (*Muted*) Don't say yes, don't say no. Compromise.

TOM: (*An instant. Then, to Western, with a social smile*) I think you love me in your own way, sir.

(*Everybody laughs admiringly—and Sophia smiles.*)

ALLWORTHY: Well, Thomas, you didn't even have one father—and now you've got three. How do you feel about that?

TOM: (*Stepping down to speak confidentially to the audience*) Shall I tell him the truth? If I do, I must say I was better off with no fathers at all than with three of them who love me only when I am rich. (*To Allworthy, telling the lie straight-facedly*) Oh, I *love* having three fathers, Squire! I don't see how people get along with only one! They must feel like utter bastards!

BELLASTON: Well said.

WESTERN: (*Howling with laughter*) Yes, well said! What a lad, what a lad!

> WAS THERE EVER A BOY LIKE YOUNG TOM JONES?
> WAS THERE EVER?
> THERE WAS NEVER!
> ALL THE WORLD IS A JOY WITH YOUNG TOM JONES,
> AND HE'S CLOVER!
> IS HE EVER?

(*Sophia smiles: she has won! Tom has learned his manners. With a glow of pleasure she moves toward Tom and takes his hand. He is bemused, but happy. Part of his quest has been accomplished: the rest will wait. . . Squire Allworthy and Mrs. Bellaston come straight downstage and sing to the audience—confidentially and bittersweetly.)*

ALLWORTHY &   WE DREAM HE IS WHAT WE WERE IN OUR YOUTH
BELLASTON: WHEN ALL OUR LIVES WERE CLOSER TO THE
          TRUTH,
          BUT NOW THAT WE ARE LONGER IN THE TOOTH—
          FAREWELL, TOM JONES!
ALL: WAS THERE EVER A BOY LIKE YOUNG TOM JONES?
     THERE'S ONE TOM JONES!
   SAY YES TO THE WORLD, SAY YES,
   YES, WORLD, YES, YES, YES!

THE END

BLUEBIRD OF HAPPINESS

A Play in Two Acts

CHARACTERS

(In the order of their appearance)

Annie Jacobs
Simon Farber
Bessie Farber
Philip Farber
Ben Farber

PLACE

The Farber residence in South Philadelphia

TIME

May, in the early 1930's

Act One

THE LIVING-DINING ROOM in a house on Hutchinson Street, near Oregon Avenue, in Philadelphia. A modest house for lower middle class people, in the early 1930's. A door to the vestibule, thence outdoors; another door to the kitchen; a stair landing for the steps that go to the second floor; a window on an alleyway, across which is a similar window of the next-door-neighbor's house, if we can see it. On the table behind the couch is a largish cardboard box, covered by an apron.

It is late afternoon, nearly dusk of a spring day. The door to the street is heard to open and shut, then Annie Jacobs enters. She is in her late twenties, attractive, frightened but brave, with an intelligently achieved gaiety. She carries two small, neatly wrapped gift packages. Setting them down, she notices the apron-covered box, lifts the corner of the apron, and smiles at what she sees under it. She calls toward the kitchen:

ANNIE: Bessie! (*No response. She goes toward the stair landing and calls up:*) Uncle Philip! Simon! (*Nobody. Puzzled by their absence, she hangs her coat on the hall rack, returns to the landing and calls again:*) Simie! (*A voice responds from the vestibule:*)
SIMON: Home! Simon's home!
(*Simon Farber enters—seventeen, part grace, part awkwardness. A burgeoning realist, he still has a trace of adolescent romantics which he ex-*

presses in histrionic style, but for the most part he is forthrightly down-to-earth. Carrying a load of books, he tosses them on the couch.)

ANNIE: Where you been, coming home so late?

SIMON: It's not late—it's only six-thirty. (*Pointing to the apron-covered box*) Hey, what's that?
(*He snatches the apron off, revealing that the box carries a legend, repeated on four sides—Do Not Touch—lettered in huge crayon strokes.*)

ANNIE: I don't know. But the neat lettering spells Bessie.

SIMON: What's she got in there?

ANNIE: I can't imagine. Maybe a present for your father.

SIMON: Oh God, I forgot his birthday! Oh God, I'll slash my wrist, I'll cut my throat, I'll do terrible things to myself! Oh God!

ANNIE: Shut up—I got him a present for you.

SIMON: You did? You honestly did? Oh, I love you, Annie. I love you with all my heart and soul. And I'll pay you back. I promise I'll pay you back. (*Hefting the present*) What is it?

ANNIE: A pipe.

SIMON: A smoking pipe?

ANNIE: No, a sewer pipe.

SIMON: But he doesn't smoke.

ANNIE: What difference does that make? He exchanges everything.

SIMON: (*Pointing to the box*) You think that's a present for him?

ANNIE: What else? What do you suppose it is? A lunch box, maybe?

SIMON: Nah—he's got one. (*Lifting an edge of the box just a hair*) It doesn't look like it contains anything, it looks like it's *covering* something.

ANNIE: (*As he lifts the other side of the box*) Her sign says Do Not Touch.

SIMON: Didn't you touch?

ANNIE: No.

SIMON: You didn't touch at all?

ANNIE: Well . . . a little bit. But then I quit. You won't. And if Bessie doesn't want you to touch, don't touch!

SIMON: What's this business with calling her Bessie? You know she hates that. Why don't you call her Mom the way I do?

ANNIE: Because she's your mom and she's my aunt. She's not even my aunt—she's my third cousin, once removed.

SIMON: *Fifteenth* cousin, once removed.

ANNIE: Tenth cousin, *twice* removed.

SIMON: You're the one who's removing yourself. If you live here like a daughter, why don't you treat her like a mother, the way she wants you to? At least, go back to calling her Aunt Bessie. I think it's dopey, calling her "Bessie." What are you doing it for?

ANNIE: Why do you have two heads?

SIMON: No, I mean it. Why did you stop calling her Aunt Bessie but you still call my father Uncle Philip?

ANNIE: (*Confused, restless; trying to laugh it off*) I don't *know*—I can't do everything at once. I think I'll quit my job.

SIMON: What? In a time like this? I thought you liked your job.

ANNIE: When I decided I was going to be a great artist, selling art supplies was a wonderful idea. But I just discovered why I can't paint. You know why? Because I see the world cockeyed.

SIMON: Well, you don't *have* to see it that way? You don't really have to paint a big red nose coming out of a belly button. The world can do without big red noses coming out of belly buttons.

ANNIE: I'm making the point that our noses are in a ridiculously prominent place. And I'm expressing my esthetic disapproval.

SIMON: You got a great cause there.

ANNIE: Never mind. I've given up painting and I've decided I'm going to be a writer.

SIMON: Uh-oh. What kind of writer?

ANNIE: The kind that wins the Pulitzer Prize and goes to Sweden to pick up the Nobel.

SIMON: I don't really think they give the Nobel Prize for writing limericks. There's nothing special about them—they aren't even dirty.

ANNIE: Go to hell, Simon.

SIMON: I've been there all afternoon.

ANNIE: Where did you go after school?

SIMON: To the basketball game.

ANNIE: *You?*

SIMON: Me.

ANNIE: I thought you hate basketball. Yesterday you said—(*Hands in prayer, imitating his theatrics*) "Dear God, don't give me basketball, give me the measles."

SIMON: Listen!—just because I'm fifteen feet tall do I have to like basketball?

ANNIE: Then why did you go to the game?

SIMON: It was a tragic blunder. Hamlet should not have killed Polonius, and I should not have gone to the basketball game.

ANNIE: Why did you?

SIMON: It was a benefit for the three teachers who got laid off.

ANNIE: Three more got laid off?

SIMON: Yeah. When Mr. Harbison said goodbye to English Three, he was so nice about it that I had a lump in my throat as big as a baseball. He said it's nobody's fault—just the depression, as if the depression was just a cold, you take two aspirins, you sneeze a lot, and a few days later it's gone. Then he read us this funny poem he made up about Herbert Hoover, and it was full of nifty jokes and we were all laughing and clapping—and suddenly he began to cry . . . Oh, dammit . . . And then, as if the day wasn't horrible enough, I went to the basketball game. And I was so sad and so mad that I rooted for the other team to win.

ANNIE: Who won?

SIMON: (*Woefully*) We did.

ANNIE: So go kill yourself.

SIMON: Yeah, I think I will. Maybe next week sometime. . . . You had a nightmare last night.

ANNIE: (*Quite still. Withdrawing*) No, I didn't.

SIMON: Yes, you did.

ANNIE: I did not have any nightmare last night.

SIMON: You were crying and shouting to somebody and I ran into your room and shook you and woke you up and you said thank you, and I went back to bed and I didn't hear you anymore.

ANNIE: You rat. You promised you would never talk about it.

SIMON: Well, you haven't had one in a long time, and I thought, if you knew about it, you could maybe make yourself stop having them—the way you did before.

ANNIE: I didn't stop them. They just stopped—that's all, they just stopped. (*Bessie Farber enters. In her mid-fifties, her prepossessing quality is strength. While she is proud of this, there is something about her valor that gives her trouble. She carries a brown paper bag, out of which protrude two loaves of bread.*)

BESSIE: Is everybody home?

SIMON: All except Poppa.

ANNIE: Where were you, Bessie?

BESSIE: Tell her I don't answer to the name Bessie.

SIMON: Where were you, Mom?

BESSIE: (*Indicating the bag*) Don't you see where I was? Bread. I went to the grocery store with a big list this morning—and I didn't forget anything! So why do I always forget bread? Bread is the most important thing in the world—right?

SIMON: Staff of life, Mom.

BESSIE: *So why do I forget bread?*

ANNIE: It's a character defect.

BESSIE: Don't get smart, young lady. It *is* a character defect. God is punishing me for some fault in my makeup. Something that I'm doing wrong—something *in* me that's missing.

ANNIE: If it's *in* you, it's not missing.

BESSIE: Don't start with me, Annie.

SIMON: (*Pointing to the cardboard box*) Hey, Mom, what's that?

BESSIE: It's your father's birthday present.

SIMON: (*Delighted, he starts for it*) Hey, let's look.

BESSIE: Don't touch. Can't you see the sign, it says Do Not Touch.

SIMON: But do you mean it?

BESSIE: Do I mean it? It's the eleventh commandment—Thou Shalt Not Touch.

SIMON: What is it, Mom? Something you bought on the installment plan?

BESSIE: Don't make jokes about the installment plan. Never in my whole life did I miss a payment on the installment plan.

SIMON: (*Faking a raid on the box*) Okay, here I go—I'm going to look at it!

BESSIE: Don't you dare! (*She re-covers the box with the apron*) It's supposed to be a surprise!

SIMON: A surprise for *him*—why should it be a surprise for us?

BESSIE: It's a surprise for everybody.

ANNIE: Why are all your presents for Uncle Philip meant for everybody? Last year you gave him the sofa which we sit in and he doesn't. The year before you gave him a new bathtub—

BESSIE: Which he sits in.

ANNIE: But it wasn't for him personally. It's not personal.

BESSIE: Something you sit in when you're naked is not personal? (*To Simon*) Where's your father?

SIMON: How do I know? He's talking to somebody.

BESSIE: To who?

SIMON: To everybody.

BESSIE: Why does he have to talk to people in his spare time? He spends the whole *working* day talking to people.

SIMON: I'd hardly call it talking, Mom. "Bulletin, Inquirer, Daily News! Read all about it!" You call that talking?

BESSIE: But it's his business—does he have to talk to people for *pleasure*?

ANNIE: An idea hits him.

BESSIE: Yeah, like a rock. And he has to throw it at somebody. So he takes aim at the first person he can see—*bang*! (*Imitating her husband*) "Hey mister, what do you think of prohibition, what do you think of short skirts, what do you think of the president?"

(*Philip Farber appears. He is a few years older than Bessie. Even when he complains, his spirit is aloft, in the zephyrs of hope. Right now he's in high spirits—he has had a good day.*)

PHILIP: What I think of the president is, if Herbert Hoover is in the head-line, you can bundle up the papers and go home! But if Al Capone is in the headlines, hoo, hoo, *hoo*!

BESSIE: Al Capone is in the headlines?

PHILIP: (*At the top of his voice*) AL CAPONE ARRESTED! And boy-chick, does that sell papers! (*Excited*) But what did they get him for? Bootlegging?—no. Prostitution?—never heard of it. Murdering a num-ber of friends and enemies?—no, God forbid! They got him because he didn't pay his income tax! *Income tax*, can you believe it?! Just think: if he had a smarter bookkeeper, they wouldn't have laid a finger on him.

BESSIE: Forget it. They got him and it sells papers—what do you care?

PHILIP: (*Angry*) I *care*! You want to hear something? Some people are not happy that he got locked up at *all*! To some people, Al Capone is not a goddamn gangster, he's a big hero! He's a leader—he pulled the cops' pants down—he's Moses in the wilderness! *Some people are not rooting for us—they are rooting for Al Capone!*

BESSIE: As your brother Arnold says, there are all kinds of dumb people in the world.

PHILIP: Sure, there are all kinds of dumb people—even smart ones! They're too smart for the rest of us—like Al Capone! I don't like it that he's so smart—I won't run up the flag for him.

ANNIE: So don't run up the flag.

PHILIP: *I want to run up the flag! For somebody!* And someday I will—I will! All of us—we will all run up the flag—all over the world—run up the flag!

BESSIE: (*Gently poking fun, she sings*) Happy days are here again, The signs of cheer are here again—

PHILIP: Why do you make fun of it? I dream about ice cream, she puts horse-radish on it.

SIMON: She don't know how to pretend the way you do, Pop.

PHILIP: No, she pretends her *own* way. Only the bad things. The Bolsheviks have invaded, Simon broke his leg, Annie's got the shingles, I got run over by a truck. (*To Bessie*) Why can't you pretend that I brought you a bunch of roses?

BESSIE: So why can't you bring me a bunch of roses?

PHILIP: (*A bit deterred*) You mean real ones?

BESSIE: Only the real ones smell good.

PHILIP: (*Kidding*) Roses have a smell to them?

BESSIE: He doesn't even know that roses have a smell. (*As they all laugh*) So where were you so late?

PHILIP: Talking to people.

BESSIE: Some day they'll throw you in the booby hatch for talking to strangers.

PHILIP: So what? I'll talk to them in the booby hatch.
(*They laugh, enjoying him.*)

SIMON: How many people did you talk to today, Pop?

PHILIP: What difference does it make? Who listens to me?

ANNIE: What would you like them to hear?

PHILIP: My object in life is to talk to every single human being on the earth, and to convince them that tomorrow things will be better.

ANNIE: Uncle Philip, do you really believe things will be better tomorrow?

PHILIP: (*A flourish of bugles*) When we'll get rid of Al Capone and prohibition and Herbert Hoover, we'll all be back in the Garden of Eden, U.S.A.! (*Pointing to the box*) What's that?

BESSIE: Nothing—it's an apron.

PHILIP: Is there somebody under it? (*Taking apron off*) Do Not Touch—what is it?

BESSIE: It's your birthday present.

SIMON & ANNIE: Happy birthday, Pop. . . . Happy birthday, Uncle Philip.

PHILIP: I got a birthday? How old am I?

BESSIE: Sixty years old.

PHILIP: Hoo-hoo, this is important, yes?

BESSIE: Yes. The next thing you know, you'll be seventy. Then eighty, then ninety. Turn around and you'll be a hundred years old.

PHILIP: So I won't turn around. What's in the box?

BESSIE: Guess. (*As he starts to touch the container*) No, don't touch. You've got to guess without touching.

PHILIP: Uh . . . what could be in there? A bunch of bananas?

BESSIE: No, dummy—take the box off.

(*Giggling, as the others do, he lifts the box. On the table, an upright telephone of the period, shining and new. Philip is overjoyed.*)

PHILIP: A telephone! A telephone! Oh, it's beautiful, a telephone! Oh, it's wonderful, Bessie! Give me a kiss! It's wonderful! It's the most wonderful present I ever had!

BESSIE: (*Pleased, but trying not to take too much credit*) I knew it would be just right for you.

ANNIE: Now you can get your object in life, Uncle Philip. You can talk to everybody in the world.

PHILIP: (*A disappointing reality strikes home*) Like who?

ANNIE: Like . . . everybody.

PHILIP: Like who, for instance? Who's got a telephone except us? Nobody I know has got a telephone. Who can I call?

ANNIE: In some neighborhoods, nearly everybody has a telephone.

PHILIP: Where—in what neighborhoods?

ANNIE: In Strawberry Mansion—where Tanta Gussie lives.

PHILIP: Who wants to talk to Tanta Gussie? I don't want to talk to her in real life, why should I talk to her on the telephone?

BESSIE: Relax. She doesn't have a telephone anymore. She made them take it out.

ANNIE: She did? Why?

BESSIE: To save money.

PHILIP: To save money? Uncle Herman left her a fortune in horsehair products.

BESSIE: Now that Uncle Herman's gone, she's stingier than ever. And mean. When the man came to take the phone out, she cursed him and the phone company and Jack Dempsey.

PHILIP: She cursed Jack Dempsey? Why?

BESSIE: Jack Dempsey invented the telephone.

PHILIP: Jack Dempsey invented the telephone?

BESSIE: Go tell her he didn't.

PHILIP: Now *that's* a dumb woman. But if she still had her telephone, I would even talk to Tanta Gussie. (*He strokes the phone lovingly*) It's beautiful. . . . I don't want to hurt your feelings, Bessie, but maybe you should've saved this present for some time when even on Hutchinson Street somebody else would have a telephone.

BESSIE: I know somebody who's got a phone right now.

PHILIP: On Hutchinson Street?

BESSIE: On Hutchinson Street.

PHILIP: Who?

BESSIE: One of our neighbors.

PHILIP: Which one?

BESSIE: Right next door.

PHILIP: (*Darkly*) You don't mean Finkelstein.

BESSIE: Yes, I mean Finkelstein. The telephone man was here—he installed two phones—one for you and one for Finkelstein.

PHILIP: (*Huffy*) If you think I'm going to talk to Finkelstein on the telephone or off the telephone, then one of us is in the cuckoo parlor.

BESSIE: Don't be stubborn, Philip.

PHILIP: He's a pig.

SIMON: He's not a pig, Pop. He's a toad.

ANNIE: Sixty percent pig and sixty percent toad.

SIMON: That's a hundred and twenty percent.

PHILIP: That's how rotten he is.

BESSIE: You're all so smart. Finkelstein is a decent hardworking man. He's not a bum, he's not a bootlegger—

PHILIP: No, he's not a bum, he's not a bootlegger, he's a thief. He steals from the poor and sells to the rich.

BESSIE: He's a pawnbroker. That's what a pawnbroker has got to do.

PHILIP: And he's a crybaby. "I'm poor, I'm poor, I'm dying of hunger, my daughter is anemic, my son's bones are rattling, my wife is so skinny she can squeeze through the hole of a bagel." Always crying—but he's got enough money to send his Leopold to college.

ANNIE: On a free scholarship.

PHILIP: No—with cash. How's that klutz going to win a free scholarship? He's got borscht in his brain.

BESSIE: So how is Simon going to win?

SIMON: (*Hotly*) I'm not, Mom! Get it out of your head. I am not going to win a free scholarship. I'm not at the top of my class, I can barely squeeze into the middle.

BESSIE: And you like it in the middle?—where nobody should know you're there?

SIMON: Don't you know I'm there?

BESSIE: If you don't, I don't!

(*Philip pinches Simon hard. The boy yowls*)

SIMON: Ow! What the hell did you do that for?

PHILIP: Your mother don't know you're there unless you let out a little scream.

BESSIE: You're so smart—so go be smart on the telephone. Call Finkelstein.

PHILIP: No! I hate him! He's mean, he's hateful! He has such a sour personality that if he looks at a cucumber it turns into a pickle.

BESSIE: Okay, so you won't use the telephone, I'll call the company tomorrow and I'll tell them to take it out. We'll save sixty cents a month.

PHILIP: (*Shocked*) We're paying sixty cents a month for an object we can't use? Bessie, I'm surprised at you. You watch every nickel and suddenly you take leave of your senses and—fwip!—sixty cents a month?

BESSIE: So what else could I give you? A man doesn't have a yearning for any object you can buy him—all he wants is to talk to everybody in the world—what do you give him for his birthday?—a half dozen handkerchiefs?

(*He is moved in a mixed-up way: surprised at Bessie's gesture, ashamed of his own misunderstanding of it, and grateful.*)

PHILIP: Thank you, Bessie. Thank you very much. Now, you know what I'm going to do for your sake—only for your sake, Bessie—I'm going to call Finkelstein.

BESSIE: Thank you. That's very nice of you.

(*She is genuinely pleased. He goes to the phone and pauses. He regrets his chivalrous gesture.*)

PHILIP: Maybe I'll do it tomorrow.

BESSIE: No—today—now.

PHILIP: I never did this before. (*Giggling in embarrassment, he lifts the receiver to his ear and speaks into the mouthpiece*) Hello. (*His face lights up with a bit of vanity*) It's a lady! She wants my number!

ANNIE: She doesn't want your number. She wants Finkelstein's number.

PHILIP: So how do I know that pig's number? (*into phone*) His name is Eli Finkelstein and he lives on Hutchinson Street. What? You will? Thank you very much. Say, listen, tell me something, did you read today's paper? . . . Uh-*huh*! . . . So what do you think about prohibition? (*She apparently likes it; he's disappointed*) Oh, you do, huh? . . . Well, all kinds of taste in the world—some people like Jell-O . . . Did you hear what Herbert Hoover said on the subject of a chicken in every pot? . . . What, you don't like chicken? . . . What? (*To the others*) She says she's not allowed to be friendly on the telephone. (*To operator*) So tell me, sweetheart, where are you friendly? . . . Yes—please—give a ring to Finkelstein. (*Delighted, laughing*) It's making a buzzing, a ringing! How do they do that? (*Into phone*) Hello. Who is this? Who? Speak louder. Ah, Finkelstein. This is Philip Farber, your next door neighbor—(*Proudly*)—calling you on the telephone. I said "Philip W. Farber!" I just called you on my new telephone to tell you to go to hell. (*An instant*) What? You can't hear me? (*With careful deliberateness*) I said go—to—hell.

THE OTHERS: Pop—don't! . . . Uncle Philip—please! . . . Are you crazy?

PHILIP: *Go to hell!* (*To the others*) He can't hear me. All my life I was afraid to tell that crazy man to go to hell, and now I got the nerve on the telephone, and he can't hear me! (*Back to Finkelstein*) If you can't hear me, then *you* talk. What? What? I can't hear you—talk louder.

Louder, you Finkelstein, louder! (*He drops the phone, runs to the open window and shouts across the areaway*) Louder, you schmuck, talk louder! (*He rushes back to the phone, lifts the receiver and listens*) What?

(*Apparently he does hear. He carefully puts the receiver on the hook. The phone call is over.*)

BESSIE: Did you hear him?

PHILIP: Yes, I heard him.

BESSIE: What did he say?

PHILIP: He said: Go to hell. (*As they laugh, he laughs at himself*) If I can't insult Finkelstein, it's sixty cents a month, wasted.

ANNIE: Don't worry about the money, Uncle Philip. When you take your other two presents back, you'll have enough for five months' telephone. (*Handing him his gift packages*) Happy birthday, Uncle.

SIMON: Happy birthday, Pop.

ANNIE: The small package is from Simon.

PHILIP: Thank you, Simon. What's in it?

SIMON: Open it and see.

PHILIP: Well, I don't want to open it, in case—uh—you know.

SIMON: You *will* have to take it back it, Pop—it's a pipe.

PHILIP: Oh, good—thank you. A pipe is just what I've always wanted to take back. (*Not opening it, he hefts the other package*) This is heavier than it looks. What's in it?

ANNIE: It's an address book.

PHILIP: A what?

ANNIE: An address book. You can write down the addresses and telephone numbers of all those people you talk to—so that they won't be strangers anymore, they'll be friends. I'm not exactly sure that's the way friendship works, but—(*Lamely*) Anyway—you can exchange it.

PHILIP: Thank you, Annie—this I won't exchange.

(*He kisses her affectionately on the cheek. For no reason—simply because it's the typical adjustment of this family—they all laugh.*)

BESSIE: And here's a birthday card—it goes with the telephone.

(*She hands him a birthday card. He holds it at arm's length because he is not wearing his reading glasses.*)

PHILIP: Happy birthday, Husband and Father. . . . What's that blue thing?

BESSIE: It's the bluebird of happiness, dope.

PHILIP: It looks like a blue chicken.

BESSIE: (*As he starts to put the card down*) No, don't put it down. There's writing inside.

PHILIP: (*He opens it but can't read it. He hands it to Simon*) Here. Either get me my glasses or read it for me.

SIMON: (*Reading*) "Dear Husband and Father. The telephone is *for* all of us— and it is also *from* all of us. We all hope that whoever you talk to will speak nice to you and you will speak nice to them. And the telephone will make you happy. Because we all love you very much and wish you the happiest birthday in the world." (*To his father*) It's signed Bessie, Annie and Simon.

PHILIP: And Ben. We mustn't leave out Ben.

BESSIE: (*Quietly, trying to hide her tension*) Ben is not included.

PHILIP: Don't spoil my birthday, Bessie.

BESSIE: Ben is not included.

SIMON: Mom, please.

BESSIE: Don't you take his side, Simon. (*To Annie*) And don't you, either.

ANNIE: I didn't say a thing.

BESSIE: Well, don't say anything. The less said about Ben the better. The more we talk about him, the more we keep him alive. And it is time for this family to come home from the funeral.

PHILIP: *There never was any funeral!*

BESSIE: I don't want to talk about this anymore. Every birthday, every damn birthday—! *I will not talk about this anymore!*

PHILIP: Our son is not dead, Bessie.

BESSIE: He's as dead as if there's a tombstone on his grave.

PHILIP: He's alive—and living in California. Or Paris. Or Baltimore, Maryland. He's alive and grown up, and on Labor Day he'll be thirty-five years old.

BESSIE: A son who does not get in touch with his parents for twelve years has to be dead somewhere. And he is dead. My cousin Albert heard that he was in a car accident when he was twenty-six years old—that place in Ohio—

ANNIE: That place in Ohio didn't exist. We wrote letters, we sent telegrams.

PHILIP: Nobody in Ohio heard of him, Bessie.

BESSIE: I heard of him. I heard he died in Chicago, I heard he died in Atlantic City, I heard he died in an airplane.

PHILIP: A person who died in a dozen places didn't die at all!

BESSIE: Wrong. A person who died in a dozen places died a dozen times.

PHILIP: Maybe never, Bessie—maybe he didn't die!

BESSIE: Maybe—always maybe! Maybe he'll arrive tonight on the 7:14. Maybe we'll hear the 7:14 screaming along the railroad track and it'll stop right in front of our door, and the conductor will make a big noise, "This stop is Benjamin Farber's house, the house of Benjamin S. Farber! Get off the train, Ben Farber—this is your house, this is your home!" And our son will get off the train, and he'll be wearing a white suit and a white Panama hat, and he'll have a white flower in his buttonhole, and he'll bring presents to all of us. It'll be a Pierce Arrow for you and a fine young bridegroom for Annie and a free scholarship to Temple University for Simon. And where did he get all that money and good fortune? By being a big lawyer or a successful pharmacist or a world-famous doctor who invented a cure for morning sickness.

PHILIP: You can make fun of me as much as you like, Bessie—but all those things are possible.

BESSIE: Stop it, Philip.

PHILIP: It's as possible for him to be a world-famous doctor as it is for him to die in Chicago, Baltimore and New York. It is *possible!*

BESSIE: It is not! The boy was a no-good and he came to a no-good end!

PHILIP: (*Angry, frustrated, hurt*) If you say that once more—if you ever say that once more—!

BESSIE: *He was a no-good!*

PHILIP: Bessie, please—

BESSIE: (*Relenting, she can't hide her ache for him*) Stop breaking your heart, Philip.

ANNIE: Can't we quit this and just celebrate Uncle Philip's birthday?

SIMON: Arguing is how we celebrate.

PHILIP: No, don't say that, Simon—let's stop being mad at one another. It's my birthday—let's smile—be happy—everything is for the best. Say it over and over again. Say it, Simon. Everything is for the best.

SIMON: Everything is for the best.

PHILIP: Now you say it, Annie. Everything is for the best.

ANNIE: (*Laughing*) Do I have to say it so—uh—pure and simple? Could I qualify it in some way?

PHILIP: What do you mean, qualify?

ANNIE: Well, could I say, for example: If this were the best of all possible worlds, and if God were in His heaven and in His right mind, everything would—perhaps—be for the best. Could I say it like that?

PHILIP: No. On my birthday, say it the way I ask you to say it. In plain words—no monkey business—*Everything is for the best!*

ANNIE: (*She laughs affectionately*) I love you, Uncle Philip—and everything is for the best.

PHILIP: *You* say it, Bessie.

BESSIE: Let's sit down and eat.

PHILIP: No—say it, Bessie.

BESSIE: I said let's eat—isn't that for the best?

PHILIP: Damn it, Bessie—say it! It won't hurt you to say it—it won't burn your tongue, you won't get a sour stomach. (*He hugs her*) Come on, honey—everything is for the best—say it.

BESSIE: (*Loosening a little*) Let me go, dummy.

SIMON: Let her alone, Pop—she can't say it!

BESSIE: Yes I can!—I can *say* anything, but it will mean nothing! (*Angrily, imitating him*) Everything is for the best!
(*They all laugh. Even Bessie . . . a little*)

PHILIP: Now I'm happy! I have converted my wife to a new religion, and now I am a happy man!
(*Outdoors, a train is going by. Loud, louder.*)

ANNIE: The 7:14!
(*The family, an automated squad, rushes to dining table, sideboard, china closet; each person has a station. They safeguard dishes, glass-*

ware, photos. The train is a crescendo of noise—and a loud whistle. The furniture shakes, the dishes clatter. The train departs; the family relaxes.)

ANNIE: I don't know why we always run to the breakables. The train never breaks anything.

SIMON: No—it just rattles the dishes.

BESSIE: From a rattle can come a break.

PHILIP: And once—years ago—before prohibition—it broke two bottles of beautiful red-cherry wine.

(At the door, Ben Farber. Nearing thirty-five, at the peak of his romantic splendor, he is dressed in a beautifully tailored brown suit, with expensive shoes, tie and hat, a wonderfully gaudy handkerchief flopping out of his breast pocket. He carries an elegant suitcase and, aloft, a bottle of champagne. The family are motionless with shock.)

BEN: Wine! Did Poppa ask for wine! Here's wine for my Poppa! Here's wine for everybody! Happy birthday, Pop!

PHILIP: *(Stillness. Then:)*

BEN? Is it you, Benny—is it you?

(He approaches his son and pats him all over—shoulders, arms, face; he is touched to tears) Is it really you?

BEN: It's me, Pop—and you look different, but you're exactly the same? Oh, Poppa, Poppa!

(Ben embraces him and kisses him on both cheeks. Then, turning to his mother:)

Aren't you going to say hello to me, Momma?

(He crosses to her. She has her left hand over her mouth and her right hand on her heart. Her body is not exactly trembling, but stirring a little from side to side. At last, quaking and unable to speak, she opens her arms and Ben hurries to be enveloped in her embrace.)

BEN: Oh, Momma, Momma.

(Abruptly she starts to shake him violently as if he were an aberrant small child.)

BESSIE: You bad boy, you bad boy, you bad boy!

(He knows this is an expression of her happiness, and it makes him weep, which he is at pains to conceal; his mission is to be happy.)

BEN: Momma—

BESSIE: I don't believe it—I don't—believe it!

PHILIP: Believe it, Bess—it's exactly like you said—a white suit and a white hat—

BESSIE: They're not white—are you color blind?—they're brown!

PHILIP: And a white flower in his buttonhole.

BESSIE: It's purple.

PHILIP: And he came in on the 7:14.

BEN: No, I didn't, Poppa. I drove.

PHILIP: You got an automobile?

BEN: Look out the window—in the alleyway. (*He stares at Simon*) Who is this—Simon?

SIMON: Hello, Ben.

BEN: (*With an outcry of delight*) I knew it—I knew it! I said to myself, "That kid was as tall as a flagpole—and now he's gonna be twice as tall as City Hall!" I knew it!
(*He pats Simon affectionately; he loves him, he hugs him*) Come on, kid—stand back to back. I bet you're almost as tall as I am! Am I right? He's almost as tall as I am, right?
(*He is bent at the knees, so that Simon will seem taller.*)

ANNIE: He's taller. Even if you stand up straight, he's taller.
(*Ben's a good sport; he laughs—appreciatively. Then, suddenly, as if seeing her for the first time.*)

BEN: My God, it's Annie! No, it's not Annie—it's some beautiful debutante that walked off the pages of the Sunday rotogravure. What's your name, Angel!—Goddess!—what's your name?

ANNIE: (*Quietly, with a wry smile*) Angel Goddess Annie Jacobs.

PHILIP: (*At the window—excited*) Look at that car! Would you look at that car? It's a Pierce Arrow! It's just like you said, Bessie, a Pierce Arrow!

BEN: It's a Stutz Bearcat, Pop.

PHILIP: You see that, Bessie? Everything about him is different than you said. No white suit—brown! No white flower—purple. No 7:14, but a Stutz Bearcat! All different! But it's all the same! It's like your wildest dream!

BESSIE: His Stutz Bearcat doesn't have a roof. Without a roof, you can get soaking wet.

BEN: (*Handing her a ring box*) Here, Momma, let this keep you warm and dry.

BESSIE: What is it? It's not my birthday. (*She opens it*) Oh, my God! It's beautiful—what is it?

BEN: It's a gold ring, Momma—with a ruby in it.

BESSIE: Oh, it's so red—it's so beautiful!
(*She puts the ring on her finger and shows it to Philip*) You talk about wine?—you want to see real wine?—give a look at this!

PHILIP: It's beautiful, Bessie—it's beautiful!

BEN: Here's something for you, Pop. Happy birthday!
(*He hands Philip a long, narrow jewel box.*)

PHILIP: What is it, a necklace? A string of pearls, maybe, to make me look sexy at the newsstand? Good God, a watch—a gold watch! What'd I do—get fired?

ANNIE: Hey, Mister, what time is it?

PHILIP: I won't tell you what time it is because I don't want to wear out the watch!

BEN: (*Noticing the telephone*) Hey, look at that!—a telephone! Poppa, you got a phone—Momma, it's a telephone!

BESSIE: He's telling me it's a telephone. What does it look like, a lox?

BEN: Is it working?—can I use it?

BESSIE: Yes—it's new—use it—you'll be the second one!

BEN: Who was the first?

PHILIP: Me. I called a very dear friend.

BEN: (*Into phone*) The number I'm calling is 3-2-1-4.
(*Waiting to be connected, he says to Simon:*) Hey, kid, open the suitcase—there's a present for you.
(*Into phone*) Hello, Marky—it's me. My parents have a telephone.
(*To the others, as Simon opens the suitcase:*) Marky says congratulations.
(*To Marky*) The number here is eight-six-two-six. Call me if necessary. Yeah—you too.
(*He hangs up*)

BESSIE: So who is Marky?

BEN: Just a guy. Friend of mine.
(*To Simon who fiddles with the suitcase lock*) What's the matter, Simie, having some trouble?

SIMON: Yeah, how do you get this open?
(*As the suitcase opens*) I got it, I got it!

BEN: You see your present?

SIMON: (*Pointing into the suitcase*) Is that it?

BEN: Yeah—take it out.
(*Simon takes it out. It's a basketball. He hides his dismay, tries to appear delighted.*)

SIMON: Great. It's a basketball. Great.

BEN: Not just "a basketball"—it's a genuine Spalding, first quality Montana steerhide. You play basketball?

SIMON: Well—uh—as a matter of fact—

PHILIP: Sure he plays—sure!

BEN: He ought to—he's got the build for it. Did you go out for the team?

SIMON: Well, not exactly.

BEN: Now, don't be bashful, kid—go out for it. You'll be wonderful! With a height like that, you can drop the ball into the basket like a lump of sugar in a glass of tea. My God, this kid's beautiful!
(*He hugs him*) I bet if you raise your hand you can poke a hole right through the ceiling of the Temple University gymnasium.

SIMON: I don't go to Temple, I'm still in high school.

BEN: That's right—you're only eighteen years old.

SIMON: Seventeen.

BEN: Of course, of course—you're not even out of Central High School yet.

SIMON: I don't go to Central, I go to South Philly.

BEN: (*Laughing*) See that? I get everything right! I knew he wasn't in college, I knew he was seventeen years old, and I knew he goes to Southern High. I know all these things because I keep in touch with what's going on! I write letters, I send picture postcards from every town I go to, I keep my fingers on the pulse of my family!

(*He is laughing at himself and it is contagious; they all laugh with him—even Bess.*)

BEN: Kid, you're marvelous, and the whole family is marvelous, and I'm marvelous too! God, what a marvelous family! I love you—I love all of you! (*Hearing Annie's laughter, he stops*) You're a totally different person when you laugh—did you know that? You're adorable when you laugh.

ANNIE: Thank you.

BEN: Did you get your present?

ANNIE: No.

BEN: It's in my suitcase. Go on—open it, sweetheart, open it.

(*Hesitantly, she goes to the suitcase, opens it, lifts up a dress. It's lovely, subtly floral-patterned, lyrical. She cannot believe her good fortune.*)

ANNIE: Is this for me?

BEN: Who else?

ANNIE: Oh, lordy!

BEN: You like it?

ANNIE: (*Quietly elated*) Oh! The flowers look so real, they—they—they have a fragrance! Oh, how wonderful!

BESSIE: What size is it?

ANNIE: (*Looking at the label*) It's an eight.
(*To Ben*) How did you know my size?

BEN: When you were four, you were this big—
(*He extends his arm to indicate her height*)—when you were eight you were this big. And now that you're twenty-five—
(*He raises his arm to the top of her head.*)

ANNIE: I'm twenty-seven.

BEN: (*An instant. He laughs engagingly*) I think you're all trying to trip me up, aren't you? First I'm a year too early and then I'm two years too late. Someday I'll be right on time. Are you really twenty-seven?

ANNIE: Yes, I am.

BEN: Have I been away so long?

BESSIE: Twelve years.

PHILIP: Thirteen, on the tenth of October.

BEN: Was it October? I thought I left in the wintertime.

SIMON: October can be very cold.

BEN: Boy, was it cold! (*Shaking the unhappy mood*)
Champagne! It's time for champagne!
(*He tosses the champagne bottle to Simon*) Here, kid. Open it.

SIMON: (*Excited*) Me? I never opened a bottle of champagne before.

BEN: Well, you gotta learn. (*Taking out a large pocket knife*) It's easy. Here—first you take this knife and—chwitt!
(*He makes a sharp, deft movement: it's a switchblade; it springs open. Everybody tightens.*)

BEN: (*Quickly full of cheer*) Here, Simie—you take this and cut away the gold foil.

SIMON: (*The switchblade alarms and attracts him*) Boy, what a knife!

BEN: Go on, kid—cut off the foil.

(*As Simon is doing it*) Good—that's the way, that's the way! You're doing it just right. This kid's got talent. Now—give me the knife, and twist off the wire. And now you take this handkerchief and you cover the cork—because there's going to be—

PHILIP: An explosion!

BEN: Right—exactly right! But only a little explosion. More like a popping sound, not much louder than a flower would make when it pops open in the springtime—pop!—like that! Now press the cork out with your thumb—that's right—turn it and press—press—and get ready for the pop, get ready for the pop.

SIMON: (*Silence. Then:*) The cork is out.

PHILIP: It's out?

(*Disappointed*) And it didn't pop?

SIMON: (*Even more disappointed*) No, it didn't pop. I thought it was supposed to pop.

BEN: (*Doing a turn*) Now, don't be disappointed, fella! Don't anybody be disappointed! If it doesn't pop, it's a good sign! It's a wonderfully special unique symbol that this is a very exceptional and notable and unparalleled vintage of champagne. Only the most extraordinary champagnes are made so that they do not pop. And because of that, they last forever. And what are they called? The Forever Effervescents! Here's to my father on his birthday—to Poppa, the Forever Effervescent!

(*He has taken the bottle out of Simon's hand and is pouring champagne in the water glasses he lifts from the dining table.*)

BESSIE: Wait! We have wine glasses somewhere.

BEN: Who needs them, Momma? These glasses are crystal—the purest crystal.

BESSIE: They're not crystal—they're just cheap glass. I got them with the free dishes at the movies.

(*Ben pours wine for everyone. They make toasts:*)

THE FAMILY: To Poppa . . . To Uncle Philip. . . . To my husband.

SIMON: Look! Look! Momma is drinking!

PHILIP: (*Joyous*) You'll get arrested, Bessie! They'll throw you in the hokey-pokey.

BESSIE: If they'll throw me in the hokey-pokey, it's better to be a little tipsy-topsy!

PHILIP: (*Exhilarated*) Did you hear that? Did you hear what your mother said? Bessie said that! (*They all laugh and tease—happy, buoyant*)

BESSIE: I can't believe it! I can't believe that we are all together again! I can't believe I could ever be so happy!

BEN: Believe everything, Momma—everything!

PHILIP: (*Taking Ben's hand and kissing it*) And it's all because of you, son! All because of you! Oh, how beautiful you look to me! And how handsome in your white-brown suit! And how rich, with your golden rings and watches and your Stutz Bearcat automobile. How did you get so rich?

BESSIE: Don't even ask him—he'll only tell you a lie.

(*She says it goodnaturedly, not intending anything too serious. But Ben takes it soberly, and is hurt by it. He pauses. Philip sees his son's distress, and tries to remedy the situation.*)

PHILIP: Don't listen to her—tell *me*—how did you get so rich?

(*Recovered now, Ben hoarsely whispers his answer as if to conspirators.*)

BEN: I stumbled on a suitcase full of diamonds in the sewers of Paree.

BESSIE: You see? I told you he would make a story out of it.

BEN: (*Smiling but serious*) No matter what I tell you, Momma, you're bound to call me a liar.

BESSIE: (*Friendly, placating*) I promise I won't call you anything. How did you get so much money?

(*He looks at her soberly, appraising her. He then looks at the others. They are on tenterhooks of curiosity. He is conflicted. Then:*)

BEN: What's the big building at Sixteenth and Spring Garden Street?

PHILIP: (*Like the others, he's puzzled*) Sixteenth and Spring Garden Street? It's the Mint.

BEN: That's right!—that's absolutely right! The Philadelphia branch of the United States Mint. Well, they've got another branch in Denver, Colorado. Where money is coined and printed. And I took two years to study it, to memorize it. Day and night, night and day, I watched the arrivals and departures. The Money Factory! And every last Thursday of the month, there was a midnight shipment that left the loading dock for points west of the Mississippi. And those particular shipments were attended by only two guards, the one who drove the truck and the one who handled the loading and locking. So on midnight of Thursday, November the 27th—you probably read about it in the papers, Pop—I stood in a dark doorway, and I watched them load the armored truck. And suddenly I got excited—I got hot, I got cold, I got all charged up. And when the driver was about to get up behind the wheel, I jumped him. I hit him a couple of times and he went down. And suddenly there was the other guy, and he was coming at me with a gun. I kicked at his gun hand and grabbed my knife—
(*He flicks his switchblade*)—and—chwitt!—I gave it to him in the gut.

ANNIE: Oh no.

SIMON: God.

BEN: I searched their clothes for the keys to the truck, and I found them. I drove to a little hidden place just outside of Manitou Springs where I had a van, and I loaded the paper money into it. There were thousands of dollars, nearly a million dollars' worth. Then I drove west to L.A. and I bought myself a summerhouse on the beautiful Malibu beach. And every evening I dressed up in white clothes and white silk shirts, and a white flower in my buttonhole.

SIMON: My God.

ANNIE: I think I'm going to be sick.

PHILIP: Don't say my God, and don't be sick. It isn't true.

BEN: Momma believes it.

BESSIE: (*Quietly*) No, I don't.

BEN: Are you sure, Momma? Wasn't it the kind of story you would make up about me in your own mind? Isn't that what you think I am, Momma? If I tell you I'm a robber and a murderer—it's not hard for you to believe that, is it, Momma? Didn't you believe that story, Momma?

BESSIE: I said I did not believe it.

BEN: Come on—tell the truth, Momma—didn't you really believe it?

PHILIP: No!—stop it! She says she didn't believe the story—and Momma does not lie!

(*Silence. Suddenly his tone softens. He is loving and gentle*) Benny—sweetheart—how could we believe that you're a thief? And a murderer—how can we believe that about you?! No! We have no murderers in the Farber family. Even my brother's son, Heskel—who was a soldier in the army—even he—with a gun—even he, a legal soldier with a legal pistol—even Heskel did not murder anybody. This could not happen in our family. Especially not you—not our Benny—the good one, the kind one, the sweet one—our Benny who cries when you throw out the dead flowers! And now you came back—you came home to us—and we will believe only the good about you, Benny—only the good! So welcome home, son—welcome home!

(*He is deeply touched, and so is Ben. They embrace and cling to one another. All the others murmur their welcomes. Then they all start embracing Ben. As they sit down to the birthday dinner, the lights fade.*)

In the darkness, Annie descends the stairs. Barely visible, she enters the living room and turns on a lamp. She is carrying the new dress that Ben has given her. She holds it lovingly but regretfully. Then, she finds the box it came in and, smoothing the dress, she puts it back in the box. She is not aware that, toward the end, Ben has come down the stairs and is watching her. Abruptly, Annie sees him. Startled, her shock makes her giggle.)

ANNIE: Oh! You scared me!

BEN: (*Smiling, he moves toward her*) What are you doing up so late? It's after midnight.

ANNIE: Time to rob a mint.

BEN: I'm sorry about that story. I hope you'll all forget it. I don't know what got into me.

ANNIE: Did it keep you awake?

BEN: Well, I'm still in California, and it's only nine o'clock.

ANNIE: (*With a vague suspicion*) I should have thought—driving across the country—you'd gradually get accustomed to the time.

BEN: Well, I didn't. What woke *you* up?

ANNIE: (*Evasively*) I don't know. The house seems strange.

BEN: With me at home.

ANNIE: It's been so long. And hardly a word.

BEN: I sent postcards from everywhere.

ANNIE: "The weather is fine. The men wear flowers in their hats."

BEN: (*He taps the telephone*) If you had one of these, I'd have called more often.

ANNIE: More often? Did you call at all?

BEN: I called the drugstore once, and I asked the phone kid to get you. When he got back, he said nobody was home, and you were having your tonsils out.

ANNIE: Adenoids.

BEN: And then—once—I was going to call again, and I ran into Uncle Arnold in Toronto, and he said you had a regular boyfriend—Ira Feldman, I think he said.

ANNIE: Goldman.

BEN: Yes, Goldman. Did that last?

ANNIE: (*Smiling*) No. Nor did Joe Marcus. They both got married. Ira has three daughters and Joe has two sons—or the other way around. (*Silence.*)

BEN: Did you try on the dress?

ANNIE: No.

BEN: I see you put it back in the box.

ANNIE: Yes.

BEN: Why?

ANNIE: (*With difficulty*) I appreciate your giving it to me. I do—I'm very grateful. But I hope you won't mind taking it back.

BEN: Why won't you try it on? (*Silence*) Please, Annie, tell me why.

ANNIE: I'm in a department store, and there's this rack of dresses—all very pretty—and there's this one—and it's the most beautiful one of all, and it's the only one on the rack that I wouldn't buy.

BEN: Why not, for God's sake?

ANNIE: Because it's for a glamorous woman. Romantic—mysterious—the opposite to what I am.

BEN: I won't for one minute believe that. (*He hurries and picks up the box. Setting it on the couch, he opens it and is taking the dress out of the box as he speaks:*) Please—do me a favor, will you? Just try it on. Don't make any judgments about anything—just slip it on for a minute. Will you do that?

ANNIE: No.

BEN: I won't watch you. (*He puts the dress on the couch, and takes out his large, colored handkerchief*) I'll blindfold myself—I won't see you changing—just tell me when you're ready.

(*As he is blindfolding himself, his spate of enthusiastic chatter does not cease.*)

BEN: I'm not looking—are you changing? Okay, I'm blind now—I can't see a thing. Just tell me when I can take the blindfold off.
(*She simply stands there, not taking her bathrobe off, not touching the new dress.*)

ANNIE: (*Quietly*) You're always playing games.

BEN: That's why everybody loves me.

ANNIE: Does everybody love you?

BEN: The minute they meet me. Love at first sight.

ANNIE: It's only on second sight that you make them sick.

BEN: You can't hurt my feelings. I bet you're going to look wonderful in that dress? Have you got it on?
(*Silence. A bit forlornly, she starts toward the stairs, to make her exit.*)

BEN: Annie—you didn't go, did you?
(*She hears something forlorn in his voice, and it stops her.*)

BEN: Annie, please don't go—I'm going to play blindman's buff and find you. I'm going to find you.
(*Still blindfolded, arms outstretched, he has been searching for her, stumbling, bumping into things. She does not smile, does not move; simply waits there. At last, his outstretched hand touches her shoulder. He quickly runs his hand down her arm and feels the texture of the material. Still blindfolded, he says quietly:*)

BEN: You didn't change.

ANNIE: No, I didn't.
(*As he takes the blindfold off*) You were expecting to touch satin and you got flannel.

BEN: (*Urgently*) You are not flannel!
(*His voice changing to a plea*) Look—Annie!—honey!—sweetheart! Let's suppose you're not a woman of glamour—romance—mystery! But if you wear that dress, you will be! It'll be so unexpected! It's the opposite to what people imagine about you!—it's exciting! A woman laughs when you expect her to cry, she scratches when you expect her to purr. And that's what's so wonderful about *you*. Your face is so sad—any minute you're gonna cry—and suddenly you smile!—and it's a great surprise!— a perfect surprise!

ANNIE: (*Amused, a bit sad, a bit ironic:*) Funny . . . all these years . . . and you're still saying the same pithy sayings.

BEN: (*Wounded, defensive*) I've never said those things in my life!

ANNIE: You said them to me a dozen years ago.

BEN: Your memory's playing tricks on you.

ANNIE: (*Quietly, almost to herself*) My memory of that occasion is correct in every detail.

BEN: What occasion?

ANNIE: On your twenty-third birthday, *you* gave *me* a birthday present.

BEN: I did? What'd I give you?

ANNIE: I was fifteen years old and you took me to the Walnut Street Theatre. It was the first time I ever saw a real play with real actors. The audience didn't like it, but I thought it was the magic of the universe! I was so happy that I cried and the tears kept streaming down my face and my nose was running and neither of us had a handkerchief, and you started to take out your shirttail, and suddenly we were screaming laughing—! And then when we got home you said, "Let's pretend this is your house but not mine, and I'm going to kiss you goodnight and go away and come back next week for another date." And we were out there, in the vestibule—and you were about to kiss me—and I caught sight of myself in the mirror and I looked awful. My nose was red from crying and my hair was a mess—and I said, "How can you kiss a thing like that?" And you said that line about the unexpected, about cry-for-joy, and sad-for-happy.

BEN: And I kissed you. Right?

ANNIE: Right.

BEN: And the sadness turned out to be happy. Just as I said. Right?

ANNIE: Right. And you never showed up for your second date.

(*They both laugh wryly*)

BEN: Well, what the hell, I left home.

ANNIE: (*Imitating his tone*) Yeah, what the hell.

BEN: But I *did* come back for my second date. Here I am! (*He stretches his arms wide*)

ANNIE: Stand still—I'm going to race across the room and fall into your arms.

BEN: I wish you would. (*When she makes no move, he lets his arms drift downward. He speaks quietly, even earnestly*) Annie . . . You don't know how many thousands of times I've thought about you. Wondering how you'd grow up. I thought: if she stays anywhere near the same as she was then, I'll fall in love with her.

ANNIE: You used to stammer when you were a kid. But you don't anymore, do you? Just now—you didn't stumble over a single word!

BEN: (*A moment. Hurt*) Please don't make fun of me. I was talking about good things—I was talking about love. Why do you want to mess things up?

ANNIE: I'm sorry . . . What've you done in all this time? Did you get married? Do you have any kids floating around somewhere?

BEN: No—nothing. No kids floating around. Not a thing. I was engaged once. Twice, as a matter of fact.

ANNIE: Clean forgot the second one, huh?

BEN: Yes, she was a lunkhead. She was goodnatured, she was pretty, but she had oatmeal in her head. But the first one was—well—kind of wonderful.

ANNIE: What happened?

BEN: She was too good for me. I couldn't make it.

ANNIE: Did you break her heart?

BEN: No. Maybe I bruised it a little.

ANNIE: You're quite a vandal, aren't you?

BEN: Me?—a vandal? Why the hell would you say a thing like that?

ANNIE: Well, I think you are. Bruising a heart here and there. Leaving a trail of sad-eyed women gazing out of their windows. Telling lies—oh, good-natured ridiculous ones—like flat champagne is Forever Effervescent—and Simon can jump through the ceiling of the college gym—and I'm the Venus di Milo of Hutchinson Street. But some of them are malicious—like robbing a mint and murdering a guard. I suspect you're quite a vicious man!

BEN: (*Getting angry*) Isn't that interesting? I tell you how beautiful you are, and how I think about you all the time, and you call me vicious! Who's the vicious one, Annie?
(*She slaps him hard. He has a flare of anger which he instantly hides. But he cannot hide his hurt.*)

BEN: There, you see? The unexpected. I expect a kiss and I get a slap. The secret of your charm.

ANNIE: You bastard. (*Miserable, wanting to weep but unable to do so, she turns away. He does not crowd her. After a while, he takes out his handkerchief.*)

BEN: If you're weeping, you can have my handkerchief.

ANNIE: I'm not weeping—and that's for champagne bottles and blindman's buff.

BEN: (*Truly troubled*) Apparently I'm doing something terribly wrong—and I don't know what it is. I don't know what happened. I come home and I bring you a present and I say nice things to you and I want to fall in love with you—and suddenly you're slapping me and I'm insulting you and you're crying—and I don't know what the hell it's all about!

ANNIE: Why did you come home?

BEN: What?

ANNIE: Twelve years—and suddenly—home! Why?

BEN: You want the truth?

ANNIE: If you can make an extra effort, I'd appreciate it.

BEN: Why did I come home!? I don't *know*! Everything's finished out there. I've been to a thousand places and I have all the money I need. Every person I ever met, and everywhere I went, I was alone. Why am I always alone—is it a sickness? Well, one day I started to wonder if it might be homesickness. So I turned my car east and started driving. And when I came into Philadelphia and was riding along the railroad track and the 7:14 came along beside me, I was so happy I could cry! And when I started to ring the doorbell and it occurred to me that we never used to lock the door, and it might still be unlocked—and it was unlocked—oh, man alive, was I happy! And the furniture all different, yet all the same, and Momma and Poppa the same, and you and Simie all grown up but still the same—and maybe there's no loneliness if you're home! Maybe that's the answer!

With my mother and father and kid brother—and someone I can fall in love with! And oh God, if she can fall in love with me—!

ANNIE: (*Silence. Then, quietly:*) I've never fallen out of love with you, Ben. . . . If you count a teen-age crush for anything.

BEN: Do you count it for anything?

ANNIE: (*Smiling ruefully*) Oh, I used to. I wrote you one romantic letter after another—full of rose petals and Emily Dickinson! And oh, the dreams I used to have!

BEN: You mean nightmares.

ANNIE: (*An instant*) I mean dreams.

BEN: You used to have nightmares. Do you have them anymore?

ANNIE: (*Laughing tightly*) I never had nightmares. I used to pretend I had them—just for attention. I was very good at pretending.

BEN: You were rotten at it. . . . You still are.

ANNIE: I'm not pretending.

BEN: Are you still having nightmares, Annie?

ANNIE: No—never anymore—never!
(*She is not a good liar. She turns away*) I had one last night.

BEN: What was it about?

ANNIE: Oh, come on—nobody wants to hear anybody else's bad dreams.

BEN: Tell me.

ANNIE: I was on a train—and it was kind of dark and scary and I—do you really want to hear this drivel?

BEN: Yes.

ANNIE: —and the train was full of shadows—people hiding—and I didn't know where I was supposed to get off—I was lost, I was terrified. And suddenly there were these two splendid people—a husband and wife—and they said, "Don't worry, little girl—we'll take care of you." And they did. They said their names were Mr. and Mrs. Erickson—and they asked me if I wanted to see where they lived. And I said yes, oh yes! And it was the most beautiful house I ever saw. In the country—soft—green—oh, the sweetness and the quiet! And a big attic—a wonderful attic full of hiding places, and lost things that were meant to be found. And music—the two of them at the piano—four hands and one heart, they used to say. So I stayed with them a long time—and how beautiful those people were!—and how I treasured them! And one evening I went up into the attic and they were suspended from a rafter.

BEN: Their name was not Erickson.

ANNIE: I know very well what their name was.

BEN: What you don't know is why they left you.

ANNIE: (*Impassioned*) That's right, that's right, that's right!

BEN: The answer to it is they didn't leave you, they left the world.

ANNIE: (*Bitterly*) Just left the world—farewell—adios! Like that! And they forgot all about their nine-year-old daughter. The little slip of a girl just a slip of the mind. So long, kid!

BEN: (*Urgently*) They didn't leave you, they left their senses. She was sick, she was dying, and he couldn't imagine living without her. They were desperate, they were out of their minds!

ANNIE: Thank you, but I've already listed all the mitigations. Once, when I went to a head doctor, I wrote them down—and I added them all up. And do you know what the total was? People leave me.

BEN: Oh, God!

ANNIE: Him too.
(*An instant. With a smile*) You see, Ben—you and I—we're opposites. You *leave* people—and people leave *me*.

BEN: I promise you—I give you my promise, Annie—I will never leave you.

ANNIE: (*With a forlorn smile*) What a clown you are.

BEN: I'm not a clown.

ANNIE: Sad and funny. Bozo at the circus.

BEN: (*Quietly*) You have to take me seriously, Annie.

ANNIE: I'll take you, but not seriously. Would you like to go to bed with me?
(*They are very still. He measures her with an appraising smile*).

BEN: You think you're taking a big chance, don't you?

ANNIE: I think you might be risky.

BEN: You put down your money and choose your chance—win, place or show.

ANNIE: There's the chance I can lose.

BEN: I never count that one.
(*She crosses to him, kisses him lightly on the mouth, and starts away. He gently brings her back, takes her in his arms and kisses her passionately.*)

PHILIP'S VOICE: (*Upstairs*) What's going on down there?

BEN: Oh, sorry, Poppa—did we wake you up?

PHILIP: (*Appearing, as he descends the stairs*) No. I was too happy to sleep.

BEN: (*Laughing*) Everybody's too happy to sleep.

PHILIP: Not Momma.

BESSIE: (*On the stairs*) Who says not Momma? I can't sleep either. What's happening in the house, what's happening? Does anybody want some cocoa?

ANNIE: I'll make it. Does everyone want cocoa?

BEN: Not me, thanks.
(*Annie goes into the kitchen to make the cocoa.*)

BESSIE: You don't want cocoa?

BEN: Nope.

BESSIE: Why?—you don't like cocoa? You used to like cocoa.

BEN: (*Smiling at the familiar*) Not in the middle of the night, Mom.

PHILIP: Schmuck!—it tastes better in the middle of the night.

BEN: (*The smile broadens*) Does it, Pop?

PHILIP: Oh yes indeed. Sometimes—two or three o'clock in the morning—your mother and me—we can't sleep. So we sneak downstairs and drink cocoa together. It's wonderful.

BESSIE: Like getting something for nothing.

BEN: (*Enjoying them*) Like stealing candy from the Five-and-Ten.

PHILIP: (*Laughing*) Yeah—perfect!

BESSIE: Nothing's perfect. You steal candy, you get caught.

PHILIP: (*Goodnaturedly mimicking her*) "Nothing's perfect. You steal candy, you get caught." She sounds exactly like Bessie.

BESSIE: *I am* Bessie. And nothing is perfect.

PHILIP: Well, Bessie—you're wrong. Some things *are* perfect.

BESSIE: Name one.

PHILIP: Ben's home.

BESSIE: Even that is not perfect. It makes me happy, but it is not perfect.

BEN: I'm sorry I told you that cock and bull story about the mint, Momma.

BESSIE: If once in your life you would tell me the truth about yourself—just once in your life—

BEN: I try, Mom. But you don't believe anything. You remember when I was in junior high school and I came home and told you I was elected vice president of my class—

BESSIE: You didn't tell me you got elected *vice* president, you told me *president*! See?—you don't even *remember* right—you want to know why? Because a liar can't remember his lies. Why did you tell me a lie?

PHILIP: He wasn't telling you a lie—he was telling you a wish!

BESSIE: And you—always making excuses for him. A wish that's not true is a lie—that's all it is—a lie! Why didn't you teach him that? What's wrong with being the vice president?
(*To Ben*) If you're elected vice president and you tell me president, then you're elected to nothing!

BEN: Which is an office you think very suitable for me.

BESSIE: I never said that you were nothing.

BEN: You said it in a thousand ways. To you I was worse than nothing! I was a criminal! Once you told me I would die in the electric chair! Do you remember that? The electric chair!

PHILIP: You're going too far, Ben. Your mother never said such a thing.

BEN: The electric chair!—she said it! We were having a fight, and she had that cut-glass fruit bowl in her hand—and I snatched it away from her and I smashed it on the floor. She started screaming that it was the most beautiful thing she ever had—and she called me a murderer and said I would die in the electric chair! I swear to God she said it!

PHILIP: Stop that—now you just stop that!

BEN: Did you say it, Mom? Tell us the truth—did you say it? *I asked you, did you say it?*

BESSIE: . . . Yes.

PHILIP: You didn't, Bessie. I don't believe you could say such a thing.

BESSIE: I said it, Philip. And I have been sorry for it every day of my life. Why is he so mean that he remembers it
(*To Ben*) Why? Why do you remember it? Why should you carry that around with you? Why can't you remember the good things?

BEN: I do remember the good things. That's why I came home—because of the good things.

BESSIE: No, the bad. Smashing fruit bowls—dying in the electric chair— that's what you came home to remember.

PHILIP: Now *you're* making it worse than it is, Bessie.

BESSIE: No I'm not. I tell things the way they happen—I don't tell any pipedreams.

PHILIP: He was a kid. A kid's allowed to have a few pipedreams.

BESSIE: *And I am not allowed the truth?*

BEN: What do you want to know, Mom?

BESSIE: Where did you get your money?

BEN: (*He is silent. Then:*) Okay, Momma . . . The truth—and I hope to God you believe it. When I left home, I couldn't get a job and I was hungry. I bummed rides to a hundred different places, I got roughed up by railroad cops, my clothes started to get rotten, I got sores all over my skin. It looked as though all your predictions would come true, Mom—I would wind up in jail or starve in a stinking alleyway. God, how miserable I was! . . . Then I had a stroke of luck. I got a cabin boy's job on a freighter that was carrying canned goods up and down the South Pacific Ocean. But it was a lousy ship, I had the trots every day I was on it, my head never stopped aching, and when we got to Tahiti, I got fired.

(*With mounting exhilaration*) Then I got another job in a little country store on the south coast of Tahiti. The owner was a grizzly old beachcomber, drunk all the time, never paid his debts, and one day a little round guy came in and took the old man's keys away and threw him out. So I asked the owner if I could run the store. And he said, "Run it? Hell, you can have it if you pay what the old bastard owes me." So, little by little, I paid him off and I did the whole store over. I made a deal to ship copra and sugar cane in exchange for canned goods. And I imported meat—and boy, was that a good item! And pretty soon, I built an addition onto the place, and I sold hardware and work clothes. And after a while, I had a whole little marketplace there—and then I had another one on another island. And on the Fourth of July—last year—I opened my third Booth W. Fields Emporium!

PHILIP: Booth W. Fields—who is that—the old man?

BEN: No, it's me—the young man—Ben Farber!

BESSIE: You changed your name?

BEN: Yes.

PHILIP: Booth W. Fields?

BEN: That's right.

BESSIE: Fields from Farber I can understand,but where did you get a name like Booth?

BEN: I read it somewhere.

PHILIP: He shot Lincoln.

BESSIE: Who shot Lincoln?

BEN: Not me, Mom.

BESSIE: Why did you change your name?

BEN: Obviously.

BESSIE: Because Farber is Jewish?

BEN: Of course.

PHILIP: Why change it? The Tahitians are anti-Semitic?

BEN: No, but I didn't want them to *become* anti-Semitic because of me.

PHILIP: Why? You did something you're ashamed of?

BEN: No, Pop, but people are inclined to dislike people if they're successful. Especially if they're Jewish.

BESSIE: Now, look at me, Ben. Look me in the eyes and tell me—truthfully—
why did you change your name? Did you do anything shameful?

BEN: No, Mom.

BESSIE: Did you do something illegal?

BEN: No, Mom.

(*Then, taking her hands in his own*) Mom—what you want to know is
whether I honestly deserve my good luck. Well, it wasn't only luck,
Momma—it was hard work, backbreaking hard work. I slaved in my business for fifteen-sixteen hours a day. No weekends, no holidays, never a
minute to catch my breath. It was *hard*! I nearly killed myself working,
Mom. That's what you want to hear, isn't it?

BESSIE: Yes, that's what I want to hear.

BEN: Well, that's what it was.

PHILIP: So who's minding the stores when you're away?

BEN: They're sold, Poppa. I sold them!

BESSIE: When?

BEN: On April first.

BESSIE: April Fool's Day? You fool, why did you sell them?

BEN: For a half million dollars, that's why I sold them.

BESSIE AND PHILIP: A half million—! . . . That's five hundred thousand dollars?

BEN: A half million down, and another half million to be paid over a five-
year period.

BESSIE: But if it was good enough for the buyer, it was good enough for
you. How could you sell such a gold mine?

BEN: Because I was homesick, Mom. I had to come home.

(*He has said it quietly, and in earnest. She is touched. She crosses to him
and lays a gentle hand on his cheek. He is deeply moved. So is Philip.
Annie comes in with cocoa on a tray.*)

ANNIE: Cocoa time.

PHILIP: Only two cups?

ANNIE: Ben didn't want any—neither do I. Good heavens, it's one o'clock—
I think I'm going to bed.

BEN: That's a great idea. I'm going to do the same.

BESSIE: (*Suspiciously*) The same as what?

BEN: Annie said she's going to bed. Well, so am I.

(*Annie has gone upstairs. Bess takes Ben's arm, detains him and speaks in an undertone so Annie won't hear.*)

BESSIE: Ben . . . Don't fool around with her, Benjamin.

BEN: Mom, what a suspicious mind! (*He goes upstairs*)

PHILIP: Did you have to say that to him? Did you have to spoil things?

BESSIE: What did I spoil—his story about Tahiti?

PHILIP: What do you mean, story? Goddamn it, what do you mean, story?

BESSIE: Anything with Tahiti in it is a story.

PHILIP: Bessie, for God's sake!

BESSIE: (*Doggedly*) It's not *real*. Why couldn't he choose a real place—like Pittsburgh, Pennsylvania or Camden, New Jersey?

PHILIP: You think the whole world is Camden, New Jersey!

BESSIE: No I don't—there's also Philadelphia. All I want to know is: Why did he choose Tahiti?

PHILIP: Because it *is* real! It's on the map—it *exists*! Can't you believe that Tahiti *exists*?

BESSIE: No, I can't. And I would give anything in the world if I could believe it, anything in the world.

(*They sit down to drink their cocoa. The lights fade.*)

END OF ACT ONE

Act Two

A FEW DAYS LATER, toward dusk of a Sunday afternoon. Outdoors, unseen by us, Simon is throwing his basketball into an empty garbage can—throwing and, for the most part, missing. Occasionally, he manages to hit the can, causing a clatter. Ben is indoors, at the open window, coaching, cheering him on. He wears a red shirt, yellow trousers, white shoes. Again, as with his homecoming costume, it is attractive.

BEN: Keep your eye on the can, kid—not on the ball—on the can!
(*Noise of ball on can*) See? You got a hunk of the can. Next time, maybe you'll get it *in*! Go on—shoot—shoot!
(*Sound of ball plumping on the ground*) To the left this time, to the left. All your shots are veering to the right—don't you notice that? To the *left*!
(*To himself, so Simon won't hear him*) Oh, shit.
(*Sound of ball hitting the can*) That's good—that's better! Any day now you'll get one in, boy—don't give up.
(*The doorbell rings. Because of his own noise and the noise from outdoors, Ben doesn't hear the ring. As it continues, augmented by a knocking sound—someone is annoyed at not being let in—he hurries into the vestibule, enroute to the door. In a moment, Ben re-enters, followed by an irritated Philip.*)
BEN: What's the big rush? Why were you ringing like a maniac?

PHILIP: I wanted to get into my own house. What's so like a maniac, what's so like a maniac?

BEN: Okay, Pop—calm down—you're in.

PHILIP: Who locked the door? The front door is never locked in this house. Why did you lock the door?

BEN: I didn't lock the door.

PHILIP: What is it, a new style?—to lock the door?

BEN: *I didn't lock the door!* And if I absentmindedly did lock it, so what, so what?

(*Clowning, putting up his fists*) Wanna make somethin' out of it? Wanna fight? Stick your dukes up. Come on—up with the dukes!

(*Instantly, he has won his father's good humor. Philip puts his fists up.*)

PHILIP: I'll give you up with the dukes. I'll give you such a dukes, your head will roll in the gutter. Like old times—but this time I'm gonna beat you, you plug-ugly! Come on, gimme your best punch, you shmaggeggi! Come on! Bang on the chin, socko in the kishkes!

BEN: (*Simultaneously with Philip*) Come on, palooka, come on! . . No kidney punches, baby, no heads up under the chin, no elbows in the clinches. Pow! Pow! Come on, honeyboy, come on! Pow, pow, pow!

(*Long ago, they used to have this mock battle. They never get anywhere near each other, but each one reacts to the other's punches as if he has been hit. A blow in the solar plexus winds one of them, a left hook gives the other one a crooked neck, a series of three jabs makes the opponent's head bob back three times. Sometimes they simply dance around each other, snorting, snuffling. Philip rubs one nostril with his thumb, clearing the pug's broken-nose obstruction; Ben wheezes and twists his mouth to one side—air, noise, snorts. It is only at the very end of the "bout" that they go into a clinch—and, as Philip is pretending to punch in close quarters, Ben spontaneously gives his father a kiss on the cheek. They hold the embrace a fleet instant, then break apart. Both men are touched. As Philip starts to sit down, he gets a bit unsteady; his hand goes to his forehead.*)

BEN: What's the matter, Pop?

PHILIP: Nothing. Just a little dizzy—it's nothing.

BEN: You okay?

PHILIP: Sure I'm okay. Doctor Lightner says I'm in great shape—I'll live to be a thousand years old.

BEN: What's Dr. Lightner say about you can't catch your breath.

PHILIP: Who can't catch my breath?—who? Listen—ten rounds with a rabbit puncher and a day with the Sunday papers, and I should be able to catch my breath?

BEN: Getting too rough, Pop?

PHILIP: Who says it's getting too rough? You won't catch me complaining. Why should I complain? I own my own stand—I'm in business for myself—I'm a rotten capitalist!

BEN: But the papers are getting heavier, right?

PHILIP: No, *the customers* are getting heavier. They're all rooting for the wrong things. Hurray for money! Hurray for speakeasies! Hurray for Al Capone!

BEN: You want to sell your stand, Poppa?

PHILIP: Why? You want to buy it?

BEN: No. Sell it to someone else.

PHILIP: And then what? I should buy the Bellevue Stratford Hotel?

BEN: Why not? I'll buy it for you! Or something else. What would you like, Pop?

PHILIP: (*Indicating Ben's clothes*) A red shirt and yellow pants.

BEN: You got 'em!

(*He starts unbuckling his belt, to take his trousers off. Philip laughs*)

PHILIP: No, no—stop it—somebody will walk in—they'll think we're yah-yah.

BEN: (*Laughing as he re-dresses*) Really, Pop—would you like some bright clothes? I'll buy them for you. You want a new car? You want a place in Florida?

PHILIP: What will I do in Florida? I hate orange juice.

BEN: You'll relax, Poppa, you'll relax.

PHILIP: When they lay me out in my coffin, I'll relax.

BEN: No coffins, Pop! I've got enough money to keep this family alive forever. Especially you, Pop. . . . If I were God, and I was choosing one person who should live forever, it would be you, Pop.

PHILIP: (*Moved*) Thank you, Ben. . . . No change—you're still so good-hearted. Remember when you were a kid—and your mother gave you the chicken liver because it was your favorite food in the whole world? Remember I used to say to you, "Would you give me your chicken liver, Benny?" And your eyes would fill up with tears—but you would take it right off your plate and give me the chicken liver. . . . Such a dumb kid.

BEN: Maybe not so dumb. I knew you'd always give it back.

PHILIP: What if I ever ate it?

BEN: Oh God, the fall of my idol!

(*They laugh. Then, seriously:*) Pop, you can have everything on my plate—and you don't have to give any of it back.

PHILIP: You're talking about money, yes?

BEN: Anything.

PHILIP: Money won't make me any happier, Ben.

BEN: What will?

PHILIP: I keep on working—Simie goes to college—your mother gets fatter and bossier—Annie gets married. . . . Maybe even you get married.

BEN: Why do you say *even* me?

PHILIP: You're a shiny bullet! You can get any girl you want. Why should you get married?

BEN: Maybe I'll surprise you.

PHILIP: Nah. You won't listen to my advice—you never did. I told you to go to college, you didn't go. I told you not to leave home—you left. So who takes my advice?

BEN: What's your advice, Poppa?

PHILIP: Settle down, you dope! Get married! Have some kids!

BEN: Well, if that's your pie in the sky—

PHILIP: Don't make fun of it! It's not such a bad dream when you're getting older. To have your children around you—married—and with children of their own—and nobody living further away than Ritner Street. Not that you can't love your kids if they're living in Australia, but Ritner Street is better. Just so they're close enough that you can touch them, *touch* them!

BEN: (*Smiling, he holds his arm out*) Touch me, Poppa.

PHILIP: (*Playfully slapping his arm*) Ah, you dumb Benjamin! . . . Some people believe in money, some people believe in God. I believe in family.

BEN: (*Gently, without criticism*) That's a small world, Pop.

PHILIP: Look, I don't mean a family only for me, I mean everybody should have a family. Even Hoover. Even *Finkelstein.*
(*They both laugh a little.*)

BEN: Maybe I *will* surprise you some day, Pop. Marriage might not be so terrible—it's better than smallpox.

PHILIP: (*With quick alarm: dead serious*) Did you have smallpox?

BEN: (*Laughing*) No, Pop. Only the black plague and leprosy.

PHILIP: (*Grinning*) Well, everything is for the best. (*Always homing to the bright side*) Maybe you *will* get married some day. Maybe later when you see your first gray hair or you feel your first pain in the back—maybe then you'll be scared enough to get married.

BEN: You mean you stop being scared of marriage when you get scared enough by life?

PHILIP: That's right.

BEN: (*Quietly*) I'm not scared yet, Poppa. I'm only restless.

PHILIP: You were always restless.

BEN: It's worse now, Pop.

PHILIP: Why?

BEN: I don't *know*, goddamn it, I don't *know*. I'm nearly thirty-five years old—time is going a little too fast—and I don't know where it went or where it's going—and I've got all this money—! Mom said I would never make it—you're a no-good, she said, and you'll never make a dollar. Well, she was wrong. I made it, son of a gun, I made it! But now that I did, nobody wants it. Mom doesn't wear the ring I gave her, and you don't wear the watch—

PHILIP: It's too good—I'm afraid I'll lose it.

BEN: —and I offer to buy her a new refrigerator so she can get rid of the old GE with that noisy monitor on top, and she says she doesn't want it—as if my money's not kosher or something. And you say you don't want my money. And I'm not sure I want it myself. I got a kick out of making it, but *having* it is nothing—it's trouble, it makes me feel guilty. And here I am at home, and I want to go away—and I *can't leave.* Home is like a last chance.

PHILIP: What does that mean, a last chance?

BEN: I don't *know* what it means. I'm afraid to stay and afraid to go. I should be seeing a *reason* for something by the time I'm this age—shouldn't I be having an answer of some kind? It's like I'm wasting my life and I don't *know* anything, Pop. Oughtn't I to know something by now?

PHILIP: You know a lot of things, Ben. You just don't know what you want.

BEN: What do I want, Pop?

PHILIP: Who knows? You think it's hard to get what you want?—it's harder to *know* what you want. Especially if you're fooling yourself.

(*The sound of the ball hitting the garbage pail.*)

PHILIP: What's that noise?

BEN: It's Simon. He's pitching his basketball into a garbage can.

PHILIP: It's got garbage in it?

BEN: (*Laughing*) No, Pop, it's empty.

PHILIP: So throwing a ball into a garbage can—this is a worthwhile activity?

BEN: It depends on what your while is worth, I guess.

(*Discouraged, Simon enters with the basketball*)

SIMON: You home, Pop?

PHILIP: No, I'll be home tomorrow—today I'm in Budapest. Why the long face? You didn't get the ball in?

SIMON: Not much. In a whole hour—twice.

PHILIP: Sunday's not a good day to get the ball in. Wait till Monday—you'll get it in five times. Tuesday's even better—ten times.

BEN: Wednesday is fifteen.

SIMON: Thanks. I'll jot down those statistics.

PHILIP: (*Calling*) Bessie! Bessie, where are you?

SIMON: Sunday's not a good day for Bessie, Pop. Wait till Monday. Tuesday is better.

PHILIP: (*Smiling*) Where is she?

SIMON: She went to see Tanta Gussie.

PHILIP: Again? She was just there a few weeks ago.

SIMON: A few months ago. Annie went with her.

PHILIP: Annie? She said she would never go to Tanta Gussie's again.

SIMON: She changed her mind.

PHILIP: Why?

SIMON: She said if she didn't go, Mom and Gussie would kill each other.

BEN: (*Laughing, enjoying himself*) I can't believe it! I can't believe that after all these years, those two women still fight with each other.

PHILIP: It's worse than ever.

BEN: Then why do they want to be together?—why do they always fight?

PHILIP: Why—he asks me why. They're mad at the whole universe, so they fight. Tanta Gussie is alone in the world, so who has she got to fight with? It's an act of mercy on your mother's part—to go fight with Aunt Gussie.

So they sit at the kitchen table and they drink tea, and Tanta Gussie says that the cookies that Momma baked for her are made from stale flour—that's why they're burned. Momma says Tanta's teapot has a sediment at the bottom because it never gets cleaned, she should get a brush and scrub it—and why is the silverware so tarnished? Tanta Gussie says to her, "So when will you ever buy a new hat?" Momma says if Tanta had taken Uncle Herman to the hospital he would never have died. Tanta Gussie says: "Your son Benny was always crazy about clothes, and if you only spent a few dollars and bought him a new suit with an extra pair of pants, he would never run away from home." They make little digs at first, then they bring up old grudges, and pretty soon there is no limit to how mean they are to each other. The worst of enemies would not be so cruel—they murder, they kill each other! Then they wash the dishes together. And sometimes—accidentally on purpose—Momma breaks a dish. Then she starts crying and Tanta Gussie starts crying. Then they hug each other as if nobody has ever said a crooked word, and they kiss, and Tanta Gussie says, "Bessie, why don't you come more often, Bessie—I love you, Bessie, why are you such a stranger?" And they both feel wonderful—they are safe with each other—they are both members of a warm and loving family. . . . And then Momma can go home.

(*With extraordinary vigor, Philip starts scratching his palms.*)

BEN: What's the matter—what're you scratching your hands for?

PHILIP: Look at them—those new roto inks—they make an itch. If you don't wash your hands right away, you have to scrape your skin off with a knife. (*He starts toward the kitchen.*)

SIMON: Don't wash in the kitchen, Pop—Momma will kill you.

PHILIP: If you see her coming, give a yell.

(*He goes into the kitchen. Simon has put the basketball on the couch. Ben lifts it and chucks it to him. Simon, surprised, makes a reach for the ball, barely gets his hands on it, drops it.*)

BEN: What'd you do—quit for the day?

SIMON: I don't know why I started. I hate basketball, I hate to play basketball, I hate to *watch* basketball. How did you ever get me to do this?

BEN: I bought you a ball—I corrupted you.

SIMON: If you bought me a pistol, would I shoot myself?

BEN: (*Laughing*) You're just like Mom. I bring you a ball, you make it a pistol. Take my advice: Just keep your eye on the ball and it'll stop being your enemy.

SIMON: When I was out there, you said don't keep your eye on the ball, keep your eye on the can.

BEN: When catching, keep your eye on the ball; when pitching, keep your eye on the can.

SIMON: I did keep my eye on it. I stared at it, I didn't blink, I hypnotized myself with that lousy can. And what happened? I missed. Nearly every time, I missed.

BEN: Because when you threw the ball, you didn't believe it would go into the basket.

SIMON: It's not a basket, it's a garbage can.

BEN: There!—that's just it! You've got to believe it's a *basket*. No! It's the gold ring on the merry-go-round, it's the big spin on the roulette wheel! And you're going to win, Simon, you're going to win!

SIMON: A garbage can is a garbage can.

(*Spoken flatly. It daunts Ben a little. Moving closer to the boy, he tries to strike sparks in Simon's imagination.*)

BEN: Simon—honeyboy!—the world's not what you *see*, it's what you make up in your *mind*!

(*An instant*) Look. I'm in an art gallery, and there's this picture of a mangy, sick, mean-looking cat. He's got blood on his mouth—yellow eyes—and he's looking at a garbage can. He's saying to me: "This garbage can is mine! Don't touch it, you son of a bitch, or I'll slash you to pieces, I'll tear your flesh off!" And I see that the can is all he's got—he'll fight me for it with all his moxie and all his heart! He'll die for it! And as I'm looking at him, I begin to imagine how desperate he is—and how *brave*! And suddenly he's *beautiful*! And I feel beautiful because I let myself go along with him in my mind.

(*An instant*) Don't you think you could do that?

SIMON: No, I'd see a cat and a garbage can. One plus one equals two—it can't equal the world.

BEN: Mmm. . . . Tell me the truth—you don't really want to go to college, do you?

SIMON: You're wrong. I want to go so badly I could die.

BEN: Why? What'll you learn there? One plus one equals two?

SIMON: That's not a bad thing to learn, Ben.

BEN: You mean you don't want to learn about the wonders of the world? I mean the big wonders. The secrets that nobody lets us in on. How it all happened—how far we can go—what our real size is—how weird we are, how wonderful, how fantastic! You don't want to know any of that?

SIMON: I want to be Simon Farber—and know the place I live in.

BEN: But you know that already.

SIMON: No, I don't. . . . And you're not making it any easier.

BEN: Me? . . . Am I mixing you up, kid?

SIMON: Yes, you are! I think I want to be myself—and suddenly I want to be like you. I want to have what you've got—all the fun and the traveling and the clothes and the girls—and I'm scared that if I go for it, I'll make a mistake, it won't be what I wanted.

BEN: What do you want, Simie?

SIMON: I want something I can understand—I want a hook I can hang my hat on!

BEN: You'll hang your*self* on it. . . . What do you want to *be*, kid?

SIMON: Oh, what the hell—!

(*He starts to go*)

BEN: No, come back, Simie—please!

(*As the boy responds to his kindness*) Tell me. I *care* about you. What do you want to be?

SIMON: I want to be a C.P.A.

BEN: A C.P.A.? That's what?—a Certified—uh—

SIMON: —Public Accountant.

BEN: (*Repressing a laugh*) You want to be a Certified Public Accountant?

SIMON: There!—you see? I knew you'd laugh at it.

BEN: I'm not laughing.

SIMON: Yes you are! Because it's not a fantastic person in a world that never existed—it's ordinary! But to me it isn't ordinary—it's very special. Especially what the title means—Certified Public Accountant—that hits me as something that's dignified and trustworthy. And if you're talking about the world, it takes into account what the world is worth!

BEN: In dollars and cents.

SIMON: (*A passionate outbreak*) In how we value one another! . . . Look! Finkelstein calls Poppa a paperboy. Poppa's not a paperboy, he's a man! And nobody would insult him if he had a title in front of his name or initials after it! And that's what I'm going to have—initials! C.P.A.! *And everybody's going to know who I am*!

BEN: (*Pause. Then, respectfully:*) When I was your age and people asked me what I wanted to be, it drove me crazy—because I didn't know. I still don't know. But you do. I envy you, kid. Simon Farber, C.P.A.! I'll be your first client.

SIMON: Forget it.

BEN: Forget it—why?

SIMON: It's not going to happen.

BEN: You want it to happen, you'll make it happen.

SIMON: You want to know something?—you make me sick!

(*Mimicking angrily*) "You want it to happen, you'll make it happen!" Presto—like that! Abracadabra! You make me sick!

(*He starts to leave. Ben calls:*)

BEN: Wait a minute, kid, wait a minute!

(*The boy comes back. Silence. Not unkindly:*) Now take it easy. Calm down.

SIMON: When I was only five or six years old, you were graduating from high school, and I was nuts about you—I followed you wherever I could. One day it was snowing and the streets were white. And I saw you go out into the alleyway, so I snuck along after you. And when I got there, you had unbuttoned your pants, and you were peeing in the snow. And then you pointed to the ground and said "B-e-n—that's my name—Ben!" And it seemed to me a wonderful thing to do. So I took my peter out and started to pee my name too. Well, I pissed all over the place, on the snow, on my shoes, on my pants, on everything. And when I was finished, I felt ashamed—and I felt as though you had tricked me.

BEN: Tricked you—how?

SIMON: You knew I couldn't write my name with a *pencil*, so how could I write it with my peter? . . . And to this day, you're making me feel ashamed for not accomplishing what I know I can't accomplish!

BEN: Button your pants—who says you can't accomplish it?

SIMON: Where the hell am I going to get the money to go to college? Pop barely makes a living. Annie barely hangs on to her job. Momma pays for her life on the installment plan!

BEN: I can put you through college twice over and half way round again.

SIMON: No, thanks—I don't want a handout.

BEN: Handout?! I'm your brother!—did you forget that?

SIMON: (*In distress*) Stop it, Benny, would you please stop it?

BEN: Stop what, for Chrissake! If I offer to pay for your college—and you turn me down—how else will you get there?

SIMON: The answer's obvious. I work my way through.

BEN: You like that idea?

SIMON: It's got nothing to do with what I "like."

BEN: So how will you go about it? You'll get a job in the daytime—say, a paper route, the way Poppa started—and go to college at night. Right?—something like that?

SIMON: Something like that.

BEN: Work by day and school by night—you know how long that'll take? You'll be a senile old man before you pass trigonometry.

SIMON: (*Angry, upset*) Don't you think I know that? Don't you think it scares the hell out of me? Look, Ben, I'm not the smartest kid in the class, the way you were. I have to work my ass off to stay in the middle. If I have to hold down a job and pass trigonometry, I'm scared to death I won't make it!

BEN: Then, come on!—it's not a handout! It's a present from a lonely man who wants to be your brother again!

SIMON: (*On the verge of tears*) My God, you know how to *get* people, don't you? You think I don't want you to pay my way? You think I don't want you to make it easy for me? You think I don't want to reach out—and hug you—and say thanks and—oh dammit, oh dammit!

(*He is crying. He turns away, humiliated. Ben, trying not to invade, puts his arm around the boy and murmurs his name a few times. Gently:*)

BEN: All right, stop crying, and tell me why you won't take it.

SIMON: (*Bringing himself under control:*) I just can't figure it out, Ben.

BEN: Yes you can. You think what Mom thinks, don't you? You think my money has a curse on it.

SIMON: I'm sure she doesn't think that, Benny.

BEN: Yes, she does.

SIMON: No, it's only . . . if she doesn't know where money comes from, she's afraid it didn't come from a good place.

BEN: And that's the way you feel about it too, huh?

SIMON: Well, you're awfully slippery about where it comes from, Ben. And in this family we're taught that the only money worth having is what you yourself work for.

BEN: Yes, and in this family we think that the only work that's honest is the work that keeps you poor.

SIMON: No! We've merely learned that there aren't any short cuts. I guess you haven't found that out yet.

BEN: (*Losing his temper*) Don't you say that to me, kid! I went the long way too! This silk shirt didn't come from a magic silkworm! I paid a lot of sweat and blood for every damn thing I own! And now I'm trying to share it with you, and you won't let me!

SIMON: (*Unhappily*) I'm sorry, Ben. I don't know what to say—I'm sorry. I didn't mean to sound ungrateful.

BEN: You *are* ungrateful!

SIMON: (*Fighting back*) Is that why you give us things? To make us grateful?

BEN: (*Exploding*) This goddamn family—I can't stand this family anymore! I offer to lend a hand in a rotten time, and what do they do?—they treat me like an outcast—like an enemy—they spit in my eye!

SIMON: Maybe that's what you're asking for.

(*Ben, for an instant, goes berserk with rage. He grabs Simon roughly.*)

BEN: You take that back, you little bastard, take it back!

SIMON: Let me go!

BEN: I said take it back!

SIMON: Okay—okay!

(*Ben lets him go. Simon, shocked by Ben's violence, views him with dread, anger. Quietly:*)

SIMON: You're a scary man, Ben.

BEN: I'm sorry I roughed you up. But you don't really think I would have hurt you, do you?

SIMON: No, I don't. I mean scary in another way.

BEN: What way?

SIMON: I think you can wreck my life, Ben—if I don't hang on to a few old slogans.

BEN: What slogans?

SIMON: (*As if engraving them on his brain*) You've got to work for what you get. Honesty is the best policy. The tortoise wins the race. The dignity of labor.

BEN: *The dignity of labor*?! There is no dignity of labor! Read your Bible, brother! Adam sinned and God punished him. You know what God said to Adam? He said: "You will earn your crusts and cookies by the sweat of your brow and the breaking of your balls!" *Is that the dignity of labor*?!

(*Bessie enters. She wears a well-worn but pleasant-looking dress-up dress. Also a hat. She has heard Ben's last words.*)

BESSIE: God didn't say any such thing.

BEN: How do you know he didn't, Mom?

BESSIE: Because God has a clean mouth—he doesn't use dirty words.

PHILIP: *(He has overheard)* That's right. When God says balls, he only means baseballs.

BESSIE: *(To Simon)* Look at your sweater—it's all covered with schmootz. How did you get so dirty?

BEN: He's been associating with me, Mom.

BESSIE: *(To Simon)* It's almost suppertime. Go and wash.

(Simon goes upstairs. Bessie starts brushing imaginary crumbs off Philip's jacket.)

PHILIP: Stop brushing me. She's always brushing crumbs off my clothes. Even on Yom Kippur, when I don't eat nothing, she brushes away the crumbs. Stop it.

BESSIE: Monster.

(She slaps him gently on the arm—a love pat. They both laugh. Ben enjoys them.)

BEN: Where's Annie?

BESSIE: She stopped at the bakery to buy chocolate éclairs for dessert.

BEN: Chocolate éclairs! You're kidding!

BESSIE: They used to call them chocolate cream puffs—and they cost three cents a piece. Now they got a French name—éclairs!—and they cost a nickel. The French people give us a lot of trouble.

BEN: *(In an ecstasy)* Oh my God, how I used to love chocolate éclairs! And I still do! I can't believe that Annie is buying chocolate éclairs!

BESSIE: *(To Philip)* I think your oldest son is going to fall down in a convulsion.

BEN: You bet I am! Chocolate éclairs—who remembered they're my favorite dessert? Who remembered? You, Momma, or Annie?

BESSIE: Who cares who remembered?

BEN: *(Delighted)* I care that you remembered! And you did remember, didn't you, Mom? You! *You* remembered that your little Benny loves chocolate éclairs! Come on, beautiful, give us a kiss!

(He grabs her. Laughing but liking it, she resists. As he dances her around the room:)

BESSIE: Stop it, meshugganer, stop it!

BEN: Come on, sweetheart, give us a kiss for Valentine's Day.

BESSIE: Valentine's Day is in February, and this is the middle of May. But anyway, here's your kiss.

(She kisses him on the cheek) Stay around until Valentine's Day, I'll give you another one.

BEN: *(He holds her a moment. Only half in jest:)* Momma, I can't tell you how I appreciate that you remembered the chocolate éclairs.

BESSIE: *(Embarrassed, disengaging herself)* Out of a nothing-little-chocolate-cream-puff he makes a whole big romantic scene in the movies.

PHILIP: Momma would like you to understand the more realistic side of a cream puff. If you're going to eat cream for dessert, you don't get meat for supper.

BESSIE: Why should you have two pleasures?

PHILIP: That's the Jewish law—you can't have two pleasures. Every pleasure has to be married to a pain. That's like your mother and me.

BESSIE: I'm the pleasure, he's the pain.

(*They all laugh*)

PHILIP: (*To Bessie*) That's what your Uncle Morris used to say.

BEN: How is Uncle Morris?

BESSIE: He's fine, he's dead.

PHILIP: That's a terrible way to say it, "He's fine, he's dead."

BESSIE: Dead is the finest that Uncle Morris ever was.

BEN: When did he die?

PHILIP: Eight, nine years ago. Cancer of the kidney.

BESSIE: Gall bladder.

PHILIP: That was Uncle Ephraim.

BEN: (*Soberly*) Uncle Ephraim's dead too?

PHILIP: And Uncle Julius.

BEN: My God. What did Uncle Julius die of?

BESSIE: A hard matzoh ball.

BEN: (*Incredulous and shocked*) He ate a hard matzoh ball and died?

PHILIP: No. He had a restaurant and *served* a hard matzoh ball, and the customer took out a pistol and shot him.

BEN: Shot him for a hard matzoh ball?!

PHILIP: Shot him dead. The moral of the story is: if you want a soft life, serve a soft matzoh ball.

BEN: I'll remember that. How's Tanta Gussie—I know *she's* not dead.

BESSIE: Why should she be dead? She's fine. When I left, she was going over her list.

BEN: What list?

BESSIE: She has a list of insults. She was checking them off to make sure she didn't miss any. . . . She's going to murder the milkman.

PHILIP: Why? What'd he do to her?

BESSIE: It's what he *didn't* do to her! And she's eighty-five years old. I tell you, she makes me sick.

BEN: Then why do you visit her?

BESSIE: Well . . . she's my tanta—she's lonely.

PHILIP: And why is she lonely?—because she won't move in with her daughter. Every time I see her, I advise her—I *beg* her—"Tanta Gussie—*please*—move in with Dave and Dora!" But does she listen to me? No!

(*Suddenly shouting*) *Nobody listens to me! They don't even hear me!*

BESSIE: They don't hear you because you talk too loud.

PHILIP: Sometimes you gotta talk loud!

(*To Ben*) Years ago, when it first came up about prohibition, I told them—I *warned* them there would be a sickness in the country. But did they listen to me? No!—*nobody listens to me!*

BESSIE: (*Raising her hand like a traffic cop*) Shah! Enough already! Shah!

PHILIP: Shah she says to me. What difference does it make if I'm shouting or I'm shah? Nobody listens to me.

BEN: How will you ever know if they're listening, Pop?

PHILIP: They will do something different than they did before. They will stop beating their dog—or they will send somebody a postal card—or they will stop biting their nails!—*something*!

BESSIE: Philip—honey—why should people listen to you? Who are you—somebody important? No. You don't *make* the newspapers, you only sell them. You expect the whole world to listen to you, because you're a good man and you listen to everybody. But everybody is not so good and kind as Philip W. Farber—so please don't expect too much from us. Don't *expect*, Philip.

(*Suddenly the noise of the train. It screams by like an explosion. Ben rushes to china closet. Philip, in frustration, screams back at it:*)

PHILIP: Shut up! Don't make so much noise! Don't interrupt quiet people when they're talking! Shut up, you son of a bitch—shut up!

(*The train is gone. Silence. Bessie, not Philip, is now at the window*)

BESSIE: Where's your auto?

PHILIP: (*Irritably*) What? What did you say?

BESSIE: I wasn't talking to you, I was talking to Ben. Where's your automobile?

BEN: I put it in a garage on Porter Street.

BESSIE: Why?

BEN: I didn't like it standing outside the house.

PHILIP: It's safe. Nobody would hurt it.

BEN: Well—the neighbors—it seemed like we were bragging.

PHILIP: For Finkelstein I would like to brag.

BEN: I'm sorry, Poppa. I'd rather have it in a garage.

BESSIE: What are you afraid of?

BEN: Afraid? Nothing.

(*Annoyed*) Everybody asks the same damn question: what am I afraid of? Nothing! I'm the least frightened person in this house! Nothing!

BESSIE: Last night when we went to bed, you locked the front door.

BEN: Habit, Mom, just plain habit.

BESSIE: We don't have that habit in this house. What are you hiding from us?

BEN: (*Starting to lose his temper*) I'm not hiding anything! Would you please quit that—I am not hiding!

BESSIE: Don't tell me! I know from your face—I know from your eyes—

BEN: Goddamn it!

BESSIE: Don't use that language—I don't like it!

PHILIP: (*Enraged*) Stop it! Both of you—stop it! I am sick of the two of you fighting with each other—I'm sick of it!

BESSIE: If you're sick of it, go for a walk—go outside!

PHILIP: (*Losing control*) I was outside all day! Now I'm inside—now I came home! Can you both remember that?—this is our home! And I want you both to stop fighting in it—stop fighting—stop!

(*He cannot summon the rest of the sentence. He goes rigid, his hand to his chest*) Bessie—

BESSIE: Oh my God!

BEN: What is it, Pop? Pop!

BESSIE: Sit down, Philip—sit down—

PHILIP: Pocket—my pocket—

(*She reaches into his vest pocket and brings out a tiny vial of nitroglycerin pills.*)

BESSIE: Open your mouth, honey—it's all right, sweetheart—it's all right—open your mouth—

PHILIP: No—give it to me—

(*He receives the pill from her, and puts it under his tongue. He tries to smile*) It'll be okay in a minute—just watch—I'll be fine—just watch—

BEN: Don't try to talk, Pop.

PHILIP: It's not so serious—don't worry—don't worry—

BESSIE: Here—let me put this pillow—

(*She shoves a pillow behind his back. He smiles.*)

PHILIP: Good—that's good.

(*He tries to keep talking, to assure them he's not as ill as they think. He is indeed breathing more naturally, smiling more easily*) Pillows are good. Pills and pillows. See? I told you. It's wonderful how those pills work. Nitro. Nitroglycerin. It's like dynamite—in fact, it *is* dynamite. I'm going to explode! Bang! Bang!

(*He laughs.*)

BEN: Pop—sh—be quiet—Pop.

PHILIP: (*Unstoppable*) I stick one tiny little pill under my tongue and in one minute—in two minutes at the most—I feel fine, I feel as good as new.

(*Faking laughter, he raises his fists at Ben*) Come on—up with the dukes, up with the dukes!

BEN: Take it easy—don't be such a smart aleck.

BESSIE: You feel dizzy, honey?

PHILIP: No—nothing—I'm telling you, I feel fine. . . . I think I'll go upstairs and take a nap.

BEN: Is he allowed to climb stairs?

PHILIP: (*Starting to rise*) What do you mean, am I allowed to climb stairs? How do I go to bed at night? On a magic carpet?

BEN: If you want to nap, you can nap on the couch.

PHILIP: I hate that couch—it's hard as a rock. Your mother bought a hard couch because it wears better. But how do *we* wear, that's the question, how do *we* wear?

(*He laughs to deny he is complaining.*)

BESSIE: I'll go up with you, honey.

BEN: No, I'll go up, Mom.

PHILIP: (*Laughing*) That's right. *You* go up with *her.*

BESSIE: Always with the bad jokes. Come on.

(*Taking him by the arm, as they ascend the stairs*) Go a few steps and rest. Not too fast, now.

(*As they go upstairs, Ben wants to follow them; starts to, but has a moment of panic. His father's illness has hit him hard. The phone rings. Reflexively, he approaches the instrument and stops, conflicted as to whether or not to answer it. It rings again. He lifts the receiver and, listening, heaves a sigh of relief.*)

BEN: Hello. Oh, I'm glad it's you, Marky. What's happening? He is? When? How did he get my number? Well, the bastard's thorough, isn't he? Yeah . . . Christ . . . No—don't do that—just do what I tell you. If he gives you a rough time again, tell him you found out where I am. I'm not in the country—I'm in Tahiti. It's a little town named Palua. P-A-L-U-A. That's right. I've got a business there—and my name is Booth W. Fields. Right. What? Yes, if he calls, I won't be here—I won't answer. That's right—I'll just let it ring. Now, don't act too smart with him. That's all you know. Okay?. . . . Okay.

(*He hangs up and is very still. His mind is caught between the two troubles, but his father is most worrisome to him. He starts up the stairs, stops, changes his mind and decides instead that he will lock the front door. As he is going toward the vestibule, Bessie is coming down the stairs. Afraid she will see what he intends to do, he comes back into the room without locking the door.*)

BESSIE: Was that the telephone?

BEN: Yes.

BESSIE: Who was it?

BEN: Nobody—a wrong number.

BESSIE: Our first telephone call, and it's a wrong number.

BEN: How is he?

BESSIE: He'll fall asleep in a little while. He usually does. And then he wakes up and he's all right.

BEN: What do you mean, he's all right? It's his heart, isn't it?

BESSIE: Yes.

BEN: So what do you mean, he'll be all right? Those pills—do they make him any better?

BESSIE: Who knows?—better—who knows?

BEN: Is there any cure in them?

BESSIE: No, they only take away the pain.

BEN: Is he taking any medicine that has any cure in it?

BESSIE: He's got a bad heart, Ben. There isn't any medicine that has a cure in it.

BEN: (*In distress, his nerves jumpy*) There has to be. My God, he shouldn't be lifting heavy bundles of newspapers every day! He's got to take care of himself—we've got to take care of him! We've got to find a cure for him—he's not that sick—he doesn't *look* that sick—my God!—what does the doctor say?

BESSIE: The doctor says there's no cure for him.

BEN: Then we'll have to go to another doctor.

BESSIE: We've been to another doctor. We've been to a half dozen doctors. A few weeks ago we went to a clinic in New York. They do all sorts of new things there—new treatments—new operations.

BEN: What did they say?

BESSIE: They said for him to take it easy. So for three days, he didn't go to his newsstand. He just stayed at home—crying. Crying is also not good for the heart.

BEN: So what did you do?

BESSIE: I let him go back to the stand—and he stopped crying.

BEN: And you started.
(*As she turns away*) We have to find some way to make him better!

BESSIE: Sick hearts don't get better, they get worse.

BEN: (*A cry of aching*) No! *He's not Uncle Morris and Julius and Herman! He's my father! I didn't come home to watch him die!*

BESSIE: What did you come home for—to see him get younger? To see his wrinkles disappear and watch his gray hair grow in black? What do you expect of a man his age?

BEN: His age? You talk about him as if he was as old as Tanta Gussie. He's only sixty years old!

BESSIE: He's sixty and I'm fifty-five. If you stay home as long as you've been away, the chances are that one of us will die in that time. Maybe both. That's what happens to parents—they die. And if you stay home and watch them die, year by year and sickness by sickness, they don't die quick, like from a gunshot—*they die slow.* It's like a watched pot never boils, a watched invalid never seems to die—ask me, I've watched a lot of them. Before they die, your love for them dies first. There's only one way for you to avoid it. Go away. It's the only way you can keep your parents alive. Alive forever. Go away.

BEN: Is that what you want me to do, Momma?

BESSIE: What I want doesn't matter.

BEN: Is that what you *advise* me to do?

BESSIE: . . . Yes.

BEN: You think if I stay home I won't be able to take it, huh?

BESSIE: That's right.

BEN: When I was a kid you called me a murderer. Now you call me a coward.

BESSIE: I didn't really mean that you were a murderer, and I don't mean you're a coward.

BEN: What other name are you calling me, Momma? If it's not coward, what name can you give a son who doesn't have the guts to watch his parents die? What name? How brave am I, Momma?

BESSIE: Why should you be brave if you don't have to be? It breaks your back if you're brave—it breaks your heart. Me, I carry my courage around inside me, like a tumor. *I hate it!*

(*A moment*) Maybe you're lucky that you don't have to see things as they are. But if you stay here, you will. So take my advice, Benny—go away! Go somewhere and dream of chocolate éclairs and how wonderful your home used to be. Because if you stay, you'll see the real picture. People get old and they get feeble and they don't know who they are. Or they get silly like Tanta Gussie. Or they drool while they're eating or soil their underwear and lose their self-respect. And they die. That's what home is. Home is a place where people get born and grow up and grow down—and die! They *die!*

BEN: (*Edgily, for something to do, he picks up the birthday card Bessie gave Philip*) What's this?

BESSIE: It was your father's birthday card. It's the bluebird of happiness.

BEN: It looks like a chicken.

BESSIE: (*With a wry smile*) That's what he said. A blue chicken.

(*Annie enters—happy, a bit giddy. She waves the bag that carries éclairs.*)

ANNIE: Éclairs! I'm sorry I took so long, but it's Sunday! Why does everybody want cakes and pies on Sunday?

BESSIE: Give me—I'll put them in the refrigerator.

ANNIE: I'll do it, Bessie.

BESSIE: (*A fierce outburst*) Do not call me Bessie! I have told you a hundred times, do not call me Bessie! I am either Aunt Bessie or I am Momma! (*Ashamed of her flareup, she entreats:*) Please—give me the bag.

(*Annie hands her the bag and Bessie starts toward the kitchen. Ben has slipped into the vestibule, to lock the front door. Almost immediately he returns. Neither Bessie nor Annie has noted this. Bessie hesitates, disoriented.*)

BESSIE: I forgot what I was thinking. I don't know what to make for supper. Should I make salmon croquettes or a lox omelette or what? What would you like, Benjamin?

BEN: How about Oysters Rockefeller, Mom?

BESSIE: (*Quietly*) You gave up all the dietary laws? You eat oysters?

BEN: But never on Friday, Mom. On Friday I eat meat—so people shouldn't think I'm Catholic.

BESSIE: And not think you're Jewish either.

BEN: Not in Tahiti.

BESSIE: What are you in Tahiti?

BEN: Nothing.

BESSIE: You go to Tahiti to be nothing? You can be nothing anywhere. Even at home you can be nothing.

BEN: I was, Mom.

(*An outburst of nervous, almost hysterical laughter, escapes him.*)

BESSIE: You say something serious, then you laugh like a hyena to pretend you didn't say it. I hate it when you do that.

BEN: (*Sober now, he says quietly*) Add that to your list, Momma.

(*Bessie goes into the kitchen*)

ANNIE: (*Quietly*) I hate it too.

BEN: (*As quiet as she is*) What else do you hate about me?

ANNIE: (*Remorseful, she rushes to him*) Nothing! I'm sorry I said that—nothing!

(*She is in his arms. They kiss with fervor.*)

BEN: Why did you sneak out while I was asleep? I thought we were going to walk on the Parkway.

ANNIE: We can't walk and sleep at the same time.

BEN: I never spent so much time in bed until I met you.

ANNIE: You met me on your fourth birthday when I was one week old.

BEN: (*Trying to lighten things*) I think I was horny for you even then. All my life.

ANNIE: Please don't say that.

BEN: In love with you, then . . . all my life.

(*He is deeply serious, deeply troubled. As she watches him soberly and in silence:*) I want you to marry me, Annie.

(*Another silence*) Is that all you're going to say?

ANNIE: I've just fainted. What happened?

BEN: I said I want you to marry me.

ANNIE: And what did I say?

(*Trying to smile it off, but frightened, she turns away. He takes this as a rejection.*)

BEN: Why didn't you tell me Poppa has a bad heart?

ANNIE: (*Startled*) Did he have an attack?

BEN: I guess it was an attack—he reached to his chest and couldn't catch his breath.

ANNIE: Where is he?—in the hospital?—where is he?

BEN: He's upstairs—in bed.

(*As she starts for the stairs, Ben stops her*) No, let him alone, he's resting.

ANNIE: Was it a bad one?

BEN: (*Unnerved*) How do I know? Is there a good one? Why didn't somebody tell me about him? Why didn't you tell me?

ANNIE: I was hoping it would . . . go away.

BEN: (*Disconnectedly*) Let's not waste time, honey—my father's sick—let's get married.

ANNIE: What does his being sick have to do with getting married?

BEN: It has to do with where I spend the rest of Poppa's life. I want to spend it right here—where he can get some pleasure out of watching me, instead of pain. I want him to see us happy. I want to have kids here—and have him and Momma help us raise them! I want to make up for all those years I've been away from both of them! My God, I didn't know what I wanted—and now I know!
(*In an ecstasy*) Oh thank God! I know what I want, I know what I want! (*Quickly, rushing to her*) Annie—honey—sweetheart—let's get married as soon as possible!

ANNIE: . . . You're . . . going too fast.

BEN: Am I making you nervous? I'll slow down—start at the beginning. Do you love me, Annie?

ANNIE: Haven't I said that?

BEN: Just once. And it could have been a slip of the tongue.

ANNIE: Don't you know I meant it?

BEN: How can I *know*? You've turned down every present I offered you. Yesterday, we stopped at that jewelry window—and that opal necklace—

ANNIE: I didn't really want it—honestly I didn't!

BEN: And the dress I gave you when I arrived—you never even tried it on.

ANNIE: I started to, Benny—a dozen times! It's the most beautiful dress I ever saw—but it's beyond me, Ben! I can't live up to that dress—it scares me!

BEN: Too many things scare you, Annie!

ANNIE: (*Unhappily*) I know—I'm sorry—I know!
(*She is having a painful difficulty. He sees this and tries to be gentler.*)

BEN: Annie . . . honey . . . the world's not a dark and terrible attic—it's a wide, sunny, open field.

ANNIE: I'm scared to go out in it.

BEN: I'll help you.

ANNIE: (*On the edge of panic*) You'll get hurt, Benny.

BEN: I'll take my chances.

ANNIE: There—you see? You've got the courage to say that—"I'll take my chances!" But I don't. And I would pull you back, Ben! I can't run as fast as you can—I can't laugh as loud—I don't have your appetite for living! It's an acquired taste, and I never acquired it.

BEN: That's bullshit! It's a taste you're born with—and if you've lost it, you can get it back!

ANNIE: How, for God's sake?—how!

BEN: By trying, goddamn it!—you've got to *care* enough to try!

ANNIE: (*An outcry*) You think I don't care? You think I don't want to be like you? And wear bright clothes and walk as if I'm dancing? Oh, what I wouldn't give to wear a hat with flowers on it! What I wouldn't give to be dressed in the colors of happiness, instead of beige and black and gray!

BEN: (*Trying to take her in his arms*) I've got enough love of life to share it with you.

ANNIE: (*Retreating*) Ben . . . don't . . .

BEN: It's catching—you'll catch if from me.

ANNIE: No . . . let me go . . .

BEN: You'll fall in love with life—you will—I promise you!

ANNIE: Ben—listen! Maybe coming back home was a terrible thing to do to yourself. I think it was. I think you ought to go away. And I mean now—before it's too late—go away!

BEN: *Will everybody stop sending me away*?! I love you, Annie! I love you more than I do myself! And you've got to say those words to me, Annie—you've got to say them often! What the hell are you saving them for?!

ANNIE: (*Trying to laugh*) A rainy day!

BEN: (*He cannot conceal the anguish*) It's a rainy day now, Annie, it's a rainy day! Maybe I did make a mistake in coming home. My father's sick—my brother dislikes me—and it's clear my mother doesn't want me here! I've tried so many places in the world . . . and . . . I . . . don't know where to go. I haven't any place to go.

ANNIE: Am I a . . . place to go?

BEN: Oh yes! *I need to go home, Annie*! And if you can't help me find a home somewhere, I'll die, Annie, I'll die!

ANNIE: I love you, Ben.

BEN: Oh God . . .

ANNIE: I love you so much that I ache all over.

BEN: When do we get married? Set the date. The sooner the better. How about ten minutes?

ANNIE: Not too fast, Ben. There are things to talk about—places to live—

BEN: I've got my eye on the perfect place, Annie! It's a beautiful house on Broad Street. The Cooper house—do you remember the Cooper House?

ANNIE: The old white one? But it's a wreck—it's all boarded up.

BEN: We'll fix it, Annie, we'll restore it! Do you remember what it was like when we were kids? It was like a mansion! Those wonderful curving stone steps—and the stained glass windows in the front door—! I used to walk up the steps to see what it would feel like—and it felt wonderful—I was just the right distance off the ground! And now the old house needs some help—and we'll help it! It'll be a mansion again!

ANNIE: (*In difficulty but trying to smile*) I . . . can't live in a mansion, Ben.

BEN: Of course you can—you *can*, Annie.

ANNIE: There's not enough of me to fill the space.

BEN: (*Gently*) Honey . . . you've got to stop talking like that.

ANNIE: (*Wavering*) Can I do it, Ben?

BEN: Not "I"—"*we*"!

ANNIE: Yes, together!—can we together?

BEN: (*Joyous, he dances her around the room*) Yes, honey, yes! We're going to bust and build and clean and decorate and put the old stain glass windows back, and we're going to make a sad old wreck into a beautiful home for ourselves and our children. And we'll have fifteen children, one for every bedroom in the house.

ANNIE: Would three be enough?

BEN: Three would be fine.

ANNIE: We're cousins.

(*Trying to laugh*) They'll be idiots.

BEN: We're twentieth cousins, twice removed.

ANNIE: We'll never be removed again.

(*With an access of joy and fear*) Oh, hold me, Ben—don't ever let me go—as tight as you can—hold me!

(*In his arms—desperately*) Oh, Benny, can I stop being frightened? Can I come out of hiding now?

BEN: (*The children's singsong*) Come out, come out, wherever you are!

ANNIE: (*On a rhapsody*) I'm never going to hide again! You watch me! I'm going to call people on the phone and tell them how happy I am! I'm going to talk to strangers on the street! I'll take ads in the Evening Bulletin. "This is my husband," I'll say. "Come and see how happy I am!"

BEN: Carry a sign in the Mummer's Day Parade.

ANNIE: And we'll win first prize!

BEN: (*Singing*) Oh, dem Golden Slippers,

Oh, dem Golden Slippers—

(*He breaks off*) Can I go to the top of your dance card, Lady?

ANNIE: You're already there!

(*She goes into his arms; they are dancing*)

BEN: Oh, dem Golden Slippers—

ANNIE: (*Joining him in the song*) Marching on parade,

Drinking lemonade—

(*They sing and dance together, making a loud noise, a gaiety. Philip is coming down the stairs.*)

PHILIP: You need another Mummer?

BEN: Pop! You all right?

PHILIP: I'm fine, I'm fine.

BEN: I'm sorry—were we too loud?—I'm sorry.

PHILIP: Sorry for what? For being happy? I read in last Sunday's Inquirer that happiness is good for every ailment.

BEN: Pop, when I give you the good news, it'll make you young again—it'll give you a brand new heart!

PHILIP: What, Doctor? Tell me, Doctor—what?

BEN: Wait—let me get Mom.

(*Calling toward kitchen, then upstairs*) Momma! Simon!

BESSIE: (*Entering from kitchen*) What's the noise out here? What's happening?

(*As Simon comes down*) What's going on? Annie—Philip—what's happening?

PHILIP: I don't know, Bessie—ask *him*.

ANNIE: He has good news for you, Momma.

BESSIE: What did you call me?

BEN: She called you Momma. You're not going to be her aunt anymore, you're going to be her mother.

PHILIP: You're going to get married?

BEN: Yes, Pop, we are.

SIMON: Hey, that's great, that's wonderful!

PHILIP: (*To Annie*) You're really going to marry this dumb fella?

ANNIE: Yes, I am.

PHILIP: I'm glad, Annie. Oh Benny, it's very good—you're doing a smart thing—a wonderful thing. Annie—
(*Philip embraces her. Then:*) You see? I told you that some nice fella would come along—a handsome young man, from a nice family, a good mother, the best father in the world, the handsomest father, the smartest—
(*They all laugh.*)

BEN: You didn't say a word, Momma.

BESSIE: (*Quietly, deeply moved and trying not to cry*) I am happy for both of you—I can't tell you how happy. I don't worry because you are cousins—you are distant, you are ten times removed—and God will be good to your children—this I know in my heart. Oh, how happy for all of us . . .

ANNIE: Once upon a time there was talk about adopting me. And it never happened. Well now, it doesn't have to happen. I'll be your daughter.

BESSIE: I loved you as a cousin, I will love you as a daughter. Oh, it's so beautiful!
(*She starts to cry a little; Philip starts to smile a lot.*)

PHILIP: Where will you live? Will you maybe live with us?

BEN: We thought we could go on living here until our house is ready.

BESSIE: House? What house?

BEN: Mom—Poppa—I'm hoping to buy the Cooper house on Broad Street—and fix it up from top to bottom—

PHILIP: The Cooper house? You mean it?

BESSIE: No, he's just dreaming a little. The Cooper house is too big—it has eighteen, twenty rooms in it.

BEN: Just the right size for our family. Right, Annie?

BESSIE: A big house like that is a terrible responsibility for Annie.
(*To Annie*) Is that what you want, honey?

ANNIE: I don't know what I want, Momma. He's crazy, but I love his kind of crazy.

BESSIE: But the Cooper house—you'll get lost in it.

ANNIE: Well, if I do, I'll just find my own little room, and curl up in it.

BEN: You will not curl up in a little room. When two people are in love and get married, they don't get littler, they get bigger!

PHILIP: (*As he applauds*) I love that boy, I love that dopey boy! Where will you get married? In the temple?

BEN: We haven't talked about it. Annie, what do you think?

ANNIE: (*Hesitantly*) I'd rather get married here—if nobody has any objection. It'll be a lot of trouble—but I'd like to have it right here at home.

BESSIE: (*Happy*) And here is where you'll have it—right here, in the living room.

BEN: But a small wedding, right? Just a few people—just us. And maybe Uncle Arnold and Aunt Helen—and who else?

ANNIE: Tanta Gussie.

PHILIP: Oh, God.

(*Imitating Gussie*) Bessie, why is the bridegroom wearing only one pair of pants?

(*They all laugh*)

BEN: Oh boy, am I going to dance at this wedding?! Hey, Simon, you wanna be my best man?

SIMON: Honest?—really? What does a best man do?

BEN: You hold on to the wedding ring—and you don't drop the ball.

ANNIE: (*To Philip*) Will you give the bride away?

PHILIP: I will never give you away—never. I will only lend you to him.

BESSIE: And what will I do?

ANNIE: You can be my maid of honor, Momma.

BESSIE: (*Touched*) Thank you, my dear. A maid of honor—it's a wonderful thing to be. And I promise you, I will always be honorable to you, Annie—always.

ANNIE: (*Also touched*) I know that, Momma.

BESSIE: And I hope *he* is.

BEN: (*Laughing*) She's got me betraying you already!

BESSIE: I didn't say that. And I don't mean that.

BEN: Then what did you mean, Mom?

BESSIE: I mean I hope you will deal honestly with her before you are married.

(*Pause.*)

BEN: Deal honestly how?

BESSIE: Tell her who you are.

BEN: She knows who I am and so do you.

BESSIE: No, I don't.

BEN: What do you want to know, Momma?

BESSIE: Two times I asked you where you got your money and both times you told me stories I couldn't believe. Now—once more—I ask you to tell the truth—not to me, but to Annie. Tell *Annie* the truth. What do you do for a living? Where did you get your money?

BEN: (*A moment of agonizing decision. Then:*) I've changed my mind, Momma—I'm not going to tell you the truth! Because no matter what I tell you, you won't believe me.

(*Desperate, a bit frenzied*) I got my money by being a banker, the owner of a railroad. Rich man, poor man, beggar man, thief! Thief, Momma! I got my money by stealing from all my friends and relatives! I won't tell you the truth, because I could break my heart telling it and you wouldn't believe me! So I won't try anymore—I'd rather leave home again—and never try, never try!

BESSIE: (*To Annie*) You see? Leave home—this is the real reason why you should think twice before you marry him. Because if he ever has to face the truth, he will run away from it—he will leave the house. No matter what house it is—here or on Broad Street.

BEN: That's not why I left this house! *You* are why I left it—*you*! You called me a murderer and drove me away! You threw me out on the street! You are the one who drove me away from home—*you*, Momma, *you*!

BESSIE: That's not true! I did not!—that's not true!

PHILIP: Bessie—Ben—

SIMON: Ben, you stop that! Stop it right this minute!

BEN: She wants the truth—well, I'm telling it!
(*To Bessie*) You made me a no-good in my home! You made me a stranger in the world! It was as if you put an infant in a basket and left him out in the winter! To die in the cold, in the loneliness! To die, Momma, to die!

BESSIE: I did what you wanted me to do! You didn't want to be one of us—*so I let you go! That's all I did to you—I let you go!*

BEN: *Now* who is the liar, Momma—*now* who is the liar!?

BESSIE: Don't you say that to me!
(*She starts for him as if to strike him, but the others intervene.*)

PHILIP: Stop it! I can't stand it! Stop it!

SIMON AND ANNIE: Momma—Momma, don't—Momma! . . . Stop it! Please! Please!
(*Cutting through the havoc, the phone rings. Bessie, closest, starts toward the phone.*)

BEN: Don't answer it!
(*She stops for the barest moment. The phone rings again. She again starts for the instrument.*)

BEN: Momma, please—don't answer it.
(*The phone rings again. Confused, conflicted, she lifts the receiver and speaks:*)

BESSIE: Hello.
(*A breath's pause. She turns to Ben*) It's for you.

BEN: (*In a panic*) Tell them I'm not here. Please, Momma, tell them I've been here and I left yesterday—I've gone to Tahiti!

BESSIE: (*An outcry of fury*) There is no Tahiti!

BEN: Momma—please—
(*A moment of tense conflict for Bessie. She makes her decision and speaks into the telephone.*)

BESSIE: He's not here—he went away. . . . What?
(*She hangs up. The room is very still. A pall, a dread*)

BESSIE: I do not lie for myself, and I do not like to lie for my children.

BEN: It was only a little lie, Momma.

BESSIE: To me all lies are the same size.
(*Indicating the caller on the telephone:*) He punished me for lying.
BEN: What did he say?
BESSIE: (*Quietly*) He said someone is on his way here to fix you up.
PHILIP: What does that mean, Ben?
BESSIE: It means somebody's going to kill him.
BEN: Nobody's going to kill me! He's only making noises—making threats. That's just the way we talk in my business!
PHILIP: What business? (*Silence*) Goddamn it, I said what business!
BEN: You're going to laugh, Pop. The most dismal, the most ordinary occupation in the world. . . . I'm a bootlegger.
PHILIP: You call this *ordinary*?
BEN: (*In an outbreak of anger at himself*) Yes—ordinary, Poppa! Thousands of people are bootlegging nowadays—millions are breaking the law—it's common, it's *ordinary*!
(*With grim humor*) I didn't come back to tell you I wrote a song or painted a picture! I came back to tell you I'm a bootlegger. Big deal, huh? What a joke!
(*In his self-disgust, he tries to laugh. Nobody joins him. Philip indicates the phone.*)
PHILIP: Who is that man?
BEN: He's a competitor of mine.
PHILIP: What did you do to him?
BEN: What others have done to me. I hijacked a truck.
PHILIP: Oh, God.
BEN: Come on, Pop—it's not that terrible. It's been done to me, and I've done it too! It's the way this business operates nowadays. Everybody's in it—the cops, the customs officers—everybody gets a cut and we all cut the whiskey! That is also ordinary! That's the way it goes, Poppa, that's the way it goes!
BESSIE: And everything for the best—right, Philip? Tell him: "It's okay, Ben: Everything is for the best."
PHILIP: (*Starting to weep*) Let me alone.
BEN: Poppa, don't cry—please, Poppa—it's no good for you—don't cry!
PHILIP: No good for me? *You* are no good for me—*you*!
BEN: Don't you say what she says, Poppa—please don't say it!
PHILIP: *You are no good for me! You are no good—you are no good for me!*
(*Philip starts beating with both fists on Ben's chest, beating and beating him. Ben does not try to resist him; he cries out in an agony:*)
BEN: Poppa, stop! You'll hurt yourself! You'll hurt yourself! Please stop! Poppa, please!
BESSIE: Philip—Philip—
(*She tears her husband away from her son. Ben cannot bear to look at anyone or at the world. He covers his face with his hands. Simon is turned away. Annie is weeping softly.*

The doorbell rings.)

SIMON: There's someone at the door!

PHILIP: (*In a rage, to Ben*) Go and unlock it!

BEN: No!

PHILIP: I'll do it myself!

BEN: No! Poppa—don't! Come back! Poppa!

(*Philip has gone into the vestibule. Ben races after him. An instant. Then, a gunshot, and another and another.*)

ANNIE: Oh, my God!

BESSIE: (*Shrieking*) Ben!

(*She streaks out into the hallway, Simon after her. Annie is too terrified to go. Her arms are clasped tightly across her breast, as if she is cold, as if she is frozen with fear.*

Philip returns. He is supporting his son, helping him walk. Ben is carrying a gun in his right hand, but his left arm has been shot; wounded in the forearm. He is bleeding a lot. Seeing him, Annie lets out a cry of relief.)

ANNIE: Oh Ben, oh Ben!

(*She rushes toward him.*)

PHILIP: Annie! Call an ambulance!

BEN: No! If you call an ambulance, you'll get the cops.

PHILIP: (*Unstrung*) Yes—yes—call Dr. Lightner!

(*She hurries to the telephone and starts speaking in an undertone.*)

PHILIP: (*To Ben*) Here—sit down—and hold your arm up—it won't bleed so bad.

(*Philip takes the gun out of Ben's hands and puts it on the table. He helps Ben into a chair.*

Bessie appears, standing in the doorway. She is in shock. Her voice is a monotone.)

BESSIE: That man on our doorstep—he's dead.

PHILIP: Help me with Ben—I need something—get me a towel or something.

(*In a daze, Bessie starts toward the kitchen. As she goes, she notices Annie on the telephone*)

BESSIE: Who are you calling?

ANNIE: Dr. Lightner.

BESSIE: Yes . . . and then call the police.

(*Silence. They hear Bessie's directive as if it were a grim court sentence. She goes into the kitchen. The lights fade.*

They come up once more about a month later, mid-day. Simon, rushing in, is out of breath, he has been running. He is yelling as he enters.)

SIMON: Mom—Pop!—Benny!—Annie! Where is everybody? Not home yet? Anybody home? Hello—hello-o-o-o!

(*Philip enters from the outdoors. He is all dressed up, hat, topcoat, everything.*)

PHILIP: Hello yourself. Stop screaming.

SIMON: Where's everybody?—what happened?

(*Bessie and Annie enter, also dressed up. Philip, Bessie and Annie are in various states of happiness.*)

BESSIE: (*To Simon*) What are you doing here?—you're out of school?

SIMON: (*Very kinetic—impatient*) It's my lunch period! For God's sake, what happened? Annie, will you please tell me what happened.

ANNIE: (*Ecstatic*) He got off! Simon, can you imagine it?—he got off!

SIMON: (*Elated*) Oh, my God!

(*They rush to one another and embrace.*)

SIMON: What do you mean, he got off? Where is he?

PHILIP: He's putting the car in the garage!

SIMON: What's that mean, he got off? You mean he's free?

BESSIE: Well, not altogether free.

SIMON: "Not altogether." What does that *mean*?

(*Turning away from his mother*) Annie, what happened, what happened?

ANNIE: Well, that man in the D.A.'s office—Mr. Colbertson—he said he would drop two of the charges, if Benny pleaded guilty to the third one.

SIMON: (*On tenterhooks*) What'd he drop, what'd he drop?

PHILIP: Murder and manslaughter.

SIMON: (*His elation increases*) No—no! You're kidding! He dropped murder and manslaughter? You're kidding!

PHILIP: What's so you're-kidding about it? He knew it was self-defense. We are all witnesses that it was self-defense. If he took it into court, what kind of chance did he have?

SIMON: How 'bout the third charge—carrying a gun without a license—what about that?

PHILIP: Ben pleaded guilty to that. He'll pay a thousand dollars fine, and six months on probation.

SIMON: (*Jumping around in a transport of joy*) Oh, I'm gonna die, I'm gonna die, I'm gonna die!

(*Ben enters, his left arm in a black sling.*)

BEN: Don't die—gimme a hug!

(*Simon rushes to embrace his brother who hugs him with one arm.*)

SIMON: Oh, I'm so happy, I'm so happy!

BESSIE: All right—too much happiness—go back to school.

SIMON: I'm gonna tell everybody, I'm gonna spread it all over! I'm gonna tell everybody—especially Finkelstein!

(*He is shouting joyously as he runs out. The briefest moment, then Annie goes to Ben.*)

ANNIE: Me too—I'm going to tell everybody how happy I am.

(*He embraces her*)

BESSIE: (*Also gentle*) Too much happiness. I don't trust too much happiness. It always has a trick in it.

BEN: What's the trick?

BESSIE: (*Deeply perturbed*) I don't know. I look at you and you are free—you are not sitting lonely in a jail. You are alive—I don't have to go to the morgue and say, "This dead thing is my son." Alive! . . . I am happy . . . But . . .

BEN: But what, Momma?

BESSIE: But a man has been killed. And my son killed him. So how can I be so happy? What has happened to me that I can stop thinking about this dead man, and I can stand here, and I can think about—what?—go into the kitchen—wash a dish—make a meal. How can I do that without going a little crazy. How can I not care that he is dead? How can I be so happy? (*She goes to him. He embraces her. Profoundly troubled, she is crying softly. In a moment, she disengages herself and goes into the kitchen. Ben is left with Annie and his father.*)

PHILIP: Happiness does not come easily to your mother. If she laughs, she thinks she's stealing something.

BEN: How about you?

PHILIP: I steal.

BEN: (*A wan smile*) How, Pop?

PHILIP: I look at the bright side, I tell myself stories with happy endings . . . I lie a little.

BEN: Like?

PHILIP: Like: this will all blow over.

ANNIE: Yes, like we will soon forget.

PHILIP: Like: your arm will get better. Like: you won't have to wear it in a sling. Like: The doctor didn't tell you that you will never be able to move your fingers again.

BEN: He didn't.

PHILIP: What do you mean, he didn't?

ANNIE: I don't understand.

(*Ben takes the sling off. Then he pulls the elastic half-glove off his hand. He slowly moves his arm this way and that way, to show it is totally usable. And he flexes his fingers to show that they too are capable. Philip watches with perplexed feelings. He is relieved, he is confused, he is perturbed.*)

ANNIE: Ben?—what happened?

PHILIP: What is it . . . this is a miracle?

BEN: No, Pop, it's not a miracle. It's just healing the way it should.

PHILIP: What are you doing now—with your hand—since when do you do this?

BEN: I've been exercising it for a week.

ANNIE: And Dr. Lightner—he didn't say you would have a crippled hand all your life?

BEN: No.

ANNIE: He didn't say that?

BEN: No, never.

PHILIP: You lied to us.

BEN: (*Pleading*) I'm sorry, Pop—but I had to do it. I had to go into the D.A.'s office with a plea of self-defense. My arm in a sling would help to prove it. And I didn't want you to lie for me.

ANNIE: You mean you didn't trust us to help you.

BEN: I didn't trust you to lie, Annie, to *lie!*

PHILIP: So you let us all think you were going to be a cripple for the rest of your life.

BEN: I'm sorry, Pop.

PHILIP: You let us all cry for you.

BEN: For a little while, yes. But you won't cry forever, Pop.

(*Philip's demeanor changes. He has grown harder, calmer. He speaks with quiet deliberateness, almost to himself.*)

PHILIP: No, we won't cry forever. We will have to stop crying for you, Ben.

BEN: Pop, it's over. Don't take it so big—it was only a little lie.

PHILIP: Little. You always say little, as if you can measure a lie in inches. Yes, you have told bigger lies—to me, to your mother, to the lawyer, to the judge. But it comes a time when one more lie is too much—even if it is a little lie. Too much—too much! So I will never believe you again, Benny.

ANNIE: Uncle Philip, don't say anymore, please.

PHILIP: Stay out of it, Annie.

ANNIE: I'm *in* it! Don't say anymore!

PHILIP: I have to make it clear to him: I want him to go away!

(*He turns to Ben. His voice is as severe as he can make it*) Did you understand me?

BEN: You mean go away forever?

PHILIP: For me, forever is a short time. But—long—short—it doesn't matter. I don't want to see you anymore, Benny. I don't want to think about you.

BEN: Please don't say that, Pop.

PHILIP: You got away from the law too easy.

BEN: Too easy?—why? Would you rather I got shot to death than that I got off without punishment?

PHILIP: It's a hard question.

BEN: (*Shocked*) My God, Pop!

PHILIP: We don't kill people in our family. Even your cousin Heskel who was a soldier didn't kill anyone. I will never be able to think about you the way I used to.

(*Trying not to weep*) I won't be able to stand it. I don't want you here— I don't want you here.

ANNIE: You can't say that to him! He's not a stranger!

BEN: I'm not your nephew Heskel, I'm your son!

PHILIP: You're a liar and a murderer. You are Al Capone!

BEN: No! I'm not!

PHILIP: He got off easy and so did you! I do not root for Al Capone!

BEN: I am not Al Capone!

PHILIP: Yes! It's a name that suits you better than Ben Farber! Change your name again, Benny—call yourself Al Capone!

BEN: You're not making sense!

PHILIP: No, I'm not. I never made sense about you. I could never bring myself to think bad things about you, Benjamin. But now I have to say them: You are Al Capone—you are the enemy! And I want you to leave the house as soon as possible.

(*Ben is stunned by the judge's sentence. It is like a death decree.*)

BEN: (*A plea; he is coming apart*)

Pop . . . I know you won't believe it . . . but I'm sorry I hurt you. I could die for hurting you, I could die for it! You're the last person in the world I want to hurt. Because I love you more than anybody, Pop—I do! All my life that was true—it was the truest thought I ever had—I love you more than anybody!

(*He is weeping. Annie goes to Ben and offers comfort. She caresses him.*)

ANNIE: Stop, Benny. Come on, Ben. The two of us—just the two of us—come on, honey.

BEN: Come on where?

ANNIE: Somewhere—just the two of us—come on!

BEN: No.

ANNIE: Ben—

BEN: He's right.

ANNIE: Whether he's right or not—you came home to have a family. And now you don't have one. So you and I—we have to make a family of our own.

PHILIP: (*Very quietly*) He doesn't have the right to have a family. A family is a precious thing—he has to deserve it. You can't keep a family together with lies—the glue doesn't hold.

ANNIE: Benny, we've got to go.

BEN: I'm going, Annie. . . . But I'm not taking you with me.

ANNIE: (*Starting to weep*) Benny, don't say that! I'm coming with you whether you want me or not—!

BEN: I do want you—I need you—I can't bear to go without you. But everything he says is true! I have no right, I have no right!

ANNIE: No—no—come on!

BEN: I can't, Annie—I can't!

ANNIE: You promised you wouldn't leave me—you promised me—!

BEN: I've never kept a promise in my life!

ANNIE: You will—you will!

BEN: When I know how to, I'll come back.

(*He turns to Philip. His voice is full of yearning*) If I do come back, Pop—the door won't be locked, will it?

PHILIP: In this house, the door is never locked.

(*Ben looks at Annie, then takes a step toward the door.*)

ANNIE: Oh Ben—no—don't go! Oh, I can't stand it!

(*She rushes to him and they embrace*)

BEN: Goodbye, my love.

(*Philip has turned away*)

BEN: Pop . . . Will you let me . . . touch you?

(*Philip turns to him a little, trying not to cry. Ben crosses the room and gently lays his hand on his father's arm. Then he removes it. And departs. Annie lets out a cry and starts to weep. Philip takes her in his arms. He comforts her softly, his words barely audible.*)

PHILIP: Shah. Shah, sweetheart, shah, shah.

(*At last she is silent and motionless. They cling to one another. Then the lights fade.*)

END OF THE PLAY

THE GREEN CLOWN

A Play in Two Acts

CHARACTERS

Carrie Campion
Lucas Campion
Delia Larkin
Joby Miller
Tully Pines

PLACE

A house on one of the Pacific palisades

TIME

The present

Act One

WE ARE ON THE PACIFIC COAST HIGHWAY. In the darkness, flashlights and car headlights glare. Lighted lanterns wave. Frenzied people scurry about. Some of the men directing traffic are expert, some amateur. A horn honks from time to time; a siren sounds off in the distance. A fire bell clangs. And voices:

VOICES: You can't go that way—it's blocked off! . . . Watch out—back up—use the side road! . . . It's a landslide, you stupid bastard—you wanna get killed? . . . The other way, the other way, you jerk, don't you see the barricade!? . . .

(*Out of the melee of motion and noises, Tully Pines steps forward. He is a deputy sheriff, in his forties, bright, overqualified for his job, a bit worn and very attractive. Right now he has lost his temper. He hurries downstage and speaks to the audience.*)

TULLY: People are crazy! They're nuts! They're out of their goddamn minds! You tell them the place is roped off, there's been a storm, there's been a landslide, half the palisade has fallen into the ocean, people have been hurt, a whole family has been killed, and they want to drive their goddamn cars right up to the brink of the palisade and have a little look-see! (*Shouting*) You'll get killed, you asshole! The whole mountainside's gonna fall on your head and you're gonna get dead and buried. The ground will collapse under your goddamn feet—you'll get swept out into the ocean! And you'll die!—do you get that?—*you'll drown, you'll die*!! (*More calmly*) It don't mean a goddamn thing to them—they're nuts! (*He rejoins the highway patrol. Flashlights. Traffic whistles. Shouts and curses*) The other way, you lunatics, the other way! Back up—take the side road—back up! (*He hurries down to address the audience again*) You think *they're* crazy? The ones that are really crazy—I mean really *really* crazy are the ones who built those goddamn houses on that goddamn cliff! It wasn't just ignorance, it was *insanity*! They knew it was dangerous!—they've been looking at maps and diagrams—they were warned!—the TV warned them, the newspapers warned them! Don't build your goddamn house on these goddamn palisades—the cliffs are crumbling! It's dangerous! Don't try to live here! Go away! Build somewhere else! Go inland! Find higher ground! Go away, you idiots, go away! Didn't you hear about Vesuvius? Hurricanes, volcanoes, earthquakes! Didn't you hear about *CATASTROPHE*?

(*Silence. Long silence. He murmurs to himself*) People want to kill themselves. They're just plain crazy.

(*He moves back to resume his policing function, and the light fades to darkness.*

A match, a blaze, a lantern light. What is revealed is chaos. A house on a cliff, overhanging the beach, the Pacific Ocean—after a storm, a flood, a landslide. This was once a study and a family room. A cozy auxiliary living area, with fireplace, books, pictures on the wall. Short days ago, a homey habitation; now, a wreck. Actually, it's not as bad as it appears at first sight. True, we see damage through the double window—a whole wing of the house has been swept down into the ocean; and, through another window, we get a glimpse of the loose-hanging structural members of a porch suspended by a thread. But the destruction appears worse than it is because the furniture and bric-a-brac have all slid to one side of the room, and some of it has been damaged. However, as the First Act proceeds, and as the characters restore some of the furnishings to their proper position, the place begins to take on some of the aspects of normalcy.

Lucas Campion appears. He's in his forties, personable, decent. He carries a lighted propane lantern. His wife, Carrie, is a bit younger. Carrying a lighted candle, she is in dismay; her hand shakes. For her sake, he is pretending to be calm.)

CARRIE: Oh no. Oh God—look at it—it's terrible—I can't bear to look—oh God.

LUCAS: I can't believe it—I can't believe it.

CARRIE: Nothing—there's hardly anything left—

LUCAS: Watch that candle—your hand is shaking.

CARRIE: It's not my hand, it's the candle. It's one of those self-shaking candles. You want to take it?

(*She extends it to him, hand trembling*)

LUCAS: No, you hold on to it. You're doing fine.

CARRIE: I'm doing what a person does when she's about to shoot herself.

LUCAS: Shoot me first.

CARRIE: There's *nothing*, Lucas. I can't see a single thing that hasn't been wrecked. I wish we had more light. Down toward the canyon they have light.

LUCAS: They probably have their own generator.

CARRIE: So have we but you wouldn't know it.

LUCAS: Shall I go down and press the button again?

CARRIE: No—it's just as stubborn as we are. Look—Delia's mantel clock—busticated. Amy's lamp. Everything I look at—everything I see—it's broken or it's gone. Where's our wedding picture?

LUCAS: It wasn't in here.

CARRIE: Yes it was—it was right on that table.

LUCAS: No, we moved it years ago.

CARRIE: No, we didn't.

LUCAS: Yes we did—when your mother died. Or was it after my father's memorial?

CARRIE: I wish you wouldn't do that.

LUCAS: Do what?

CARRIE: Reckon Time by who died when. Circa dead and destruction.

LUCAS: Don't complain—it's history. It's your own subject.

CARRIE: History can be cheerier than that. So can you. Look how cheery you were with the TV man.

LUCAS: Was I cheery with the TV man?

CARRIE: I thought you were wonderful.

LUCAS: What'd I say?

CARRIE: "Anyway, we've got each other."

LUCAS: Did I say that?

CARRIE: Yes you did.

LUCAS: Self-fulfilling crock.

CARRIE: No. It was dear, Lucas, it was sweet.

(*She starts to cry. He embraces her.*)

LUCAS: You want a handkerchief?

CARRIE: I have one.

LUCAS: You're dingo. You look at the whole calamity—the house wrecked—the furniture destroyed—the memories all shot to hell—and you don't cry, you don't whimper, you're as brave as a marine. And then we find a major consolation—that we've got each other—and you bawl like a baby.

CARRIE: I know—I don't cry logical.

(*She is laughing and crying as the lights go on—a table lamp, a hallway light, a wall bracket. The return of illumination excites them.*)

CARRIE: The lights, the lights!

LUCAS: Presto-changeo!

CARRIE: There are great wonders left! Hey—look!

LUCAS: Look at what?

CARRIE: With the light on, it's not as bad as I thought it was.

LUCAS: It's worse.

CARRIE: No, really, Luke—it only *looks* terrible because all the furniture's jammed up against that one wall. But if we were to push things back to where they belong—

LUCAS: Carrie, we lost the whole bedroom wing of the house—the side porch is hanging by a thread—windows are shattered—the furniture's crippled—things are broken that we've been trying to break for years—

CARRIE: (*She smiles wryly*) Yes. and we can never replace them. (*She has already started to work*) Here—help me—

LUCAS: Carrie, it's useless—

(*Since he is not helping her, she starts to lift a large, heavy wingchair.*)

LUCAS: Don't lift that damn thing by yourself!

(*He annoyedly helps her move the chair into approximately the center of the room.*)

CARRIE: There! It looks better already!

LUCAS: Sure! Better Homes and Gardens!

(*They laugh at the ridiculousness of it. She resumes her task: to rearrange the furniture.*)

CARRIE: Let's move the coffee table. Dammit, the leg's broken.

LUCAS: (*With quiet deliberateness*) Would you please stop pushing things around.

CARRIE: (*Losing her temper*) I'm not just "pushing things around"—I'm trying to make order out of this damn wreckage! How did it happen, for God's sake!? Who did it? Who the hell did this when our backs were turned? What treacherous bastard did this?!

(*She turns, hurries downstage, faces the audience. She is momentarily out of control.*)

CARRIE: *Treacherous bastard! Treacherous son of a bitch bastard! Treacherous bastard!*

(*She brings herself under control. She is still speaking to the audience.*)

CARRIE: I don't know exactly what person or thing I'm calling a treacherous bastard, but being a thinking person, I have to know why things happen—it's my *duty* to know! I am an Associate Professor of American History from the Settling of Jamestown to the Battle of Panama, and I try to teach my students not only the facts and footnotes of history but how to turn a scream of rage into a disciplined and constructive exercise in our search for a viable future. How to prevent a nuclear disaster, how to make war without packing a bullet or raising a voice. I hope one day to give a course called History and Accommodation. I think, if the human race is to survive, we must learn to accommodate to anything—illness, cruelty, injustice, stupidity, violence, even death. Accommodating to disaster. Personally I have not yet learned to do this. But this is just another lesson that must be learned—and by God, I'm going to learn it! (*In the spirit of high resolve, she resumes the task of putting things where they belong*) Come on!—we've got to do it!—help me!

LUCAS: Are you cuckoo?

CARRIE: We've got to clean up or slit our throats? Which?

LUCAS: Can we do both?

CARRIE: In what order?

(*Energizing herself, she claps her hands as if bringing a class to order; she is a cheery schoolteacher*) Okay, down to work, down to work!

LUCAS: (*Quietly*) This is dumb, honey.

CARRIE: Let's clean up, sweetheart! Pull the pieces together!

(*Clapping her hands again*) Quickly now—and no complaints!—get the job done! Order out of chaos!

(*Stillness. She stops pumping up her enthusiasm. Nobody moves. He speaks as soothingly as possible.*)

LUCAS: Honey . . . this place is probably not salvageable.

CARRIE: Don't say "this place" as if it were inanimate.

LUCAS: It *is* inanimate.

CARRIE: It's our home.

LUCAS: It was. But it's perched on the tip of a palisade that's about to fall into the ocean.

CARRIE: I'm not giving it up, Lucas.

LUCAS: We'll build somewhere else, honey. More inland. Safer. Everybody told us not to build so close to the ocean. Well, now we know—and we won't do it again. We'll take our insurance money and build on higher ground this time—

CARRIE: —and write the rest of this off.

LUCAS: Yes—we have to.

CARRIE: How about the memories?

LUCAS: You don't have to write them off—you take the good ones with you.

CARRIE: You taught Amy to swim in the ocean. That was quite a feat—learning to swim in the ocean—! And we had a swing on the beach—(*She shouts to the imaginary Amy*) Don't swing so high, honey! Amy—stop—don't swing so high! Oh, look at you, look at you, up in the clouds! Not so high, honey, not so high! (*Back to Lucas, with slight worry and vast pride*) Isn't she splendid? She's fearless—that little tiger is fearless. (*Quietly*) Can't we save part of it, Lucas? This side of the house doesn't look too bad. We can board up the entrance to the porch. Can't we save just the *living* part of it?

LUCAS: (*Carefully*) If any part can be saved, we're not the ones to make that judgment.

CARRIE: Who makes it?

LUCAS: The honchos.

CARRIE: It's our house—we're the honchos.

LUCAS: No, I mean the insurance guys, the contractors, the zoning board.

CARRIE: They'll drag their feet.

LUCAS: Patience, lovey, patience.

CARRIE: I wish I could talk to my sister. She's smart about these things—and very experienced. I'll try to get her. Where's my phone? What'd that sonofabitching storm do with my telephone—where's my phone?

LUCAS: The phones aren't working.

(*But she is not listening. She is single-mindedly, compulsively searching through the debris and at last—hurray!—she finds the telephone.*)

CARRIE: *Voila!*

LUCAS: Honey, the phones aren't working.

CARRIE: She has a new number. Do you have Delia's new number?

LUCAS: Carrie—listen to me—the phones are dead. They are not working.

CARRIE: Or Amy—I wish I could call Amy. (*She comes to terms with the fact. She speaks mostly to herself*) But the phones aren't working. (*She slowly puts the phone down, then carefully surveys the desolation*) Well, no use stalling. We've already helped the place. Let's push some more stuff around.

LUCAS: You're just kidding yourself, Carrie. Let's just go.

CARRIE: (*With subdued dismay*) What do you mean, "let's just go"?

LUCAS: Leave it.

CARRIE: (*Unable to face the despair*) *Leave it?*—leave the place to looters and vandals?

LUCAS: There aren't any looters and vandals. Dozens of state troopers are policing the Highway.

CARRIE: Good. Then, it'll be a safe place to sleep.

LUCAS: Sleep? Where?

CARRIE: Here.

LUCAS: But the whole bedroom wing is gone.

CARRIE: (*A bit helter skelter*) Who says we need a bedroom wing? Is that an absolute requirement, a bedroom wing? Is it a sacred law that we can't lie down and shut our eyes in anything but a bedroom wing? What happens if we do? Do we get arrested?

LUCAS: (*With careful deliberateness*) There's no place to sleep, Carrie.

CARRIE: We can sleep on the floor. My God, didn't you ever go camping? *Camping!* (*Singing*) Ol' MacDonald had a farm, ee-i-ee-i-o! *Camping!* We can clear a little space—right here on the floor, and before you know it—being as tired as we are—we'll be fast asleep, and thank God this day is over! Now come on, Lucas!

(*She has been shoving furniture around. She is not being particularly systematic about it, just energetic. The energy of desperation.*)

LUCAS: Carrie, stop it. You know damn well we can't sleep here tonight. Let's try to be sensible.

CARRIE: What's more sensible?—that sickening motel?—the Oxnard What?

LUCAS: Oxnard Sea and Surf—it wasn't so terrible.

CARRIE: It had bedbugs, Lucas.

LUCAS: Honey, you decided you wouldn't like that motel when we were still a mile away from it.

CARRIE: I made my mind up when I saw the trashcans overflowing on the sidewalk and the red necks throwing beer cans. And then I made my mind up when we entered the bedroom and saw the condoms on the bedposts.

LUCAS: Placed there, I'm sure, by a civically responsible management—in the spirit of public hygiene.

(*Silence*) It's okay—we'll find another place.

CARRIE: We tried, Luke. They're all filled up. There are hundreds of people who are worse off than we are. We'll just have to make do with what we've got.

LUCAS: There isn't even any water to brush our teeth with.

CARRIE: Bottled water!

LUCAS: Yes—we forgot.

CARRIE: The bar!—there might be some seltzer in the bar.

LUCAS: The bar's gone. It went with the bedrooms.

CARRIE: (*Calling to a nonexistent bartender*) Make mine a martini!

LUCAS: A Gibson!

CARRIE: With an extra little onion in it.

LUCAS: I'll settle for the onion. Story of my life: settle for the onion.

CARRIE: Well, for tonight, we'll just have to settle for the floor. Now come on, Lucas—help me clear away some of this stuff.

(*Lucas turns to the audience.*)

LUCAS: I helped her clear a space for sleeping on the floor. Having been married to Carrie for twenty-three years, I have learned to make my peace with a number of irrational ideas. Not that she's crazy—she's not. Well, not certifiably. In fact, she's a very rational woman. She's reliable, she's there on time, she loses her temper only when it's justifiable, she's still quite wonderful in bed, she attends faculty meetings. Her students are in love with her. They go to her for advice, not about the Sherman Act or the Dred Scott Decision but about what keeps them awake at night. She agonizes with them, and sometimes it does make her seem a little crazy. And she has other madnesses. . . . But so do I. My major craziness is Carrie. I adore her. She is my whole life. The more difficult our lives together, the more I love her. If you ask me if I would die for her—that's quite a question—yes, I think I would.

CARRIE: Guess what—there's some good news.

LUCAS: Really?—what is it?

CARRIE: My files—in the alcove—they're mostly intact.

LUCAS: Oh, good, Carrie—everything?

CARRIE: The top drawers—the Kentucky days—youth and education—they're both bone dry. But the middle years with Lincoln are a little damp, and so is the early time in the White House. But they're all safe.

LUCAS: Are you relieved or disappointed?

CARRIE: If anything had to be swept off the cliff, why couldn't it be Mary Todd Lincoln?

LUCAS: You can still give her a push.

CARRIE: You mean by actually writing it.

LUCAS: Yes.

CARRIE: Did you know that ever since the beginning of time, none of the research for works unwritten is ever thrown away? It's all on file on the Internet. You look it up under Stillborn. Just think of all those research babies that never had a chance.

LUCAS: If you're that guilty about it, you'd better write it.

CARRIE: I guess I'll have to—I've had a directive.

LUCAS: A disaster happens, and you look for a directive—it's got to *mean* something. But it doesn't. It's wanton and it's meaningless. It's just a freak of nature—it doesn't signify a goddamn thing. Zilch.

CARRIE: Then why do I have the feeling I've been warned?

LUCAS: Warned?—oh, come on.

CARRIE: No—really, Luke. I've had a clear and imperative warning: Either throw the stuff away or *use* it! No more shit-kicking! Clear your desk and write the goddamn biography!

LUCAS: Bravo! Sit down—I'll bring you a pencil. (*Everything stops. She looks at him; she sees him.*)

CARRIE: Do you know how angelic you are?

LUCAS: Is this a new subject or variations on the old?

CARRIE: Putting up with my idiocies, my moods, my poking around in sloppy alternatives—like a rat in a garbage dump. Do you know what a wonderful person you are?

LUCAS: I say that to myself every single day—before lunch. I go down to the men's room of the Artcraft Commercial Design Product Studio and I look at my shining visage in the mirror and I say, "What a wonderful person you are, what an angel, what a cherub out of the sacred reaches of heaven!" And then I flush the john.

CARRIE: (*Pointing*) What's that?

LUCAS: What's what?

CARRIE: Sticking up there—behind the couch.
(*She goes for it*) Oh my goodness! Oh my goodness, goodness—honey, look at it!
(*She lifts the object. It is an oil painting on canvas. The Green Clown. Realistic, primitive, not very good. It has been torn, a single cut, as if—purposely—damaged.*)

LUCAS: Holy Moses—The Green Clown.

CARRIE: Look at it—it's been slashed.

LUCAS: Jesus . . . right across the face.

CARRIE: Oh Luke—he's wrecked, he's ruined!

LUCAS: No, honey, it's only a tear.

CARRIE: The word "tear" is spelled the same way as tear.
(*She makes the distinction between the sounds "tare" and "teer"*) Poor Amy. She'll cry like a baby when she sees what's happened to it.

LUCAS: No need for tears, honey. It's a clean cut, it can be mended.

CARRIE: No it can't . . .

(*A moment*) . . . and I'm going to tell you why. Because I hate that picture. I've always hated it.

LUCAS: Tell you a secret—me too.

(*A moment of realization, then they start laughing; they howl with laughter. As they do, Delia Larkin appears. She is Carrie's older sister, modish without being silly about it, more striking without being beautiful.*)

DELIA: What the hell's so freakin' funny?

CARRIE Deelie!

DELIA: Hello, babe. Hi, Lucas!

LUCAS: Hello, Delia.

CARRIE: Oh, Deelie, Deelie!

(*Carrie and Delia are embracing and weeping and laughing in a kind of controlled hysteria.*)

DELIA: Your phone is dead. I've been trying to reach you for hours—but it's dead.

LUCAS: Yes, we know.

DELIA: (*She looks around*) Oh murder, what a wreck! How about yourselves—are you having breakdowns and collapses?—you don't seem to be. Let me look at you—are you fat, are you thin?—is there anything about you I can criticize? No, not a damn thing. You're as perfect as peaches and I'm proud of you both.

(*Looking around*) My God, look at this place! Who's your interior decorator? Tell him that his new decor is not going to be widely popular. My God, what a mess!—what a hellforsaken mess!

CARRIE: Are you speaking as my sister or as my insurance agent?

DELIA: (*In a huff*) I am not an insurance agent—I am an insurance *broker*!

CARRIE: Oh, I'm sorry.

DELIA: No you're not. If you were really sorry you'd remember what I've told you a thousand times—*broker! B-r-o-k-e-r!*

CARRIE: Broker, broker, broker! I don't know why I always forget—and I promise you, the next time I make the same mistake, I'll cut my tongue out.

DELIA: Don't overdo it, sweetie. It's not really a point of ego.

(*She hurries downstage to address the audience. She is angry at Carrie and at herself.*)

DELIA: I'm lying—it *is* a point of ego. Everything's a point of ego. I'm a broker, not an agent—a *broker*. An agent works for a company—I work for myself! I'm an independent—I don't grovel, I don't make forms out in quadruplicate and I don't kiss ass. I make deals for all sorts of people with all sorts of money. I earn big fat commissions. I cheat, I take kickbacks, I am very very rich, and I would sell my soul for a weekend of quiet love and sweet contentment.

(*Adopting her happiest manner, she addresses them with high good cheer*)
Well, goddamn it, no fucking landslide's gonna beat my family!—look at
you, you're both marvelous!

CARRIE: Thank you, Deelie. We're not—but thanks.

LUCAS: Is Howard with you?

DELIA: No, Lucas, Howard is not *with* me—Howard is *against* me.

CARRIE: Oh no.

DELIA: Oh yes.

CARRIE: Why?

DELIA: Why—she asks me why. Why did the storm happen? Why can't I
find somebody I can tell my right age to?

CARRIE: I'm sorry, baby. What happened?

DELIA: I sent him back to his wife, that's what happened.
(*She turns and talks to the audience*) And good riddance to him! We've been
banging around for four years now, and suddenly one night—New Year's
Eve—he calls me and says he has finally left his wife. Happy New Year! I'm
so happy I can walk barefoot on the air! I'm a beautiful kite and he's sail-
ing me up in the bright blue sky! Happy days, I don't have to live alone anymore—he's going to move in with me! God knows, my house is big and luxo
and it's in the Sunday section of the San Diego Tribune. But then—oh murder, this is where the kite string breaks!—he tells me that he has taken an
apartment of his own, and he's not moving in with me—he's decided he's
the kind of person who should live alone, and watch the hockey game when
he feels like it, and leave the seat up. So I get very desperate and I start running down to Armand Gautier's torture salon and I lose thirty-two pounds
and change my hair and get a new makeup and learn to lower my voice so
I don't break people's eardrums. And what do you think?—he doesn't even
notice I've been changing. So we go on a weekend to the Eldorado, and I'm
whispering so low, he has to go like this with his ear—
(*She cups her ear with her hand*)—and at last I'm talking so low that I
can't talk at all. And I've got laryngitis from *not talking*! So we had a big
fight with him shouting and me going eek-eek-eek-eek! And I realize he
doesn't love me, he doesn't even like me, so that same week I go out and
get myself a new shrink. And one afternoon he's listening to me and I see
this sickly look on his face, like he's been eating rotten shrimp, and I realize that I am a widely disliked individual, and *even my shrink* doesn't
like me! And I wake up to the fact that the only person who really gives
a damn about me is my sister Carolyn—the only one—and I'm so grateful to her for hanging in there—and for loving me a little—and I love her
so much—!
(*She halts, to forestall tears*) I hate that she's unhappy and I hate that she's
in this dangerous house, and by Christ I'm going to do my best to get her
out of it!
(*With studied brightness, to Carrie*) So here's to love and kisses! How's
your book?

CARRIE: What book?

DELIA: That biography you were working on. About the president's wife. Molly Madison.

CARRIE: In the first place, I haven't started *writing* the book, I'm still on research. In the second place, her name is not *Molly* Madison, it's *Dolly* Madison. And in the third place, I wasn't writing about Dolly Madison, I was writing about Mary Todd Lincoln.

DELIA: Isn't she the same as Molly Madison?

(*As they all laugh*) Well, I figure if you can switch from Molly to Dolly, and if you can switch from Dolly to Mary, why don't you switch from Mary to Hillary?

CARRIE: What for?

DELIA: Sex. Where there's sex, there's bucks.

CARRIE: I don't think that's the first consideration of a historical biography.

DELIA: You're dead wrong, kid. The first consideration for anything is that it should sell. Who cares whether it's Molly or Dolly or Mary or Hillary?— as long as it's a best seller. Did you ever notice that "best seller" has the same first initials as "bullshit"?

CARRIE: I'll make a note of that.

DELIA: (*Busy, busy*) Outta here! I gotta get you both outta here! My car's parked just the other side of the police barrier. I've got an empty suitcase and a duffel bag in it. I'll go get them. Meanwhile, you guys—pull together whatever you need, whatever you can find—and we'll be off for San Diego.

CARRIE: No, wait—

DELIA: No waiting. It's dangerous here—we could all go slippity-doo-dah right into the ocean—so let's get the hell out.

(*In a rush*) I adore you, sweetie, now please do as I say.

(*She hurries off. Silence.*)

CARRIE: "I adore you, sweetie, now do as I say."

LUCAS: She said "please." Now, come on, honey, don't make it sound like tyranny. She wants to be generous.

CARRIE: And she loves me.

LUCAS: Well, she does. She's a good, warm soul, and she's not committing an actionable crime by inviting us to her house for a few days.

CARRIE: A few days. That's what they said to the Count of Monte Cristo when they threw him in the dungeon for thirty years.

LUCAS: I wouldn't say her house is exactly a dungeon. A freezer full of Häagen-Dazs, a TV on every wall, four sea-water jacuzzis, and fresh air pumped down from Oregon. Just think, if we go to San Diego, you can turn on the TV, and have a jacuzzi with Peter Jennings while guzzling chocolate and peanut brittle.

CARRIE: (*Unamused*) Yum, yum.

LUCAS: I think she's being very kind—and she's lonely—and it's a good-hearted offer in a time of emergency—and we ought to take her up on it.

CARRIE: Do we have to go on and on about leaving the house? I think that's what scares me the most.

LUCAS: Okay, hon. But sooner or later—

CARRIE: Sooner or later may never come.

LUCAS: Sooner or later is always here.

(*They smile wryly over this minor difference. She is facing alternatives, and quietly issues her article of faith:*)

CARRIE: I'm going to do my best to hang on to the house, Lucas.

LUCAS: (*With difficulty*) Let's not make a resolution we can't keep, sweetheart.

CARRIE: I'm going to keep it. Forever.

LUCAS: I don't know what forever means. I'm trying to figure out the next ten minutes.

CARRIE: (*Muted*) It's our dream house, Luke.

LUCAS: Yes, it was.

CARRIE: And it will continue to be. Luke, listen. After the first shock is over, it's really not as bad as it appeared to be. Take this room, for example: it's already better than it was when we first walked in here. What I mean— it's not a total loss. We can fix the house, Luke. We owe it something— we've got an obligation to it! We'll mend it—we'll heal it!

LUCAS: (*Carefully*) We may not be able to rebuild a ruined dream, honey. We may have to start a new one.

CARRIE: (*A battle with tears*) I don't think I can, Lucas. Oh, Luke, it was so beautiful once!

(*In a sudden shift*) Right there!—right there, where you're standing is where Amy stood when we played that game she made up—what was the name of it?

LUCAS: Whirligig.

CARRIE: Yes—that's it! (*To the imaginary Amy*) No, Amy, it's against your own rules! You've got to go *somewhere*—it doesn't matter where—but *somewhere*! Nowhere is not a destination!

LUCAS: (*Suddenly, without cue*) Sand-colored!

CARRIE: That was something else.

LUCAS: (*Arguing*) You're damn right it was something else! It was the perfect color!

CARRIE: Yes, but not for the terrace room!

LUCAS: You're wrong!—perfect for the terrace room!

CARRIE: You've got no taste!

LUCAS: Sand color! People come off the beach right onto the terrace. The terrace room should be an extension of the beach—that's all, just an extension!

(*A battle cry*) Sand color! What could be better than sand color?

CARRIE: Yellow.

LUCAS: No! A warm tawny buff. A seaside illusion. A beach. Sand color!

CARRIE: Yellow. A lovely, golden sunshiny yellow.

LUCAS: Peepee!

CARRIE: Not peepee—sunshine. Van Gogh. Fields of sunflowers in the sunshine. A Van Gogh yellow.

LUCAS: Van Gogh peepee.

(*Silence*)

CARRIE: I've forgotten. What color did it turn out to be?

LUCAS: A sandy shade of peepee yellow.

CARRIE: Awful, wasn't it?

LUCAS: Aren't compromises terrible?

CARRIE: Amy said compromises were neither here nor there—they're like getting ready to vomit.

(*They are suddenly convulsed with laughter. Which ceases on a dying fall. They are bereft; they are beaten. She is weeping silently as she looks down at the ocean; and so—hiding it—is he.*)

CARRIE: Look at that damn ocean. So sweet, so calm, so innocent. Like a baby under a blanket. That's what Amy said. (*Restless, unhappy*) Why doesn't she get in touch with us?—why doesn't she phone?

LUCAS: (*Muted*) The phones are down, honey.

(*Joby appears. Not yet middle-aged he appears older. A little man, dressed in worn and second-hand clothes. Homeless, but not exactly a beggar. The camera he carries, a Polaroid on a leather strap around his neck, does not exist. It is, like much that Joby "owns," imaginary. If allowed only one word to give him identity, the word is "happy." He laughs a lot; he giggles. But there's another side of him: his temper. He loses it from time to time.*)

JOBY: Hold it! Stand still! Don't move! Gonna take yer pitcher! Don't move now, don't move! Bbbbblllllbbbbb-bip!

(*He giggles delightedly*) Gonna be a fine pitcher! Now you just wait and see how nice and fine this pitcher gonna be! All my pitchers come out lookin' good. It's the nature of Joby's pitchers—smile and feel good—that's what people look like—smile and feel good! Now then—let's look and see what we got here.

(*He talks to the picture as he is extracting it—with care, with solicitude, much like a baby being born*) Come on now, sweetheart. Now come out nice and easy. Nice and shiny and easy. Now then—here we are!

(*He removes the imaginary snapshot from the imaginary camera. He looks at it with swooning delight*) Oh my God! Dear Lord above, ain't that a pretty pitcher? Dear Father in heaven, ain't they the smilin'est, sassiest two people that ever came out of a pitcher box!

(*He hands Carrie the picture*) Now you look at it and enjoy yourself, and then show it to him. Now tell me the truth—tell me God's truth—ain't that the prettiest pitcher you ever saw? *And free!* Absolutely *free*! You don't have to pay a nickel for it. It's all free—for old times' sake! Ain't that right—old times' sake?

CARRIE: (*Vaguely—does she know him?*) Yes . . . old times' sake.

JOBY: You don't reco'nize me, do you?

CARRIE: . . . Not really.

JOBY: And he don't, neither.

LUCAS: You look very familiar to me, but—uh—

JOBY: But you don't know me, huh? Well, why should you? It's been a number of years and you didn't see me but once or twice—and I guess I've changed a lot. I'm dirtier'n I used to be, and older and I guess I could do with a shave. But anyways, I'da thought you'd remember me because I saved your daughter's life.

(*A tight pause.*)

CARRIE: Amy?

JOBY: Yes—that was her name—Amy. I pulled her outta that wrecked car, I did. All bleedin' and cut by the windshield. And I called the Highway Patrol and the Sheriff—and they all went zoom! right off to the hospital. And saved that sweet girl's life!

CARRIE: (*Remembering him*) Joby.

JOBY: (*Laughing, giggling, and delighted*) Yep—that's me—Joby.

CARRIE: Yes—I remember you now.

LUCAS: I do too.

JOBY: Nice people! That's what you was then and that's what y'are now—nice people. And I heard you was having a little trouble again, with the lan'slide and all, so I thought I'd have a look at you and say, "Courtesy of the house! You can come and stay with me—courtesy of the house!"

CARRIE: (*Carefully*) Well, that's very kind of you, but what do you mean, stay with you?

JOBY: Which word don't you understand?

CARRIE: Do you have a house now, Joby?

JOBY: Do I need a house if I wanna say "Come and stay with me?" What I mean is I like you and I wanna do for you, and you're homeless—just like me.

CARRIE: We're not exactly homeless—well, at least only temporarily.

LUCAS: We're going to build somewhere else—more inland.

JOBY: That's a very good spirit, Mister. Like that bird, you know, comin' up outta the ashes. What was it now—some kind of an ostrich, wa'n't it?

LUCAS: Look, as you see we're very upset right now—

CARRIE: —we don't know which way to go—trying to save whatever we can—

LUCAS: But we don't need any help, really.

CARRIE: No, we don't.

LUCAS: But if we can help *you*—say with a dollar or two—

JOBY: (*Warning*) Now you keep your hand in your pocket. Money!—did I ast you for money?

LUCAS: No, not really.

JOBY: Not only "not really"! Not at all!

(*To Carrie*) Did I ast him for a few dollars? Did I ast him for a goddamn nickel? Now, come on—let's get to work.

(*He reaches for a drawing stand, picks it up and is starting to move it.*)

CARRIE: Don't touch that!

JOBY: I ain't stealin' it, I'm just movin' it.

CARRIE: It belongs to Amy. It's her drawing table.

JOBY: Well, she ain't drawin' on it now—and if you guys want a place to sleep—

LUCAS: What my wife means is that we don't really want any help.

CARRIE: (*Genuinely grateful*) Yes—thank you very much.

(*Silence. He doesn't go. They are a bit tense. Then Joby speaks quite lovely.*)

JOBY: You know the worstest thing about bein' homeless? It ain't that you don't have a good place to sleep—you can git a lot of good places—an empty store, a train station, a bench at the airport—. And it ain't that you can't get nothin' to eat. I picked some better meals outta garbage cans than my wife used to cook when she was sober. No, them ain't the things that's baddest about bein' homeless. What's baddest is nobody'll let you *do* for them. They don't trust you to do somethin' right or somethin' good. They think you turned stupid or lost the use of yer hands. Or they think you'll cheat 'em or fuck 'em over, or run off with their goddamn drawin' table.

CARRIE: No, no, it wasn't that—

JOBY: (*Angry*) Well, what the hell was it, then? I can move that table from this side of the room to that side just as good as you can. And I know a hell of a lot more about sleepin' in a junkyard than you do. In fact, you might say that after a storm or a tornado or an earthquake, I'm better fitten to be *alive* than you are! So why don't we start all over? Why don't you innerduce yourself to me and I'll innerduce myself to you, and we'll make a house outta this ungodly mess! My name is the same as it was five-six years ago—Joby Miller. What's yours, Mister?

(*Silence. Joby turns to Carrie*) I guess he's a little backward in tellin' his name. Can you step forward for him?

CARRIE: His name is Lucas. Lucas Campion.

JOBY: And what's yours?

CARRIE: Carrie Campion.

JOBY: Just like it used to be, right?

CARRIE: Just like it used to be.

JOBY: Pleased to meet yez again, both of you. And I forget now—what do you do for a livin'?

(*Quickly*) Just in case he's backward about that too, I'll tell you what *I* do. I'm a pitcher guy—what you might call a low-cost photographer. But what I used to be—I used to be an odd-jobs man. Fix anything. Light switch. Broken bicycle. New washers in old plumbing. My God, I spelled out my life in faucet washers. And I worked for a guy—he said I was the best damn odd-jobs-man he ever had. And I was too. But then one day somethin' rotten happened—I got fired. My boss says to me, "The reason I'm lettin' you go—it ain't that the *jobs* are odd—*you* are!"

(*Abruptly, he turns from them and directs himself to the audience*) He said

I was odd, and that hurt me. It really did—it hurt me bad. If I was doin' my work, what difference did it make if I was odd? What is this odd stuff that makes so much difference? Ain't the difference itself a pretty goddamn odd thing? What's wrong with bein' odd? Well, I been thinkin' about that over the years—and I seen a funny thing. As between the odds and the evens, I'm makin' out better bein' one of the odds than one of the evens. And, tell you the truth, tryin' to *act* like one of the evens is the oddest job of all.

(*With strong determination*) So I won't do it!

(*A moment*) Now. What do *you* do?

(*Silence*) Why ain't he talkin'? He do something bad for a livin'? Like a Mafia man?

CARRIE: He's what he used to be. He's still an artist.

JOBY: Stonecutter, right?

LUCAS: (*Uncomfortable with this*) Well, I used to be a sculptor, yes. But I don't do that anymore.

JOBY: What do you do?

LUCAS: I—uh—I'm a commercial designer.

JOBY: Is that better or worse than bein' a stonecutter?

LUCAS: (*His discomfort increasing*) Well—it's different. For one thing, I no longer work for myself, I work for a company. And the object isn't to make something *I* like, but something *they* like.

JOBY: Somethin' useful.

LUCAS: Yes—exactly. Not that something useful can't also be something beautiful, but it appears you sell more *of* them if they're ugly.

JOBY: Like what?

LUCAS: Like—uh—well, like a one piece plastic toilet brush—or a garbage compactor that whistles when it's full.

JOBY: Whistles a song?

LUCAS: (*Amused*) No, just whistles. But "whistles a song"—that might be a new gimmick. We'll have to look into that.

JOBY: (*Also amused; having a good time*) I'll buy it if it whistles a song. And the terlet brush too. But *it* don't have to whistle. I figure if a terlet brush can be kinda pretty, that's plenty good enough—even if it can't whistle. That's my philosophy of life. Don't expect too much. Never expect a terlet brush to whistle.

LUCAS: That sets a very sensible limit, I think.

JOBY: Yes it does.

(*To Carrie*) How's Amy?

CARRIE: She's fine—she's just fine.

JOBY: Still paintin' them pitchers?

CARRIE: Oh yes—and more talented than ever! She'll be getting her Master of Fine Arts degree any day now—and guess what—tomorrow's her twenty-first birthday.

JOBY: Twenty-one years old—my-oh-my-oh-my! I'll have to go and git her

somethin'. A present—a real nice present—have to bring her somethin'.
(*He grins*) Write any books lately?

CARRIE: No, not lately, no.

JOBY: Teacher, ain't you?

CARRIE: Yes. I teach history.

JOBY: You teach history what?

(*He bursts into laughter again*) You get it? I just made a joke. She said she
teaches history, and I said—

LUCAS: (*Affably*) We got it, Joby.

JOBY: (*Turning to Carrie*) I'm sorry if you think I was makin' fun of you teachin'
history. I wasn't. I like history. I like it a lot. So long as nobody tells me I gotta
believe it—there's nothin' I like better than a good juicy hunka history. It's like
a story—you know?—it's like a fairy tale. I just love the hell out of a fairy tale.

CARRIE: (*Quietly*) Me too.

JOBY: You mean you don't have to believe it?

CARRIE: Not as much as I used to.

JOBY: You sound a little sad about that.

CARRIE: Yes, I guess I am.

JOBY: Then why do you go on doin' it?

CARRIE: It's . . . complicated.

JOBY: Not to me it ain't. You mean you wake up every mornin' and you go
down there to that high school—

CARRIE: College.

JOBY: —and you teach history out of a book you don't believe what it says?
Well, why do you do that? What's in it for you?

(*She doesn't know the answer, but she doesn't want to slough him off.*)

CARRIE: Continuity.

JOBY: I don't know what that means.

CARRIE: It doesn't matter.

JOBY: (*A sudden and surprising outburst of anger*) Yes, it does matter! You
took the trouble to say somethin' to me, I guess you want me to understand it. Don't you?

CARRIE: Yes, I guess I do.

JOBY: Then whyn't you talk with words I know what they mean? What the
hell is "continuity"?

CARRIE: It's my notion of history.

JOBY: I still don't get it.

LUCAS: It means if she can become part of the past, she might become part
of the future.

JOBY: Yeah . . . I think I know what that means, I think I do.

(*To Carrie*) Is that what you mean?

CARRIE: Yes, kind of.

JOBY: So that's what we ain't got between us, right? We ain't got no continuity. No history. We didn't go to the same school, we didn't learn how
to spell *cat* from the same blackboard, and your old lady didn't steal no

food stamps. Hell, man, I didn't even get no education. I got thrown out of the Consolidated High School of South Hillsbury for takin' my peter out in the schoolyard.

LUCAS: .... Is that what you did?

JOBY: (*Angry*) No I didn't! It was a big lie!

LUCAS: In—uh—what way was it a lie?

JOBY: I didn't take my peter out, I took my *finger* out!

LUCAS: You took your finger out of where?

JOBY: My pants! Like this!

(*He puts his arm in his trousers and sticks his finger out where his penis was meant to be seen. He wiggles his finger*) Now that looks like my peter, don't it? But it ain't—it's only my finger. And that's a whole different story! It don't really *look* like no peter—and it don't act like it. It'll wiggle and point, but it won't do what a peter will do! And there ain't no law says you can't stick your own finger outta yer own pants— never *was* no law like that! A fella's got a constitutional right to stick his finger out of his pants! But I got throwed outta school. Now I bet you never got throwed outta nothin'—right?—never got throwed outta nothin'.

LUCAS: Well, not for the same reason.

JOBY: But you *feel* like you got thrown out because you ain't chippin' stone no more, you're makin' terlet brushes. Is that it?

LUCAS: (*Wryly*) I don't think it's quite that simple, but it'll do.

JOBY: And she's tellin' lies about Roosevelt and Lincoln and why the hell we was in a war with guys that was littler than we are. Right?

CARRIE: More or less.

JOBY: So we're all different and we're all the same, and that means we're all mixed up because we got no history together, we got no past, we ain't even got the same *words*! so I think we better take and fix that right now!

LUCAS: (*Amused, interested*) How do we fix it?

JOBY: Well, if we ain't got a history together, we just make one.

CARRIE: Just make it?

JOBY: Make it—from scratch.

LUCAS: (*Trying to hide his amusement*) How do we do that?

JOBY: We act like we're kids together. We go back to the first grade—to kindygarden—to dancin' around in a circle—takin' hands! Take my hand, Carrie—come on, Lucas, take my hand!

LUCAS: (*Smiling*) What'll I do with it?

JOBY: Just *take* it, man—grasp a-hold of it.

CARRIE: (*Muted*) Take it, Lucas.

(*She quietly crosses and takes Joby's hand*) Come on, Luke.

JOBY: Yeah, come on, Luke. It ain't gonna hurt you to take my hand. Ain't nothin' wrong with it. It ain't got no disease or nothin'.

LUKE: Oh, I didn't mean—

JOBY: And it's clean! You can't count the number of times I go down to the ocean and wash my pinkies in the nice cool salt water of the Pacific Ocean. Take it—you can *feel* how clean it is—take it!

CARRIE: Luke—be a sport—

(*Lucas comes down to speak to the audience. He is amused, but also—not understanding why—agitated.*)

LUCAS: What are we doing, for Pete sake?—this is ridiculous. Is he making fools out of us—are we making fools of ourselves? Are we getting flipped out? What the hell are we doing, taking this kook's hand? Did our common sense break away with the cliff? What are we doing?

(*Carrie also hurries down and addresses the audience.*)

CARRIE: Why am I calling him crazy? Because he wants us to *believe* he is? What if he wants us to believe he's sane—would that be more convincing? Is there some absolute level of eccentricity you get to, and after you've reached it people call you a lunatic? Or is it all a play on words? What play? What game are we playing? Who's *It*?

(*Carrie and Lucas have been addressing the audience separately. Now, the next two speeches, they speak simultaneously.*)

LUCAS: What's going on here?—we have to hang on to something—hang on to something—what are we doing?

CARRIE: Ride with it—ride with it—play along as if you believe it—play the game— ride along with it!

(*As they emerge from the hectic shouting, they are all holding hands making, a circle, as gently, as innocently as if they were kindergarten children. And as they move around in the circle, they sing:*)

CARRIE, JOBY & LUCAS:
Ring around a rosie,
Pocket full of posies,
Sitting on a cozy,
All fall down!

(*The singing is shy, innocent, with an edge of embarrassment. Odd, idyllic. They are enjoying themselves.*

Delia appears, carrying a suitcase and a duffel bag. She looks at the eccentric spectacle. Puzzled, off balance, she's determined to be a good sport. She adopts a baby voice:)

DELIA: I brought milk and cookies—c'n I play too?

JOBY: (*His amiable self*) Sure—join in!—anybody can play!

CARRIE: (*Embarrassed*) We were—well—I don't know what we were doing, but—

(*Introducing*) This is my sister, Delia—and this is Joby.

DELIA: (*A big friendly smile*) Hey—hi there!

JOBY: (*Holding up his imaginary camera*) You're pretty—hold still.

DELIA: (*Goodnaturedly*) "You're pretty hold still" is what the guy says when he pushes you into the trunk of the car.

JOBY: Oh, not me—I just wanna take your pitcher! Bbbbbllllllbbbbb-*birk*!

Now you just wait a little half second of a minute and you'll see the purtiest pitcher you ever saw in your whole life.

DELIA: (*Cordial, friendly*) If you guys would please tell me the rules of this game I promise I'll follow every one of them.

CARRIE: (*Lamely, but smiling*) It's just your picture, honey—that's all, just your picture.

JOBY: And here it is! Pitcher of a beautiful lady on enterin' a house nearly gone to the waves!

(*Handing her the imaginary picture*) With the compliments of Joby Miller.

DELIA: (*Genuinely confused, but playing the cheery good sport*) I don't know how to thank you for this. As an expression of gratitude, I can do a back-flip double somersault—or will you think I'm a nut?

JOBY: Why did you say that?

DELIA: Say what?

JOBY: Nut.

DELIA: Did I say that? I meant cuckoo—and I was saying it about myself.

JOBY: I know how that works. You say those bad things about yourself, but you really mean me, don't you?

DELIA: (*Conciliating*) I didn't mean that and I certainly didn't *say* that.

JOBY: (*Starting to give in to his anger*) I didn't *say* what you *said*, I *said* what you *meant*.

DELIA: (*Innocent and trying to stay friendly*) Somewhere along the road, did I go to Cleveland?

JOBY: (*Getting angrier*) See that?—she's makin' fun of me. Calls me a nut and *treats* me like a nut!

DELIA: (*Nonplused and upset*) I didn't call you anything, for God's sake, nothing!

JOBY: Now she's callin' me *nothin'*! Now you take that back! Take it back, do you hear me?—take it back!

DELIA: (*Frightened*) Is this something we should do something about?

JOBY: I know what you mean by that—you mean am I dangerous!

DELIA: I didn't *say* that!

JOBY: (*Apoplectic*) No, I ain't dangerous and I ain't no nut! Now you take it back or I'll break somethin'!

(*He lifts Amy's lamp off the table.*)

LUCAS: Don't bother breaking that—it's already broken.

JOBY: (*His rage is unabated*) I'll break it again! I am not a nut! I am a friend of the family! I am a very good friend of the family! Better than she is!

DELIA: I don't have to be a friend—I'm her sister!

JOBY: Yeah, and you're Amy's aunt. And as an aunt, you ain't worth two beans and a fart! Where the hell were you when Amy had her accident? Why di'n't you show? Why di'n't you make a phone call or send a flower? No, you was somewhere the hell-and-gone in upstate Africa or the South Pole of Portugal!

DELIA: (*Defensive*) I was in the Greek city of Athens, tending to a very sick love affair!

(*Suddenly turning to Carrie and Lucas*) Why the hell do I have to excuse myself to this dingaling? What the hell's going on here?

CARRIE: Exactly what you see. We're in serious trouble. We were in serious trouble once before and Joby was very helpful. He's offered to be helpful again.

DELIA: In return for which?

JOBY: In return for which you c'n kiss my kazoo.

(*Suddenly realizing he's making a botch of it, he starts hitting himself*) Oh dammit, dammit! Why can't I learn how to talk to you people? I don't know how to answer yer questions! I don't know how to fight you off so you'll let me alone! I don't know how to *give* nothin' without I get conked on the head for it! I don't know how to *be* or what to *say*?

(*Deeply distressed, he is on the verge of tears. They are surprised by this genuine show of emotion, and touched by his frank inability to handle his mental difficulty. Also, they are namelessly ashamed. Silence for a moment. . . . Now Carrie takes over.*)

CARRIE: Joby, would you move that coffee table back against that wall over there—what remains of it, the wall I mean? Would you do that, please?

JOBY: (*Relieved, grateful*) Sure I will.

CARRIE: Lucas, help me with this couch, will you?

(*Carrie, Lucas and Joby start rearranging the furniture.*)

DELIA: Wait a minute. Just hold everything, everybody just hold everything. What the devil are we doing?

CARRIE: We're making ourselves a place to sleep. The couch is still wet, unfortunately, but we can get the floor dry enough—and I'm hoping the pillows in the hallway closet won't be too damp. Also, there are some blankets in the trunk—or I *think* there are some blankets—and an old quilt, as I remember—

DELIA: Wait a minute—hold it—you've *got* a place to sleep. A nice warm dry ballroom-sized bedroom in a huge imitation Frank Lloyd Wright type house in one of the snobbier sections of San Diego. And right outside your humongous plate glass window there's the biggest fucking pink camellia bush you ever laid your eyes on! Now, stop all this stupid nonsense and this dipsydoodle ring-around-a-rosie and let's pack a few things and get the hell out of here!

CARRIE: (*Placating*) Delia—honey—I do appreciate your coming—and your sweet invitation—and you know how I love camellias—but it doesn't seem we're going to make it to San Diego—not tonight anyway—

(*Delia hurries down to speak to the audience. She is more deeply upset than she wants Carrie to see.*)

DELIA: Why is she turning me down? She's in terrible trouble—and I came here to help her—why is she giving me the lumps? Maybe I was wrong about her liking me—maybe she doesn't. Why should she be any different from the rest of the world? But what has she got against me, when I can't bear to see her hurt? Are we still holding grudges against one another? How long can we quarrel about who gets the blue dress with the pearl buttons and who gets the ugly brown one with the eggplant collar and cuffs? She's pretty and she doesn't *need* the pretty dress, but I do. Oh, do I need it! What if she doesn't really like me—who've I got left? If she only loved me half as much as I love her—!

(*An instant*) These days, there's a lot of talk about contagious diseases—and how important it is not to get too close to somebody who's got something that's catching. Well, the most contagious disease of all is unhappiness—and boy, am I infected with it! No wonder nobody wants to come near me. Not only the others—even my sister, when she really *needs* me! Keep your distance, everybody—that Delia gal has broken out into a bad case of unhappiness!—she's dying of it!

(*On the verge of falling apart, she starts to reassemble herself. She is now her normally brash self—raucous, studiedly vulgar. Loudly, to Carrie:*) All right, kiddo—pull your shit together because you're coming with me! I bought that fucking camellia bush expressly because it's your favorite flower—come and take a look at it! And I mean now! So you waltz yourself off to the bathroom right this minute, little sister, you wash your pretty face, you brush your pearly teeth, you take a leak, and off we go to safety and San Diego. (*Silence. Nobody moves.*)

DELIA: What's happening?

(*Another pause*) What's happening is that nothing's happening, that's what's happening.

(*Another pause*) Why do I exert my maximum generosity and my minimum bad temper, and nobody is listening to me?

JOBY: She's not going.

DELIA: You stay out of it.

JOBY: She wants you to know that she appreciates the camellia bush, but she ain't going.

DELIA: (*Under utmost control*) Carolyn, I haven't been able to figure out who this standby is, but you certainly don't expect me to deal with him, do you?

CARRIE: No, I don't. Joby, please. Delia, I appreciate your coming—honestly I do—but we're staying here. So please go.

DELIA: No. I will not go anywhere without you. This house is dangerous. Any hour now, it's gonna slide into the friggin' ocean!

JOBY: No, it ain't!

DELIA: No it ain't what?

JOBY: No it ain't gonna slide into no friggin' ocean. It's got five pilin's. Four of 'em are okay. And the fifth one was wobbly, so I put sandbags under it. Seven sandbags—swiped 'em myself and lugged 'em myself, and now the pilin' is as tight as a pig's ass!

DELIA: You may be a specialist on pig's asses, but I'm a specialist on houses. I'm an insurance broker. I've paid off two fallen palisades and one earthquake. I know faults—I am a top guru on faults—I am a heart-kidney-and-lung man where faults are concerned. And this house has a dozen of them. It has the added complication of belonging to my sister and brother-in-law for whom I have a deep concern and an undeserved affection. So would you please leave the premises.

JOBY: No, I won't.

TULLY'S VOICE: I'm afraid you'll have to, Joby.

(*Tully Pines, the deputy sheriff, has appeared at the doorway.*)

TULLY: Get going, Joby. Hello, Carrie—hi, Luke.

(*Pointing to Delia*) Who's this?

CARRIE: My sister, Delia Larkin. Sheriff Pines.

TULLY: *Deputy* Sheriff. (*Turning to Joby*) I told you to get moving, Joby.

JOBY: I ain't *got* to get movin' just because you *tell* me to get movin', Tully. I di'n't do nothin' wrong. I ain't trespassin' and I ain't sleepin' on no public property, and I ain't got my dick out in no public places. So you don't have to whack me across the soles of my feet and tell me to wake up and get goin'!

TULLY: They tell me you've just swiped eight sandbags off the town embankment.

JOBY: Seven.

TULLY: (*To the others*) You all heard him admit to swipin' seven sandbags.

(*To Joby*) I can lock you up for theft of county and federal property.

JOBY: I didn't theft nothin'!

(*Holding his arms up in the air*) You can search me—I ain't got no seven sandbags on my person.

(*He turns to Carrie and Lucas*) I don't have to go if you don't tell me to go. And I hope you won't do that. Because I can help you.

CARRIE: (*On the edge of hope*) How, Joby?

JOBY: You didn't lose the whole house, you just lost part of it. And I can help you save what's left. Take that side porch, for example. It's standin' there like a cripple on one leg! But I can shore up the other ones! All it'll take is a few two-by-fours, a hammer and some nails. And I can do it!

LUCAS: Don't get her hopes up, Joby.

JOBY: Why shouldn't I get her hopes up? I ain't sayin' I can bring back what's gone into the ocean, but I can save what's left.

(*Brightly, energetically*) Get the spirit goin', that's what I can do—get the spirit goin'!

(*A silent instant.*)

CARRIE: Do it, Joby.

JOBY: Thank you. I'll go and find some two-by-fours.

(*He hurries out. A pause.*)

LUCAS: I'm afraid that was a mistake.

TULLY: Yes, I think so.

CARRIE: Why?—what harm can he do?

LUCAS: What's the line? "A false hope is a false friend."

TULLY: Look—Carrie—Lucas—I think it's a bit too late to be hopin' for anything. I don't know what the hell you're still doin' in this house. You should be a long way out of here.

DELIA: (*To Carrie and Lucas*) There—you see?

(*To Tully*) I'm glad you came by, Officer. I'm handling their insurance on this residence. And I've been telling them exactly what you're telling them. Only now it's official. I take it you're condemning the property?

CARRIE: You take it wrong, Delia—he's not condemning anything! We've known Tully for a long time. He's our friend. He helped us with Amy's accident—and we see him often. He's not about to condemn our house. Are you, Tully?

DELIA: Wait a minute! It's to your *advantage* if he condemns it!

LUCAS: How so?

DELIA: If the town or the county or the federal government condemns your property, the insurance company has no recourse. Read your policy, for Pete sake! If your residence is totally condemned, they've got to pay you every last dollar you ever put into it.

CARRIE: We don't want every last dollar. We just want enough money to help us fix it up, restore it to what it used to be.

DELIA: Then you're at the mercy of contractors and appraisers and insurance investigators and lawyers. And you don't wind up getting what you lost, you wind up with a signed quit claim and twenty cents! So I beg you—Carrie—Luke—stand aside and let this nice sheriff man post his condemned notice, and let's all clear out with our skins.

CARRIE: (*Anxious*) You're not going to condemn the house, are you, Tully?

TULLY: (*Quietly*) You don't see me postin' a sign, do you?

CARRIE: Thank you, Tully, thank you.

TULLY: I don't say it won't happen. If the building board says it's condemned, well then the zoning board will condemn it. And there's not a helluva lot I can do about it.

DELIA: But you can have an influence, Sheriff, you know very well that you can change a few people's minds.

TULLY: Sometimes maybe. Not often.

DELIA: Well, if you're a friend of the family—

CARRIE: (*Upset*) Delia, I wish you wouldn't start *working* people.

DELIA: (*Also upset*) What the devil do you mean, "working people"? I'm not doing it to be mean, Carrie. I'm doing it for you and Luke—you're my *family*! And it's not as though I'm doing something behind your back—I'm being perfectly aboveboard about it. I'm just trying to help you, that's all, just trying to help you.

CARRIE: (*Relenting*) I know you are. I'm sorry, honey.

DELIA: You don't really mean you're going to sleep here?

CARRIE: We're going to try, Deelie.

TULLY: You're welcome to come over to my place, you guys.

CARRIE: Thank you, Tully—that's very kind—but—I know it's crazy—but I don't want to leave—I can't leave—

TULLY: You'll have to face it, Carrie.

CARRIE: (*An outburst*) "You'll have to face it!" I think those words are the ugliest words in the English language!

TULLY: (*Angry but quiet*) You'll have to face it—the time can come when this house will have to go.

CARRIE: (*Losing her temper*) Don't *say* that, don't *say* that!

TULLY: I'm not sayin' it—Nature's sayin' it!

CARRIE: The hell with Nature!

TULLY: You know, you environmentalists make me sick. You're all on the side of Nature—you're Nature's friend, you're Nature's goodbuddy. You're on a dozen committees—Save the Land, Save the Atmosphere, Save the Red-crested Tiddlymouse, Save the Triple-eyed Wallabus. But when it comes down to it, you don't respect Nature at all. Nature wants to take this land back from you—and why shouldn't it?—it's got a damn good right to it! It's giving you a clear and fair warning to get the hell out of here! Why don't you respect it? Why don't you just get up and go?! No, you just hang on to your little handful of dirty mud on the legal principle of Knucklehead's Domain—until you wreck the land and freak out your fortunes and break your goddamn hearts!

DELIA: Why don't you make them go?

TULLY: Because the law hasn't told me to—not yet. And until it does—they're my friends. But it ain't my business to fight some good sense into them. Because maybe their sense is smarter than mine—and maybe they *can* fix this house. But even if they're putting up a foolish fight, I respect the dumb guts it takes to fight it.

CARRIE: Thank you, Tully.

TULLY: I got a trial in the morning, but I'll drop by in the afternoon.

(*To Delia*) Pleased to meet you, I think.

DELIA: Likewise, I think.

(*He departs.*)

CARRIE: Go home, Deelie. Thanks for coming, but go home.

DELIA: If you think I'm going back to my Kingdom Come in San Diego before I get you crackpots settled in this hellhole, you're just bankrupt in the brain.

LUCAS: Don't worry about us, Deelie—we can take care of ourselves.

DELIA: Oh, you can, can you? The investigators will be here tomorrow, and the appraisers. Do you know who they are—they're the Gestapo, they're the KGB. They'll eat your heart out, they'll make liars out of both of you. They'll make you feel that you're not *victims* of the storm, but that you *perpetrated* it! . . . I'm hanging around—I'll find a room somewhere.

CARRIE: Stay away from Oxnard. There's a motel called the Sea and Surf. It caters to creeps.

DELIA: Tonight I qualify.

(*She goes. Silence. Utter stillness. Carrie changes the position of a side chair—changes it just a little. Lucas adjusts the coffee table—barely a hair. At last, out of their desolation:*)

CARRIE: I wish Amy would call.

(*Pause. Silence. Stillness*) I hope she comes home for her birthday.

(*He is responding, but almost invisibly, and in silence. He continues to move things around, to make a little order out of the chaos. Carrie has lifted up the torn picture of The Green Clown. She is looking at it forlornly. The stillness lengthens. The light fades.*

The state troopers and the Sheriff's deputies are blowing their whistles, flashing their flashlights, shouting at the rubbernecking drivers while the latter yell and honk their horns as a retort to the officers' commands. A siren sounds, getting further and further away. The lights and sounds dwindle and retreat.

When the lights come up again, there are some blankets on the floor. It is late in the afternoon. Delia sits in a wooden armchair, waiting. Tully enters. He carries a large bulging shopping bag, and a good-sized object that looks like a plastic picnic box.)

TULLY: Hi, anybody home?

DELIA: (*Weary with waiting*) I'm home.

TULLY: Carrie's last class on Thursday is generally over at five o'clock. And Lucas should be home by now.

DELIA: Well, guess what—they're not.

TULLY: You been waitin' long?

DELIA: Since the Civil War, I think. What've you got in the bag?

TULLY: Food.

DELIA: That's nice. Very thoughtful. And what's that huge, economy-size plastic thing?—a piano?

TULLY: It's for heatin' up the food. Runs on house current or on batteries, take your choice.

DELIA: Steak delmonico flambé.

TULLY: With fries. Comin' up.

DELIA: You're very—uh—outgoing with them.

TULLY: (*Studiedly casual*) Oh, I'll go out for friends.

DELIA: You see them often?

TULLY: Yeah, kinda. I drop in. Just for a beer, you know.

DELIA: Beer—is that allowed?

TULLY: Non-alcoholic beer. . . . The insurance guys been around?

DELIA: Appraiser and investigator.

TULLY: Wha'd they say?

DELIA: Oh, they say this won't hurt any more than a pinprick, then behind your back they give you a mastectomy.

TULLY: Behind your back?—is it a new kind?

DELIA: . . . Did you bring a condemned sign with you?

TULLY: No, I didn't.

DELIA: If you're really their friend, don't you think you ought to nudge that along a little?

TULLY: No, I don't.

DELIA: Then maybe you're *not* really a friend.

TULLY: (*With quiet dignity*) I don't think I have to do any provin' around here.

DELIA: Which of them is really your friend—Carrie or Lucas?

TULLY: Either or? Only one to a customer?

DELIA: I suspect, from the way you look at her, it's really Carrie.

TULLY: Yeah, I'm nuts about her. The minute she leaves her husband, I'll tear her clothes off and jump her like a rabbit.

DELIA: You think if you admit it, you'll disarm me into thinking you wouldn't?

TULLY: Jesus, you're so lost in your head, you need a road map.

DELIA: (*Bridling a little*) I don't need a road map to figure out that if you were really their friend, you would herniate yourself to see that this house is condemned.

TULLY: Just jam a padlock on their life, right?

DELIA: Not on their life, on their house.

TULLY: This house is her life—I wouldn't have the heart.

DELIA: Have the heart, did you say? Is that a common expression among law enforcement officers?

TULLY: It's not a common expression anywhere.

DELIA: (*Studiedly intellectual*) What I mean is, I always heard that police officers and constables and sheriffs—the way they became cops—and how they derived their authority—was by not referring to their hearts. And that helped them to become first class bullies and sadists, which is what they want to be. I always heard that.

TULLY: And I always heard that what insurance brokers broke was wind. In church.

DELIA: Strange, what people hear, isn't it?

TULLY: Very strange.

DELIA: In church, huh?

TULLY: That's what I heard.

DELIA: It hasn't happened yet. Not in church.

TULLY: You're younger than you look. Are you only five years older than your sister?

DELIA: Go to hell.

TULLY: Is that where you spent the night?

DELIA: You could say that. Oxnard Sea and Surf.

(*He whistles.*)

DELIA: A whistle doesn't describe it.

TULLY: They still got condoms on the bedposts?

DELIA: Twin beds, four bedposts on each, eight condoms.

TULLY: I guess the management puts them there as a kind of public accommodation, like ice for your Pepsi.

DELIA: Oddly enough, I didn't really mind them. They're all different colors. Some of them are pretty.

TULLY: What's your favorite?

DELIA: (*She looks at him a moment*) Is this going to make any difference in our relationship?

TULLY: It might.

DELIA: I think I favor the shocking pink.

TULLY: That's kind of like a healthy flesh color, right?

DELIA: Reasonably healthy.

TULLY: Yeah, that's my favorite color too.

DELIA: Yes, I can imagine it being worn with flattering effect.

TULLY: Thank you—that's quite a compliment.

DELIA: Are you married?

TULLY: No, I'm not. I used to be married, but my wife got sick and passed away. So I never got married anymore.

DELIA: You figure if they're going to blow the whistle on you and get sick and die—the hell with them.

TULLY: Well, I wouldn't put it that crudely, but yes, that's my opinion.

DELIA: You don't think—all things considered—and vis-a-vis humanity— that's rather a tight anus?

TULLY: Could be, could be.
(*A moment. He is interested in her*) You were beginning to turn on, and suddenly you turned off. Right?

DELIA: Yes, kind of.

TULLY: Why?

DELIA: Because you're single.

TULLY: You mean you're more interested in me married than single?

DELIA: Yes, that's right.

TULLY: How does that work out?

DELIA: I don't go with single men—only married ones. Somehow, I get better mileage out of married men than bachelors. They last longer and they hold up better—talking obsolescence, depreciation and wear-and-tear. My average with bachelors is seventeen months and three days—and then they start to get moldy. My average with married men is four and a half years. The married ones come to me looking sad and droopy and end-of-the-line. And guilty, for some reason, as though it's the first day of school and they've just wet their pants. So I dry 'em out and giggle 'em up and I buy them a few bright ties, and I screw five or ten years off them and send them back to their wives. It works out very well. I get Christmas cards.

TULLY: (*Quietly*) You do, huh?

DELIA: Sure do.

TULLY: (*A statement, not a question*) You feel good about it.

DELIA: Oh yes I do. I figure I'm performing a public service. Filling a vacancy in the marriage cycle. I'm a reconditioner of men. I lube out their squeaks, I smooth out their dents, I give 'em a paint job. Then I send them back to their garages—with a short-term guarantee.

TULLY: Shame I don't have a garage to go back to.

DELIA: Yes it is. How about you?—things working out okay?—getting along with the womenfolk?—having a ball? I mean that in the plural, of course.

TULLY: I get along.

DELIA: How do you treat them? What do you talk about? Condoms?

TULLY: I'm sorry I started that line of discussion.

DELIA: What "line of discussion" would you start with?

TULLY: Food, I think. That's my best subject—food.

DELIA: Oh yes, food's a good subject. You can work up quite a rolling discussion on the subject of food.

TULLY: Yeah, quite a roller. Natural foods especially. There's a lot of dialog in natural foods.

DELIA: Fake butter versus honest-to-God margarine.

TULLY: Nice clean lake fish versus dirty bottom feeders. Free range chickens—ducks that still got the quack in them.

DELIA: And enzymes.

TULLY: Oh yes—enzymes. I'm very big on enzymes and how they'll catalyze your gizzard! And when I've proved that not only my heart's in the right place, but so are my taste buds and my intestines—I'm then ready to go in for the payoff.

DELIA: How do you do that?

TULLY: It's my best move.

DELIA: What is?

TULLY: I ask for a recipe.

DELIA: A recipe?

TULLY: Yeah, a recipe. Do you know how magical it is for a man to ask a woman for a recipe? In the first place, it's flattery—it's the finest hunk of flattery a man can dream up in his head. You're tellin' a woman that you like what she's put on the table for you, what she's doin' to your mouth and your guts and your balls and your belly. But it's more than that. You're tellin' the lady that you don't know how to cook that thing up for yourself. You're only a man in a kitchen, and you're fumblin' around with your sustenance, and you're makin' good ingredients taste like shit—and will she help you, will she be kind and talented enough to help you out of the garbage dump and into high heaven. And last of all you're telling her that you're eating alone-in-the-world and you're dying to have a woman around the house—and you're lonely.

(*She hears him wind up on a partially serious, quite genuine note, and isn't sure what to do with it. She goes the casual way.*)

DELIA: And that about does it, huh?

TULLY: That about does it.

DELIA: One easy step—kitchen to kip.

TULLY: That's a neat way of puttin' it.

DELIA: I guess you're too busy to notice, but there's a faintly unpleasant odor of sexism in the air.

TULLY: Sexism? How am I sexist?

DELIA: I don't know . . . watching you manipulate your pots and pans to that cunning masculine purpose . . .

TULLY: (*With a reserve of dignity*) I'll tell you about "that cunning masculine purpose." Before my wife got sick, I didn't know how to boil an egg. When the sickness hit her, I learned to cook so that I could feed her and tempt her to eat, and do my best to keep her alive. I didn't for one minute resent cooking for her and doing the dishes. What I resented was that she didn't get better. And after a while I had to face the fact that I could tear my heart out and cook it for her and she still wouldn't get better. . . . So . . . ultimately—as a cook—I failed. She died on me.

(*An instant*) I guess it was foolheaded of me to think that what I did in the kitchen would have the slightest effect on what happened in the bedroom, but what was sexist about it?

DELIA: I'll have to think about that. Give me a minute—or a month.

TULLY: Take whatever time you need.

(*Lucas enters. He's loaded up with a briefcase, a large brown envelope and three tubes of rolled-up plans, drawings and diagrams.*)

LUCAS: You know what the world is?—the world is a great big pit full of rattlesnakes and copperheads, and they're squirming and hissing and slithering around in there and they're gorging on these tiny little mice and the tiniest mice of them all are us!

DELIA: Had a great day, huh?

LUCAS: Oh, joyous!

(*Referring to the load he is carrying; there's no place to put it*) What the hell do I do with all this creepy crud?

(*Delia hurries to Amy's drawing board, removes her purse and briefcase from it, and the morning newspaper and the* New Yorker.)

DELIA: Here—put it here. Any special calamity?

LUCAS: No, just the normal nine to five. Design directors, clients, an assorted variety of hit men and enforcers. They start by telling you how sorry they are that your house has just slid into the ocean, and they wind up by strangling your grandmother. Hi, Tully.

TULLY: Anybody want me to lock up, I got the cuffs.

(*We hear Carrie's voice. It is lofty, loud and dithering with happiness.*)

CARRIE: Guess what! Guess what! Everybody, guess what! Amy's coming home!

(*She enters, still rocketing. She carries a huge bunch of daffodils and a bag that contains two bottles of champagne.*)

CARRIE: I got through to her—I finally got through to her. And she's coming home! She's cutting a few classes and she's on her way right now! Not tomorrow, not next month—*now!*—Amy's on her way home *right now!*

DELIA: (*Muted*) Take it easy, Carolyn.

CARRIE: *You* take it easy!

(*Handing her the daffodils*) Here—put these in water—keep them fresh! Find a vase somewhere or an empty coffee can—anything—aren't they beautiful, aren't they just fantab-beautiful?!

(*Handing Lucas the wine*) Here, Lucas—find some way to keep these cool, will you be a darling. If you can't find any ice, call Alaska—make a snow-drift—anything, everything—Amy's coming home! And what I thought was, we'd have a little champagne right here at home, and then we'd all traipse down to Santa Monica and go someplace for dinner—spicy stuff—hot peppers and chili—Amy loves chili—

TULLY: I brought you a lot of food.

CARRIE: Oh my goodness—you didn't! We can have her birthday dinner right here at home! Oh Tully, what a honey-bun you are!

TULLY: Chicken fricassee—I figure everybody likes chicken fricassee. And potato croquettes and garlic-broccoli. And a little raspberry custard desert. And if you want to warm the food and cool the dessert, you use this thing. It's called a Portokitch. It's a broiler and a refrigerator, both at once, and it's even got a little tiny microwave.

(*To Lucas*) I'll show you know it works.

LUCAS: I know how it works. I designed the case for it.

(*For Tully, the slightest sign of deflation, then elaborate, good-natured delight.*)

TULLY: You did?—well, hold my foot, that's wonderful! I hope it's real successful, Lucas. It's a real good product and I hope you hit the jackpot on it.

LUCAS: We're not making a dime on it. It costs too much. It's a dump.

TULLY: Well, dammit—no justice in the world. Unless you got a trick, some-way.

(*An instant*) I gotta leave now—night duty. But I brought you somethin' else. There's gonna be a Zoning Board Meeting on Tuesday night, and if you want to hang on to your house, you gotta convince them that you got a sensible way to fix it. Now there are a couple of ways—there's cantilevering and there's cement pilings into the palisades. They cost as much as you can count, but there's always a way of doin' it—and a few people have saved their houses. So I brought a couple of leaflets for you to study up on—here's one put out by the Portland Cement people—and this one's on cantilevers. Here—I brought two copies of each—for both of you. But most important—this.

(*He hands him a four-page official form*)

LUCAS: What is it?

TULLY: It's a questionnaire—for the Zoning Board. Now put your mind to it—be careful what you say. If you got any questions, give me a call.

LUCAS: (*Not too convincingly*) Thank you, Tully.

CARRIE: Oh, Tully, you're a dear. Did I call you a honey-bun?

TULLY: (*Pleased but embarrassed*) Quit it.

DELIA: With all gratitude for your food, and with all due respect for the neatness of your uniform, I think you're a first class shit.

TULLY: (*Pretending to write in his time book*) Do you? I'll put that on the report—how do you spell it?

DELIA: You know goddamn well that there's no way in the world they can rebuild this place. You know that their only decent chance is for you to condemn the place so they can start all over again! And all you're doing is sucking up to my sister's idiocy!

TULLY: (*Evenly and genuinely*) I don't call it idiocy. I call it bravery. She's trying to save some important part of her life. It's a dream. Now, I don't have anything to do with people's dreams—that ain't my job. But the law hasn't expressed itself as yet, and until it does, I can be an accessory to whatever she's hopin' for.

(*He departs.*)

CARRIE: What a lovely man.

DELIA: He's a shit—he's exactly what I called him, he's a shit. And if you think he's a lovely man, let *him* talk to the insurance vultures—not me!

LUCAS: Were they here today?

DELIA: Yes—and they've started to hack away at you.

LUCAS: What'd they say?

DELIA: For an overture, they said you were doing something a little heavy here. Running what they call "an illegal enterprise."

CARRIE: Sounds like a whorehouse.

DELIA: They said you had an office over your garage.

LUCAS: It's not an office—it's a studio. Or it was.

DELIA: Typewriter—computer—fax—printer—two desks—

LUCAS: One desk and a drawing table. It was my studio at home, damn it, it was my studio!

DELIA: And right down here—those files.

CARRIE: They're Mary Lincoln, for heaven's sake!

DELIA: They don't care if it's Mary Mother of God, honey—if it's a a file, it's an office. Files are the worst. They took pictures of them. They took pictures of everything. They even took a picture of me—I looked like a garbage truck.

CARRIE: Next time they come, I'll talk to them myself.

DELIA: You think you'll do better than I did? Lucas—please—talk some sense into her.

LUCAS: I'm not so sure what the sensible thing is, Delia. Let me study these leaflets a while.

CARRIE: And we can all go to the Zoning Board.

DELIA: I'm not going to that meeting, and I don't want you to. Let them condemn it. Please, Luke—Carrie—let them condemn it.

CARRIE: I don't want to talk about this anymore. Amy will be coming home soon, and I want to get ready for her party. Now, come on, you guys—help me.

DELIA: I'm not going to help you, and I'm not going to join your party, and I'm not going to eat any of the deputy's food. I'm going down to the diner, I'm gonna have a cheese hamburger with onions, and go back to the motel.

And I beg you, Lucas, read her some reality, for God's sake, or things will get more and more catastrophic around here.
(*She goes. Silence. Carrie is unnerved.*)

CARRIE: She has a sexual lust for catastrophe!

LUCAS: We have to listen to her, Carrie.

CARRIE: (*An outbreak*) I won't listen to her, I refuse to listen to her! She's a gravedigger, she's a spoilsport. She wants to ruin our evening, she wants to wreck Amy's party! Well, we won't let her!—we won't! We're going to shake her out of our minds and have fun tonight! Now—where are we going to eat? We need surfaces—
(*Seeing Lucas's tubes and briefcase on the drawing board*) Whose stuff is this?

LUCAS: It's my stuff.

CARRIE: Would you remove it, please.

LUCAS: (*Quietly*) No, I will not remove it.

CARRIE: It's Amy's drawing board.
(*Suddenly, hectored, at his temper's end, he flies off:*)

LUCAS: It's my drawing board! Tonight, it's my drawing board. I have no other place to work—my studio's gone—it's my drawing board!

CARRIE: Easy, Lucas.

LUCAS: Don't tell me "easy"—I've got to work!—I've got to work!
(*Flurried, he comes down and addresses the audience.*)

LUCAS: It's a lie—I have no necessity to work. It won't make any difference if I do—not a goddamn bit of difference!
(*An instant. He tries to collect himself*) I'm going to get fired. I can see it in everything John McCandless doesn't say to me. I'm going to lose my job. So I don't think I can be sociable tonight. God knows I've been sociable in this house. More than I ever wanted, more than I ever expected I could be. Parties on the beach—out-of-town executives for the weekends—noisy celebrations—procurement and pimping—the wives and the bimbos—all the working-rich, and how long since I've really worked, rich or poor, how long since I've taken a chisel to a block of stone?—how long?!
(*A moment*) Not as if I were talented. Carrie's wrong—I haven't got it. I can take my hammer and chisel to the work, I can split the stone, but no breath comes out of it—nothing—no eyelid moves. Oh Christ, what to do with this mediocre talent? Make plastic mock-ups, that's what to do with it. Pour synthetics into molds and watch them alchemize into money and Jaguars and Concorde airplanes and great big yellow tents on the Fourth of July, commemorating someone's Independence. So why do I give the finger to Delia's money and her cars and her vulgarities, when we drive the same Ferrari and serve the same champagne? . . . Well, something, you've got to have *something*! How about success?—will that do?—can it stand for what is wanted? Can anything?
(*A moment*) The house is as good as gone. Who are all those sane and sober-minded people who did not build on cliffs and beaches? How do

they do it? How do they keep it all together?

(*He returns to Carrie. He is under control. He speaks with as much equanimity as he can manage*) A party, did you say?

CARRIE: I don't want to make things difficult for you, Luke—and I won't, I promise I won't. But when Amy arrives, we'll have to do *something* with her. So why don't we just have a *little* party—just a short one—a glass of wine and a bite to eat—and then you can go to work afterward. We'll make ourselves scarce—we'll go to sleep in the hallway, and you know Amy, she'll just curl up like a little puppydog, and before you know it—

LUCAS: It doesn't matter whether Amy is coming or not. What we remember of her won't be here.

CARRIE: Now, come on, Lucas. She's fine. I just spoke to her a few hours ago.

LUCAS: You didn't speak to her and she didn't speak to you.

CARRIE: I can tell you her very words.

LUCAS: She doesn't *have* any words. She doesn't talk anymore. She can't brush her teeth—she can't feed herself. She doesn't understand what we say.

CARRIE: Yes, she does. The last time I saw her, she recognized me. She said my name, she said "Mother." And when I got up to go she said no, I swear to God she didn't want me to go and she said no to me. So I stayed until she fell asleep. And she knew me, Lucas, she knew me!

(*They are both very still. They simply stare at one another. At last, she cannot meet his gaze. She breaks down and starts to cry. He takes her in his arms. He caresses her gently. At last, in better control of herself, she extricates herself from his embrace and stands looking out at the ocean. He starts to unroll his design sheets.*

Offstage, a sound of singing. It is Joby's voice. The words of his song are:)

JOBY: Happy birthday to you, Happy birthday to you, Happy birthday, dear Amy, Happy birthday to you.

(*Joby enters. He is carrying a white birthday cake with twenty-one candles and one for good luck. He is as happy as usual.*)

JOBY: Birthday girl not here yet? Good! Let's get things ready for her. Let's light the candles on the cake. Shall we light the candles on the cake?

(*He has started to light the candles. Lucas watches, spellbound. Carrie gazes at Joby as he lights one candle, then another. Slowly, as if hypnotically drawn, she moves toward Joby and the candles. He hands her the box of matches. A long moment she does nothing. Then she strikes a match. As she is starting to light the candles, the illumination fades to blackness.*)

END OF ACT ONE

Act Two

IT IS LATE AFTERNOON, the following day. The light is changing from early dusk to evening. Carrie, Lucas, Delia and Tully are playing Scrabble. Amy's drawing board has been let down to its lowest position, and the players sit on the floor, with or without blankets under them, and play the game. The only oddity about this undertaking is that a cardboard stand has been improvised for a fifth player, although the game makes no provision for a fifth. The imaginary player—with a rack and real tiles in front of her—is, of course, Amy. For the moment the four real players play as if there's nothing unusual about the game. Lucas has been drinking a little; Delia has been drinking a lot. Neither of them is drunk. Carrie has been abstinent, as has Tully.

TULLY: Your turn, Delia.

DELIA: I'm thinking, I'm thinking, I'm thinking.

CARRIE: (*Imitating Delia's singsong*) You're drinking, you're drinking, you're drinking.

DELIA: (*Laughing*) I better hurry up and play because any minute now my sister is going to say I'm drunk.

CARRIE: You're drunk.

DELIA: So are you.

CARRIE: Me? Neither the grape nor the grain has touched my pure, abstaining lips.

DELIA: The nice economical thing about my sister is that she can get cock-eyed without drinking a drop.

LUCAS: Play the game, please.

CARRIE: It's Amy's turn.

TULLY: She just played. She finished the word "protocol."

CARRIE: It's still Amy's turn, it's Amy's turn!

(*Abruptly, as if at the end of his patience, Tully rises and hurries down to speak to the audience, and give vent to his irritation.*)

TULLY: What are we doin'?—what the goddamn hell are we doin'? In the middle of a house that's falling into the ocean, we're playing Scrabble. Four real people and one imaginary one. With Amy! We're playing Scrabble with Amy, for Chrissake! Why? What for?

(*An instant*) For Carrie, that's what for. To help her erase what she calls the hard, sharp lines. Between what's really *out-there* and what we make up in our heads. Between yesterday and tomorrow. To help her believe that life goes on. It *continues*. Like she says, it doesn't require big events to give it continuity—little ones will do. Little chores and habits, little routines, little games we play with one another. Yesterday, today and tomorrow—if we flow with the time-stream, things get better. We become accustomed to the rules, we follow them, we get to know our addresses and phone numbers, we learn how to behave with one another, so we can stand what we gotta go through, *so we can bear it*!

(*A pained smile*) We all know that games are a lot of crap, but we go along. Because we want to believe what Carrie believes. We love her, we admire her, we want to be on her side! We want her to keep her goddamn house even if it doesn't make sense, even if it turns out to be against the law, we want Carrie to get her way, we want her to win, we want her to be happy.

(*A passionate exhortation*) Be happy, Carrie, be happy!

(*An instant*) So we play Scrabble.

(*He laughs in an uncharactistically uncontrolled way*) We're a pack of dingleheads!—we play Scrabble!

(*He rejoins the game.*)

LUCAS: Play the game, Delia.

DELIA: You know what I was thinking? I was thinking I'm sick to death of playing Scrabble.

LUCAS: The alternative is conversation.

DELIA: I'll play Scrabble.

(*Setting a tile on the board*) There! That at least gets me a double-letter score.

CARRIE: You'd score more points if you drank less wine.

DELIA: You can say that about Life—but I hope you won't.

CARRIE: (*To the others*) All that alcohol and very little food.

(*To Delia*) When did you eat last, idiot? Did you go to bed hungry?

DELIA: No, I didn't. I had a hamburger at Dooney's Diner. It was made of old Nikes—it was very good.

(*She looks at the Scrabble board*) Who's winning?

TULLY: Carrie's way ahead.

CARRIE: No I'm not. Amy's ahead of all of us.

DELIA: Do you have to keep saying that?

CARRIE: Well, she is.

(*Joby comes in from the kitchen. He is cleaner, neater than before, wearing a makeshift apron and carrying a ragged-edged piece of plyboard which functions as a serving tray. Besides the porch-carpentry he's been engaged in, he is making himself useful as household help. On the serving tray is a nearly depleted box of saltines, and there's a dish of what will pass as a cocktail dip.*)

JOBY: I found some more crackers that're only a little bit soggy, and I made some more dip.

CARRIE: Oh great—I'm nuts about your dip. How'd you ever make it?

DELIA: If you ask for a recipe, the sheriff will say you're making a pass.

(*They all laugh.*)

JOBY: Gonna tell you how to make it. You take all the mayonnaise you got and you mix in all the peanut butter you got and then you look around and see, have you got any anchovies and sweet pickles. And then you take and you squoosh everything up and you add a little orange marmalade, and it's done.

CARRIE: And delicious.

DELIA: (*Ironically*) Scrumptious. A gourmet's delight.

CARRIE: Where'd you get the anchovies and pickles?—you found all that stuff in the refrigerator?

JOBY: Oh no. It ain't no trick to make a dip outta what's in the refrigerator. The trick is to make a dip outta what's in the garbage bag.

CARRIE: (*Hiding her dismay*) You mean this is made out of garbage?

DELIA: Oh my God!

(*She makes a monumental barfing sound and hides behind the couch.*)

JOBY: (*Insulted*) I said it came out of the garbage bag, but it ain't garbage! If something gets found and you make use of it, it ain't garbage! And if some-*body* gets found, he ain't garbage either. He may be homeless but he ain't garbage!

DELIA: Who said anything about homeless?

JOBY: You're pissed off at me because I'm homeless!

DELIA: (*Flaring*) It's got nothing to do with homeless! I'm pissed off at you because you nearly made me throw up!

JOBY: Don't you dare to call me homeless!

DELIA: Jesus, I didn't use that word—you did. You said it!—you rammed it down our throats!

JOBY: Because you were *thinkin'* it! I could see it in your face! In your eye!—you had "homeless" in your eye!

DELIA: Which eye?

JOBY: You were thinkin' *homeless*—you were *against* me and you were *thinkin'* it!

(*In a flare of pride*) Anyway, I got no time for you! I gotta go and finish my porch! Hey, Lucas, put your foot on this!

(*He has brought forth an eight-foot length of two-by-four, a stud that is still attached to two unkempt, broken pieces of siding. He has spread it all out on the floor, and means for Lucas to stand on the stud while Joby, with hammer in hand, prises the scraps of siding loose from the two-by-four.*)

JOBY: Now hold still, Luke, while I lift this sucker loose!

(*Muttering as he works*) I'da had this job finished if I had some nice clean two-by-fours.

LUCAS: I told you to buy them and I'd pay for them.

JOBY: I know you did, I know you did.

LUCAS: (*Goodnaturedly*) Well, stop beefin'.

JOBY: You don't get the point! Don't none of you get the point! Ain't no trick to buy brand new two-by-fours. The trick is to use what's out there— what's left after the storm—what Nature couldn't kill!

LUCAS: Good work, Joby. You'll be written in the Holy Book of Reclamation.

JOBY: I sure hope so. I think Jesus, bein' a carpenter, always used old studs instead of new ones.

DELIA: I'm sure he did, but I got another idea. Why don't you get your studs where you got your camera?

JOBY: (*To the others*) Just when we get the day goin' so we can stand it, somebody comes up with a logical question.

(*He is gathering his usable lumber*) I'm goin' back there to the porch, and when I finish fixin' it it's gonna be the prettiest porch you ever laid your friggin' eyes on.

(*Sheer victory!*) Happy days!

(*On a high, he goes out with the stud. An instant:*)

DELIA: Did I insult that little bastard?

LUCAS: You came pretty close. The word "homeless" got a little workover.

DELIA: I didn't *say* it! And even if I did, who says the word homeless is an insult?

CARRIE: It's a cheap shot!

DELIA: Now, wait a minute! That tricky little monster! In one minute he switched me from a goodhearted liberal left-of-center Democrat into a heartless persecutor of the poor-and-homeless and a redneck one-eyed sonofabitch.

CARRIE: Well, you certainly didn't reach to him with an open heart.

DELIA: You don't reach with your heart, you reach with your hand.

CARRIE: (*Brandishing a fist*) And boy, you reached!

DELIA: (*Hotly*) I can't believe you're doing this!

CARRIE: Doing what, for God's sake?!

DELIA: Taking his side against your sister.

CARRIE: I'm not taking anybody's side, and your being my sister is beside the point.

DELIA: What is the point? Is he your ally against me? Is he your brother? Are all men brothers? How about sisters? No, you're not a sister, you're a mother! You're a "mother," Carolyn Larkin Campion, you're an A-number one "mother."

CARRIE: (*To the others*) She can turn any word in the language into an obscenity. Even the word mother becomes a scuz!

DELIA: So's your ass!

CARRIE: Why do you have to turn into a mean drunk? Of all the drunks you could be, why do you want to be a mean one? You could be kind, you could be sweet, you could be philosophical, you could be quizzical, you could be sentimental, *you could be LOVABLE!*

DELIA: (*Angry*) I *am* lovable, you stupid jerk, I *am* lovable! And I'm sweet, goddamn it, I am sweet! I am whipped cream, I am butterscotch and caramels! I'm so sweet, you shake hands with me you get diabetes!

LUCAS: (*He laughs, enjoying her idiocy*) She's wonderful!

(*Hugging her*) You're wonderful, hon!

DELIA: What'd I say that suddenly made me wonderful. Tell me what it was—I'll say it again!

(*Now Tully laughs. Carrie catches it and joins the hilarity. Tipsy in one way or another, they are all on the verge of enjoying themselves and each other.*)

CARRIE: (*To Delia*) You see how adorable you are when you're not angry?

DELIA: Who says I'm angry? Joby? He's got me wrong. I'm not angry at Joby—swear to God I'm not angry at him!

CARRIE: You certainly did a down-in-one angry act.

DELIA: How should I act? What shall I do for him? Knit him a scarf? Give him a pedicure? Hey, Joby, bring me your poor, your tired, your hungry, your naked feet!

(*More soberly:*) You're putting the wrong gloss on this, Carrie. I've got nothing against that little creep. I just don't want him in the family.

CARRIE: Can't you pretend?

DELIA: No! Why should I?

CARRIE: Because he needs us! Because he's all alone in the world, and he needs somebody. And why shouldn't he *have* somebody? He's a good-hearted soul and he *does* things for people. He's been going to see Amy all these years. Not often, but more frequently than *we* go. He heard we were in trouble, he came running!—mending things!—cleaning up! For all those acts of kindness, what do I do?—punch him in the face and run him out of town?

DELIA: Who says you should run him out of town?

CARRIE: You were certainly hinting in that direction!

DELIA: Then you read me wrong, Sister! I'm Mrs. Magnanimous! I'm the Red Cross, I'm the Salvation Army!

CARRIE: Will you stop that!

DELIA: I am the American Federation of Charities!

CARRIE: I hate you when you get like this!

DELIA: You hate me at other times as well!

CARRIE: Yes, I do—I admit it, I do! Especially when you're drunk!

DELIA: (*Rage, heartbreak*) *Drunk!* I can't stand that word anymore! Is that all I am, a drunk? You look at me and all you see is a *drunk*?! Is that all I am?! Is that all you can see? You look at me and all you see is a woman who is drunk?! Is that all I am in your eyes? Is that all?!

(*She is weeping and hysterical, and trying to bring herself under control. She comes rushing downstage, to get the aid of the audience.*)

DELIA: Will somebody please turn me off?—the button's on the left.

(*An instant*) They've got me all wrong. I'm a good, kind, helping person. That's what I want to be with my sister, that's what I meant to be with Joby. I'm on his side! I'm like him—I'm homeless! I've got a big fucking house in San Diego and I'm as homeless as he is! I've got eight bedrooms and six baths. And windows all over the place, windows! But who's looking in on me?—*who knows I'm there*?!

(*An outcry*) *All I've got is windows!*

(*The wine has taken its toll: she is weeping. Silently, Carrie goes to her, strokes her arm gently, consoles her.*)

CARRIE: It's all right, honey—it's all right.

DELIA: (*Muttering*) Monster . . . that's what I am . . . monster.

CARRIE: Sh . . . hush.

DELIA: Why am I so disgusting . . . so disgusting . . .?

(*She moves away from Carrie's comfort. She is trying to pull herself together. With an effort toward levity*) I feel like I used to feel when I was wearing the dress with the eggplant collar and cuffs.

CARRIE: Oh God, she's going to make me feel guilty.

DELIA: Well, you just appropriated the other one—you *were* guilty!

CARRIE: (*Losing her temper; angry at Delia and at herself*) All right—I'm guilty! Shall I pull out my fingernails, shall I chop off my hands? I'm guilty, I'm guilty, I'm guilty, I'm guilty!

LUCAS: Of what?

CARRIE: (*Flaring*) Of everything! Do I have to be guilty of only one thing? Can't I have a variety? Can't I mix 'em all up? An egg plant dress, and a biography I can't write, and my daughter in a wheelchair, and my husband unhappy with his life, and a house that is slipping out of my hands and into the sea! All my fault! Mea culpa! Guilty! Guilty of everything!

(*Silence. She has unnerved them all, mostly herself.*)

TULLY: I think we should go back to the game.

LUCAS: Whose turn is it?

CARRIE: (*Quietly*) Amy's.

DELIA: (*Quietly*) I want her out of the game.

CARRIE: She can't be out of the game. It's her Scrabble set and she has a right to play it.

DELIA: She's cheating.

CARRIE: She is not cheating. You say that because she's winning. She's beating all of us.

DELIA: Yes, she certainly is.

CARRIE: I meant that without a double meaning.

DELIA: But it *has* a double meaning—she's wrecking our lives! She's part of a better life we had together, and she won't let us start a new one! She's confusing us! She's trying to make us feel that the past is part of the present—that we *owe* something to it. But we don't owe it anything! It's over, it's finished!

CARRIE: It's never finished—and we owe everything to it! We're part of it, and it's part of us! It's the only lifeline we can count on—it's continuous! And I'm doing my best to keep it from being broken! I'm stepping over the bounds of rationality to keep it alive! I'm devoting my goddamn life to it.

DELIA: (*Muttering*) Amy, Amy, Amy, Amy.

CARRIE: (*Silence. Then, quietly:*) You want to know something, Delia?— you're a mean-spirited bitch. You sit here and play Scrabble, a game that means absolutely nothing to you—in fact, you dislike it very much. You've got nothing invested in it—no dream, no love of any kind, nothing precious to tie you into this stupid and irrelevant pastime. Still—good sport that you are—you play the game and pretend to be a part of it. But you refuse to play the game of "Amy's Home" when all our hearts and hopes are deeply, seriously, *painfully* a part of it!

DELIA: (*Quiet. Ashamed, she turns to Lucas*) If your wife weren't such a self-righteous shit, I'd tell her she was right.

LUCAS: Tell her anyway.

DELIA: (*Not unkindly*) You're a self-righteous shit.

LUCAS: (*Affectionately*) No, dummy—not that part—the other part.

DELIA: And you're right. I take it all back about Amy being in the game. I apologize. I'll go sit in the rear of the room, I'll crouch in the water closet. I'll do acts of penance. I'll pick all the lint out of my navel and donate it to the poor.
   (*To Amy—the empty spot at the table*) Amy!—goddamn it, get your ass together, and let's go back to this brainbustin' game!

LUCAS: No, I'm sick of it—let's tell jokes.

DELIA: Clean or dirty?

TULLY: There aren't any clean jokes anymore. Anybody know a clean one? (*Silence. Then:*)

DELIA: I know a clean joke—but it *is* about fucking.

CARRIE: I like fucking. Why is it subject to so much ridicule?

DELIA: Because it's ridiculous.

LUCAS: Dying's more ridiculous, but most of those jokes fall flat. I tried one at the start of my presentation this afternoon—about an old man who bought a plot in the cemetery as an act of defiance. He went there every day and pissed on his own grave.

(*A moment. He gets no laugh*) See? Nothing. I get absolutely nothing on it. Why not?—isn't it a good joke?

DELIA: (*Dryly*) Boy, it's a pisser.

LUCAS: Well, it deserves *something*—a little grin—a titter. But I knew I was dead. It was a ba-a-ad, ba-a-ad omen.

CARRIE: It was not such a bad omen. You told me you got one out of three.

LUCAS: (*Self-deprecating sarcasm*) Oh yes, my big triumph! The Big Wow of Lucas W. Campion!

TULLY: One out of three—what's that mean?

LUCAS: I presented three objects for approval. Two of them got shot down, bleeding on the threshold. The third was a very weak maybe.

TULLY: What was the weak maybe?—an actual object?

LUCAS: You really want to know?—it's called a HappiToner.

TULLY: What's that?

LUCAS: It's more ridiculous than fucking or dying.

TULLY: But what *is* it?

LUCAS: A HappiToner—doesn't the name itself smell like a scam? Doesn't it suggest a dead rat, decomposing in the closet?

TULLY: (*To Carrie*) Why doesn't he tell me what it is?

CARRIE: He's like all of us—first he has to say his mea culpas.

LUCAS: Well, it *is* awful—it's an awful *object*. And the proof that it's awful is that those three vice-presidential cockroaches think it's going to make an Olympic improvement in our dedicated destinies. And what is this glorious contraption?—it's a massaging machine!

(*He hurries downstage to harangue the audience. He is a pitchman, a carnival barker, a con man. Nearby, an imaginary HappiToner, the size of a coffin*) Yessirree, folks, that's what it is—a massaging machine! Step right up, step right in! The HappiToner, ladies and gentlemen—the Hap, Hap, HappiToner! Step in closer, Mr. McCandless—here's a seat, Mr. Galloway! Now you see this box here—ain't it a pretty one?—no, it don't look like no coffin, it's just the opposite. You get inside and you *come to life, you come to living, you come to zestful, power-packed living*! It's computerized happiness, that's what it is! It takes your measurements and it writes down all your aches and all your troubles! Where you hurt and where you stiffen! Like a Charley horse or a twisted neck or a pain in the boopus or a ruction in the rumpy-dump! And then those magical rubber fingers come out and excite all your *lazy-happy* joints—massage, massage!—the dexterous fingers of Sweden, the love-stroking manipulators of shiatsu—and you feel like you're a *maker* in the world and you've got a V.I.P. table in heaven, and you're high-muscle-toned and merry-go-lucky, and you're honeymooning on the Bay of Paradise!

(*He is rhapsodic. Now his voice is his own—dealing with the realities*) And then it's over and out. Time passes. The ecstasy goes gray, as gray as a fog. Gradually you become aware that you still hurt. Some hidden ganglion in your mind, some beating of your heart tells you that you ache. Deep, deep inside you, you know that the agony will worsen. You ask around about the Bay of Paradise, but nobody has heard of it—and the agonizing tortures are all coming back. These torments are not referred to in the catalog, and they've not been programmed into the machine. And you know that no matter how you try to computerize your heartache, you will never compose an electronic description of it. And the HappiToner just stands there—a waste, a mockery and an immorality. And the pain becomes unbearable and you become more and more . . . afraid.

TULLY: And you designed this . . . object?

LUCAS: No, I just did the box. It was originally made of a sickly brown plastic and I re-designed it to look like a big cradle, a soft, goosedown, faintly-fragranted cradle. Available in pale pink or celestial blue. And I put a little cassette player in it. And when you open the door—very distantly—like a sweet recollection of reclaimable youth—it plays "Some Enchanted Evening."

(*Silence.*)

DELIA: (*Mocking*) That's nice. I like "Some Enchanted Evening." I like it a lot.

LUCAS: (*Also mocking*) Yes. I thought you would.

DELIA: The HappiToner, did you say? Let me know when it becomes available.

LUCAS: Oh, don't buy it retail. I can get a value on it.

CARRIE: Yes, get her a value.

TULLY: You know, I may be a cornball, but I'd really like to have one of those machines.

(*Silence. One by one, they look at him: the disenchanted versus the single naif who may honestly believe in the commercial miracle.*)

DELIA: (*To Lucas*) Well, there you go—there's your market.

TULLY: (*Catching the slur, he is defensive*) Yes, I *am* his market! And I *do* get stiff necks and Charley horses and tortures in the back—and I frequently experience pains in the ass called Delia!

DELIA: If one of your pains is a Delia, a HappiToner won't help.

TULLY: You know, I can't figure it. Sometimes I latch on to you guys, and sometimes I walk into a conversation and it's like a mine field—booby traps all over the place—*va voom!* What's *wrong* with him designing a machine like that? What's wrong with him helpin' people get a little relief from their aches and pains? Even if it's only a passing moment—even if it's only a few minutes of relief—what the hell is wrong with it?

LUCAS: (*In a sudden rage*) It's a fake! It's a fake, it's a cure-all, it's a fixit, *it's a fake!* People will buy that contraption the way they buy an exercise machine, then shove it away in the attic. They'll squander a couple thousand bucks on something they'll use six-and-a-half times—then they'll forget about it. And is there anything the HappiToner can do that a half hour's ping-pong game with your son or daughter can't do better? *Why do we brown-nose the gadgetry—why do we idolize the goddamn technology?*

TULLY: Why shouldn't we idolize it? It does things better than we do—and a damn sight faster! It saves time—and our time is limited! It's valuable!

LUCAS: No! Time is not valuable! It's a tyrant, it's our enemy! It ties us into knots of past, present and future. It reduces us to short distances and high velocities! It petrifies us with milestones and gravestones. It segmentizes us into ages and birthdays and rituals. And finally, when it's bored with us, it cancels us like a dead sitcom! We are very good at ending things— oh yes, we are great killers and terminators!—but the one thing we cannot terminate is time. It is the ultimate technology—an unstoppable, remorseless machine without a battery or a button. It is the worst dragon in our lives—and it is indestructible!

TULLY: What bugs me about what you say is not that I don't understand it—but that you don't, either.

LUCAS: You're quite right, Tully—I don't.

TULLY: You sound like the carpenter who couldn't drive a nail with his hammer, so he hit it with his head.

LUCAS: It's a very apt analogy.

TULLY: What two pieces are you trying to nail together?

CARRIE: His life and his work.

TULLY: Seems like he's doing better at his work than he thinks he is.

CARRIE: He doesn't have any respect for that. He was a very promising sculptor.

TULLY: (*Challenging*) Yeah?—what'd he promise? That he'd be better? That he'd be the best?

CARRIE: He had three fine shows. Some real recognition in the papers. Two prizes.

TULLY: Why did he quit?

CARRIE: Ask him.

TULLY: (*To Lucas*) Why did you quit?

LUCAS: I'm my father's son. I'm hooked on money.

CARRIE: Not as hooked as your father was.

DELIA: No, he was a money-louse. Meanest, cruelest, tightest asshole in the Amalgamated Assholes of America.

LUCAS: That's enough, Delia.

CARRIE: She's right. Lucas did a head of him in granite. It was strong, it was rugged. And alive—oh, so wonderfully alive! He gave it to his father on his seventieth birthday. The old man put it alongside the fireplace. He used to strike matches on it.

LUCAS: Maybe that's all it was good for.

CARRIE: Good for?—what a stupid remark!—good for? You've been mugged by the creeps of utility, my friend!—*good for*? It was beautiful! And so were the three abstracts and The Scarecrow and the head of Amy. That one especially—you're going to finish the head of Amy one of these days—you're going to do that—you promised.

LUCAS: I never made such a promise.

CARRIE: Yes you did, Lucas. But even unfinished, I love it. It's like what I felt the first time I saw those entombment figures of Michelangelo. Those half-finished people—struggling to pull themselves out of the marble.
(*To the non-present Michelangelo statues*) Come on!—out of the stone!—out!—pull yourselves out of the dead rock! Come alive!—breathe!—take a deep breath!
(*To the others*) They're dying to climb into the future!—dying to be born!
LUCAS: (*Dryly*) Dying to be born—it's a phrase.
CARRIE: It's more than a phrase, Lucas. There's that solemnly-given promise that one day they will breathe!
(*To the statues again*) And you will too! Your eyelids will flutter, your lips will move, your faces will glow—and you will smile!—yes, you will smile! *You will be created!*
(*To Lucas*) And so will Amy! She'll come home and she'll sit quietly for you on the top of that little stepladder, and you'll stand before that wonderfully-veined marble and you'll chip away at it. And then one day it will be finished and you will show us the quiet happiness in Amy's life, and we'll all gaze at the beautiful soul of our beatified daughter.
LUCAS: Carrie—please—it's never going to happen. I haven't got it! I can't download Michelangelo! It's gone—even the marble is gone.
CARRIE: You'll find it—we'll all help you find it. It's not lost, Lucas! A piece of living art doesn't get washed out to sea like a piece of rubbish. And it does not disappear! Nor has our daughter disappeared. She's *alive*!
DELIA: (*Quietly but firmly*) Yes . . . she's alive. And the question is: Should she be?
(*Dead silence.*)
LUCAS: Gently, Delia.
DELIA: Gently doesn't do it, Luke.
(*She turns squarely to Carrie*) Amy's in a nursing home, Carolyn. She's sick—she has a damaged brain. She has to be dressed and bathed and fed. She can do nothing for herself, literally nothing. Sometimes she seems to stop breathing and she has to be slapped so that she will take a breath. Frequently she doesn't swallow her food, and they have to reach into her mouth and dig it out again. She can't talk—no words can find their way to her lips—she doesn't know anybody.
CARRIE: Yes, she does. She knows me. The last time I saw her, she smiled. She kept on smiling at me.
DELIA: I don't believe it.
CARRIE: But it's true! Ask her night attendant—that nice Mrs. Templeton—ask her about the last time I was there. Ask Joby.
LUCAS: No need to ask Joby.
CARRIE: Yes—ask him. He visits her more often than any of us!
(*Calling*) Joby!
LUCAS: Carrie, stop it.
CARRIE: Joby, come here!

(*Joby enters, happy to be summoned, giggling.*)

CARRIE: Joby, tell them what you told me after you saw Amy the last time. Tell them.

JOBY: (*Grinning*) Well, she's improvin'. Gettin' better. Amy's improvin'.

LUCAS: (*Gently*) You keep saying that, Joby, but you know you're making it up.

JOBY: (*Stricken*) Oh no, not makin' anything up. Swear to God—swear to the Almighty—not makin' nothin' up! She's improvin'!

DELIA: How is she improving?

JOBY: She's learnin' how to count.

DELIA: Count what?

JOBY: Count her fingers!

(*He chuckles delightedly—he has scored a victory*) You say to her, "Amy, count to five." And she raises her hand up in the air. And she goes like this with her fingers—one, two, three, four, five. She doesn't *say* nothin', unnerstand. She just makes this movement with one finger at a time. And she never makes no mistake—she can count to ten and never make no mistake! Hell, that's as good as *I* can do!

(*He laughs giddily over his joke*) How d'you like that?—ain't that great, what she can do now, ain't that great?

(*He looks from one to another of them, hoping to see a smile or hear a word of approval—and belief. But, as gently as possible, they turn away from him; nobody meets his eye, nobody believes him. Even Carrie is a bit disappointed, troubled. Joby realizes he has not come off as well as he hoped. He tries further to ingratiate himself.*)

JOBY: I can tell you other ways she's improvin'—you wanna hear them?— how she's learnin' to talk—and how she's learnin' the words to a song . . . and . . .

(*No takers. He too is disappointed in himself. Woefully distressed, he is brave-spirited and does not give up: he means to leave them on a hopeful note.*)

JOBY: Well, the *good* news is that the porch is almost finished. There's only a little wobble on the far side, and that'll tighten up with a spike and a spit. And then I'm gonna get rid of some of them loose boards in the kitchen, and get rid of a lot of broken stuff—and the place is gonna look real good, real good—you bet your soul-and-body—*real good*!

(*He has recovered his optimism and good cheer as he leaves the room. Silence.*)

LUCAS: (*Restrained*) I spoke to her primary doctor on Thursday of last week. He didn't say a word about any progress of any kind. He did not mention counting.

CARRIE: Perhaps Joby is exaggerating a little, but I'm not. Last week I brought her a new toy. A pretty little hand-painted rattle. And she smiled at me and said, "Carrabell." Remember how she used to call me Carrabell? I could see her crossing the bridge from what she had forgotten into what she remembered. And she smiled at me—I swear that she smiled at me.

LUCAS: She doesn't know what she's smiling at.

CARRIE: How do you know that? How do you know that she isn't starting to think and to recognize? How do you know she's not getting better? How do you know that some miracle mightn't happen—a machine, perhaps—a wonderful machine—!

(*A sudden inspiration*) Maybe *your* machine, Lucas—maybe the HappiToner—

LUCAS: No—

CARRIE: It might, Lucas—it might help! You can never tell about these things.

LUCAS: It won't work, Carrie.

CARRIE: It won't hurt to *try*, Lucas—just to *try*!

LUCAS: (*Frustrated, in pain*) The machine is not meant to do that, Carrie. It's not meant to do anything but make money! The machine is a fake!

CARRIE: (*She turns to Tully*) Tully, you talk to him. He doesn't believe in technology, but I think you do—so tell him, talk to him.

TULLY: I don't believe everything I hear or read—but last week, in the L.A. Times there was this machine for cystic fibrosis—

CARRIE: (*Eagerly*) Yes—yes—these kids who couldn't breathe—strangling in their own mucus—and suddenly this miracle machine—

TULLY: —and they can breathe again—they go to school and they take gym classes and play games in the schoolyard.

CARRIE: And how about the dialysis machines and the Pacemakers that save the heart? And there was that article in the Harvard Health Letter—did you read it?—there's this research doctor at Harvard who's working on a little electronic device no bigger than a child's hand and you strap it to the back of her head and it enhances her mind. It makes connections—people who were shadows in the dark become all lighted up in her brain—and suddenly she's recognizing us. And she laughs at an old joke and she remembers where she lives and she calls me Carrabell and she can paint a picture. You read about that device, Lucas—remember?—you read about it.

LUCAS: (*Quietly*) No, I didn't. And neither did you.

CARRIE: (*Fiercely*) Yes I did—and so did you! I showed it to you!

LUCAS: You didn't, Carrie.

CARRIE: Yes I did! You were on the porch—reading the Sunday magazine section—

LUCAS: You dreamed it—you're making it up!

CARRIE: You bastard! You son of a bitch, I *did* show it to you! You goddamn son of a bitch, you don't believe it because you're afraid to believe it! You're afraid to tie the past to the future! You want to forget what we all were together. You want to cut all the traces and write everything off— our child, our marriage—and this house—and the whole world!—you want to write it all off as if it never happened!

LUCAS: (*With the utmost kindness*) We have bad memories in this house, Carrie.

CARRIE: But we have good ones too. Think of the good ones!

(*Suddenly entreating*) The good ones, Lucas. The birthday parties and the anniversaries! And the Sunday you got your first review in the New York Times! And the day I got tenure and we had a big cookout on the terrace! And Amy's graduation from high school and the party on the beach. And the dancing—everybody always seemed to be dancing in this house!—oh, the dancing!

(*Suddenly*) I want to dance! I want to dance! Somebody, dance with me!

DELIA: And she ain't drunk a drop.

CARRIE: Dance with me! Lucas—Tully—*please!*—dance with me!

DELIA: (*With a slightly tipsy abandon*) I'll dance with you, kid!

(*Singing*) Some enchanted evening—

(*They are dancing together. Delia continues singing "Some Enchanted Evening."*)

CARRIE : I want to dance with Amy! Not with you—with Amy!

DELIA: Sorry, sweetheart, her card is full.

CARRIE: I want to teach Amy how to dance!

(*She slips away from Delia and continues dancing with the imaginary Amy. Delia, meanwhile, does not stop dancing even if she has no partner.*)

CARRIE: (*To the imaginary Amy*) It's easy, honey. You just make a square, that's all, make a square!

DELIA: Some enchanted evening

You will see a stranger . . .

(*Joby enters and watches the festivity. Delia sees that he has no partner and, to make amends, takes him in her arms and dances with him. Happy, he wants to dance to a livelier rhythm. So he starts singing "Do, do, do"*)

JOBY: Do, do, do what you do to me—

Do, do!

CARRIE: (*To Amy*) Amy, honey, you're wonderful—you're so beautifully graceful—you move like a ballet dancer.

(*Her arms empty, she dances around the room, and winds up near Tully. He extends his arms and she unthinkingly slips into them. Delia continues singing "Some Enchanted Evening," and Carrie sings with her. Joby sings "Do, Do, Do," and Tully sings "Mountain Greenery." It is a dissonance of music, but a dance of pleasure. For all its grimness, they are having a good time. Not, however, Lucas. He is watching, deeply troubled. At last the pleasure has been used up. Carrie faces Lucas.*)

CARRIE: That's a memory of good times in this house—and you don't even try to recall them.

LUCAS: (*In pain but under self-control*) I recall a dear, lovable glad-hearted child who smashed her car up on the Pacific Coast Highway, and when they put her all together again, she had no brain.

CARRIE: So you don't want one either.

LUCAS: (*The pain breaking through*) I can't help having one!

CARRIE: You don't want any memories, Lucas—not even the good ones!

LUCAS: The good ones hurt the most.

CARRIE: So you don't want *any*! The hell with history—you don't want to tie your future to your past. You don't want to be tied to the house or Amy or our marriage or that young Lucas who was a fervent, talented sculptor. You don't want yesterday to have anything to do with tomorrow.

DELIA: What's wrong with wanting a new start?

CARRIE: We're not finished with the old one! We've got a big salvage job to do!

TULLY: And if you're going to do it, you'll have to start it right now. The Zoning Board meets tomorrow night.

LUCAS: I can't wait.

TULLY: Don't just scoff it off, Lucas. If you want a permit to rebuild—and if you don't want your house condemned—you better fill out that questionnaire I gave you. Have you done that?

LUCAS: Not yet, no.

TULLY: Please do it in pencil so I can have a look at it first. I've been to hundreds of these meetings. They can ask tricky questions.

LUCAS: I don't think I can even answer the questions that aren't tricky. They asked for my name and address. That ain't easy. It'll take extensive research.

TULLY: It won't help to be a smartass, Lucas. You've got to take this on the level. And answer on the level too. When they get you in person, they're going to ask you some direct questions. And some of them are tough.

LUCAS: Like what?

TULLY: Well, completion money. When they see the extent of the restoration, they'll want to know if you've got enough money to finish the job.

CARRIE: Well, we'll have the insurance money.

DELIA: It's never as much as you think, Carrie—unless the house is condemned, of course.

CARRIE: We'll make up the difference. Won't we, Lucas?

(*Lucas doesn't answer. Tully takes up the slack.*)

TULLY: There are a number of questions that are too personal for them to put in a written form. But they will ask you for certain private assurances.

CARRIE: What do they want to know?

TULLY: Do you have the will to see it through?

CARRIE: Yes we do.

DELIA: Don't be so hasty, Carolyn.

TULLY: Yes, you've got to be careful. They're asking something that's got to do with plain old-fashioned guts. Do you have the heart to finish the job? They don't want to be giving out a permit to rebuild a house that should really be condemned—and halfway through, the owner gets discouraged and takes a hike, and suddenly the town is left with a wreck. So you've got to examine yourself—square—no excuses.

CARRIE: We won't take a hike—we'll see it through.

TULLY: You say "we." I haven't heard a word from Lucas.

LUCAS: Because I don't know what word to say.

(*Quietly, almost to himself*) I . . . envy . . . all of you. Each of you knows exactly what your own personal choice is. Carrie wants to stay here and rebuild the old house, and maybe the old life. Delia wants us to get the hell out of here and not get swept into the ocean—she wants family. I don't know why Tully wants us to stay, but it's quite clear that that's what he wants. In fact, every choice is clear—except mine. I've got one foot in the house and one foot on the highway. What's that story about Lucky Pierre who's caught in bed with his wife and his mistress and can't get an erection because he doesn't know which way to turn. Some people think that's funny, but I don't. It's a choice of hapless hopes—and that's not funny to me. And when I go to that Zoning Board tomorrow night, I don't want the right to salvage something that's hopeless.

DELIA: And it is hopeless.

CARRIE: (*Upset*) Are you talking about the house or about Amy or our life together, or what?

DELIA: I'm a specialist on houses, not human relations—so I'll stick to real estate. When the zoning board meets tomorrow—you listen to me—don't you beg for a permit. Let the house go. Let it be condemned, and then you take your insurance money—and I'll find you a new place to live. A good safe place—inland—on high ground—not subject to washout and flood. If you want to build from scratch, I'll help you find a nice, secure, dependable piece of land. I won't charge you for the service. Sister-to-sister stuff—no commissions.

TULLY: Don't sell so hard.

DELIA: (*Hotly*) I am not selling hard, I'm selling sensible! What the hell are *you* selling?

TULLY: (*Controlled, defensive*) What should I be selling?

DELIA: Safety! You're a police officer—sell safety! Tell them the number of people who've gotten hurt by this disaster, tell them about the family that got swept out to sea. Tell them the next storm will be their last storm! Tell them, tell them!

TULLY: They're grown up—they don't need to be told.

DELIA: (*In a rage*) Why are you feeding them this bullshit about holding up this hillside?! Cement pilings! Cantilevers! Why don't you tell them to get out of here! Why don't you help them load the goddamn moving van!

TULLY: (*Also angry*) If they want to stay, I'm gonna help them stay!

DELIA: Of course you are! Because you don't *want* them to move! You don't want her to slip away, do you? You don't want them to drive off some morning and never see her again! Because you're so nuts about her, you can't tell your badge from your zipper!

CARRIE AND LUCAS: (*Together*) Slow down, Deelie . . . Easy, Delia, please.

DELIA: He's a double-talking son of a bitch!

(*He slaps her. Carrie gasps. Lucas steps toward them to prevent further violence. Tully is dismayed at himself.*)

TULLY: Fifteen years in a uniform . . . never laid a hand on a woman. . . . never.

(*Pause*) I'm very sorry.

DELIA: (*Muted*) You can't hide behind an apology.

TULLY: There's nothing to hide.

DELIA: (*To Tully as she points to Lucas*) He knows better than that!

LUCAS: I know very little, and I don't want to know any more.

DELIA: You *do* know more, Lucas! Why the hell are you denying it?

CARRIE: (*To Lucas*) She's only guessing at what you already know. . . . Tully and I had an affair a number of years ago.

DELIA: And for all we know it's still going on.

TULLY: It's not going on now, and it didn't go on then. Carrie was lying.

CARRIE: I was not! I never lied about you—never!

TULLY: (*Quietly*) She stayed at my house for two days and two nights. It was immediately after Amy's accident. In the hospital, after they did the first operation on the girl, Carrie went berserk. She started drinking. For two days she didn't have a sober moment. She couldn't bear to go home. I told Lucas I was hiding her from people who had questions to ask. Which indeed I was. I took care of her. I sobered her up. On the third day, I drove her to see Amy at the hospital. Carrie seemed less alive than Amy did. I stayed with her—at the hospital—all day. Toward evening, I drove her home. When we got to the house, I didn't even go indoors with her. . . . I never slept with her.

LUCAS: That story is probably not true. But it is what I was told—and it is what I believe.

TULLY: Thank you, Lucas. Everything I've said is the absolute truth. But I don't want to take credit for honesty—unless the rest of it is told.

LUCAS: What is the rest?

(*A moment of stillness.*)

DELIA: He's in love with her.

TULLY: Yes, that's the rest. I thought—in the aftermath of the flood—we'll be discarding a lot of debris. This is a good time for me to get rid of some of mine. The worst hunk of jetsam is that I'm the family friend. That's only partly true—the rest of it is junk. I've been in love with her for all these years. There's not a helluva lot I can do about it because I know how attached they are to each other. But—telling how I feel—at least I don't have to carry it all alone. I don't expect to be doing anything about it. I'm just in love with her, that's all, I'm just in love with her—and it hurts. But I make do with what I've got. If I see her two or three times a week, that's kind of a pain killer, and I appreciate it. Once in a while I bring her something—a few flowers, maybe, or some candy—and by accident—we're unwrapping something together—our hands might touch. I can feel it for hours.

(*An instant*) Well . . . now . . . there's the question. Will they move away or will they stay? If they stay, I guess we'll just have to leave things as they are. Making do with what we've got. Bein' grateful for staying close, and not hurting so much as we get older. But if they move—I don't know how I'll stand it if they move. I think I'll die of loneliness . . . of thinking about her . . . lonely . . . die of it.

(*Without making more of it, he drifts out of the room. It is as though his absence has left a hole in the atmosphere. Silence. Lucas starts to assemble the Scrabble game. He tries not to sound too desolate.*)

LUCAS: I guess we scratch the Scrabble . . .

CARRIE: (*Absently*) . . . Yes.

LUCAS: Where'd the board come from—one of the hallway closets?

CARRIE: Yes, the hallway.

(*He has put all the pieces in the Scrabble box. He now puts the lid on the box and takes it out into the hallway. Without looking at one another, Carrie and Delia are intently aware of one another. Stillness. Then:*)

DELIA: You lied to me.

CARRIE: No, I didn't.

DELIA: Yes. I remember distinctly what you said.

CARRIE: I don't want to talk about it.

DELIA: You lied to me. You told me that you slept with him.

CARRIE: I made a mistake. I was drunk.

DELIA: I don't think you've ever been drunk in your whole life. You don't have to be.

CARRIE: He told you how drunk I was. I imagined we slept together. Imagination can go a lot of ways. Forward—backward—lots of ways. Maybe I did sleep with him, maybe I didn't! I don't know. I didn't know then and I don't know now. But I wanted to—oh God, I wanted us to make love! I wanted it from the first day I saw him. And I still do—and I don't know how to turn the clock around—so that it'll happen sometime—sometime—!

(*She is miserable, valiantly fighting time and tears. Delia is very still. The lights fade.*

The highway patrol is directing traffic at night. The men's voices have lost their urgency. Even the waving of the lanterns is not so frantic.)

VOICES: Detour . . . Detour . . . Use the inland roads . . . Use the side road, fella, the side road. Detour . . . detour.

(*Darkness. When the lights come up again, it is Wednesday morning, toward ten o'clock. Joby has turned the drawing board into a breakfast table. There are three place settings, a pot of coffee, a plateful of paper napkin-covered toast, a few oranges. Joby adjusts the place settings a bit more neatly. He lifts the glass coffee pot and feels it to see if it has become too cold. He decides that it's still hot enough to drink, and sets it down again. Lucas comes in by way of the damaged side of the house.*)

JOBY: Did you find 'er?

LUCAS: No. You sure she said she was going for a walk?

JOBY: Oh yes—said it right out.

LUCAS: Along the beach?

JOBY: That's what she said.

LUCAS: How come I didn't notice?

JOBY: You were tryin' to use the phone.

LUCAS: I looked both directions. Did she say she was going toward Oxnard or Malibu?

JOBY: She di'n't say.

(*Carrie enters. She looks cheery enough, but it is fake; she is working hard at it.*)

CARRIE: The beach is beautiful. Even with all that wreckage, it's just beautiful.

LUCAS: How far did you go?

CARRIE: Oh, just toward the end of the row. Four of the houses have been condemned. But the end one—the house with the blue shutters—they got a permit. They're already working on it. He's jacking things up, and she's hammering away—and cursing. Their name is Thaxos. She asked me if we had just moved in. Can you imagine that? We've been living here for nearly twenty years, and we've just learned each other's names. Two earthquakes we've gone through but—because neither of them caused us any damage—we hardly said hello at the Supermarket. But the minute we get smashed by the same fist, we want to know who's hurting, and how much. How do we measure it? . . . Thaxos their name is. They got a permit.

JOBY: We will too. You wait an' see—we gonna get a permit.

CARRIE: Have we heard from the Zoning Board?

LUCAS: You mean Tully?—no, not yet.

JOBY: He gonna come walkin' in here wit' a blue paper. Did you all know that a permit is a blue paper?

CARRIE: (*Dryly but not unkindly*) Thank you, Joby—that's important information. And I hope you're right.

JOBY: I *know* I'm right. I sat in that Zonin' Board room last night, and I listened to you and Lucas and you near made me cry. And I looked at the Zonin' Board and I thought what kind of mean sonsabitches is gonna say no to you, and I didn't see no mean sonsabitches on that Zonin' Board, and so I know Tully's gonna walk right in here with a blue paper. And we'll go on fixin', and start hangin' pitchers on the walls.

(*Delia enters.*)

DELIA: Well?—any news? God, I need coffee! Will somebody inject it into an artery, please.

(*She is pouring herself some coffee*) Any news from the Zoning Board?

CARRIE: Not yet.

DELIA: I know you'll want to kill me for what I'm going to tell you, but before any such homicide takes place, I want you to be assured that you're in no way obligated to accept what I've planned for you.

CARRIE: What purgatory have you planned, Sister?

DELIA: I realized that if your house is condemned, you will need a place to live. Immediately. Not tomorrow, not yesterday—*today*! And I don't want to push San Diego one step further. So I made a few calls and I did a little visiting. And I found a three-bedroom nicely furnished apartment that you can rent on a month-to-month basis. It's only a fairly nice neighborhood—an ever-so-slightly wrong block in Santa Monica—but not bad, really, and after all, it's only a temporary expedient and you can move in right this minute.

CARRIE: You didn't sign anything, did you?

DELIA: No, of course not.

CARRIE: Or give them a deposit?

DELIA: Oh no, no, no, what sort of amateur do you think I am? But I did give her my card, and wrote down my insurance license number, and you can sign the forms the minute you move in.

(*Tully enters.*)

TULLY: Good morning.

LUCAS: (*To Joby*) I don't see any blue paper, Joby.

TULLY: What did you say?

LUCAS: Joby was telling us that if we get a permit, it will be printed on blue paper.

TULLY: Joby's got it wrong. A permit is on ordinary white paper—and I don't have one to give you.

CARRIE: (*Muted*) Oh, God.

TULLY: I'm sorry, Carrie—Luke—the property's been condemned.

CARRIE: (*An outburst*) It's not a "property," it's a house! And it is not "condemned"!

LUCAS: Carrie—

CARRIE: It is not condemned! Who's got the right to use a word like that? Who's allowed to condemn anything or anybody! What arrogance!—what brutality! Condemned! This house is not condemned—we can strike that word right out of the index! It is not condemned!

TULLY: I really can't tell you how sorry I am, Carrie. And you mustn't blame them—and certainly not yourself. You were wonderful at the meeting—both of you. I was certain that you had won them over last night. But afterward—you know how it is when the board is sitting by itself, and looking at the investigator's reports, and reviewing the code—and I'm sure they wanted to give you a fair shake . . .

DELIA: It's not that terrible, Carrie—really—you'll see. I know it hurts, but it's only a temporary hurt.

CARRIE: (*As controlled as she can be*) No comforts, please.

DELIA: Well, there *are* comforts. After a while, you'll have the insurance money, and you can go somewere and build yourself a beautiful dream house. On higher ground.

CARRIE: This is my highest ground.

TULLY: Please don't fight it anymore, Carrie.

CARRIE: I *will* fight it, I *will*! We must have some recourse left. We're not little mice that get scared out of our nests, and we just go scurrying off in all directions! We can have another hearing, can't we? I can hire a lawyer—I can pay a contractor to draw up a set of plans—

DELIA: You can spend a fortune and prejudice your insurance and empty your bank account and break your heart.

(*Tully reaches into his envelope and pulls out a few copies of a Condemnation Notice. He speaks more formally than usual:*)

TULLY: I am instructed to post copies of this Condemnation Notice indoors and outdoors—a minimum of six places—three outdoors and three in. I am also instructed to inform you that this house is dangerous, and you are ordered to vacate it within twenty-four hours.

CARRIE: I am not vacating anything.

LUCAS: (*Gently*) Let's do it together, sweetheart.

CARRIE: I am not leaving this house. I am not leaving this room.

TULLY: I brought my station wagon. You can put the larger objects in it. The smaller objects can go in Lucas's car—

(*To Delia*)—and yours, if you don't mind.

DELIA: (*She assents. Then, to Joby:*) Joby, there's a Queen Anne chair in what used to be their bedroom. Can you help me rassle that out of here?

JOBY: No. I'm stayin' here with her.

DELIA: Please, Joby.

JOBY: And I'm gonna finish that porch.

TULLY: No you're not.

JOBY: I got work to do—don't get in my way, Tully.

TULLY: No permit has been issued—and you're not allowed to do any more work on this house.

JOBY: I don't need no permit. All I need is my two hands and a hammer.

(*He pulls his hammer out of his carpenter's belt and starts to go out on the porch. Tully stops him.*)

TULLY: Stay here, Joby—give me that hammer!

JOBY: It don't belong to you, it belongs to them!

TULLY: Give it to me!

(*He starts to wrest the hammer out of Joby's hand. Joby raises the hammer threateningly.*)

JOBY: I'll give it to you across your head!

TULLY: You're under arrest, Joby!

(*They struggle over the hammer. The others try to bring the fight under control. The following five speeches are shouted in unison.*)

JOBY: Across the head—across the head—

TULLY: Let go—let go!

CARRIE: Tully, don't hurt him!

LUCAS: Let him alone—don't hurt him—let him alone!

DELIA: Give him the hammer, you idiot!

(*The battle is over. Tully has the hammer. Joby has been overcome, but not in spirit: he is still proud.*)

JOBY: You said I'm arrested.

TULLY: Get out of here, Joby.

JOBY: (*Challenging*) Go on—arrest me!

TULLY: I said get going. But I warn you, Joby—no more workin' on the house.

JOBY: I'm not promisin' nothin'. I ain't licked yet, Tully.

(*He goes out. A moment of silence.*)

TULLY: Please don't encourage him anymore. You're only gettin' him into trouble. He was better off on his own—believe me, he was better off.

(*Tully, still carrying the hammer, leaves the room. Pause.*)

DELIA: (*To Carrie*) You've got some skirts and slacks in a bureau drawer. Everything seems dry. Shall I pack them?

CARRIE: (*Abstracted, she still has not made up her mind*) I don't know . . . whatever . . .

(*Delia goes out. Another stillness.*)

LUCAS: Come on, honey. Let's start with your books. A lot of these didn't even get wet. Here—I'll load you up—start with an arm full—

CARRIE: I'm not moving.

LUCAS: Please, Carrie. This place is dangerous.

CARRIE: You're betraying me.

LUCAS: No I'm not—believe me I'm not—

CARRIE: This is the only house I've ever been happy in. This is the only place I've ever deeply loved anybody. My sister, you, and my parents—but not the way I've loved you and Amy—you're the only ones I'd die for—and I still love you both—and here is where I love you—right here—at home—and all that love—it'll all be gone if we leave here—all gone if we desert this house—all that love—all gone—all gone—

LUCAS: No, it won't, Carrie. We'll just start all over again—somewhere else—we will, Carrie . . .

(*He takes an armload of books and goes out. She remains very still. Then she takes one step and, as if it was a mistake, steps back onto the spot she just occupied. Delia enters. She hangs back so that Carrie won't see her until Delia is ready. She is having a difficulty she may not be able to manage. At last she musters her courage:*)

DELIA: May I . . . could I have one last chance with you, Carrie?

CARRIE: Last chance to do what?

DELIA: (*Her difficulty increasing*) I—it upsets me—the picture of you guys settling into a sublet house with a transparent plastic slipcover on the living room couch.

CARRIE: I haven't settled for that, Deelie.

(*Mostly to herself*) I haven't settled for anything.

DELIA: Then one last try, Carolyn.

(*An entreaty*) Please—you and Lucas—please come home with me.

CARRIE: (*Also having difficulty*) I—how do I say this?—you don't know how I appreciate—oh, Deelie . . . !

DELIA: Please don't say "appreciate" anymore. I'm not doing it for you— I'm doing it for myself!

(*Long moment. They gaze at one another.*)

DELIA: I used to think you loved me—and even liked me a little. But I guess I was mistaken. But I'm not mistaken about myself—I love you very much, Carrie. I've always loved you—and admired you—and envied you. But most of all, loved you. And I want you to move in with me. And I'll just have to pretend you love me as much as you used to when we were kids, and I was easier to love.

CARRIE: But I do, Deelie—and more!

DELIA: Please—it's late—you don't have to say it.

CARRIE: I swear to God, Deelie—I swear! I've always loved you—and looked up to you! You're my only sister, for God's sake—there's so much we *feel* about each other! When Mom died, you were the only family I had. And if you need someone to live with—and someone to love you—we don't nec- essarily have to come and live with *you*, you can come and live with us!

(*A critical moment. The whole relationship seems to change. Delia can- not believe this alteration in her fortune, she cannot believe what she is hearing.*)

DELIA: What did you say?

CARRIE: I don't know where we'll be living—here—Santa Monica—some- where on higher ground—! And I'm sure Lucas will agree—sometimes I think he likes you better than he likes me—

(*Trying to make Delia smile*)—and you and I can go on fighting just the way we used to. Okay, Deelie—okay?

DELIA: . . . You mean it?

CARRIE: Of course I mean it!

DELIA: You really mean it?

(*She starts to cry. Carrie takes her in her arms.*)

CARRIE: Hush, baby, hush.

DELIA: Oh Carrie, oh Carrie—

CARRIE: Hush, honey.

(*Delia comes out of the embrace. They are suddenly shy with one another. They smile a little, they weep a little.*)

DELIA: I can go back to San Diego now. It won't hurt a bit.

CARRIE: We'll come and visit. We'll come for the Fourth.

DELIA: That means Thanksgiving.

CARRIE: Maybe both.

DELIA: I'll pester you.

(*A moment*) Goodbye, honey.

CARRIE: Goodbye, babe.

DELIA: (*At the door*) You can stop feeling guilty about the dress with the eggplant collar and cuffs. I secretly preferred it. I wore it to shreds.

(They both try to smile. Delia departs. The smile on Carrie's face becomes fixed for a moment. Then it's gone. Her seeming self-possession with Delia was all assumed: she is trying not to quake. From a distance, there is a sound of someone hammering. It is Tully tacking up the exterior Condemned sign. He now appears. He carries a number of signs, the hammer and a few nails. He finds a section of wooden paneling and starts hammering a sign in place. The hammering puts her in a panic.)

CARRIE: *(An outburst)* Stop that! That is burr-walnut paneling! Stop that!

TULLY: I've got to do it, Carrie.

CARRIE: Stop it! Haven't you got any feeling? Stop it, stop it, stop it!

(She is trying to get the hammer and signs away from him. He is resisting, trying to calm her down. They are grappling with one another.)

TULLY: Carrie—quit it—Carrie—who the hell are you?—Joby!? Please—for God's sake!—*please!*

CARRIE: Don't you have any feelings?—stop that!

(The skirmish over, she has achieved nothing: he still has the hammer and signs.)

CARRIE: Can't you feel what's happening to us?—haven't you got a heart?

TULLY: *(Restrained)* I'm trying to get you to go.

CARRIE: Why do you want me to go? You said that you love me—why are you trying to get rid of me?—why have you been lying to them!

TULLY: *(Quietly)* I haven't lied to anybody, Carrie.

CARRIE: Why are you telling them we never made love together?

TULLY: Because we didn't.

CARRIE: What are you trying to do—make me believe I'm crazy? You think I don't remember every moment? We're standing in the back corridor of the hospital. The doctor has told us about Amy. No hope, no hope. I'm coming apart—no help, no hope! And then that unfailing question—do we let her live or shut off the lines and let her die. And Lucas—I can't believe he would let our child die—I can't believe it! Can we be quarreling about the same thing? We're losing our minds—we're shouting—we're screaming in the hospital corridor—and suddenly I can't look at him, I can't bear the sight of him, I can't go home—

(Screaming at the remembered Lucas) Go away!—don't touch me!—I hate you—let me alone!

(More quietly) The whole world is gone, the whole world! I'm cold—terrified—I'm shaking—out of my wits. So you take over. Everything—you're doing everything. You move and you point and give orders and get things done. And I'm in your car—we're riding—I don't know where—and we're walking up the steps of your house—and suddenly you're holding me, you're caresssing me—and we're at each other like animals—I'm laughing, I'm crying—I'm screaming the walls down. . . .

TULLY: It never happened.

CARRIE: It happened again the next day. I stayed in your house and we made love again—if you can call it love—it was teeth and rage and fingernails—

and it never happened to me before you came along and it never happened after—

TULLY: It never happened at all.

CARRIE: Why are you saying that?—why are you denying it!

TULLY: Because none of it occurred. You came home with me, yes. And I gave you a drink. And then I gave you another. And then I couldn't stop you—you kept on drinking—and you turned and turned—trying to keep your balance—and suddenly you slumped to the floor and I picked you up and got some of your clothes off and put you to bed. That's all that happened. Nothing more—I didn't touch you. You didn't awaken until early afternoon of the next day. I put hot and cold compresses on your wrists and your forehead, and at dawn the next morning, I drove you home. And that was it.

CARRIE: Why do you have to tell it that way. Why do you lie about it?

TULLY: It's not a lie, it's the truth!

CARRIE: Only because you tell it very well that way!

TULLY: (*Sharply*) All right! Let's pretend that it happened the way you tell it. It *didn't* happen that way, but let's pretend we agree on your story. What's the use of it? What possible kindness can it serve?

CARRIE: (*Fiercely*) I'm not talking about kindness!

TULLY: *I am!* After we've told it your way, what do we do? Do we then get into your little Honda convertible and ride off into the dawnlight with our hair blowing in the balmy breeze? Was there enough between us that would sustain even that one romantic scene? No, not a goddamn bit of it! You loved Lucas then and you love him now. You never denied that to me— you still don't deny it! Your past was with him and so is your future. And you and I—what'd *we* have? We shared that one brief moment in time when the watch is just about to stop running. Well, it stopped. Even by your story, it stopped. In my story, it never started.

(*A moment*) What I don't understand is: why do you want to believe it happened the way you tell it?

CARRIE: Because, love or no love, it was the most alive few hours of my life. Alive!—all of me—alive! I don't want to lose that time.

TULLY: All right, you imagined it. You don't have to lose it—you can still imagine it!

CARRIE: No, I need to know that it happened! Not in my imagination but in my memory. Something that actually occurred!—to me!—a fact in history—part of my living life!

TULLY: (*Mostly to himself*) Something else you can feel guilty about.

CARRIE: (*The thought is provocative to her*) Yes, maybe. Something to replace my guilt over Amy.

TULLY: (*With an ironic smile*) You don't have to replace it. The reliable thing about life is that you don't have to make do with only one guilt, you can have a lot of them.

(*Lucas enters.*)

LUCAS: Tully—sorry to bother you—could I borrow your car keys. I'd like to move your station wagon closer to the house.

TULLY: Oh—yes—I meant to do that.

(*Without giving Lucas his keys, Tully goes out. There is a tense moment between Lucas and Carrie.*)

LUCAS: We're almost finished. There's surprisingly little to carry.

(*She doesn't respond. He continues*) We didn't take any of your personal things. We thought you'd make your own choices.

(*Another silence*) There's not much time.

(*Joby enters carrying the The Green Clown painting.*)

JOBY: This pitcher was on the rubbish pile. I figured you don't want it no more?

LUCAS: No, we don't.

JOBY: Then if you don't want it, c'n I have it?

LUCAS: Yes, but it's shot, Joby. Look—it's ripped—it's torn.

JOBY: I can fix it. I'll turn it over and take some of your sticky tape that you got in the kitchen there—and I'll tape them damages so nobody'd ever notice. It'll be as good as new.

LUCAS: But you can't fix this part—look—some of the paint is gone.

JOBY: I'll fix it. I promise you, I c'n fix it, I can mend it! No matter what Tully says, no matter what that Zoning board says, everything is mendable.

(*His remark gives her pause. Quietly:*)

CARRIE: You really believe that?

JOBY: Sure I believe it.

CARRIE: (*She releases her hold on the painting*) Then you can have it.

JOBY: Thank you. I'm much obliged to you.

(*Touched, he takes the painting off with him. There is a tight stillness.*)

LUCAS: If you're making that painting a metaphor for this house, you're making a big mistake. Joby is wrong. Not everything can be mended.

CARRIE: If you believe in it, you can repair it.

LUCAS: Not everything.

CARRIE: Everything.

LUCAS: A bad painting?—a house that's practically gone?—a child in a nursing home?

CARRIE: (*Passionately*) Everything! Everything! If you believe in the dream, you can rescue it. It doesn't have to die. It doesn't have to get dumped into the ocean! It doesn't have to live its life in a nursing home—saying nothing, mute, silent! If you believe in the dream—

LUCAS: *I don't believe in it! I don't believe in the dream!* I never did! My dream was not to have a large house on the Pacific Ocean, but to have a small room with an easel and a block of stone. And why did I give it up? It wasn't that I lacked the talent! I lacked the courage to fail! *I lacked the courage!*

(*A painful quiet*) And so I settled for three cars and two mortgages and HappiToners and plastic toilet brushes and beach parties for vice presidents.

(*An instant*) And you lacked the courage too. Your dream was not four
filing drawers full of research on a woman you don't give a damn about.

CARRIE: You're wrong! I do care about her—and I'll get around to writing
her story one of these days!

LUCAS: Yes—just like I'll get around to visiting Amy one of these days.

CARRIE: You *have* been visiting her.

LUCAS: No. It's not true. I haven't seen her in nearly ten months.
(*A difficult moment.*)

CARRIE: But you've been telling me . . . you say you visit her.

LUCAS: I've been lying. I can't bear to be in the same room with her. I can't
stand the emptiness in her eyes. I can't stand the smell of her half-digested
food. I can't stand the nothing—the nothing—!

CARRIE: You're wrong about her. She's getting better. You don't see it because you're not looking for it! But Amy is improving—I see improvement
every time I visit her—a smile that wasn't there before—a little gesture
with a hand—I see it, I see her getting better.

LUCAS: (*Muted*) Amy is our worst lie of all.

CARRIE: (*The onset of panic*) No lie—none—never!

LUCAS: (*Quietly*) Amy was a sweet child with a quite ordinary mind—and
she had no special talent of any sort. But we told her she was the prettiest in her class, and the most graceful. We praised the little stories she
wrote, but they were as banal as everybody else's. And then the most hurtful lie of all—we told her she was a talented artist. We took her to gal-
leries and museums, and we groomed her for academies. And all the time
we were perpetrating a heinous cruelty on her.

CARRIE: (*An outburst*) No! I won't let you say that! We were never cruel to
her—never!

LUCAS: We were cruel in every kind word we said to her! We made her think
she deserved our love only if she was talented, only if she was successful!
Well, she *wasn't* talented and she wasn't successful! So our love was a
mean and ugly abuse! And in retribution she lied to us. Lies of omission.
She never mentioned the minor fact that she was on drugs.

CARRIE: She did not try to kill herself! It was an accident! She always drove
too fast, and she tried to avoid a car that was in the wrong lane—it was
an accident!

LUCAS: She was stoned, Carolyn. Tully found heroin in her car, and a hypodermic.

CARRIE: No heroin—no hypodermic—not a word of it in the report.

LUCAS: (*Quietly*) Tully was protecting you. He says he was protecting all of
us. We've all lied in one way or another, all of us!

CARRIE: No! I can't stand it! I can't stand it!
(*She starts to weep uncontrollably. At last Lucas goes to her and takes her
in his arms.*)

CARRIE: I want things as they used to be. I don't care if they were all lies—
I want to be connected with that woman who had a happy family. I want

to be married to that man who had a dream. I want to be part of the history of happiness. I don't want our history to stop and have to start all over again. I want it all to continue, to go on forever, to continue. If it takes pretending, I'll pretend—if it takes lying, I will lie! I want the past, Lucas, I want the past, I am dying for the past!

(*She weeps softly now. He holds her. Then:*)

LUCAS: Come on now—we've got to go.

CARRIE: Do we really have to go?

LUCAS: Yes.

CARRIE: (*Unsteady*) I don't know if I can do it, Lucas.

LUCAS: (*Gently*) Come on—I'll help you—come on.

CARRIE: I'll leave if I can make a deal with you.

LUCAS: What's the deal?

CARRIE: The next time I go to visit Amy, you come with me. You never go alone—and I never go alone. We visit her together.

(*A long moment.*)

CARRIE: Is it so difficult?

LUCAS: Yes.

CARRIE: Will you do it?

LUCAS: Yes.

CARRIE: Do you promise?

LUCAS: I promise.

CARRIE: (*Muted*) I'm ready then.

(*They get to the door. She turns to look at the room once more.*)

CARRIE: It was such a pretty room.

LUCAS: Yes it was.

CARRIE: On that table—didn't we used to have our wedding picture on that table?

LUCAS: Yes. A long time ago.

CARRIE: I wonder what ever happened to it.

LUCAS: We'll find it.

(*A moment of stillness. They go out. Joby, unseen by them, has entered by the other door. When they depart, he comes in out of the shadows, and we see he is carrying the painting of The Green Clown. Presumably, he has, for better or worse, mended it. He looks at the painting, looks around the room: which wall to hang it on? He notes the Condemned sign that hangs from a nail in the paneling. He carries the painting to it, suspends The Clown from the nail the sign hangs on, thus covering the Condemned sign. Seeing the picture hung, Joby steps back from it a few paces. He stands there, studying it, admiring it. He is very still. To Joby it is very beautiful . . . Slowly, ever so slowly, the lights fade.*)

END OF THE PLAY

THE LOSS OF D-NATURAL

A Play in Two Acts
by
JOHN ROC

(Pseudonym for N. Richard Nash)

CHARACTERS

JOHN . . . . .A man in his late fifties
EMILY . . . . .His wife
JESSICA . . . . .Their daughter
CHARLES . . . . .Emily's brother
PAUL . . . . .Jessica's husband
CARLA ⎫
FRANK ⎭ . . . . .Children of Paul and Jessica

Act One

A PLACE TO INHABIT, with an upstairs and downstairs, the steps disappearing into nowhere. Part of the outdoors is visible, enough to know that distances go far.

John, a man in his fifties, approaches his own house as if he were a stranger. He enters and calls.

JOHN: Hello! I'm home!

EMILY: (*Her voice, calling from upstairs*) Who's there?

JOHN: It's me. I'm home.

EMILY: Who?

JOHN: Me. John. Your husband. Home.

EMILY: Who? Wait a minute—I'll be there presently. Who did you say it was?

JOHN: (*To himself*) I ought not to stand for this again. Bloody nuisance. (*Holding up his fist*) I ought to give her a jolt in the mouth. Beat the damn-fool bewilderment out of her.

EMILY: What?

JOHN: Go to hell—go to goddamn hell!
(*Emily appears. She is John's age.*)

EMILY: Now then. Who did you say you are?

JOHN: I'm John. Your husband. Home.

EMILY: Home from where?

JOHN: Home from the office or the field. You don't believe that? The factory, the building site. The whorehouse.

EMILY: Is someone building anything?

JOHN: No.

EMILY: Then I suppose it's the office or the factory you're home from. Not the field, certainly. My—uh—husband, did you say?

JOHN: I hinted, yes.

EMILY: He isn't here just now.

JOHN: I'll wait for him. Perhaps he'll be coming in as I go out.

EMILY: Perhaps. What did you say your name was?

JOHN: John. The same name as your husband. In fact, I am your husband. Shall I repeat the name?

EMILY: Oh, my husband, yes—he's late again. He always worries me when he's late. These days, you know—anything can happen. It's dangerous, don't you think?

JOHN: I think there's danger, yes.

EMILY: At his age especially.

JOHN: Why? What is his age?

EMILY: (*Laughing*) Oh, it's this—the one we're living in—it's this!

JOHN: I mean how old is he?

EMILY: (*Bargaining*) Is a thousand too much?

JOHN: I think so. Could you make it less?

EMILY: I really don't see how I can, not without taking a substantial loss. Is a hundred all right?

JOHN: A hundred is fine.
(*Gently*) I appreciate all you've tried to do.

EMILY: I do my best—I really do my best.
(*Pause*) You *look* like my husband.

JOHN: I also do my best. Even in this wind.

EMILY: (*After a troubled silence*) You—uh—don't really think there's a wind. Do you?

JOHN: . . . Yes, I do, Emily.

EMILY: You said that yesterday.
(*Trying to laugh*) You have your little . . . revenge.

JOHN: No.

EMILY: Is spite your only pleasure nowadays?

JOHN: N-no, I have another pleasure now and then.

EMILY: It blew everything away, you said. Something preposterous about chairs. And flower pots, right off the window sill. And all the black keys right out of the piano.
(*She laughs. He doesn't. As he watches her, measuring:*) I think you're very comical sometimes. Especially when you don't mean to be. Especially when you mean to be . . . terrifying.

JOHN: I don't.

EMILY: Yes you do. You mean to throw me into a state of witless panic—but you won't.

JOHN: I don't try, Emily.

EMILY: Oh yes—don't tell me. I watch you—I see you do it. You just let loose a scarifying little hint. A little gray mouse—and you lock me in the room with it.

JOHN: Emily, I don't—I never do.

EMILY: Oh, don't you? How about the last time Charles was here? Why, you built it up and built it up—! It's right here, you said—whirling about!—yesterday, today and tomorrow! You stormed it about my head! And the truth of it is, you made it all up!

JOHN: (*Restrained*) I didn't make it up, Emily.

EMILY: Everybody knows you made it up.

JOHN: Who's everybody?

EMILY: Charles! He caught you at it! He caught you red-handed!

JOHN: Charles makes me sick.

EMILY: Don't you start on my brother now!

JOHN: (*Deliberately, facing her*) He's disgusting and he makes me sick.

EMILY: You're squeamish, that's all. Just because you can't stand people with false teeth—! Lots of people have false teeth!

JOHN: Nobody but your brother Charles wears his false teeth on a chain around his neck.

EMILY: That's not disgusting—it's merely eccentric.

JOHN: The sight of a man's choppers on a chain around his neck is disgusting.

EMILY: Not if they're clean. You can't keep the teeth in your mouth as clean as Charles keeps his teeth around his neck. Now, can you—can you?

JOHN: That's a challenging question, and I'd like to face it head-on, four-square. When your brother puts his false teeth in his mouth with one brass chain dangling at this side and another brass chain dangling at the other side, and when he gets his fork hand tangled with *this* chain and his knife hand tangled with *that* chain, and when he starts eating and cannot manage to keep his chains, teeth, knife, fork and provender all in his mouth at the same time, the disgorging that happens in naked view of all of us is enough to make me *vomit—VOMIT!*

EMILY: (*Blandly*) There you go—fabricating. You've never seen him eat with his false teeth in his mouth. You've made up a myth.

JOHN: I haven't seen him *eat* with them, but I've seen the *teeth*. And *they're* not a myth—they're a *fact!*

EMILY: Like your story about the wind. Was that a fact too?

JOHN: Oh, worse—the truth.

EMILY: You made it up.

JOHN: (*Losing his temper*) No, not again!—you know it was the truth! You still quicken out of bed at night. My God, things are gone that we still know the names of! How far can we look? Where are the things that used to have motion? What do we do with our closets full of old words? We lost D-Natural—and the two little boys—

EMILY: (*Defensive*) That wasn't my fault!

JOHN: (*Angry*) I've said it wasn't! What do you want me to do?—goad you into blaming the loss of the two boys on you? What an appetite for guilt you have!

EMILY: (*She turns away, distressed*) I can barely remember them. I quarrel so I *will* remember. The quarrel comforts me—I wish you wouldn't mind it. (*Trying to shake it off. More cheerfully:*) I do remember Jessica. Everything about her. Her voice. The way she wore her hair. Her silver equanimity.

JOHN: (*Gently*) No equanimity.

EMILY: (*Ignoring it*) But no wonder I recall her so well. She's still alive.

JOHN: We . . . don't know that for certain. Do we?

EMILY: Oh yes we do! I wouldn't remember her so clearly if she weren't, would I?

JOHN: You don't remember her as clearly as you did.

EMILY: You're wrong! There's not a thing about Jessica that's faded—not a bit! Why, when she comes to visit us I'll—

JOHN: Emily, she won't!

EMILY: —know her before I see her! Why, if she were to come into this room and stand behind my back and not say a word—silent as a cat—I'd know she was there!

JOHN: You frequently do when she isn't.

EMILY: Don't you dare to say she won't come back!

JOHN: She will not, Emily.

EMILY: She will—she promised!

JOHN: On the contrary. She warned you—she clearly warned you she'd never set foot inside this house again.

EMILY: She may have said such things to you. But not to me—never!

JOHN: What *did* she say? What were her exact *words*?

EMILY: Oh, come now, come now.

JOHN: No!—exact words!—tell me!—words!

EMILY: She said . . . she loves me . . . us . . . Because we're her—what word did she use?—her parents! Yes! And that she'll come again—any time we want her.

JOHN: Any time we want her?

EMILY: Yes.

JOHN: All we have to do . . . want her?

EMILY: Yes—yes!

JOHN: (*Not unkindly*) Well . . . I do. Don't you?

EMILY: . . . Yes.

JOHN: Then . . . why isn't she here?

EMILY: (*Apprehensive. In flight:*) Oh, little gray mouse, gray mouse!

JOHN: (*An outburst*) I am *not* trying to frighten you! I simply want you to tell me: why isn't she here?

EMILY: I don't want any more of this!

JOHN: You know why she's not, don't you?

EMILY: I said I don't want any more!

JOHN: Jessica's not here—and she's not coming back—

EMILY: Enough—that's enough!

JOHN: —because every time she comes, you kill her!

EMILY: No—I don't—no! Don't you start that all over again!

JOHN: The last time—you don't remember the last time? She was holding that thing in her hands—

EMILY: I know what you're going to say!

JOHN: —and she fell. You don't remember how she fell? Right there—at the foot of the stairs—

EMILY: No, it's not true!

JOHN: —with a few stairs above her—

EMILY: I was trying to help!

JOHN: —and she kept crying up to you to make you stop, make you stop—

EMILY: John—no!

JOHN: —and she was bleeding and she fell and still you wouldn't stop—

EMILY: I won't listen to any more—I won't!

JOHN: —and we all came running—and I tried to stop you and I couldn't! (*Pause*) Then you were still . . . and so was she . . . And I couldn't do a thing for her, couldn't do a thing . . .
(*Stillness*) You don't . . . remember that?

EMILY: . . . Yes.

JOHN: (*With a failing effort at composure*) And when she left she said she'd never come again.

EMILY: (*Quiet, composed*) That's where your memory goes soft.

JOHN: If it consoles you to have a different thought, you hang on to it.

EMILY: I will hang on. Because I'm sure she'll turn up one of these days. She's bound to—she knows I won't hurt her anymore. Good grief, where dying is concerned, there has to be a last time—that's the saving grace of it!

JOHN: (*Compassionately*) No saving grace, my dear. None.

EMILY: You dress in black.

JOHN: (*Pointing to his clothes*) This is brown, I think. And these are gray. You dress in pretense.

EMILY: No pretense, John. But no hair shirts either.

JOHN: The truth is a hair shirt. The truth is another earthquake. It's a fire, a freeze.

EMILY: Stop that, stop that!

JOHN: Why don't you go down There and hear what they say.

EMILY: (*Her terror mounting*) I don't want to hear what they say!

JOHN: Catastrophe, they say! They say another wind, they say a plague of many-mouthed animals. They say dusk, they say unending dusk, they say dusk will fall like a blindness!

EMILY: Stop it—stop it!

(*In an intense fury*) You want to spoil all I've done, don't you?

JOHN: What have you done?

EMILY: (*In a rage*) *I've done my housekeeping!* I've taken to the shovels and the pails and the brooms and the brushes! Housekeeping, yes—I've done my housekeeping! I've cleaned up all the debris of my faults and my weaknesses! I've hidden all my meaner prejudices in dark drawers, in attics, in closets! I've hidden my hatreds behind a screen of affection. You can search high and low and you won't find a speck of spite or an untidy grudge or a mote of malice. I've polished up my best manners and I've dusted off my artificial flowers of kindness. Look at me! I'm bathed and well-assembled and my house shines like a rainbow!

(*Turning on him with fury*) And I won't let you lay a turd of terror in the middle of my living room!

JOHN: (*With grim irony*) The schedule is therefore changed: There will be no catastrophe.

EMILY: (*In grim quiet*) I hate that about you, John.

JOHN: Hate what?

EMILY: You tell the truth as if it were a lie.

JOHN: We're even. I hate your pretenses. I try to go along with them, and there I am—I'm trapped. You leave me there to chew the leg off some bloody fantasy.

EMILY: Why do you ask questions?

JOHN: Why can't you treat them as rhetorical?—why do you feel called upon to answer?

EMILY: How can you stand the vacuum? Jessica, for instance—if we don't *know* about her, we have to make up answers.

JOHN: No!

EMILY: And if the lie turns true—

JOHN: I said no, Emily—no more!

(*Abruptly, he grabs her arms and holds them to her side.*)

JOHN: Hold still! Someone's coming! Someone's there!

EMILY: What? Let go of me.

JOHN: No—don't move—don't talk! Someone's coming!

EMILY: Let go! I want to see!

JOHN: No! Don't look outdoors! Someone's there!

EMILY: There's no one! I don't believe you!

JOHN: Whisper! Don't let them hear you!

(*A voice offstage calls: "Hello! Hello!"*)

EMILY: It's Charles! It's my Charlie!

JOHN: Sh—quiet. Don't let him know we're here.

(*Charles appears. He is younger than his sister. He's a glutton, with his false teeth, emblem of his appetite, hung around his neck by a brass necklace. He carries a huge birdcage, covered now, unidentifiable. He sets it on the ground and stops a little way from the door. He calls again:*)

CHARLES: Hello-o-o-o-o!

EMILY: Charlie—Charlie—

JOHN: (*Restraining her*) No—don't go—don't let him in!

EMILY: He's my brother—he's a visitor!

JOHN: Please be quiet—he'll hear you!

CHARLES: Hello—is anybody here? Emily? John? Emily! It's your dear brother. Anybody there?

(*Angry*) I know you're there! You've got to be there—where else can you be? I know you're there, you devils! You miserable, selfish, sons of bitching devils—I know you're there!

(*Suddenly he weeps*) Oh please—let me in—please! You can't make me stay out here! Please!

EMILY: Oh, listen! I can't bear it when he cries.

JOHN: He's faking.

EMILY: Yes I know—but I can't bear it! He fools me every time!

JOHN: Don't *let* him fool you! Turn away! Don't listen to him!

EMILY: Help me—help me! I'm going to call to him! Stop me—please stop me!

(*John puts his hand over Emily's mouth. Charles' entreaties grow more pitiful.*)

CHARLES: Please—oh please—I'll get sick again—I'll die out here—Emily—John!

(*Emily can't stand Charles' supplications. She moans, she struggles to wrest herself away from John's hold.*)

JOHN: No! Be still—hold still!

CHARLES: Oh please—Em-i-leee!

EMILY: (*Breaking away with an outcry*) Charlie!

(*With an outcry, she breaks away, rushes to the door and tears it open.*)

JOHN: No—come back, you chickenheart! You weak-kneed wetness!

EMILY: (*Tearing the door open*) Charlie!—come in!—we're home!

(*Charles, leaving the birdcage on the ground, comes charging indoors. His desperation is gone—he's jubilant with relief and victory.*)

CHARLES: I knew you'd let me in! I knew it!

JOHN: Get out of here!

CHARLES: (*Joyous*) Hello, Emily! Hello, John, dear John! Hello, my family! Hello, my beloved family!

JOHN: I said get out, get out!

CHARLES: (*Ignoring John*) I'm glad you let me in! I'm especially glad *you* let me in, John. That was nice of you, very nice. And clever—oh, how clever it was of you. Because if you hadn't, I'd have shouted louder and louder—shouted the bloody walls down! And if that had failed, I'd've started to howl—wail and rail and set up such a marrow-chilling bone-freezing howling as would turn your blood to urine, that's what I'd've done! And then—oh miserable day—I'd take my clothes off! Hat, coat and shirt—shoes, socks and underwear—with my chest hair blowing in the memory of the old wind and my bollocks out in the nowhere—oh murder, what a wonderful horrible sight! And then, by God, you'd've opened the goddamn door after all—and've offered me a great big juicy gut-filling dinner!

(*With enraged definition*) Now then!—where's the food? I'm hungry! Anybody offering me a little bloody-red morsel to eat? I've got my chow-chompers all ready here—and my stomach dry and empty—*and I am perishing of hunger*!

JOHN: Get out.

CHARLES: Hungry. I said hungry.

JOHN: There's nothing here to eat. Nothing for you. Get out.

CHARLES: She called me in. She. That's my sister. Called me in. Us—we—brother and sister—sister and brother. Flesh and blood, heart of heart. Squeezed out of the same cave, we were. Sucked the same nipple, peed in the same potty. She told me: *IN*!

JOHN: I tell you out.

CHARLES: (*He wheels about, to face Emily*) You going to let him throw me out?

EMILY: No.

JOHN: Out, I said. Out!

CHARLES: No. I won't. We're *Family*!

JOHN: Go on and shout while I toss you—

CHARLES: (*Shouting*) *Family*! *Love*! *Understanding*!

JOHN: —into the gutter!

CHARLES: *Comfort*! *Devotion*! *Family*!

(*An instant*) HUNGER!!

(*John has been manhandling him toward the door. Now, as they get closer to it, Charles's bones go to jelly, and he falls on the floor.*)

CHARLES: Please be kind! Don't be unkind to me, John—I love you, John—you're my family—

JOHN: Get up, hog, get up!

CHARLES: No!

(*He starts to undress*) Coat, shirt and underwear.

EMILY: John—please—John!

JOHN: Go on, take your clothes off. You know when I'll throw you out?—when you're naked as an eyeball.

(*Helping him undress*) Here, I'll lend a hand. Off-sy goes the shirt-sy, then the undershirt-sy. Now the trousers, laddy-boy.

(*Charles suddenly stops undressing. He pulls himself together. He is lofty with pride.*)

CHARLES: No! To hell with you! I shall remain fully clothed in my dignity. You have convinced me that I am something less than welcome here. Therefore, I go. And I take my present with me.

EMILY: (*Ears up*) Present? What present?

JOHN: Emily, I forbid it!

EMILY: I want the present!

CHARLES: (*Smugly*) There—you see? You can always count on family affection—and greed.

JOHN: Emily, if you let him stay because of some mean wretched little charity—

EMILY: I don't really *want* the present. I simply want to know what it is. What, Charles—tell me—what?

CHARLES: (*Lording it*) Ah, no—sorry, Emily. Grieved that I can't accept your kind invitation to stay—your generous, gracious invitation to remain in this warm, welcoming haven of sweet refuge. Must go, alack-aday, simply must go. Pressing engagements elsewhere. Au 'voir!

EMILY: No —stop!—what's the present?

CHARLES: It's so loving of you both to want me as your guest. So heartwarming! Yes indeed, it warms my cockles. Oh, warms them—heats up my little old chilly cockles! But I simply must decline your invitation! Dearbeloved Brother Charles—Regrets!

JOHN: Nobody's inviting you—nobody.

EMILY: (*Nakedly*) I want the present! Give me the present!

CHARLES: Oh, impossible! Not at all the way things are done. House gift, you know—token of gratitude for hospitality.
(*His dignity is gone. A spit of rage*) Hospitality, you miserable bastards, *hospitality!*

EMILY: *Stay!*

JOHN: No! Emily—no!
(*He reaches to pull her away from Charles. She shakes him off violently.*)

EMILY: Take your scabby hands off! You don't bring me presents!
(*To Charles*) You stay!—where's my present?

CHARLES: Thank you. I reluctantly accept.

EMILY: I don't see any present. Are you trying to cheat me? Where is it?

CHARLES: It's outside. Don't trust me, do you?

EMILY: No, I don't. Go and get it.
(*Charles hurries outdoors.*)

JOHN: Whatever it is, I hope it's no good.

EMILY: Whatever it is, I'll want it. It'll change the order of things.

JOHN: I hope it doesn't fit. I hope the color is wrong. I hope it doesn't taste good. I hope it brings you bad luck. Bad dreams! I hope it brings you bad dreams!
(*Charles returns with the covered birdcage. He does not uncover it.*)

CHARLES: Here you are—it's a bird!

EMILY: Oh, happiness—a bird, a bird! What kind? Take the cover off! No—wait—please wait—don't let the moment slip away too fast—let me guess what kind it is! Oh, lovely, a bird—is it a canary?

CHARLES: (*Enjoying the game*) I don't think it's a canary, n-no.

EMILY: Oh, take the cover off!
(*As he starts to do so*) No—wait! Is it a finch, is it a little golden finch?

CHARLES: N-no, not really, not really a finch.

EMILY: A mynah-bird, a parrot, a little blue and purple parakeet?—oh, I can't stand it!—take it off, take the cover off!

(*With a flourish, Charles whips the cover off. In the cage, a hideous, bloody, wounded cockerel.*)

EMILY: What's that? Oh no!—how ugly it is!

JOHN: (*Quietly*) What did you expect?

EMILY: Oh, ugly. What is it?

CHARLES: Why, bless you, it's a cockerel.

EMILY: Hideous, disgusting. What's that all over him?

CHARLES: Come now, you know what it is—it's blood.

EMILY: Oh, take it away. Loathsome—take it away!

(*As he starts to remove the cage, she stops him*) No—wait a minute.

(*Slowly, in the stillness, she forces herself to look inside the cage*) Is it really blood?

CHARLES: Of course it is.

EMILY: It's—all—different kinds.

CHARLES: Some is wetter, some is dryer.

EMILY: . . . Some is thicker.

(*Without loathing now. Interested*) How ugly it is.

(*Whirling on Charles, in a rage*) You filthy beast, you cheated me again!

CHARLES: How?—no I haven't!—how?!

EMILY: You said it was a bird!

CHARLES: It is a bird!

EMILY: A real bird—flying and singing and splashing in its bath and making a cry of happiness!

CHARLES: You should have heard the cry of happiness this one made!

EMILY: Where, you liar? How? When?

CHARLES: In the fight, in the battle!

EMILY: (*Pause. Caught. Quietly*) This has been in a fight?

CHARLES: Certainly. Cockfight. White cock, red cock.

JOHN: Is that true?

CHARLES: True?—of course it's true. And you should've heard the cry out of this little cock.

(*He makes a crowing sound*) Hi cockalorum!

EMILY: What's that?—do it again!

CHARLES: Hi cockalorum—battle of happiness! I kill you, red cock! Blood, I lame you—blood, I maim you—blood, I pluck your eye out! Kill, I kill you, guts and entrails! Happiness—hi cockalorum!

EMILY: Was it brave—was it really brave?

(*She is excited*)

CHARLES: Yes—brave!—hi cockalorum!

(*Going to the cage, Emily speaks to the cock as if it were a baby.*)

EMILY: Hello, brave cockalorum. Hello, dear brave darling cockalorum. Hello cockalorum, cockalorum, darling, darling.

(*Turning to the others*) What shall we do with him?

(*Silence*) He's so untidy—shall we wash him?

(*Silence*) We must do something with him. But what, but what?

(*She sees Charles throw a quick glance at John who is impassive, watching the other two. Charles looks smilingly to her. She understands.*)

EMILY: *No!*

CHARLES: Now Emily—

EMILY: *No—no!*

CHARLES: Please—I'm hungry!

EMILY: No—I won't do it!

CHARLES: You needn't do it—I'll do it *for* you.

EMILY: No—he's mine. You gave him to me as a present! A house present!

CHARLES: Suppose I'd brought you a bottle of wine. What would we do?—just wash it and read the label? No—we'd consume it!

EMILY: But this is alive! John—stop him! You won't let him do it, will you, John?

JOHN: (*Smiling wryly*) Yes, why not? Got my wish, didn't I? It doesn't fit. Color's wrong. Bad dreams.

CHARLES: But it'll taste good—it certainly will taste good.

EMILY: No—I won't let you!

CHARLES: Now, come on, Emily, you know it *is* going to be done.

EMILY: No—I won't let you! Hi cockalorum—you said that—cockerel, brave cockerel—fought a brave fight—brave cockalorum!

CHARLES: When fighting, he's brave—when cooked, he's delicious.

EMILY: *No!*

CHARLES: Now, Emily, don't fret it up too much, my dear. A little of this delicacy is becoming in a woman. But I know you—you like to eat, you have a healthy appetite.

JOHN: (*Perversely enjoying this. Quietly*) Yes, and if you carry this queasiness too far, you won't—without being shamefaced about it—bring yourself to eat the chickabiddy.

CHARLES: Oh, she'll eat him—right down to the cock-a-doodle-doo. And why not?—that's what he's for. And the whole damn thing won't hurt him—not much anyway. Not the way I do it.

EMILY: Stop it!

CHARLES: (*Continuing as if uninterrupted*) Why, I'll just take the knife and draw it across his neck. You don't have to saw away at it, or anything like that. You don't even have to cut, not really. You just draw the knife gently across the jugular—gently—like a bow across a fiddle string. A little spurt of blood—he lets out a bit of a squawk—hi cockalorum! And it's done. (*He takes up the birdcage and starts for the kitchen*) Not to worry, take my word for it. Hi cockalorum—and the bird is still.

(*Charles goes into the kitchen.*)

EMILY: He . . . not now . . . He's not going to do it now, is he?

JOHN: Just a bow across a fiddle string.

EMILY: (*Starting to panic*) Not now! I don't want it now! Not here!

JOHN: (*Evenly*) Then stop him, if you like. Go on.

EMILY: (*Calling lamely*) Charles! Not now!

(*Charles' voice comes from the kitchen, elated.*)

CHARLES: Here we go!

(*We hear the squawk of the cockerel. Simultaneously, Emily shrieks:*)

EMILY: *Hi cockalorum!*

(*She rushes to John*) Oh, hold me—no more killing, no more dying—hold me!

JOHN: For Pete sake, control yourself—it's only a chicken!

EMILY: I'm shaking—I'm going to fall—hi cockalorum—going to fall!

(*Charles returns carrying the slaughtered cock. He smiles*)

CHARLES: There you are. Quick as I promised. Here, Emily—all yours now. Cook it.

EMILY: Take it away!—no!

CHARLES: Nothing to be frightened of. Only a dead cock. Go on—cook it. Cook the cock.

EMILY: I don't want it. Take it away.

(*Slowly he moves toward her. His voice is seductive, but there is also a threat in it, an ominousness.*)

CHARLES: It's only a chicken, Emily. How many times have you ever cooked a chicken, dear girl? Now, you've cooked many's the succulent chicken, haven't you? Certainly you have. Of course, I don't blame you for screaming it up when that chicken-fellow was alive and scratching, so to speak, when he was a bold bad cockerel, hi cockalorum and all that. But he's dead now, getting colder every minute, no good as a brave cockerel, no goddamn good at all. No good to a woman, certainly. Got to be alive to be a good cockerel, right? But dead, he's only a chicken.

(*The menace is getting clearer*) Now you're alive. At least right now you are. So you're good as a woman and you're good as a wife. Now, you be good as a sister and a cook. Now—take it, Emily.

(*As she takes it, his voice goes cruel*) Now, no more nonsense out of you, understand? You go and take that bloody dead thing and do like a goddamn woman!

(*Silent, frightened, Emily takes the bird into the kitchen. With a contemptuous smile, John confronts Charles.*)

JOHN: You cruel pig.

CHARLES: Are you speaking, sir, or having an emission?

JOHN: You're a cruel pig, aren't you?

CHARLES: Why? You think what I just did—it's going to mark her for life? Think she'll live in a dark shadow because of this black bloody experience, do you? Bruise her Miss Piss sensibilities? *What sensibilities*?!

(*Then, less vehemently*) None! Don't worry about her. When she comes back in this room, she'll be wiping her hands on her dear little apron and dabbing the sweat off her pert little nose—and she'll be as merry as if you were tickling her titties! Because these women, they don't give a belch about the dead, they don't! Something's dead, all they want to do is skin it down, cook it and eat it. Makes them cozy in the heart, warm in the belly and as merry as a tickle tit!

(*Emily enters. As Charles predicted, she is cheery. She wipes her hands on her apron and sings.*)

EMILY: What a lovely bird! Lots of good flesh on it and the cleanest, whitest fat I've ever seen! A nice roly-poly chicken—just like the old days!

CHARLES: See that? Merry as a tickle tit.

EMILY: Merry as what?

CHARLES: Wipe the sweat off your nose. Don't want it dripping into the bubbling broth, do we?

EMILY: Oh heavens, there's no broth as yet. Haven't even plucked it and taken out its entrails. It'll be hours.

CHARLES: (*Shaking with nerves; blabbering*) Hours?—no!—I can't stand it! I'm dying of hunger. Take the liver out, Emily—a liver cooks in a jiffy—just throw it in a little water. Cook the liver, Emily!

EMILY: Shall I?—what a nuisance—set the table. You and John—you set the table—and try to be friendly. If you want to enjoy eating chicken together, you've got to be friendly.

(*Happy to be cooking, she flounces back into the kitchen. Charles and John start setting the table.*)

CHARLES: It's the most spiritual canon of morality.

JOHN: What is?

CHARLES: If you want to enjoy eating chicken together, you've got to be friendly.

JOHN: I think I'd rather forgo chicken.

CHARLES: Emily wouldn't. You don't bounce her around enough.

JOHN: I don't? How do you know?

CHARLES: All that wiggling of ass. If she did more of that in bed, she'd do less down here.

JOHN: That's a penetrating observation.

CHARLES: You're setting the table all wrong.

JOHN: I'm setting it right.

CHARLES: You're setting it for three.

JOHN: You don't mean to set it for one, do you? You want to leave us out and eat the bird all by yourself?

CHARLES: Seven.

JOHN: What?

CHARLES: Set it for seven.

JOHN: How do you figure seven?

CHARLES: Don't ask questions. Seven.

JOHN: I'll set it for three.

CHARLES: (*With a quiet threat in his voice*) You're not being friendly, John. Now you do as I say. You think I'd say seven if I didn't know there'll be seven people eating? You think I *want* to share that fowl with six other people when I could be sharing it with only two?! *Seven!*

(*Pause. John weighs a decision. Then, deliberately.*)

JOHN: I think . . . I'll have to cut your tongue out on this visit.

(*Pause. They measure each other.*)

CHARLES: You think that, do you?

JOHN: Yes, I think that.

CHARLES: Well, if you do, give it back to me—to eat!

(*He howls with laughter. John does not. Emily enters.*)

CHARLES: Did you bring me my liver?

EMILY: My goodness, Charlie, I just put it in the pot.

CHARLES: It takes a lot less time to cook a liver than people are likely to imagine. I hope you put some herbs in the water—spices—things like that—at least salt and pepper. It should make a lovely soup. Oh, I can smell it! Oh, dear festival, I can smell it!

(*He starts for the kitchen.*)

EMILY: Stay out of there—and finish that table! Good heavens, you're doing it all wrong! Clear those extra plates—clear them!

CHARLES: You let them alone. I'm setting seven places for seven people!

JOHN: He's amuck.

CHARLES: (*Flaring*) I am not amuck! I know what I'm talking about! I was down There today—even while you were down There! And while you were just poking around and looking lost and discovering nothing, I discovered everything!

(*Emily and John, silent, furtively glance at one another. Emily speaks under restraint.*)

EMILY: What did you discover?

CHARLES: (*Pointing to the table*) Seven is correct. In addition to the three of us, there will be four dinner guests. Seven is the proper number.

EMILY: Oh, my goodness. Will one chicken be enough?

CHARLES: One chicken is never enough.

JOHN: It'll do. There will only be the three of us. He's telling lies.

CHARLES: (*With dignity*) I'm only telling what I heard.

JOHN: You heard lies.

CHARLES: (*Hiding his anger*) Very well, I heard lies. I also heard lies when I told you, on my last visit, that the streets would get narrower. Then how does it happen that they *did* get narrower? I said we would start losing our windows. Well, it happened, didn't it?—one window at a time—and now all yours are gone—you have no windows anymore. Was that a lie? And the bridge—remember when I told you the children would be chased off the bridge?

EMILY: (*Quietly, frightened*) And have they been?

CHARLES: This morning.

EMILY: (*A whisper*) Oh no—oh no!

CHARLES: And they all ran off in many directions. And some of them cannot be found.

EMILY: Oh no. What will we do? Will they let us go and look for them?

CHARLES: Look where? Who knows where the bridge goes to?

EMILY: *They* know, and they'll tell *you.*
(*Tremulous*) They will, Charlie—won't they?—won't they?

JOHN: (*Quietly*) Yes, they will. Because he works for them.

CHARLES: I don't! I do not work for them! I swear to you I don't!

JOHN: Yes you do, Charles. You're an informer, you're a toad. You tell them what we do and what we say and what we think. You betray us.

CHARLES: No! I give you my word—I swear to you—

JOHN: The last time you were here, you told them we were hoarding things.

CHARLES: No—it wasn't me—I didn't tell them!

JOHN: And they came storming in here and took a little bag of crackers and a cup of raisins that we were saving for a midnight binge—

EMILY: —and they tore open all our private things and ripped out our thoughts and purged us of our kindest memories. "Don't recall your happiness!" they said. "It's not allowed, it's not allowed!"
(*She is weeping softly. Charlie's entreaty sounds altogether genuine.*)

CHARLES: Please—please don't blame me for that. I had nothing to do with it. I swear to you by everything I once held dear—I had nothing to do with it.

JOHN: You're an insider down There, Charlie—you're one of the insiders.

CHARLES: No I'm not—no!

JOHN: Listen, Charlie, one night about a year ago, you slipped away and went down There, and I followed you. You went under the bridge and you walked a narrow alleyway to the house that used to be the inn. You went inside and I could hear a lot of people there—laughing—talking—a clatter of dishes. And there was a smell—a wonderful smell of food inside—like the old days—onions being cooked—and garlic and spices—oh, the delicious aroma of spices—! Slowly, step by step, I got as close to the door as I could. And once—when it stayed open for a bit—I got a glimpse of all the insiders sitting around the biggest round table I had ever seen. And you were one among them. You were right there in the midst of them. And what a feast it was! Oh, blessed memory, there was a great shining golden goose upon the table, and a crown roast of pork and a fat and gleaming fish on a bed of green things—was it thyme or marjoram? And the cornucopias of fruit—where did they all come from?—oh the fruit, so many fruits!
(*A moment*) How did you get there, Charlie—an insider among insiders—and where did all that food come from?

CHARLES: (*Quietly*) It was a fake.

JOHN: Yes, you are. What do you mean, it was?

CHARLES: *It was a fake*! It was a banquet made of plaster and of paint! It was a mock-up of old memories! It was art, Johnny, it was art! Not the culinary art, but *art*! The painter paints, the sculptor makes a wooden fish so real that it swims in the stream of consciousness. The whole groaning board of food—a fake! A recollection of a festive meal we had so long ago! Mouth memory!—nostalgia in the hall of food!—a delectable dining pleasure in the past!

JOHN: A Memorial to a Dear-departed Meal.

CHARLES: Yes—why not? We have memorials for dead people we do not care about—why not a memorial for a meal we loved? Some of the corpses I have mourned—I'd rather have a rack of spareribs any day!

JOHN: You see what a liar he is? It was art, he says, it was make-believe. Well, why did that splendid visual mockup *smell* so good? Where did it get its wonderful mouthwatering *aroma*?

CHARLES: It was art, Johnny-boy, it was art! Art lets you smell what isn't there—art fills in the spaces! And we've still got artists, Johnny—they take a long time dying! *It was art*!!

EMILY: If pretense satisfies you, we'll let you pretend to eat the liver.

CHARLES: (*Angry*) The liver is real and that cock is real! Down to the very squawk—he's real!

JOHN: Where did you get it?

CHARLES: There's a man who deals in contraband. In his cellar, he fattens animals for food. He has two squirrels, a few rats, a cat or too, and chickens. He's breaking the law—he's hoarding. I told them about him—and I was given a chicken for my loyalty.

EMILY: I'll never eat that chicken, never.

CHARLES: Oh yes you will.

EMILY: Not a mouthful, not a morsel.

CHARLES: Yes, she will. Won't she, Johnny?

JOHN: You know more about hunger than I do.

CHARLES: I do—I admit it. I know more about hunger than anybody. I know more than has been written. Right now, I could eat that whole chicken by myself. Do you think the liver could be done by now?

EMILY: Probably.

CHARLES: (*Dithering*) Could I have it, do you suppose? Do you think I could have the liver now?

EMILY: I'll go and see.

(*She goes into the kitchen. As she disappears, Charles calls after her.*)

CHARLES: Oh, Emily—you're the only one! The only one that's good to me—the only one! That's why I bring you presents. I don't bring him presents—only you! Better than cockerels too!

(*Emily appears at the kitchen door, a cooking fork in hand.*)

EMILY: You've got another present for me?

CHARLES: You bet I have. Go on—get the liver.

EMILY: Oh, lovely! Another present—lovely!

(*She goes back into the kitchen.*)

CHARLES: Aren't you curious about my present?

JOHN: No—alarmed. I hate your presents. You can spell that both ways.

CHARLES: This is a gift of very special merit.

JOHN: How do we get rid of it?

CHARLES: You won't. I think you will like it.

(*Emily enters with a cooked chicken liver on a fork.*)

EMILY: Here you are, Charlie. Now, what's the present? Careful now—it's hot.

CHARLES: Oh, delicious! Shall I use my choppers? No, it's so soft, I don't need them! I'm going to faint—it's delicious!

EMILY: The present—I'll have my present now.

CHARLES: Oh, hot, delicious, hot! What would you like best in the world?

EMILY: . . . Best?

CHARLES: Yes—what?

EMILY: (*A whisper*) Oh no.

(*She knows what the present is, and begins to tremble. John also knows, and turns violently on Charles.*)

JOHN: You monster! To awaken her dream this way!

CHARLES: It's not a dream!

JOHN: To give her even the vaguest hope that Jessica will come home!

CHARLES: She will be here.

EMILY: Oh heaven, I can't believe it—I can't believe it!

JOHN: Don't believe it! This cruel bastard—! At the last minute—when she doesn't arrive—he'll say he got the times confused—the schedule was changed—the bridge was closed—there was some mixup in the realities!

CHARLES: No mixup—none!

JOHN: Don't listen to him! She said she would never come again, and she won't!

CHARLES: Yes, she will! I wrote her a letter and she said yes!

(*Silence.*)

EMILY: (*In wonderment*) You wrote her a letter?

CHARLES: Yes I did. Oh, this juicy thing—last bite—goodbye, farewell. Yes, I wrote her a letter and I said, "Your mother yearns for you." I said, "She pines. Come quickly before it is too late. Your father's dying."

JOHN: (*Turning quickly*) You said I'm dying?

CHARLES: Yes, I did.

JOHN: I'm not dying—why the hell did you tell her I'm dying?!

CHARLES: We're all dying, aren't we? Besides, it gave the letter some urgency. And I said to her, "Bring your husband, bring the children."

JOHN: She hasn't any husband.

EMILY: And no children.

CHARLES: But it gave the letter—*sincerity*. If you really want a guest to come, why, say it open-handed: "Bring your husband, bring the children, bring the kittens and the dog."

JOHN: She hasn't any kittens and she—

CHARLES: Oh, damn you, John—is she welcome or not?

EMILY: Yes, she's welcome! Oh heavens, she is welcome!

JOHN: (*Turning on her*) How can you be so goddamn gullible! Do you believe what this monstrosity is saying?

CHARLES: Why shouldn't she? It's all true! I believe it myself! Look at those plates! Why do you think I've set those four extra plates?!

JOHN: To hell with your four extra plates! Here's one of them!

(*He picks up a plate and smashes it.*)

EMILY: No—stop—stop!

JOHN: And here's another one!

(*He breaks another plate.*)

EMILY: Oh do stop—please—please!

CHARLES: Go on—break them all! They're not mine, they're yours!

(*Handing him the third plate*) Here, break another one!

JOHN: Yes, I will, I will!

(*He breaks it.*)

CHARLES: Now—here—the last one—break it, break it!

(*He hands the plate to John, unaware that the visitor has come: Jessica. She stands outdoors, looking at the house, her manner cool, detached. Or seemingly so. Now, during the breaking of the plates, she advances toward the house, opens the door and stands there, watching, impassive.*)

CHARLES: Go on—break it.

(*But John arrests the action. For he alone sees Jessica. Stillness.*)

JESSICA: Good evening, Father.

(*Emily and Charles turn. Emily lets out a cry.*)

EMILY: Oh no. Oh, Jessica—is it you? Is it really you?

JESSICA: Good evening, Mother.

EMILY: Oh my dear!

JOHN: Jessica—Jessica!

EMILY: Oh, daughter—welcome—welcome home!

JESSICA: Am I really? Welcome home?

CHARLES: Jessica—me—say hello to me—don't you remember me?

JESSICA: (*Studying him coolly*) Have I ever seen you before? No, I think not. (*She turns away*) How are you, Mother? Father, are you well? And how is Uncle Charles?

CHARLES: (*Titillated*) But that's me! Me—I'm Uncle Charles—that's me!

JESSICA: (*Turning slowly to examine him. Distantly*) How loathsome he is. Wouldn't we do better without him?

CHARLES: No we wouldn't. I'm here!

JESSICA: Why?

CHARLES: (*Blatant*) Because I belong here! This is my family!

JESSICA: Quietly. Answer the question quietly.

CHARLES: It's the only family I have! No one else—and nowhere to go!

JESSICA: Not so close. Stand back a bit.

(*To John*) Does he really have to stay? Is he in the order of things?

EMILY: Yes, he is, my dear.

JESSICA: (*With a tight smile*) I was talking to Father.

CHARLES: (*To Emily*) Watch her now. You better keep an open eye on her. She'll freeze us out, that's what she'll do.

(*To Jessica*) But not me, you won't. I'm on to you.

JESSICA: (*Measuring him*) Are you, then?

CHARLES: Don't believe me, do you? Well, see those broken plates? Who knew to set seven places? Who knew you weren't alone? I did!

EMILY: Is there someone with you, my dear?

JOHN: Was he telling the truth, then?

CHARLES: Of course I was! I know everything.

JESSICA: Do you indeed . . . know everything?

CHARLES: A husband and two children.

EMILY: (*Agog*) Where? Oh, where?

JOHN: They're here? With you?

ALL: (*In a spill of excitement*) Where?—outdoors? . . . Let's go and bring them in! . . . Where are they?—where?!

(*In commotion, they start for the door. For the first time, Jessica loses control:*)

JESSICA: No!—wait!—stop! I say stop!

(*As they go silent*) Not yet.

(*As Charles starts to move*) I said not yet!

(*She pauses; fixes upon him*) You say you know everything. That's quite a responsibility. I hope you're up to it. How did I get here?

CHARLES: If you think I'll submit to your testing me—

JESSICA: (*Summarily*) Answer the question. How did I get here?

CHARLES: By the bridge.

JESSICA: (*With a smile*) Yes, I thought you'd know that . . . Are you sorry you told me?

CHARLES: No, not a bit. You don't frighten me, Jessica.

JESSICA: Let's get on with it. My husband—you know of him?

CHARLES: Of course I do—he doesn't say very much.

EMILY: What do you mean, he doesn't say very much? What does he leave out?

JESSICA: (*Gently*) Be quiet, please.

CHARLES: Or hear—he doesn't hear very well. Does he, does he?

JESSICA: That's as it may be. My children now. How many?

CHARLES: Two.

JESSICA: How . . . old are they?

(*Charles is perturbed. Seeing this, she is insistent*) I said how old?

CHARLES: I—it's—they're both the same—I know that much—twins!

JESSICA: How old?

CHARLES: Three months—born three months ago.

JESSICA: (*Smoothly*) That makes it simple, then—they're three months old.

CHARLES: (*Quickly, as if avoiding capture*) I said three months ago.

JESSICA: (*In pursuit*) How old, *how old*?!

CHARLES: They're fully grown!

(*Tense pause.*)

JESSICA: Precisely. They're fully grown. Shall I ask you any more questions?

CHARLES: (*Giving up, he turns away*) No.

JESSICA: One can't know everything . . . or anything.

(*As Emily moves toward the door, as if to escape, Jessica bars her way*) No—please—a little patience, Mother. And don't be frightened, please. Oh my, it's so bright in here. Even without the windows, it's much too bright. And louder than I remember it.

(*Remembering*) That other time . . . some place . . . also loud and light. Well, such places weren't meant for shade and quiet. It's a pity all pain can't be borne in the dark. Did I say born?

(*With a quiet smile*) Bearing and borning. It's a little pun. They gave me all they had and went away. "Try to stay awake," they said. Then they had others to attend to. The light got whiter and whiter. There were always pains in pairs—the near one and the far one. One I loved and one I hated. Too exposed under the white light—and not naked enough. When every stitch of clothes was gone, I kept wanting to take more off— my skin, my hair. I tore with my fingernails, I bit myself. And then they started coming. Oh, more than two, than three, than four—there were so many of them! Whatever they were—too many. And all of them more pulpy than they should have been. Too moist—I could shape them too easily. If I pressed a form, the form would stay. For something human, too obedient. I can't recall how many. Or how I came to judge. If it didn't pulse a little . . . and move . . . I suppose you could call it "move." Or if it was too soft—one had to say no to it. Two—only two—were somewhat firm. Not perfect, as one thinks of perfect, but capable of holding . . . shape . . . identity. Those two I kept. They grew. They grew faster than the old surprises: "Oh my, you've grown! I'd never have known you!"

(*As if to herself*) I never have.

(*She laughs a little, quietly. Then, more darkly:*) They grew the way terror grows. At night.

(*Silence. Then:*) I'll call them now.

(*She goes to the door, opens it and summons them with a gesture. The man appears first: Paul. He is tall, lean, with distance in his eyes. Just slightly behind him are the girl and boy: Carla and Frank. They are of adolescent stature. The boy is blind. The girl has no arms. All are mute. They enter the house*)

JESSICA: This is my husband. He is nearly blind but he is not deaf. He will understand what you say. His name is Paul. This is my daughter Carla. She understands. How much I don't know. More than the others. As you see, she has no arms. This is my son Frank. He is blind. Except in the matter of size, he is backward and, I suspect, nearly always afraid. Yet, for some reason I do not comprehend, he smiles more than the others do. I am not at all sure I know what it means when any of them smile. They are all mute.

(*To Paul, Carla and Frank*) This is my mother. This is my father.

EMILY: How . . . do you do.

JOHN: Welcome . . . to you all.

EMILY: (*Starting toward them*) I would like to—

JESSICA: Do not embrace them. You don't really want to do it—

EMILY: Jessica—

JESSICA: —and they won't understand.

CHARLES: You didn't introduce me.

(*To the children*) I am your great-uncle—Charles.

JESSICA: One would hope that they would treat each of us differently. For example, smile at my parents and snarl at you. But they treat us all the same. I grieve over that.

JOHN: How do we say to them that we . . .?

JESSICA: I wouldn't try, Father.

JOHN: But I would like to tell them.

EMILY: (*Quickly: the habituated hostess*) Perhaps we could all sit down. Get acquainted. Have a little chat!

(*They all sit. John gestures to a rocking chair and Paul sits in it. Long silence. Emily speaks with studied cheeriness.*)

EMILY: Now then—here we are together. And my dear Jessica a mother! What a delightful surprise!

(*Silence. Jessica appraisingly watches her mother. Emily sails onward.*)

EMILY: Two such lovely children! And you did it all on your own, didn't you? No calling for comfort or for counsel. Didn't worry your mother with any of the pesky preliminaries! None of the nuisances of baby clothes, of layouts and layettes, and shall I purchase pink or blue, and what kind of nipples should I put on the bottles, real rubber or synthetic? And here they are, without any help from grandmama—safe and sound—healthy, wealthy and wise! Just went off and did it all by yourself, didn't you, dear Jessica?—there's a brave girl!—and brought home two fully grown three-month-old children!

JOHN: Careful, Emily.

EMILY: (*Heedless of his warning; unstoppable*) Two of them—a pair!—a litter, in fact.

(*She giggles. Charles, the troublemaker, smiles. Jessica is composed. Her husband and children are inscrutable.*)

JOHN: Emily, please stop it.

EMILY: Oh come now, let's not be evasive about it, John. They're here and we're grandparents and these are ours! Now, which of us do they look like?

JOHN: They don't look like either of us.

EMILY: You're not really looking. I think the boy looks like you and the girl looks like me.

CHARLES: And that's exactly the way it should be.

EMILY: Boys with the boys—

CHARLES: —and girls with the girls!

EMILY: Yes! And whichever of us they look like, they're very pretty children in their way. Pretty, I mean, if you see them without prejudice.
(*To the children, loudly, as if they're deaf*) You're pretty! You're—both—very—pretty!

JESSICA: They're not deaf, Mother.

EMILY: Oh, aren't they? How nice. I thought they had everything.

JESSICA: They don't "have" anything, Mother. They're not diseased, they're not ill in any way.

EMILY: Oh, I'm delighted! Just a couple of perfectly healthy, average, normal children!

JOHN: Will you stop it?!

EMILY: Stop what, for heaven's sake?

JESSICA: (*Quietly*) He means if you want to be cruel to them—or to me—

EMILY: I don't want to be cruel to anybody!

CHARLES: She's not being cruel, Jessica.

JESSICA: Yes she is. She's not so stupid as to say those things—unless she means to hurt me with them.

EMILY: (*Angry and wounded*) I don't mean to hurt you!

JESSICA: You're mocking!

EMILY: I'm not mocking—I'm pretending! I mean to like your children! To love them, in fact—to take them to my heart—and to see them as my own!

JESSICA: (*An instant. Then, muted:*) Why need you love them?

EMILY: (*Taken aback*) Why need I . . . ?

JESSICA: Yes. You needn't love them at all.

EMILY: Then why did you bring them home?
(*She has said it quietly. Jessica is caught by the question. Charles laughs almost inaudibly. Jessica whirls on him.*)

JESSICA: You be quiet!

CHARLES: Oh, I will be! I won't say a word.

JOHN: (Indicating the children) Are *they* saying anything?

JESSICA: Father, don't *you* start up.

JOHN: (*Trying to sound reasonable*) I'm not trying to hurt anybody's feelings, Jessica. But you said they understand. Or this one does. Whom do they understand? You? Us? Each other? If they understand each other, how do they manage it?
(*He walks to the children and smiles diffidently*) I—forgive me—do you talk to one another? Do you? If you do, will you—one day—speak to me? I would like that. You needn't really *say* anything. I certainly won't. . . . Just speak to me.
(*Silence.*)

CHARLES: Nothing.

JOHN: How do you know there's nothing!
(*He flares, then looks to his daughter*) Was there nothing, Jessica?
(*As she turns away, John points to Frank*) That one smiled.

JESSICA: I told you—he smiles at anything.

EMILY: Who says we need to talk?

JOHN: I do.

EMILY: You have a horror of silence.

JOHN: Because silence is horrible. Something dangerous might drop into it.

EMILY: Well, I have no horror of it—none at all. There are lots of things we can do together, the children and I—and never say a word to one another. Games, for example! Why, I'll find so many games—! And toys—and throwing one's self about—and laughing! I hope they know what laughing's got to do with things!—and if they don't, I'll tell them! My God, it's old times, isn't it?

CHARLES: What's old times?

EMILY: Having children in the house.

(*She is touched by the remembrance*) Just like those days . . . long ago . . . when there was almost enough to go around, and we would wait for the mailman, and a thought was not wrapped in darkness but lofted like a kite—there!—look at it!—my thought—in the sky—up there—how beautiful it is! In the days before we lost D-Natural.

JOHN: Do you think of it much?

EMILY: Yes, but I can't hear it.

CHARLES: It's gone. Forget it—it's all gone.

JESSICA: I think he's right . . . it's gone.

(*Emily goes to the children. She mouths her words carefully.*)

EMILY: I'm going outdoors now. Will you come?

JESSICA: (*Cautious*) Outdoors?—why?—what for?

EMILY: We've got to be together. Do you mind?

JESSICA: What will you do together?

EMILY: We'll—I don't know—we'll watch.

JESSICA: Watch what?

EMILY: Each other. We'll start that way.

(*An instant*) What else is there to do?

(*Silence. Jessica decides:*)

JESSICA: All right. Go, children, go.

JOHN: (*Hesitantly, to Emily*) May I come with you?

EMILY: Oh, will you?—how nice!

CHARLES: (*With mock gaiety*) Go, kiddies!—everybody out!—go and watch! (*Warning with a laugh*) Watch out!

(*Emily, John and the children go outdoors. Jessica's glance follows them until they're out of sight. She is namelessly apprehensive. She turns to see Charles studying Paul. The latter, heedless of Charles' fixed stare at him, continues rocking. Jessica watches Charles watching Paul. At last:*)

JESSICA: Let him alone.

CHARLES: (*Startled*) What?—me? I haven't touched him.

JESSICA: Don't stare at him.

CHARLES: They're watching something—so am I. What's he watching?

JESSICA: Us.

CHARLES: He's not even looking at us.

JESSICA: He sees us without looking at us.

CHARLES: Do you see me without looking at me?

JESSICA: I see as much of you as I can bear.

CHARLES: You think you make me uncomfortable, choosing to look at nothing rather than at me. But I'm on your mind. You asked for me the instant you arrived.

JESSICA: Yes, I looked at you and said, "Where is Uncle Charles?"

CHARLES: That didn't hurt. It didn't prove to me I don't exist.

JESSICA: What did it prove?

CHARLES: Only that, for the moment, you did not choose to discuss the subject of Me.

JESSICA: That moment or any moment.

CHARLES: (*Busy, busy*) Let's have empty talk, let's be sociable, let's talk about others. Do you know my friend?

JESSICA: Have you got a friend?

CHARLES: If I had, would you know him?

JESSICA: What name?

CHARLES: Any name. Harry Bardell. Bill Wormsley. Clavis Jones. You know Clavis Jones?

JESSICA: I know all of them. They say you make them sick. They say you give them cankers and acnes and abscesses. They say you are diseased.

CHARLES: You know what they say about you?

JESSICA: Oh yes, all of them. And others too. Shall I make some others up?

CHARLES: Please do.

JESSICA: Willie Moke. Big Johnson. Halliwell, the Man with the Chest.

CHARLES: Yes, I know. They told me.

JESSICA: What do they say?

CHARLES: They say you have cankers and acnes and abscesses. They say you are diseased.

JESSICA: Yes, that's what I tell them.

CHARLES: Why do you tell them that?

JESSICA: It keeps them away.

CHARLES: Not me. I know you say those things for spite.

(*Silence. She is appraising him somewhat differently than before. He suspects this.*)

CHARLES: Do you have a palm?

JESSICA: A palm?

CHARLES: On your hand.

JESSICA: Shouldn't I have two of them?

CHARLES: If you were looking at someone's palm, which would you rather see, a raisin or a roach?

JESSICA: Are those the only choices?

CHARLES: That's all.

JESSICA: I'll have to give it thought.
CHARLES: I've thought about it, lots of times.
JESSICA: Which, then?
CHARLES: I don't know. Hold out your palm.
JESSICA: No.
CHARLES: Please.
JESSICA: I said no.
CHARLES: You know you will, sooner or later. You're too curious not to.
   (*She weighs this moment. Slowly, she holds out her palm. He looks at it*
   without touching her.)
JESSICA: Well?
CHARLES: I knew that's what I'd see.
JESSICA: I knew it too.
   (*They are five feet apart. He is not touching her.*)
JESSICA: Stop stroking my palm.
CHARLES: I thought you might enjoy it.
   (*He goes to Paul*) I'm not really stroking her palm, my friend. We're just
   having a little truce.
   (*Turning back to Jessica*) What a lovely hand you have. Skin smooth and
   touched with pink. And beautiful fingernails—I must beware of them.
JESSICA: Stop stroking my palm.
CHARLES: In a little while I'll stop. How do you spell "home"?
JESSICA: Home?
CHARLES: Yes. H - o - m - e—home—how do you spell it?
JESSICA: You just spelled it.
CHARLES: I spell it often—because this is my home—did you know that?
JESSICA: No, I didn't.
CHARLES: It's absolutely true. This is the only home I have.
JESSICA: It's not your home—my father detests you. And truth to tell, I'm
   sure my mother is frequently disgusted by you.
CHARLES: And you don't help me very much. No matter how kind I am to
   your parents—no matter how much I bring them food and medicine and
   news of the outside world—you don't call that to their attention. You
   never tell them I am generous. You never have a sympathetic word to say
   about me. You never say to them, "He's not so bad—he's really quite all
   right." You never say you've come to like me more than you used to—or
   understand me better.
JESSICA: I don't lie very well.
CHARLES: (*Nakedly*) There's too much world! I need a home to come to!
JESSICA: (*Without sympathy*) Too bad, too bad.
CHARLES: I need a place to leave my stomach pills and my foot powder! I
   need a bed that has the imprint of my body!
JESSICA: There's nothing we can say or do that can make your home here
   more secure than it already is.
CHARLES: Oh, yes there is! I could make children!

JESSICA: (*Puzzled and alarmed*) . . . Children?

CHARLES: Healthy ones.

JESSICA: (*Flaring*) My children are not unhealthy! They are malformed but they are not unhealthy!

CHARLES: (*Derisively*) Malformed but not unhealthy!—what a pretty distinction! I could make children that are healthy but *not* malformed! (*Pointing to Paul*) I could make better children than he did!

JESSICA: Those are visions you'd better not be seeing.

CHARLES: If I had healthy children here, they would be easier to love than yours are! And far more welcome to your parents! And I would be welcome too. We would all be a family—all goodhearted and loving and welcoming to one another.

JESSICA: Stop maundering. It'll never happen.

CHARLES: Why not? No strings attached. Just rutting like healthy animals. Why not?

JESSICA: Why not, he says—my God, why not?

CHARLES: *Yes—why not?* Outmoded laws?—old customs?

JESSICA: Perennial hatreds!

CHARLES: Uncles?—nieces?—all that drivel?

JESSICA: Nothing to do with it!

CHARLES: Think new, think current practice! Women lie abed with their sons—men impregnate their daughters!

JESSICA: Stop it—take your hands away! (*He is nowhere near her, certainly not within arm's length*)

CHARLES: Where? Where are they?

JESSICA: Take your hands away!

CHARLES: Tell me where they are! Tell me where my hands are!

JESSICA: No! Take them away!

CHARLES: They're on your breasts, aren't they? My hands are on your breasts! Aren't they, aren't they? (*Silence. Her stillness is the admission. She is visibly perturbed. He smiles. Then he goes to Paul and speaks in the friendliest spirit.*)

CHARLES: No harm done, my friend. Didn't touch her, didn't lay a finger on her pink-white skin. Mouth unkissed and breasts inviolate. . . . Lovely shirt you're wearing. (*John enters. He is elated.*)

JOHN: They watch things—they truly watch things! Even the boy—without his sight—he watches. (*A moment. His mood sobers*) Doesn't he?

JESSICA: It's arbitrary.

JOHN: (*Insistent*) But doesn't he?

JESSICA: Sometimes I think he does. (*Emily enters. She too is exhilarated.*)

EMILY: If I didn't have the dinner to make—! Oh, I'd much rather be with them, you know! Ah, such dears—such darling children! The boy—oh heavens, he's so sweet! And Carla—I'm sure she's bright! Why, in scarcely a minute, I taught her how to laugh! Dear thing, there she was laughing—laughing away! Did you hear her, Jessica?

JESSICA: No.

EMILY: (*Defensively*) Well, she *was* laughing! Tell her, John—she was, wasn't she? Carla did laugh—didn't she?

JOHN: I . . . think so.

EMILY: (*Hotly*) What do you mean, you think?—you heard her as clearly as I did!

JESSICA: (*Quietly. Flatly*) The children are mute.

EMILY: Oh, I suspect the boy is—though I'm not even sure about him. But Carla—make no mistake about it—she laughed aloud.

JESSICA: Carla is mute.

EMILY: (*Her resentment rising*) I didn't say I heard her *speak*—I said she laughed.

JESSICA: She makes a sound occasionally. As if something were caught in her throat. It is not a laugh—it has no pleasure in it.

EMILY: (*An outburst of rage*) I didn't say it was a pleasurable laugh! (*Silence. The two women are openly confronted. There is old fury in both of them.*)

JESSICA: If it wasn't pleasurable, what sort of laugh are you trying to teach her, Mother?

EMILY: (*Out of control*) Whatever there is! Whatever sound she can make! Whatever can be heard! Whatever will be answered!

JESSICA: Like the sound you're making now?

EMILY: No! Clearer! Louder! One that's heard! And answered!

JESSICA: *Why don't you give it up?!*

EMILY: No! I won't give it up! I won't!

JOHN: Emily, please. Control, my dear, control!

EMILY: What did she come home for?

JOHN: Emily—Jessica—

EMILY: (*To her daughter*) What did you come home for?

CHARLES: To make trouble! She's always making trouble!

JESSICA: (*To her father, desperately*) Why don't you tell her how things are?!

CHARLES: Go on—make trouble, make trouble!

JESSICA: (*Wheeling on Charles*) Or you!—why don't you tell her?!

CHARLES: Tell her what, you lunatic, tell her what?!

JESSICA: (*A torrent of rage*) We can't walk in the streets anymore! Our children cannot speak to us! There are no kites in the air! We've lost D-Natural! Tell her! Why don't you tell her?!

EMILY: (*Meeting rage with rage*) You think I don't know? Well, I do—just as well as you do! And a few things you don't know—which I have spared you! But no more! I'll whip you with them now! I'll have you down on your knees crying for me to let up!

JESSICA: (*Challenging*) Tell me—tell me now!

EMILY: I'll kill her—I'll kill her!

JOHN: Let her alone! Emily! Let her alone!

EMILY: I'll kill her! Oh, help me, help me!

(He clutches her to him, half to comfort, half to stifle.)

JOHN: Sh . . . be still . . . Emily . . . be still.

JESSICA: Tell me—tell me now!

EMILY: (*Weeping, murmuring*) Kill her . . . kill her . . .

CHARLES: (*Quietly*) Yes . . . Kill her, Emily. Teach her a lesson. Kill her.

(He laughs, almost enjoying it. Stillness now, except for Emily's low, convulsive sobbing. John, holding her in his arms, caresses her gently, silently. Jessica stands alone, isolated. Paul, in the rocking chair, rocks a little, slowly.

The lights fade, but not too quickly.)

END OF ACT ONE

Act Two

AFTER DINNER. Frank and Carla sit together, John and Emily sit together, Paul and Jessica sit together. Charles sits alone. Charles sighs. He belches. He sighs again, deeply contented.

CHARLES: That was a most delicious chicken.

JOHN: Yes, indeed. Delicious. Most.

CHARLES: Best I ever had. And done to a turn. Wasn't it done to a turn?

JOHN: Done to a turn. I'd certainly agree that's what it was done to.

CHARLES: A turn—an absolute turn.
  (*He smacks his lips*)

JESSICA: He's still eating it.

CHARLES: I wish I were. Oh, dreams!

JESSICA: You may resume eating it, if you like. There's a sliver of it on your chin.

CHARLES: (*Alert*) Sliver of what? Chicken?

JESSICA: On your chin.

CHARLES: Oh, I know you—you're titillating me.

JESSICA: You're quite welcome—but not at all. It's there. If you don't eat it, it'll go dry. Or rot. Or drop off. And be lost forever.

CHARLES: She's teasing, isn't she, John? Emily?

EMILY: No, Charles—there *is* a sliver there.

(*Charles looks quickly from one to another. Satisfied they are telling the truth, he snakes his tongue out and around, now this side, now that. They watch him with a lively, partisan interest. Will his tongue reach?*)

EMILY: Ah, there! It dropped to the floor.

CHARLES: Where, where?

(*He goes down on all fours*) I don't see it—where? Ah, here it is!

(*He pops it in his mouth*) Ah, delicious! The lagniappe. I thank you all for calling it to my attention.

EMILY: You make me feel dreadful, Charles—knowing there wasn't enough to eat. Of course, there never is. But I do try to make it seem there is. I beat a lot of air into everything. I heat the plates up so they're too hot to hold—and I keep the serving dishes in motion. If there isn't enough food, the next best thing is fuss. And, of course . . . dessert.

CHARLES: (*Alerted*) Dessert?

EMILY: I've been saving it for just such an occasion as this.

CHARLES: (*Enthusiastic*) Dessert?—really?—what is it?

EMILY: A few days ago, I found a fig.

CHARLES: A fig?

EMILY: Yes, it was windy, and the sand shifted, and there it was. The stem of it was rotten but the rest of it was dry. Dried fig!—do you remember dried figs? So tonight I cut it into seven equal parts—and we've got dessert! (*Emily produces a board with pieces of fig on it, The others are festive. They exclaim gaily:*)

JOHN, JESSICA, CHARLES: Emily, what a wonder you are!. . . . Presto-changeo, Mother finds a fig! . . . Dessert!—a fig, a fig!

(*Somehow, during the serving, Jessica, serving her husband and children, winds up with the serving board. On it remains a section of fig—Charlie's share.*)

CHARLES: (*In a dither*) Where's mine?—why do I get served last?—where's my fig?

JESSICA: Here it is. But you can't have it yet.

CHARLES: Can't have it?—of course I can!—it's mine!

JESSICA: Not yet.

CHARLES: Emily!—isn't that mine?—what's she doing to me?—isn't that my dessert?

(*To Jessica*) Give it to me!

JESSICA: You can't have it until you put your false teeth in your mouth.

CHARLES: What?

JESSICA: Put your false teeth in your mouth.

CHARLES: My false teeth are my false teeth—and my fig is my fig!

JESSICA: You ate your whole dinner without using your false teeth. I've never seen you use them. I don't think you use them at all.

CHARLIE: Yes I do—I do!

JESSICA: Has anybody seen him use them? Mother, have you? Father?

EMILY & JOHN: No . . . I haven't, no.

JESSICA: Nobody has seen you use them. Why do you say that you do?

CHARLES: (*Getting more and more nervous*) Because I do—I do! When I'm alone I use them all the time.

JESSICA: Use them now. Put them in your mouth.

CHARLES: No—no—give me my fig—no!

JESSICA: You see?—you don't use them at all! You just hang them around your neck to offend us, to nauseate us, to turn our stomachs, to make us sick!

CHARLES: No! They're my emblem! They tell me how hungry I am! They tell you too! They say it to everybody! Charlie's hungry!—give him something to eat!—give him a handout! Please!—help him!—he's hungry!—give him a fig!

JESSICA: (*Quietly*) Take that chain off.

CHARLES: No, I won't, I won't!

EMILY: (*Quietly*) Go on, Charlie—peace in the family—take it off.

CHARLES: (*Frightened*) . . . Take it off?

JESSICA: Give it to me.

CHARLES: (*Starting to whimper*) . . . No.

JESSICA: Give it to me and you'll have your fig.

CHARLES: (*Softly, as if to himself*) No . . . Shall I do it, Emily?

EMILY: Yes, Charlie.

CHARLES: And she'll give me the fig?

EMILY: Yes, Charlie.

CHARLES: (*To Jessica*) Will you?

JESSICA: Yes.

(*Trembling, as if giving up one of his life supports, Charlie takes the chain off and hands it to Jessica. Trying to hide her disgust, she accepts the appurtenance and puts it in the pocket of her dress. She thereupon extends the board so Charlie can have his share of the fig.*)

CHARLES: Thank you, Jessica. Oh, delicious!—oh my, this is delicious! (*To Emily*) Are you sure there isn't any more of it?

EMILY: I wish there were, Charlie. For your sake—and for the children. (*To Jessica*) Do you really think they had enough to eat?

JESSICA: Oh yes, don't fret over them.

EMILY: Considering they eat so little, they *are* so *big* . . . for their age.

JESSICA: Yes.

EMILY: Three months, did you say?

JESSICA: Yes.

EMILY: All the children nowadays are bigger than their parents. It's the nutrition. Don't you think it's the nutrition, Charles?

CHARLES: Oh yes, the nutrition, yes.

EMILY: I do hope they had enough nutrition.

CHARLES: The hell with nutrition—the trick is to have enough to eat.

EMILY: I'll ask them. Did you, children?—did you have enough to eat? (*With a smile to the others*) They say they had plenty, thank you.

CHARLES: Did *they* say thank you or did you add that little touch yourself?

EMILY: (*With a laugh*) I confess I added it myself.

(*An instant*) How did you know I added it myself? Are you beginning to
hear them too?

(*Before he can answer. Excited*) Charles is beginning to hear them too!

JESSICA: (*Gently warning*) Mother . . .

EMILY: He is! Ask him! Charles, you are beginning to hear them, aren't you?

JOHN: (Muted) I think . . . I am.

(*This is unexpected. Silence. They turn to John.*)

JESSICA: You're not.

JOHN: (*Guardedly*) I didn't say I actually hear them—

EMILY: Don't let her talk you out of it, John.

JOHN: —I said I think I'm beginning to hear them speak.

EMILY: There!—you see?

JESSICA: (*To John*) How can you, if they don't speak?

CHARLES: How can they speak?—they're only three months old.

JESSICA: (*An outburst, pointing to Paul*) It isn't age! Why can't *he* speak?

CHARLES: How old is *he*?

EMILY: Oh heavens, is he an infant too?!

JESSICA: Stop it! There'll be no ridicule!

CHARLES: (*With thick mockery*) Why, who'd think to ridicule a little babykins?
Gone and married an infant, has she? A little babykins infant, that's what he is.
(*Teasing, to Paul*) Hello, little addle-dee-daddle-ookums. What are we
crying for, little oddle-de-doodle-mooshkins? Peed in our pantaloons, have
we? Oogle dee woogle, wig with the waggle!

(*Emily and Charles are beside themselves with glee. John and Jessica try
to put a halt to it.*)

JOHN: No—don't—he doesn't like it—don't!

JESSICA: Stop it—please stop!

CHARLES: Urgle, gurgle, making a little goop-up, are you?

JESSICA: Stop it, stop it!

(*Carla springs from her chair, rushes to Charles and starts kicking him.*)

CHARLES: Why, you nasty little tart, you!

(*He grabs Carla. She bites and kicks with unabated fury.*)

JOHN: Stop it—both of you!

EMILY: Charles! Charles, please!

JESSICA: Carla—stop! Carla, he'll hurt you! Carla!

(*Pulling them apart, she vents her fury on Charles.*)

JESSICA: Get away! Don't you dare to touch her!

(*As Carla goes at Charles again*) And you—you stop it! I'm ashamed of
you! No, I don't care if he is a dirty hog—when I say stop, you stop! I am
not on his side! And don't you dare say such a thing!

(*Attention quickens. She is clearly being "spoken to" by Carla. The others are stone still, watching. Now Jessica turns her anger to Frank.*)

JESSICA: And you stay out of it! Of *course* you had something to do with it! If you hadn't laughed, she'd've never kicked him! Don't lie to me—I distinctly heard you!

(*Suddenly turning on Paul who is also soundless and immobile*) It certainly *is* serious. And if you took a hand in the bringing up of the children—! Carla, stop it—I've heard enough from you. Out—both of you—out! Frank, did you hear me?—out! Paul—please!

(*To the children*) No, I don't care what you do—you'll have to amuse yourselves! Go somewhere—watch something—go to bed! Paul, send them to bed!

(*Pause. The children go upstairs. Silence. Jessica turns to see all eyes tensely fixed on her.*)

EMILY: (*Very low*) There—you see? They were talking to her.

CHARLES: (*To Emily, in a hoarse whisper*) She's a liar. They were *not* talking to her. She made it up. She's trying to confuse us. She says they're deaf and dumb, and suddenly they're having this conversation? It's a lie!

(*Turning on Jessica*) You're a liar!

JESSICA: About what?

CHARLES: That argument! The whole family squabble—you made it all up!

JESSICA: Of course I did.

EMILY: No, you didn't! We heard it—every word you said!

CHARLES: No! That girl didn't say a word—neither did the boy! And her husband—he was absolutely silent! All silent, weren't they?

(*Shouting at Jessica*) Weren't they?

(*She doesn't answer, but John says, quietly.*)

JOHN: And you didn't get kicked in the shin, did you?

CHARLES: It's not the same thing!

JOHN: And when she sent them upstairs—when *he* sent them upstairs—they didn't go, did they?

CHARLES: Yes they did, but it's not the same!

(*To Jessica*) Tell them it's not the same!

JESSICA: (*Quietly, not looking at him*) Yes it is—it's all the same!

CHARLES: (*Passionately*) No it's not! When you arrived here a few hours ago, you said they were deaf and dumb. Even ten minutes ago—deaf and dumb! And suddenly they speak! What is this change of rules? What did you bring home?—a lie or a confusion?

JESSICA: What difference does it make? We can't handle either one.

EMILY: (*Quietly*) Don't make so much of it, Charles. She has simply changed her mind.

CHARLES: (*An angry charge*) No!—you! You changed it for her! You couldn't bear that those children were unreachable, so you made them hear and speak!

(*He turns quickly to Jessica*) But they *don't* hear and speak! You say they do to please your mother! She's trapped you in a lie! She always traps you!

Every time you come, she tricks you into some picture she has of you, some dream she wants you to match up to! *Tell her your children do not speak!*

EMILY: (*Quietly*) You fool. Don't you see that she needs to believe that they do? Why do you make trouble? You want to be at home here, but you make trouble. You have a difficulty with lies and confusion. But Charlie— dear Charlie—things don't have to be clear—nor even truthful. Just pleasant and bearable. That's what the secret of home is . . . pleasant and bearable. Now then: do you want to be home?

(*Long silence. He is under great strain.*)

CHARLES: (*Abject*) . . . Yes . . . Yes, I do.

EMILY: Then say something pleasant, Charlie. There's a good lad—say something pleasant.

CHARLES: (*With difficulty*) I . . . like you . . . very much. I am your brother and you are my sister—and I like you very much.

EMILY: That's very good.

(*Pointing to John*) And he is my husband and I am his wife. And she is my daughter and I am her mother.

CHARLES: (*Trying to be happy*) We're a family, aren't we?

(*Pointing to Jessica and himself*) Niece and uncle—uncle and niece!

JOHN: Yes—look at us—look at all the pleasant idiots—grandfather, grandmother, uncle—

EMILY: —wife, mother, grandmother—

CHARLES: Family—family! And I am uncle, grand-uncle, brother, brother-in-law—I am so many pleasant people, it makes me dizzy!

EMILY: Oh, let's be dizzy and dance!

(*To John*) Will you dance with me, my dear?

CHARLES: (*On a note of high hilarity*) Cutting in, cutting in! I'll dance with you, Emily!

(*He takes his sister in his arms and starts dancing her around the room*)

JOHN: I think I have a beautiful daughter in the vicinity! Dance, Jessica? I hear it's very pleasant? Will you dance?

JESSICA: (*Formally*) A pleasure—a true pleasure!

(*They are all dancing about, having an idiotically pleasant time. Laughter, chatter.*)

EMILY: You see, Charlie?—you see how it's done? Jessica, do you see?

JESSICA: Yes, Mama—it's very pleasant!

(*Strange music—without D-Natural—has eased into the background. Everybody is making an eerily merry time of it. A strange gaiety pervades the atmosphere. As the dance starts turning a bit wild, with a hint of pandemonium, Paul slowly rises from his rocking chair. He stands statuesquely motionless. The others don't at first notice he has risen. Now Jessica sees him. She stops dancing with an outcry.*)

JESSICA: Look!

(*As the others go still*) Look at him—he's dancing!

(They look at the motionless man and at one another.)

JOHN: Is he dancing?

EMILY: *(In an ecstasy)* Yes! He's dancing—he's dancing!

CHARLES: *(In a tight, constrained voice)* No he's not.

EMILY: *(With whispered urgency)* Yes, he is, Charlie—believe me, he is.

JESSICA: Oh, look at him! Look at him leap!

JOHN: What a turn—what a lovely turn!

EMILY: Isn't he beautiful when he dances!

CHARLES: *He's not dancing!*

JESSICA: Higher, Paul! Faster and higher!

JOHN: Do it again!—do the turn again!

CHARLES: *No! He's not moving! He's absolutely still!*

JESSICA: Oh beautiful!—what a lovely leap!

EMILY: Beautiful! So beautiful I can't stand it!

CHARLES: *(Rushing from one to another)* John—he's not dancing! Emily—Jessica—he's not dancing—you know it!

JOHN: Out of the way—we can't see him!

CHARLES: Liars! You're all liars! It's just like the old days! The poem is beautiful except it doesn't make sense! The painting is exquisite, but there's nothing on the canvas! *There's nothing there!* He isn't dancing! It's lies! It's Art all over again—it's lies!

(The music dies away. The dancing ceases. Paul sits down. There is a mood of deep seriousness, of worry . . . The quiet holds. Charles is deeply upset, trying not to weep.)

CHARLES: *(A muted entreaty)* He wasn't dancing . . . was he?

(Nobody responds. His entreaty deepens) Please tell me the truth. You all lied . . . didn't you?

JOHN: . . . Yes. I did.

JESSICA: I did too.

EMILY: *(Quietly strong)* Speak for yourselves. I didn't lie.

(To Charles) You've spoiled things.

CHARLES: I tried not to. Believe me, I tried.

EMILY: I'm not going to forgive you. You'll go hungry for this. No matter how much food you bring us, I'll see that you go hungry for this.

CHARLES: *(His crafty self again)* Is that why you stole it, then?

EMILY: Stole what?

CHARLES: You know what.

EMILY: What did I steal?

CHARLES: You think I don't know what happened?

EMILY: I don't know what you're talking about.

(Charles is back in command of himself—and of the circumstance. But he reconnoiters—the terrain demands caution. He has been a bear; he is now a fox. He circles. To Emily:)

CHARLES: You want us to be a family. Very well—I want that too. Now I feel—I strongly feel—if we're to be a family—then, no secrets. Everything out in the open, the bright strong sunlight. Visible. Audible. Clear. Need something?—ask for it. Feel something?—tell it. No subterfuges.

(Then, zeroing in) Especially at the dinner table.

EMILY: *(To John)* Ask him what the devil he's talking about.

CHARLES: You ask me.

(He waits as she slowly turns to face him) How many heads on a chicken?

EMILY: Go to hell.

CHARLES: All right, then: How many wings?

EMILY: I'm going to bed.

CHARLES: How many *legs* on a chicken?

EMILY: *(To John)* Are you going to let him speak to me like this?

JOHN: Is there something pornographic in the question?

CHARLES: *(Forging ahead)* How many legs on a chicken?—how many legs?

EMILY: *(With dignity)* There are two legs on a chicken and I dislike you very much.

CHARLES: Two legs!—that's right!—two legs on a chicken! Where's the second one?

EMILY: Very much indeed!

CHARLES: You served only one leg. I brought you a chicken that was—

(He looks at Jessica)—normal. In every respect—normal! It had the proper number of eyes and the proper number of wings. It also had the proper number of legs—two of them. Why did you serve only one? Did you eat it beforehand? Have you taken to the lowest form of female perfidy?—pilfering out of the pot? Gobbling the goodies beforehand?

EMILY: Nonsense! Absolutely not!

CHARLES: You've been sneaking chicken legs!

EMILY: No I haven't!

CHARLES: Where is it, then?

EMILY: John, will you let him badger me like this?

JOHN: *(After an instant. Reservedly)* Where is it, Emily?

CHARLES: She ate it.

EMILY: No, I didn't! You may not have noticed—any of you—that I ate hardly anything at dinner. No!—and that's not because I ate a chicken leg beforehand. It's because when there's only one chicken and seven of us to eat, I abstain. I abstain! I add water to the broth and I eke things out. I do not eat, I eke!

CHARLES: Then why did you eke the chicken leg?

EMILY: I saved it! I wrapped it up and saved it!

CHARLES: Ah, now we hear the truth. Where is it?

EMILY: You think I'll tell you that?

CHARLES: Yes! It was my bird that fed the family! Now, where the hell is it?

EMILY: Go and find it!

CHARLES: I will!—you bet on that!—I will!

(He rushes into the kitchen. She yells to him.)

EMILY: Find a truffle while you're at it! Root under the oak tree with your ugly snout! Dig up a truffle!

(*Hushed, to the others*) He'll never find it—not a sniff of it. Will he, Jessica?

JESSICA: (*Exchanging a conspiratorial glance with Emily.*) No, he won't, Mother.

JOHN: But he'll wreck your kitchen, looking for it.

EMILY: What do I care?

JOHN: Your sacred domain—not care?

EMILY: (*Irritable, distressed*) No—not care!

JOHN: (*Goading her*) Where you're a priestess?—not care?

EMILY: (*Starting for the stairs*) Goodnight.

JOHN: (*To irritate and to seduce*) A lovely priestess!—radiant and well-formed.

(*He touches her. She speaks a quiet warning.*)

EMILY: Take your hands away. I'm going to bed.

JOHN: Yes, do. But don't go right to sleep.

EMILY: Hands off. The priestess says hands off. What ignominy.

JOHN: What, my dear?

EMILY: (*With disaffection*) Hands in the pot and in the groin. Cooking, lovemaking, chicken legs. You men and your hungers. What a lie it is!—to speak of love and cookery as if they were something more than a gross abomination. Gross, gross abomination! Priestess of the sacred flame—what jiggery-pokery! Priestess of the pot and chamber pot. Priestess of thirty feet of entrails, sucking drains and cloaca! Priestess of your slimy pipes and protuberances! How ignominious! . . . I'm off. To sleep.

(*Emily goes up the stairs.*)

JESSICA: Now she's really at it.

JOHN: Not at you. At me.

JESSICA: At me tomorrow, then.

JOHN: (*His eyes narrowing*) That's what you came for, isn't it?

JESSICA: I beg your pardon?

JOHN: To go at her—and her at you.

JESSICA: What an unconscionable thing to say.

JOHN: Steady. I know the time of day. What did you come for?

JESSICA: Nostalgia. The scent of bureau drawers.

JOHN: Ah yes, old lavender. I don't believe it.

JESSICA: To test a memory or two. To count your wrinkles.

JOHN: To quarrel.

JESSICA: No . . . All right—that too.

JOHN: You clod, you think you'll settle old disputes? You won't, you know. Better keep the scab on.

JESSICA: It stinks, it's festering.

JOHN: Get out of here. Please, Jessie, go! Don't spend the night!

JESSICA: Last time you said the same.

JOHN: And I was right. To count our wrinkles, did you say? More wrinkles than last time. Did you come to see us die?

JESSICA: The dying's always been on the other foot.

JOHN: Revenge, is that it? Jess, you can't settle that old score—she's way ahead of you!

JESSICA: Oh, don't I know! My whole childhood, ahead of me! But I'll catch up!

JOHN: (*More gently*) Could I be the one you want to catch up with, Jessica?

JESSICA: (*It's a new thought, a dark one*) You could be . . . yes.

JOHN: A death in the family . . . that's what you'll settle for.

JESSICA: If that's a settlement.

JOHN: Whose death, Jess? Hers? Yours? Mine?

JESSICA: I wouldn't kill you, Father. You don't know that?

JOHN: No, I don't, Jess. You don't either.

JESSICA: (*In pain*) I don't want to . . . anyone. And if I did, I couldn't.

JOHN: I think you could.

JESSICA: Oh, please.

JOHN: Then what did you come for? Please go.
(*Indicating Paul*) Take him and your children and please go.

JESSICA: They're what I came for!

JOHN: For what? Are you so proud?—to show them off to us?

JESSICA: What a bastard you are.

JOHN: Are you?!

JESSICA: (*An outcry*) To show *me* off! To *you*! Whatever they are, they're progeny—and mine! And better than I ever thought I could—! Oh murder! To show *me* off! To *them*! To show them who I was! And am. And you, you son of a bitch, you're helping not one bit!

JOHN: What? What do you want me to do?

JESSICA: (*Pointing to Paul*) Tell him something!

JOHN: Tell him what?

JESSICA: Something of me. Something you remember. Something good.

JOHN: (*A moment Then, to Paul*) She had a temper. And selfish. She was always selfish.

JESSICA: No!—something good!

JOHN: She lied. She was a child that lied.

JESSICA: (*Tormented*) I'll kill you for this—I will!

JOHN: I said you might.

JESSICA: (*Beseeching*) *Tell him!*

JOHN: She made trouble—she had a lust for trouble.
(*An instant. Then*) But I loved her very much. She made me cry at night. I loved her. I said she lied—well, so did I. We had a good many lies between us. Perhaps that's all we had. Perhaps, if the truth were known . . . if it could be known . . . we're strangers. And we've had what strangers have.

JESSICA: What lies?—what?

JOHN: (*Pointing to Paul*) Here comes another one! Like admiring your infant scrawls and saying they were pictures! It's what you want of me! Like telling me to talk to him. But how? He's deaf! Or stupid. Doesn't get a word I say—

JESSICA: He *understands*! He does everything we ask him to.

JOHN: Want me to agree to that?—I will. Why not? You said he danced— I said I saw him do it! Your mother said he spoke—I said I heard him! We lie—we all pitch in—we make a community of lies!

JESSICA: Tell him something good.

JOHN: Ah, but you want it true as well. How's that possible?

JESSICA: If not about me, then about yourself! Tell him about yourself! Tell him *something*!

JOHN: Yes—something—there must be something.
(*Finding it. To Paul*) Go away.

JESSICA: Father—please—

JOHN: Get out of here! Go now!
(*John starts for the stairs. She grabs him.*)

JESSICA: No—please—I beg you. There must be some kindness to give him— some comfort—some memory of the past—what it was like in those days— what *you* were like—

JOHN: (*This at last arrests him*) What I was like . . .
(*Silence. Then*) I awaken in the morning. Go to work. I scribble the imprecise word, I drive the rusty nail, I draw the line not crooked but not straight. I measure the money and myself. I close the safety door, I flee from the discovery. I imagine someone's looking for me—I don't know who—it may be me-myself. But nobody will find me—I'll see to that. I'll turn out all the lights—and we'll all search for me, and we'll find no one! Ah, but there's the hitch! There's always *someone* in the dark, there's always *something*! There's loss of breath, there's coldness in the heart.
(*Pause*) No one's been searching for me, no one's *really* searching. There's no one there but me.

JESSICA: (*She is crying softly*) That's not true.

JOHN: It was true then and it's true now.

JESSICA: Things change!

JOHN: Nothing changes! Catastrophe or good fortune—nothing changes!

JESSICA: (*A sob*) It's not true! It can't be true! I love you, Father—it's not true!

JOHN: (*Gently*) Try not to cry.
(*Silence. She gathers herself together.*)

JESSICA: Are we making it up, then? What we had in those good old days— are we making it all up?

JOHN: Not entirely, I suppose. There was a time when we were not afraid of everything—of each other, of the air, of the very atmosphere. We had some rituals, as I recall, we had a poem here and there, we had D-Natural, although I suspect it was never as beautiful as we say it was. And assurances—we had a number of vast and wonderful assurances. Love, for example. Everyone had a right to it and, with some luck and effort, everyone could have it. And Tomorrow. Remember how we used to say the word, "Tomorrow"—like an incantation—Tomorrow!—the most perfect day!—indestructible—going on forever! . . . And God. What a sublime fiction!—how did we ever invent him?—the grandest assurance of them all! . . . All gone now. All gone. And I think—since you want the truth— I miss them.

JESSICA: We can resurrect them, Father—every one of them—we can resurrect them!

JOHN: There isn't time. And—since the game we're playing is The Truth— they may have caused our worst catastrophes.

(*He starts up the stairs.*)

JESSICA: No! Father, come back! No, no!

(*But he continues inexorably upward. When he is gone, she is in despair, not knowing where to turn. Her attention turns to her husband.*)

JESSICA: You, there. Say something. I tell them that you understand—but I'm not sure you do. I tell them that you speak—I know you don't. But what do you *think*? You're from another world—give us some advice, since we've made such a wreck of this one! Who are you? Are you a savant or are you a vegetable? Are you what we have to look forward to? *Tell us who you are!*

(*Paul rises and goes up the stairs. Silent, hopelessness deepening, she watches him go. She doesn't notice that Charles has entered, by way of the kitchen. He has been watching her, biding his time. He now speaks measuredly.*)

CHARLES: He won't talk to you, but I will.

(*She turns, sees him. With main force, she takes control of herself.*)

JESSICA: Go away.

CHARLES: No, I think not. You've got your clothes off.

(*As she starts for the stairs, he bars her way*) No—wait! What did you do with it?

JESSICA: Let me go by. Do with what?

CHARLES: The chicken leg.

(*She breaks into grim, ironic laughter.*)

JESSICA: My God, is that what it's all about?—a chicken leg? Is that what you reduce it all to?—a goddamn chicken leg?!

CHARLES: Give it to me. What did you do with it?

JESSICA: I stole it.

CHARLES: I know you did that. I saw you and your mother making eyes about it. Where is it?

(*Alarmed*) You haven't eaten it?

JESSICA: I'm saving it.

CHARLES: What for?

JESSICA: What from, you mean.

CHARLES: You mean from me?

JESSICA: Yes. To watch you starve. Right here in front of me. I wish it weren't such a slow-pokey process. I'd like it all sped up—time-accelerated—so I can watch you perish right here—right now, skin getting flabbier, flesh hanging from the bones, and then, at last—a dry, wasted transparency! (*Charmingly*) Could you manage it for me, do you think?

CHARLES: Give me the chicken leg.

JESSICA: Are you perishing now?

CHARLES: You're a spider. Give it to me. An ugly spider.

JESSICA: Both loathsome, aren't we?

CHARLES: (*Shrewdly*) You don't *have* to see yourself in me.

JESSICA: (*Unsettled*) Me?—in you?

CHARLES: Loathsome—quite so—I am—even to myself. Why are *you* to *you*?

(*Flat out*) Give me my chicken leg.

JESSICA: Don't you dare to say I see myself in you.

CHARLES: Give me what I need and go to bed.

JESSICA: I warn you, Charles, you'd better leave—you better not stay here.

CHARLES: Ah, it's chasing away time, is it? Your father chases you and you chase me.

JESSICA: You listened, of course.

CHARLES: And I heard you say you weren't going. Well done—you shouldn't. Neither should I. Must keep the family together!—got to!—must!

JESSICA: Not with you here, no!

CHARLES: Then you surrender to the enemy.

JESSICA: What enemy?

CHARLES: Whatever pulls us apart. This one's not good enough—that one's not pretty—he's got no eyes, she's got no arms!

(*Pointedly, to himself*) And this one's too hungry. The enemy! Pulls us apart!

(*With mounting excitement*) Drives us out—whirls us off into space— flings us away from the center—centrifugal—centrifugal—

JESSICA: You want us sucked homeward!

CHARLES: Well put!

JESSICA: Centripetal!

CHARLES: Sucked homeward! As you were! Just like me! To be together again!

JESSICA: Not with you!

CHARLES: With all of us! We need each other—we all need each other—you even need me!

(*Silence*) So we must submit to that. We must be pliant. Yield. To one another. That way, we will give one another an easier time . . . a breath . . . a relief against the enemy.

(*Then, cunning, wary*) Can you guess why I'm sure that's how it will be? Because I hear things . . . down There.

JESSICA: We always knew you were a member.

CHARLES: I'm more than that—I'm a carrier.

JESSICA: As in disease.

CHARLES: I carry harms and benefits. How do you think your parents are alive? It's not only the occasional chicken that sustains them. It's me. It's Charlie or it's manacles. It's death and dungeons. They're old, they're useless, they're seditious, they complain too much, they *think*. I could inform on them, or simply leave them here to waste away. But I share chickens with them! Now you, goddamn you, you give me my chicken leg!

JESSICA: (*Amazed*) My God, you're desperate. A measly chicken leg, and you're reckless for it!

CHARLES: I'm starving!

JESSICA: Stop trembling—you disgust me!

CHARLES: Help me! Call me by my name! Say Charles!

JESSICA: Keep your distance now, keep your distance.

CHARLES: Help me! Take my hand—say Charles—take my hand!

JESSICA: No—no!

CHARLES: I warn you—be kind! Oh, please!

JESSICA: No!

CHARLES: Please! I'm fat and my sweat puts me in bad odor and I cry too much! Be kind to me!

JESSICA: I'll see you die.

CHARLES: No! I'll eat and eat—and be called by my name! I'll go to bed with you—I'll be loved and loved and—

JESSICA: Take your hands away1

CHARLES: —and touch you—kiss you—touch every part of you—kiss—touch—kiss—

(*He clutches at her. She forces her way to the table and picks up a knife. He wrests it from her; he drops it. As he tries to retrieve it, she struggles with him. He tears at her and at her clothes, her body. She breaks away, picks up the knife and taunts him:*)

JESSICA: (*Brandishing the knife*) No—don't stop—come after me! Come—don't give up!

CHARLES: You mean bitch! You teasing bitch!

(*He goes after her again. They struggle for the knife. She breaks away and taunts him to return.*)

JESSICA: Come! Come! Don't give up—there's a little breath in you yet—come, boy—come!

(*He grabs her. She struggles and, knowing she has the best of it, she screams with laughter as he cries out in pain. Suddenly, he starts getting the best of it, and the knife clatters free. Their outcries are heard. Paul comes rushing down the stairs, followed by John and Emily. Paul violently tears them apart. Before he can inflict savagery, Emily and John separate them from Charles.*)

EMILY: No—stop! Everybody, stop! An end to this!

(*The violence ceases. John picks up the knife.*)

EMILY: What? Tell me! What is this? What?

JOHN: Can't you see it? Look at them! And this!

(*He holds up the knife. Paul starts for Charles again.*)

EMILY: Stop him!

JESSICA: No! Let him go for his throat!

(*Emily and John stand in Paul's way. Emily speaks to Paul.*)

EMILY: No! I said no!

(*To Jessica*) Make him understand! What, then? Charles—Jessica—what?

CHARLES: She drove me! She tantalized me crazy!

JESSICA: Why didn't you let me deal with him?!

EMILY: How deal? Do what?

JESSICA: Kill him!

JOHN: Why didn't you, then? You're fitter than he is!

(*Holding up the knife again*) And there was this.

JESSICA: Give it to me—give me a second chance with it!

EMILY: No! No more!

JESSICA: Give me!

EMILY: I said no more!

CHARLES: Oh, thank you, Emily, thank you—you're the only one—

EMILY: Silence!

(*With loathing*) You know what you've done for yourself, don't you? Do you know?

CHARLES: Emily—please—she—I was half crazy—she's a teasing whore!

JESSICA: All right, Mother—no knives—and we won't tear him apart, member by member. What will we do with him?

JOHN: Yes—what now? He attacked our daughter. Does he get away with it?

EMILY: Yes. Quite away.

CHARLES: Oh, thank you, Emily, thank you!

EMILY: Yes—away. Away so far he'll never find his way back.

CHARLES: (*He freezes*) What do you . . . ? Away where?

JOHN: You're driven out, my friend.

CHARLES: NO! She didn't say—! Emily, you didn't say that!

EMILY: Go away. Don't come back. Not ever, back.

CHARLES: Emily—?!

(*With uncontrolled laughter*) She doesn't mean it! She's a tease—she's like her daughter—teasing—tantalizing—! Wouldn't drive me away, not her! Not ever—no! She's—that's my sister—she loves me—wouldn't do a thing—!

(*A wild outcry*) Emily!

EMILY: And not tomorrow. Now.

CHARLES: No! It's late at night—I wouldn't know where to—! We'll think this over—we'll all think it over—and sometime—in the morning maybe—

JOHN: Not the morning.

JESSICA: She said now.

JOHN: (*Opening the door*) Get out.

(*Charles charges to the door and throws his body against it, slamming it shut.*)

CHARLES: No! Emily—please—I need a moment with you! Got to talk to you alone. A moment, a moment!

EMILY: See that you go.

(*To the others*) Lock the door after him.

CHARLES: No—wait! You can't leave me alone with them! I'll get nowhere with them!

(*With a flash of desperate cunning*) And you won't either! Never thought of that, did you? They're the left-handed ones. Weak—incompetent—let their scruples cripple their actions! Can't rely on them, can you? No, not for food and for your protection. It's me—it's brother Charles you've got to count on! Drive me out, will they? Why, that's a funny turn, that is! Ha, ha, ha, ha—what a funny turn! Don't you dare to go upstairs and leave your life in the hands of these *fumblefingers!*

(*He sees her momentary indecision. Then she moves past him and, with dignity, ascends the staircase. He panics.*)

CHARLES: No—wait—Emily—stop—I'm sorry—I didn't mean to—! Emily, come back! I'm sorry for everything! Emily! *EMILY!*

(*She is gone. He turns to the others*) I said I was sorry! I say it to everybody! I know somebody here is going to say a word of forgiveness. You're not as cruel as she is! She's a cold, hard stone, that one is. And nobody in the family's like that—nobody like her—nobody! None of us! Are we?

(*Cold silence. He twists back to the stairway*) E-M-I-L-Y! No—you can't do it! Where will I go? I can't go down There because—I'll tell you a secret—they're out to get me. They're out to get me everywhere. Except at home! The only place that I'm not scared is home—it's here at home! *EMILY!*

(*As they start to move away from him*) No—please—don't everybody send me away! I can't go out alone! Oh please—John—you! I beg you—let me stay!

(*Paul passes him and goes up the stairs. Jessica starts to follow. So does John. Charlie goes down on his knees and clutches John's hand.*)

CHARLES: No—John—please—I beg you!

JOHN: Get up. You're disgusting. Get up.

CHARLES: No, I can't get up! This is my natural position!

JOHN: (*Trying to tear his hand away*) Let me go! Get up!

CHARLES: No! I'm too fat to get up! I'm too old! My legs are full of water and they've begun to swell! My kidneys don't work very well—not well at all! I can't go wandering, you know—I simply can't do that! I have to sit—I have to sit somewhere! And lie down often! *I need home!*

(*Then, a deep hoarse secret*) And you know something? I hear noises in the night, and I awaken thinking that the wind has come again. But it's only me, gasping for breath! I get fewer and fewer breaths, it seems to me—is there less air at night? Isn't there enough to go around? I have to save a little extra so I can call somebody! But what if no one's there? (*Wild, a heartbreak*) E-M-I-L-Y! I'm dying of hunger—and I am hungry for home! Home! I am famished for it! *I am hungry for home!*

(*John has wrested himself away from Charles. He now points to the door. Laboriously, Charles gets to his feet. He looks from John to Jessica. She is as inexorable as her father. Charles slowly makes his way to the door, and goes out into the night. John closes the door behind him, and locks it. As John and Jessica make their way upstairs, the lights indoors go to near blackness.*

Outdoors, in cold moonlight, Charles wanders about in circles, agonized with fright, maddened with hysteria, crying, mumbling, moaning to himself. As he gets lost in his own circles, dizzy now, he subsides onto the ground, heaving and softly sobbing. Now, in the near-darkness inside the house, we see Frank come down the stairs. The blind boy falters in the double darkness. Making his way to the front door, he fumbles with the lock and the doorknob, and opens the door. Uncertainly he crosses the threshold. He stands there, dead still, facing the figure of Charles. The boy is "watching." Now, at last, slowly, quite slowly, he advances to the prostrate man. He remains motionless, unseen by Charles. At this point, Carla comes spilling down the stairs. Nimble, soundless, fleet, she darts into every dark corner of the room, searching for her brother. She is in an ague of terror. Now she sees the door slightly ajar, shoulders it open and hurries outdoors. Catching sight of her brother, she lets out a muted sound and hurries to him. The utterance quickens Charles to alertness. He raises his head from the ground. Carla, with her torso, is trying to push the boy indoors, to safety. Too late. With predatory agility, Charles' hand darts out and seizes the boy. The large animal has snatched small prey. The boy utters strangled noises of terror. So does Carla. She kicks and throws her whole body into the assault. Suddenly the boy is free—rushing about, flailing sightlessly in the night, making agonized half-formed noises, not knowing where to flee. At last he makes off, away from the house, into outer darkness. But Carla is caught. Charles has seized her. Armless, she twists, writhes, contorts herself, trying to break loose, and to cry out. Now she falls, still shuddering to be free. He pins her down, beating and thrashing, struggling with the small game run to earth. A few crippled twitches of her body, then she is spent and still. . . . The lights fade.

When the lights come up again, there is nobody to be seen, neither indoors nor outdoors. It is morning. Emily comes downstairs with a basketful of cloth remnants. John enters the house from outdoors.)

EMILY: You've found them?

JOHN: No. Neither of them.

EMILY: Paul? Jessica?

JOHN: I don't know where *he's* gone looking. She's gone down There.

EMILY: They may as well give over.

(*With a start*) Down There, you said?

JOHN: Yes.

EMILY: Jessica?

JOHN: Yes—I told you yes.

EMILY: What for?—it's dangerous!—what does she think she'll make of it?

JOHN: Ask her.

EMILY: I ask you. Why?

JOHN: (*Unevenly*) She thinks—perhaps—if Charles is there—or has been there—or if there's talk, if Charles is talking—! She knows that it is dangerous. She thinks perhaps the children . . .

EMILY: You're maundering.

JOHN: Yes, I am, I suppose.

EMILY: They won't say—down There—where the children are. Even if they know, they won't say.

JOHN: Why are you so sure? You know about them?

EMILY: I know what you know.

JOHN: Then you know nothing.

EMILY: All the more reason you should've stopped her.

JOHN: How?—she's your daughter.

EMILY: Where is he? The other one?

JOHN: Don't call him "the other one." If you mean Paul, say Paul. Say her husband—anything.

EMILY: Where's Anything?

JOHN: I told you—searching. Beating every bush. Investigating shadows. Calling out their names.

EMILY: Calling, did you say?

JOHN: Did I say calling? No, I didn't. I said beating every bush.

EMILY: You said calling.

JOHN: *I* did the calling. I called the children's names.

(*Mostly to himself*) Good grief, I must have thought he called. Or why . . . ? I didn't say he called—you invented that.

EMILY: (*After a pause*) Down There, you say? What a fool she is.

JOHN: She's not. She tries.

EMILY: I said that. Fool.

JOHN: Be kind to fools.

EMILY: Why? If our lives depend on them . . .

JOHN: That's why. The better part of wisdom, I'll tell you that.

EMILY: Caution, you mean.

JOHN: It's a fine line where extinction is involved . . . unless you've got a taste for it.

EMILY: Likely, I have.

JOHN: She hasn't. Don't trap her, Emily. Be kind, I say. One of us, at least. I failed her last night.

EMILY: It was a night for that. You failed me too.

JOHN: I think not, dear soul. You were asleep.

EMILY: Awake! You told me to stay awake. I'm compliant.

JOHN: I thought asleep.

EMILY: You thought no such thing.

JOHN: Tell me what I thought. I'm lying, then?

EMILY: Yes, you are.

JOHN: (*Angry*) I'm not! I reached for you. You didn't move—you weren't there!

EMILY: You reached as if to say: I'm trespassing—don't notice.

JOHN: But you did notice, didn't you? And pretended not to. Who's lying, then?

EMILY: Oh, was that you?

JOHN: Me!—this very me!

EMILY: *You*, what do you think I am, a smooth-assed virgin that you reach for me like that? You, lad—you keep your tenderness, you hear?—you keep it! My God, your delicate fingertips, the skin worn thin! How thin-skinned *are* you?—how thin-skinned do you think I am?

JOHN: No tenderness? What a guilty thing you've got between your legs!

EMILY: Yes—guilty!—wants no tenderness! Only pain! And penalty!

JOHN: Penal and penis—the same root, aren't they?—to hear you tell it.

EMILY: They are—oh yes, they are!

JOHN: (*In a rage*) You do your penance elsewhere—not with me!

EMILY: You want to make me weep? Or rut?

JOHN: Weep and rut, as virgins do!

EMILY: I won't weep for you!

JOHN: You'll weep all right! One night you'll weep!

EMILY: (*Laughing*) Oh, is it dying I'm to weep about?—what else is new?—how's *your* dear family?—the summer's late this year.

JOHN: (Quietly) It's bigger talk than that, my dear.

EMILY: (*Soberly*) Dying is the smallest talk I know.

(*Jessica enters. She is a confusion of terror and wrath. By might and main, she controls herself.*)

JOHN: You found them?

JESSICA: Where's Paul? No, I didn't. Where is he?

JOHN: Still searching.

EMILY: You—your father says—is it true you went down There?

JESSICA: Yes.

EMILY: What lunacy.

JOHN: Well?—what happened?—well?

JESSICA: . . . Name one truth.

JOHN: I beg your pardon.

JESSICA: Well, that's one. It's cheap. You always beg somebody's pardon, Father—it costs you very little to use good manners to escape. I mean a truth that costs you something. One—just one!—from either of you!

(*Silence. Then*) Damn you both—one truth!

EMILY: (*Gently*) Who's down There, Jessica?

JESSICA: (*With a mirthless laugh*) Oh gracious day, that is the biggest lie of all! You tell *me*! Who's There?

JOHN: (*Apologetically*) We . . . don't know, my dear.

JESSICA: But you're certain someone is.

EMILY: There always has been.

JESSICA: Who?

EMILY: The fools. Like you.

JESSICA: The fools? In charge?

EMILY: Oh come now, it doesn't matter who's in charge—now, does it really? If a mess is inevitable, it's tiddlywinks who makes it.

JESSICA: (*Insistent, driving*) But someone's There! You do say so!

JOHN: . . . Yes.

JESSICA: You know it for certain?

JOHN: There always has been. Someone to—someone at least to—to—

JESSICA: To what, Father?

JOHN: To be afraid of.

JESSICA: Do you need a special someone for that purpose?

(*An instant*) I'll tell you what there is. There's dust. And quantities of quiet. Old flags. Old, dry, vermiculated flags, and bunting. There's a torn surplice. And scrolls. And oh, so many books that the words have flown from, like moths. And registers of names. Wheels that have gone crooked and medicines dry in bottles. Paintings that have flaked away, statues turned powdery, with a leg gone or a breast. No sound—yet, echoes. Dry, everything dry. Blood, spittle, sweat, urine, all dry. Hardly a stain or a stench. A little incense.

(*A sudden outcry*) Where are you? Is no one There?—where are you? Isn't there someone to dispense something?—a drop of wine, a wafer, an aphrodisiac, a sedative?! Isn't there someone who will help me find my children? Will someone talk to me? Will someone give me a form to fill out? Will someone take my name? Is there a map of the terrain? Where do I go to seek myself—or someone—or my children? *Where are my children?*!

EMILY: You're looking my way, then?

JESSICA: Yes—tell me! Where are my children?!

EMILY: Am I supposed to know?—what do you want of me?

JOHN: *Do* you know where they are?

EMILY: How could I know?

(*Violently, to Jessica*) Is that what you want at last?—to charge me with your children? Or to blame me for the dust? Well, blame yourself, girl, for whatever you've had that's lost! Or for whatever you've never had you'll never find. Why should you have anything?—you never learned your catechism.

JESSICA: What catechism?

EMILY: The questions about mind, soul, heart, truth! And all those queries about love. Why, think back, girl—all those times you nodded yes—when you should have been shaking yourself to pieces, crying no! Why, love, girl—even if you leave all those minor concupiscent lusts—even the best of it is only itching powder! It makes small pustules and it's gone—not even a raging scar! Pus-and-pockmark—even motherhood! Child lost, you say?—why bother?

JOHN: *(To Emily)* If you know, you tell her!

EMILY: Even if I knew, I wouldn't! They're gone. Sooner or later it had to be. What does she want, prolonged farewells?

JESSICA: Where are they?—please!

EMILY: Sad departures?

JESSICA: You have to tell me!

EMILY: Long lingering goodbyes?—with the tears and the snot running out of every aperture? And nothing left of your children but some toy, some small obscenity in a bathroom cupboard? And nothing ever after—until their need for you is new again?!

JESSICA: My need is new, Mother!—where are they?! Oh, please!

EMILY: I—do—not—know!
(A wrenching outcry) Why did you bring them here? Next time, you bring perfect children, do you hear?! *You hear me?!—perfect children!*

JESSICA: They're the best I could do!

EMILY: No—perfect children! I don't want to see forgotten frailties again! Your burns and bruises, your weeping on the stairs, the soil in your bed, your sighs, regrets, discharges, rages—no! I want well-made children, clean and well-proportioned, perfect children who smell nicely on my bosom, call me grandmama and love me better than they love you!

JESSICA: *(An outcry of triumph)* Love, you said! You said the magic word! Mother, you said love!

EMILY: You brought me monsters!

JESSICA: No—no—

JOHN: Emily—stop it!

EMILY: Monsters!
(Her assault is too much for Jessica. She breaks down.)

JESSICA: No—please—oh, stop—my children—oh, my children—where are my children?

EMILY: *Monsters!*

JOHN: Enough! You stop it, do you hear?
(He grabs her roughly) I said enough! Now then, take it back—every word you said.

EMILY: No—nothing!

JOHN: You take it back—I warn you—! Go to her. Touch her. Comfort her!

EMILY: No—no comfort!

JOHN: Touch her, I said!

JESSICA: *(Starting to recover)* No—I don't want her near me.

JOHN: Jessica—

JESSICA: Nor you either.

(*She rises, stopping his advance. Her strength is growing*) They—are—not—monsters. I'm only one remove from them. Not monsters. You're two removes. Perhaps *you* are the monster.

(*Pointing to John*) Or him. Why blame me?

EMILY: Because you should have lost them. Somewhere on the way, you should have lost them!

JESSICA: Why? They're sweet—they're peaceable. What harm do they do?

EMILY: They jeopardize the rest.

JESSICA: What rest, *what*?

EMILY: You—me—us. They imperil us. Bring us all our ailments. Headache, heartache, shame. Horror and loneliness.

(*Hard*) It's good if they get lost. Adrift. Set adrift or killed. We had two others once—before you came. Adrift. I can't recall their names—how's that for how it hurts?

(*Then, almost gently*) You—in the light—in the pain—with the baby sac broken—those, how many did you say? Can you recall their names?—why, bless you, they hadn't any! What had they, then? Which of those squashy, mushy things had dignity, do you suppose?

JESSICA: Which of us has?

EMILY: (*As if uninterrupted*) Which would have learned to read the best or smile the merriest, which would have sung a song? Which one looked like you, like me, like him? *Which pulp was your dream?*!

(*More quietly*) Adrift, then. Adrift and down the drain? The strong ones—dry them off and let them stay! The weak ones—down the drain!

(*Abruptly, without warning, John starts to laugh. They turn and observe him.*)

EMILY: What struck your father?

(*To John*) Is the moon too bright?

JOHN: It's daylight—no moon. The weak ones down the drain, you say?

(*Exulting*) I've got you, you mean bitch, got you dead to rights! At last! Oh, Jessica—at last I've got her!

EMILY: Turn down the moon.

JOHN: Oh no—I don't mind the light—I love it!

(*Pointing to Jessica, he confronts Emily*) Her—your daughter—Jessica—how would you call her?—weak or strong?

EMILY: Strong, but not enough.

JOHN: She's as strong as you are—you know it.

EMILY: One day perhaps—not yet.

JOHN: Right now. Easily your match—quite easily—and one day—

EMILY: One day, one day—who'll see one day?

JOHN: You've seen it.

EMILY: What? The moon, the moon.

JOHN: You've seen it many times.

EMILY: What, what?

JOHN: And each time you've seen it, you have killed her!

EMILY: (*A fugitive now*) No—never—not ever—don't you dare to say—

JOHN: You've killed her many times!

(*Triumphantly*) Oh woman, I've got you now. Yes, many times! The weak ones down the drain, you say? Why her?! Why not Charles? Oh happy day, he's weakness—why not him? Or me! You've made no bones about how weak *I* am—why not me? And killing *me* would be a children's game— I wouldn't give a bit of trouble, dying. One two three! Just cook me a strong savory—a little extra pepper in my soup—I'd sneeze to death! (*Then, quieter and more deadly*) Or—best of all—oh yes, this is best of all—you didn't kill our little boys. You lied about that—you didn't kill them! Those weakling boys with narrow chests and mucus in their eyes— you cozened them for years, sang them sweet lullabies, gave them your titties till they were eight years old! Eat, little weaklings, drink and eat, suckle Mama, oh suckle me!

EMILY: It's lies—I let them die!

JOHN: (*To Jessica*) This woman—she hoards guilts—she invents them! (*To Emily*) They died!—in spite of you!

EMILY: Lies—all lies—

JOHN: Suckle Mama—suckle, suck! (*With an outcry of contempt*) You!—are you the woman who's been ter- rorizing me? Why, it's never been the catastrophe at all! Nor whatever's left down There. Not even hunger! It's you—the terror has been you! And look at you! Why, I can rub you out of my eyes like an eyelash! (*He spits at her.*)

EMILY: Now—I'll kill him now— (*Bent on murder, she starts for him. Jessica goes between them.*)

JESSICA: No—stop! The two of you—stop, I say!

JOHN: (*Quietly*) Jessica—a needless thing—to stop her, I mean. She'd have stopped herself. She'd never have harmed a hair—of me. Why, I'm her prize weakling. She needs me more than I need her. Suck, Mama—suck. (*His laughter is subdued. Paul comes rushing in. He has Frank under phys- ical restraint. The boy is flailing and thrashing about, trying to shake off his father's hampering hands. He is in an agony of distress, his clothes torn, his eyes wild, his movements a torment of terror.*)

JESSICA: Paul—Frank—oh what, oh what?

JOHN: Hold him—he'll hurt himself—hold him!

EMILY: No—let him go!

JESSICA: Oh, please—what happened?—where's your sister?

EMILY: Let him go!

JOHN: What's he saying? Is he speaking?—what's he say?

JESSICA: Your sister—where's your sister?! Paul—where is she?! (*Abruptly, Frank's flailing ceases. The boy's body goes rigid. No sound except for the muted pain in the boy's throat. He and he alone is looking toward the door. What he sees there is Charles . . . an abomination of blood, vomit, excrement and self-loathing. Bereft now of his wits.*)

CHARLES: No—let *me*! I'll tell you—let me!

JESSICA: Oh, God!

CHARLES: Oh, kill me! Somebody—oh, somebody—please!—oh, kill me!

JESSICA: What?—my daughter—?!

CHARLES: Oh, kill me! I ate and vomited! Oh, look—I'm blood and vomit!— oh, kill me!—oh please, please!

JESSICA: Oh no—oh, somebody—!

CHARLES: Kill! Kill me!

(*An instant of silence. Jessica turns to her mother.*)

JESSICA: He's yours—he always has been. Do it.

EMILY: (*A whisper*) . . . No.

JESSICA: There—on the table—take it.

EMILY: (*Recoiling from the knife*) No!

(*Jessica picks up the knife, crosses the room and hands the knife to her mother.*)

JESSICA: I said yes. Now. Do it.

EMILY: No—I won't—I can't!

JESSICA: (*Quietly*) Kill him, Mother. Him, this time. Not me.

EMILY: No—no one! Ever! No more!

JESSICA: Kill him! The family, Mother! Violated! The family!

(*With hypnotic insistence*) Go on. Courage, Mother. Adrift, you said. Remember? Down the drain, the weak ones. They must. You're right— they must. Go on now. Go on.

(*Emily, as if under Jessica's spell, takes the knife. She moves only one step toward Charles, but cannot move further. She drops the knife with an outcry.*)

EMILY: I can't!

(*Charles sobs. Instantly, Jessica retrieves the knife and rushes to her mother to put the knife back in Emily's hand.*)

JESSICA: I say yes!—you kill him!

EMILY: (*Struggling to break away from Jessica*) Please—oh, let me go!

JOHN: Let her go!

JESSICA: Kill him!

EMILY: Oh, please!

JOHN: Let her go—have mercy—let her go!

JESSICA: Kill!

EMILY: *No!*

(*Jessica plunges the knife into Emily's body. Emily clings to her daughter as if in an embrace.*)

EMILY: Oh no!—oh yes! Oh Jessica—oh my dear! Oh daughter—oh thank you—oh my dear!

(*Silence. Then, very gently*) Now then . . . my dear one . . . let me down. No need to hold me anymore. You may . . . let me down. Oh, love! Oh, my daughter!

(*Jessica helps Emily to lie down*) Down? Have you let me down?

JESSICA: (*Kneeling beside her*) Yes, Mother.

EMILY: How kind you are.

(*Silence.*)

JOHN: She's dead.

JESSICA: Dead? I—never—I never have before.

JOHN: It starts now.

JESSICA: But I never—oh no!

(*Jessica emits a sound, an utterance of pure anguish, an unearthly scream— a note of final despair, a note of purest music.*)

CHARLES: (*Slowly, as from a dream, coming out of his madness*) That sound? Who made that sound?

(*Silence. John looks at Jessica.*)

JOHN: Was it D-Natural?

(*Charles half nods in awe and wonderment. Jessica arises and emits the horrifying wail again. Her father goes to her.*)

JOHN: (*With deep compassion*) Yes, D-Natural. Be still. Be still, my dear, be still.

(*He holds her in his arms, he comforts her. In a moment, she moves away from him, as if in a trance. John goes to Emily, and speaks to her.*)

JOHN: Very well, then, Emily.

(*Slowly, Emily arises. Her face is washed clean.*)

EMILY: Ah . . . is it time, then?

JOHN: Yes.

EMILY: Jessica, is it time?

JOHN: (*To the abstracted Jessica*) Your mother's speaking to you, my dear.

JESSICA: Oh?

EMILY: (*Tenderly*) I said is it time?

JESSICA: Time? Ah, yes.

EMILY: (*Forlornly*) You mean right now? You've only just arrived.

JESSICA: We'll come again, Mother.

EMILY: Oh, soon, I hope.

JESSICA: Oh, yes indeed—quite soon.

JOHN: It's been a lovely visit, my dear.

EMILY: Oh, lovely, yes indeed!

JESSICA: And such a fine dinner last night. Such a lovely chicken.

EMILY: Yes, you must thank your Uncle Charles.

JESSICA: (*Like a dutiful child*) Thank you, Uncle Charles.

CHARLES: A lovely chicken, yes.

JOHN: (*Embracing Jessica*) You must promise to be kind to yourself, my dear.

JESSICA: And you too, Father—be kind.

(*Social chatter*)

I must say, you're both looking very well this time. I think maybe things are a little better nowadays. Don't you agree?

EMILY: Oh yes, much better.

JESSICA: Don't you think times are changing, Father?

(*With her direct question to her father, the chitchat ceases. They are serious.*)

JOHN: Well, we've gotten back D-Natural.

EMILY: (*Hoping, but hardly daring to believe it*) Was it really D-Natural, do you think?

JOHN: Yes. I think it was.

EMILY: Did it always sound that way?

JOHN: What way?

EMILY: So painful.

JOHN: I don't know. What do you think, Jessica?

JESSICA: I don't know. I can hardly remember it.

    (*A moment*) Well—time to go. Come, Paul—come, Frank. Where's Carla?

JOHN: I just saw her. She's out there somewhere.

JESSICA: (*Calling*) Carla! Carla, honey, we're going now!

EMILY: What's she doing out there, anyway?

JESSICA: Just watching.

    (*Lightly*) G'bye, Mom—G'bye, Dad!

EMILY AND JOHN: Goodbye, sweetheart. G'bye, love!

JESSICA: Take care, now.

JOHN: You too—take care!

    (*Paul departs first. Then Frank. Jessica remains on the threshold a moment, surveying the room and her parents, as if to commit them to memory. When the registry seems complete, she raises her fingertips to her lips and gently blows them a kiss. They smile with deep benignity. The lights dim to darkness.*)

END OF THE PLAY

ABOUT THE AUTHOR

After a brief stint of professional boxing, N. Richard Nash settled down to being a teacher of philosophy, and then—he calls this a natural segue—of drama. He has taught at Bryn Mawr College, Haverford, Brandeis, the University of Pennsylvania, and has lectured at Yale and Princeton.

Nash has written with distinction in a number of media—the theater, television, motion pictures, the musical stage, poetry and fiction. Best known for his work in the theater, he has had many plays produced on and off Broadway, and throughout the world. Certainly his most famous play is *The Rainmaker* which is now regarded as a classic. It has been translated into nearly forty languages, including an African tongue which has no written form—the actors learned their translated lines by rote.

In television, he is one of that select half dozen writers whose names have now gone down in media history as The Golden Age of Television: Nash, Gore Vidal, Paddy Chayefsky, Robert Alan Aurthur, Horton Foote and Rod Serling.

Nash wrote the screenplay for *Porgy and Bess*, and the libretti for *The Happy Time* and *110 in the Shade*.

Among his novels, which have won admiring reviews, two have been bestsellers—*East Wind, Rain* and *The Last Magic*.

Nash has had an honored career, and has won a great number of American and international awards, among them The American Dramatists Award, the Maxwell Anderson Verse Drama Award, the Orbéal Prize, the Wilhelm Gosse Award, the Cannes Prize for Literature and Drama, the Geraldine Dodge Award and the New American Play Award.

He is currently at work on a nonfiction book about creativity and criticism, and has just completed a new novel, *The Wildwood*.